Indian Himalaya Handbook

Vanessa Betts &
Victoria McCulloch

To the north of the plains stand the Himalaya, what a 19th-century Surveyor General of India described as "the finest natural combination of boundary and barrier that exists in the world. It stands alone. For the greater part of its length only the Himalayan eagle can trace it. It lies amidst the eternal silence of vast snowfield and icebound peaks". In the eastern foothills of the Himalaya, for example, are some of the wettest regions in the world, still covered in dense rainforest, while in their western ranges are the high-altitude deserts of Ladakh. Similarly the Gangetic plains stretch from the fertile and wet delta of Bengal to the deserts of North Rajasthan. Even the peninsula ranges from the tropical humid climate of the western coast across the beautiful hills of the Western Ghats to the dry plateau inland.

Inspiring religious awe, philosophical contemplation and imperial ambition throughout human history, the Himalaya are quite literally as close as we can get to the heavens. Sacred to Hindus, Muslims and Buddhists alike, the wealth of cultural heritage is matched only by astonishing biodiversity; Ladakh's high-altitude plateau, where semi-nomadic tribesmen have hewn a living along ancient trade routes and ribboned rivers reveal verdant terraced villages; the lush tea plantations of North Bengal beneath the austere Kangchendzonga mountain; the remote, magical cloud forests of Arunachal Pradesh; the rhododendron- and azalea-swathed valleys of Sikkim; the jungles of Uttarakhand where tigers once roamed; the apple orchards and pine-clad hills of Himachal Pradesh and the lotus-fringed lakes of Kashmir; it's truly a region of magic and myth.

For the visitor the experience is just as diverse, whether trekking amid the most spectacular mountains in the world, pursuing a spiritual path through meditation and yoga or seeking adrenalin highs from the wide range of extreme sports activities on offer. No matter where you go, from the colonial hill stations of Darjeeling and Mussoorie, the Buddhist enclaves of Dharamshala and Tawang, the old hippy haunt of Manali, the clarified air of Leh, the ashrams of Rishikesh or the source of the sacred River Ganges in Gangotri, expect humbling hospitality, jaw-dropping vistas and memories to last a lifetime. Sab kuch milega! Everything is possible.

**THIS PAGE** Colourful boats on Naini lake, in the hill resort of Nainital, Uttarakhand
**PREVIOUS PAGE** Buddhist monk at Tsuglagkhang complex in McLeodganj

# Don't miss...

**1 Haridwar** ▸▸ page 93
The spectacular Ganga Arti fire *puja* against a stunning sunset backdrop.

**2 Corbett National Park** ▸▸ page 133
Tiger- and elephant-spotting in scenic rugged terrain.

**3 Sarahan** ▸▸ page 149
Evening prayers at this impressive Bhimakali Temple.

**4 McLeodganj** ▸▸ page 189
Walking the Kora around the Dalai Lama's residence.

**5 Srinagar** ▸▸ page 227
A magical night on a houseboat on Dal Lake.

**6 Nubra Valley** ▸▸ page 259
A lush green valley dotted with remote and friendly villages.

**7** **Darjeeling** ▶▶ page 307
Terraced tea gardens, mountain views
and exceptional trekking opportunities.

**8** **Kurseong** ▶▶ page 315
Low-key town set in tea
estates and orange groves.

**9** **Pemayangtse** ▶▶ page 346
An ancient monastery in an
awe-inspiring setting.

**10** **Kaziranga National Park** ▶▶ page 363
A UNESCO World Heritage Site, famed
for its Asian one-horned rhinos.

**11** **Tawang Monastery** ▶▶ page 376
A monastery surrounded by mountains
and ice-cold lakes.

**12** **Ziro Valley** ▶▶ page 378
Tribal life in pretty villages set in
paddy fields.

Kolkata

100 km
100 miles

The Government of India states that
"the external boundaries of India
are neither correct nor authenticated"

TIBET
(CHINA)

ARUNACHAL
PRADESH

SIKKIM    BHUTAN    **11** Tawang    Ziro **12**    Saikhoa
                                                       Ghat
Pemayangtse **9**  Gangtok        Itanagar    Dibrugarh
         **7** Darjeeling
         **8** Kurseong          **10** Kaziranga
            Siliguri              National Park
                         ASSAM
                    Guwahati                NAGALAND
BIHAR   WEST                                        MYANMAR
        BENGAL      Shillong                        (BURMA)
                MEGHALAYA        MANIPUR
        BANGLADESH

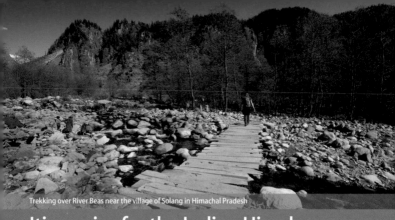

Trekking over River Beas near the village of Solang in Himachal Pradesh

# Itineraries for the Indian Himalaya

First-time visitors are often at a loss when faced with the vast possibilities for travel in the Indian Himalaya. We have made suggestions for two- to three-week trips on the basis that some journeys will be flown and that air or rail tickets have been booked in advance. Air tickets can be difficult to get at short notice for some trips, for example Delhi–Leh–Delhi, so try to book them in advance online. For visiting the Western Himalaya, the most convenient access from abroad is by flying into Delhi and for the Eastern Himalaya, by flying into Kolkata.

Sunrise in Corbett National Park, Uttarakhand

Entrance to the Rumtrek Monastery, Sikkim

## ITINERARY ONE
### The Foothills
Arrive in Delhi and visit Agra by train to see the splendour of the Taj. Travel by road or train to Dehra Dun and onward to the place of the sages, Rishikesh, for a few days by the Ganga, which gives access to some of Hinduism's holiest places of pilgrimage. Next stop is at Corbett National Park, rich in both flora and fauna (tigers are occasionally seen), before heading for Almora, surrounded by wonderful scenery and with several old temples nearby. Experience the hill station of Nainital for a few days, before returning to Delhi.

## ITINERARY TWO
### The Old Hindustan–Tibet Road
Start in Delhi as above and take the *Himalayan Queen*, which connects with the narrow-gauge Shivalik train from Kalka to Shimla. Travel by road along the old Hindustan–Tibet Road eastwards, stopping at Sarahan for a few nights, with its Bhimakali temple, Sangla and Kalpa before continuing into Spiti and the remote Buddhist settlements of Tabo and Kaza. The road through the wide Spiti Valley and over the Kunzum La and the Rohtang Pass in Upper Lahul brings you down to Manali. From there return to Delhi. The route through Spiti and Lahul may not be open during the monsoon and in winter.

## ITINERARY THREE
### Ladakh–Little Tibet
Arrive in Delhi and travel up by road to Manali via Mandi or Nalagarh. From July to September the Manali–Leh road is

### TRAVEL TIP
Treks are easily arranged on arrival, but first-time visitors to India are recommended to book a tour in advance through a reputable agent.

usually open so you can travel by 4WD or bus to Sarchucamp through the spectacular high-altitude desert. A 12-hour drive through Taglang La (the second highest motorable pass in the world) takes you to Leh. While in Leh visit some monasteries and Pangong Tso or Nubra. Fly back to Delhi and visit Agra for the Taj Mahal by train.

## ITINERARY FOUR
### The Valley of the Gods

Arrive in Delhi and travel via Pathankot on the Kangra Valley mountain railway to Kangra and visit Palàmpur and Andretta. Experience the Tibetan Buddhist presence in McLeodganj (Upper Dharamshala) for a few days then travel to Kullu or Naggar with rewarding walks and unspoilt Pahari villages and temples in the surrounding area. Return by road via Mandi, Pragpur or Nalagarh to Delhi or fly back from Bhuntar near Kullu.

Snow-covered mountains at Rohtang Pass at 3985 m

Buddha statue in the Nubra Valley, Ladakh

## ITINERARY FIVE
### North Bengal and Sikkim

Arrive in Delhi or Kolkata. Fly to Bagdogra, the airport for the hill station of Darjeeling, which you can reach by the steam Himalayan Railway or by road. Drive through tea gardens and along the Tista Valley on the way to Kalimpong. Continue your journey into Sikkim where Gangtok is a good base for a few days or visit the important Buddhist monastery at Rumtek and, via a precipitous road, the beautiful Changu Lake. You can then go west to Pelling, a base from which to see the awe-inspiring Pemayangtse Monastery, then on to Yuksom for day treks and a visit to the Khecheopalri 'Wishing' Lake. Return to Bagdogra for the flight back to Kolkata or Delhi.

Trekking in the Darjeeling area or in Sikkim is best October-December and in April-May, avoiding the monsoon.

### TRAVEL TIP

Always carry your passport, plus photocopies. These might be required at checkpoints, especially in Jammu and Kashmir and Arunachal Pradesh.

## ITINERARY SIX
### The northeastern hills

Start in Kolkata or Delhi. Fly (or take the train) to Guwahati. Take the hill road (or catch a helicopter) to Shillong in the 'Abode of the Clouds'. From there visit Cherrapunji, in perpetual mist or rain, with high waterfalls, caves and tribal markets. Stop at Kaziranga National Park and see rhinos. Then travel on to Tezpur and Dirang via Tipi with its orchids. Continue to the rarely visited Tawang for its ancient Buddhist monastery and the high-altitude lakes nearby. Return via Nameri Eco Camp to Guwahati for a flight back to Kolkata.

Darjeeling, producer of a quarter of India's tea, is surrounded by terraced tea gardens

The 16th-century monastery of Dankar Gompa perches precariously in the high-altitude Spiti Valley

The ancient Bhimakali Temple, in Sarahan, Himachal Pradesh, has strikingly elaborate carvings

# Contents

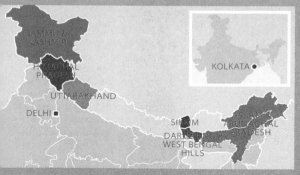

# Contents

Essentials

# Planning your trip

## Best time to visit the Indian Himalaya

In most of India, by far the most pleasant time to visit is from the end of the monsoon in November to the end of March. However, there are important exceptions. The hill stations in the Himalaya are beautiful in the hot weather months of April to early June. Parts of the western Himalaya can be excellent through to September though it can be very cold and sometimes wet in spring.

Because local variations are important, the handbook gives an idea of the most comfortable times to visit for many places.

Peak season differs across the Himalayan region depending on monsoon (low season) and mid-winter (low season). Hill stations, like Shimla, have peaks during the summer holiday months (May and June) when they are incredibly busy as well as during the Pujas (September and October). The Leh peak season is July to September. Jumping-off points (Almora, Nainital, etc) will raise prices during these times.

Some of the country's great festivals such as **Dasara** and **Diwali** are celebrated in October and November. See also Festivals in the Indian Himalaya, page 26.

## What to do in the Indian Himalaya

The Himalaya have perhaps the greatest potential for sport and adventure travel in the world, yet the opportunities are as yet still little developed. Mountaineering itself has been by far the most important single sporting activity during the last century, and trekking has now become popular in several areas of the Indian Himalaya. Today specialist operators offer activities ranging from skiing – near Manali or Kufri, for example – to hang-gliding, whitewater rafting and mountain biking. With the exception of a few trekking routes it is essential to seek advice and to go as part of a group or organized tour (see below).

### Birdwatching
The country's diverse and rich natural habitats harbour over 1200 species of birds of which around 150 are endemic. Visitors can enjoy spotting oriental species whether they are in towns, in the countryside or more abundantly in the national parks and sanctuaries. On the plains, the cooler months (Nov-Mar) are the most comfortable for a chance to see migratory birds from the hills, but the highlands themselves are ideal in May-Jun and again after the monsoons when visibility improves in Oct-Nov. Bodies of water of all sizes draw visiting waterfowl from other continents during the winter. **The Great Himalayan National Park** in Himachal Pradesh is a great place to see birds and wildlife.

It is quite easy to get to some parks from the important tourist centres. *A Birdwatcher's Guide to India* by Krys Kazmierczak and Raj Singh (Prion Ltd, Sandy, Bedfordshire, UK, 1998), is well researched and comprehensive with helpful practical information and maps.

See also Birds, page 432, and www.delhi bird.net, www.kolkatabirds.com and www. orientalbirdclub.org.

### Cycling
Cycling offers a peaceful and healthy alternative to cars, buses or trains. Touring on locally hired bicycles is possible along country roads – ideal if you want to see village life in India and the lesser-known wildlife parks. Consult a good Indian

## Packing for the Indian Himalaya

You can buy most essentials in larger cities, but the more you get off the beaten track into the Himalayas the smaller the range, although you can get good cold weather gear.

At altitude, wear a stronger high-factor sun screen than you would normally use and have a sun hat. Earplugs and an eyemask are also essential, as is a good torch for frequent power cuts. Indian pharmacies can be very cheap but aren't always reliable, so take a supply of medicines from home, including inhalers and anti-malarial drugs. For protection against mosquitoes, take repellent. See also Health, page 32.

Photocopies of documents, passport ID and visa pages, and spare passport photos are useful when applying for permits or in case of loss or theft.

Take a good padlock to secure your budget room too, though these are cheaply bought in India.

For trekking equipment, see page 8.

agent for advice. Expert guides, cycles and support vehicle and accommodation in simple resthouses or tents, are included, see page 39.

### Fishing

Fishing is popular in both the western and the eastern Himalaya, the famous mahseer being found all the way from the Indus system to the Brahmaputra. The rivers Beas and Jhelum in Himachal, and Jammu and Kashmir respectively, the Ganga above Tehri in Uttarakhand, and the Bhoreli in Arunachal all offer excellent fishing opportunities for trout and mahseer. Check out the lovely Himalayan Trout House (www.mountainhighs.com) in Himachal Pradesh.

### Motorcycling

For those keen on moving faster along the road, by travelling on the 2 wheels of a motorbike (preferably a 'Bullet'), see page 20.

### Trekking

Naturally, the Himalayas invite trekkers of all levels. See page 6.

### Whitewater rafting

The rivers can be dangerous except when low in Aug and Sep.

The snow-fed rivers that flow through Kashmir, Himachal, Uttar Pradesh and Sikkim offer excellent whitewater rafting. The options range from a half-day trip to one lasting several days, and allow a chance to see scenery, places and people off the beaten track. The trips are organized and managed by professional teams who have trained abroad. The Ganga and its tributaries offer the most developed whitewater rafting in the Indian Himalaya. Between Oct and Apr, from a base camp at Beasi-Shivpuri just 70 km from Rishikesh, is a set of Grade III and IV rapids. Further into the mountains near Deoprayag there are Grade IV and V rapids on the Alaknanda and Bhagirathi, tributaries of the Ganga itself. Much further north in the arid regions of Ladakh and Zanskar you have to wait until the monsoon season from Jul-Sep for the Indus and Zanskar rivers to become accessible, and further west the Chenab has nearly 230 km of superb Grade IV and V rafting, open Nov-Mar. In the east, the Tista and Rangit have excellent stretches open after the monsoon, between Oct and Apr. In Arunachal, the Siang (Upper Brahmaputra) River has Grade III-IV navigable rapids and trips run Nov-Dec each year.

### Yoga and meditation

There has been a growing Western interest in the ancient life disciplines in search of physical and spiritual wellbeing, as practised in ancient India. Yoga is supposed to regulate the nervous system and aims to attain the union of body, mind and spirit through the practice of *asanas* (body postures), breath control, discipline, cleansing, contemplation and awareness. It seeks to achieve moral purification through abstinence and restraint (dietary and sexual). Meditation, which complements yoga to relieve stress, increase awareness and bring inner peace, prescribes the practice of *dhyana* (purposeful concentration) by withdrawing oneself from external distractions and focusing one's attention to consciousness itself. This leads ultimately to *samadhi* (release from worldly bonds). Hatha yoga has captured the Western imagination as it promises good health through postural exercises, while the search for inner peace leads others to learn meditation techniques.

Centres across the country offer courses for beginners and practitioners. Rishikesh in Uttarkhand is seen as the home of yoga and there are many ashrams offering courses. Another popular place for Westerners to try yoga is around Mcleod Ganj and Bhagsu in Himachal Pradesh. Whether you wish to embark on a serious study of yoga or sample an hour's introductory meditation session, India offers opportunities for all, though you may need to apply in advance for some popular courses. The **International Yoga Festival** in Rishikesh is held annually in Feb/Mar. In Rishikesh, there are also opportunities for satsang with enlightened masters such as Mooji. Most courses in Rishikesh are held in the winter months and are quieter from Apr to Oct.

## Trekking

The Himalaya offers unlimited opportunities to view the natural beauty of mountains, rare flora and fauna and the diverse groups of people who live in the ranges and valleys, many of whom have retained unique cultural identities because of their isolation. The treks described in this book are only for guidance. They try to give you a flavour of an area or a destination. Some trails fall within the 'Inner Line' for which special permits are required (see page 10 and box, page 335). For books on Trekking, see page 438.

**Independent trekking** There are some outstandingly beautiful treks, though they are often not through the wilderness sometimes conjured up. However, trekking alone is not recommended as you will be in unfamiliar territory where you may not be able to communicate with the local people and if injured you may not have help at hand. Independent trekkers should get a specialist publication with detailed route descriptions and a good map. Remember, mountain topography is subject to constant change, and tracks and crossings can be affected very rapidly. Speak to those who know the area well and have been trekking to the places you intend visiting.

**Backpacking camping** Hundreds of people arrive each year with a pack and some personal equipment, buy some food and set off trekking, carrying their own gear and choosing their own campsites or places to stay. Serious trekkers will need a framed backpack. Supplies of fuel wood are scarce and flat ground suitable for camping rare. It is not always easy to find isolated and 'private' campsites.

**Trekking without a tent** Although common in Nepal, only a few trails in India offer the ease and comfort of this option. Exceptions are the Singalila Ridge trail in the Darjeeling area and the Sikkim Khangchendzonga trek. On these, it is often possible to stay in trekking huts or perhaps in village homes. You carry clothes and bedding and for not much money a night you get a space on the floor, a wooden pallet or a camp bed, or in the more luxurious inns, a room and shower. The food is simple, usually vegetable curry, rice and dhal which, although repetitive, is healthy and can be tasty. This approach brings you into more contact with the local population, the limiting factor being the routes where accommodation is available.

**Locally organized treks** Porters can usually be hired through an agent in the town or village at the start of a trek. Porters hired in the bazar can be cheaper than agency porters but may be unreliable. They will help carry your baggage, often cook for you, and communicate with the local people. A good porter will know the area and some can tell you about local customs and point out interesting details en route. Away from roads, the footpath is the principal line of communication between villages. Tracks tend to be very good, well graded and in good condition. In remoter areas away from all habitation, tracks may be indistinct and a local guide is recommended. Although some porters speak a little English, you may have communication problems. Remember, you may be expected to provide your porter's warm clothing and protective wear including shoes, gloves and goggles on high-altitude treks.

Hiring a *sardar* and crew is more expensive but well worthwhile since he will speak some English, act as a guide, take care of engaging porters and cooks, arrange for provisions and sort out all logistical problems. A *sardar* will cost more and although he may be prepared to carry a load, his principal function will be as a guide and overseer for the porters. Make sure your *sardar* is experienced in the area you will be travelling in and can show good references that are his own and not borrowed.

**Using a trekking agent** Trekking agents based in Delhi or Kolkata or at hill stations (eg Leh, Darjeeling, Gangtok) will organize treks for a fee and provide a *sardar*, porters, cooks, food and equipment, but it requires effort and careful thought on your part. This method can be excellent and is recommended for a group, preferably with some experience, that wants to follow a specific itinerary. You have to follow a pre-arranged itinerary in some areas, as required by the government, and also as porters expect to arrive at certain points on schedule. You can make arrangements from abroad in advance: often a protracted business with faxes and emails. Alternatively, wait until you get to India but allow at least a week to make arrangements.

**Fully organized and escorted trek** A company or individual with local knowledge and expertise organizes a trip and sells it. Some or all camp equipment, food, cooking, planning the stages, decision-making based on progress and weather conditions, liaison with porters, shopkeepers, etc are all taken care of. When operating abroad, the agency may take care of all travel arrangements, ticketing, visas and permits. Make sure that both you and the trekking company understand exactly who is to provide what equipment. This has the advantage of being a good, safe introduction to the country. You will be able to travel with limited knowledge of the region and its culture and get to places more easily which as an individual you might not reach, without the expense of completely kitting yourself out. You should read and follow any advice in the preparatory material you are sent, as your enjoyment greatly depends on it.

An escorted trek involves going with a group; you will camp together but not necessarily all walk together. If you are willing to trade some of your independence for careful, efficient organization and make the effort to ensure the group works well together, the experience can be very rewarding. Ideally there should be no more than 20 trekkers (preferably around 12). Companies have reputations to maintain and try to comply with Western concepts of hygiene. Before booking, check the itinerary – is it too demanding, or not adventurous enough? Also find out whether the leader is qualified and is familiar with the route and what equipment is provided.

## Local agents

Tourist offices and government-approved trekking agents in Delhi and the hill stations will organize fairly inexpensive treks. Tour operators and travel agents are listed in each town. See also Tour operators, page 38. The following are recommended:

**Above 14000 ft**, Log Huts area, Manali, Himachal Pradesh, T(0)9816-544803, www.above14000ft.com. Expert, environmentally conscious adventure organizers, specializing in treks, mountain biking, climbing expeditions and mountaineering courses throughout Uttarkhand, Ladakh and Himachal. Paperless office. Highly recommended.

**Adventure Quests**, www.adventure quests.net. Run by ex-servicemen, with a range of adventurous trekking and rafting trips in Arunachal Pradesh.

**Aquaterra Adventures**, S-507, ground floor, Greater Kailash II, New Delhi, T011-2921 2641/2760, www.treknraft.com. Award-winning outfit offering trekking, rafting, kayaking, etc in all Indian Himalayan states. Highly recommended.

**Ibex Expeditions**, see page 40.

**Mountain Adventures**, A-51, SFS Mount Kailash, New Delhi, T011-2622 2202, www.mountainindia.com.

**Rimo Expeditions**, Hotel Kanglhachen Complex, Leh, T01982-253348, www.rimoexpeditions.com. Great local outfit based in Leh.

**Spiti Ecosphere**, www.spitiecosphere.com. Exceptional trekking agent that also organizes homestays and volunteering projects in the Spiti Valley, Himachal Pradesh.

**Terralaya Travels**, Gangtok, Sikkim, T03592-252516, www.terralaya.com. Specialists in the Northeast states, with interesting sleeping options (including homestays); biking, trekking, spiritual, nature, etc journeys offered.

**Touching Cloud Base**, T(0)9816-544803, www.touchingcloudbase.com. Exceptional paragliding opportunities in Bir and Manali in Himachal Pradesh.

**Wanderlust**, G-18, 2nd floor, Masjid Moth, Greater Kailash II, New Delhi 110048, T011-4053 7115, www.wanderlustindia.com.

## Foreign operators

### Australia and New Zealand
**Adventure World**, see page 12.
**Himalayan Travellers**, Wellington, T04-863325.
**Peregrine Adventures**, see page 12.

### UK
**Exodus**, see page 38.
**Explore Worldwide**, T0845-291 4541, www.explore.co.uk.
**High Places**, T0845-257 7500, www.highplaces.co.uk.
**KE Adventure**, T01768-773966, www.keadventure.com.
**Snow Lion Expeditions**, T0800-525 8735, www.snowlion.com.
**Trans Himalaya**, T01764 650604, www.trans-himalaya.com.

### USA
**Air Treks**, T1877-247 8735, www.airtreks.com
**Mountain Travel Sobek**, T1888-831 7526, www.mtsobek.com.

**Equipment and clothing** If you have good equipment, it is worth taking it, especially your own boots. Mountaineering and trekking equipment can sometimes be hired from hill stations. Ask the tourist offices there. Guard against cold, wet, sudden changes of temperature, strong sun and wind! Waterproof jacket with hood and over-trousers (windproof, waterproof and 'breather' type); warm sweater; fleece jacket; tracksuit; hiking trousers or shorts (knee length but not cycling); cotton T-shirts; cotton underwear; thermal underwear (vests, long johns); gloves; balaclava or ski toque; sun hat; swimwear. Try to carry lightweight, quick-drying fabrics that can be easily washed in cold-water streams. (After the trek, you might consider offering clothes you can part with to your porter.) Good lightweight walking boots with ankle support should be comfortable and well worn in, as blisters can ruin a trek; spare laces, good trainers (for resting the feet; also suitable for many low-level treks except in snow and off-the-trails); polypropylene undersocks, heavy walking socks. Sunglasses (with UV filter), snow glasses if you are planning to go above the snow line, high-factor sun block (SPF 50+), lip cream, a good sleeping bag (cheap ones from a local market are unsuitable above 4000 m) plus cotton liner, a Thermarest pad or a double thickness foam sleeping mat, 2-m-sq plastic sheet (sold locally), torch (flashlight) with replacement batteries or a Petzl headtorch, a compass, binoculars, insulated bag water-bottle (to also take to bed!), a day pack, a tent (in certain areas). Those expecting to climb high, cross glaciers, etc may need to hire crampons, ice axes, snow gaiters, ropes, etc as well as a silver survival blanket and a reinforced plastic 'bivouac bag'. A kerosene stove and strong fuel container suitable for high altitudes (kerosene is widely available); water filter and containers; nesting cooking pots (at least two); enamel mug and spoon and bags for provisions. Be sure to eat a balanced diet. Local foods will be available along the trail, and in fact the porters' meal of chapati or rice, vegetables, dhal and sweet milky tea is quite nutritious. Some shops stock limited amounts of dry goods for trekkers (noodles, chocolate bars, canned foods, fruit, nuts, porridge oats, etc). You might prefer to take some freeze-dried packs of favourites from home. Remember to thoroughly boil the fresh (unpasteurized) local milk.

**Maps** Survey of India has started producing trekking maps, scale 1:250,000; but at present these cover only the Himachal and Uttarakhand areas; none are available for the Northeast. For information on Sikkim trekking maps, see page 354.

**Trekking seasons** These vary with the area you plan to visit and the elevation. Autumn is best in most parts of the Himalaya though March to May can be pleasant. The monsoons (mid-June to end-September) can obviously be very wet and localized thunderstorms can occur at any time, particularly in the spring and summer. Start your trek early in the morning as the monsoon approaches. It often continues to rain heavily up to mid-October in the Eastern Himalaya. The Kullu Valley is unsuitable for trekking during the monsoons but areas beyond the central Himalayan range, eg Ladakh, Zanskar, Lahul and Spiti, are largely unaffected. Be prepared for extremes in temperatures in all seasons so come prepared with light clothing as well as enough waterproof protection. Winters can be exceptionally cold; high passes can be closed and you need more equipment. Winter treks on all but a few low-altitude ones (up to 3200 m) are recommended only for the experienced trekker accompanied by a knowledgeable local guide.

**Garhwal and Kumaon Himalaya** (pages 113-122): This is an all-season trekking destination because of its variety of climate and terrain. It is perhaps best in May and June when days are cool and clear. Even with the onset of the monsoons when mist covers the mountains you may get breaks in the rain of three or four days. Clouds can lift to give you some good mountain views but equipment may feel a little damp. The mountains are best for flowers in July and August. Late September to mid-November is again good for trekking.

**Himachal** (pages 210-215): The best times are as in Garhwal and Kumaon. The monsoon (mid-July to mid-September) is generally very wet and offers no mountain views. Trekking is usually possible from May to October when most passes are open (the Parvati Pass may be blocked until early July). In July to September high-altitude flowers are in bloom including summer rhododendrons.

**Kashmir** (Kashmir, currently risky because of the political situation; Ladakh, page 246 and Zanskar, page 235): Trekking is ideal between April and November. In Ladakh (the area open to trekkers), the motorable road from Manali to Leh is normally open from mid-June to October though flights to Leh from Delhi operate all year round. Most treks cross passes above 4500 m and are passable from early July to September.

**Darjeeling area** (pages 311-314): April and May has a chance of occasional showers but the rhododendrons and magnolias are in full bloom; October and November are usually dry with excellent visibility. Early December is possible but very cold.

**Sikkim** (pages 354-356): Mid-February to late May and again October to early December are possible; April, May, October and November are best.

**Arunachal** October to February is best for trekking in this remote wilderness, although nights are extremely cold.

**Trekking permits** Trekking is permitted in all areas other than those described as Restricted or Protected and within the 'Inner Line', so that you may not go close to the international boundary in many places. Often, destinations falling within these 'sensitive' zones, which have recently been opened for trekking, require treks to be organized by a recognized Indian Travel Agent for groups of at least four, travelling on a specified route, accompanied by a representative/liaison officer. Sometimes there are restrictions on the maximum number of days, season and type of transport used. The 'Inner Line' runs parallel and 40 km inside the international boundary; Kaza (Himachal Pradesh), however, is now open to group trekkers though overnight stay is not allowed at Puh, Khabo or Sumdo. Other areas now open to tourists include Kalindi Khal (Garhwal), Milam Glacier (Kumaon), Khardung La, Tso Moriri and Pangong (Ladakh), Tsangu Lake, Lachung and Yumthang (Sikkim) and Kameng Valley (Arunachal Pradesh).

On arrival in India, government-approved trekking agencies can obtain permits relatively easily, usually within three or four days. It can be much slower applying for trekking permits from abroad and may also slow down your visa application.

Some restricted areas are still totally closed to foreigners. For other restricted areas, permits are issued at the Foreigners' Regional Registration Offices in Delhi and Kolkata (and sometimes at a local FRRO), from immigration officers at some points of entry, or arranged by a travel agent (the easiest option). See box, page 335.

There are also entrance fees for the various national parks and conservation areas, which can be as much as Rs 600.

**Being prepared Health**: You will probably experience mountain sickness in its mildest form if you go much over 3000 m (very occasionally at lower altitudes). It is best to move at a slow pace and take plenty of rest and fluids. See also page 32.

**Security**: Thefts and muggings are very rare but on the increase. Be particularly careful of pickpockets at the start of a trek. Thieves sometimes hang around groups of trekkers knowing that many will be carrying all their money for the trek in cash. Guard your money at the point of departure. Keep your valuables with you at all times, make sure the tent 'doors' are closed when you are going for meals, and lock your room door in lodges. Be particularly careful with rucksacks carried atop buses on long journeys – always keep a watch on them when other passengers are loading/unloading their belongings.

Mountaineering courses **Himalayan Mountaineering Institute** ① *Darjeeling, T0354-225 4083/225 4087, www.himalayanmountaineeringinstitute.com*, offers information on mountaineering and runs one-month beginners' and advanced mountaineering courses. **Indian Mountaineering Foundation** ① *New Delhi, T011-24111211, www.indmount.org*, funds serious mountaineering, skiing, high-altitude trekking expeditions. Their permission is required for scaling any of India's peaks.

# Getting to the Indian Himalaya

## Air

India is accessible by air from virtually every continent. Most international flights arrive in Delhi or Mumbai, both of which have good internal connections to Kolkata and other airports in Northeast India. Some carriers permit 'open-jaw' travel, arriving in and departing from different cities.

### Buying a ticket
**Discounts** The cheapest fares from Europe tend to be with Central European, Central Asian or Middle Eastern airlines. You can also get good discounts from Australasia, Southeast Asia and Japan. International air tickets can be bought in India in airline offices, or over the internet.

**Ticket agents** Companies dealing in volume and taking reduced commissions for ticket sales can offer better deals than the airlines themselves. The national press carry their advertisements. **Trailfinders** ① *www.trailfinders.co.uk*, has worldwide agencies; **STA** ① *www.statravel.co.uk*, offers special deals for under-26s; **Travelbag** ① *www.travelbag.co.uk*, quotes competitive fares and is part of ebookers.

**From Europe** Despite the increases to Air Passenger Duty, Britain remains the cheapest place in Europe for flights to India. From mainland Europe, major European flag carriers including **KLM** and **Lufthansa** fly to Delhi and/or Mumbai from their respective hub airports. In most cases the cheapest flights are with Middle Eastern or Central Asian airlines, transiting via airports in the Gulf. Several airlines from the Middle East (eg **Emirates**, **Gulf Air**, **Kuwait Airways**, **Qatar Airways** and **Oman Air**) offer good discounts to Indian regional capitals from London, but fly via their hub cities, adding to the journey time. Consolidators in the UK can quote some competitive fares, such as www.skyscanner.net; www.ebookers.com; and **North South Travel** ① *T01245-608291, www.northsouthtravel.co.uk* (profits to charity).

**From North America** From the east coast, several airlines including **Air India**, **Jet Airways**, **Continental** and **Delta** fly direct from New York to Delhi and Mumbai. **American** flies to both cities from Chicago. Discounted tickets on **British Airways**, **KLM**, **Lufthansa**, **Gulf Air** and **Kuwait Airways** are sold through agents although they will invariably fly via their country's capital cities. From the west coast, **Air India** flies from Los Angeles to Delhi and Mumbai, and **Jet Airways** from San Francisco to Mumbai via Shanghai. Alternatively, fly via Hong Kong, Singapore or Bangkok using one of those countries' national carriers.

**Air Canada** operates between Vancouver and Delhi. **Air Brokers International** ① *www.airbrokers.com*, is competitive and reputable. **STA** ① *www.statravel.co.uk*, has offices in many US cities, Toronto and Ontario. Student fares are also available from **Travel Cuts** ① *www.travelcuts.com*, in Canada.

**From Australasia** Qantas, **Singapore Airlines, Thai Airways, Malaysian Airlines, Cathay Pacific** and **Air India** are the principal airlines connecting the continents, although Qantas is the only one that flies direct, with services from Sydney to Mumbai. Singapore Airlines, with subsidiary **Silk Air**, offers the most flexibility. Low-cost carriers including **Air Asia** (via Kuala Lumpur), **Scoot** and **Tiger Airways** (Singapore) offer a similar choice of arrival airports at substantial savings, though long layovers and possible missed connections make this a slightly more risky venture than flying with the mainstream airlines. **STA** and **Flight Centre** offer discounted tickets from their branches in major cities in Australia and New Zealand. **Abercrombie & Kent** ① *www.abercrombiekent.co.uk*, **Adventure World** ① *www.adventureworld.net.au*, **Peregrine** ① *www.peregrineadventures.com*, and **Travel Corporation of India** ① *www.tcindia.com*, organize tours.

**Airport information** The formalities on arrival in India have been increasingly streamlined during the last few years and the facilities at the major international airports greatly improved. However, arrival can still be a slow process. Disembarkation cards, with an attached customs declaration, are handed out to passengers during the inward flight. The immigration form should be handed in at the immigration counter on arrival. The customs slip will be returned, for handing over to the customs on leaving the baggage collection hall. You may well find that there are delays of over an hour at immigration in processing passengers who need help with filling in forms. When departing, note that you'll need to have a printout of your itinerary to get into the airport, and the security guards will only let you into the terminal within three hours of your flight. Pre-paid taxis to the city are available at all major airports. Insist on being taken to your chosen destination even if the driver claims the city is unsafe or the hotel has closed down.

    **Departure tax** Rs 500 is payable for all international departures other than those to neighbouring SAARC countries, when the tax is Rs 250 (not reciprocated by Sri Lanka). This is normally included in your international ticket; check when buying. (To save time 'Security Check' your baggage before checking in at departure.) Some airports have also begun charging a Passenger Service Fee or User Development Fee to each departing passenger. This is normally included in international tickets, but some domestic airlines have been reluctant to incorporate the charge. Keep some spare cash in rupees in case you need to pay the fee on arriving at the terminal.

## Road

Crossings between India and its neighbours are affected by the political relations between them. Get your Indian visa in advance, before arriving at the border. Several road border crossings are open periodically, but permission to cross cannot be guaranteed. Those listed below are the main crossings, which are usually open all year to tourists.

### From Bangladesh
To **Kolkata** from Dhaka is possible on the Maitree Express train, which restarted services in 2008. It runs twice a week in each direction (from Dhaka on Wednesday and Friday; to

Dhaka on Tuesday and Saturday) taking around 10-11 hours. Buses also run daily between the two cities. To **Tripura** from Dhaka is only four hours by road from the border crossing, just 2 km from the centre of Agartala, with flights to Kolkata. The border post is efficient when open but arrive there before 1500, as formalities often take time. Regulations are subject to change so find out in advance.

## From Bhutan
The nearest airport at **Bagdogra** is four or five hours' drive from Jaigaon, the rather untidy and unkempt Indian border town. The Indian Immigration checkpost is on the main street, about 1 km from the 'Bhutan Gate' at the border town of Phuntsholing where it is possible to spend a night. To enter Bhutan you need to go through an authorized travel agent and arrange the full visit in advance; the daily fee is currently US$200.

## From Burma/Myanmar
The recently reopened Moreh/Tamu border crossing links Myanmar with the state of Manipur. However, foreigners have reported great difficulty in securing permission to either leave or enter Myanmar by land.

## From Nepal
Four crossings are in common use: To **Delhi via Banbassa** is the shortest direct route between Kathmandu and Delhi, via the Nepali town of Mahendranagar and Banbassa. To **Varanasi via Gorakhpur** you must go to the **Sonauli-Bhairawa** crossing, the shortest and fastest route to Varanasi; many continue to Delhi from there. From Kathmandu or Pokhara you can get to Bhairawa, 6 km inside the Nepal border, Sonauli on the border itself, and Nautanwa on the Indian side. From there, buses take 3½ hours to Gorakhpur, with train connections for Delhi, or 5½ hours by bus to Varanasi. To **Patna via Raxaul-Birganj** several buses run daily from Raxaul to Patna (five to seven hours) but timings are unreliable and the buses are crowded and uncomfortable. The bus journey between Kathmandu or Pokhara and the border takes about 11-12 hours. Tourist minibuses are the only moderately comfortable option. To **Darjeeling via Kakarbhitta**; Kakarbhitta is on the Nepalese side of a wide river which forms the border between India and Nepal. A kilometre-long road bridge links it to the Indian town of Raniganj on the east bank. Cycle rickshaws run between the two. The larger Indian town of Bagdogra is 15 km away. For details see under Siliguri, page 307.

# Transport in the Indian Himalaya

## Air

India has a comprehensive network linking the major cities of the different states. Deregulation of the airline industry has had a transformative effect on travel within India, with a host of low-budget private carriers offering sometimes unbelievably cheap fares on an ever-expanding network of routes in a bid to woo the train-travelling middle class. On any given day, booking a few days in advance, you can expect to fly between Delhi and Kolkata for around US$100 one way including taxes, while a month's notice and flying with a no-frills airline can reduce the price to US$50-70. Although flying is comparatively expensive, for covering vast distances or awkward links on a route it is an option worth considering. For shorter distances and on routes where you can sleep during an overnight journey (eg Delhi–Amritsar) it makes more sense to travel by train.

The best way to get an idea of the current routes, carriers and fares is to use a third-party booking website such as **www.makemytrip.com** or **www.yatra.com**. Tickets booked on these sites are typically issued as an email ticket, which you will need to print out in order to show a paper ticket at the airport to be allowed into the terminal.

Be prepared for delays, especially during the winter. Nearly all northern routes originate in Delhi where from early December to February smog has become a common morning hazard, sometimes delaying departures by several hours. The same problem is common in Kolkata.

### Domestic airlines

The following airlines were well established at the time of writing, though the pace of change is rapid:

**Air India**, www.air-india.com, is the nationalized carrier with a wide network of domestic routes.

**Indigo**, T099-1038 3838, www.goindigo.in. Comparable to **SpiceJet**.

**Jet Airways**, T1800-225522, T011-3989 3333, www.jetairways.com. The longest-established of the private airlines, offering full-service domestic flights.

**Jetlite**, www.jetlite.com. Comprehensive coverage of the country.

**SpiceJet**, T1800-180 3333, www.spicejet.com. No-frills service between major cities.

## Rail

Trains can still be the cheapest and most comfortable means of travelling long distances saving you hotel expenses on overnight journeys. It gives access to booking station Retiring Rooms, which can be useful from time to time. Above all, you have an ideal opportunity to meet local travellers and catch a glimpse of life on the ground. For schedules and availability see www.indianrail.gov.in and www.erail.in.

There are several air-conditioned 'high-speed' *Shatabdi* (or 'Century') *Express* for day travel, and *Rajdhani Express* ('Capital City') for overnight journeys. These cover large sections of the network but due to high demand you need to book them well in advance (up to 90 days). Meals and drinks are usually included.

For rail enthusiasts, the steam-hauled narrow-gauge train between Ghoom and Darjeeling in North Bengal (a World Heritage Site) is an attraction. Currently the diesel narrow-gauge line is only running between Kurseong and Darjeeling, rather than the full route from Siliguri.

**Classes** **A/c First Class**, available only on main routes, is very comfortable with two- or four-berth carpeted sleeper compartments with washbasin. As with all air-conditioned sleeper accommodation, bedding is included, and the windows are tinted to the point of being almost impossible to see through.

**A/c Sleeper**, two and three-tier configurations (known as 2AC and 3AC), are clean and comfortable and good value. **A/c Executive Class**, with wide reclining seats, is available on many *Shatabdi* trains at double the price of the ordinary **a/c Chair Car** which is equally comfortable. **First Class (non-a/c)** is gradually being phased out (now rather run down but still pleasant if you like open windows). **Sleeper Class** provides basic upholstered seats and is a 'Reserved' class though tickets are sometimes 'subject to available accommodation'. **Second Class** (non-a/c), two and three-tier (commonly called Sleeper), provides exceptionally cheap and atmospheric travel but can be crowded and uncomfortable, and toilet facilities can be unpleasant; it is nearly always better to use the Indian-style squat loos rather than the Western-style ones as they are better maintained. At the bottom rung is **Unreserved Second Class**, with hard wooden benches. You can travel long distances for a trivial amount of money, but unreserved carriages are often ridiculously crowded, and getting off at your station may involve a battle of will and strength against the hordes trying to shove their way on.

## Indrail passes
These allow travel across the network without having to pay extra reservation fees and sleeper charges but you have to spend a high proportion of your time on the train to make it worthwhile. However, the advantages of pre-arranged reservations and automatic access to 'Tourist Quotas' can tip the balance in favour of the pass for some travellers. Tourists (foreigners and Indians resident abroad) may buy these passes from the tourist sections of principal railway booking offices and pay in foreign currency or by major credit card. Fares range from US$57 to US$1060 for adults or around half that for children. Rail-cum-air tickets are also to be made available. Indrail passes can also conveniently be bought abroad from special agents. For people contemplating a single long journey soon after arriving in India, the half- or one-day pass with a confirmed reservation is worth the peace of mind; two- or four-day passes are also sold. The UK agent is **SD Enterprises Ltd** ① *103 Wembley Park Drive, Wembley, Middlesex, HA9 8HG, UK, T020-8200 9549, www.indiarail.co.uk*. They make all necessary reservations and offer excellent advice.

## Cost
A/c First Class costs about double the rate for two-tier, and non a/c Second Class about half. Children (5-12) travel at half the adult fare. The young (12-30 years) and senior citizens (65 years and over) are allowed a 30% discount on journeys over 500 km (just show your passport). Fares for individual journeys are based on distance covered and reflect both the class and the type of train. Higher rates apply on the Mail and Express trains and the air-conditioned *Shatabdi* and *Rajdhani Expresses*.

## Rail travel tips
**Bedding** It can get cold in air-conditioned coaches when travelling at night. Bedding is provide on second class air-conditioned sleepers. On others it can be hired for Rs 30 from the station baggage office for second class.

**Berths** It is worth asking for upper berths, especially in second class three-tier sleepers, as they can also be used during the day when the lower berths are used as seats. Once the middle berth is lowered for sleeping the lower berth becomes too cramped to sit on.

**Delays** Always allow plenty of time for booking and for making connections. Delays are common on all types of transport. The special *Shatabdi* and *Rajdhani Express* are generally quite reliable. Ordinary Express and Mail trains have priority over local services and occasionally surprise by being punctual, but generally the longer the journey time, the greater the delay. Delays on the rail network are cumulative, so arrivals and departures from mid-stations are often several hours behind schedule. Allow at least two hours for connections, more if the first part of the journey is long distance.

**Food and drink** It is best to carry some, though tea, bottled water and snacks are sold on the platforms (through the windows). Carry plenty of small notes on long journeys. Rs 100 notes can be difficult to change when purchasing small items. On long-distance trains, the restaurant car is often near the upper-class carriages (bogies).

**Internet services** Much information is now available online via the websites **www.erail.in**, **www.indianrail.gov.in** and **www.trainenquiry.com**, where you can check timetables, numbers, seat availability and even the running status of your train. Internet tickets can theoretically be bought on **www.irctc.co.in**, though a credit card is required; foreign cards are accepted, but persistence is needed with the website when registering. An alternative is to seek out a local agent who can sell e-tickets, which can cost as little as Rs 50, and can save hours of hassle; simply present the printout to the ticket collector.

**Left luggage** Bags can be left for up to 30 days in station cloakrooms. These are especially useful when there is time to go sightseeing before an evening train. The bags must be lockable and you are advised not to leave any food in them (rats!).

**Ladies' compartments** A woman travelling alone, overnight, on an unreserved second class train can ask if there is one of these. Lone female travellers may feel more comfortable in air-conditioned sleeper coaches, which require reservations and are used extensively by Indian families.

**Ladies' and seniors' queues** Separate (much shorter) ticket queues may be available for women and senior citizens. Travellers over 60 can ask for a 30% discount on the ticket price.

**Overbooking** Passengers with valid tickets but no berth reservations are sometimes permitted to travel overnight, causing great discomfort to travellers occupying lower berths. Wait-listed passengers should confirm the status of their ticket in advance by calling enquiries at the nearest computerized reservation office. At the station, check the reservation charts (usually on the relevant platform) and contact the station manager or ticket collector.

**Porters** These can carry prodigious amounts of luggage. Rates vary from station to station (usually listed on a board on the platform).

**Pre-paid taxis** Many main stations have a pre-paid taxi (and auto-rickshaw) service, which offers a reliable service at a fair price. Search these out on arrival, they can save you from nasty disagreements.

**Security** Keep valuables close to you, securely locked, and away from windows. For security, carry a good lock and chain to attach your luggage.

**Tickets and reservations** It is now possible to reserve tickets for virtually any train on the network from one of the 1000 computerized reservation centres across India. It is always best to book as far in advance as possible (usually up to 60 days). To reserve a seat on a particular train, note down the train's name, number and departure time and fill in a reservation form while you line up at the ticket window; you can use one form for up to four passengers. At busy stations the wait can take an hour or more. You can save a lot of time and effort by asking a travel agent to get your tickets for a fee of Rs 50-100. If the class you want is full, ask if special 'quotas' are available under any of Indian Rail's special quotas. Foreign Tourist Quota reserves a small number of tickets on popular routes for overseas travellers; you need your passport. The other useful special quota is Tatkal, which releases a last-minute pool of tickets at 1000 on the day before the train departs. If the quota system can't help you, consider buying a 'wait list' ticket, as seats often become available close to the train's departure time; phone the station on the day of departure to check your ticket's status. If you don't have a reservation for a particular train but carry an Indrail Pass, you may get one by arriving three hours early. Be wary of touts at the station offering tickets, hotels or exchange.

**Timetables** Regional timetables are available cheaply from station bookstalls. The handy *Trains at a Glance* (Rs 30) lists popular trains likely to be used by most foreign travellers and is available at stalls at Indian railway stations.

## Road

Road travel is sometimes the only choice for reaching many of the places of outstanding interest, particularly national parks or isolated tourist sites. In the absence of trains, buses are often the only budget option into the Himalaya. For the uninitiated, travel by road can also be a worrying experience because of the apparent absence of conventional traffic regulations. Vehicles drive on the left – in theory. Routes around the major cities are usually crowded with lorry traffic, especially at night, and the main roads are often poor and slow. There are a few motorway-style expressways, but most main roads are single track. Some district roads are quiet, and although they are not fast they can be a good way of seeing the country and village life if you have the time.

**Bus** Services are run by the State Corporation from the State Bus Stand (and private companies which often have offices nearby). The latter allow advance reservations, including booking printable e-tickets online (check www.redbus.in) and, although tickets prices are a little higher, they have fewer stops and are a bit more comfortable. There are also sleeper buses (a contradiction in terms) – if you must take a sleeper bus, choose a lower berth near the front of the bus. The upper berths are almost always really uncomfortable on bumpy roads.

**Bus categories** Though comfortable for sightseeing trips, apart from the very best 'sleeper coaches' even **air-conditioned luxury coaches** can be very uncomfortable for really long journeys. Often the air conditioning is very cold so wrap up. Journeys over 10 hours can be extremely tiring so it is better to go by train if there is a choice. **Express buses** run over long distances (frequently overnight), these are often called 'video coaches' and can be an appalling experience unless you appreciate loud film music blasting through the night. Ear plugs and eye masks may ease the pain. They rarely average more than 45 km per hour. **Local buses** are often very crowded, quite bumpy, slow and usually poorly maintained. However, over short distances, they can be a very cheap, friendly and easy way of getting about. Even where signboards are not in English someone will usually give you directions. Many larger towns have **minibus** services, which charge a little more than the buses and pick up and drop passengers on request. Again very crowded, and with restricted headroom, they are the fastest way of getting about many of the larger towns.

**Bus travel tips** Some towns have different bus stations for different destinations. Booking on major long-distance routes is now computerized. Book in advance where possible and avoid the back of the bus where it can be very bumpy. If your destination is served only by a local bus you may do better to take the Express bus and 'persuade' the driver, with a tip in advance, to stop where you want to get off. You will have to pay the full fare to the first stop beyond your destination but you will get there faster and more comfortably. When an unreserved bus pulls into a bus station, there is usually an unholy scramble for seats, whilst those arriving have to struggle to get off. In many areas there is an unwritten 'rule of reservation' using handkerchiefs or bags thrust through the windows to reserve seats. Some visitors may feel a more justified right to a seat having fought their way through the crowd, but it is generally best to do as local people do and be prepared with a handkerchief or sarong. As soon as it touches the seat, it is yours! Leave it on your seat when getting off to use the toilet at bus stations.

**Car** A car provides a chance to travel off the beaten track, and gives unrivalled opportunities for seeing something of India's great variety of villages and small towns. Until recently, the most widely used hire car was the Hindustan Ambassador. However, except for the newest model, they are often very unreliable, and although they still have their devotees, many find them uncomfortable for long journeys. Ambassadors are gradually giving way to more efficient (and boring) Tata and Toyota models with mod-cons like optional air-conditioning and seat belts. A handful of international agencies offer self-drive car hire (Avis, Sixt), but India's majestically anarchic traffic culture is not for the faint-hearted.

**Car hire** Hiring a car and driver is the most comfortable and efficient way to cover short to medium distances, and although prices have increased sharply in recent years car travel in India is still a bargain by western standards. A car shared by three or four can be very good value. Even if you're travelling on a modest budget a day's car hire can help take the sting out of an arduous journey, allowing you to go sightseeing along the way without looking for somewhere to stash your bags. Local drivers often know their way around an area much better than drivers from other states, so where possible it is a good idea to get a local driver who speaks the state language, in addition to being able to communicate with you. The best way to guarantee a driver who speaks good English is to book in advance with a professional travel agency, either in India or in your home country. You can, if you choose, arrange car hire informally by asking around at taxi stands, but don't expect your driver to speak anything more than rudimentary English.

On pre-arranged overnight trips the fee you pay will normally include fuel and interstate taxes – check before you pay – and a wage for the driver. Drivers are responsible for their expenses, including meals (and the pervasive servant-master culture in India means that most will choose to sit separately from you at meal times). Some tourist hotels provide rooms for drivers, but they often choose to sleep in the car overnight to save money. In some areas drivers also seek to increase their earnings by taking you to hotels and shops where they earn a handsome commission; these are generally hugely overpriced and poor alternatives to the hotels recommended in this book, so don't be afraid to say no and insist on your choice of accommodation. If you feel inclined, a tip at the end of the tour of Rs 100 per day is perfectly acceptable. Be sure to check carefully the mileage at the beginning and end of the trip.

|  | Tata Indica non-a/c | Tata Indigo non-a/c | Hyundai Accent a/c | Toyota Innova |
|---|---|---|---|---|
| 8 hrs/80 km | Rs 1200 | Rs 1600 | Rs 2200 | Rs 2500 |
| Extra km | Rs 8 | Rs 10 | Rs 15 | Rs 15 |
| Extra hour | Rs 80 | Rs 100 | Rs 200 | Rs 180 |
| **Out of town** | | | | |
| Per km | Rs 8 | Rs 10 | Rs 15 | Rs 15 |
| Night halt | Rs 200 | Rs 200 | Rs 300 | Rs 250 |

## Taxi

Taxi travel in India is a great bargain, and in most cities you can take a taxi from the airport to the centre for under US$10. Yellow-top taxis in cities and large towns are metered, although tariffs change frequently. Increased night-time rates rates apply in some cities, but there should not be any extra charge for luggage. Insist on the taxi meter being flagged in your presence. If the driver refuses, the official advice is to contact the police. This may not work, but it is worth trying. When a taxi doesn't have a meter, you will need to fix the fare before starting the journey. Ask at your hotel desk for a guide price.

At stations and airports it is often possible to share taxis to a central point. It is worth looking for fellow passengers who may be travelling in your direction and get a pre-paid taxi. At night, always have a clear idea of where you want to go and insist on being taken there. Taxi drivers may try to convince you that the hotel you have chosen 'closed three years ago' or is 'completely full'. Say that you have a reservation.

## Rickshaw

**Auto-rickshaws** (autos) are almost universally available in towns across India and are the cheapest and most convenient way of getting about. It is best to walk a short distance away from a hotel gate before picking up an auto to avoid paying an inflated rate. In addition to using them for short journeys it is often possible to hire them by the hour, or for a half or full day's sightseeing. In some areas younger drivers who speak some English and know their local area well may want to show you around. However, rickshaw drivers are often paid a commission by hotels, restaurants and gift shops so advice is not always impartial. Drivers often refuse to use a meter, sometimes quote a ridiculous price. Tariffs are shown on a fare chart which should be read in conjunction with the kilometre reading shown on the meter.

**Cycle-rickshaws** and **horse-drawn tongas** are more common in the more rustic setting of a small town or the outskirts of a large one. You will need to fix a price by bargaining. The animal attached to a tonga usually looks too undernourished to have the strength to pull the driver, let alone passengers.

Kolkata holds the dubious honour of being the only city in the world where **hand-pulled rickshaws** remain an essential means of transport; in the monsoon, they are often the only vehicles that can get through the flooded streets. The government periodically tries to ban them, but until another form of employment can be found for 18,000 men, they are likely to remain. Always agree a price before getting on board and expect a very bumpy ride.

## Cycling

Cycling is an excellent way of seeing the quiet byways of India. It is easy to hire bikes in most small towns for about Rs 50 per day. Indian bikes are heavy and without gears, but on the flat they offer a good way of exploring comparatively short distances outside towns. In the more prosperous tourist resorts, mountain bikes are now becoming available, but at a higher charge. It is also quite possible to tour more extensively by bike, for which you may want to buy a cycle.

There are shops in every town and the local Hero brand is considered the best, with Atlas and BSA good alternatives; expect to pay around Rs 1200-1500 for a second-hand Indian bike but remember to bargain. At the end of your trip you could sell it easily at half price. Imported bikes have lighter weight and gears, but are more difficult to get repaired and carry the much greater risk of being stolen or damaged. If you wish to take your own, it is quite easy if you dismantle it and pack it in its original shipping carton; be sure to take all essential spares including a pump. It is possible to get Indian spares for 26" wheel cycles. All cyclists should take bungy cords (to strap down a backpack) and good lights from home, although cycling at night is not recommended; take care not to leave your bike parked anywhere with your belongings. Bike repair shops are universal and charges are nominal.

It is possible to cover 50-80 km a day quite comfortably. One cyclist reported that the national highways are manic but country roads, especially along the coast, can be idyllic, if rather dusty and bumpy. You can even put your bike on a boat for a backwater trip or on top of a bus. If you want to take your bike on the train, allow plenty of time for booking it in on the brake van at the parcels office and for filling in forms.

It is best to start a journey early in the morning, stopping at midday and then resuming your journey in the late afternoon. Night riding, though cooler, can be hazardous because of lack of lighting and poor road surfaces. Try to avoid major highways as far as possible. Fortunately foreign cyclists are usually greeted with cheers, waves and smiles and truck drivers are sometimes happy to give lifts to cyclists (and their bikes). This is a good way of taking some of the hardship out of cycling round India.

## Motorcycling

This is a particularly attractive way of getting around. It is easy to buy new Indian-made motorcycles including the 350cc Enfield Bullet and several 100cc Japanese models, including Suzukis and Hondas made in collaboration with Indian firms; Indian Rajdoots are less expensive but have a poor reputation for reliability. Buying new at a fixed price ensures greater ease and reliability. Buying second hand in rupees takes more time but is quite possible (expect to get a 30-40% discount) and repairs are usually easy to arrange and quite cheap. You can get a broker to help with the paperwork involved (certificate of ownership, insurance, etc) for a fee (see also Insurance, page 33). They charge about Rs 5000 for a No Objection Certificate (NOC), essential for reselling; it's easier to have the bike in your name. Bring your own helmet and an international driving permit. Vespa, Kinetic Honda and other makes of scooters in India are slower than motorbikes but comfortable for short hauls of less than 100 km and have the advantage of a 'dicky' (small, lockable box) for spares, and a spare tyre.

## Hitchhiking

Hitchhiking is uncommon, partly because public transport is so cheap. If you try, you are likely to spend a very long time on the roadside. However, getting lifts in vehicles and trucks in areas with little public transport (such as Ladakh) is more likely, whilst those riding motorbikes or scooters in tourist areas can be expected to pick up the occasional hitchhiking policeman! It is not recommended for women on their own.

## Maps

For anyone interested in the geography of India, or even simply getting around, trying to buy good maps is a depressing experience. For security reasons it is illegal to sell large-scale maps of areas within 80 km of the coast or national borders, and it is illegal to export any large-scale maps.

The **Bartholomew** 1:4 m map sheet of India is the most authoritative, detailed and easy-to-use map available. It can be bought worldwide. **GeoCenter World Map** 1:2 m, covers India in three regional sections and is clearly printed. **Nelles'** regional maps of India at the scale of 1:1.5 m offer generally clear route maps, though neither the road classifications nor alignments are wholly reliable.

State and town plans are published by the **TTK Company**. These are often the best available though they are not wholly reliable. For the larger cities they provide the most compact yet clear map sheets (generally 50 cm by 75 cm format).

The **Survey of India** publishes large-scale 1:10,000 town plans of approximately 70 cities. These detailed plans are the only surveyed town maps in India, and some are over 30 years old. The Survey also has topographic maps at the scale of 1:25,000 and 1:50,000 in addition to its 1:250,000 scale coverage, some of which are as recent as the late 1980s. However, maps are regarded as highly sensitive and it is possible to buy these only from main agents of the Survey of India.

**Stanfords** ① *12-14 Long Acre, London, WC2, T020-7836 1321, www.stanfords.co.uk*, offers a mail order service.

# Where to stay in the Indian Himalaya

India has an enormous range of accommodation. You can stay safely and very cheaply by Western standards right across the country. In all the major cities there are also high-quality hotels, offering a full range of facilities; in small centres hotels are much more variable. In Kashmir and Sikkim, old Maharajas' palaces have been converted into comfortable, unusual hotels. At the top end, alongside international chains, India boasts several home-grown hotel chains, best of which are the exceptional heritage and palace hotels operated by the Taj group.

In the peak season (October to April) bookings can be extremely heavy in popular destinations. It is sometimes possible to book in advance by phone, fax or email, but double check your reservation, and always try to arrive as early as possible in the day.

**Hotels →** *For hotel price codes, see box, opposite.*
**Price categories** The category codes used in this book are based on prices of double rooms excluding taxes. They are **not** star ratings and individual facilities vary considerably. The most expensive hotels charge in US dollars only. Expect to pay more in Delhi and, to a lesser extent, in Kolkata for all categories. Prices away from large cities tend to be lower for comparable hotels.

**Off-season rates** Large reductions are made by hotels in all categories out-of-season in many resorts. Always ask if any is available. You may also request the 10-15% agent's commission to be deducted from your bill if you book direct. Clarify whether the agreed figure includes all taxes.

**Taxes** In general most hotel rooms rated at Rs 3000 or above are subject to a tax of 10%. Many states levy an additional luxury tax of between 10 and 25%, and some hotels add a service charge of 10% on top of this. Taxes are not necessarily payable on meals, so it is worth settling your meals bill separately. Most hotels in the $$ category and above accept payment by credit card. Check your final bill carefully. Visitors have complained of incorrect bills, even in the most expensive hotels. The problem particularly afflicts groups, when last-minute extras appear mysteriously on some guests' bills. Check the evening before departure, and keep all receipts.

**Hotel facilities** You have to be prepared for difficulties which are uncommon in the West. It is best to inspect the room and check that all equipment (air conditioning, TV, water heater, flush) works before checking in at a budget hotel. Many hotels try to wring too many years' service out of their linen, and it's quite common to find sheets that are stained, frayed or riddled with holes. Don't expect any but the most expensive or tourist-savvy hotels to fit a top sheet to the bed. Modest hotels may not have their own **restaurant** but will often offer 'room service', bringing in food from outside. In temple towns, restaurants may only serve vegetarian food. Many hotels operate a 24-hour **checkout** system. Make sure that this means that you can stay 24 hours from the time of check-in.

In some states **power cuts** are common, or hot water may be restricted to certain times of day. The largest hotels have their own generators but it is best to carry a good torch.

In some areas **water supply** is rationed periodically. Keep a bucket filled to use for flushing the toilet during water cuts. Occasionally, tap water may be discoloured due to

## Price codes

**Where to stay**

| | | | |
|---|---|---|---|
| $$$$ | over US$150 | $$$ | US$66-150 |
| $$ | US$30-65 | $ | under US$30 |

Unless otherwise stated, prices are for two people sharing a room in the high season, including taxes and service charges.

**Restaurants**

| | | | | | |
|---|---|---|---|---|---|
| $$$ | over US$12 | $$ | US$6-12 | $ | under US$6 |

Prices refer to the cost of a meal for one person with a drink, not including service charge.

rusty tanks. During the cold weather and in hill stations, hot water will be available at certain times of the day, sometimes in buckets, but is usually very restricted in quantity. Electric water heaters may provide enough for a shower but not enough to fill a bath tub. For details on drinking water, see page 25.

At some times of the year and in some places **mosquitoes** can be a real problem, and not all hotels have mosquito-proof rooms or mosquito nets. If you have any doubts check before confirming your room booking. In cheap hotels you need to be prepared for the presence of flies, cockroaches, spiders, ants and geckos (harmless house lizards). Poisonous insects and scorpions are extremely rare in towns. Hotel managements are nearly always prepared with insecticide sprays. Remember to shut windows and doors at dusk. Electrical mats and pellets are now widely available, as are mosquito coils that burn slowly. Dusk and early evening are the worst times for mosquitoes so trousers and long-sleeved shirts are advisable, especially outdoors.

Hotels close to temples can be very **noisy**, especially during festivals. Music blares from loudspeakers late at night and from very early in the morning, often making sleep impossible. Mosques call the faithful to prayers at dawn. Earplugs are invaluable.

Some hotels offer 24-hour checkout, meaning you can keep the room a full 24 hours from the time you arrive – a great option if you arrive in the afternoon and want to spend the morning sightseeing.

Hotels in hill stations often supply **wood fires** in rooms. Usually there is plenty of ventilation, but ensure that there is always good air circulation, especially when charcoal fires are provided in a basket.

Where staff training is lacking, the person who brings up your cases may proceed to show you light switches, room facilities, TV tuning, and hang around waiting for a **tip**. Room boys may enter your room without knocking or without waiting for a response to a knock. Both for security and privacy, it is a good idea to lock your door when you are in the room. At the higher end, you should expect to tip bellboys a little for every favour.

## Tourist 'bungalows'

The different state tourism development corporations run their own hotels and hostels, which are often in places of special interest. These are very reasonably priced, though they may be rather dated, restaurant menus may be limited and service is often slow.

## Railway retiring rooms
Railway stations often have 'Retiring Rooms' or 'Rest Rooms' which may be hired for periods of between one and 24 hours by anyone holding an onward train ticket. They are cheap and simple though often heavily booked.

## Government resthouses
Resthouses may be available for overnight stays, especially in remote areas. They are usually very basic, with a caretaker who can sometimes provide a simple meal, with notice. Check the room rate in advance as foreigners can be overcharged. Government officials always take precedence, even over guests who have booked.

## Indian-style hotels
These, catering for Indian businessmen, are springing up fast in or on the outskirts of many small- and medium-sized towns. Most have some air-conditioned rooms and attached showers. They are variable in quality but it is increasingly possible to find excellent value accommodation even in remote areas.

## Hostels
The Department of Tourism runs 16 youth hostels, each with about 50 beds, usually organized into dormitory accommodation. The YHA also have a few sites all over India. Travellers may also stay in religious hostels (*dharamshalas*) for up to three days. These are primarily intended for pilgrims and are sometimes free, though voluntary offerings are welcome. Usually only vegetarian food is permitted; smoking and alcohol are not.

## Homestays
At the upmarket end, increasing numbers of travellers are keen to stay in private homes and guesthouses, opting not to book large hotel chains that keep you at arm's length from a culture. Instead, travellers get home-cooked meals in heritage houses and learn about a country through conversation with often fascinating hosts. Delhi has many new and smart family-run B&Bs springing up. Tourist offices have lists of families with more modest homestays. Companies specializing in homestays include **Home & Hospitality** ① *www.homeandhospitality.co.uk* and **Sundale Vacations** ① *www.sundale.com*.

## Camping
Mid-price hotels with large grounds are sometimes willing to allow camping. Regional tourist offices have details of new developments. For information on YMCA camping facilities contact: **YMCA**, The National General Secretary, National Council of YMCAs of India, PB No 14, Massey Hall, Jai Singh Rd, New Delhi 1.

# Food and drink in the Indian Himalaya

**Food** → *See box, page 23, for restaurants price codes. For a glossary of food and drink, see page 440.*

You find just as much variety in dishes and presentation crossing India as you would on an equivalent journey across Europe. Different combinations of spices give each region its distinctive flavour. The food in Himachal Pradesh for example is mildly spiced and flavoured with yoghurt in many dishes.

The larger hotels, open to non-residents, often offer **buffet** lunches with Indian, Western and sometimes Chinese dishes. These can be good value (Rs 400-500; but Rs 1000 in the top grades) and can provide a welcome, comfortable break in the cool. The health risks, however, of food kept warm for long periods in metal containers are considerable, especially if turnover at the buffet is slow. We have received several complaints of stomach trouble following a buffet meal, even in five-star hotels.

It is essential to be very careful since food hygiene may be poor, flies abound and refrigeration in the hot weather may be inadequate and intermittent because of power cuts. It is best to eat only freshly prepared food by ordering from the menu (especially meat and fish dishes). Avoid salads and cut fruit, unless the menu advertises that they have been washed in mineral water.

If you are unused to spicy food, go slow! Stick to Western or mild Chinese meals in good restaurants and try the odd Indian dish to test your reaction. Popular local restaurants are obvious from the number of people eating in them. Try a traditional *thali*, which is several preparations, placed in small bowls, surrounding the central serving of wholewheat chapati and rice. A vegetarian *thali* would include *dhal* (lentils), two or three curries (which can be quite hot) and crisp poppadums, although there are regional variations. A variety of pickles are offered – mango and lime are two of the most popular. These can be exceptionally hot, and are designed to be taken in minute quantities alongside the main dishes. Plain *dahi* (yoghurt) or *raita* usually acts as a bland 'cooler'.

Many city restaurants and backpacker eateries offer a choice of so-called **European options** such as toasted sandwiches, pancakes, apple pies, fruit crumbles and cheesecakes. Italian favourites (pizzas, pastas) can be very different from what you are used to. Western confectionery, in general, is disappointing. **Ice creams**, on the other hand, can be exceptionally good; there are excellent Indian ones as well as some international brands.

India has many delicious tropical **fruits**. Some are seasonal (eg mangoes, pineapples and lychees), while others (eg bananas, grapes and oranges) are available throughout the year. It is safe to eat the ones you can wash and peel.

## Drink

**Drinking water** used to be regarded as one of India's biggest hazards. It is still true that water from the tap or a well should never be considered safe to drink since public water supplies are often polluted. Bottled water is now widely available although not all bottled water is mineral water; most is simply purified water from an urban supply. Buy from a shop or stall, check the seal carefully (some companies now add a second clear plastic seal around the bottle top) and avoid street hawkers; when disposing of bottles puncture the neck, which prevents misuse but allows recycling for storage. There is growing concern over the mountains of plastic bottles that are collecting and the waste of resources needed to produce them, so travellers are encouraged to use alternative methods of getting safe drinking water. It is strongly suggested you take your own reusable, steel water bottle and fill it up at the numerous restaurants and hotels that provide filtered water, or you may wish to purify water yourself. Always carry enough drinking water with you when travelling. It is important to use purified water for cleaning your teeth.

**Tea** and **coffee** are safe and widely available. Both are normally served sweet, and with milk. If you wish, say 'no sugar' (*chini nahin*), 'no milk' (*dudh nahin*) when ordering. Alternatively, ask for a pot of tea and milk and sugar to be brought separately. Freshly brewed coffee is a common drink in South India, but in the North, ordinary city restaurants will usually serve the instant variety. Even in aspiring smart cafés, espresso or cappuccino may not turn out quite as you'd expect in the West.

Bottled **soft drinks** such as Coke, Pepsi, Limca and Thums Up are universally available but always check the seal when you buy from a street stall. There are also several brands of fruit juice sold in cartons, including mango, pineapple and apple. Don't add ice cubes as the water source may be contaminated. Take care with fresh fruit juices or *lassis* as ice is often added.

Indians rarely drink **alcohol** with a meal, water being on hand. In the past wines and spirits were generally either imported and extremely expensive, or local and of poor quality. Now, the best Indian whisky, rum and brandy (IMFL or 'Indian Made Foreign Liquor') are widely accepted, as are good wines from Maharashtra. If you hanker after a bottle of imported wine, you will find it only in the top restaurants or specialist liquor stores and have to pay at least Rs 1000-1500.

For the urban elite, refreshing Indian beers are popular when eating out and so are widely available. 'Pubs' have sprung up in the major cities. Elsewhere, seedy, all-male drinking dens in the larger cities are best avoided by women travellers, but can make quite an experience otherwise – you will sometimes be locked into cubicles for clandestine drinking. If that sounds unsavoury then head for the better hotel bars instead; prices aren't that steep. In rural India, local rice, palm, cashew or date juice *toddy* and *arak* is deceptively potent, and the Sikkimese *chhang* makes a pleasant change, drunk out of a wooden tankard through a bamboo straw.

Most states have alcohol-free dry days or enforce degrees of prohibition. Some upmarket restaurants may serve beer even if it's not listed, so it's worth asking.

# Festivals in the Indian Himalaya

The Himalaya host an extraordinary wealth of festivals every year, many specific to a particular state or community or even a particular temple. The biggest festival of all, and the largest gathering of humanity on the planet, is the **Kumbh Mela**, which draws millions of pilgrims to four holy sites in India in a rotation system. One of these sites is Haridwar in Uttarakhand, where the Ardha (half) Kumbh Mela will be held in 2016. The last Maha (great) Kumbh Mela (which occurs every 144 years) was in Allahabad, in Uttar Pradesh, in 2013.

Festivals tend to fall on different dates each year depending on the Hindu lunar calendar, so check with the tourist office. Some major festivals are given below; details of these and others appear under the particular state or town.

A few count as national holidays: **Republic Day** (26 January); **Independence Day** (15 August); **Mahatma Gandhi's Birthday** (2 October); and **Christmas Day** (25 December). 1 January (when following the Gregorian calendar) is accepted officially as **New Year's Day**, but there are regional variations that fall on different dates, often coinciding with spring/harvest time, such as **Naba Barsha** in Bengal (14 April) and **Rongali Bihu** in Assam (mid-April). **Makar Sankranti** always falls on 14 January and is highly auspicious in Bengal, when the huge **Gangasagar Mela** sees the gathering of pilgrims at the mouth of the Ganga to mark the end of winter. During the spring festival of **Vasant Panchami** (January/February) people wear bright yellow clothes to herald the advent of the season with singing, dancing and feasting. In Bengal this festival is commonly called **Saraswati Puja**, as the goddess of learning is worshipped, and it is a state holiday.

**Maha Sivaratri** (February/March) marks the night when Siva danced his celestial dance of destruction; it is celebrated with feasting and fairs at Siva temples, but preceded by a night of devotional readings and hymn singing. Varanasi sees Siva devotees collect en masse, when the ghats become a camping ground for *sadhus*, *naga babas* and their followers. A good place to experience Sivaratri is Rishikesh.

**Holi**, the festival of colours, occurs at the end of February or the start of March and is particularly vibrant in North India. On the first night, bonfires are lit symbolizing the end of winter (and conquering of evil). People have fun throwing coloured powder and water at each other and in the evening some gamble with friends. If you don't mind getting covered in colours you can risk going out, but celebrations can sometimes get very rowdy (and unpleasant, especially for lone women) in urban areas, even though alcohol is not for sale during the festival.

**Buddha Jayanti**, the first full moon night in April/May, marks the birth of the Buddha, and Bodh Gaya attracts pilgrims from all over the world to celebrate in its temples. There are also celebrations in Mcleod Ganj in Himachal Pradesh.

The September/October festival of **Dasara** has many local variations. The **Kullu Dasara** in particular attracts spectators from all over the country and abroad; throughout summer over 300 village idols have paid loud and colourful visits to one another, born aloft on volunteers' shoulders and accompanied by trumpets, drums, holy men and elders. The final festival in October brings all of them together for a raucous festival lasting several days.

In North India, celebrations for the nine nights (*navaratri*) are marked with **Ramlila**, various episodes of the Ramayana story (see page 411) being enacted with particular reference to the battle between the forces of good and evil.

In Kolkata, the focus is on Durga's victory over the demon Mahishasura and **Durga puja** is celebrated in a massive way, with huge *pandals* erected in public spaces, often themed to reflect current events or mimic world monuments, containing images of the goddess, her consorts and her enemies.

The Goddess Lakshmi is venerated all over India with **Diwali/Deepavali**, the festival of lights, which falls on the dark *chaturdasi* (14th) night (the one preceding the new moon) in October/November, when rows of lamps or candles are lit in remembrance and *rangolis* are painted on the floor as a sign of welcome. Fireworks have become an integral part of the celebrations, often set off days before Diwali. In Bengal, **Kali Puja** is celebrated the day before Diwali but is a distinct festival.

**Christmas Day** sees Indian Christians celebrate the birth of Christ in much the same way as in the West; many churches hold midnight masses and decorations go up.

In the Northwest, Ladakh in particular hosts spectacular **Buddhist festivals**, many during winter but some during the short period of the year when the passes are open (July-October). Of these the tourism department's **Ladakh Festival**, in and around Leh at the beginning of September, is the most accessible, and provides an opportunity to watch archery, polo and masked dances, plus an insight into Ladakhi costume, music and culture.

Religious festivals occur all year round, often at varying times, and those at the *gompas* (monasteries) of **Hemis** (June), **Lamayaru** (July) and **Karsha** (July) celebrating the triumph of good over evil are a feast of colour, with whirling priests and elaborately painted *thankas*, the intricate Buddhist paintings for which the region is famous. Every three years (the next is 2016) an enormous *thanka* is ceremoniously unveiled at Phyang Monastery during the **Phyang Tsedup festival** (July), attracting many pilgrims.

Meanwhile in Himachal Pradesh, Dharamshala enthusiastically celebrates the **Dalai Lama's birthday** on 6 July with special seminars, musical performances, feasts and temple services, and the mountains reverberate with the emotive sound of Tibetan horns and drums. There is also a **Shoton Opera** (*llamo*) festival in March, and at the Tibetan Institute for Performing Arts you can catch regular traditional events throughout the year aimed at keeping the culture alive in exile.

**Losar**, the Tibetan New Year, is celebrated widely at Buddhist centres throughout the region during the first three days of the first lunar month of the year.

### Muslim holy days

These are fixed according to the lunar calendar. According to the Gregorian calendar, they tend to fall 11 days earlier each year, depending on the sighting of the new moon. **Ramadan** (28 June-27 July 2014, 18 June-16 July 2015, 6 June-5 July 2016) is the start of the month of fasting when all Muslims (except young children, the very elderly, the sick, pregnant women and travellers) must abstain from food and drink from sunrise to sunset. **Id-ul-Fitr**, with much gift-giving, is the three-day festival that marks the end of Ramadan. **Id-ul-Zuha/Bakr-Id** (4 October 2014, 23 September 2015) is when Muslims commemorate Ibrahim's sacrifice of his son according to God's commandment; this is the main time of pilgrimage to Mecca (the Hajj). It is marked by the sacrifice of a goat, feasting and alms giving. **Muharram** is when the killing of the Prophet's grandson, Hussain, is commemorated by Shi'a Muslims.

# Responsible travel in the Indian Himalaya

## Local customs

Most travellers experience great warmth and hospitality. With it comes an open curiosity about personal matters. You should not be surprised if total strangers ask for details of your job, income and family circumstances or discuss politics and religion.

### Conduct
Respect for the foreign visitor should be reciprocated by a sensitivity towards local customs and culture. How you dress is how people will judge you; cleanliness, modest clothes and a smile go a long way. Scanty, tight clothing draws unwanted attention. Displays of intimacy are totally inappropriate in public places. You may at times be frustrated by delays, bureaucracy and inefficiency, but displays of anger and rudeness will not achieve anything positive, and often make things worse. People's concept of time and punctuality is also often rather vague so be prepared to be kept waiting.

### Courtesy
It takes little effort to learn common gestures of courtesy and they are greatly appreciated. The greeting when meeting or parting, used universally among the Hindus across India, is

the palms joined together as in prayer, sometimes accompanied with the word *namaste* (North and West) or *namoshkar* (East). Muslims use the greeting *assalām aleikum*, with the response *waleikum assalām*, meaning 'peace be with you'; 'please' is *mehrbani-se*; 'thank you' is often expressed by a smile, or with the somewhat formal *dhannyabad* or *shukriya* (Urdu). For useful Hindi phrases, see page 440.

## Hands and eating

Traditionally, Indians use the right hand for giving, receiving, shaking hands and eating, as the left is considered to be unclean since it is associated with washing after using the toilet. In much of rural India cutlery is alien at the table except for serving spoons, and at most humble restaurants you will be offered only small spoons to eat with. If you visit an ashram or are lucky enough to be invited to a temple feast day, you will almost certainly be expected to eat with your hands. Watch and copy others until the technique becomes familiar.

## Women → *See also page 41.*

Indian women in urban and rural areas differ in their social interactions with men. To the Westerner, Indian women may seem to remain in the background and appear shy when approached. Yet you will see them working in public, often in jobs traditionally associated with men in the West, in the fields or on construction sites. It is not considered polite for men to photograph women without their consent, so ask before you start snapping.

Women do not usually shake hands with men as physical contact between the sexes is not acceptable. A Westernized city woman, however, may feel free to shake hands with a foreign visitor. In certain, very traditional rural circles, it is still the custom for men to be offered food first, separately, so don't be surprised if you, as foreign guest (man or woman), are awarded this special status when invited to an Indian home.

## Visiting religious sites

Visitors to all religious places should be dressed in clean, modest clothes; shorts and vests are inappropriate. Always remove shoes before entering (and all leather items in Jain temples). Take thick socks for protection when walking on sun-baked stone floors. Menstruating women are considered 'unclean' and should not enter places of worship. It is discourteous to sit with one's back to a temple or shrine. You will be expected to sit cross-legged on the floor – avoid pointing your feet at others when attending prayers at a temple. Walk clockwise around a shrine (keeping it to your right).

Non-Hindus are sometimes excluded from the inner sanctum of **Hindu** temples and occasionally even from the temple itself. Look for signs or ask. In certain temples and on special occasions you may enter only if you wear unstitched clothing such as a *dhoti*.

In **Buddhist** shrines, turn prayer wheels in a clockwise direction. In Sikh *gurudwaras*, everyone should cover their head, even if it is with a handkerchief. Tobacco and cigarettes should not be taken in. In **Muslim** mosques, visitors should have only their face, hands and feet exposed; women should also cover their heads. Mosques may be closed to non-Muslims shortly before formal prayers.

Some temples have a register or a receipt book for **donations**, which equate to an obligatory entry fee. The money is normally used for the upkeep and services of the temple or monastery. In some pilgrimage centres, priests can become unpleasantly persistent. If you wish to leave a donation, put money in the donation box; priests and Buddhist monks often do not handle money. It is also not customary to shake hands with a priest or monk. *Sanyasis* (holy men) and some pilgrims depend on donations.

## Begging

Beggars are found on busy street corners in large Indian cities, as well as at bus and train stations where they often target foreigners. Visitors can find this distressing, especially the sight of severely undernourished children or those displaying physical deformity. You may be particularly affected when some persist in making physical contact. In the larger cities, beggars are often exploited by syndicates, which cream off most of their takings. Yet those seeking alms near religious sites are another matter, and you may see Indian worshippers giving freely to those less fortunate than themselves, since this is tied up with gaining 'merit'. How you deal with begging is a personal choice but it is perhaps better to give to a recognized charity than to make largely ineffectual handouts to individuals. Young children sometimes offer to do 'jobs' such as call a taxi, carry shopping or pose for a photo. While travelling, some visitors prefer to hand out fruit than money to the many open-palmed children they encounter.

## Charitable giving

A pledge to donate a part of one's holiday budget to a local charity could be an effective formula for 'giving'. Some visitors like to support self-help cooperatives, orphanages, refugee centres, disabled or disadvantaged groups, or international charities like **Oxfam**, **Save the Children** or **Christian Aid** which work with local partners, either by making a donation or by buying their products.

**Concern India Foundation**, 6K Dubash Marg, Mumbai, T022-2202 9708, www.concernindia.org. An umbrella organization working with local charities. **Salaam Baalak Trust**, www.salaambaalak trust.com. Set up by the team who made *Salaam Bombay* 25 years ago; they offer food, shelter, education and vocational training. Inspiring work.

**SOS Children's Villages**, A-7 Nizamuddin West, New Delhi 110013, T011-2435 9450, www.soscvindia.org. Over 30 children's projects in India, eg opposite Pital Factory, Jhotwara Rd, Jaipur 302016, T0141-228 0787. **Trek-Aid**, 2 Somerset Cottages, Stoke Village, Plymouth, Devon, PL3 4AZ, www.a38.com/trekaid. Health, education, etc, through self-help schemes for displaced Tibetan refugees.

## Photography

Many monuments and national parks charge a camera fee ranging from Rs 20-100 for still cameras, and as much as Rs 500 for video cameras (more for professionals). Special permits are needed from the Archaeological Survey of India, New Delhi, for using tripods and artificial lights. When photographing people, it is polite to first ask – they will usually respond warmly with smiles. Visitors often promise to send copies of the photos – don't unless you really mean to do so. Photography of airports, military installations, bridges and in tribal and 'sensitive border areas' is not permitted.

# Essentials A-Z

## Accident and emergency

Contact the relevant emergency service (police T100, fire T101, ambulance T102) and your embassy (see Directory in Delhi, page 80, and Kolkata, page 304). Make sure you obtain police/medical reports for insurance claims.

## Children

Children of all ages are widely welcomed. However, care should be taken when travelling to remote areas where health services are primitive. Diarrhoea and vomiting are the most common problems, so take the usual precautions. In the big cities you can get safe baby foods and formula milk. Wet wipes and disposable nappies are difficult to find. The biggest hotels provide babysitting. See also Health, page 32.

## Customs and duty free

Tourists are allowed to bring in all personal effects 'which may reasonably be required', without charge. The official customs allowance includes 200 cigarettes or 50 cigars, 0.95 litres of alcohol, a camera and a pair of binoculars. Valuable personal effects and professional equipment including jewellery, special camera equipment and lenses, laptop computers and sound and video recorders must in theory be declared on a Tourist Baggage Re-Export Form (TBRE) in order for them to be taken out of the country, though in practice it's relatively unlikely that your bags will be inspected beyond a cursory x-ray. Nevertheless, it saves considerable frustration if you know the equipment serial numbers in advance and are ready to show them on the equipment. In addition to the forms, details of imported equipment may be entered into your passport. Save time by completing the formalities while waiting for your baggage. It is essential to keep these forms for showing to the customs when leaving India, otherwise considerable delays are very likely at the time of departure.

## Disabled travellers

India is not specially geared up for less able-bodied travellers. Access to buildings, toilets (sometimes squat type), pavements and public transport can prove frustrating, but it is easy to find people to give a hand to help with lifting and carrying. Provided you are prepared to pay for at least mid-price accommodation, car hire and taxis, travel in India should be fairly accessible.

Some travel companies specialize in exciting holidays, tailor-made for individuals depending on their level of disability. **Global Access**, Disabled Travel Network, www.globalaccessnews.com, provides travel information for 'disabled adventurers' and includes a number of reviews and tips. **Special Tours India**, www.specialtoursindia. com, specializes in eco-holidays and has a jeep trip to Ladakh tailored to the needs of disabled travellers.

## Drugs

Be aware that the government takes the misuse of drugs very seriously. Anyone charged with the illegal possession of drugs risks facing a fine of Rs 100,000 and a minimum 10 years' imprisonment. Several foreigners have been imprisoned for drugs-related offences in the last decade.

## Electricity

India's supply is 220-240 volts AC. There may be pronounced variations in the voltage, and power cuts are common. Power back-up by generator or inverter is becoming more widespread, though it may not cover a/c. Socket sizes vary so take a universal adaptor; low-quality versions are available locally. Many hotels, even in the higher categories, don't have electric razor sockets.

## Embassies and consulates

For information on visas and immigration, see page 40. For a list of Indian embassies and consulates abroad, see http://meaindia. nic.in/ onmouse/mission.htm.

## Gay and lesbian travellers

Indian law forbids homosexual acts for men (but not women) which carry a maximum sentence of life imprisonment. Although it is common to see young males holding hands in public, this very rarely indicates a gay relationship and is usually an expression of friendship. Overt displays of affection between homosexuals (and heterosexuals) can offend and should be avoided. Nevertheless, Kolkata celebrated its 7th Gay and Lesbian Film Festival in 2013, a sign that in the cities at least, attitudes may be starting to shift. Check out www.timeoutdelhi.net/ gay-lesbian for events in Delhi.

## Health

See your GP or travel clinic at least 6 weeks before departure for general advice on travel risks and vaccinations. Try phoning a specialist travel clinic if your own doctor is unfamiliar with health conditions in India. Make sure you have sufficient medical travel insurance, get a dental check, know your own blood group and if you have a long-term condition such as diabetes or epilepsy obtain a Medic Alert bracelet/necklace (www.medicalert.co.uk). If you wear glasses, take a copy of your prescription.

Confirm your primary **vaccination** courses and boosters are up to date. It is advisable to vaccinate against diphtheria, tetanus, poliomyelitis, hepatitis A and typhoid. Yellow fever is not required in India but you may be asked to show a certificate if you are entering from an area with risk of yellow fever transmission.

Vaccination against rabies is advised for those going to risk areas that will be remote from a reliable source of vaccine. Even when pre-exposure vaccines have been received urgent medical advice should be sought after any animal bite.

**Malaria** is a danger in India and, although it has some seasonality, it is too unpredictable not to take prophylaxis. Specialist advice should be taken on the best anti-malarials to use.

### Health risks
**Altitude sickness** can creep up on you as just a mild headache with nausea or lethargy during your visit to the Himalaya. The more serious disease is caused by fluid collecting in the brain in the enclosed space of the skull and can lead to coma and death. The best cure is to descend as soon as possible. It is essential to get acclimatized before undertaking long treks or arduous activities.

The standard advice for **diarrhoea** prevention is to be careful with water and ice for drinking. If you have any doubts about where the water came from then boil it or filter and treat it. Bottled water is readily available and cheap. Food can also transmit disease. Be wary of salads, re-heated foods or food that has been left out in the sun. There is a simple adage that says wash it, peel it, boil it or forget it. Also be wary of unpasteurized dairy products as these can transmit a range of diseases. Diarrhoea may be also caused by viruses, bacteria (such as E-coli), protozoa (such as giardia), salmonella and cholera. It may be accompanied by vomiting or by severe abdominal pain. The key treatment with all diarrhoea is rehydration. Try to keep hydrated by taking the right mixture of salt and water. This is available as Oral Rehydration Salts (ORS) in ready-made sachets or can be made up by adding a teaspoon of sugar and a half teaspoon of salt to a litre of clean water. You can also use flat carbonated drinks. If the symptoms persist, consult a doctor.

**Mosquitoes** are more of a nuisance than a serious hazard but some, of course, are carriers of serious diseases such as **malaria** so it is sensible to avoid being bitten as much as possible. Sleep off the ground and use a mosquito net and some kind of insecticide. Mosquito coils release insecticide as they burn and are available in many shops, as are tablets of insecticide, which are placed on a heated mat plugged into a wall socket.

**Rabies** is endemic throughout certain parts of India, so avoid dogs that are behaving strangely and cover your toes at night to protect them from vampire bats, which also carry the disease. If you are bitten by a domestic or wild animal, do not leave things to chance: scrub the wound with soap and water and/or disinfectant, try to at least determine the animal's ownership where possible and seek medical assistance at once. The course of treatment depends on whether you have already been vaccinated against rabies.

The range of visible and invisible **sexually transmitted diseases** is awesome. Unprotected sex can spread HIV, hepatitis B and C, gonorrhea (green discharge), chlamydia (nothing to see but may cause painful urination and later female infertility), painful recurrent herpes, syphilis and warts, just to name a few. You can cut down the risk by using condoms, femidoms or avoiding sex altogether.

Make sure you protect yourself from the **sun** with high-factor sun screen and don't forget to wear a hat.

### If you get sick

Contact your embassy or consulate for a list of doctors and dentists who speak your language, or at least some English. Doctors and health facilities in major cities are also listed in the Directory sections of this book. Make sure you have adequate insurance (see below).

### Useful websites

**www.cdc.gov** US government site that gives excellent advice on travel health and details of disease outbreaks.
**www.fitfortravel.scot.nhs.uk** A-Z of vaccine/health advice for each country.
**www.numberonehealth.co.uk** Travel screening services, vaccine and travel health advice, email/SMS text vaccine reminders and screens returned travellers for tropical diseases.

## Insurance

Buying insurance with your air ticket is the most costly way of doing things. For advice, see www.dh.gov.uk/policyandguidance/healthadvicefortravellers.

If you are carrying expensive equipment you may need to get separate cover for those items (claims for individual items are often limited to £250) unless they are covered by existing home contents insurance.

Check exactly what your medical cover includes, eg ambulance, helicopter rescue or emergency flights back home, and check for exclusions: you may find that activities such as mountain biking are not covered. Also check the payment protocol. You may have to pay first before the insurance company reimburses you.

Always carry with you the telephone number of your insurer's 24-hr emergency helpline and your insurance policy number.

## Internet

India is at the forefront of the technology revolution and is the the third largest internet user in the world. Most hotels and many backpacker places, including restaurants and cafés, have Wi-Fi, and internet cafés are plentiful (where you may have to produce ID).

In small towns there is less internet access and it is recommended to take precautions: write lengthy emails in Word, save frequently, then paste them into your web-based email server rather than risking the loss of missives home when the power fails or the connection goes down. Browsing costs vary dramatically depending on the location: these can be anything from Rs 20-100, with most charging somewhere in between.

## Language

Hindi, spoken as a mother tongue by over 400 million people, is India's official language. The use of English is also enshrined in the Constitution for a wide range of official purposes, notably communication between Hindi and non-Hindi speaking states. The most widely spoken Indo-Aryan languages are: Bengali (8.3%), Marathi (8%), Urdu (5.7%), Gujarati (5.4%), Oriya (3.7%) and Punjabi (3.2%). Among the Dravidian languages Telugu (8.2%), Tamil (7%), Kannada (4.2%) and Malayalam (3.5%) are the most widely used. Most of these languages have their own scripts. In all, there are 15 major and several hundred minor languages and dialects.

English now plays an important role across India. It is widely spoken in towns and cities and even in quite remote villages it is usually not difficult to find someone who speaks at least a little English. Outside of major tourist sites, other European languages are almost completely unknown. The accent in which English is spoken is often affected strongly by the mother tongue of the speaker and there have been changes in common grammar which sometimes make it sound unusual. Many of these changes have become standard Indian English usage, as valid as any other varieties of English used around the world. It is possible to study a number of Indian languages at language centres.

See also page 437. For Hindi words and phrases, food and drink and a glossary of terms, see page 440.

## Media

International **newspapers** (mainly English language) are sold in the bookshops of top hotels in major cities and occasionally by booksellers elsewhere. India has a large and lively English-language press.

The best known are the traditionalist *The Hindu*, www.hinduonline.com/today; the slightly more tabloid-establishment *Times of India*, www.timesofindia.com; and *The Statesman*, www.thestatesman.org. *The Economic Times* is good for world coverage. *The Asian Age* is now published in the UK and India simultaneously and gives good coverage of Indian and international affairs. Some of the most widely read current affairs weeklies are *India Today*, *Frontline* and *The Week*, which are journals in the *Time* or *Newsweek* mould. *Business Today* is of course economy-based, while *Outlook* has a broader remit and has good general interest features.

## Money

**Exchange rates** (Jan 2014)
UK£1 = Rs 100; €1 = Rs 84; US$1 = Rs 61; AUS$1 = Rs 56; NZ$1 = Rs 51.
Indian currency is the Indian rupee (Re/Rs). It is **not** possible to purchase these before you arrive. If you want cash on arrival it is best to get it at the airport bank. Rupee notes are printed in denominations of Rs 1000, 500, 100, 50, 20, 10. The rupee is divided into 100 paise. Coins are minted in denominations of Rs 10, Rs 5, Rs 2 and Rs 1. **Note** Carry in a money belt worn under clothing. Have a small amount in an accessible place.

**Credit cards**
Major credit cards are accepted in the main centres, but rarely in small towns. It is easy to obtain a cash advance against a credit card. Payment by credit card can sometimes be more expensive than payment by cash and some credit card companies charge a premium on cash withdrawals. Some railway

reservation centres are now taking payment for train tickets by Visa, which can be very quick as the queue is short, but they cannot be used for Tourist Quota tickets.

Another option is to use a pre-paid currency card (such as **Caxton Card**, www.caxtonfxcard.com), which is equivalent to but more practical than traditional traveller's cheques.

## ATMs

By far the most convenient method of accessing money, ATMs are prevalent all over India, usually attended by security guards. Banks with ATMs for Cirrus, Maestro, Visa and MasterCard include: **Bank of Baroda, Citibank, HDFC, HSBC, ICICI, Punjab National Bank** and **State Bank of India** (SBI). A withdrawal fee is usually charged by the issuing bank on top of the various conversion charges applied by your own bank. Fraud prevention measures may result in travellers having their cards blocked by the bank when unexpected overseas transactions occur; advise your bank of your travel plans before leaving.

## Changing money

The **State Bank of India** and several others in major towns are authorized to deal in foreign exchange. Some give cash against Visa/MasterCard. The larger cities have licensed money changers with offices usually in the commercial sector. Changing money through unauthorized dealers is illegal. Premiums on the currency black market are very small and highly risky.

Large hotels change money 24 hrs a day for guests, but banks often give a much better rate of exchange. It is best to exchange money on arrival at the airport bank or the Thomas Cook counter. You should be given a foreign currency encashment certificate when you change money through a bank or authorized dealer; ask for one if it is not automatically given. It allows you to change Indian rupees back to your own currency on departure. It also enables you to use rupees to pay hotel bills or buy air tickets. The certificates are only valid for 3 months.

## Cost of travelling

Most food, accommodation and public transport, especially rail and bus, is exceptionally cheap, although the price of basic food items such as rice, lentils, tomatoes and onions have skyrocketed. There is a widening range of moderately priced but clean hotels and restaurants outside the big cities, making it possible to get a great deal for your money. Budget travellers sharing a room, taking public transport, avoiding souvenir stalls, and eating nothing but rice and dhal can get away with a budget of Rs 400-600 (about about US$7-11 or £6-7) a day. This sum leaps up if you drink alcohol (still cheap by European standards at about US$2, £1 or Rs 80 for a pint), smoke foreign-brand cigarettes or want to have your own wheels (you can expect to spend between Rs 150 and 200 to hire a Honda per day). Those planning to stay in fairly comfortable hotels and use taxis sightseeing should budget at US$50-80 (£30-50) a day. India can be a great place to pick and choose, save a little on basic accommodation and then treat yourself to the type of meal you could only dream of affording back home. Also, be prepared to spend a fair amount more in Delhi, where not only is the cost of living significantly higher but where it's worth coughing up extra for a half-decent room. A newspaper costs Rs 5 and breakfast for 2 with coffee can come to as little as Rs 100 in a basic 'hotel', but if you eat banana pancakes or pasta in a backpacker restaurant expect to pay more like Rs 80-150 a dish.

## Opening hours

**Banks** Mon-Fri 1030-1430, Sat 1030-1230. Top hotels sometimes have a 24-hr money changing service. **Post offices** Mon-Fri 1000-1700 and Sat mornings. **Government**

**offices** Mon-Fri 0930-1700, Sat 0930-1300 (some on alternate Sat only). **Shops** Mon-Sat 0930-1800. Bazars keep longer hours.

## Post

The post is fairly unreliable, and it's unwise to send anything of value. It is best to use a post office where you can hand over mail for franking across the counter, or a top hotel post box. Government emporia or shops in the larger hotels will send purchases home if the items are difficult to carry.

Airmail services to Europe, Africa and Australia take about a week and a little longer for the Americas. Speed post (which takes about 4 days to the UK) is available from major towns. Courier services (eg DHL) are available in the larger towns. At some main post offices you can send small packages under 2 kg as **letter post** (rather than parcel post), which is much cheaper. Check that the post office holds the necessary customs declaration forms (2-3 copies needed). Write 'No commercial value' if returning used clothes, books, etc. Sea Mail has been phased out to be replaced by SAL (Surface Air Lifted). The prices are fractionally lower than airmail, delivery can take up to 2 months.

## Safety

### Personal security

In general the threats to personal security for travellers in India are remarkably small. However, incidents of petty theft and violence directed specifically at tourists have been on the increase so care is necessary in some places, and basic common sense needs to be used with respect to looking after valuables. Follow the same precautions you would when at home. There have been much-reported incidents of severe sexual assault in Delhi, Kolkata and some more rural areas in 2013. Avoid wandering alone outdoors late at night in these places. During daylight hours be careful in remote places, especially when alone. If you are

under threat, scream loudly. Be cautious before accepting food or drink from casual acquaintances, as it may be drugged – although note that Indians on a long train journey will invariably try to share their snacks with you, and balance caution with the opportunity to interact.

Some parts of India are subject to political violence. The Vale of Kashmir and Jammu remain under tight military control. Even when the border area is relatively quiet, the army is massively deployed and on constant alert.

Following a major explosion on the Delhi to Lahore (Pakistan) train in 2007 and the Mumbai attacks in 2008, increased security has been implemented on many trains and stations. Similar measures at airports may cause delays for passengers so factor this into your timing. Also check your airline's website for up-to-date information on luggage restrictions.

### Travel advice

Seek advice from your consulate before you travel. Also contact: British Foreign & Commonwealth Office Travel Advice Unit, T0845-850 2829, www.fco.gov.uk. US State Department's Bureau of Consular Affairs, Overseas Citizens Services, Room 4800, Department of State, Washington, DC 20520-4818, USA, T202-647 1488, http://travel.state.gov. Australian Department of Foreign Affairs Canberra, Australia, T02-6261 3305, www.smartraveller.gov.au. Canadian official advice is on www.voyage.gc.ca.

### Theft

Theft is not uncommon. Keep passports and valuables with you at all times. Don't regard hotel rooms as being automatically safe; even hotel safes don't guarantee secure storage. Avoid leaving valuables near open windows even when you are in the room. Use your own padlock in a budget hotel when you go out. Pickpockets and other thieves operate in the big cities. Crowded areas are particularly high risk. Take special care of your belongings when getting on or off public transport.

If you have items stolen, they should be reported to the police as soon as possible. Keep a separate record of vital documents, including passport details. Larger hotels will be able to assist in contacting and dealing with the police. Dealings with the police can be very difficult, the paperwork involved in reporting losses can be time consuming and irritating and your own documentation (eg passport and visas) may be demanded. In some states the police themselves sometimes demand bribes, though you should not assume that if procedures move slowly you are being expected to offer a bribe.

Confidence tricksters are common around railway stations or places where tourists gather.

### Travel safety
The traffic police are tightening up on traffic offences in some places. They have the right to make on-the-spot fines for speeding and illegal parking. If you face a demand for a fine, insist on a receipt. If you have to go to a police station, try to take someone with you.

If you face really serious problems, for example in connection with a driving accident, you should contact your consular office as quickly as possible. Always ensure you have your international driving licence and vehicle documentation with you.

**Motorcycles** don't come fitted with helmets and accidents are commonplace so exercise caution, the horn and the brake.

Thefts on **trains** are on the rise. First-class compartments are self-contained and normally completely secure, although nothing of value should be left near open train windows. Most thefts occur in non-a/c sleeper class carriages. Luggage should be chained to a seat for security overnight. Locks and chains are available at main stations and bazars. If you put your bags on the upper berth during the day, beware of fellow passengers climbing up for a 'sleep'. Be guarded with new friends on trains who show particular interest in the contents of your bag and be extra wary of accepting food or drink from casual acquaintances; travellers have reported being drugged and then robbed.

## Senior travellers

Travellers over the age of 60 can take advantage of several discounts on travel, including 30% on train fares and up to 50% on some air tickets. Ask when booking, as these will not be offered automatically. See www.asparkholidays.com, based in New Delhi, for tours designed for senior citizens.

## Smoking

Smoking is banned in all public places including transport, but permitted in open spaces nationwide. Bars and discos often have a designated smoking area. To avoid fines, check for notices.

## Telephone

The international code for India is +91. The IDD prefix for dialling out of India is 00. International Direct Dialling is available in privately run call booths, usually labelled on yellow boards with the letters 'PCO-STD-ISD', although these are becoming far less common. You dial the call yourself, and the time and cost are displayed on a screen. Cheap rate is 2100-0600. Calls from hotels are usually much more expensive, though some will allow local calls free of charge. Internet phone booths are the cheapest way of calling overseas.

A double ring repeated means it is ringing. Equal tones with equal pauses means engaged, similar to in the UK.

Due to the tremendous pace of the telecommunications revolution, millions of telephone numbers go out of date every year. Current telephone directories are often out of date and some of the numbers given in this book will have been changed even as we go to press. **Directory enquiries**, T197, can be helpful but works only for the local area code.

**Mobile phones** are for sale everywhere, as are local SIM cards that allow you to make calls within India and overseas at much lower rates than using a 'roaming' service – sometimes for as little as Rs 0.5 per min. Private companies include **Airtel**, **Vodafone** and **Idea**. To connect you'll need to complete a form, have a local address (a hotel receipt with your name on will do), and present photocopies of your passport and visa plus 2 passport photos. Most phone dealers will be able to help. India is divided into a number of 'calling circles' or regions, and if you travel outside the region where your connection is based (eg from Delhi into Himachal Pradesh), you will pay higher 'roaming' charges for calls. In the northeast states, sim cards from other states do not work at all, and every state has its own network for security reasons. Likewise for Jammu and Kashmir.

## Time

GMT +5½ hrs. India doesn't change its clocks, so from the last Sun in Oct to the last Sun in Mar it is UK time +5½ hrs, and the rest of the year it's +4½ hrs (USA, EST +10½ and +9½ hrs; Australia, EST -5½ and -4½ hrs).

## Tipping

A tip of Rs 10 to a luggage porter in a modest hotel (Rs 20 in a higher category) would be appropriate. In upmarket restaurants, a 10% tip is acceptable when service is not already included; in cheaper places round off the bill. Indians don't normally tip taxi drivers but a small extra amount over the fare is welcomed. Porters at airports and railway stations often have a fixed rate displayed but will usually press for more. Ask fellow passengers what a fair rate is.

## Tourist information

There are Government of India tourist offices in the state capitals, as well as state tourist offices (sometimes Tourism Development Corporations) in the major cities and a few important sites. They produce their own tourist literature and some also have lists of city hotels and guesthouses. The quality of material is improving though maps are often poor. Many offer tours of the city and sights, and overnight and regional packages. Some run modest hotels and can arrange car hire and guides. The staff in the regional and local offices are usually helpful.

## Tour operators

### UK
**Colours Of India**, www.partnershiptravel. co.uk. Tailor-made cultural, adventure, spa and cooking tours.
**Cox & Kings**, www.coxandkings.co.uk.
**Dragoman**, www.drago man.com. Overland, adventure, camping.
**Exodus**, www.exodus.co.uk. Small group overland and trekking tours.
**Greaves Tours**, www.greavesindia.com. Luxury, tailor-made tours using only scheduled flights. Traditional travel such as road and rail preferred to flights between major cities.
**Kuoni**, Kuoni House, Dorking, Surrey, RH5 4AZ, T01306-747002, www.kuoni.co.uk, and subsidiary upmarket brand. **Voyages Jules Vernes**, www.vjv.co.uk. Run week-long culture and relaxation tours.
**On the Go Tours**, 68 North End Rd, London, W14 9EP, T020-7371 1113, www.onthe gotours.com. Legendary tours and tailor-made itineraries at amazing prices.
**Select Connections**, www.selectconnections. co.uk. Excellent tailor-made tours throughout India, with great homestays.
**Shakti**, www.shaktihimalaya.com. Bespoke, all-inclusive walking, rafting and cultural

experiences in the foothills of the Himalaya with English-speaking guides and their own lodge (see page 130).

**Steppes Discovery**, www.steppesdiscovery.co.uk. Wildlife safaris, tiger study tours and cultural tours with strong conservation ethic.

**Trans Himalaya**, 16 Skye Crescent, Crieff PH7 3FB, T01764-650604, www.trans-himalaya. com. Under the direction of Gyurme Dorje, a Tibetologist and Tibet travel writer, they organize travel throughout the Himalaya (Bhutan, Sikkim, Nepal and Ladakh).

**Travel the Unknown**, www.travelthe unknown.com. Eco-conscious and off-the-beaten track tours, award-winning company, with regular trips to the northwest and northeast each year. Recommended.

## India

**Aquaterra Adventures**, www.treknraft.com. Trekking, rafting, kayaking, etc in all Indian Himalayan states. Excellent reputation.

**The Blue Yonder**, www.theblueyonder.com. Highly regarded and award-winning sustainable and community tourism operators, active in Sikkim and other states.

**Classic Bike Adventures**, www.classic-bike-india.com. An Indo-German company which arranges high-octane tours around South India, Rajasthan and the Himalaya and Nepal on Enfield motorbikes.

**Help Tourism**, www.helptourism.com. Eco-tours in Assam, Arunachal and North Bengal, involving local communities.

**Ibex Expeditions**, www.ibexexpeditions.com. Award-winning eco-aware tour operator for tours, safaris and treks.
**Indebo India**, www.indebo.com. Customized tours and travel-related services throughout India.
**Purvi Discovery**, www.purviweb.com, www.assamteatourism.com. Experienced in tours to Arunachal, Assam and other northeast destinations, a quality outfit with quality accommodation.
**Royal Expeditions**, www.royalexpeditions.com. Specialist staff for customized trips, knowledgeable about options for senior travellers. Luxury 4WD escorted self-drive adventures in the Himalaya.
**Shanti Travel**, www.shantitravel.com.

### North America
**Adventures Abroad**, T1-800-665 3998, www.adventures-abroad.com.
**High Asia**, 33 Thornton St, Hamden, Connecticut, T609-269-5332. Adventurous and exploratory tours in Assam and Arunachal Pradesh, including elephant trekking, tribal culture tours and trips linking India to China via the Burma Rd.
**Myths and Mountains**, T1-800-670 6984, www.mythsandmountains.com. Culture, crafts and religion.
**Spirit of India**, USA T1-888-3676147, www.spirit-of-india.com. General and spirituality-focused tours, local experts.

### Australia and New Zealand
**India Unbound**, www.indiaunbound.com.au. Intriguing range of small-group trips and bespoke private tours.
**Intrepid Travel**, www.intrepidtravel.com. Cookery courses to village stays and treks. Very socially and environmentally responsible outfit.

## Visas and immigration

For embassies and consulates, see page 32. Virtually all foreign nationals, including children, require a visa to enter India. The rules regarding visas change frequently and arrangements for application and collection also vary from town to town so it is essential to check details and costs with the relevant embassy or consulate. These remain closed on Indian national holidays. Now many consulates and embassies are outsourcing the visa process, it's best to find out in advance how long it will take. For example, in London where you used to be able to get a visa in person in a morning if you were prepared to queue, it now takes 3-5 working days and involves 2 trips to the office.

At other offices, it can be much easier to apply in advance by post, to avoid queues and frustratingly low visa quotas. Postal applications can take 10-15 working days to process.

Visitors from countries with no Indian representation may apply to the resident British representative, or enquire at the Air India office. An application on the prescribed form should be accompanied by 2 passport photographs and your passport which should be valid 6 months beyond the period of your visit. Note that visas are valid from the date granted, not from the date of entry. For up-to-date information on visa requirements visit www.india-visa.com.

Currently the following visa rules apply:

**Transit** For passengers en route to another country (no more than 72 hrs in India).
**Tourist** 3-6 month visa from the date of issue. Multiple entries permitted; request this on the application form if you wish to visit neighbouring countries.
**Business** 3-6 months or up to 2 years with multiple entry. A letter from the company giving the nature of business is required.
**5 year** For those of Indian origin only, who have held Indian passports.
**Student** Valid up to 1 year from the date of issue. Attach a letter of acceptance from Indian institution and an AIDS test certificate. Allow up to 3 months for approval.
**Visa extensions** Applications should be made to the Foreigners' Regional Registration Office (FRRO) in New Delhi or Kolkata, or an office of the Superintendent of Police in the District Headquarters. After 6 months, you must leave India and apply for a new visa – the Nepal office is known to be difficult. Anyone staying in India for a period of more than 180 days (6 months) must register at a convenient Foreigners' Registration Office.

#### Permits and restricted and protected areas

Some areas are politically sensitive and special permits may be needed to visit them, though the government is relaxing its regulations. The border regions, tribal areas and Himalayan zones are subject to restrictions and special permits may be needed to visit them. For permits to Arunachal Pradesh, Ladakh and Sikkim, see pages 374, 246 and 335, respectively.

## Weights and measures

Metric system has come into universal use in the cities. In remote areas local measures are sometimes used. One lakh is 100,000 and 1 crore is 10 million.

## Women travellers

Independent travel is still largely unheard of for Indian women. Although it is relatively safe for women to travel around India, most people find it an advantage to travel with a companion. Even then, privacy is rarely respected and there can be a lot of hassle, pressure and intrusion on your personal space. Backpackers often meet like-minded travelling companions at budget hotels. Cautious solo women travellers recommend wearing wedding rings, but the most important measure is to dress appropriately, in loose-fitting, non-see-through clothes, covering shoulders, arms and legs (such as *salwaar kameez*). In mosques women should be covered from head to ankle. See www.independenttraveller.com and www.wanderlustandlipstick.com for women-only tours to India.

'Eve teasing' is an unfortunate result of the sexual repression latent in Indian culture, combined with a young male population whose only access to sex education is via the dingy cybercafés. Unaccompanied women are most vulnerable in major cities, crowded bazars, and tourist centres where men may follow them and touch them; festival nights are particularly bad for this. If you are harassed, it can be effective to make a scene. Be firm and clear if you don't wish to speak to someone. The best response to staring, whether lascivious or curious, is to avert your eyes down and away. This is not the submissive gesture it might seem, but an effective tool to communicate that you have no interest in any further interaction.

Aggressively staring back or verbally confronting the starer can be construed as a come-on. It is best to be accompanied at night, especially when travelling by rickshaw or taxi in towns. Be prepared to raise an alarm if anything unpleasant threatens.

Most railway booking offices have separate women's ticket queues or ask women to go to the head of the general queue. Take advantage of the gender segregation on public transport, both to avoid hassle and talk with local women. Some buses have seats reserved for women, and there is a separate women's carriage on the Delhi metro. See also page 29.

## Contents

Delhi

### At a glance

**Getting around** Metro, taxi and bus (the latter off peak only). Hiring a car and driver saves much haggling with rickshaw drivers.
**Time required** At least 3 days to explore Old Delhi and the key museums and archaeological sites.
**Weather** Cold winters and foggy mornings, staggeringly hot in May and Jun. Oct and Mar are best.
**When not to go** It's too hot to enjoy Delhi in the weeks prior to the monsoon.

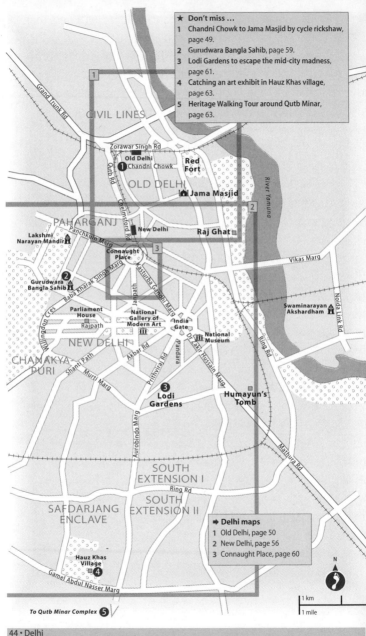

★ Don't miss ...

1 Chandni Chowk to Jama Masjid by cycle rickshaw, page 49.

2 Gurudwara Bangla Sahib, page 59.

3 Lodi Gardens to escape the mid-city madness, page 61.

4 Catching an art exhibit in Hauz Khas village, page 63.

5 Heritage Walking Tour around Qutb Minar, page 63.

Grand Trunk Rd

CIVIL LINES

Zorawar Singh Rd

Old Delhi

1 Chandni Chowk

Red Fort

Qutb Rd

OLD DELHI

Chelmsford Rd

Jama Masjid

River Yamuna

PAHARGANJ

Panchkuin Marg

New Delhi

Raj Ghat

Lakshmi Narayan Mandir

Connaught Place

3

Vikas Marg

Gurudwara Bangla Sahib

Baba Kharak Singh Marg

Kasturba Gandhi Marg

Jantar

Swaminarayan Akshardham

Mandir Marg

Parliament House

Rajpath

National Gallery of Modern Art

India Gate

National Museum

Noida Link Rd

NEW DELHI

Akbar Rd

Pandara

CHANAKYA-PURI

Shanti Path

Murti Marg

Prithviraj Rd

Dr Zakir Hussain Marg

Ring Rd

3

Lodi Gardens

Humayun's Tomb

Aurobindo Marg

SOUTH EXTENSION I

Mathura Rd

Ring Rd

SAFDARJANG ENCLAVE

SOUTH EXTENSION II

➡ Delhi maps

1 Old Delhi, page 50
2 New Delhi, page 56
3 Connaught Place, page 60

Hauz Khas Village

4

Gamel Abdul Nasser Marg

To Qutb Minar Complex 5

N

1 km

1 mile

Delhi can take you aback with its vibrancy and growth. Less than 60 years ago the spacious, quiet and planned city of New Delhi was still the pride of late colonial British India, while to its north, the lanes of Old Delhi resonated with the sounds of a bustling medieval market. Today, both worlds have been overtaken by the rush of modernization. As Delhi's population surges, its tentacles have spread in all directions – from both the ancient core of Shahjahan's city in the north and the late British capital of New Delhi to its south.

Close to New Delhi Railway Station, the cheap hotels and guesthouses of Paharganj squeeze between cloth merchants and wholesalers. In Old Delhi, further north, with the Red Fort and Jama Masjid, the old city is still a dense network of narrow alleys and tightly packed markets and houses. Your senses are bombarded by noise, bustle, smells and apparent chaos. A 'third city' comprises the remorselessly growing squatter settlements (*jhuggies*), which provide shelter for more than a third of Delhi's population. To the south is another, newer, chrome-and-glass city, the city of the modern suburbs and urban 'farms', where the rural areas of Gurgaon have become the preserve of the prosperous, with shopping malls, banks and private housing estates. Old and new, simple and sophisticated, traditional and modern, East and West are juxtaposed. Whatever India you are looking for, the capital has it all – getting lost in warrens of crowded streets, wandering through spice markets, eating kebabs by the beautiful Jama Masjid, lazing among Mogul ruins, listening to Sufi musicians by a shrine at dusk or shopping in giant shining malls, drinking cocktails in glitzy bars and travelling on the gleaming Metro.

### Getting there

Delhi is served by **Indira Gandhi International (IGI) Airport**, which handles both international and domestic traffic. The new T3 (International Terminal) has one of the longest runways in Asia and is connected to the city centre by Metro. It is about 23 km from the centre. During the day, it can take 30-45 minutes from the Domestic Terminal and 45 minutes to an hour from the International Terminal to get to the centre. With the Metro, it should take 20 minutes. A free shuttle runs between the terminals. To get to town take a pre-paid taxi (see Transport, page 77) or an airport coach, or ask your hotel to collect you.

The **Inter State Bus Terminus (ISBT)** is at Kashmere Gate, near the Red Fort, about 30 minutes by bus from Connaught Place. Local buses connect it to the other ISBTs.

There are three main railway stations. The busy **New Delhi Station**, a 10-minute walk north of Connaught Place, can be maddeningly chaotic; you need to have all your wits about you. The quieter **Hazrat Nizamuddin** (which has some south-bound trains) is 5 km southeast of Connaught Place. The overpoweringly crowded **Old Delhi Station** (2 km north of Connaught Place) has a few important train connections. ▶▶ *See Transport, page 77.*

### Getting around

The new Metro is making the sprawling city very navigable: it's now possible to get from Connaught Place to Old Delhi in a cool five minutes; while Connaught Place to Qutb Minar is about 30 minutes, and all the way down to the final stop in Gurgaon is about one hour. It is a strange experience to go from air-conditioned high tech to the bustling streets of Chandi Chowk. There is a women-only carriage at the front of each train, clearly marked inside and on the platform – this prevents women from having to succumb to the crush of the other carriages. There is a fine of Rs 250 for men ignoring all the signs in pink and, in early 2011, a posse of women made men do sit-ups on the train for trespassing into the pink zone! Like any city Metro service, try and avoid rush hour if you can. At each Metro station you have to go through airport-like security and have your bag x-rayed, etc.

Auto-rickshaws and taxis are widely available, and new rate cards mean that drivers will now use their meters, even with foreigners. It's best to use pre-paid stands at stations, airport terminals and at the junction of Radial Road 1 and Connaught Place if possible. The same applies to cycle rickshaws, which ply the streets of Old Delhi. City buses are usually packed and have long queues. Be on your guard from thieves around New Delhi Station. State Entry Road runs from the southern end of Platform 1 to Connaught Place. This is a hassle-free alternative to the main Chelmsford Road during the day (gate closed at night). Also watch your change or cash interactions even at the pre-paid booths – sometimes they do a switch of a Rs 100 note for a Rs 10 for example. Fleets of Radio Taxis are the newest additions to the city's transport options. These include: **Delhi Cab** ① *T011-4433 3222*; **Easy Cab** ① *T011-4343 4343*; **Mega Cabs** ① *T011-4141 4141*; and **Quick Cab** ① *T011-4533 3333*. ▶▶ *See Transport, page 77.*

### Orientation

The **Red Fort** and **Jama Masjid** are the focal point of Old Delhi, 2 km northeast of Connaught Place. Chandni Chowk, the main commercial area, heads west from the fort. Around this area are narrow lanes packed to the rafters with all different types of wares for sale. To the southeast are **New Delhi Railway Station** and the main backpackers' area **Paharganj**, with **Connaught Place**, the notional 'centre' of New Delhi, about 1 km south.

Running due south of Connaught Place is **Janpath** with small shops selling craft products, and hotels like the **Imperial**. Janpath is intersected by **Rajpath** with all the major state buildings at its western end. Immediately south is the diplomatic enclave, **Chanakyapuri**. Most of the upmarket hotels are scattered across the wide area between Connaught Place and the airport to the southwest. As Delhi's centre of gravity has shifted southwards, a series of new markets has grown up to serve extensive housing colonies such as **South Extension**, **Greater Kailash** and **Safdarjang Enclave**. This development has brought one of the major historic sites, the **Qutb Minar**, within the limits of the city, about half an hour by taxi south of Connaught Place. **Gurgaon**, which is strictly not in Delhi but in Haryana, is the new business hub with many shopping malls to boot.

## Tourist information

Most tourist offices are open Monday-Friday 1000-1800, www.delhitourism.com. **The Government of India Tourist Office** ① *88 Janpath, T011-332 0005, Mon-Sat 0900-1800; also at the international airport*, is helpful and issues permits for visits to Rashtrapati Bhavan and gardens. There are several branches of **Delhi Tourism** ① *N-36 Connaught Pl, T011-2331 5322 (touts pester you to use one of many imposters; the correct office is directly opposite 'Competent House')*; the branch at **Coffee Home Annexe** ① *Baba Kharak Singh Marg, T011-336 5358*, offers hotel, transport and tour bookings (T011-2462 3782, 0700-2100). There are also branches at the airport terminals, the Inter-State Bus Terminal; **New Delhi Railway Station** ① *T011-2373 2374*; and **Nizamuddin Railway Station** ① *T011-2251 1083*. Also contact the **India Tourism Development Corporation (ITDC)** ① *L-1 Connaught Circus, T011-2332 0331*.

## Best time to visit

October to March are the best months to visit, but December and January can get quite cold and foggy at night. Pollution can affect asthma sufferers – in fact a lot of people develop respiratory problems and sore throats if they spend more than a few days in Delhi; echinacea can help. Monsoon lasts from the end of June to mid-September. May and June are very hot and dry and, with the whole city switching on its air-condioning units, power cuts are suffered more frequently at this time. Even the malls in Saket were having to keep their air conditioning on low during the summer of 2012.

## Background

In the modern period, Delhi has only been India's capital since 1911. It is a city of yo yo-ing fortunes and has been repeatedly reduced to rubble. There have been at least eight cities founded on the site of modern Delhi.

According to Hindu mythology, Delhi's first avatar was as the site of a dazzlingly wealthy city, Indraprastha, mentioned in the Mahabharata and founded around 2500 BC. The next five cities were to the south of today's Delhi. First was Lalkot, which, from 1206, became the capital of the Delhi Sultanate under the Slave Dynasty. The story of the first Sultan of Delhi, Qutb-ud-din Aybak, is a classic rags-to-riches story. A former slave, he rose through the ranks to become a general, a governor and then Sultan of Delhi. He is responsible for building Qutb Minar, but died before its completion.

The 1300s were a tumultuous time for Delhi, with five cities built during the century. Siri, the first of these, has gruesome roots. Legend has it that the city's founder, Ala-ud-din, buried the heads of infidels in the foundation of the fort. Siri derives its name from the

Hindi word for 'head'. After Siri came Tughlaqabad, whose existence came to a sudden end when the Sultan of Delhi, Muhammad Tughlaq, got so angry about a perceived insult from residents, he destroyed the city. The cities of Jahanpanah and Ferozebad followed in quick succession. Delhi's centre of gravity began to move northwards. In the 1500s Dinpanah was constructed by Humayun, whose wonderful tomb (1564-1573) graces Hazrat Nizamuddin. Shahjahanabad, known today as Old Delhi, followed, becoming one of the richest and most populous cities in the world. The Persian emperor Nadir Shah invaded, killing as many as 120,000 residents in a single bloody night and stealing the Kohinoor Diamond (now part of the British royal family's crown jewels).

The next destroyers of Delhi were the British, who ransacked the city in the wake of the Great Uprising/Mutiny of 1857. The resulting bloodbath left bodies piled so high that the victors' horses had to tread on them. For the next 50 years, while the port cities of Calcutta and Bombay thrived under the British, Delhi languished. Then, in 1911, King George, on a visit to India, announced that a new city should be built next to what remained of Delhi, and that this would be the new capital of India. The British architect Edwin Lutyens was brought in to design the city. You could argue that the building hasn't stopped since ...

The central part of New Delhi is an example of Britain's imperial pretensions. The government may have been rather more reticent about moving India's capital, if it had known that in less than 36 years time, the British would no longer be ruling India. Delhi's population swelled after the violence of partition, with refugees flooding to the city. In 10 years the population of Delhi doubled, and many well-known housing colonies were built during this period.

The economic boom that began in the 1990s has lead to an explosion of construction and soaring real estate prices. Delhi is voraciously eating into the surrounding countryside. It is a city changing at such breakneck speed that shops, homes and even airports seem to appear and disappear almost overnight.

# Places in Delhi

The sites of interest are grouped in three main areas. In the centre is the British-built capital of **New Delhi**, with its government buildings and wide avenues. The heart of **Shahjahanabad** (Old Delhi) is about 2 km north of Connaught Circus. Some 10 km to the south is the **Qutb Minar** complex, with the old fortress city of **Tughluqabad**, 8 km to its east. Across the Yamuna River is the remarkable new Akshardham Temple. You can visit each separately, or link routes together into a day-tour to include the most interesting sites.

## Old Delhi → *For listings, see pages 68-80.*

Shah Jahan (ruled 1628-1658) decided to move back from Agra to Delhi in 1638. Within 10 years the huge city of **Shahjahanabad**, now known as Old Delhi, was built. The plan of Shah Jahan's new city symbolized the link between religious authority enshrined in the Jama Masjid to the west, and political authority represented by the Diwan-i-Am in the Fort, joined by Chandni Chowk, the route used by the emperor. The city was protected by rubble-built walls, some of which still survive. These walls were pierced by 14 main gates. The **Ajmeri Gate**, **Turkman Gate** (often referred to by auto-rickshaw wallahs as 'Truckman Gate'), **Kashmere Gate** and **Delhi Gate** still survive.

## Chandni Chowk

Shahjahanabad was laid out in blocks with wide roads, residential quarters, bazars and mosques. Its principal street, Chandni Chowk, had a tree-lined canal flowing down its centre which became renowned throughout Asia. The canal is long gone, but the jumble of shops, alleys crammed with craftsmen's workshops, food stalls, mosques and temples, cause it to retain some of its magic. A cycle rickshaw ride gives you a good feel of the place. Make sure you visit **Naughara Street**, just off Kinari Bazar; it's one of the most atmospheric streets in Delhi, full of brightly painted and slowly crumbling *havelis*.

The impressive red sandstone façade of the **Digambar Jain Mandir** (temple) standing at the eastern end of Chandni Chowk, faces the Red Fort. Built in 1656, it contains an image of Adinath. The charity bird hospital (www.charitybirdshospital.org) within this compound releases the birds on recovery instead of returning them to their owners; many remain within the temple precincts. Beyond Shahjahanabad to the north lies Kashmiri Gate, Civil lines and the Northern Ridge. The siting of the railway line which effectively cut Delhi into two unequal parts was done deliberately. The line brought prosperity, yet it destroyed the unity of the walled city forever. The Northern Ridge was the British cantonment and Civil Lines housed the civilians. In this area the temporary capital of the British existed from 1911-1931 until New Delhi came. The Northern Ridge is a paradise for birds and trees. Follow the **Mutiny Trail** by visiting Flagstaff Tower, Pir Ghaib, Chauburj, Mutiny Memorial. Around Kashmire Gate and Civil Lines, you can discover the Old Residency, St James Church, Nicholson's Cemetery and Qudsia Bagh.

## Red Fort (Lal Qila)

ⓘ *Tue-Sun sunrise to sunset, Rs 250 foreigners, Rs 10 Indians, allow 1 hr. The entrance is through the Lahore Gate (nearest the car park) with the admission kiosk opposite; keep your ticket as you will need to show it at the Drum House. There are new toilets inside, best to avoid the ones in Chatta Chowk. You must remove shoes and cover all exposed flesh from your shoulders to your legs.*

Between the new city and the River Yamuna, Shah Jahan built a fort. Most of it was built out of red *lal* (sandstone), hence the name **Lal Qila** (Red Fort), the same as that at Agra on which the Delhi Fort is modelled. Begun in 1639 and completed in 1648, it is said to have cost Rs 10 million, much of which was spent on the opulent marble palaces within. In recent years much effort has been put into improving the fort and gardens, but visitors may be saddened by the neglected state of some of the buildings, and the gun-wielding soldiers lolling around do nothing to improve the ambience. However, despite the modern development of roads and shops and the never-ending traffic, it's an impressive site.

**The approach** The entrance is by the Lahore Gate. The defensive barbican that juts out in front of it was built by Aurangzeb (see page 394). A common story suggests that Aurangzeb built the curtain wall to save his nobles and visiting dignitaries from having to walk – and bow – the whole length of Chandni Chowk, for no one was allowed to ride in the presence of the emperor. When the emperor sat in the Diwan-i-Am he could see all the way down the chowk, so the addition must have been greatly welcomed by his courtiers. The new entrance arrangement also made an attacking army more vulnerable to the defenders on the walls.

**Chatta Chowk and the Naubat Khana** Inside is the **Covered Bazar**, which was quite exceptional in the 17th century. In Shah Jahan's time there were shops on both upper and

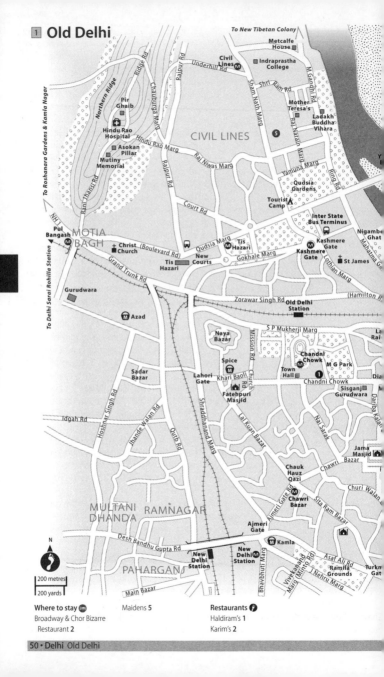

To New Tibetan Colony

Metcalfe House

Civil Lines

Indraprastha College

Underhill Rd

Ridge Rd

Chauburja Marg

Raipur Rd

Sham Nath Marg

M Gandhi Rd

Shri Ram Rd

Mother Teresa's

Ladakh Buddha Vihara

Pir Ghaib

Northern Ridge

Hindu Rao Hospital

Asokan Pillar

Mutiny Memorial

Hindu Rao Marg

Raj Narain Marg

CIVIL LINES

To Roshanara Gardens & Kamla Nagar

Raj Niwas Marg

Raipur Rd

Court Rd

Yamuna Marg

Qudsia Gardens

Tourist Camp

Ring Rd

Ram Jhans Rd

NH-1

Pul Bangash

MOTIA BAGH

Christ (Boulevard Rd) Church

New Courts

Qudsia Marg

Tis Hazari

Inter State Bus Terminus

Nigambo Ghat

Kashmere Gate

Kashmere Gate

St James

Mahatma Ga

Tis Hazari

Gokhale Marg

Lothian Marg

To Delhi Sarai Rohilla Station

Grand Trunk Rd

Gurudwara

Azad

Zorawar Singh Rd

Old Delhi Station

(Hamilton R

Naya Bazar

Mission Rd

S P Mukherji Marg

La Rai

Spice

Sadar Bazar

Lahori Gate

Khari Baoli

Church

Chandni Chowk

Town Hall

M G Park

Chandni Chowk

Dia

Hoshnar Singh Rd

Jhande Walan Rd

Qutb Rd

Shraddhanand Marg

Fatehpuri Masjid

Lal Kuan Bazar

Sisganj Gurudwara

Dariba Kalan

Idgah Rd

Nai Sarak

Jama Masjid

Bazar

Chauk Hauz Qazi

Churi Walan

MULTANI DHANDA

RAMNAGAR

Chawri Bazar

Sita Ram Bazar

Ajmeri Gate

Ajmeri Gate Rd

Desh Bandhu Gupta Rd

New Delhi Station

New Delhi Station

Kamla

Asaf Ali Rd

Ramlila Grounds

Turkn Gat

PAHARGANJ

Bhavbhuti Marg

Vivekanand Marg (Minto) Rd

J Nehru Marg

200 metres

200 yards

Main Bazar

**Where to stay** 🛏  Maidens 5

Broadway & Chor Bizarre Restaurant 2

**Restaurants** 🍴

Haldiram's 1

Karim's 2

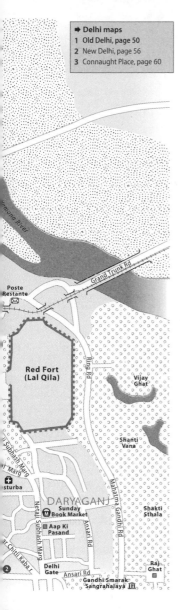

Poste
Restante

Red Fort
(Lal Qila)

Vijay
Ghat

Shanti
Vana

DARYAGANJ

Sunday
Book Market

Aap Ki
Pasand

Shakti
Sthala

Delhi
Gate

Ansari Rd

Raj
Ghat

Gandhi Smarak
Sangrahalaya

Grand Trunk Rd

Ring Rd

Subhash Marg

Marg

sturba

Chitli Kabar L

Netaji Subhash Marg

Ansari Rd

Mahatma Gandhi Rd

Yamuna River

lower levels. Originally they catered for the Imperial household and carried stocks of silks, brocades, velvets, gold and silverware, jewellery and gems. There were coffee shops too for nobles and courtiers.

The **Naqqar Khana** or **Naubat Khana** (Drum House or music gallery) marked the entrance to the inner apartments of the fort. Here everyone except the princes of the royal family had to dismount and leave their horses or *hathi* (elephants), hence its other name of **Hathi Pol** (Elephant Gate). Five times a day ceremonial music was played on the kettle drum, *shahnais* (a kind of oboe) and cymbals, glorifying the emperor. In 1754 Emperor Ahmad Shah was murdered here. The gateway with four floors is decorated with floral designs. You can still see traces of the original panels painted in gold or other colours on the interior of the gateway.

**Diwan-i-Am** Between the first inner court and the royal palaces at the heart of the fort, stood the **Diwan-i-Am** (Hall of Public Audience), the furthest point a normal visitor would reach. It has seen many dramatic events, including the destructive whirlwind of the Persian Nadir Shah in 1739 and of Ahmad Shah the Afghan in 1756, and the trial of the last 'King of Delhi', **Bahadur Shah II** in 1858.

The well-proportioned hall was both a functional building and a showpiece intended to hint at the opulence of the palace itself. In Shah Jahan's time the sandstone was hidden behind a very thin layer of white polished plaster, *chunam*. This was decorated with floral motifs in many colours, especially gilt. Silk carpets and heavy curtains hung from the canopy rings outside the building; such interiors were reminders of the Mughals' nomadic origins in Central Asia, where royal durbars were held in tents.

At the back of the hall is a platform for the emperor's throne. Around this was a gold railing, within which stood the princes and great nobles separated from the lesser nobles inside the hall. Behind the throne canopy are 12 marble panels inlaid with motifs of fruiting trees, parrots and cuckoos. Figurative workmanship is very unusual in Islamic buildings, and these panels are the only example in the Red Fort.

As well as matters of official administration, Shah Jahan would listen to accounts of illness, dream interpretations and anecdotes from his ministers and nobles. Wednesday was the day of judgement. Sentences were often swift and brutal and sometimes the punishment of dismemberment, beating or death was carried out on the spot. The executioners were close at hand with axes and whips. On Friday, the Muslim holy day, there would be no business.

**Inner palace buildings** Behind the Diwan-i-Am is the private enclosure of the fort. Along the east wall, overlooking the River Yamuna, Shah Jahan set six small palaces (five survive). Also within this compound are the Harem, the Life-Bestowing Garden and the Nahr-i-Bihisht (Stream of Paradise).

**Life-Bestowing Gardens (Hayat Baksh Bagh)** The original gardens were landscaped according to the Islamic principles of the Persian *char bagh*, with pavilions, fountains and water courses dividing the garden into various but regular beds. The two pavilions **Sawan** and **Bhadon**, named after the first two months of the rainy season (July-August), reveal something of the character of the garden. The garden used to create the effect of the monsoon and contemporary accounts tell us that in the pavilions – some of which were especially erected for the **Teej** festival, which marks the arrival of the monsoon – the royal ladies would sit in silver swings and watch the rains. Water flowed from the back wall of the pavilion through a slit above the marble shelf and over the niches in the wall. Gold and silver pots of flowers were placed in these alcoves during the day whilst at night candles were lit to create a glistening and colourful effect.

**Shahi Burj** From the pavilion next to the Shahi Burj (**Royal Tower**) the canal known as the **Nahr-i-Bihisht** (Stream of Paradise) began its journey along the Royal Terrace. The three-storey octagonal tower was seriously damaged in 1857 and is still unsafe. In Shah Jahan's time the Yamuna lapped the walls. Shah Jahan used the tower as his most private office and only his sons and a few senior ministers were allowed with him.

**Moti Masjid** To the right are the three marble domes of Aurangzeb's 'Pearl Mosque' (shoes must be removed). Bar the cupolas, it is completely hidden behind a wall of red sandstone, now painted white. Built in 1662 of polished white marble, it has some exquisite decoration. All the surfaces are highly decorated in a fashion similar to rococo, which developed at the same time as in Europe. Unusually the prayer hall is on a raised platform with inlaid outlines of individual *musallas* ('prayer mats') in black marble. While the outer walls were aligned to the cardinal points like all the other fort buildings, the inner walls were positioned so that the mosque would correctly face Mecca.

**Hammam** The **Royal Baths** have three apartments separated by corridors with canals to carry water to each room. The two flanking the entrance, for the royal children, had hot and cold baths. The room furthest away from the door has three basins for rose water fountains.

**Diwan-i-Khas** Beyond is the single-storeyed **Hall of Private Audience**, topped by four Hindu-style *chhattris* and built completely of white marble. The *dado* (lower part of the wall) on the interior was richly decorated with inlaid precious and semi-precious stones. The ceiling was silver but was removed by the Marathas in 1760. Outside, the hall used to have a marble pavement and an arcaded court. Both have gone.

This was the Mughal office of state. Shah Jahan spent two hours here before retiring for a meal, siesta and prayers. In the evening he would return to the hall for more work before going to the harem. The hall's splendour moved the 14th-century poet Amir Khusrau to write the lines inscribed above the corner arches of the north and south walls: *"Agar Firdaus bar rue Zamin-ast/Hamin ast o Hamin ast o Hamin ast"* (If there be a paradise on earth, it is here, it is here, it is here).

**Royal palaces** Next to the Diwan-i-Khas is the three-roomed **Khas Mahal** (Private Palace). Nearest the Diwan-i-Khas is the **Tasbih Khana** (Chamber for the Telling of Rosaries) where the emperor would worship privately with his rosary of 99 beads, one for each of the mystical names of Allah. In the centre is the **Khwabgah** (Palace of Dreams) which gives on to the octagonal **Mussaman Burj** tower. Here Shah Jahan would be seen each morning. A balcony was added to the tower in 1809 and here George V and Queen Mary appeared in their Coronation Durbar of 1911. The **Tosh Khana** (Robe Room), to the south, has a beautiful marble screen at its north end, carved with the scales of justice above the filigree grille. If you are standing with your back to the Diwan-i-Khas you will see a host of circulating suns (a symbol of royalty), but if your back is to the next building (the Rang Mahal), you will see moons surrounding the scales. All these rooms were sumptuously decorated with fine silk carpets, rich silk brocade curtains and lavishly decorated walls. After 1857 the British used the Khas Mahal as an officer's mess and sadly it was defaced.

The **Rang Mahal** (Palace of Colours), the residence of the chief *sultana*, was also the place where the emperor ate most of his meals. It was divided into six apartments. Privacy and coolness were ensured by the use of marble *jali* screens. Like the other palaces it was beautifully decorated with a silver ceiling ornamented with golden flowers to reflect the water in the channel running through the building. The north and south apartments were both known as **Sheesh Mahal** (Palace of Mirrors) since into the ceiling were set hundreds of small mirrors. In the evening when candles were lit a starlight effect would be produced.

Through the palace ran the **Life-bestowing Stream** and at its centre is a lotus-shaped marble basin which had an ivory fountain. As might be expected in such a cloistered and fossetted environment, the ladies sometimes got bored. In the 18th century the **Empress of Jahandar Shah** sat gazing out at the river and remarked that she had never seen a boat sink. Shortly afterwards a boat was deliberately capsized so that she could be entertained by the sight of people bobbing up and down in the water crying for help.

The southernmost of the palaces, the **Mumtaz Mahal** (Palace of Jewels) ① *Tue-Sun 1000-1700*, was also used by the harem. The lower half of its walls are of marble and it contains six apartments. After the Mutiny of 1857 it was used as a guardroom and since 1912 it has been a museum with exhibits of textiles, weapons, carpets, jade and metalwork as well as works depicting life in the court. It should not be missed.

## Spice market

Outside the Red Fort, cycle rickshaws offer a trip to the spice market, Jama Masjid and back through the bazar. You travel slowly westwards down Chandni Chowk passing the town hall. Dismount at Church Road and follow your guide into the heart of the market on Khari Baoli where wholesalers sell every conceivable spice. Ask to go to the roof for an excellent view over the market and back towards the Red Fort. The ride back through the bazar is equally fascinating – look up at the amazing electricity system. The final excitement is getting back across Netaji Subhash Marg. Panic not, the rickshaw wallahs know what they are doing. Negotiate for one hour and expect to pay about Rs 100. The spice laden air may irritate your throat. Also ask a cycle rickshaw to take you to Naughara Street, just off Kinari Bazar, a very pretty street amidst the chaos of Old Delhi.

## Jama Masjid (Friday Mosque)

ⓘ *Visitors welcome from 30 mins after sunrise until 1215; and from 1345 until 30 mins before sunset, free, still or video cameras Rs 150, tower entry Rs 20.*

The magnificent Jama Masjid is the largest mosque in India and the last great architectural work of Shah Jahan, intended to dwarf all mosques that had gone before it. With the fort, it dominates Old Delhi. The mosque is much simpler in its ornamentation than Shah Jahan's secular buildings – a judicious blend of red sandstone and white marble, which are interspersed in the domes, minarets and cusped arches.

**The gateways** Symbolizing the separation of the sacred and the secular, the threshold is a place of great importance where the worshipper steps to a higher plane. There are three huge gateways, the largest being to the east. This was reserved for the royal family who gathered in a private gallery in its upper storey. Today, the faithful enter through the east gate on Fridays and for **Id-ul-Fitr** and **Id-ul-Adha**. The latter commemorates Abraham' (Ibrahim's) sacrificial offering of his son Ishmael (Ismail). Islam (unlike the Jewish and Christian tradition) believes that Abraham offered to sacrifice Ishmael, Isaac's brother.

**The courtyard** The façade has the main *iwan* (arch), five smaller arches on each side with two flanking minarets and three bulbous domes behind, all perfectly proportioned. The *iwan* draws the worshippers' attention into the building. The minarets have great views from the top; well worth the climb for Rs 10 (women may not be allowed to climb alone). The **hauz**, in the centre of the courtyard, is an ablution tank placed as usual between the inner and outer parts of the building to remind the worshipper that it is through the ritual of baptism that one first enters the community of believers. The **Dikka**, in front of the ablution tank, is a raised platform. Muslim communities grew so rapidly that by the eighth century it sometimes became necessary to introduce a second *muballigh* (prayer leader) who stood on this platform and copied the postures and chants of the *imam* inside to relay them to a much larger congregation. With the introduction of the loudspeaker and amplification, the *dikka* and the *muballigh* became redundant. In the northwest corner of the mosque there is a small shed. For a small fee, the faithful are shown a hair from the beard of the prophet, as well as his sandal and his footprint in rock.

## New Delhi → For listings, see pages 68-80.

Delhi's present position as capital was only confirmed on 12 December 1911, when George V announced at the Delhi Durbar that the capital of India was to move from Calcutta to Delhi. The new city, New Delhi, planned under the leadership of British architect Edwin Lutyens with the assistance of his friend Herbert Baker, was inaugurated on 9 February 1931.

The city was to accommodate 70,000 people and have boundless possibilities for future expansion. The king favoured something in form and flavour similar to the Mughal masterpieces but fretted over the horrendous expense that this would incur. A petition signed by eminent public figures such as Bernard Shaw and Thomas Hardy advocated a ndian style and an Indian master builder. Herbert Baker had made known his own views even before his appointment when he wrote "first and foremost it is the spirit of British sovereignty which must be imprisoned in its stone and bronze". Lutyens himself despised ndian architecture. "Even before he had seen any examples of it", writes architectural historian Giles Tillotson, "he pronounced Mughal architecture to be 'piffle', and seeing it did not disturb that conviction". Yet in the end, Lutyens was forced to compromise.

## India Gate and around

A tour of New Delhi will usually start with a visit to India Gate. This war memorial is situated at the eastern end of **Rajpath**. Designed by Lutyens, it commemorates more than 70,000 Indian soldiers who died in the First World War. Some 13,516 names of British and Indian soldiers killed on the Northwest Frontier and in the Afghan War of 1919 are engraved on the arch and foundations. Under the arch is the Amar Jawan Jyoti, commemorating Indian armed forces' losses in the Indo-Pakistan War of 1971. The arch (43 m high) stands on a base of Bharatpur stone and rises in stages. Similar to the Hindu *chhattri* signifying regality, it is decorated with nautilus shells symbolizing British maritime power. Come at dusk to join the picnicking crowds enjoying the evening. You may even be able to have a pedalo ride if there's water in the canal.

## National Gallery of Modern Art

*Jaipur House, near India Gate, 1011-2338 4640, www.ngmaindia.gov.in, Tue-Sun 1000-1700, Rs 150 foreigners, Rs 10 Indians.*

There is now a new air-conditioned wing of this excellent gallery and select exhibits in the old building housed in a former residence of the Maharaja of Jaipur. The '*In the Seeds of Time...*' exhibition traces the trajectory of modern Indian art. Artists include: Amrita Shergil, with over 100 exhibits, synthesizing the flat treatment of Indian painting with a realistic tone; Rabindranath Tagore (ground floor) has examples from a brief but intense spell in the 1930s; The Bombay School or Company School (first floor) includes Western painters who documented their visits to India. Realism is reflected in Indian painting of the early 19th century represented by the schools of Avadh, Patna, Sikkim and Thanjavur; The Bengal School (the late 19th-century Revivalist Movement) showcases artists such as Abanindranath Tagore and Nandalal Bose have their works exhibited here. Western influence was discarded in response to the nationalist movement. Inspiration derived from Indian folk art is evident in the works of Jamini Roy and YD Shukla. Prints from the gallery shop are incredibly good value – up to Rs 80 for poster-size prints of famous works.

## National Museum

*Janpath, T011-2301 9272, www.nationalmuseumindia.gov.in, daily 1000-1700, foreigners Rs 300 (including audio tour), Indians Rs 10, camera Rs 300; free guided tours 1030, 1130, 1200, 1400, films are screened every day (1430), marble squat toilets, but dirty.*

The collection was formed from the nucleus of the Exhibition of Indian Art, London 1947). Now merged with the Asian Antiquities Museum it displays a rich collection of the artistic treasure of Central Asia and India including ethnological objects from prehistoric archaeological finds to the late Medieval period. Replicas of exhibits and books on Indian culture and art are on sale. There is also a research library.

**Ground floor Prehistoric**: seals, figurines, toy animals and jewellery from the Harappan civilization (2400-1500 BC). **Maurya Period**: terracottas and stone heads from around the

**N**

700 metres
700 yards

### Where to stay
Amarya Haveli **24** *F2*
Claridges **5** *C3*
Jyoti Mahal **1** *A3*
K One One **28** *D4*
Life Tree **12** *E4*
Manor **13** *E5*
Master **14** *B2*
Oberoi **15** *C4*
Prince Polonia **3** *A3*
Rak Internacional **4** *A3*
Taj Mahal **19** *C3*
Tree of Life **16** *F3*
Vivanta by Taj **2** *C4*
Youth Hostel **22** *C2*

### Restaurants
Baci **21** *C4*
Bukhara **1** *C1*
Café Sim Tok **2** *A3*
Dum Pukht **1** *C1*
Grey Garden & Gunpowder **3** *F2*
Indian Accent **13** *D5*
Kainoosh **34** *E1*
Khan Cha Cha **33** *C4*
Latitude **27** *C3*
Lodi **10** *D3*
Magique **35** *F2*

Naivedyam & Elma's **4** *F2*
Nathu's & Bengali Sweet
 House **18** *B4*
Olive at the Qutb **12** *F2*
Park Baluchi **6** *E2*
Sagar Ratna **8** *E4*
Tadka **14** *A3*
Triveni Tea Terrace **5** *B4*

### Bars & clubs
Blue Frog **36** *F2*
Café Morrisons **38** *E3*
Living Room **7** *F2*
Stone **45** *D4*
Urban Pind **47** *E4*
Zoo **48** *F2*

Metro Stops (Yellow Line)
Metro Stops (Videt Line)

➡ **Delhi maps**
1 Old Delhi, page 50
2 New Delhi, page 56
3 Connaught Place, page 60

third century BC include the *chaturmukha* (four-faced) *lingam*. **Gandhara School**: stucco heads showing the Graeco Roman influence. **Gupta terracottas** (circa AD 400): including two life-size images of the river goddesses Ganga and Yamuna and the four-armed bust of Vishnu from a temple near Lal Kot. **South Indian sculpture**: from Pallava and early Chola temples and relief panels from Mysore. Bronzes from the Buddhist monastery at Nalanda. Some of Buddha's relics were placed in the Thai pavilion in 1997.

**First floor Illustrated manuscripts**: include the *Babur-i-nama* in the emperor's own handwriting and an autographed copy of Jahangir's memoirs. **Miniature paintings**: include the 16th-century Jain School, the 18th-century Rajasthani School and the Pahari schools of Garhwal, Basoli and Kangra. **Aurel Stein Collection** consists of antiquities recovered by him during his explorations of Central Asia and the western borders of China at the turn of the 20th century.

**Second floor Pre-Columbian and Mayan artefacts**: anthropological section devoted to tribal artefacts and folk arts. **Sharad Rani Bakkiwal Gallery of Musical Instruments**: displays over 300 instruments collected by the famous *sarod* player.

## Rashtrapati Bhavan and Nehru Memorial Museum

Once the Viceroy's House, Rashtrapati Bhavan is the official residence of the President of India. The Viceroy's House, New Delhi's centrepiece of imperial proportions, was 1 km around the foundations, bigger than Louis XIV's palace at Versailles. It had a colossal dome surmounting a long colonnade and 340 rooms in all. It took nearly 20 years to complete, similar to the time it took to build the Taj Mahal. In the busiest year, 29,000 people were working on the site and buildings began to take shape. The project was surrounded by controversy from beginning to end. Opting for a fundamentally classical structure, both Baker and Lutyens sought to incorporate Indian motifs, many entirely superficial. While some claim that Lutyens achieved a unique synthesis of the two traditions, Tillotson asks whether "the sprinkling of a few simplified and classicized Indian details (especially *chhattris*) over a classical palace" could be called a synthesis. The Durbar Hall, 23 m in diameter, has coloured marble from all parts of India.

To the south is **Flagstaff House**, formerly the residence of the commander-in-chief. Renamed Teen Murti Bhawan it now houses the **Nehru Memorial Museum** ① *T011-2301 4504, Tue-Sun 1000-1500, planetarium Mon-Sat 1130-1500, library Mon-Sat 0900-1900, free*. Designed by Robert Tor Russell, in 1948 it became the official residence of India's first prime minister, Jawaharlal Nehru. Converted after his death (1964) into a national memorial, the reception, study and bedroom are intact. A *Jyoti Jawahar* (torch) symbolizes the eternal values he inspired and a granite rock is carved with extracts from his historic speech at midnight on 14 August 1947; an informative and vivid history of the Independence Movement.

The **Martyr's Memorial**, at the junction of Sardar Patel Marg and Willingdon Crescent, is a magnificent 26-m-long, 3-m-high bronze sculpture by DP Roy Chowdhury. The 11 statues of national heroes are headed by Mahatma Gandhi.

## Eternal Gandhi Multimedia Museum

① *Birla House, 5 Tees Jan Marg (near Claridges Hotel), T011-3095 7269, www.eternal gandhi.org, closed Mon and 2nd Sat, 1000-1700, free, film at 1500.*
Gandhi's last place of residence and the site of his assassination, Birla House has been converted into a whizz-bang display of 'interactive' modern technology. Over-attended by young guides

eager to demonstrate the next gadget, the museum seems aimed mainly at those with a critically short attention span, and is too rushed to properly convey the story of Gandhi's life. However, a monument in the garden marking where he fell is definitely worth a visit.

Other museums in the city related to Gandhi include: **National Gandhi Museum** ⓘ *opposite Raj Ghat, T011-2331 1793, www.gandhimuseum.org, Tue-Sat 0930-1730*, with five pavilions – sculpture, photographs and paintings of Gandhi and the history of the *Satyagraha* movement (the philosophy of non-violence); **Gandhi Smarak Sangrahalaya** ⓘ *Raj Ghat, T011-2301 1480, Fri-Wed 0930-1730*, displays some of Gandhi's personal belongings and a small library includes recordings of speeches; and the **Indira Gandhi Museum** ⓘ *1 Safdarjang Rd, T011-2301 0094, Tue-Sun 0930-1700, free*, charting the phases of her life from childhood to the moment of her death. Exhibits are fascinating, if rather gory – you can see the blood-stained, bullet-ridden sari she was wearing when assassinated.

## Parliament House and around
Northeast of the Viceroy's House is the **Council House**, now **Sansad Bhavan**. Baker designed this based on Lutyens' suggestion that it be circular (173 m diameter). Inside are the library and chambers for the Council of State, Chamber of Princes and Legislative Assembly – the **Lok Sabha**. Just opposite the Council House is the **Rakabganj Gurudwara** in Pandit Pant Marg. This 20th-century white marble shrine, which integrates the late Mughal and Rajasthani styles, marks the spot where the headless body of Guru Tegh Bahadur, the ninth Sikh Guru, was cremated in 1657. West of the Council House is the **Cathedral Church of the Redemption** (1927-1935) and to its north the Italianate Roman Catholic **Church of the Sacred Heart** (1930-1934), both conceived by Henry Medd.

## Connaught Place and Connaught Circus → *See map, page 60.*
Connaught Place and its outer ring, Connaught Circus (now officially named **Rajiv Chowk** and **Indira Chowk**, but still commonly referred to by their old names), comprise two-storey arcaded buildings, arranged radially around a circular garden that was completed after the Metro line was installed. Designed by Robert Tor Russell, they have become the main commercial and tourist centre of New Delhi. Sadly, the area also attracts bands of insistent touts.

## Lakshmi Narayan Mandir
To the west of Connaught Circus is the Lakshmi Narayan **Birla Temple** in Mandir Marg. Financed by the prominent industrialist Raja Baldeo Birla in 1938, this is one of the most popular Hindu shrines in the city and one of Delhi's few striking examples of Hindu architecture. Dedicated to Lakshmi, the goddess of well-being, it is commonly referred to as **Birla Mandir**. The design is in the Orissan style with tall curved *sikharas* (towers) capped by large *amalakas*. The exterior is faced with red and ochre stone and white marble. Built around a central courtyard, the main shrine has images of Narayan and his consort Lakshmi while two separate cells have icons of Siva (the Destroyer) and Durga (the 10-armed destroyer of demons). The temple is flanked by a *dharamshala* (rest house) and a Buddhist *vihara* (monastery).

## Gurudwara Bangla Sahib
ⓘ *Baba Kharak Singh Rd, free.*
This is a fine example of Sikh temple architecture, featuring a large pool reminiscent of Amritsar's Golden Temple. The 24-hour reciting of the faith's holy book adds to the atmosphere, and there's free food on offer, although don't be surprised if you're asked

to help out with the washing up! You must remove your shoes and cover your head to enter – suitable scarves are provided if you arrive without.

Further northeast on Baba Kharak Singh Marg is **Hanuman Mandir**. This small temple was built by Maharaja Jai Singh II of Jaipur. **Mangal haat** (Tuesday Fair) is a popular market.

## ③ Connaught Place

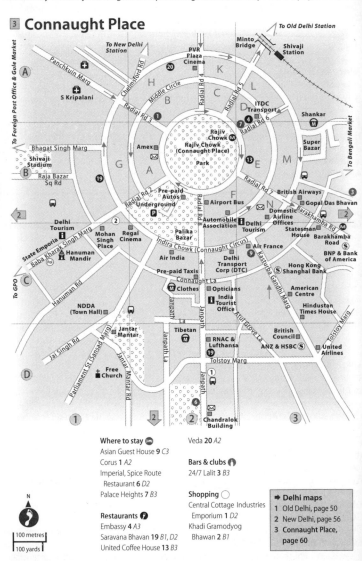

**Where to stay** 🛏
Asian Guest House **9** C3
Corus **1** A2
Imperial, Spice Route
   Restaurant **6** D2
Palace Heights **7** B3

**Restaurants** 🍴
Embassy **4** A3
Saravana Bhavan **19** B1, D2
United Coffee House **13** B3

Veda **20** A2

**Bars & clubs** 🍸
24/7 Lalit **3** B3

**Shopping** ◯
Central Cottage Industries
   Emporium **1** D2
Khadi Gramodyog
   Bhawan **2** B1

➡ **Delhi maps**
1 Old Delhi, page 50
2 New Delhi, page 56
3 Connaught Place,
   page 60

## Jantar Mantar

Just to the east of the Hanuman Mandir in Sansad Marg (Parliament Street) is Jai Singh's **observatory** (Jantar Mantar) ① *sunrise to sunset, Rs 100 foreigners, Rs 5 Indians*. The Mughal Emperor Mohammad Shah (ruled 1719-1748) entrusted the renowned astronomer Maharaja Jai Singh II with the task of revising the calendar and correcting the astronomical tables used by contemporary priests. Daily astral observations were made for years before construction began and plastered brick structures were favoured for the site instead of brass instruments. Built in 1725 it is slightly smaller than the later observatory at Jaipur.

## Memorial Ghats

Beyond Delhi Gate lies the **Yamuna River**, marked by a series of memorials to India's leaders. The river itself, a kilometre away, is invisible from the road, protected by a low rise and banks of trees. The most prominent memorial, immediately opposite the end of Jawaharlal Nehru Road, is that of Mahatma Gandhi at **Raj Ghat**. To its north is **Shanti Vana** (Forest of Peace), landscaped gardens where Prime Minister Jawaharlal Nehru was cremated in 1964, as were his grandson Sanjay Gandhi in 1980, daughter Indira Gandhi in 1984 and elder grandson, Rajiv, in 1991. To the north again is **Vijay Ghat** (Victory Bank) where Prime Minister Lal Bahadur Shastri was cremated.

## South Delhi → *For listings, see pages 68-80.*

South Delhi is often overlooked by travellers. This is a real pity as it houses some of the city's most stunning sites, best accommodation, bars, clubs and restaurants, as well as some of its most tranquil parks. However be warned, South Delhi can be hell during rushhour when the traffic on the endless flyovers comes to a virtual standstill. But with the Metro, you can explore all the way down to Gurgaon with relative ease.

## Lodi Gardens

These beautiful gardens, with mellow stone tombs of the 15th- and 16th-century Lodi rulers, are popular for gentle strolls and jogging. In the middle of the garden facing the east entrance from Max Mueller Road is **Bara Gumbad** (Big Dome), a mosque built in 1494. The raised courtyard is provided with an imposing gateway and *mehman khana* (guest rooms). The platform in the centre appears to have had a tank for ritual ablutions.

The **Sheesh Bumbad** (Glass Dome, late 15th century) is built on a raised incline north of the Bara Gumbad and was once decorated with glazed blue tiles, painted floral designs and Koranic inscriptions. The façade gives the impression of a two-storeyed building, typical of Lodi architecture. **Mohammad Shah's Tomb** (1450) is that of the third Sayyid ruler. It has sloping buttresses, an octagonal plan, projecting eaves and lotus patterns on the ceiling. **Sikander Lodi's Tomb**, built by his son in 1517, is also an octagonal structure decorated with Hindu motifs. A structural innovation is the double dome which was later refined under the Mughals. The 16th-century **Athpula** (Bridge of Eight Piers), near the northeastern entrance, is attributed to Nawab Bahadur, a nobleman at Akbar's court.

## Safdarjang's Tomb

① *Sunrise to sunset, Rs 100 foreigners, Rs 5 Indians*.

Safdarjang's Tomb, seldom visited, was built by Nawab Shuja-ud-Daulah for his father Mirza Mukhim Abdul Khan, entitled Safdarjang, who was Governor of Oudh (1719-1748), and Wazir of his successor (1748-1754). Safdarjang died in 1754. With its high enclosure walls, *char bagh* layout of gardens, fountain and central domed mausoleum, it follows the tradition of Humayun's tomb. Typically, the real tomb is just below ground level. Flanking the mausoleum are pavilions used by Shuja-ud-Daulah as his family residence. Immediately to its south is the battlefield where Timur and his Mongol horde crushed Mahmud Shah Tughluq on 12 December 1398.

## Nizamuddin's Tomb
ⓘ *Dress ultra-modestly if you don't want to feel uncomfortable or cause offence.*
At the east end of the Lodi Road, Hazrat Nizamuddin Dargah (Nizamuddin's Tomb) now tucked away behind the residential suburb of Nizamuddin West, off Mathura Road, grew up around the shrine of Sheikh Nizamuddin Aulia (1236-1325), a Chishti saint. This is a wonderfully atmospheric place. *Qawwalis* are sung at sunset after *namaaz* (prayers), and are particularly impressive on Thursdays – be prepared for crowds. Highly recommended.

West of the central shrine is the **Jama-at-khana Mosque** (1325). Its decorated arches are typical of the Khalji design also seen at the Ala'i Darwaza at the Qutb Minar. South of the main tomb and behind finely crafted screens is the grave of princess Jahanara, Shah Jahan's eldest and favourite daughter. She shared the emperor's last years when he was imprisoned at Agra Fort. The grave, open to the sky, is in accordance with the epitaph written by her: "Let naught cover my grave save the green grass, for grass suffices as the covering of the lowly". Pilgrims congregate at the shrine twice a year for the **Urs** (fair) held to mark the anniversaries of Hazrat Nizamuddin Aulia and his disciple Amir Khusrau, whose tomb is nearby.

## Humayun's Tomb
ⓘ *Sunrise to sunset, Rs 250 foreigners, Rs 10 Indians, video cameras Rs 25, located in Nizamuddin, 15-20 mins by taxi from Connaught Circus, allow 45 mins.*
Eclipsed later by the Taj Mahal and the Jama Masjid, this tomb is the best example in Delhi of the early Mughal style of tomb. Superbly maintained, it is well worth a visit, preferably before visiting the Taj Mahal. Humayun, the second Mughal emperor, was forced into exile in Persia after being heavily defeated by the Afghan Sher Shah in 1540. He returned to India in 1545, finally recapturing Delhi in 1555. The tomb was designed and built by his senior widow and mother of his son Akbar, Hamida Begum. A Persian from Khurasan, after her pilgrimage to Mecca she was known as Haji Begum. She supervised the entire construction of the tomb (1564-1573), camping on the site.

**The approach** The tomb enclosure has two high double-storeyed gateways: the entrance to the west and the other to the south. A *baradari* occupies the centre of the east wall, and a bath chamber that of the north wall. Several Moghul princes, princesses and Haji Begum herself lie buried here. During the 1857 Mutiny Bahadur Shah II, the last Moghul emperor of Delhi, took shelter here with his three sons. Over 80, he was seen as a figurehead by Muslims opposing the British. When captured he was transported to Yangon (Rangoon) for the remaining four years of his life. The tomb to the right of the approach is that of Isa Khan, Humayun's barber.

**The dome** Some 38 m high, the dome does not have the swell of the Taj Mahal and the decoration of the whole edifice is much simpler. It is of red sandstone with some white marble to highlight the lines of the building. There is some attractive inlay work, and some *jalis* in the balcony fence and on some of the recessed keel arch windows. The interior is austere and consists of three storeys of arches rising up to the dome. The emperor's tomb is of white marble and quite plain without any inscription. The overall impression is that of a much bulkier, more squat building than the Taj Mahal. The cavernous space under the main tombs is home to great colonies of bats.

## Hauz Khas

ⓘ *1-hr cultural show, 1845, Rs 100 (check with Delhi Tourism, see page 47).*
South of Safdarjang's Tomb, and entered off either Aurobindo Marg on the east side or Africa Avenue on the west side, is Hauz Khas. Ala-ud-din Khalji (ruled 1296-1313) created a large tank here for the use of the inhabitants of Siri, the second capital city of Delhi founded by him. Fifty years later Firoz Shah Tughluq cleaned up the silted tank and raised several buildings on its east and south banks which are known as Hauz Khas or Royal Tank.

Firoz Shah's austere tomb is found here. The multi-storeyed wings, on the north and west of the tomb, were built by him in 1354 as a *madrasa* (college). The octagonal and square *chhattris* were built as tombs, possibly to the teachers at the college. Hauz Khas is now widely used as a park for early-morning recreation – walking, running and yoga *asanas*. Classical music concerts, dance performances and a *son et lumière* show are held in the evenings when monuments are illuminated by thousands of earthen lamps and torches. Wandering the streets of Haus Khaz village, you can almost forget that you are in India. Labyrinthine alleys lead to numerous galleries, boutiques, restaurants and a lot of little design studios.

## Qutb Minar Complex

ⓘ *Sunrise to sunset, Rs 250 foreigners, Rs 10 Indians. The Metro goes to Qutb Minar. Bus 505 from New Delhi Railway Station (Ajmeri Gate), Super Bazar (east of Connaught Circus) and Cottage Industries Emporium, Janpath. Auto Rs 110, though drivers may be reluctant to take you. This area is also opening up as a hub for new chic restaurants and bars.*
Muhammad Ghuri conquered northwest India at the very end of the 12th century. The conquest of the Gangetic plain down to Benares (Varanasi) was undertaken by Muhammad's Turkish slave and chief general, Qutb-ud-din-Aibak, whilst another general took Bihar and Bengal. In the process, temples were reduced to rubble, the remaining Buddhist centres were dealt their death blow and their monks slaughtered. When Muhammad was assassinated in 1206, his gains passed to the loyal Qutb-ud-din-Aibak. Thus the first sultans or Muslim kings of Delhi became known as the **Slave Dynasty** (1026-1290). For the next three centuries the Slave Dynasty and the succeeding Khalji (1290-1320), Tughluq (1320-1414), Sayyid (1414-1445) and Lodi (1451-1526) dynasties provided Delhi with fluctuating authority. The legacy of their ambitions survives in the tombs, forts and palaces that litter Delhi Ridge and the surrounding plain. Qutb-ud-din-Aibak died after only four years in power, but he left his mark with the **Qutb Minar** and his **citadel**. Qutb Minar, built to proclaim the victory of Islam over the infidel, dominates the countryside for miles around. Visit the *minar* first.

**Qutb Minar** In 1199 work began on what was intended to be the most glorious tower of victory in the world and was to be the prototype of all *minars* (towers) in India. Qutb-ud-din-Aibak had probably seen and been influenced by the brick victory pillars in Ghazni in Afghanistan, but this one was also intended to serve as the minaret attached to the Might of Islam Mosque. From here the muezzin could call the faithful to prayer. Later every mosque would incorporate its minaret.

As a mighty reminder of the importance of the ruler as Allah's representative on earth, the Qutb Minar (literally 'axis minaret') stood at the centre of the community. A pivot of Faith, Justice and Righteousness, its name also carried the message of Qutb-ud-din's (Axis of the Faith) own achievements. The inscriptions carved in Kufi script tell that "the tower was erected to cast the shadow of God over both east and west". For Qutb-ud-din-Aibak it marked the eastern limit of the empire of the One God. Its western counterpart is the Giralda Tower built by Yusuf in Seville.

The Qutb Minar is 73 m high and consists of five storeys. The diameter of the base is 14.4 m and 2.7 m at the top. Qutb-ud-din built the first three and his son-in-law Iltutmish embellished these and added a fourth. This is indicated in some of the Persian and Nagari (North Indian) inscriptions which also record that it was twice damaged by lightning in 1326 and 1368. While repairing the damage caused by the second, Firoz Shah Tughluq added a fifth storey and used marble to face the red and buff sandstone. This was the first time contrasting colours were used decoratively, later to become such a feature of Mughal buildings. Firoz's fifth storey was topped by a graceful cupola but this fell down during an earthquake in 1803. A new one was added by a Major Robert Smith in 1829 but was so out of keeping that it was removed in 1848 and now stands in the gardens.

The original storeys are heavily indented with different styles of fluting, alternately round and angular on the bottom, round on the second and angular on the third. The beautifully carved honeycomb detail beneath the balconies is reminiscent of the Alhambra Palace in Spain. The calligraphy bands are verses from the Koran and praises to its patron builder.

**Quwwat-ul-Islam Mosque** The Quwwat-ul-Islam Mosque (The Might of Islam Mosque), the earliest surviving mosque in India, is to the northwest of the Qutb Minar. It was begun in 1192, immediately after Qutb-ud-din's conquest of Delhi and completed in 1198, using the remains of no fewer than 27 local Hindu and Jain temples.

The architectural style contained elements that Muslims brought from Arabia, including buildings made of mud and brick and decorated with glazed tiles, *squinches* (arches set diagonally across the corners of a square chamber to facilitate the raising of a dome and to effect a transition from a square to a round structure), the pointed arch and the true dome. Finally, Muslim buildings came alive through ornamental calligraphy and geometric patterning. This was in marked contrast to indigenous Indian styles of architecture. Hindu, Buddhist and Jain buildings relied on the post-and-beam system in which spaces were traversed by corbelling, ie shaping flat-laid stones to create an arch. The arched screen that runs along the western end of the courtyard beautifully illustrates the fact that it was Hindu methods that still prevailed at this stage, for the 16-m-high arch uses Indian corbelling, the corners being smoothed off to form the curved line.

**Screens** Qutb-ud-din's screen formed the façade of the mosque and, facing in the direction of Mecca, became the focal point. The sandstone screen is carved in the Indo-Islamic style, lotuses mingling with Koranic calligraphy. The later screenwork and other extensions (1230) are fundamentally Islamic in style, the flowers and leaves having been replaced by more arabesque patterns. Indian builders mainly used stone, which from the fourth century AD had been intricately carved with representations of the gods. In their first buildings in India the Muslim architects designed the buildings and local Indian craftsmen built them and decorated them with typical motifs such as the vase and foliage, tasselled ropes, bells and cows.

**Iltutmish's extension** The mosque was enlarged twice. In 1230 Qutb-ud-din's son-in-law and successor, Shamsuddin Iltutmish, doubled its size by extending the colonnades and prayer hall – 'Iltutmish's extension'. This accommodated a larger congregation, and in the more stable conditions of Iltutmish's reign, Islam was obviously gaining ground. The arches of the extension are nearer to the true arch and are similar to the Gothic arch that appeared in Europe at this time. The decoration is Islamic. Almost 100 years after Iltutmish's death, the mosque was enlarged again, by Ala-ud-din Khalji. The conductor of tireless and bloody military campaigns, Ala-ud-din proclaimed himself 'God's representative on earth'. His architectural ambitions, however, were not fully realized, because on his death in 1316 only part of the north and east extensions were completed.

**Ala'i Minar and the Ala'i Darwaza** To the north of the Qutb complex is the 26-m **Ala'i Minar**, intended to surpass the tower of the Qutb, but not completed beyond the first storey. Ala-ud-din did complete the south gateway to the building, the **Ala'i Darwaza**; inscriptions testify that it was built in 1311 (Muslim 710 AH). He benefited from events in Central Asia: since the early 13th century, Mongol hordes from Central Asia fanned out east and west, destroying the civilization of the Seljuk Turks in West Asia, and refugee artists, architects, craftsmen and poets fled east. They brought to India features and techniques that had developed in Byzantine Turkey, some of which can be seen in the Ala'i Darwaza.

**Iltutmish's Tomb** Built in 1235, Iltutmish's Tomb lies in the northwest of the compound, midway along the west wall of the mosque. It is the first surviving tomb of a Muslim ruler in India. Two other tombs also stand within the extended Might of Islam Mosque. The idea of a tomb was quite alien to Hindus, who had been practising cremation since around 400 BC. Blending Hindu and Muslim styles, the outside is relatively plain with three arched and decorated doorways. The interior carries reminders of the nomadic origins of the first Muslim rulers. Like a Central Asian *yurt* (tent) in its decoration, it combines the familiar Indian motifs of the wheel, bell, chain and lotus with the equally familiar geometric arabesque patterning. The west wall is inset with three *mihrabs* that indicate the direction of Mecca.

## Tughluqabad

① *Sunrise to sunset, foreigners Rs100, Indians Rs 5, video camera Rs 25, allow 1 hr for return rickshaws, turn right at entrance and walk 200 m. The site is often deserted so don't go alone. Take plenty of water.*

Tughluqabad's ruins, 7.5 km east from Qutb Minar, still convey a sense of the power and energy of the newly arrived Muslims in India. From the walls you get a magnificent impression of the strategic advantages of the site. **Ghiyas'ud-Din Tughluq** (ruled 1321-1325), after ascending the throne of Delhi, selected this site for his capital. He built a massive fort around his capital city which stands high on a rocky outcrop of the Delhi Ridge. The fort is roughly octagonal in plan with a circumference of 6.5 km. The vast size, strength and obvious solidity of the whole give it an air of massive grandeur. It was not until Babur (ruled 1526-1530) that dynamite was used in warfare, so this is a very defensible site.

East of the main entrance is the rectangular **citadel**. A wider area immediately to the west and bounded by walls contained the **palaces**. Beyond this to the north lay the **city**. Now marked by the ruins of houses, the streets were laid out in a grid fashion. Inside the citadel enclosure is the **Vijay Mandal tower** and the remains of several halls including a long underground passage. The fort also contained seven tanks.

A causeway connects the fort with the tomb of Ghiyas'ud-Din Tughluq, while a wide embankment near its southeast corner gave access to the fortresses of **Adilabad** about 1 km away, built a little later by Ghiyas'ud-Din's son Muhammad. The tomb is very well preserved and has red sandstone walls with a pronounced slope (the first Muslim building in India to have sloping walls), crowned with a white marble dome. This dome, like that of the Ala'i Darwaza at the Qutb, is crowned by an *amalaka*, a feature of Hindu architecture. Also Hindu is the trabeate arch at the tomb's fortress wall entrance. Inside are three cenotaphs belonging to Ghiyas'ud-Din, his wife and son Muhammad.

Ghiyas'ud-Din Tughluq quickly found that military victories were no guarantee of lengthy rule. When he returned home after a victorious campaign the welcoming pavilion erected by his son and successor, Muhammad-bin Tughluq, was deliberately collapsed over him. Tughluqabad was abandoned shortly afterwards and was thus only inhabited for five years. The Tughluq dynasty continued to hold Delhi until Timur sacked it and slaughtered its inhabitants. For a brief period Tughluq power shifted to Jaunpur near Varanasi, where the Tughluq architectural traditions were carried forward in some superb mosques.

## Baha'i Temple (Lotus Temple)

ⓘ *1 Apr-30 Sep 0900-1900, 1 Oct-31 Mar Tue-Sun 0930-1730, free entry and parking, visitors welcome to attend services, at other times the temple is open for silent meditation and prayer. Audio-visual presentations in English are at 1100, 1200, 1400 and 1530, remove shoes before entering. Bus 433 from the centre (Jantar Mantar) goes to Nehru Place, within walking distance (1.5 km) of the temple at Kalkaji, or take a taxi or auto-rickshaw.*

Architecturally the Baha'i Temple is a remarkably striking building. Constructed in 1980-1981, it is built out of white marble and in the characteristic Baha'i temple shape of a lotus flower – 45 lotus petals form the walls – which internally creates a feeling of light and space (34 m high, 70 m in diameter). It is a simple design, brilliantly executed and very elegant in form. All Baha'i temples are nine-sided, symbolizing 'comprehensiveness, oneness and unity'. The Delhi Temple, which seats 1300, is surrounded by nine pools, an attractive feature also helping to keep the building cool. It is particularly attractive when flood-lit. Baha'i temples are "dedicated to the worship of God, for peoples of all races, religions or castes. Only the Holy Scriptures of the Baha'i Faith and earlier revelations are read or recited".

## East of the Yamuna → *For listings, see pages 68-80.*

Designated as the site of the athletes' village for the 2010 Commonwealth Games, East Delhi has just one attraction to draw visitors across the Yamuna.

## Swaminarayan Akshardham

ⓘ *www.akshardham.com, Apr-Sep Tue-Sun 1000-1900, Oct-Mar Tue-Sun 0900-1800, temple free, Rs 170 for 'attractions', musical fountain Rs 20, no backpacks, cameras or other electronic items (bag and body searches at entry gate). Packed on Sun; visit early to avoid crowds.*

Opened in November 2005 on the east bank of the Yamuna, the gleaming Akshardham complex represents perhaps the most ambitious construction project in India since the foundation of New Delhi itself. At the centre of a surreal 40-ha 'cultural complex' complete with landscaped gardens, cafés and theme park rides, the temple-monument is dedicated to the 18th-century saint Bhagwan Swaminarayan, who abandoned his home at the age of

11 to embark on a lifelong quest for the spiritual and cultural uplift of Western India. It took 11,000 craftsmen, all volunteers, no less than 300 million hours to complete the temple using traditional building and carving techniques.

If this is the first religious site you visit in India, the security guards and swarms of mooching Indian tourists will hardly prepare you for the typical temple experience. Yet despite this, and the boat rides and animatronic shows which have prompted inevitable comparisons to a 'spiritual Disneyland', most visitors find the Akshardham an inspiring, indeed uplifting, experience, if for no other reason than that the will and ability to build something of its scale and complexity still exist.

**The temple** You enter the temple complex through a series of intricately carved gates. The Bhakti Dwar (Gate of Devotion), adorned with 208 pairs of gods and their consorts, leads into a hall introducing the life of Swaminarayan and the activities of BAPS (Bochasanwasi Shri Akshar Purushottam Swaminarayan Sanstha), the global Hindu sect-cum-charity which runs Akshardham. The main courtyard is reached through the Mayur Dwar (Peacock Gate), a conglomeration of 869 carved peacocks echoed by an equally florid replica directly facing it.

From here you get your first look at the central monument. Perfectly symmetrical in pink sandstone and white marble, it rests on a plinth encircled by 148 elephants, each sculpted from a 20-tonne stone block, in situations ranging from the literal to the mythological: mortal versions grapple with lions or lug tree trunks, while Airavatha, the eight-trunked mount of Lord Indra, surfs majestically to shore after the churning of the oceans at the dawn of Hindu creation. Above them, carvings of deities, saints and *sadhus* cover every inch of the walls and columns framing the inner sanctum, where a gold-plated *murti* (idol) of Bhagwan Swaminarayan sits attended by avatars of his spiritual successors, beneath a staggeringly intricate marble dome. Around the main dome are eight smaller domes, each carved in hypnotic fractal patterns, while paintings depicting Swaminarayan's life of austerity and service line the walls (explanations in English and Hindi).

Surrounding the temple is a moat of holy water supposedly taken from 151 sacred lakes and rivers visited by Swaminarayan on his seven-year barefoot pilgrimage. A total of 108 bronze *gaumukhs* (cow heads) representing the 108 names of God spout water into the tank, which is itself hemmed in by a 1-km-long *parikrama* (colonnade) of red Rajasthani sandstone.

## Delhi listings

*For hotel and restaurant price codes and other relevant information, see pages 22-26.*

### 🛏 Where to stay

Avoid hotel touts. Airport taxis may pretend not to know the location of your chosen hotel so give full details and insist on being taken there. Around Paharganj particularly, you might be followed around by your driver trying to eek a commission out of the guesthouse once you have checked in. It really saves a lot of hassle if you make reservations. Even if you change hotel the next day, it is good to arrive with somewhere booked especially if you are flying in late at night. Hotel prices in Delhi are significantly higher than in most other parts of the country. Smaller **$$** guesthouses away from the centre in **South Delhi** (eg Kailash, Safdarjang) or in **Sunder Nagar**, are quieter and often good value but may not provide food. **$** accommodation is concentrated around **Janpath** and **Paharganj** (New Delhi), and **Chandni Chowk** (Old Delhi) – well patronized but basic and usually cramped yet good for meeting other backpackers.

**Old Delhi and beyond** *p48, map p50*
**$$$$ Maidens**, 7 Sham Nath Marg, T011-2397 5464, www.maidenshotel.com. 54 large well-appointed rooms, restaurant (slow), barbecue nights are excellent, coffee shop, old-style bar, attractive colonial style in quiet area, spacious gardens with excellent pool, friendly welcome, personal attention. One of Delhi's oldest hotels. Recommended.
**$$$ Broadway**, 4/15A Asaf Ali Rd, T011-4366 3600, www.hotelbroadwaydelhi.com. 36 rooms, some wonderfully quirky. Interior designer Catherine Levy has designed some of the rooms in a quirky kitsch style, brightly coloured with psychedelic bathroom tiles. The other rooms are classic design. **Chor Bizarre** restaurant and bar is highly regarded,

as is the 'Thugs' pub. Walking tours of Old Delhi. Easily one of the best options.

**New Delhi** *p54, maps p56 and p60*
**Connaught Place**
**$$$$ Imperial**, Janpath, T011-2334 1234, www.theimperialindia.com. Quintessential Delhi. 230 rooms and beautiful 'deco suites' in supremely elegant Lutyens-designed 1933 hotel. Unparalleled location, great bar, antiques and art everywhere, beautiful gardens with spa and secluded pool, amazing **Spice Route** restaurant. Highly recommended.
**$$$ Hotel Corus**, B-49 Connaught Pl, T011-4365 2222, www.hotelcorus.com. Comfortable hotel right at the heart of things. Good value rooms. You get 15% discount in their onsite **Liffe Caffe.**
**$$$ Palace Heights**, D26-28 Connaught Pl, T011-4358 2610, www.hotelpalace heights.com. Recently given a complete facelift, the bright, modern rooms with good attention to detail, represent the best choice in Connaught Pl in this price bracket. There's also an attractive glass-walled restaurant overlooking the street.
**$ Asian Guest House**, 14 Scindia House, off Kasturba Gandhi Marg, the sign is hidden behind petrol pump, T011-2331 0229, www.asianguesthouse.com. Friendly faces greet you here, although it's a bit tricky to find – call ahead for directions. Great central location. Clean basic rooms, some with a/c, some with TV.

**Paharganj**
Paharganj is where backpackers congregate. Sandwiched between the main sights and near the main railway station, it's noisy, dirty and a lot of hassle.
**$$$$-$$$ Jyoti Mahal**, 2488 Nalwa St, behind Imperial Cinema, T011-2358 0524, www.jyotimahal.net. An oasis in Paharganj with large and atmospheric rooms in a beautiful converted *haveli* and new deluxe

rooms in stylish new wing. Top-notch rooftop restaurant serving continental and Indian dishes. It's a very atmospheric place to dine. Nice boutique **Pink Safari** too. Highly recommended.

**\$\$ Prince Polonia**, 2325-26 Tilak Gali (behind Imperial Cinema), T011-4762 6600, www.hotelprincepolonia.com. Very unusual for Paharganj in that it has a rooftop pool (small, but good for a cool down). Breezy rooftop café. Attracts a slightly more mature crowd. Safe, clean. Recently refurbished.

**\$ Rak International**, 820 Main Bazar, Chowk Bowli, T011-2358 6508, www.hotelrak international.com. 27 basic but clean rooms. Professionally run. Quiet, friendly hotel with a rooftop restaurant and water feature.

### Rajendra Nagar

**\$\$\$-\$\$ Master Guest House**, R-500 New Rajendra Nagar (Shankar Rd and GR Hospital Rd crossing), T011-2874 1089, www.master bedandbreakfast.com. 3 beautiful rooms, a/c, Wi-Fi, rooftop for breakfast, *thalis*, warm welcome, personal attention, secure, recommended. Each room has the theme of a different god, complete with appropriate colour schemes. Very knowledgeable, caring owners run excellent tours of 'hidden Delhi'. They make Delhi feel like home. Recommended.

### South Delhi *p61*

Most of the city's smartest hotels are located south of Rajpath, in a broad rectangle between Chanakyapuri and Humayun's Tomb.

**\$\$\$\$ Claridges**, 12 Aurangzeb Rd, T011-3955 5000, www.claridges.com. 138 refurbished, classy rooms, art deco-style interiors, colonial atmosphere, attractive restaurants (**Jade Garden** is good), slick **Aura** bar, impeccable service, more atmosphere than most. Recommended.

**\$\$\$\$ Manor**, 77 Friends Colony, T011-2692 5151, www.themanordelhi.com. Contemporary boutique hotel with 10 stylish rooms, heavenly beds, polished stone surfaces and chrome, relaxing garden, a haven.

Beautiful artwork and relaxed vibe. Acclaimed restaurant **Indian Accent**. Charming service.

**\$\$\$\$ Oberoi**, Dr Zakir Hussain Marg, T011-2436 3030, www.oberoihotels.com. 300 rooms and extremely luxurious suites overlooking golf club, immaculate, quietly efficient, beautiful touches, carved Tree of Life in lobby, all 5-star facilities including 2 pools and spa, superb business centre, good restaurants – **360°** gets rave reviews.

**\$\$\$\$ Taj Mahal**, 1 Mansingh Rd, T011-2302 6162, www.tajhotels.com. 1 of 3 Taj hotels in Delhi. 300 attractive rooms, comfortable, new club levels outstanding, excellent restaurants and service, lavishly finished with 'lived-in' feel, friendly 1920s-style bar. There is also a **Vivanta by Taj** hotel close to Khan Market with a more business mood.

**\$\$\$\$-\$\$\$ Amarya Haveli**, P5 Hauz Khas Enclave, T011-4175 9268, www.amarya group.com. Luxury, boutique, hip guesthouse, run by 2 Frenchmen. Unique, bright, en suite rooms, with TV, Wi-Fi. Fantastic roof garden. Great home cooked food. Book ahead. They have a sister property **Amarya Villa** in Safdarjung Enclave – the decor there is inspired by *Navratna* (nine gems) – both properties are effortlessly chic. Highly recommended.

**\$\$\$ K One One**, K11, Jangpura Extn, 2nd floor, T011-4359 2583, www.parigold.com. Homely guesthouse in quiet, central residential area. Run by wonderful ex-TV chef, who also gives cooking lessons. All rooms en suite with a/c, minibar, Wi-Fi, some with balconies. Wonderful roof terrace with views of Humayan's Tomb. Rooftop room is lovely. Book ahead.

**\$\$\$-\$\$ Tree of Life B&B**, D-193, Saket, T(0)9810-277699, www.tree-of-life.in. Stylish B&B with beautifully decorated rooms, simple but chic. Kitchen access, excellent on-site reflexology and yoga – really good atmosphere. The owner also runs **Metropole Tourist Service** (page 78). Close to Saket Metro station and to **PVR** cinema and malls.

**\$\$ Life Tree**, G 14 Lajpat Nagar Part II, T(0)9910-460898, lifetreebnb@gmail.com. A more simple but charming B&B from the

Tree of Life family – well located for Khan Market and centre.

**$ Youth Hostel**, 5 Naya Marg, Chanakyapuri, T011-2611 6285, www.yhaindia.org. Wide range of room from a/c doubles to a basic dorm (a/c dorms much better). Meals available at restaurant if ordered in advance. Soulless but clean and comfortable. Great location. You need YHA membership to stay (Rs 250 foreigners, Rs 100 Indians).

### Airport

Unless you can afford a 5-star, hotels around the airport are overpriced and best avoided.
**$$$-$$ Sam's Snooze at My Space** T3 IGI Airport, opposite Gate 17, T(0)8800-230013, www.newdelhiairport.in. You can book a snooze pod for $9 per hr – only if you are flying out of T3. There's Wi-Fi, TV and DVD, work stations.

## 🍴 Restaurants

The larger hotel restaurants are often the best for cuisine, decor and ambience. Buffets (lunch or dinner) cost Rs 700 or more. Sun buffets are becoming quite the thing in the top-notch hotels. Others may only open around 1930 for dinner; some close on Sun. Alcohol is served in most top hotels, but only in some non-hotel restaurants eg **Amber**, **Ginza** and **Kwality**.

The old-fashioned 'tea on the lawn' is still served at the **Imperial** and in **Claridges** (see Where to stay, pages 68 and 69). **Aapki Pasand**, at 15 Netaji Subhash Marg, offers unusual tea-tasting in classy and extremely professional surroundings; it's quite an experience.

### Old Delhi *p48, map p50*

In **Paranthewali Gali**, a side street off Chandni Chowk, stalls sell a variety of *paranthas* including *kaju badam* (stuffed with dry fruits and nuts). Other good places to try local foods like *bedmi aloo puri* with spiced potato are **Mahalaxmi Misthan Bhandhar** at 659 Church Mission St and

Natraj Chowk 1396 Chandni Chowk for *dahi balli* and *aloo tikki*. For sweets you have to seek out **Old Famous Jalebi Wala**, 1797 Dariba Corner, Chandni Chowk – as they are old and famous.

**$$$-$$ Chor Bizarre**, Broadway Hotel (see Where to stay, page 68), T011-4366 3600. Tandoori and Kashmiri cuisine (Wazwan, Rs 500). Fantastic food, quirky decor, including salad bar that was a vintage car. Well worth a visit.

**$ Haldiram's**, 1454/2 Chandni Chowk. Stand-up counter for excellent snacks and sweets on the run (try *dokhla* with coriander chutney from seller just outside), and more elaborate sit-down restaurant upstairs.

**$ Karim's**, Gali Kababiyan (south of Jama Masjid), Mughlai. Authentic, busy, plenty of local colour. The experience, as much as the food, makes this a must. Not a lot to tempt vegetarians though.

### New Delhi *p54, maps p56 and p60*
### Connaught Place and around

**$$$ Sevilla**, Claridges Hotel (see Where to stay, page 69). Beautiful restaurant with lots of outdoor seating serving up specialities like tapas and paella as well as wood fired pizza and the dangerous house special sangria.

**$$$ Spice Route**, Imperial Hotel (see Where to stay, page 68). Award-winning restaurant charting the journey of spices around the world. Extraordinary temple-like surroundings (took 7 years to build), Kerala, Thai, Vietnamese cuisines, magical atmosphere but food doesn't always thrill.

**$$$ Veda**, 27-H, T011-4151 3535, www.vedarestaurants.com. Owned by fashion designer Rohit Bal with appropriately beautiful bordello-style decor, done out like a Rajasthani palace with high-backed leather chairs and candles reflecting from mirror work on ceilings. Food is contemporary Indian. Great atmosphere at night. There is another branch at DLF Vasant Kunj.

**$$ Embassy**, D-11, T011-2341 6434. International food. Popular with artistic-intellectual-political crowd, good food, long-standing local favourite.

**$$ United Coffee House**, E-15 Connaught Pl, T011-2341 1697. Recommended more for the colonial-era cake-icing decor than for the fairly average food. Often someone waxing lyrical over a Casio keyboard. Always attracts a mixed crowd, well worth a visit.

**$ Nathu's**, and **Bengali Sweet House**, both in Bengali Market (east of Connaught Pl). Sweet shops also serving vegetarian food. Good dosa, *iddli*, *utthapam* and North Indian *chana bathura*, *thalis*, clean, functional. Try *kulfi* (hard blocks of ice cream) with *faloodu* (sweet vermicelli noodles).

**$ Saravana Bhavan**, P-15/90, near McDonalds, T011-2334 7755; also at 46 Janpath. Chennai-based chain, light and wonderful South Indian, superb chutneys, unmissable *kaju anjeer* ice cream with figs and nuts. Can take hours to get a table at night or at weekends. Highly recommended.

**$ Triveni Tea Terrace**, Triveni Kala Sangam, 205 Tansen Marg, near Mandi House Metro station (not Sun). Art galleries, an amphitheatre and this little café in quite an unusual building close to CP – the tea terrace is a bit of an institution.

### Paharganj

The rooftop restaurants at **Jyoti Mahal** and **Shelton** are great locations for a bite to eat.
**$$-$ Café Sim Tok**, Tooti Chowk, above Hotel Navrang, near Hotel Rak, T(0)9810-386717. Tucked away little gem of a Korean restaurant. No signage, ask for **Hotel Navrang** and keep going up stairs to find delicious *kimbab* (Korean sushi), *kimchi* and all sorts of soups, in a sweet little café.
**$ Tadka**, off Main Bazar. Good option for tasty food in this area. Great range of all the usual Indian favourites, with nice decor, friendly staff and good hygiene levels.

### South Delhi *p61*

**$$$ Baci**, 23 Sunder Nagar Market, near HDFC Bank, T011-4150 7445. Classy, top-quality Italian food, run by gregarious Italian-Indian owners. There are also branches of her cheaper café **Amici** springing up in Khan Market and Hauz Khas.

**$$$ Bukhara**, ITC Maurya Sheraton, Sardar Patel Marg, T011-2611 2233. Stylish Northwest Frontier cuisine amidst rugged walls draped with rich rugs (but uncomfortable seating). Outstanding meat dishes and dhal. Also tasty vegetable and *paneer* dishes, but vegetarians will miss out on the best food.

**$$$ Dum Pukht**, ITC Maurya Sheraton, Sardar Patel Marg, T011-2611 2233, www.itcwelcomgroup.com. Open evenings; lunch only on Sun. Voted one of the best restaurants in the world, it marries exquisite tastes and opulent surroundings.

**$$$ Grey Garden**, 13a Hauz Khaz Village, near the lake, T011-2651 6450. New kid on the block in the lovely Hauz Khaz village, this boho chic little number serves up a small menu but with great attention to detail. Delicious banana-wrapped fish or thin-crust pizzas, lotus stem chips and other assorted goodies. Book ahead at weekends. Highly recommended.

**$$$ Indian Accent**, at The Manor, 77 Friends Colony West, T011-4323 5151. With a menu designed by Manish Mehotra, who runs restaurants in Delhi and London, this acclaimed restaurant offers up Indian food with a modern twist. Your *dosas* will reveal masala morel mushrooms, rather than the traditional Goan prawns *balchao* here you will find it with roasted scallops. The menu reflects the changing of the seasons and there is live fusion music on Sat. Highly recommended.

**$$$ Kainoosh**, 122-124 DLF Promenade Mall, Vasant Kunj, T(0)9560-715544. Under the watchful eye of celebrity chef Marut Sikka, delicious *thalis* marry the traditional and modern faces of Indian food. This is *thali* with a difference – bespoke with giant morel mushrooms, sea bass mousse and chicken cooked in orange juice and saffron in a terracotta pot.

**$$$ Latitude**, 9 Khan Market, above Good Earth, T011-2462 1013. Like sitting in someone's very posh, very chic living room and getting served delicious Italian numbers like bruschetta, yummy salads and pastas. Topped off with top-notch coffees.

**$$$ Lodi**, Lodi Gardens, T011-2465 5054. Continental lunch, Indian dinner menu in pleasant, Mediterranean-style surroundings, nice terrace and garden. Come more for the setting than the food which can be mediocre.

**$$$ Magique**, Gate No 3, Garden of 5 Senses, Mehrauli Badarpur Rd, T97175-35533. High-class quality food, in a magical setting. Sit outside among the candles and fairy lights. One of Delhi's most romantic restaurants.

**$$$ Olive at the Qutb**, T011-2957 4444, www.olivebarand kitchen.com. Branch of the ever popular Mumbai restaurant and some people say the Delhi version wins hands down. Serving up delicious platters of Mediterranean food and good strong cocktails. Or head to their sister restaurant in the Diplomat Hotel – Olive Beach especially for their legendary blow-out Sun brunches: for Rs 2195 you get open access to a mind-boggling buffet and as many martinis as you can drink.

**$$$ Park Baluchi**, inside Deer Park, Hauz Khas Village, T011-2685 9369. Atmospheric dining in Hauz Khas Deer Park. The lamb wrapped in chicken served on a flaming sword comes highly recommended. Can get crowded, book ahead.

**$$ Elma's**, 24/1 Hauz Khas Village, T011-2652 1020. Lovely little café serving up all manner of tea and cakes and more hearty options like shepherd's pie! Mismatched china and funky furniture make this a great little hang-out.

**$$ Naivedyam**, Hauz Khas Village, T011-2696 0426. Very good South Indian, great service and very good value in a very beautiful restaurant. Highly recommended.

**$ Khan Cha Cha**, Khan Market, 75 Middle Lane. This no-frills joint serves some of the best kebabs in the city from a window in the middle lane of Khan Market. Fantastic value. You can recognize the place from the crowd clamouring at the counter.

**$ Sagar Ratna**, 18 Defence Colony Market, T011-2433 3110. Other branches in Vasant Kunj, Malviya Nagar and NOIDA. Excellent South Indian. Cheap and "amazing" *thalis* and coffee, very hectic (frequent queues). One of the best breakfasts in Delhi.

## Bars and clubs

Many national holidays are 'dry' days. Delhi's bar/club scene has exploded over the last few years. Expect to pay a lot for your drinks and, when in doubt, dress up; some clubs have strict dress codes. Delhi's 'in' crowd is notoriously fickle; city magazines (*Time Out, First City*) will point you towards the flavour of the month. For more insight into Delhi check out the website www.bringhomestories.com.

**South Delhi** *p61*

**24/7**, Lalit Hotel, Barakhamba Av, Connaught Pl. Boasting molecular mixology with their cocktails and regular turns by prominent DJs and more alternative acts, 24/7 is putting itself in the scene.

**Blue Frog**, near Qutb Minar, www.blue frog.co.in. For years, **Blue Frog** has been the best venue in Mumbai with supreme live acts and star DJs doing a turn and now it's coming to Delhi.

**Café Morrisons**, Shop E-12, South Extension Part II, T011-2625 5652. Very popular rock bar. Come for live bands or to mosh to the DJ.

**The Living Room**, 31 Haus Khaz, T011-4608 0533, www.tlrcafe.com. Recently done-up, this place has a funky laid-back atmosphere day and night over 3 floors. By day there's cosy armchairs and sofas. By night, things kick up a gear with live music, open mics and DJs spinning electronica and dubstep, and all manner of themed nights. Recommended.

**Rick's**, Taj Mahal Hotel, 1 Mansingh Rd, T011-2302 6162, www.tajhotels.com. Suave Casablanca-themed bar with long martini list, a long-time fixture on Delhi's social scene.

**Urban Pind**, N4, N-block market, GK1, T011-3951 5656. Multi-level bar, with large roof terrace, popular. Hosts a controversial expat/journalist night on Thu with an 'all-you-can-drink' entry fee, unsurprisingly this normally features a lot of drunk foreigners.
**Zoo**, at **Magique** (see Restaurants, page 72), one of the latest and most popular places on the scene serving up big portions of beats in a beautiful location.

## 🎭 Entertainment

**Delhi** *p48, maps p50, p56 and p60*
For advance notice of upcoming events see www.delhievents.com. Current listings and reviews can be found in *First City* (monthly, Rs 50) and *Time Out* (fortnightly, Rs 50). For programmes see cinema listings in the daily *Delhi Times*.

### Music, dance and culture
**Goethe Institute**, 3 Kasturba Gandhi Marg, T011-2332 9506. Recommended for arts, film festivals, open-air cinema, plays and events.
**India Habitat Centre**, Lodi Rd, T011-2468 2222. Good programme of lectures, films, exhibitions, concerts, excellent restaurant.
**Indian International Centre**, 40 Lodhi Estate, Max Mueller Marg, T011-2461 9431, www.iicdelhi.nic.in. Some fantastic debates and performances, well worth checking the 'forthcoming programmes' section of their website.
**Kingdom of Dreams**, Great Indian Nautanki Company Ltd. Auditorium Complex, Sector 29, Gurgaon, Metro IFFCO, T0124-452 8000, www.kingdomofdreams.in. Ticket prices Rs 750-3000 depending on where you sit and more pricey at the weekend. The highlight is a much acclaimed all-singing, all-dancing Bollywood style performance. A little like an Indian Disneyland showcasing Indian tastes, foods, culture, dress and dance all in one a/c capsule, but done impeccably.
**Triveni Kala Sangam**, 205 Tansen Marg (near Mandi House Metro station),

T011-2371 8833. Strong programme of photography and art exhibitions, plus an excellent North Indian café.

### Son et lumière
**Red Fort** (see page 49), Apr-Nov 1800-1900 (Hindi), 1930-2030 (English). Entry Rs 50. Tickets available after 1700. Take mosquito cream.

## 🎉 Festivals

**Delhi** *p48, maps p50, p56 and p60*
For exact dates consult the weekly *Delhi Diary* available at hotels and many shops and offices around town.

Muslim festivals of **Ramadan**, **Id-ul-Fitr**, **Id-ul-Zuha** and **Muharram** are celebrated according to the lunar calendar.

### January
**26 Jan** Republic Day Parade, Rajpath. A spectacular fly-past and military march-past, with colourful pageants and tableaux from every state, dances and music. Tickets through travel agents and most hotels, Rs 100. You can see the full dress preview free, usually 2 days before; week-long celebrations during which government buildings are illuminated.
**29 Jan** Beating the Retreat, Vijay Chowk, a stirring display by the armed forces' bands marks the end of the Republic Day celebrations.
**30 Jan** Martyr's Day, marks the anniversary of Mahatma Gandhi's death; devotional *bhajans* and Guard of Honour at Raj Ghat. Kite Flying Festival, Makar Sankranti above Palika Bazar, Connaught Pl.

### February
**2 Feb** Vasant Panchami, celebrates the 1st day of spring. The Mughal Gardens are opened to the public for a month. Thyagaraja Festival, South Indian music and dance, Vaikunthnath Temple.

## April
**Amir Khusrau's Birth Anniversary**, a fair in Nizamuddin celebrates this with prayers and *qawwali* singing.

## August
**Janmashtami**, celebrates the birth of the Hindu god Krishna. Special *puja*, Lakshmi Narayan Mandir.

**15 Aug  Independence Day**, Impressive flag-hoisting ceremony and prime ministerial address at the Red Fort.

## October-November
**2 Oct  Gandhi Jayanti**, Mahatma Gandhi's birthday; devotional singing at Raj Ghat.
**Dasara**, with over 200 Ramlila performances all over the city recounting the *Ramayana* story.
**Ramlila Ballet**, the ballet, which takes place at Delhi Gate (south of Red Fort) and Ramlila Ground, is performed for a month and is most spectacular. Huge effigies of Ravana are burnt on the 9th night; noisy and flamboyant.
**Diwali**, the festival of lights; lighting of earthen lamps, candles and firework displays.
**National Drama Festival**, Rabindra Bhavan.
**Oct/Nov  Dastkar Nature Bazaar**, working with over 25,000 crafts people from across India, **Dastkar's** main objective is to empower rural artisans and keep alive the traditional crafts of India. They hold many events each year, but this is the pinnacle. Knowing that shopping here will bring a difference to the lives of rural people.

## December
**25 Dec  Christmas**, Special Christmas Eve entertainments at major hotels and restaurants; midnight mass and services at all churches.

## ⚬ Shopping

**Delhi** *p48, maps p50, p56 and p60*
There are several state emporia around Delhi including the **Cottage Industries Emporium (CIE)**, a huge department store of Indian handicrafts, and those along Baba Kharak Singh Marg (representing crafts from most states of India). In this stretch, there are several places selling products from women's collectives or rural artisans, like **Mother Earth** and **Hansiba**). Shops generally open 1000-1930 (winter 1000-1900). Food stores and chemists stay open later. Most shopping areas are closed on Sun.

### Art galleries
Galleries exhibiting contemporary art are listed in *First City*.
**Delhi Art Gallery**, Hauz Khas Village. A newly expanded gallery with a good range of stunning contemporary art.
**Nature Morte**, A-1 Neethi Bagh, near Kamla Nehru College, www.naturemorte.com. With a twin gallery in Berlin, you can expect the most profound and inspiring of contemporary art here.
**Photo Ink**, Hyundai MGF building, 1 Jhandewalan Faiz Rd, www.photoink.net. Close to Paharganj, this gallery offers up top notch contemporary photography.

### Books and music
Serious bibliophiles should head to the Sun book market in Daryaganj, Old Delhi, when 2 km of pavement are piled high with books – some fantastic bargains to be had.
**Central News Agency**, P 23/90, Connaught Pl. Carries national and foreign newspapers and journals.
**Full Circle**, 5 B, Khan Market, T011-2465 5641. Helpful knowledgeable staff. Sweet café upstairs for a quick drink – food is hit and miss though.
**Kabaadi Bazaar**, Netaji Subhash Marg, Old Delhi. Sun market with thousands of very cheap used books, great for browsing.
**Manohar**, 4753/23 Ansar Rd, Daryaganj, Old Delhi. A real treasure trove for books on South Asia and India especially, most helpful knowledgeable staff. Highly recommended.
**Munshiram Manoharlal**, Nai Sarak, Chandni Chowk. Books on Indology.

**Rikhi Ram**, G Block Connaught Circus, T011-2332 7685. This is the place to come if you've wondered about how easy it is to learn to play and travel with a sitar. Has a range of guitars and other stringed instruments too.

## Carpets

Carpets can be found in shops in most top hotels and a number round Connaught Pl, not necessarily fixed price. If you are visiting Agra, check out the prices here first.

## Clothing

For designer wear, try **Ogaan** and for more contemporary, less budget blowing try **Grey Garden** both in **Hauz Khas Village**, **Sunder Nagar Market** near the Oberoi hotel, or the Crescent arcade near the Qutab Minar.

For inexpensive (Western and Indian) clothes, try shops along Janpath and between Sansad Marg and Janpath; you can bargain down 50%.

The **Central Cottage Industries Emporium** (see below) has a good selection of clothing and fabrics. The **Khadi shop** (see Emporia, below) has Indian-style clothing. **Fab India**, 14N-Gt Kailash I (also in B-Block Connaught Pl, Khan Market and Vasant Kunj). Excellent shirts, Nehru jackets, *salwar kameez*, linen, furnishing fabrics and furniture. The most comprehensive collection is in N block.

## Earthenware

Unglazed earthenware *khumba matkas* (water pots) are sold round New Delhi Railway Station (workshops behind main road).

## Emporia

Most open 1000-1800 (close 1330-1400). **Central Cottage Industries Emporium**, corner of Janpath and Tolstoy Marg. Offers hassle-free shopping, gift wrapping, will pack and post overseas; best if you are short of time.

**Dilli Haat**, opposite INA Market. Rs 15, open 1100-2200. Well-designed open-air complex with rows of brick alcoves for craft stalls from different states; local craftsmen's outlets

(bargaining obligatory), occasional fairs (tribal art, textiles, etc). Also good regional food – hygienic, safe, weighted towards non-vegetarian. Pleasant, quiet, clean (no smoking) and uncrowded, not too much hassle.

**Khadi Gramodyog Bhawan**, near the Regal building, Baba Kharak Singh Marg. For inexpensive homespun cotton *kurta pajama* (loose shirt and trousers), cotton/silk waistcoats, fabrics and Jaipuri paintings.

## Jewellery

Traditional silver and goldsmiths in Dariba Kalan, off Chandni Chowk (north of Jama Masjid). Cheap bangles and along Janpath; also at Hanuman Mandir, Gt Kailash I, N-Block. Also Sunder Nagar market. Bank St in Karol Bagh is recommended for gold. **Amrapali**, Khan Market has an exceptional collection from affordable to mind-blowing. **Ashish Nahar**, 1999 Naughara St, Kinari Bazaar, Chandni Chowk, T011-2327 2801. On quite possibly the prettiest street in Delhi, full of brightly painted and slowly crumbling *havelis*, you will find a little gem of a jewellery shop.

## Markets and malls

Beware of pickpockets in markets and malls. **Hauz Khas village**, South Delhi. Authentic, old village houses converted into designer shops selling handicrafts, ceramics, antiques and furniture in addition to luxury wear. Many are expensive, but some are good value. A good place to pick up old Hindi film posters with many art galleries and restaurants. **Khan Market**, South Delhi. Great bookshops, cafés, restaurants and boutiques. Full of expats so expect expat prices. **Sarojini Nagar**, South Delhi. Daily necessities as well as cheap fabric and clothing. Come for incredible bargains. This is where a lot of the Western brands dump their export surplus or end-of-line clothes. Haggle hard. **Select City Walk**, Saket. An enormous, glitzy mall for the ultimate in upmarket shopping. Lots of chains, cinemas, etc. **Shahpur Jat**, is a new up and coming shopping area, south of **South Extension**.

**Tibetan Market**, North Delhi. Stalls along Janpath have plenty of curios – most are new but rapidly aged to look authentic.

## Souvenirs

**Aap ki Pasand**, opposite Golcha cinema, Netaji Subhash Marg, Old Delhi. Excellent place to taste and buy Indian teas.

**Dastkari Haat**, 39 Khan Market, www.indian craftsjourney.in. Charming selection of conscious crafts from around India working with rural artisans and women's collectives.

**Gulabsingh Johrimal Perfumers**, 467 Chandni Chowk, T011-2326 3743. Authentic *attars* (sandalwood based perfumes), perfumes and incense. High-quality oils are used.

**Haldiram's**, Chandni Chowk near Metro. Wide selection of sweet and salty snack foods.

**Khazana India**, 50A Hauz Khaz Village. Little treasure trove of Bollywood posters, old photographs and all sorts of interesting bric-a-brac.

**People Tree**, 8 Regal Building, Connaught Pl. Handmade clothing, mostly T-shirts with arty and people conscious slogans. Great posters made up of all those weird signs that you see around India and wide-range of ecological books. A real find.

**Playclan**, F51 Select Citywalk, Saket, www.theplayclan.com. Fantastic shop selling all manner of clothes, notebooks, lighters and pictures with great colourful cartoon designs created by a collective of animators and designers – giving a more animated view of India's gods, goddesses, gurus, Kathakali dancers and the faces of India.

**Purple Jungle**, 16 Hauz Khaz Village, T(0)9650-973039, www.purple-jungle.com. Offering up kitsch India with bollywood pictures and curious road signs refashioned onto bags, clothes, cushions, etc.

## ⏱ What to do

### Body and soul

**Integral Yoga**, Sri Aurobindo Ashram, Aurobindo Marg, T011-2656 7863. Regular yoga classes (Tue-Thu and Sat 0645-0745 and 1700-1800) in *asana* (postures), *pranayama* (breathing techniques) and relaxation.

**Laughter Club of Delhi**, various locations, T011-2721 7164. Simple yogic breathing techniques combined with uproarious laughter. Clubs meet early morning in parks throughout the city.

**Sari School**, Jangpura Extension, near Lajpat Nagar, T011-4182 3297. Author of *Saris in India* Rta Christi Kapur holds classes every Sat in different styles of sporting a sari.

**Tree of Life Reflexology**, T(0)9810-356677. Reflexology with acclaimed teacher Suruchi. She also does private and group yoga classes on the roof and in the park.

**The Yoga Studio**, Hauz Khaz, www.the yogastudio.info. Regular yoga classes with Seema Sondhi, author of several yoga books, and her team

**Yogalife**, Shapur Jat main market, T(0)9811-863332, www.yogalife.org. Closed Mon. Bright, friendly centre.

### Tours and tour operators
### Delhi Tourism tours

Departs from **Delhi Tourism**, Baba Kharak Singh Mg near State Govt Emporia, T011-2336 3607, www.delhitourism.nic.in. Book a day in advance. Check time.

**Evening Tour** (Tue-Sun 1830-2200): Rajpath, India Gate, Kotla Firoz Shah, Purana Qila, *son et lumière* (Red Fort). Rs 150.

**New Delhi Tour** (0900-1400): Jantar Mantar, Qutb Minar, Lakshmi Narayan Temple, Baha'i Temple (Safdarjang's Tomb on Mon only).

**Old Delhi Tour** (1415-1715): Jama Masjid, Red Fort, Raj Ghat, Humayun's Tomb. Both Rs 100 plus entry fees.

### ITDC Tours

Guides are generally good but tours are rushed, T011-2332 0331. Tickets booked from **Hotel Indraprastha**, T011-2334 4511.

**New Delhi Tour**: departs from L-1 Connaught Circus and **Hotel Indraprastha** (0800-1330), Rs 125 (a/c coach): Jantar Mantar, Lakshmi Narayan Temple, India

Gate, Nehru Pavilion, Pragati Maidan (closed Mon), Humayun's Tomb, Qutb Minar.
**Old Delhi Tour**: departs **Hotel Indraprastha**. (1400-1700), Rs 100: Kotla Firoz Shah, Raj Ghat, Shantivana, Jama Masjid and Red Fort.

## Taj Mahal tours

Many companies offer coach tours to Agra (eg **ITDC**, from L1 Connaught Circus, Sat-Thu 0630-2200, Rs 600, a/c coach). However, travelling by road is slow and uncomfortable; by car, allow at least 4 hrs each way. Train is a better option: either *Shatabdi* or *Taj Express*, but book early.

## Walking tours

**Chor Bizarre**, Hotel Broadway, T011-2327 3821. Special walking tours of Old Delhi, with good lunch, 0930-1330, 1300-1630, Rs 350 each, Rs 400 for both.
**Delhi Metro Walks**, T(0)9811-330098, www. delhimetrowalks.com. With the charismatic Surekha Narain guiding your every step, informative heritage walks around Delhi. Opt for a tour of Old Delhi or venture south to Qutb Minar and nearby Mehrauli.
**Master Guest House** (see Where to stay, page 69). Highly recommended walking tours for a more intimate experience.
**Salaam Baalak Trust**, T(0)9873-130383, www.salaambaalaktrust.com. NGO-run tours of New Delhi station and the streets around it, guided by Javed, himself a former street child. Your Rs 200 goes to support the charity's work with street children.

## Tour operators

There are many operators offering tours, ticketing, reservations, etc, for travel across India. Many are around Connaught Circus, Parharganj, Rajendra Pl and Nehru Pl. Most belong to special associations (IATA, PATA) for complaints.
**Ibex Expeditions**, 30 Community Centre East of Kailash, New Delhi, T011-2646 0244, www.ibexexpeditions.com. Offers a wide range of tours and ticketing, all with an eco ledge. Recommended.

**Kunzum Travel Café**, T-49 Hauz Khaz Village, T011-2651 3949. Unusual travel centre and meeting place for travellers. Free Wi-Fi, walls lined with photos, magazines, and buzzing with people. Also hosts photography workshops and travel writing courses.
**Namaste Voyages**, I-Block 28G/F South City, 2 Gurgaon, 122001, T0124-221 9330, www. namastevoyages.com. Specializes in tailor-made tours, tribal, treks, theme voyages.
**Paradise Holidays**, 312 Ansal Classique Tower, J block, Rajouri Garden, T011-4552 0736, www.paradiseholidays.com. Value for money. Highly recommended.
**Shanti Travel**, F-189/1A Main Rd Savitri Nagar, T011-4607 7800, www.shantitravel. com. Tailor-made tours throughout India.

## ⊖ Transport

### Air

All international flights arrive at the shiny new terminal of **Indira Gandhi International Airport**, 20 km south of Connaught Pl. Terminal 1 (Domestic) enquiries T011-2567 5126, www.newdelhiairport.in; Terminal 3 (International) T0124-377 6000. At check-in, be sure to tag your hand luggage, and make sure it is stamped after security check, otherwise you will be sent back at the gate to get it stamped.

The domestic air industry is in a period of massive growth, so check a 3rd-party site such as www.cleartrip.com or www.makemytrip.com for the latest flight schedules and prices.

The most extensive networks are with **Indian Airlines**, T140/T011-2562 2220, www.airindia.com; and **Jet Airways**, T011-3989 3333, airport T011-2567 5404, www. jetairways.com. **Indigo**, T(0)9910-383838, www.goindigo.in, has the best record for being on time etc, and **Spicejet**, T(0)9871-803333, www.spicejet.com.

### Transport to and from the airport

The Metro is up and running and it is now possible to travel from New Delhi train station to the airport in 20 mins. There is a booth just outside 'Arrivals' at the International and Domestic terminals for the **bus** services. It is a safe, economical option. A free **shuttle** runs between the 2 terminals every 30 mins during the day. Some hotel buses leave from the Domestic terminal. Bus 780 runs between the **airport** and **New Delhi Railway Station**.

The International and Domestic terminals have **pre-paid taxi** counters outside the baggage hall (3 price categories) which ensure that you pay the right amount (give your name, exact destination and number of items of luggage). Most expensive are white 'DLZ' **limousines** and then white 'DLY' **luxury taxis**. Cheapest are 'DLT' **ordinary Delhi taxis** (black with yellow top Ambassador/Fiat cars and vans, often very old). 'DLY' taxis charge 3 times the DLT price. A 'Welcome' desk by the baggage reclamation offers expensive taxis only. Take your receipt to the ticket counter outside to find your taxi and give it to the driver when you reach the destination; you don't need to tip, although they will ask. From the International terminal DLT taxis charge about Rs 240 for the town centre (Connaught Pl area); night charges double 2300-0500.

## Bus
### Local
The city bus service run by the **Delhi Transport Corporation (DTC)** connects all important points in the city and has more than 300 routes. Information is available at www.dtc.nic.in, at DTC assistance booths and at all major bus stops. Don't be afraid to ask conductors or fellow passengers. Buses are often hopelessly overcrowded so only use off-peak.

### Long distance
Delhi is linked to most major centres in North India. Services are provided by **Delhi Transport Corporation (DTC)** and State Roadways of neighbouring states from various **Inter-State Bus Termini (ISBT)**.

Allow at least 30 mins for buying a ticket and finding the right bus. If any of the numbers below have changed since writing check www.delhitourism.gov.in.

**Kashmere Gate**, north of Old Delhi, T011-2296 0290 (general enquiries), is the main terminus, with a restaurant, left luggage, bank (Mon-Fri 1000-1400; Sat 1000-1200), post office (Mon-Sat 0800-1700) and telephones (includes international calls). The following operators run services to neighbouring states from here: **Delhi Transport Corp**, T011-2386 5181. **Haryana Roadways**, T011-2296 1262; daily to **Agra** (5-6 hrs, quicker by rail), **Varanasi** and many others.

**Sarai Kale Khan Ring Rd**, smaller terminal near Nizamuddin Railway Station, T011-2469 8343 (general enquiries), for buses to Haryana, Rajasthan and UP: **Haryana Roadways**, T011-2296 1262. **Rajasthan Roadways**, T011-2291 9537. For **Agra**, **Gwalior**, etc.

**Anand Vihar**, east side of Yamuna River, T011-2215 2431, for buses to Uttar Pradesh, Uttarakhand and Himachal Pradesh.

### Car hire
The main roads out of Delhi are very heavily congested; the best time to leave is in the very early morning.

Hiring a car is an excellent way of getting about town either for sightseeing or if you have several journeys to make.

Full day local use with driver (non a/c) Rs 900 and for (a/c) is about Rs 13-1600, 80 km/8 hrs, driver overnight *bata* Rs 150 per day; to Jaipur, about Rs 6 to 8000 depending on size of car The **Tourist Office**, 88 Janpath, has a list of approved agents. We highly recommend **Metropole** see below. **Cozy Travels**, N1 BMC House, Middle Circle, Connaught Pl, T011-4359 4359, cozytravels@vsnl.net.com.

**Metropole Tourist Service**, 224 Defence Colony Flyover Market (Jangpura Side), New Delhi, T011-2431 2212, T(0)9810-277699, www.metrovista. co.in. Car/jeep (US$45-70 per day), safe, reliable and recommended, also hotel bookings and can help arrange homestays around Delhi. Highly recommended.

## Metro
The sparkling new Metro system (T011-2436 5202, www.delhimetrorail.com) is set to revolutionize transport within Delhi. For travellers, the yellow line is the main aorta and useful as it stops Chandni Chowk, Connaught Pl and Qutb Minar. The blue line connects to Paharganj. The violet line for Khan Market. And the Orange Line linking airport to New Delhi train station.

**Line 1 (Red)** Running northwest to east, of limited use to visitors; from Rithala to Dilshad Garden.

**Line 2 (Yellow)** Running north–south through the centre from Jahangipuri to Huda City via Kashmere Gate, Chandni Chowk, New Delhi Station, Connaught Pl (Rajiv Chowk), Hauz Khaz, Qutb Minar and Saket – probably the most useful line for visitors.

**Line 3 (Blue)** From Dwarka 21 to Valshall or City Centre (splits after Yamuna Bank) intersecting with Line 2 at Rajiv Chowk and running west through Paharganj (RK Ashram station) and Karol Bagh.

**Line 4 (Orange)** Just 4 stations for now including I.G.I Airport to New Delhi Train Station.

**Line 5 (Green)** From Mundka to Inderlok.

**Line 6 (Violet)** From Central Secretariat to Badarpur, including Khan Market and Lajpat Nagar. Useful.

Trains run 0600-2200. Fares are charged by distance: tokens for individual journeys cost Rs 6-19. **Smart Cards**, Rs 100, Rs 200 and Rs 500, save queuing and money. **Tourist Cards** valid for 1 or 3 days (Rs 70/200) are useful if you plan to make many journeys. Luggage is limited to 15 kg; guards may not allow big backpacks on board. Look out for the women-only carriages at the front of each train, clearly marked in pink. For an insight into the construction of the Metro, there is a Metro museum at **Patel Chowk** on the yellow line.

## Motorcycle hire
**Chawla Motorcycles**, 1770, Shri Kissan Dass Marg, Naiwali Gali, T(0)9811-888918. Very reliable, trustworthy, highly recommended for restoring classic bikes.

**Ess Aar Motors**, Jhandewalan Extn, west of Paharganj, T011-2367 8836, www.essaarmotors.com. Recommended for buying Enfields, very helpful.

Also for scooter rentals **U Ride**, T(0)9711-701932, find them on facebook.

## Rickshaw
**Auto-rickshaws** Widely available at about half the cost of taxis. Normal capacity for foreigners is 2 people (3rd person extra); the new fare system is encouraging rickshaw wallahs to use the meter. Expect to pay Rs 30 for the shortest journeys. Allow Rs 150 for 2 hrs' sightseeing/shopping. It is best to walk away from hotels and tourist centres to look for an auto.

**Cycle-rickshaws** Available in the Old City. Be prepared to bargain: Chandni Chowk Metro to Red Fort. They are not allowed into Connaught Pl.

## Taxi
Yellow-top taxis, which run on compressed natural gas, are readily available at taxi stands or you can hail one on the road. Meters should start at Rs 13; ask for the conversion card. Add 25% at night (2300-0500) plus Rs 5 for each piece of luggage over 20 kg.

**Easy Cabs**, T011-4343 4343. Runs clean a/c cars and claim to pick up anywhere within 15 mins; Rs 20 per km (night Rs 25 per km). Waiting charges Rs50/30 mins.

## Train
Delhi stations from which trains originate have codes: **OD** – Old Delhi, **ND** – New Delhi, **HN** – Hazrat Nizamuddin, **DSR** – Delhi Sarai Rohilla. The publication *Trains at a Glance*' (Rs 30) lists important trains across India, available at some stations, book shops and newsagents.

New Delhi Railway Station and Hazrat Nizamuddin Station (500 m north and 5 km southeast of Connaught Pl respectively) connect Delhi with most major destinations. The latter has many important southbound trains. **Old Delhi Station**, 6 km north of the centre, has broad and metre-gauge trains. **Delhi Sarai Rohilla**, northeast of CP, serves Rajasthan.

Train enquiries T131. Reservations T1330. Each station has a computerized reservation counter where you can book any Mail or Express train in India.

**International Tourist Bureau (ITB)**, 1st floor, Main Building, New Delhi Station, T011-2340 5156, Mon-Fri 0930-1630, Sat 0930-1430, provides assistance with planning and booking journeys, for foreigners only; efficient and helpful if slow. You need your passport; pay in US$, or rupees (with an encashment certificate/ATM receipt). Those with **Indrail** passes should confirm bookings here. At the time of writing the station was under renovation, so the layout may change, but be wary of rickshaw drivers/ travel agents who tell you the ITB has closed or moved elsewhere. (There are also counters for foreigners and NRIs at **Delhi Tourism**, N-36 Connaught Pl, 1000-1700, Mon-Sat, and at the airport; quick and efficient.)

New Delhi and Hazrat Nizamuddin stations have pre-paid taxi and rickshaw counters with official rates per km posted: expect to pay around Rs 25 for 1st km, Rs 8 each km after. Authorized *coolies* (porters), wear red shirts and white *dhotis;* agree the charge, there is an official rate, before engaging one. For left luggage, you need a secure lock and chain.

For the purpose of this guide, some useful services are: **Agra**: *Shatabdi Exp 12002*, ND, 0600, 2 hrs; *Taj Exp 12280*, HN, 0710, 2¾ hrs. **Kolkata**: *Rajdhani Exp 12314*, ND, 1630, 17½ hrs. **Chandigarh**: *Kalka Shatabdi 12011*, 0740, 3½ hrs (NDLS), goes onto **Kalka** for Shimla 4 hrs. **Pathankot** (for Dharamsala) *Jammu Mail 14033*, 2010, 10 hrs (goes onto **Jammu**, 15 hrs).

## ⓘ Directory

**Delhi** *p48, maps p50, p56 and p60*
**Embassies and consulates** Most are in the diplomatic enclave/Chanakyapuri. For details, go to embassy.goabroad.com.
**Medical services** Ambulance (24 hrs): T102. **Hospitals:** Embassies and high commissions have lists of recommended doctors and dentists. Doctors approved by IAMAT (International Association for Medical Assistance to Travellers) are listed in a directory. Casualty and emergency wards in both private and government hospitals are open 24 hrs. **Ram Manohar Lohia**, Willingdon Crescent, T011-2336 5525, 24-hr A&E. **Bara Hindu Rao**, Sabzi Mandi, T011-2391 9476. **JP Narayan**, J Nehru Marg, Delhi Gate, T011-2323 2400. **Safdarjang General**, Sri Aurobindo Marg, T011-2616 5060. **S Kripalani**, Panchkuin Rd, T011-2336 3728. **Chemists:** Many hospitals have 24-hr services: **Hindu Rao Hospital**, Sabzi Mandi; **Ram Manohar Lohia Hospital**, Willingdon Crescent; **S Kripalani Hospital**, Panchkuin Rd. In Connaught Pl: **Nath Brothers**, G-2, off Marina Arcade; **Chemico**, H-45. **Useful contacts** Fire: T101 Foreigners' Registration Office: East Block-VII Level 2, Sector 1, RK Puram, T011-2671 1443. Police: T100.

# Contents

## Footprint features

# Uttarakhand

## At a glance

⊖ **Getting around** Trains reach the foot of theHimalaya; use buses, share jeeps or car hire on mountain routes.

◑ **Time required** 1-2 weeks for eastern hill stations and a retreat around Rishikesh; 12 days for Char Dham pilgrimage; 3-4 days for Corbett NP; 7 days for the Kumaon hill stations.

☼ **Weather** Warm to steamy in the lowlands, cool and fresh to snowy in the mountains.

✗ **When not to go** During the rambunctious Siva festival in Aug, when towns by the Ganges become crowded beyond belief.

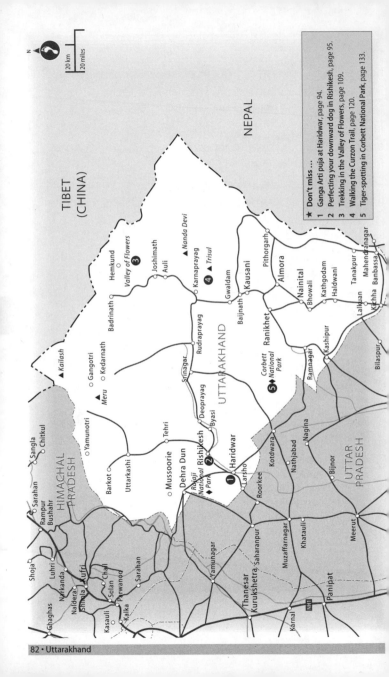

N

20 km
20 miles

TIBET (CHINA)

NEPAL

★ Don't miss ...
1  Ganga Arti puja at Haridwar, page 94.
2  Perfecting your downward dog in Rishikesh, page 95.
3  Trekking in the Valley of Flowers, page 109.
4  Walking the Curzon Trail, page 120.
5  Tiger-spotting in Corbett National Park, page 133.

▲ Kailash

○ Gangotri
○ Kedarnath
▲ Meru

○ Badrinath
Hemkund ○
Valley of Flowers ③
Joshimath ○
Auli ○
▲ Nanda Devi

Karnaprayag ○
④ ▲ Trisul
Gwaldam ○

Rudraprayag ○

Srinagar ○

Deoprayag ○
Byasi ○

Baijnath ○
Kausani ○
Pithoragarh ○

Almora ○
Nainital ○
Bhowali ○
Kathgodam ○
Haldwani ○

Ranikhet ○
Corbett National Park ⑤

Ramnagar ○

Kashipur ○

Tanakpur ○
Lalkuan ○
Kichha Banbassa ○
Mahendranagar ○

UTTARAKHAND

○ Yamunotri
○ Barkot
○ Uttarkashi
○ Tehri
○ Mussoorie
○ Dehra Dun
Rajaji National Park
Rishikesh ②
① Haridwar
Larsho ◆

Bilaspur ○

HIMACHAL PRADESH

Ghaghas ○
Shoja ○
Luhri ○
Narkanda ○
Rampur Bushahr ○
Sarahan ○
Sangla ○
Chitkul ○

Naldera ○
Kufri ○
Chail ○
Shimla
Solan ○
Parwanoo ○
Sarahan ○
Kasauli ○
Kalka ○

Roorkee ○
Yamunanagar ○
Saharanpur ○

Kotdwara ○
Nathaijabad ○
Nagina ○
Bijnor ○

UTTAR PRADESH

Thanesar ○
Kurukshetra ○
Khataulic ○
Muzaffarnagar ○
Meerut ○

Karnal ○
Panipat ○
NH1

With Himachal Pradesh to the west, Tibet to the north and Nepal to the east, it's small wonder that the Himalayan hill-state of Uttarakhand holds some of India's most magnificent mountain scenery.

Garhwal and Kumaon's thickly wooded hillsides break softly towards a stunning range of snow-capped Himalayan peaks, including India's second highest mountain Nanda Devi, forming one of the world's most awesome natural borders. Were it not for travel restrictions imposed following hostilities between India and China in the 1960s, trekking in this remote and still relatively untouched region might now be as popular as in Nepal, whose natural beauty and variety of routes it easily matches.

Many of Uttarakhand's most stunning treks are in fact age-old pilgrimage routes (or 'yatra' routes). As the source of the Ganga and Yamuna rivers, the state looms large in India's mythological history – it is the setting for much of the Mahabharata – and contains some of India's holiest shrines.

On the banks of the Ganga, the holy cities of Haridwar and Rishikesh have served as spiritual magnets for millennia, and receive a continuous stream of pilgrims from all over India seeking to fill plastic bottles with precious holy water, and foreign visitors who come to study yoga or the vedas.

Further east, Almora and Nainital have long served as charming, cool holiday resorts in the hills, while the great tiger reserve of Corbett National Park stands as a beacon of successful wildlife management. With India's whitewater rafting capital just north of Rishikesh at Shivpuri, and the development of skiing facilities at Auli, Uttarakhand is now establishing a reputation for adventure sports, too.

## The land

**Geography** The extraordinarily contorted geology of the Garhwal and Kumaon Himalaya reflects the fierce uplifting and the complex movements that have happened since the great mountain range first started to form. The outer ranges of the Shiwaliks, generally less than 2500 m high, are a jumble of deeply dissected sediments. In places these are separated from the Lesser Himalayan ranges by great longitudinal valleys, or *duns*, such as Dehra Dun. The Lesser Himalayan towns immediately to the north of the Shiwaliks, such as Mussoorie, Almora and Nainital, offer coolness from the overpowering summer heat of the plains. Forming a massive barrier to their north are the permanent snows of **Nanda Devi** (7816 m), **Shivling** (6543 m) and other peaks over 6000 m. The high peaks are surrounded by deep valleys, with some of the world's largest glaciers at their heads. Some meteorologists predict that the Himalaya will be glacier-free within 30 years or so. Although partly attributed to a 10,000-year retreat of the last northern hemisphere Ice Age, the speed of glacial melt has accelerated since the 1970s. The Gangotri Glacier, one of the 'water towers' of the River Ganga, is receding at a rate of 23 m per year, a pattern repeated across all of the great Himalayan ice sheets. The resultant loss of river flow threatens irrigation and drinking water supplies to 500 million people in the Gangetic Basin.

**Climate** The climate of Uttarakhand is dominated by the monsoon, with over three quarters of the rainfall coming between June and September, but temperature is controlled both by height and by season. In the lower valleys, such as Dehra Dun, summers are hot and sticky and temperatures reach 45°C. Towns on the ridges up to 2000 m, such as Almora and Ranikhet, experience maximum summer temperatures of 34°C, while in winter they experience snow, and temperatures even in the outer valleys fall to as low as 3-4°C. June and September are uncomfortably humid in the foothills, despite lower temperatures. The high peaks are under permanent snow and in the higher hills the air can be very cold. Late April to early June and September to October tend to be the best times for trekking.

## Culture

Ethnically, the people of the plains are largely of Indo-Aryan origin, with stronger Mongoloid influences closer to the border with Tibet. Hindi and Urdu are widely spoken, but there are numerous local dialects such as Garhwali and Kumaoni (hill) dialects.

## History

The 14th century ruler Ajai Pal (1358-1370) consolidated a number of petty principalities that made up Garhwal (Land of the Forts) to become the region's raja. The area was a popular plundering ground for Sikh brigands. The **Gurkhas** overran it in 1803, taking women and children into slavery and conscripting men into their army. Gurkha encroachments on the land around Gorakhpur prompted the British to expel them from Garhwal and Kumaon in 1814. They took the eastern part of Garhwal as British Garhwal and returned the western part, Tehri Garhwal, to the deposed raja. The hillsmen here have long resented their political domination by the plainsmen of Uttar Pradesh, so the creation of Uttarakhand (Sanskrit for 'northern section', but initially called Uttaranchal) on 9 November 2000 was the fulfilment of a long cherished dream. In the first state elections, held in February 2002, the Congress swept the BJP from power, and the veteran Congress leader ND Tiwari became chief minister. The question of the capital is still contentious. Dehra Dun has initially been given the status of 'interim capital', but there are still demands that it should be transferred to Gairsain, a hill town in the heart of the new state.

In the State Assembly elections of February 2007 the BJP took 34 of the state's 70 seats against the Congress party's 21 and the BSP's eight, and the BJP formed a government under the Chief Minister B C Khanduri. Uttarakhand has five members of the Lok Sabha (India's lower house), all of which went to the Congress in the 2009 elections.

## Economy

Scattered farming villages among picturesque terraces show the skill with which Uttarakhand's mountain people have adapted to their environment. Agriculture is still by far the most important economic activity for people in the hills, often carried out with considerable sophistication, both of engineering and of crop selection. On many of the hillsides terracing is wonderfully intricate, and a wide variety of crops are grown: paddy, wheat, barley, hemp and lentils on the low-lying irrigated terraces; sugar cane, chilli, buckwheat and millet higher up. Market gardening and potato cultivation have spread around all the townships. Rotation of crops is widely practised and intensive use of animal manure helps to fertilize the soil. The terraces themselves, sometimes as high as 6 m, may have as many as 500 flights, and some villages have up to 6000 individual terraces. Given that it takes one man a day to build a wall 1 m high and 2 m long, it is easy to see the vast amount of labour that has gone into their construction, and how much care is lavished on their maintenance. Drought-like conditions in 90% of the state since November 2008 have devastated farmers, whose irrigation entirely depends on rain.

The forests supply vital wealth. Apart from the timber itself, resin is often a valuable export, and woodcarving is a widely practised skill. Horticulture, fruit cultivation and the production of medicinal plants are potentially of great value, though transport remains a huge problem. Today tourism is an increasingly important source of income, thought to bring in over US$50 million a year from domestic and foreign visitors. Development of the new state's massive hydroelectric potential is highly controversial. The Tehri Dam, at over 250 m high the eighth tallest dam in the world, was the focus of intense opposition from environmental campaigners for more than 30 years. The lower tunnels were closed in 2001 and the upper tunnel in October 2005, allowing the first electricity to be generated in 2006. The stored water provides little benefit to the state, being primarily used to enhance irrigation and supply urgent water needs of Delhi and other rapidly growing cities on the plains. In 2009, a 77-year-old retired academic, GD Agrawal, staged a month-long hunger strike in his fight to halt work on the Lohari Nag Pala hydroelectric project, a series of six dams and numerous tunnels, which environmentalists argued would dry up 125 km of the Bhagirathi River, the source stream of the Ganges, between Gangotri and Uttarkashi. The central government has now established a Ganga River Basin Authority to manage the basin's development, and Environment Minister Jairam Ramesh has declared that "India is a civilization of rivers, and it should not become a land of tunnels", yet work is nearly complete on a huge new dam on the Alaknanda, the second of the Ganges' two key tributaries, with plans in place for up to 30 more dams in the Ganga basin, which if completed would see several of the sacred confluences inundated under metres of water. The protests and investigations have magnified since the devastating flash floods in Uttarakhand in June 2013 where over 10,000 people lost their lives, which many blamed on the increasing number of dams in the area.

# Eastern hill stations

*The quickest cool escape from Delhi's sweltering summer, the old Raj hill stations of Mussoorie and Landour still make a popular getaway, with their crumbling bungalows, pine-scented pathways and grand Himalayan panoramas. The state capital, Dehra Dun, sprawls across the valley below and is home to some of India's most important educational, research and military facilities.* ▶ *For listings, see pages 89-92.*

## Dehra Dun → *For listings see pages 89-92. Colour map 1, B4. Phone code: 0135.*
*Population: 578,000. Altitude: 640 m.*

Dehra Dun (*dera* – camp; *dun* – valley, pronounced 'doon'), lies in a wooded valley in the Shiwalik Hills. In Hindu legend the Dun Valley was part of Siva's stamping ground. Rama and his brother are said to have done penance for killing Ravana, and the five Pandavas stopped here on their way to the mountains. It makes a pleasant and relaxing stop on the way to the hills, and its mild climate has made it a popular retirement town. The cantonment, across the seasonal Bindal Rao River, is spacious and well wooded, while the Mussoorie road is lined with very attractive houses.

There is not much to recommend the town other then a place to stay if you are caught late at night on your way to a hill station. It is busy, with some international chain stores and coffee shops recently opened on the Rajpur road up to Mussoorie. If you happen to be caught in traffic on your way through, keep your eyes open for the very unique miniature suits of armour displayed in the iron shops along the main roads.

### Arriving in Dehra Dun
**Getting there** The railway station, off Haridwar Road to the south of town, has trains from Delhi, Varanasi, Rajasthan and Kolkata. Buses and shared taxis heading for the Mussoorie and the Garhwal hills use the Mussoorie Bus Stand, just outside the station, while those bound for the plains and the Kumaon hills use the new inter-state bus terminal (ISBT, often referred to as the 'New' Delhi Bus Stand) 5 km southwest of the centre. Shared *tempos* and rickshaws (Rs 50-60) can take you into town.

**Getting around** The City Bus Stand, also used by private buses, is just north of the clock tower in the busy town centre, about 10 minutes on foot from the railway station. Although the town centre is compact it is best to get a taxi or auto-rickshaw for visiting the various sights, which are between 4 km and 8 km away. ▶ *See Transport, page 92.*

**Tourist information** GMVN ① *74/1 Rajpur Rd, T0135-274 7898.* **Uttarakhand Tourism** ① *45 Gandhi Rd, next to Drona Hotel, T0135-265 3217, Mon-Sat 1000-1700.*

### Background
A third century BC Asoka rock inscription found near Kalsi suggests that this area was ruled by the emperor. During the 17th and 18th centuries Dehra Dun changed hands several times. The Gurkhas overran it on their westward expansion from Kumaon to Kangra, finally ceding it in 1815 to the British, who developed it as a centre of education and research. It is still a major centre for government institutions like the Survey of India and the Royal Indian Military College, and in November 2000 it became the provisional state capital of

Uttaranchal (re-named in 2007 as Uttarakhand), but there is still no sign of agreement of an alternative state capital.

## Places in Dehra Dun

The **Survey of India** (founded 1767), has its headquarters on Rajpur Road, 4 km north of the clock tower. **Robber's Cave** (8 km), **Lakshman Sidh** (12 km), the snows at **Chakrata** (9 km) and sulphur springs at **Shahasradhara** (14 km) are also within easy reach. The springs were threatened by limestone quarrying until the High Court forced the closure of the quarries. Replanting of the deforested hills has been allowing the water table to recover.

In the west of town, off Kaulagarh Road, the **Doon School**, India's first public school, is still one of its most prestigious. Further along, the highly regarded **Forest Research Institute** (1914), an impressive red-brick building which was designed by Lutyens, is surrounded by the fine lawns of the **Botanical Gardens** and forests. It has excellent **museums** ① *Mon-Fri 0900-1730*. The **Tapkesvar Cave Temple** ① *5 km northwest of town, open sunrise to sunset*, is in a pleasant setting with cool sulphur springs for bathing. There is a simple Indian café nearby. Buses stop 500 m from the temple.

Six kilometres south of town, close to the ISBT, the Tibetan enclave of Clement Town is home to **Mintokling Monastery**, with a striking new 60-m-high *stupa*. The nearby **Dhe Chen Chokhor Kagyupa Monastery** has a similarly tall statue of the Buddha.

## Mussoorie and Landour → *For listings see pages 89-92. Colour map 1, B4.*

Mussoorie, named after the Himalayan shrub mansoor, has commanding views over the Doon Valley to the south and towards the High Himalaya to the north. It is spread out over 16 km along a horseshoe-shaped ridge up to which run a series of buttress-like subsidiaries. Being the nearest hill station to Delhi, it is very popular with Indian tourists though no longer as clean as it was once, and it has nothing over other hill stations. Landour, 300 m higher and away from the crowds, by contrast has fresh, pine-scented air.

### Arriving in Mussoorie → *Phone code: 01362. Population: 30,000. Altitude: 1970 m.*

**Getting there** Other than a 7-km trek, the 30-km road from Dehra Dun (just under 1¾ hours by bus) is the only way to the town. Buses arrive at the library (west end of the long Mall) or the Masonic Lodge Bus Stand (east end). Buses from Delhi take six to seven hours.

**Getting around** Taxis are available for longer journeys, including the steep climb to Landour. For local trips cycle rickshaws are available or you can hire a bike. ▸▸ *See Transport, page 92.*

**Tourist information** GMVN ① *Library Bus Stand, T0135-263 1281*. **Uttarakhand Tourism** ① *The Mall, T0135-263 2863*.

## Places in Mussoorie

Captain Young 'discovered' Mussoorie in 1826 and it developed as an escape from the heat of the plains for the British troops. To the east, **Landour**, at 2270 m, has the old barracks area. The first British residence was built here, followed by The Mall, Club, Christ Church (1837) and the library. It's a very pleasant walk up through the woods and away from the crowds of The Mall. There are good views, though the weather can change quickly. 'Char Dukan' is a small junction in the cantonment area with two snack bars/shops and a post office; the road to the right leads to the **International Language School** and the one to the left to **Lal Tibba** – a nice view point (take binoculars). The Woodstock School and the Language School are in a magnificent location, and some of the guesthouses have stunning views. To the west are **Convent Hill**, **Happy Valley** (where Tibetan refugees have settled; the school may welcome volunteers to teach English), and the pleasant **Municipal Garden**.

### Walks
From the tourist office, it is 5 km to **Lal Tibba** and nearby **Childe's Lodge** on the highest hill. **Gun Hill**, where before Independence a midday gun fire enabled residents to set their watches, has a stunning view of snow-capped peaks, best at sunrise. It can be reached in around half an hour on foot or horseback by a bridle path leaving from the Kutchery on The Mall, or by a 400-m **ropeway** ⓘ *0900-1900, Rs 75 return*. However, the mess of souvenir stalls, cafés and photographers later in the day may not appeal to all. The **Camel's Back Road**, from Kulri to the library, is a pleasant 3-km walk.

### Excursions from Mussoorie
**Kempty Falls**, 15 km away on the Chakrata Road, is a rather dispiriting 'beauty spot', with fabulous ribbon-like falls spoiled by mounds of rubbish and a pair of resorts gaudily advertising soft drink brands. A taxi is about Rs 300 with a one-hour stop. Heading to

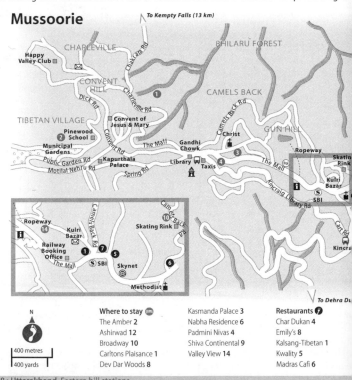

## Mussoorie
↑ To Kempty Falls (13 km)

|  | Where to stay 🛏 | Kasmanda Palace 3 | Restaurants 🍴 |
| --- | --- | --- | --- |
|  | The Amber 2 | Nabha Residence 6 | Char Dukan 4 |
|  | Ashirwad 12 | Padmini Nivas 4 | Emily's 8 |
| 400 metres | Broadway 10 | Shiva Continental 9 | Kalsang-Tibetan 1 |
|  | Carltons Plaisance 1 | Valley View 14 | Kwality 5 |
| 400 yards | Dev Dar Woods 8 |  | Madras Cafi 6 |

**Dhanolti**, 25 km away, you can go on a further 3 km to find the **Surkhanda Devi Temple** at 3030 m. There are superb views of several high peaks over 6500 m. A taxi is Rs 800 with a two-to three-hour stop. Buses between Mussoorie and Chamba take you within 2 km of the hill top.

## ⊙ Eastern hill stations listings

*For hotel and restaurant price codes and other relevant information, see pages 22-26.*

### ⊙ Where to stay

**Dehra Dun** *p86*
There are good discounts out of season (Aug-Feb). The cheaper hotels are near the station and the clock tower; the upmarket ones are north, along **Rajpur Rd**.
**$$$$ Vishranti**, Lower Kandoli Village, Doon Valley, T0135-3987750, www.vishranti

Rice Bowl **7**
Tavern **2**
Whispering Windows **3**

resorts.com. Beautiful resort and spa – a good getaway, although its popular with weddings; Indian cricket legend MS Dhoni got married here.
**$$$$-$$$ Shaheen Bagh**, Upper Dehradun, T0135-210 8199, T(0)9897-046353, www.shaheenbagh.in. Price includes breakfast and dinner. Beautiful guesthouse on a 3-ha property by the river, with lovely interior spaces in grand country-house style, large canopied beds, pretty gardens (370 bird species recorded) with mountain views in the Ton River valley, fruit trees and pool. Distant from town; a refuge. Service has gone downhill under new ownership but it's still recommended.
**$$$ Ajanta Continental**, 101 Rajpur Rd, T0135-274 9595, www.hotelajanta dehradun.com. 29 clean rooms, good restaurant/bar, pleasant family-run.
**$$ President**, 6 Astley Hall, Rajpur Rd, T0135-265 7082, www.hotelpresident dehradun.com. Has 22 smallish a/c rooms, excellent restaurant, bar, coffee shop, exchange, travel, golf and riding arranged, pleasant service.
**$$-$ Deepshikha**, 57/1 Rajpur Rd, T()99999-89548. 22 Basic rooms (some a/c) that overlook a busy road. Restaurant.
**$ Private guesthouses**, Clement Town (Tibetan Colony), 6 km south of centre near ISBT. Spacious, clean rooms (Rs 250). Quiet and peaceful atmosphere, but somewhat ad hoc; no phone for bookings, so best to show up and ask at the monasteries.

**Mussoorie and Landour** *p87, map p88*
Some hotels are old-fashioned but full of character. There are also a string of modern moderately priced hotels west of Gandhi Chowk on **The Mall** and **Motilal Nehru Rd**.

The Mall is closed to cars and buses. You may have to walk to your hotel; porters are available at the bus stands. Prices are based on high-season tariffs, which are often quite ridiculous; most offer big off-season discounts. The options below are situated in Mussoorie unless otherwise stated.

**$$$$ The Amber**, near Company Bagh, Hathi Paon Rd, T0135-2630202, www.the amber.in. Epic views from this resort. A beautiful deck overhangs the valley and all rooms and the restaurant share the view of the rolling hills.

**$$$$-$$$ Nabha Residence** (Claridges), Airfield, Barlow Ganj Rd, 2 km from town centre, T0135-263 1426, www.claridges.com. 22 rooms with veranda arranged around attractive garden in converted hill palace, superb views, Raj-style but with all mod cons. Very good family rooms with lofts. Includes half-board.

**$$$ Kasmanda Palace Hotel**, near The Mall, T0135-263 2424, www.kasmanda palace.com. 14 comfortable rooms, once Basset Hall of the Christ Church complex (built 1836), a British sanatorium, then royal guesthouse from 1915, interesting furnishings (hunting trophies, amazing photo history on walls), peaceful, spacious grounds. Steep climb from Mall Rd so call for jeep transfer. Highly recommended.

**$$$-$$ Carltons Plaisance**, 1.5 km from main mall, Charleville Rd, T0135-263 2800, T(0)9358-120911, www.carltonplaisance. com. Victorian house converted into a hotel with period furniture, peaceful, spacious, 12 rooms (some with fine views), pretty suites, good restaurant (includes Tibetan).

**$$$-$$ Cloud End Forest Resort**, 7 km from town, in the forest, T(0)96340-96861, www.cloudend.com. Rustic, fabulous views, 7 rooms with bath in colonial-period lodge, there are some tents on-site too. Home-cooked meals.

**$$$-$$ The Hermitage**, Kanatal, on a ridge near Surkhanda Devi Temple, 35 km north of Mussoorie, T(0)991-767 4830, www.kanatal hermitage.com. 16 comfortable rooms,

pleasant lawns and restaurant, nightly bonfire with music. Price includes breakfast and dinner

**$$$-$$ Padmini Nivas**, Library, The Mall, T0135-263 1093. 27 rooms in former palace with character, some with good views, also (**$$$**) cottages, not grand but pleasant ambience, good restaurant (pure vegetarian Gujarati). Car parking and access before the gated mall area. Highly recommended.

**$$ Broadway**, 3 km from main mall, Camels Back Rd, next to rink, T0135-263 2243, www.hotelbroadwaymussoorie.com. Renovated 19th-century hotel, 10 rooms with bath, best with views and geyser, some with bucket hot water, Indian meals, cheap and atmospheric.

**$$ Hotel Shiva Continental**, next to clock tower, The Mall, Kulri, T0135-263 2174, www. shivacon.in. Pretty patio, some rooms with views, basic rooms but relatively clean.

**$$-$ Valley View**, The Mall (Kulri) near Ropeway, T0135-263 2324. Friendly, with 14 clean rooms (some with kitchenette), Great open-air terrace and all the rooms have a shared balcony, restaurant, bakery, garden, good service.

**$ Ashirwad**, Clocktower, T(0)93581-31281, www.hotelashirwadmussoorie.com. Good location with basic rooms and friendly reception. Although try and make sense of their tagline 'Ayurveda Nature Avalanches'!

**$ Hotel Dev Dar Woods**, Fair View, Sisters Bazaar, Landour Cant, T0135-263 2644. A great trekkers' hotel, clean rooms in a period house, budget hotel in woods, secluded but next to a well-stocked shop with local honey, jam and cheese. Surprisingly good pizza is the only thing on the menu.

## 🍴 Restaurants

### Dehra Dun p86

**$$ Kabila**, 447 Rajpur Rd, T(0)135-65999, Come up the stairs and find a Rajasthani village – excellent, but pricey Rajasthani *thali*.

**$$ Kumar**, 15B Rajpur Rd (towards **Kwality**, see below). Tasty Punjabi dishes, friendly staff.

**$$ Orchard**, 3-D, Dak Patti, near MDDA Park, Rajpur Road. Great location with good valley views. They serve Chinese, Tibetan and Thai food here. Great chicken *momos*.
**$ Osho**, 111 Rajpur Rd. Good snacks in roadside café.
**$ Sheetal Restaurant**, west of town on canal bank. Attractive setting.

### Bakeries
**Ellora** and **Grand**, both on Rajpur Rd, Paltan Bazar. Fresh bread, biscuits and sticky toffees.

### Mussoorie and Landour *p87, map p88*
**$$$ Emily's**, Landour (Rokeby Manor). Excellent breakfast buffet and good range of foods.
**$$$ Kasmanda Palace Hotel** (near the mall, past the Anglican church) has affordable and delicious Western and Indian food. Eat on the grass terrace and enjoy views over the valley. Very pleasant ambience and friendly service.
**$$ Char Dukan**, Landour (above Woodstock School). Great sandwiches and omelettes.
**$$ Hotel Dev Dar Woods** (see Where to stay). A lovely stop for a fantastic pizza, which is the only thing on the menu but worth it for the mountain views and pine-scented air.
**$$ Kwality**, above Bank of Baroda, Kulri. International. Dependable quality.
**$$ Tavern**, Kulri. Respectable Thai and roasts, live music and dancing some nights.
**$$ Whispering Windows**, Library Bazar, Gandhi Chowk. International. Popular bar.
**$ Kalsang-Tibetan Restaurant**, near bank on main mall. Tasty Tibetan food, lively ambience. Recommended.
**$ Madras Cafi**, Kulri. Very good South Indian.
**$ Rice Bowl**, The Mall. Tibetan and Chinese.

## ⊙ Shopping

### Mussoorie and Landour *p87, map p88*
The main areas are Library, Kulri and Landour Bazars and Shawfield Rd near Padmini Niwas. Several shops on The Mall sell handcrafted walking sticks. For woollen goods try **Garhwal Wool House**, near GPO; **Natraj**, Picture Palace; or the **Tibetan market**, near Padmini Nivas.
**Banaras House**, The Mall. Silks.
**Baru Mal Janki Dass**. Tribal silver jewellery.

## ⊙ What to do

### Dehra Dun *p86*
**GMVN**, Old Survey Chowk, 74/1 Rajpur Rd, T0135-274 6817, www.gmvnl.com. Runs the following tours: City sights, 1030, Rs 120; Mussoorie and Kempty Falls, 1000, Rs 150; Haridwar and Rishikesh, 1000, Rs 200.
**President Travel**, T0135-265 5111, prestrav@sancharnet.in. Ticketing and general travel arrangements.

### Mussoorie and Landour *p87, map p88*
**Fishing**
Fishing is popular in the Aglar and Yamuna rivers for mahseer and hill trout. A permit is required; available from Division Forest Officer, Yamuna Division.

### Horse riding
1-hr ride (7 km) around Camels Back Rd, Rs 250. Off-season, Rs 100.

### Language classes
**Landour Language School**, 41/2 Landour Cantt, Mussoorie, T0135-263 1487, www.landourlanguageschool.com. One of the best schools in India, including Urdu, Garhwali and Sanskrit as well as Hindi. Courses for all levels and timescales. Rs 325 per class (one-to-one tuition), Rs 210-240 per person for group classes; max 4 lessons per day. Standard of teachers varies so try a few till you are happy.

### Paragliding
**Snowbird Flying Club**, near the lake, T0135-263 1366. Open 1000-1700.

### Tours and tour operators
Tours operated by **GMVN**. Kempty Falls: Rs 50, at 0900, 1200, 1500 (off-season:

1000, 1300). Dhanolti, Surkhanda Devi
Temple, Mussoorie Lake: full day (0900),
Rs 130, season only. Tickets from KMVN
and Uttarakhand Tourism.
**Garhwal Alpine Tours**, Masonic Lodge,
T0135-263 2507.
**Kulwant Travels**, Masonic Lodge Bus Stand,
T0135-263 2717.

### Yoga
**Yog Ganga Centre**, 101 Old Rajpur, near
Shahenshah Ashram, Dehra Dun, T0135-273
3653, www.yog-ganga.com. Highly regarded
Iyengar yoga school established by a couple
who have advised the Indian government on
the yogic syllabus for India's education system.

## ⊙ Transport

### Dehra Dun p86
**Air** Jolly Grant air strip (24 km), enquiry
T0135-241 2412; limited flights to/from
**Delhi** with Jet Airways.
**Bus** Local buses leave from Rajpur Rd, near
clock tower. Long-distance buses leave from
New Delhi Bus Stand (ISBT), Clement Town,
T0135-213 1309, for most hill destinations
and the plains, including **Chandigarh** (5 hrs),
**Delhi** (7-8 hrs), **Dharamshala** (14 hrs),
**Haridwar** (1 hr) **Kullu/Manali** (14 hrs),
**Nainital** (12 hrs); **Ramnagar** for **Corbett**
(7 hrs), **Rishikesh** (1 hr; board inside terminal
as buses fill to bursting at the main gate),
**Shimla** (8-9 hrs). Mussoorie Bus Stand,
outside the railway station, T0135-262 3435.
Half hourly to **Mussoorie**, 0600-2000, tickets
from counter No 1, Rs 22. Private buses from
City Bus Stand, Parade Ground. Regular
services to **Mussoorie**, 1 hr. Drona Travels
(GMVN), 45 Gandhi Rd, T0135-265 3309, or
Doon Tours & Travels, 16 Bhatt Shopping
Complex, 1 Haridwar Rd, T(0)9760-008687.
Rs 800-1000 per day, friendly, professional.
**Taxi/rickshaw** Taxi, T(0)9412-325257.
Auto-rickshaw Rs 50 from station to centre.
Cheaper but crowded vikrams easily available.
**Train** Railway Station, T0135-262 2131.
Reservations opposite, 0800-2000, Sun

0800-1400; book early for Haridwar. **New
Delhi**: *Shatabdi Exp 12018*, 1700, 6 hrs, :
*Jan Shatabdi 12056* 0510, 6hrs; *Dehradun
Exp 19020*, 1035, 10 hrs. **Allahabad**: *Link
Exp 14114*, 1320, 19 hrs. **Kolkata**: *Doon Exp
13010*, 2020, 34 hrs (via **Varanasi**, 19 hrs).
**Varanasi**: *Dehra Dun-Varanasi Exp 14266*,
1815, 21 hrs.

### Mussoorie and Landour p87, map p88
**Bus** Long-distance stands: Library (Gandhi
Chowk), T0135-263 2258; Masonic Lodge
(Kulri), T0135-263 2259. Frequent service
to **Chamba**, scenic trip via **Dhanolti**, 3 hrs;
**Dehra Dun** through Ghat roads, Rs 22,
1 hr. Private buses **to Delhi**, are Rs 200-250
depending on a/c facility. Direct buses **from
Delhi** ISBT, dep 0515, 2230, 6-7 hrs, about
Rs 120; stop for snacks at **Cheetal Grand**. Also
buses from **Saharanpur Railway** and **Tehri**.
**Taxi/rickshaw** Cycle rickshaws for
The Mall, fixed-fare chart from tourist office.
Taxi stand at Library, T0135-263 2115;
stand at Masonic Lodge, T0135-261 0002;
Kulwant Travels, Masonic Lodge Bus Stand,
T0135-263 2717. To **Dehra Dun**, Rs 400;
**Delhi** Rs 2800.
**Train** See above for trains from **Dehra
Dun**. Railway Out Agency (computerized
all-India reservations), near GPO, **Kulri**,
0800-1100, 1200-1500, Sun 1800-1400,
T0135-263 2846.

## ⊙ Directory

### Dehra Dun p86
**Medical services** Doon Hospital,
Amrit Kaur Rd, T0135-265 9355. **Useful
contacts** Rajaji National Park, 5/1 Ansari
Marg, T0135-262 1669. For permits. Wildlife
Institute of India, PO Box 18, Chandrabani,
T0135-264 0111, www.wii.gov.in.

### Mussoorie and Landour p87, map p88
**Medical services** Civil Hospital at
Landour, T0135-263 2891. **Community**,
South Rd, T0135-263 2053. **St Marys**,
Gun Hill Rd, T0135-263 2891.

# Haridwar, Rishikesh and around

*The sacred cities of Haridwar and Rishikesh abound in Hindu religious history and seethe with modern-day pilgrims. Yet, although only a few kilometres apart, they share little in tempo or atmosphere. One of the oldest cities in the world, dilapidated, heady Haridwar, fabled for holding Vishnu's footprint and the site of numerous scenes from the Mahabharata, is one of Hinduism's seven holiest cities and correspondingly overrun with Indian pilgrims – in 2013 over 55 days nearly 100 million devotees arrived as the city played host to the epic Kumbh Mela festival. Meanwhile, ashram and swami-filled Rishikesh, upriver, is much more geared towards Western spiritual seekers: a place one writer summed up as a hybrid of Blackpool and Lourdes. Along with an array of sound hatha yoga and vedanta classes come all the accoutrements of international budget travel: internet cafés, self-help bookshops, clothes and mantra CD shops. Further upstream, the sacred Ganga has a new following, hungry for adventure not enlightenment: they are drawn to Shivpuri in its role as India's unofficial whitewater rafting capital. The Char Dham pilgrimage route begins at Rishikesh, and the town makes a good base from which to arrange treks in the Garhwal Himalaya or elephant-spotting trips into the nearby Rajaji National Park.* ➤➤ *For listings, see pages 97-103.*

## Haridwar → *For listings see pages 97-103. Colour map 1, C4. Phone code: 0133. Population: 175,000.*

Haridwar lies at the base of the Shiwalik Hills where the River Ganga begins a 2000-km journey across the plains. In setting foot on the western bank here (Hari-Ki-Pairi), Vishnu made it one of Hinduism's seven holy cities (see Hindu Holy places, page 407), a place where pilgrims bathe to cleanse themselves of sins, where *swamies* sermonize, Brahmin priests preside over spectacular sunset ceremonies, *sadhus* sit at makeshift shelters under trees and beggars huddle and urchins dart between the crowds.

### Arriving in Haridwar

**Getting there and around** The nearest airport is at Jolly Grant, 30 km away on the Dehra Dun road. Haridwar is connected by rail to all major cities. It is 214 km from Delhi by road on NH45, but the train is much faster. Locally there are private buses, tempos, autos, *tongas*, cycle rickshaws and taxis. Haridwar is also the stepping off point for Rishikesh. ➤ *See Transport, page 101.*

**Tourist information** **Uttarakhand tourist office** ⓘ *Motel Rahi, T T0133-4226430, Mon-Sat 1000-1700.* **GMVN** ⓘ *Lalta Rao Bridge, T01334-424240, 1000-1700.* **UP Tourism** ⓘ *Lalta Rao Bridge, T01334-227370.* **Ganga Sabha** ⓘ *near Hari-ki Pairi, T01334-227925.* Only vegetarian food is available in town and there is no alcohol.

### Background

Seventh-century Chinese traveller Hiuen Tsang mentioned the city in his writing, and Timur (Tamburlaine) sacked it in AD 1399, see page 391.

**Hari-ki-Pairi**, where Vishnu trod, is now where some of the Ganga is drawn off as irrigation water for the Upper Ganga Canal system and for a hydroelectric power station.

## Places in Haridwar

Near the steps at Hari-ki-Pairi is a modern clock tower and some temples, none particularly old. Further down, foodstalls and shrines line alleyways leading off into the bazar. There are six bridges to take you across the river, where it is quieter. A new footbridge leads directly to Hari-ki-Pairi. Foreign visitors are likely to be approached for donations for its construction and upkeep. There are many *ashrams* here, including Shatikunj, Ananda Mayee Ma, said by some to have the most authentic Ganga arti, and Premnagar. Many have herb gardens producing Ayurvedic medicines.

**Moti (Lower) Bazar**, parallel to the Jawalapur–Haridwar road, is interesting, colourful, invariably crowded and surprisingly clean and tidy. Stalls sell coloured powder piled high in carefully made cones (for *tikas*). Others sell saris, jewellery, brass and aluminium pots, sweets and snacks. **Mansa Devi Temple** is worth visiting for the view. Set on the southernmost hill of the Shiwaliks, it is accessible on foot or by the crowded cable car (0630-2030, Rs 80 return; or take the package ticket to include Chanda Devi temple, 4 km away on the other side of the Ganga). Towards Rishikesh, 5 km from Haridwar, are the newer temples: **Pawan Dham** with a Hanuman temple, its spectacular glittering glass interior and the seven-storey **Bharat Mata Mandir** to Mother India.

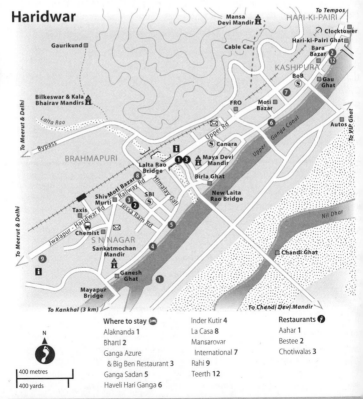

Haridwar

| Where to stay | | Restaurants |
|---|---|---|
| Alaknanda 1 | Inder Kutir 4 | Aahar 1 |
| Bharti 2 | La Casa 8 | Bestee 2 |
| Ganga Azure | Mansarovar | Chotiwalas 3 |
| & Big Ben Restaurant 3 | International 7 | |
| Ganga Sadan 5 | Rahi 9 | |
| Haveli Hari Ganga 6 | Teerth 12 | |

N

400 metres
400 yards

**Kankhal**, 3 km downstream, with the **Temple of Dakseshwara**, is where legend holds that Siva's wife, Sati, burned herself to death, irked at her father Daksa's failure to invite her husband Siva to a grand sacrifice. Siva temporarily destroyed the sacrifice, and gave Daksa (himself a son of Brahma) the head of a goat. Professor Wendy Doniger says that when Siva learned that of Sati's suicide, "he took up her body and danced in grief, troubling the world with his dance and his tears until the gods cut the corpse into pieces. When the *yoni* fell, Siva took the form of a *linga*, and peace was re-established in the universe".

## Rajaji National Park → *For listings see pages 97-103. Colour map 1, B4. Altitude: 302-1000 m.*

① *The park can be reached from Haridwar, Rishikesh and Dehra Dun (see Transport, page 102). Permits from Director 5/1 Ansari Rd, Dehra Dun, T0135-262 1669, Mohan's Adventure, T01334-265543, or at the Chilla park office, T01382-266757. Open 15 Nov-15 Jun between sunrise and sunset. Entry first 3 days: foreigners Rs 600, Indians Rs 150; camera Rs 50; video, Rs 5000. Car permit Rs 2500-500. Jeep hire from Haridwar, Rishikesh or Dehradun.*

Uttarakhand's largest park, 820 sq km, is named after C Rajagopalachari, the only Indian to hold the post of governor general. Spread across the rugged and dangerously steep slopes of the Shiwaliks, the park's vegetation ranges from rich *sal, bhabbar* tracts, broad-leaf mixed forest to *chir* pine forests interspersed with areas of scrub and pasture which provide a home for a wide variety of wildlife including over 23 mammal and 438 species of bird. On foot, however, you are likely to see very little. Even by car or jeep many are disappointed as few animals are spotted.

A large number of **elephants**, together with the rarely seen **tiger**, are found, here at the northwest limit of their range in India. The elephants move up into the hills when the water holes are dry. A census taken in 2001 recorded 453 elephants, 30 tigers and 236 **leopards** in the park. Other animals include spotted deer, sambar, muntjac, nilgai and ghoral. Along the tracks, you may spot wild boar, langur and macaque; the Himalayan yellow-throated marten and civet are rare. Peacocks, jungle fowl and kaleej pheasants can be spotted in the drier areas, while waterbirds attracted by the Ganga and the Song rivers include many kinds of geese, ducks, cormorant, teal and spoonbill, among others.

## Rishikesh → *For listings see pages 97-103. Colour map 1, B4. Phone code: 01350. Population: 72,000.*

Rishikesh stands on the banks of the Ganga where it runs swiftly through a forested gorge in the southernmost foothills of the Shiwaliks. The quiet of these hills has drawn sages for centuries, including many of the greatest luminaries of 20th-century yoga, such as Swami Sivananda, founder of the Divine Life Society, Swami Satyananda of the Bihar school, and perhaps most famously Maharishi Mahesh Yogi, whose Western-tinged spiritual patter captured the imagination of the Beatles and paid for a then space age, now abandoned, ashram. Today it's a mixed bag of ashrams, sadhus, Ayurveda clinics and globetrotting teachers, yet, Rishikesh still has a certain magic. In the evening, chants of *Om Namoh Shivaya* drift on the air, as the last whitewater rafters of the day paddle in to shore, in what must be one of the most surreal endings to a rafting trip anywhere in the world. Some find it disappointing and lacking in atmosphere; others stay for weeks. A vegetarian temple town, meat and alcohol are prohibited; eggs are only eaten in private.

**Clean Himalaya** ① *www.cleanhimalaya.org*, is an award-winning environmental group, established by members of the Divine Life Society (contact Susan T(0)9897-946696) running local rubbish collections and campaigning for greater public awareness of green issues. Volunteer, donate, and encourage local businesses to sign up.

## Arriving in Rishikesh

**Getting there** From Haridwar, buses are both quicker and far more frequent than trains. Buses from Delhi and Dehra Dun arrive at the main bus stand in the town centre.

**Getting around** The compact town centre, with the bus stands and bus station, is 1 km from the river. But it is the ashrams further north, concentrated around Ram Jhula and Lakshman Jhula (the two pedestrian suspension bridges), that are where most foreigners consider Rishikesh proper to be. Frequent shared taxis (Rs 5-10) go between the Bazar and the bridges, or you can cross by boat near Ram Jhula (Rs 10). Shared jeeps link the quarters on the east bank (Rs 5-10). ▶▶ *See Transport, page 102.*

**Tourist information Garhwal Mandal Vikas Nigam (GMVN)** ① *Shail Vihar, Haridwar Bypass Rd, T0135-243 2648,* also at **Yatra Office** ① *Kailash Gate, Bypass Rd, T0135-243 1793,*

# Rishikesh

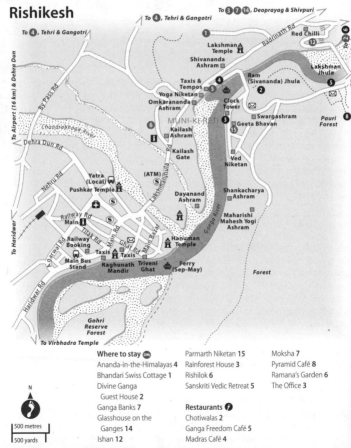

**Where to stay** 🛏

Ananda-in-the-Himalayas **4**
Bhandari Swiss Cottage **1**
Divine Ganga
 Guest House **2**
Ganga Banks **7**
Glasshouse on the
 Ganges **14**
Ishan **12**

Parmarth Niketan **15**
Rainforest House **3**
Rishilok **6**
Sanskriti Vedic Retreat **5**

**Restaurants** 🍽
Chotiwalas **2**
Ganga Freedom Café **5**
Madras Café **4**

Moksha **7**
Pyramid Café **8**
Ramana's Garden **6**
The Office **3**

*yatra@gmvnl.com*, organizes trekking, mountaineering, rafting and the Char Dham tour (four to 12 days). **Uttarakhand Tourism** ① *162 Railway Rd, T0135-243 0209*, is helpful. During the *yatra* season, tourist information is also available from the **Uttarakhand Guest House** ① *next to the Yatra Bus Stand, T094-1010 6800*.

## Places in Rishikesh

Many travel to Rishikesh (Hair of Sages) to study in one of its numerous ashrams, seats of spiritual learning often housed in bizarrely colourful architectural curiosities. As a result, the town has become something of a yoga supermarket. Evening *aarti* is popular at Parmath Niketan, but the Triveni ghat (which has striking statues of Siva) is where local pilgrims perform the ritual. The trees along the east bank between Lakshman and Ram Jhula shade scores of bungalows, the homes to the ubiquitous saffron-robed sadhus you'll find sitting at every pathside, swinging tiffins and sparking up chillums. Follow the track northeast, beyond Lakshman Jhula, to reach beautiful, secluded swimming beaches.

Rishikesh is the base for several pilgrimages and treks, including the **Char Dham Pilgrimage**, or going to the Garhwal hills and Hemkund Sahib.

---

## ⓦ Haridwar, Rishikesh and around listings

*For hotel and restaurant price codes and other relevant information, see pages 22-26.*

## ⓦ Where to stay

**Haridwar** *p93, map p94*
Many offer off-season discounts outside Jun and Jul, up to 50% Nov-Feb.
**$$$$ Ganga Sadan**, opposite Chintamani Ashram, Sharvan Nath Nagar, T01334-228322, www.gangasadan.com. Sleek new boutique hotel right on the Ganga, with a private bathing ghat and atmospheric rooftop café. The more expensive of the well-equipped rooms boast a wonderful unobstructed view of the river; avoid the cheaper inside rooms, which are windowless and not worth the asking price.
**$$$-$$$ Haveli Hari Ganga**, Pilibhit House, 21 Ramghat, T01334-226443, www.havelihariganga.com. Attractively restored *haveli* with exclusive bathing ghat on the Ganga, rooms decorated along mythological themes, old-world charm and modern luxury, Ayurvedic treatments and yoga.
**$$-$$ Alaknanda** (UP Tourism), Belwala (east bank), By-pass Rd, T01334-226379, www.up-tourism.com. 32 rooms, best a/c

with bath, restaurant (simple vegetarian), small garden, on riverbank, quiet.
**$$ La Casa**, Bilkeshwar Rd, close to Hari-ki-Pairi Rd, T01334-221197. Great value rooms at this stylish hotel where they have put some imagination into the decor with jewelled colour walls and stenciling.
**$$ Mansarovar International**, Upper Rd, towards Hari-ki-Pairi, T01334-226501. Clean, 64 simple rooms, dorm (Rs 100), restaurant.
**$$ Rahi** (Uttarakhand Tourism), opposite railway station, T01334-4226430. Hotel with 19 rooms (some a/c), restaurant, tourist info.
**$$ Teerth**, Subhash Ghat, Hari-ki-Pairi, T01334-228506. Excellent central location, great views over ghats, 32 reasonable rooms, some air-cooled, but not the value it once was.
**$$-$ Ganga Azure**, Railway Rd, T01334-227101, www.hotelgangaazure.com. 32 adequate rooms, TV, hot water, some a/c, decent restaurant. They have also opened the **Ganga Heritage** which has lovely decor.
**$ Bharti**, Hari ki Pairi, T01334-224396, hotel_ bharti@yahoo.co.in. Basic but very well-kept rooms with bucket hot water, family atmosphere.
**$ Inder Kutir**, Niranjani Akhara Rd, SN Nagar, T01334-226336. A good new budget option, with bright and airy rooms opening on to a

terrace. One room has a balcony from which you can peep through to the river. It's in a family home and friendly.

### Rajaji National Park *p95*
For reservation of a guesthouse, contact Rajaji National Park, 5/1 Ansari Marg, Dehra Dun, T0135-262 1669. To stay in a tribal village, contact **Mohan's Adventure**, T01334-220910, see page 100.

**$$ Tourist Bungalow**, Chilla, T1334 951382. With rooms, dorm (Rs 150) and tents.
**$ Forest Rest Houses**, near all the gates. All have at least 2 suites. Those at Chilla (apparently best spot for wildlife) and Motichur cost Rs 1000. Others at Asarodi, Beribara, Kansrao, Kunnao, Phandowala, Ranipur and Satyanarain are Rs 600. All have electricity and water supply except Beribara and Kansrao. Very basic, 'concrete boxes', self-catering (utensils provided), not good value.

### Rishikesh *p95, map p96*
The noisy and congested town around the bazar and Triveni ghats couldn't be further from the spiritual calm for which many travel to Rishikesh, but it does hold some good accommodation if you're less eager to immerse yourself in *sadhus* and *swamis*. The best options across Ram Jhula Bridge, in Swargashram, are within ashrams themselves, which can be safe and clean but impose curfews and some moderate constraints on behaviour. The best independent hostels and guesthouses are dotted on either riverbank of Lakshman Jhula, 30 mins north of Ram Jhula on foot (unadvisable at night).

**$$$$ Ananda-in-the-Himalayas**, The Palace, Narendra Nagar, T01378-227500, www.ananda spa.com. Exclusive destination spa with 75 rooms (including a literally palatial suite in the Viceregal Palace, which has its own open-air hot tub and 3 cottages with their own infinity pools and saunas), in a superb location 30 mins above Rishikesh with panoramic views across the valley. Winner of many international awards.

**$$$$ Atali Ganga**, Atali Dogi, Milestone 30, Badrinath Rd, T(0)9756-611114, www. ataliganga.com. Pioneering responsible tourism in the area, Atali Ganga is run by the excellent **Aquaterra Adventures** who organize exceptional treks and rafting expeditions. This beautiful property is 30 km up river of Rishikesh and as well as stunning rooms, there is a great pool, climbing wall and fantastic food. Recommended.
**$$$$ Glasshouse on the Ganges**, 23rd Milestone Rishikesh–Badrinath Rd, Gular Dogi District, T(0)99171-91115, www. neemranahotels.com, 23 km from Rishikesh towards Badrinath. A lovely riverside retreat in lychee and mango tree garden once used by the Rajas of Garwhal. Rooms either in main block or cottages. The property has its own beach and yoga is complimentary.
**$$$ Camp Silver Sands**, Beach No 12 Rishikesh, Badrinath Rd, T011-29212760 (Delhi), www.aquaterra.in. The best tent option along the banks of the Ganga. With a close eye kept on the environment and conscious tourism, they run exceptional rafting expeditions. The tents are simple but comfortable and the food is great – dinner under the stars by the rushing river. Meals included. Highly recommended.
**$$$ Ganga Banks**, Shivpuri, contact Wanderlust in Delhi, T011-4163 6896, www.wanderlust india.com. A 'green' resort with 28 comfortable, eco-friendly cottages with bath, built using local raw materials, restaurant, pool, health spa, in natural surroundings employing recycling techniques (no plastics), solar heating, well placed for trekking, rafting, etc.
**$$$ Rainforest House**, below Neer Gaddu forest *chowkie*, Badrinath Rd, 3 km from Tapovan, T(0)97191-43013, www.rainforest-house.com. Charming, isolated guesthouse upstream from Rishikesh on the Ganga with 9 rustic but beautifully designed double rooms set around a central court. Very peaceful forested retreat without phones or TVs, run by English and Indian husband and wife. Lovely relaxed restaurant serving delicious

Indian and Italian food, delicious salads and great pizzas. There is a beautiful yoga space as well. Whole-heartedly recommended.

**$$ Divine Ganga Cottage**, Tapovan village, T0135-2442175, www.divinegangacottage. com. Quiet location away from Laxman Jhula with newly renovated rooms and a friendly atmosphere. In the winter months, you can enjoy good at **Ramana's Garden** a project set up to help orphans, Recommended.

**$$ Sanskriti Vedic Retreat**, Swarg Ashram, www.sanskritivedicretreat.com. Sadly at the time of writing in 2013 they were renovating following a serious fire – check their website for their progress. Great place for conscious healthy food, good rooms and lovely yoga shala.

**$$-$ Rishilok** (GMVN), Badrinath Rd, Muni-ki-Reti, T0135-243 0373. Within walking distance of Ram Jhula, set far enough from the main road and taxi stand to be quiet, is this charming 1970s government guesthouse. Although its fading upholstery is as old as the building, it holds 46 clean rooms, some with bath, in blocks set around a beautifully kept garden of bamboo, bougainvillea and butterflies. Excellent service.

**$ Bhandari Swiss Cottage**, High Bank, off Lakshman Jhula Rd, T0135-243 2939. Most rooms here are gifted with a heavenly view over the Ganga and to the hills beyond. Big rooms, clean and basic and a tranquil setting. Internet café and little restaurant.

**$ Ishan**, west end of Lakshman Jhula, T0135-243 1534. Clean and pleasant rooms, some with balconies overlooking river, internet downstairs and an excellent restaurant.

**Ashrams and yoga shalas**
There are scores of visiting teachers, both of hatha yoga and of meditation. Check fly posters and ask fellow travellers for the latest details.

**Dayananda**, Purani Jhadi near Chandrabhaga River, T0135-243 0769, www.dayananda.org. Has daily lectures on Vedanta, and rooms with marble floors and tiled bathrooms.

**Parmarth Niketan**, Swargashram, T0135-243 4301, www.parmarth.com/home. Large scale ashram, with well attended sunset *aarti* on the Ganga. Tidy rooms in blocks set around pleasant leafy gardens full of stucco deities and friezes of passages from the *Gita*.

## 🍴 Restaurants

**Haridwar** *p93, map p94*
Cheap stalls on Railway Rd provide simple food for pilgrims.

**$$ Aahar**, Railway Rd. Punjabi, Chinese and continental. Excellent meals.

**$$ Big Ben**, Ganga Azure (see Where to stay). Decent, large range of Indian, Chinese and continental.

**$ Bestee**, Railway Rd. Mughlai and South Indian. Stuffed *parathas* are recommended.

**Rishikesh** *p95, map p96*
Madras Café, on the West Bank, and Chotiwalas, on the East Bank, are Ram Jhula's 2 long-running, cheap fast food joints. Amrita Little Italian Café is a sweet stop off for proper espresso coffee to the right of the boat jetty crossing on the West bank. Safe drinking water is sold to refill bottles near the Ram Jhula, and the mini-markets all sell prized international supplies including Lindt dark chocolate, 'yogi' bread, cakes and home-made peanut butter.

**$$ Ramana's Garden**, uphill from Lakshman Jhula then right at **Tapovan Resort**, 5 mins' walk, www.friendsoframanasgarden.org. Open 1100-1530 and Sat, 1830-2100 (closed May-October). If the organic home-grown salad plates and scrumptious cakes weren't enough in themselves, this pleasant garden restaurant funds a school for local orphan children, who spill out across its grounds during breaks and help Ramana's multinational team of volunteers in the kitchen. Film nights on Sat.

**$ Ganga Freedom Café**, behind Dr Kothari clinic, Lakshman Jhula. Easily the tastiest scran on the East Bank – serving the likes of rosemary roast tatties and ratatouille, a little pricier than some local *dabhas* but food comes in big portions. Lovely atmosphere and views along the river.

**$ Moksha**, near Goa Beach, Lakshman Jhula, T(0)9897-460487. Chilled-out bamboo café heading north on the east bank of the Ganga serving up the usual travellers fare.

**$ Mount Valley Mama Cottage**, next to Bhandari Swiss Cottage. All-you-can-eat *thalis* are much famed among travellers. Delicious and highly recommended.

**$ The Office**, Swargashram ghats near clock tower. Although tiny, this is so much more than a chai joint: it has excellent specials, such as fresh chick pea salad or houmous and apple and chocolate banana samosas. Minimalist bulletin board for upcoming courses, yoga cookery, Ayurveda. Plus a teeny balcony on the Ganges. Lovely.

**$ Pyramid Café**, Lakshman Jhula. Offers all sorts of veggie and vegan health food, such as tofu brown rice *kombucha* and spirulina. The atmosphere and soundtrack in the mellow tipi garden make it well worth the short walk up the hill for. There's Wi-Fi too.

## ❊ Festivals

### Haridwar *p93, map p94*
Thousands of pilgrims visit the city when the birth of the river (*Dikhanti*) is celebrated in spring. **Kumbh Mela**, held here every 12th year (next in Mar-Apr 2021), and **Ardha Kumbh** also every 12 years (next in 2016), attract millions of devotees who come to bathe in the confined area near Hari-ki-Pairi.

### Rishikesh *p95, map p96*
**Feb-Mar** International Yoga Festival, hosted by the Parmarth Niketan ashram. An opportunity to meet and learn from some of the leading lights in the yoga community.

## ◎ Shopping

### Rishikesh *p95, map p96*
Rishikesh has several excellent bookshops specializing in yoga and the spiritual life,

especially the one by Laxman Jhula bridge and German Bakery; good places to rummage for reading material are on the east bank of the Ganga near Ram Jhula and the west bank at Lakshman Jhula. The central market area around Dehra Dun, Haridwar, Ghat and Railway Rds has markets and curio shops.

**Gecko**, under **Hotel Ishan**, Lakshman Jhula. Intriguing and colourful range of Nepali-made dresses and winter jackets.

**Pundir General Store**, Badrinath Rd, Tapovan Sarai. Whether you are hankering for Korean *miso*, V8 juice, European chocolate or a new yoga mat – this place has a bit of everything. Little café upstairs too.

## ◷ What to do

### Haridwar *p93, map p94*
**Body and soul**
**Patanjali Yogpeeth**, near Bahadarabad, Delhi–Haridwar National Highway, T01334-240008, www.divyayoga.com. Simple rooms. Enormous and exceptionally well-equipped ashram/yogic hospital, offering yoga camps and treatments for diseases from diabetes to impotence. However, daily yoga classes are taught in Hindi only

### Tours and tour operators
Daily tours of Haridwar-Rishikesh, 0930, Rs 80; Dehra Dun--Mussoorie, 0800, Rs 140; Rajaji National Park, 1000, 1430.
**Ashwani Travels**, 3 Railway Rd, T01334-224581, ashwanitravels@hotmail.com. Official agent of GMVN, specializing in pilgrimage tours, also trekking.
**Mohan's Adventure**, next to Chitra Cinema, Railway Rd, T01334-265543, www.mohans adventure.in. Very reliable trips run by Sanjee Mehta. Trekking, jeep safaris, rafting. Jungle trips into Rajaji National Park, with night stay in tribal village. Highly recommended.

### Rishikesh *p95, map p96*
**Boat rides**
On the Ganga from from Lakshman Jhula. Fix rates with local boatmen.

## Body and soul

Yoga classes, meditation courses and instruction in Ayurveda and Vedanta are Rishikesh's stock-in-trade. Most hotels can put you in touch with courses, though both style and quality are highly variable. The following institutions are well-established and reliable.

**Omkarananda Ashram** (Durga Mandir) above Yoga Niketan, Ram Jhula, T0135-243 0713. Good Iyengar yoga courses, also offers music and classical dance.

**Parmarth Niketan**, T0135-243 4301 (see Where to stay).

**Sivananda Ashram** (Divine Life Society), T0135-243 0040. Short to 3 month courses (apply 1 month ahead); holds music classes and produces herbal medicines. Forest Academy open to male students; non-Indians can attend classes informally, but are not given certificates.

**Swami Rama Sadhaka Grama**, south of town centre on Virbhadra Rd, T0135-245 0093, www.sadhakagrama.org. Yoga training with a strong focus on meditation, based on the Himalayan tradition laid out by Sankaracharya. There's a rigorous 600-hr yoga teacher training program, or you can simply use the cottages for a few days' retreat. There is an exceptional ayurvedic hospital too.

**Ved Niketan**, south end of Swargashram ghats, T0135-2430279. Has a flexible programme of yoga; also Hindi, Sanskrit, music and dance classes and basic rooms.

## Music

**Sivananda Ramesh**, towards Muni-ki-Reti Taxi Stand, T(0)98971-73406. Lessons in tabla, sitar, santoor, singing, etc.

## Rafting and trekking

There are more than 60 whitewater rafting outfits in town, and Shivpuri, 17 km north, has become an adventure sports playground. You can book onto daily trips on the Grade I waters the day before, or go for more adventurous, longer-haul expeditions with meals and overnights at camps. Below are 3 companies known for their sound environmental records. Ask the government office for a full list of operators.

**Aquaterra**, T011-29212641, www.aqua terra.in. Based in Delhi with an outpost 30 km north of Rishikesh, Aquaterra is the only Indian company to be included in the *National Geographic's* Best Adventure Travel Companies on Earth. With impeccable safety standards and fantastic guides, they offer many rafting and trekking opportunities in the area. Highly recommended.

**De-N-Ascent Expeditions**, Tapovan Sarai T0135-244 2354, www.kayakhimalaya.com. Excellent equipment and stringent safety, with a background in kayaking. Runs day trips and more adventurous routes through less charted waters.

**Red Chilli**, Tapovan, above Lakshman Jhula, T0135-243 4021, www.redchilli adventure.com. Enthusiastic local outfit with good environmental standards. Recommended.

## Tour operators

**Garhwal Himalayan Exploration**, Muni Ki Reti, T0135-244 2267, www.thegarhwal himalayas.com. Wide range of trekking and rafting trips.

**GMVN**, Yatra Office, T0135-243 1793, www.gmvnl.com. Char Dham pilgrimage tours, plus 4-to 5-day adventure tours and yoga at **Parmarth Niketan**.

## ⊙ Transport

**Haridwar** *p93, map p94*
**Bus** The long-distance bus stand is opposite the railway station. Frequent buses to/from **Delhi** (5-7 hrs) and **Dehra Dun** (1¾ hrs). Buses for Rishikesh leave irregularly and only when enough passengers turn up; better to take a tempo or taxi.

**Rickshaw, jeep and taxi** The taxi stand is outside railway station, rates negotiable. To **Rishikesh** costs Rs 600-800. Tempos shuttle around town and to nearby destinations; to **Rishikesh**, Rs 25 (more for Lakshman Jhula). Catch them outside the railway station where the chance of getting a seat is highest. **Taxi Union**, outside bus stand, T01334-227338, has share jeeps to **Joshimath** (Rs 320 a seat) via **Deoprayag**, **Rudraprayag** (Rs 180) and **Karanprayag** (Rs 220). Private jeeps (for up to 9 passengers) cost around Rs 2500 per day in May-Jun, or around Rs 1800 outside pilgrimage season.

**Train** Railway Station, T131. Reservation office 0800-2000. 3 trains per day to **Rishikesh**, 0515, 0845, 1715, better to take road transport; **Delhi** (**OD**): *Dehra Dun Exp 19020*, 1255, 8½ hrs (**HN**); *Mussoorie Exp 14042*, 2310 (**DSR**), 9 hrs (beware of thieves); *Shatabdi Exp 12018*, 1810, 4½ hrs (**ND**). **Dehra Dun**: *Shatabdi Exp 12017*, 1125, 1¼ hrs, among several others. **Varanasi**: *Dehra Dun Varanasi Exp 14266*, 2035, 20 hrs. For **Nainital (Kathgodam)**: *Dehradun-Kathgodam Exp 14120*, 0020, 7 hrs. For **Shimla**, travel via Ambala and Kalka (train is better than bus).

### Rajaji National Park *p95*

The park has 8 entry gates. From **Dehra Dun**: **Mohan** (25 km on Delhi–Dehra Dun highway, 5-hr drive from Delhi), **Ramgarh** (14 km, Delhi–Dehra Dun highway, via Clement Town) and **Lachhiwala** (18 km, Dehra Dun–Haridwar route, right turn before Doiwala). From **Haridwar**: **Chilla** (7 km, via private bus route to Rishikesh), **Motichur** (9 km, Haridwar–Rishikesh or Dehra Dun–Haridwar highways) and **Ranipur** (9 km, Haridwar–BHEL–Mohand Rd). From **Rishikesh**: **Kunnao** (6 km, via private bus route on Rishikesh–Pashulok route). From **Kotdwara**: **Laldhang** (25 km, via private bus route Kotdwara to Chilla).

### Rishikesh *p95, map p96*

Rishikesh is the main staging post for visiting the Himalayan pilgrim centres of **Badrinath** (301 km); **Gangotri** (258 km); **Kedarnath** (228 km); **Uttarkashi** (154 km); **Yamunotri** (288 km).

**Bus** Long-distance buses use **main bus stand**, Haridwar Rd, T0135-243 0066.

Various State Government bus services (DTC, Haryana Roadways, Himachal RTC, UP Roadways serve destinations including: **Chandigarh** (252 km), **Dehra Dun** (42 km, every 30 mins), **Delhi** (238 km, 6 hrs), **Haridwar** (24 km, every 30 mins), **Mussoorie** (77 km). For **Shimla**, stay overnight in Dehra Dun and catch 0600 bus. Share taxis for Dehra Dun and Haridwar leave from outside the bus stand.

The **Yatra Bus Stand**, Dehra Dun Rd, has buses for local destinations and the mountain pilgrimage sites. Reserve tickets the day before (especially during *yatra* season, May-Nov); open 0400-1900, 0400-1400 out of season. To **Char Dhams**: buses leave early for the very long routes to Hanuman Chatti (for Yamunotri), **Badrinath**, **Gangotri**, **Gaurikund** (for Kedarnath); best to take a luxury bus, and break your journey. For **Badrinath** and **Hemkund** stop overnight at Joshimath (after 1630 road to Govindghat is southbound only). Although the *yatra* season ends in late Oct (Yamunotri, Gangotri, Kedarnath) to mid-Nov (Badrinath), bus frequency drops drastically during Oct. Even light rains can cause severe road blocks, mainly due to landslides. Bus for Badrinath departs from **Tehri Bus Stand** (100 m right from station), 1600, Rs 180, but noisy, crowded and uncomfortable. **Garhwal Motor Owners Union**, T0135-243 0076; **Tehri Garhwal MOU**, **Triveni**, Haridwar Rd, T0135-243 0989. Also worth a try, though no cheaper than buses, are 'Newspaper taxis', eg Joshimath, Rs 200 per person; ask at **Sanjay News Agency**, Main Rd (before turn-off to Ghat Rd) or travel agent.

**Ferry** Ferry boat from near Ram Jhula for river crossing, Rs 10, return Rs 15.

**Jeep** Hire for **Badrinath** (1-way), Rs1500-2000, is the best option. Book the night before.

**Motorbike** Motorbike mechanic at **Bila**, opposite Ganga View Hotel, Lakshman Jhula

**Rickshaw** Auto-rickshaw rates are negotiable; allow around Rs 30 to **Ram Jhula**, Rs 35-40 for **Lakshman Jhula**.

**Taxi** Fixed rates from from taxi stands south of **Ram Jhula** and in the market near **Lakshman Jhula**.

**Tempo** Mostly fixed routes. From Ram Jhula shared, to Rishikesh Bazar Rs 5; from Lakshman Jhula Rs 10; to **Haridwar** Rs 25, 50 mins. Foreigners may be asked for more.

**Train** There is a branch line from **Haridwar** to **Rishikesh**, but the bus is quicker.

## ● Directory

**Haridwar** *p93, map p94*
**Medical services** District Hospital, Upper Rd, T01334-226060. RK Mission, Kankhal, T01334-247141. Chemists: on Railway and Upper Rd. **Useful contacts** Police: T01334-227775.

**Rishikesh** *p95, map p96*
**Medical services** Ambulance: T102. Govt Hospital, Dehra Dun Rd, T0135-243 0402. Nirmal Ashram, T0135-243 2215. Sivananda, Muni-ki-Reti, T0135-243 0040.

# Garhwal and the Pilgrimage (Yatra)

*The shrines of Kedarnath, Yamunotri, Gangotri and Badrinath are visited by hundreds of thousands of Hindu pilgrims each summer. They come from all corners of the subcontinent to engage in what William Dalrymple calls "a modern-day Indian Canterbury Tales". Garhwal's fragmented political history gives no clue as to the region's religious significance. The sources of the Yamuna and the Ganga, and some of Hinduism's holiest mountains, lie in the heart of the region. Since the seventh-century Tamil saint Sankaracharya travelled north on his mission to reinvigorate Hinduism's northern heartland, some have been watched over permanently by South Indian priests. The most famous is the Rawal – head priest – at the Badrinath temple, who to this day comes from Kerala. Badrinath is one of the four* dhams, *'holiest abodes' of the gods. Along with Dwarka, Puri and Ramesvaram, they mark the cardinal points of Hinduism's cultural geography. After a ritual purificatory bathe in the Ganga at Haridwar and, preferably, Rishikesh, the pilgrim begins the 301-km journey to Badrinath. The purpose is to worship, purify and acquire merit. Roads go all the way to Gangotri and Badrinath, and to within 5 km of Yamunotri and 14 km of Kedarnath. The correct order for pilgrims is to visit the holy places from west to east: Yamunotri, Gangotri, Kedarnath and Badrinath. The floods of June 2013 where over 10,000 people were killed badly affected Kedarnath and the roads leading up to these pilgrimage places. They managed to get the yatra routes open again by October for limited numbers of pilgrims. Vaibhav Kala, who has been leading treks and expeditions in the Himalayas for many years, says: "Rebuilding is on, it's painfully slow. The lives that have changed will take years to get back to normal."* ›› *For listings, see pages 110-113.*

## Arriving in Garhwal and the Pilgrimage

Temples and trekking routes open from the end of April to mid-November (October for Badrinath). June is very crowded; heavy rains from July to mid-September may trigger landslips. The best time to visit is May and mid-September to mid-October. *Yatra* tourists on public buses are required to register with the Yatra Office at the Yatra (Local) Bus Stand, Rishikesh (0600-2200). A certificate of immunization against cholera and typhoid is needed. In practice, 'Registration' is often waived, but the immunization certificate is checked. Accommodation prices are higher than average. **GMVN** (www.gmvnl.com) organizes 12-day pilgrimage tours from Delhi and Rishikesh during season.›› *For trekking, see page 113.*

Yamunotri can be reached from Rishikesh or from Dehra Dun via Yamuna Bridge and Barkot. The former is the more popular. From Rishikesh it is 83 km to Tehri, or 165 km via Deoprayag. **Tehri**, northeast of Rishikesh, the capital of the former princely state, will eventually be submerged by the waters behind the controversial and still unfinished Tehri Dam. **New Tehri**, 24 km from the original town, is a 'planned' town and the new district headquarters. Note that it is an offence to photograph sensitive installations, troop movements and bridges on most routes. Offenders can be treated very severely.

### Yamunotri → *Colour map 1, B4. Altitude: 3291 m.*
Dominated by **Banderpunch** (6316 m), Yamunotri, the source of the Yamuna, is believed to be the daughter of Surya (the sun) and the twin sister of Yama (the 'Lord of Death'). Anyone who bathes in her waters will be spared an agonizing death.

To begin the trek to reach the temple take a jeep from **Hanuman Chatti** (large vehicles also stop here and pick up) to **Janki Chatti**, 8 km further up, which is more pleasant and where you can leave luggage. The trek along the riverbank is exhilarating with the mountains rising up on each side, the last 5 km somewhat steeper. The source itself is a difficult 1-km climb from the 19th-century **Yamunotri Temple** ① *0600-1200, 1400-2100*, with a black marble deity. The modern temple was rebuilt this century after floods and snow destroyed it. There are **hot springs** nearby (the most sacred being Surya Kund) in which pilgrims cook potatoes and rice tied in a piece of cloth. The meal, which takes only a few minutes to cook, is first offered to the deity and then distributed as *prasad*. On the return to Hanuman Chatti, you can visit the **Someshwar Temple** at **Kharsali**, 3 km across the river from Janki Chatti. The temple is one of the oldest and finest in the region.

### Uttarkashi and around → *Colour map 1, B4. Altitude: 3140 m.*
This busy town, en route to Gangotri, 155 km from Rishikesh, has several places to stay but all are full during the season. There's a **tourist office** ① *T01374-222290*, the **Nehru Institute of Mountaineering** offers courses and you can trek to **Dodital** (see page 116); porters can be hired. You can buy provisions from the bazar near the bus stand. If you are in town on 14 January you will see the **Makar Sankranti Garhwal festival** of music and dance. Uttarkashi was badly affected by the floods and landslides in June 2013.

If you can, make a detour at Saur, a small village between Rishikesh and Uttarkashi. Abandoned when the residents moved to nearby towns four decades ago, it has since become a responsible tourism project set up by **DueNorth**. You can stay in beautifully restored cottages (see page 111) with stunning scenery.

### Gangotri and around → *Colour map 1, B5. Altitude: 3140 m.*
Gangotri, 240 km from Rishikesh, is the second of the major shrines in the Garhwal Himalaya. A high bridge now takes the road across the Jad Ganga River, joining the Bhagirathi which rushes through narrow gorges, so buses travel all the way. The 18th-century granite **temple** is dedicated to the goddess Ganga, where she is believed to have descended to earth. It was built by a Gurkha commander, Amar Singh Thapa, in the early 18th century and later rebuilt by the Maharaja of Jaipur. Hindus believe that Gang (here Bhagirathi) came down from heaven after **King Bhagirath**'s centuries-long penance. He wanted to ensure his dead relatives' ascent to heaven by having their ashes washed b the sacred waters of the Ganga. When the tempestuous river arrived on earth, the force o

# Ganga

The magnificent River Ganges is the spiritual heart of Hinduism and the blood that flows through its veins. Running from a high mountain glacier in Uttarakhand and flowing out at the Bay of Bengal, the river, worshipped as the goddess Ganga attracts people from all over the world to pray and make purification *pujas*.

The story goes that when the goddess Ganga came to earth she fell upon the head of Lord Shiva, the first man of yoga, was caught in his hair and let out in small streams to spread across the earth. Lord Shiva sat and received her at Gangotri in Uttarakhand, which is considered to be the source of the Ganges and is now one of the most sacred places to dip in the holy waters.

Over time, the actual source has receded a further 18 km to the Gaumukh glacier and you can find *sadhus* (holy men) and pilgrims along the route to the glacier.

Other auspicious places to dip are at Rishikesh and Haridwar in Uttarakhand, and then further downstream at Allahabad and Varanasi. They are seen as *tirthas* – places where the veil between the physical and spiritual world is at its thinnest. People come to pray, to leave offerings of flowers and to bring the ashes of their dead. Haridwar and Allahabad (see page 93) both play host to the **Kumbh Mela**, the largest spiritual gathering on earth, attracting nearly 100 million people. Spectacular Ganga Arti fire *pujas* are performed by Brahmin priests every evening in Rishikesh, Haridwar and Varanasi.

The Ganges river basin – the most heavily populated in the world – is inhabited by 37% of India's mighty 1.2 billion population and this has evidently impacted on the river itself. This is a place where people bathe, perform *pujas*, do their laundry and bring the ashes of the dead. On top of that are the contamination of municipal and industrial waste and the impact of dams. Indeed, the pollution is shocking, with coliform bacteria levels reaching 5500, a level too high to be safe for agricultural use, let alone drinking and bathing. While the Ganga as a celestial being enjoys immortality, the river itself is struggling.

An action plan is in place targeting industry, but progress is slow. Individuals are reacting too: Nagnath, a *sadhu* in Varanasi, has been on a fast since 2008 to protest against the environmental devastation of the Ganges.

---

...er flow had to be checked by Siva who received her in the coils of his hair, lest she sweep ...ll away. A submerged lingam is visible in the winter months.

**Rishikund**, 55 km from Uttarkashi, has hot sulphur springs near **Gangnani** suitable for ...athing, and a 15th-century temple. The **Gaurikund waterfall** here is one of the most ...eautiful in the Himalaya. Below Gangotri are **Bhojbasa** and **Gaumukh**, which are on a ...radual but scenically stunning trek. You can continue to trek another 6 km to Nandanvan ...4400 m), base camp for Bhagirathi peak, and continue 4 km to Tapovan (4463 m), known ...or its meadows that encircle the base of Shivling peak.➤➤ *For trekking, see page 113.*

## Rishikesh to Kedarnath → *For listings, see pages 110-113. Colour map 1, B4-B5.*

...rom Rishikesh the road follows the west bank of the Ganga and enters forest. At the ...3rd milestone, at **Gular-dogi village**, is the orchard and garden of the Maharaja of Tehri ...arhwal, close to a white-sand and rock beach, which is now home to a luxury hotel.

The section up to **Deoprayag** (68 km) is astonishingly beautiful. The folding and erosion of the hills can be clearly seen on the mainly uninhabited steep scarps on the opposite bank. Luxuriant forest runs down to the water's edge which in many places is fringed with silver sand beaches. In places the river rushes over gentle rapids. A few kilometres before Byasi is **Vashisht Gufa** (the cave where the saint meditated) which has an ashram. About 5 km after **Byasi** the road makes a gradual ascent to round an important bluff. At the top, there are fine views down to the river. The way tiny fields have been created by terracing is marvellous. Jeeps can be hired from here to Badrinath or Rishikesh.

**Deoprayag** is the most important of the hill *prayags* because it is here, where the frothing Bhagirathi from Gangotri joins the calm Alaknanda flowing down from Badrinath, that the Ganga herself is born. The town tumbles down the precipitous hillside in the deeply cut 'V' between the rivers, with houses almost on top of one another. Where the rivers meet is a pilgrims' bathing ghat, artificially made into the shape of India. From Deoprayag, the road is flat as far as Srinagar (35 km) and the land is cultivated. The Siva and Raghunath temples here attract pilgrims.

The old capital of Tehri Garhwal, **Srinagar** was devastated when the Gohna Lake dam was destroyed by an earthquake in the mid-19th century. The most attractive part of Srinagar, which is a university town, runs from the square down towards the river. There are some typical hill houses with elaborately carved door jambs. The 35-km route from Srinagar to **Rudraprayag**, at the confluence of the Mandakini and Alaknanda, passes through cultivated areas, wild ravines, and the vast construction works for a new dam. Halfway, an enormous landslip indicates the fragility of the mountains. Some 5 km before reaching Rudraprayag, in a grove of trees by a village, is a tablet marking the spot where the 'man-eating leopard of Rudraprayag' was killed by Jim Corbett. Rudraprayag with its temples is strung out along a narrow part of the Alaknanda Valley.

For Kedarnath, leave the Pilgrim road at Rudraprayag, cross the Alaknanda River, and go through a tunnel before following the Mandakini Valley through terraced cultivation and green fields. The road goes past **Tilwara**, 9 km, then **Kund**, to **Guptakashi** where Siva proposed to Parvati. If time permits and you have hired a jeep from Guptakashi stop at **Sonprayag**, 26 km, a small village at the confluence of the Mandakini and Son Ganga rivers, to visit the **Triyuginarayan Temple** where the gods were married. Enjoy the viewpoint here before continuing to **Gaurikund**, 4 km away, where the motorable road ends. Hundreds of pilgrims bathe in the hot sulphur springs in season. From here you either trek (start early) or ride a mule to **Kedarnath**, 14 km away. The ascent, which is steep at first, is through forests and green valleys to **Jungle Ghatti** and **Rambara** (over 1500 m), the latter part goes through dense vegetation, ravines and passes beautiful waterfalls. Beyond Rambara the path is steep again. At intervals tea stalls sell refreshments.

## Kedarnath Temple and around → *For listings, see pages 110-113. Colour map 1, B5.*

The area around Kedarnath is known as Kedarkhand (the Abode of Siva). Kedarnath has one of the 12 *jyotirlingas* (luminous energy of Siva manifested at 12 holy places, miraculously formed lingams). In the *Mahabharata*, the **Pandavas** built the temple to atone for their sins after the battle at Kurukshetra.

### Kedarnath Temple → *Altitude: 3584 m. 77 km from Rudraparyag. Pujas at 0600 and 1800.*
The Kedarnath Temple is older and more impressive than Badrinath. Some claim is originally more than 800 years old. Built of stone, unpainted but carved outside,

comprises a simple, squat, curved tower and a wooden-roofed *mandapa*. Set against an impressive backdrop of snow-capped peaks, the principal one being the Kedarnath peak (6970 m), the view from the forecourt is ruined by ugly 'tube' lights. At the entrance to the temple is a large Nandi statue.

## Vasuki Tal → *A guide is necessary. Altitude: 4235 m.*

Vasuki Tal, about 6 km away, the source of Son Ganga, is to the west up along a goat track. It has superb views of the Chaukhamba Peak (7164 m). A short distance northwest is the beautiful Painya Tal where through the clear water you can see the rectangular rocks which form the lake bottom.

## Kedarnath Musk Deer Sanctuary

① *Permits to visit from DFO, Kedarnath Wildlife Division in Gopeshwar, T01372-252149, dfokedarnath@rediffmail.com; Rs 100, Indians Rs 40.*

The area bounded by the Mandal–Ukhimath road and the high peaks to the north (the Kedarnath Temple is just outside) was set aside in 1972 principally to protect the endangered Himalayan musk deer – the male carries the prized musk pod. There is a **breeding centre** at Khanchula Kharak about 10 km from Chopta. The diversity of the park's flora and fauna are particular attractions. Dense forested hills of chir pine, oak, birch and rhododendron and alpine meadows with the presence of numerous Himalayan flowering plants, reflect the diverse climate and topography of the area while 40% of the rocky heights remain under permanent snow. Wildlife includes jackal, black bear, leopard, snow leopard, sambar, *bharal* and Himalayan tarh, as well as 146 species of bird. A 2-km trek from Sari village near Chopta leads to Deoriatal, at 2438 m, overlooking Chaukhamba Peak.

## The Panch Kedars

There are five temples visited by pilgrims: Kedarnath, Madhmaheswar, Tungnath, Rudranath and Kalpeshwar. These vary in altitude from 1500 m to 3680 m in the Rudra Himalaya and make an arduous circuit. Kedarnath and Badrinath are 41 km apart with a tiring *yatra* (pilgrim route) between the two; most pilgrims take the longer but easier way round by bus or car. The myth of the 'five Sivas' relates how parts of the shattered Nandi Bull fell in the five places: the humped back at Kedarnath, the stomach at Madhmaheswar, the legs at Tungnath, the face at Rudranath and the hair at Kalpeshwar. Since all but Kalpeshwar and Tungnath are inaccessible in winter, each deity has a winter seat in a temple at Ukhimath. The images are brought down in the autumn and returned to their temples in the spring.

## Panch Kedars trek

If you wish to undertake the 170 km, 14-day trek, start at Rishikesh, visiting Kedarnath first (see above). Return to Guptakashi and proceed to Kalimath to start the 24-km trek to **Madhmaheswar** from Mansuna village. You can stop overnight at **Ransi**, 1 km southwest of Madhmaheswar, and continue following the Ganga through the Kedarnath Musk Deer Sanctuary (see above). From near the temple at 3030 m, which has three streams flowing by it, you can see Chaukhamba Peak (7164 m).

**Tungnath**, at 3680 m the highest temple, is surrounded by the picturesque Nanda Devi, Neelkanth and Kedarnath mountains. You reach it by a 3-km trek from Chopta, on a driving route from Ukhimath to Gopeshwar, passing through villages, fields and wooded hills before reaching meadows with rhododendrons. The two-hour climb, though steep, is not difficult since it is along a good rocky path with occasional benches.

For **Rudranath**, at 3030 m, get to Gopeshwar by road and then on to Sagar (5 km) for the 24-km trek covering stony, slippery ground through tall grass, thick oak and rhododendron forests. Landslides are quite common. The grey stone Rudranth temple has the Rudraganga flowing by it. The views of the Nandadevi, Trisul and Hathi Parbat peaks and down to the small lakes glistening in the surroundings are fantastic.

**Kalpeshwar**, at 2100 m, near Joshimath, is the only one of the Panch Kedars accessible throughout the year. Its position, overlooking the Urgam Valley, offers beautiful views of the Garhwal's most fertile region with its terraced cultivation of rice, wheat and vegetables. Trekking across the Mandakini starts from Tangni.

## Rudraprayag to Badrinath → *For listings, see pages 110-113.*

### The road to Joshimath → *Colour map 1, B5.*
Along the Pilgrim road, about midway between Rudraprayag and Karnaprayag, you pass **Gauchar**, famous locally for its annual cattle fair. The valley is wider here providing the local population with very good agricultural land. The beautiful Pindar River joins the Alaknanda at **Karnaprayag**, 17 km, while **Nandaprayag** is the confluence with the Nandakini River. All these places have **GMVN** accommodation. **Chamoli**, 40 km further on, is the principal market for the Chamoli district though the administrative headquarters is at Gopeshwar on the hillside opposite. By this point, the valley walls have become much higher and steeper and the road twists and turns more. Troop movements up to the border with Tibet/China are common and military establishments are a frequent sight on the Pilgrim road. From Chamoli onwards the road is an impressive feat of engineering.

### Joshimath → *Colour map 1, B5. Phone code: 01389. Altitude: 1875 m.*
Joshimath is at the junction of two formerly important trans-Himalayan trading routes. Travellers to Govindghat and beyond may be forced to spend a night here as the road closes to northbound traffic at 1630. Joshimath is now the base for India's longest and highest **cable car route** ⓘ *generally begins 0800 or 0900, Rs 200 one way to Auli Ski Resort,* with beautiful views of Nanda Devi, Kamet, Mana Parvat and Dunagiri peaks, all above 7000 m. There is a restaurant in the meadow. The **tourist office** ⓘ *in the annexe above Neelkanth Motel, T01389-222181,* is helpful.

### Vishnuprayag
Vishnuprayag is at the bottom of the gorge at the confluence of the Alaknanda and Dhauliganga rivers. Some 12 km and a steep downhill stretch brings the road from Joshimath to the winter headquarters of the Rawal of Badrinath. Buses for Badrinath along the narrow hair-raising route start around 0600, the one-way flow regulated by police. You travel through precipitous gorges, past another Hanuman Chatti with a temple and climb above the tree-line to reach the most colourful of the *Char Dhams*, in the valley.

The **Bhotias** (Bhutias), a border people with Mongoloid features and strong ties with Tibet, live along these passes (see page 335). The women wear a distinctive Arab-like headdress. Like their counterparts in the eastern Himalaya, they used to combine high altitude cultivation with animal husbandry and trading, taking manufactured goods from India to Tibet and returning with salt and borax. When the border closed following the 1962 Indo-Chinese War, they were forced to seek alternative income and some were resettled.

**Auli** → *Colour map 1, B5. Altitude: 2519 m. By road it is 16 km from Joshimath, or a 5-km trek; there is also a cable car (see Transport, page 113).*

The extensive meadows at Auli, on the way to the Kauri Pass, had been used for cattle grazing by the local herders. After the Indo-Chinese War (1962), a road was built from Joshimath to Auli and a Winter Craft Centre set up for the border police in the 1970s. With panoramic views of mountains, particularly Nanda Devi and others in the sanctuary, and Mana and Kamet on the Indo-Tibet border, and good slopes, Auli has been developed as a **ski** resort by **GMVN** and **Uttarakhand Tourism** operating from mid-December to early March. Though not a spectacularly equipped resort by world standards, Auli offers a 500-m ski lift (Rs 30) and 800-m chair lift (Rs 200), and has cheap lessons and gear hire.

---

## Badrinath and around → *For listings, see pages 110-113. Colour map 1, B5.*
*Phone code: 01389. Altitude: 3150 m.*

According to Hindu Shastras, no pilgrimage is complete without a visit to Badrinath, the abode of Vishnu. Along with Ramesvaram, Dwarka and Puri, it is one of the four holiest places in India, see page 407. Guarding it are the Nar and Narayan ranges and in the distance towers the magnificent pyramid-shaped peak of Neelkanth, at 6558 m; a hike to its base takes two hours. Badri is derived from a wild fruit that Vishnu was said to have lived on when he did penance at Badrivan, the area which covers all five important temples including Kedarnath. Shankaracharya, the monist philosopher from South India, is credited with establishing the four great pilgrimage centres in the early ninth century AD, see page 407.

### Badrinath Temple
The main Badrinath Temple is small and brightly painted in green, blue, pink, yellow, white, silver and red. The shrine is usually crowded with worshippers. The *Rawal* (Head Priest) always comes from a Namboodri village in Kerala, the birthplace of Shankaracharya. Badrinath is snowbound over winter, when the images are transferred to Pandukeshwar, and is open late April to October. Along with worshipping in the temple and dispensing alms to the official (sometimes wealthy) temple beggars outside, it is customary to bathe in **Tapt Kund**, a hot pool nearby below the temple. This is fed by a hot sulphurous spring in which Agni (the god of fire) resides by kind permission of Vishnu. The temperature is around 45°C. **Badrinath Festival** takes place 3-10 June.

### Hemkund and the Valley of Flowers → *Colour map 1, B5.*
ⓘ *Permits to enter the park are issued at the police post at the road head of Govindghat and the Forest Check Post at Ghangharia, Rs 600 (Indians Rs150) for a 3-day permit. Camping overnight in the valley or taking back plants or flowers is prohibited.*
**Govindghat**, 20 km from Joshimath, is on the road to Badrinath. A bridle track leads to Ghangharia, for the Valley of Flowers, 19 km further on, and Hemkund Sahib. This trail-head is very crowded in peak season (May-June). You can trek or hire mules for the two-day journey; there are several tea-stalls along the route.

**Ghangharia**, at 3048 m, is a 14-km walk from Govindghat. May to June are very busy. Those arriving late without a reservation may only find floor space in the Sikh Gurudwara.

To reach **Hemkund** (6 km further on, 4329 m) after 1 km from Ghangharia leave the main Valley of Flowers track, up a path to the right. **Guru Gobind Singh** is believed to have sat here in meditation during a previous incarnation, see page 422. It is an important Sikh pilgrimage site. On the shore of the lake where pilgrims bathe in the icy cold waters is a modern *gurudwara*; well worth the long trek though some may suffer from the high altitude. Hemkund is also a Hindu pilgrimage site, referred to as **Lokpal**. Lakshman, the younger brother of Rama, meditated by the lake and regained his health after being severely wounded by Ravana's son, Meghnath. A small Lakshman temple stands near the *gurudwara*. Despite its ancient connections, Hemkund/Lokpal was 'discovered' by a Sikh *Havildar*, Solan Singh, and only became a major pilgrimage centre after 1930.

The 14-km trail from Govindghat to Ghangharia runs along a narrow forested valley past the villages of **Pulna** and **Bhiyundar**. The **Valley of Flowers** (3000-3600 m; best July-August), is a further 5 km. **Hathi Parbat** (Elephant Peak), at 6700 m, rises dramatically at the head of the narrow side valley. Close views of mountains can be seen from Bhiyundar. The trek has beautifully varied scenery. After crossing the Alaknanda River by suspension bridge the winding path follows the Laxman Ganga as its constant companion, passing dense forests and commanding panoramic views of the lovely Kak Bhusundi Valley on its way to the hamlet of **Ghangaria** (Govind Dham), the base for the Valley of Flowers, nestling amidst giant deodars. As the path from Ghangaria gradually climbs to the Valley of Flowers, glaciers, snow bridges, alpine flowers and wildlife appear at intervals. The 6-km-long and 2-km-wide U-shaped valley is laced by waterfalls. The River Pushpati and many other small streams wind across it, and its floor, carpeted with alpine flowers during the monsoons, is particularly beautiful. It is especially popular because of its accessibility. The valley was popularized by **Frank Smythe**, the well-known mountaineer, in 1931. Local people had always kept clear of the valley because of the belief that it was haunted, and any who entered it would be spirited away. A memorial stone to Margaret Legge, an Edinburgh botanist, who slipped and fell to her death in 1939 reads, "I will lift up mine eyes unto the hills from whence cometh my strength".

## Satopanth → *25 km from Badrinath. Take a guide.*

Satopanth, a glacial lake, takes a day to reach from Badrinath via the track along the Alaknanda Valley; it's a gentle climb up to **Mana** village (6 km north) near the border, inhabited by Bhotias. Foreigners need to register here and deposit their cameras since they are not permitted to take photographs. Nearby is the cave where Vyasa is said to have written the epic *Mahabharata*. The track disappears and you cross a snowbridge, trek across flower-filled meadows before catching sight of the impressive 144-m **Vasudhara Falls**. The ascent becomes more difficult as you approach the source of the Alaknanda near where the Satopanth and Bhagirathi Kharak glaciers meet. The remaining trek takes you across the **Chakra Tirth** meadow and over the steep ridge of the glacier till you see the striking green Satopanth Lake. According to legend its three corners mark the seats of Brahma, Vishnu and Siva. The peaks of **Satopanth** (7084 m) from which the glacier flows, **Neelkanth** (6558 m) and **Chaukhamba** (7164 m) make a spectacular sight.

## ◉ Garhwal and the Pilgrimage (Yatra) listings

*For hotel and restaurant price codes and other relevant information, see pages 22-26.*

### ● Where to stay

Contact **GMVN**, T0135-243 1793, www.gmvnl. com, for reservations in their **$$-$** resthouses along the routes. Some have 'deluxe' rooms which are still basic, with toilet and hot water, and most have dorms (Rs 200). There are also simple guesthouses in places. Room prices everywhere blow out during *yatra* season, and advance reservations are essential; GMVN places may only be available if you book their organized tour. Carry bottled water or a filter and take a good torch. This book was researched before the terrible flooding in Jun 2013, please check ahead with GMVN Rishikesh to check on roads and guest house availability (number and website above). They had the Char Dam roads open by Oct 2013 for small groups of pilgrims. Uttarkashi was particularly badly hit – where Hotel Akash Ganga and the Manikarnika temple were washed away.

### Yamunotri *p104*
There are other lodges and *dharamshalas* and also places to eat.
**$ Rest House**, Janki Chatti, GMVN, T01375-235639. Closed Dec-Mar.
**$ Rest House**, Yamunotri, GMVN. On a hill.
**$ Tourist Rest House**, by the river, Hanuman Chatti. Closed Dec-Mar. GMVN, clean, simple rooms, dorm (Rs 200), hot water in buckets, the only decent place.

### Uttarkashi and around *p104*
**$$$ Saur Project**, south of Tehri, between Uttarkashi and Rishikesh, T(0)9899-061383, www.duenorth.in. Amazing restoration project of local cottages in the 'ghost' village of Saur which was abandoned 4 decades ago. With stunning views, terraced fields, this is a place to connect to nature and conscious farming. Food is included in price and you can learn to cook local foods – delicious. More village cottages are being restored using local traditions. Recommended.
**$$$ Shikhar Nature Resort**, 5 km out of town, by the Bhagirathi River, T01374-223762, www.naturecampsindia.com. Luxury tents with pretty furnishings with mod cons in scenic setting.
**$$-$ Sahaj Villa**, Gangotri Highway, Gyansu, Uttarkashi, T01374-222783. Basic, clean rooms. Restaurant on-site.

### Dodital
**$ GMVN Tourist Bungalow**, near bridge, T01374-222 271. Small, 33 rooms with bath, few a/c, vegetarian meals.

**$ Monal Tourist Home**, near Kot Bungalow, T01374-222270, www.monaluttarkashi.com. Pleasant rooms and atmosphere, a little out of town. Friendly owner leads good day treks, plus yoga and Hindi classes.
**$ Shivam**, T01374-222 525. Some a/c.

### Gangotri *p104*
Expect very basic accommodation here with erratic electricity.
**$$ Tourist Rest House** (GMVN), T01377-238021, across the footbridge. 20 rooms and dorm, meals.
**$ Ganga Niketan**, across the road bridge. Good rooms and a simple terrace restaurant.
**$ Gangotri Guest House**, near bus stand. T(0)75790-57689. Simple rooms.

### Rishikesh to Kedarnath *p105*
**$$-$ New Tourist Bungalow**, on a hill 1 km south of village centre, Rudraprayag, T01364-233347, www.gmvnl.com. 25 rooms with bath, all with excellent views of prayag, plus dorm.
**$$-$ Tourist Rest House**, near bus stop in central square, Srinagar, T01346-252199, www.gmvnl. com. 90 rooms, deluxe en suite, cabins and dorm, restaurant, tourist office, clean and quiet.
**$ Chandrapuri Camp**, north Rudraprayag, T01364-283207. By the river. 10 safari-type tents for 4.
**$ Tourist Bungalow**, Gaurikund, T01364-269202, www.gmvnl.com. May-Nov. 10 rooms.
**$ Tourist Bungalow**, Guptakashi, T01364-267221, www.gmvnl.com. 6 basic, clean rooms.
**$ Tourist Bungalow**, on a hillside, 1.5 km from the main bazar and bus stand, Deoprayag, T01378-266013, www.gmvnl. com. 16 rooms, some with bath, meals.

### Kedarnath Temple *p106*
**$ Tourist Rest House**, T01364-2632280. 16 rooms, some with bath, and dorm.

### The road to Joshimath *p108*
**$ Tourist Bungalow**, Gauchar, T01363-240611, www.gmvnl.com. Open all year.
**$ Tourist Bungalow**, Nandaprayag, T01372-261215, www.gmvnl.com. Open all year. Small but clean rooms.
**$ Tourist Bungalow**, Karnaprayag, T01363-244210, www.gmvnl.com. Open all year. Attractive setting.

### Joshimath *p108*
Hotel prices rise in high season.
**$$$-$$ Himalayan Abode**, Upper Mall, by bus stand, T(0)9412-082247. Attractive homestay with wall-to-wall views and great home-cooked food.
**$$ Dronagiri Hotel**, T01389-222622. Comfortable hotel with restaurant.
**$$ Nanda Inn**, Auli Rd, 3 km from Joshimath, T(0)98379-37948. Away from the bustle of the bazaar, this homestay is on the way to Auli. Friendly family.
**$ Kamet**, by Ropeway, Lower Mall, T01389-222155. Not great value but cheaper rooms in annexe.
**$ Tourist Rest House (New)**, T01389-222226. OK rooms in ugly block.

### Auli *p109*
**$$ Devi Darshan Lodge**, near Helipad T(0)9719-316777, Simple rooms, but epic views. Good restaurant.
**$$-$ Tourist Bungalow**, T01389-223208, www.gmvni.com. Wide range, including huts and a dorm (Rs 150), large restaurant.

### Badrinath *p109*
For pilgrims: *dharamshalas* and *chattis* (resthouses), T01381-225204.
**$$ Devlok** (GMVN), near bus stand, T01381-222212. The best option in the trekking area with 30 large rooms and a restaurant.

### Hemkund and Valley of Flowers *p109*
Ghangaria was badly affected by the floods in 2013, although the Hemkund Yatra did start again in Oct 2013.

**$$$ Himalayan Eco Lodges**, Ghangharia, T01244-081500 (Gurgaon), www.himalayan ecolodges.com. Good tents with attached bathrooms, price includes meals and tea.
**$$-$ Hotel Bhagat**, at the far end of Govindghat, T(0)94129-36360, www.hotel bhagat.com. Good clean rooms – a cut above the rest.
**$$-$ Tourist Lodge**, Ghangharia. Overpriced rooms, dorm (Rs 100), tent (Rs 60).
**$ Krishna**, Ghangharia. Rooms with bath.
**Forest Rest House** and **Govind Singh Gurudwara**, Govindghat, free beds and food to all (donations accepted) and reliable cloakroom service for trekkers.

## ⊕ What to do

### Uttarkashi and around *p104*
**Mount Support**, Gangotri Rd, near bus stand, T01374-222419. Foreign exchange at monopoly rates. Hire guides and porters.

### Joshimath *p108*
**Eskimo Travels**, next to GMVN, T01389-221177. Recommended for trekking, climbing and skiing.
**Garhwal Mountain Services**, T01389-222288. For porters.
**Mountain Shepherds**, Lata village, T(0)971-931 6777, www.mountainshepherds.com. Unique community tourism venture, with treks around the Nanda Devi region led by properly trained guides, plus unusual options including the chance to accompany local shepherds on their daily rounds.

## ⊕ Transport

For further details of getting to the region, see Rishikesh Transport, page 102.

### Yamunotri *p104*
**Bus** Early bus (0600) best from Rishikesh to **Hanuman Chatti** (210 km, 9 hrs).

**Uttarkashi and around** *p104*
**Bus** Frequent buses from Dodital to
**Rishikesh** (140 km) and **Gangotri** (100 km)
during the *yatra* season.

**Kedarnath Temple** *p106*
**Bus** From **Rishikesh** to **Rudraprayag**
and **Gaurikund**.

**Joshimath** *p108*
**Bus** Frequent buses to **Badrinath**, 4 hrs, via
**Govindghat**, 1 hr, Rs 15; to **Kedarprayag**,

1300, 4 hrs; **Rishikesh**, 0400, 0600, 10 hrs;
**Rudraprayag**, 1100, 5 hrs.

**Auli** *p109*
**Bus** Regular buses from **Rishikesh** (253 km),
**Haridwar** (276 km) up to **Joshimath**.
**Cable car** A modern 25-seater cable
car carries people from Joshimath. It costs
Rs 300 return in season, Rs 200 off season.
**Jeeps/taxis** Between **Joshimath** and Auli.

# Trekking in Garhwal and Kumaon Himalaya

*This region contains some of the finest mountains in the Himalaya and is highly accessible and yet surprisingly very few Westerners visit it, many preferring to go to Nepal. Of the many treks available, eight routes are included here. The scenic splendour of these ranges lies partly in the fact that the forests around the big peaks are still wonderfully untouched and the local population unaffected by the ravages of mass tourism. It is easy to get up into the mountain ranges of Garhwal and Kumaon, enabling a feeling of intimacy with the alpine giants. The mountains have been described as "a series of rugged ranges tossed about in the most intricate confusion" (Walton, 1910).*

## Arriving in Garhwal and Kumaon Himalaya
Reliable local agents who will make all arrangements including accommodation and porters are in Haridwar, Dehra Dun and Rishikesh. Porter agents in Uttarkashi, Joshimath, Munsiari, etc, who act as trekking agents, may not be as reliable; negotiate rates for specific services and insist on reliable porters. The Forest Office charges an entry fee and a camping fee that varies for each trek. Different months offer different things: at lower altitudes in February and March there are spectacular displays of rhododendrons; April and May allows access to higher altitudes but can get very hot and views can be restricted due to large-scale burning; July and August sees the monsoon and is good for alpine flowers but wet, humid and mostly cloudy. If the monsoon is heavy, roads and tracks can become impassable; in September the air is beautifully rain-washed, but early morning clear skies can give way by 1000 to cloud, and views may completely disappear; in October and November temperatures are lower, the skies clearer and the vegetation greener following the monsoon.

## Background
This region had been open since the British took over in 1815 but it was closed in 1960 due to political troubles with China, and during this period Nepal became popular with climbers and trekkers. Garhwal and Kumaon Himalaya have gradually been opened to explorers since 1975, though parts bordering Tibet remain closed. Much of the early Himalayan exploration was undertaken here. **Trisul**, 7120 m, after it had been climbed by Doctor Tom Longstaff in 1906, remained the highest mountain climbed for the next 30 years.

## Trekking

Trekking in this region is not highly organized so you need to be well prepared. Topographical maps are not available locally. A good map for the area is Leomann's *Indian Himalaya Sheet 8, Kumaon Garhwal*. On most treks you need a tent (though not for the Pindari Glacier trek, for example). Very few villagers speak English, and the rewards for the well-equipped trekker, who has planned carefully, are great – especially the feeling of being far from the madding crowd. If you are travelling in small groups of three to four it is often possible to find lodgings in villagers' houses but despite their hospitality, this is uncomfortable. Where available, **GMVN** and **KMVN** lodges provide rustic but clean rooms and some have deluxe rooms with bath. Caretakers cook simple meals. If you would like to leave the logistics to someone else, hire a government-recognized specialist tour operator.

Around **Gangotri** and **Yamunotri** in Garhwal there are a number of good treks, some suitable for the independent or 'go-it-alone' trekker. **Nanda Devi** is the other area and this forms a ring that includes both Garhwal and Kumaon. There are many more treks than

# Garhwal & Kumaon treks

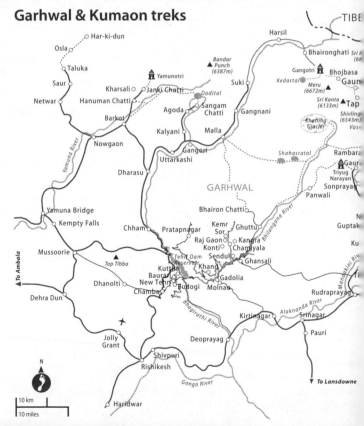

those indicated here. The lower part of the Niti Valley, and the Darma Valley, are open to groups of four with requisite permits. You are not allowed to go beyond Badrinath.

### Gangotri to Gaumukh

The best-known trek here is to Gaumukh (Cow's Mouth) and, if desired, beyond onto the Gangotri Glacier. Gaumukh can easily be managed in three days with minimal equipment but carry provisions. Before setting off for Gaumukh or beyond you must register with the District Forest Office in Uttarkashi (not the easiest office to find – 3 km north of Uttarkashi with no signage! Keep asking.) It's Rs 600 for foreigners (Rs 150 for Indians) for two day permit. You can also pay extra day charges of Rs 250 a day if you want to stay longer which is really necessary if you want to do a leisurely trek to Gaumukh. Also on entry to Gaumukh trek, just outside of Gangotri, you pay a deposit of Rs 200 for all your plastic – you will need to count up all your potential wrappers and bottles and you get the money back on your return when you show all your wrappers. This is making the trekking route much cleaner than before and should be applauded.

From Gangotri, at 3046 m, follow the well-defined, gradually ascending path for 14 km to **Bhojbasa** at 3792 m. It takes about five hours. There is a **Tourist Rest House** here which has four rooms and a dorm without bedding (at the time of writing, accommodation was just in tents as the dorm had been destroyed by a glacier). This is, however, often full. You can hire good-value two-person tents for Rs 160 a night. There is also an *ashram* where trekkers and pilgrims can stay and there is tented accommodation at **Chirbasa**, 5 km before Bhojbasa.

The 4 km to **Gaumukh** (the last section is across boulder scree and moraine), takes about one hour so it is quite feasible to go from Bhojbasa to Gaumukh, spend some time there, then return the same day. There are plenty of tea houses en route. Gaumukh, the present source of the Bhagirathi (Ganga) River, is at the mouth of the Gangotri Glacier where blocks of glacier ice fall into the river and pilgrims cleanse themselves in freezing water. There are breathtaking views. There is basic tent accommodation.

Beyond Gaumukh more care and camping equipment is required. The **Gangotri Glacier** is in an amphitheatre of 6500- to 7000-m peaks which include Satopanth (7084 m), Vasuki (6792 m), Bhagirathi (6556 m), Kedar Dome and the prominent trio of Bhagirathi I, II and III; Shivling (6543 m), standing alone, is one of the most spectacular peaks in the Himalaya.

## Tapovan → *Altitude: 4463 m.*

In a breathtaking setting in a grassy meadow on the east bank of the Gangotri Glacier, this is the base camp for climbing expeditions to the stunningly beautiful **Shivling** (6543 m), Siva's lingam and the 'Matterhorn of the Himalaya'. You can either return the same way or make a round trip by crossing over the glacier for 3 km to **Nandanvan**, at 4400 m, and continuing upwards for a further 6 km to Vasuki Tal beneath **Vasuki** peak (6792 m). Since the trek involves crossing a glacier crossing, it is recommended that you go with a guide. The return is via Nandanvan, the west bank of the Gangotri Glacier crossing the Raktvarn Glacier to Gaumukh-Raktvarn, so called because of the rust-coloured boulders in its moraine. Full camping equipment is necessary on this trek.

## Gangotri to Kedartal

This is an excellent short trek with scenic variety and spectacular views but be aware of the problems associated with altitude and allow time for acclimatization. It requires a tent, stove and food. It is 17 km to Kedartal (5000 m), a small glacial lake surrounded by Meru (6672 m), Pithwara (6904 m) and Bhrigupanth (6772 m).

Leaving Gangotri you proceed up the gorge of the Kedar Ganga (Siva's contribution to the Bhagirathi River). It is 8 km to Bhoj Kharak and then a further 4 km to Kedar Kharak, passing through some beautiful Himalayan birch forest en route. The bark from the trees (*bhoj* in Garhwali) was used by sages and hermits for manuscripts. From Kedar Kharak, where you can camp, it is a laborious 5-km ascent to Kedartal. Besides the peaks surrounding the lake you can also see the Gangotri range.

You return to Gangotri the same way. **Rudugaira Kharak** is the base camp for the peaks at the head of the Rudugaira Valley. Coming down towards Gangotri you must cross to the opposite bank near Patangnidhar to avoid the cliffs on the west bank. Nearer Gangotri cross back to the west bank.

## Gangotri to Yamunotri via Dodital

This is a beautiful trek between Kalyani and Hanuman Chatti, a distance of 49 km. You can do a round trip from either end. It takes five days.

From **Uttarkashi** take a local bus to Kalyani via **Gangori**, 3 km away, or walk it. At **Kalyani**, 1829 m, the recognized starting point of the trek, you take a track to the right. From here it gets steeper as the path climbs through forest to **Agoda**, 5 km away. There is a suitable camping or halting place 2 km beyond Agoda. The next day carry on to **Dodital**, 16 km away at 3024 m, picturesquely set in a forest of pine, deodar and oak. This is the source of the Asi Ganga and is stocked with trout. There is a dilapidated **Forest Rest House** and several cheap lodges. Above the lake there are fine views of Bandar Punch (Monkey's Tail, 6387 m). To reach **Hanuman Chatti** at 2400 m, walk for 6 km up to the Aineha Pass, 3667 m, which also has splendid views. Then it is a 22-km walk down to Hanuman Chatti, the roadhead for Yamunotri.

## Har-ki-Dun Trek

Har-ki-Dun (God's Valley) nestles in the northwest corner of Garhwal near the Sutlej-Yamuna watershed. The people of the area have the distinction of worshipping **Duryodhana**, head of the crafty royal family in the *Mahabharata*, rather than siding with the pious Pandavas. The valley is dominated by Swargarohini (6096 m) and Kalanag. From **Nowgaon**, 9 km south of Barkot, take a bus to the roadhead of **Sankri**. From here it is a gradual ascent over 12 km to **Taluka**, and **Osla** (2559 m), 11 km further. Another 8 km and 1000 m higher is **Har-ki-Dun** (3565 m), an ideal base for exploring the valley. Allow three days to Har-ki-Dun. There are **Forest** and **Tourist Rest Houses** at all these places.

You can return to Nowgaon or, if properly equipped and provisioned, trek for 29 km on to **Yamunotri** via the Yamunotri Pass (5172 m). You will need to allow time for acclimatization. The views from the pass are well worth the effort.

## Nanda Devi area → *Colour map 1, B5.*

Nanda Devi (7816 m), named after the all-encompassing form of the female deity, dominates the Garhwal and Kumaon Himalaya. With its two peaks separated by a 4-km-long ridge, the second-highest mountain in India is incredibly beautiful. She is also the most important of Garhwal's deities, protected by a ring of mountains, 112 km in circumference, containing 12 peaks over 6400 m high. In only one place is this defensive ring lower than 5500 m, at the **Rishi Gorge**, one of the deepest in the world. It is the place of ascetic sages (*rishis*). The Nanda Devi Sanctuary is a World Biosphere Reserve.

### Pindari Glacier Trek

This trek along the southern edge of the Sanctuary is an 'out and back' trek, ie you return by the same route. **KMVN Tourist Lodges** ⓘ *www.kmvn.gov.in, some with only 4 beds, none with telephones*, are dotted along the route so this trek can be done with little equipment, although a sleeping bag is essential. Book your accommodation early or take your own tent. The trek is 66 km from Song, which has the last bus terminus.

From **Bageshwar**, see page 127, take a local bus to **Bharari**, at 1524 m, which has a PWD Rest House, a cheap hotel and **Tourist Bungalow** ⓘ *T01372-260465, www.gmvnl.com*; open all year. From here you can walk 16 km along the Saryu Valley to **Song** or take another bus. It is just over 1.5 km further to **Loharkhet**, at 1829 m, which also has a PWD Bungalow in the village and a basic **KMVN Tourist Rest House** overlooking it. There are good views of the hillside opposite and the head of the Saryu Valley. It is 11 km from Loharkhet to **Dhakuri** via the Dhakuri Pass (2835 m) which has a wonderful view of the south of the Nanda Devi Sanctuary including Panwali Dhar (6683 m) and Maiktoli (6803 m). The walk to the pass is mostly through forest on a well-graded path. About 100 m below the pass on the north side is a clearing with a **PWD Bungalow** and a **KMVN Tourist Rest House**. The views are great, especially at sunrise and sunset.

In the Pindar Valley you descend to **Khati**, 8 km away at 2194 m, first through rhododendron, then mixed forests dominated by stunted oak. Khati is a village with over 50 households situated on a spur that runs down to the river, some 200 m below. There is a **PWD Bungalow**, **KMVN Tourist Rest House** and a village hotel. You can buy biscuits, eggs and chocolate, brought in by mule from Bharari.

From Khati follow the Pindar 8 km to **Dwali**, 2580 m, which is at the confluence of the Pindar and the Kaphini rivers. Here there is a **KMVN Travellers' Lodge** and a run-down **PWD Bungalow**. If you have a tent, camp in front. The next stop, 6 km on, is **Phurkiya**, 3260 m, which also has a **KMVN Travellers' Lodge**. This can be used as a base for going up to Zero Point (4000 m), a viewpoint from where the steep falling glacier can be seen (it is difficult for trekkers to go up to the snout of the glacier itself). On either side there are impressive peaks, including **Panwali Dwar** (6683 m) and **Nanda Kot** (6876 m). Return to Bharari the same way.

From Dwali, however, a side trip to the **Kaphini Glacier** is worthwhile. Alternatively, you could trek up to **Sundar Dhunga Glacier** from Khati. Including either of these, the trek can be accomplished in a week but for comfort allow nine days.

# Nanda Devi area treks

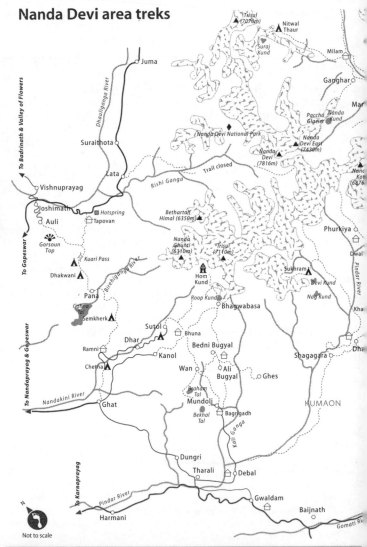

## Roopkund Trek → *Altitude: 4800 m. Kund means lake in Garhwali.*

A legend relates Nanda Devi, the wife of Siva, to this small lake. When her sister Balpa accompanied her husband King Jasidhwal of the medieval Kingdom of Kanauj on a pilgrimage to Kailash (Mount Trisul), she delivered a child at Balpa de Sulera (adjoining Bhagwabasa), thus polluting the entire mountain. Nanda Devi's herald Latu (who has a temple at Wan), at the command of the goddess, hurled the royal pilgrimage party into the small tarn called Roopkund; hence the remains of the 300 bodies found in the lake. Thirty years ago the Indian anthropologist DN Majumdar discovered a number of frozen bodies around this small mountain tarn, the remains of a party of pilgrims on a *yutra* who died when bad weather closed in. Carbon-dating suggests the bones are 600 years old.

This is a highly varied and scenic trek which can be undertaken by a suitably equipped party. A week is sufficient – nine days if you want to take it more comfortably with a rest day for acclimatization. The road now goes all the way to Lohajung pass, so you can start the trek there. Debal and Gwaldamare good places along the way to pick up provisions.

**Gwaldam** → *Colour map 1, C5. Altitude: 1950 m.* Gwaldam is a small market strung out along a ridge surrounded by orchards. The British established tea plantations which have since been abandoned. **GMVN Tourist Bungalow** ① *T01363-274244, www.gmvnl. com*, has splendid views from the garden, especially at dawn and dusk, of Trisul (7120 m) and Nanda Ghunti (6310 m).

**Debal**, at 1350 m, is a further 8 km on through pine forest and there is another **KMVN Tourist Rest House**, a **Forest Rest House** and *dharamshalas*. From here you can either walk 12 km along a dirt road through villages with views of Trishul (6855 m), or drive to **Lohajung Pass** (2350 m) where there is an attractive **GMVN Travellers' Lodge** and two cheap lodges, right on the ridge beside a pretty shrine. The best option is **Patwal Tourist Lodge**, PO Mundoli, Chamoli, which has spotless, comfortable rooms, immaculate toilet and showers (bucket hot water), and treks arranged by a retired army officer. From **Lohajung** you walk down through stunted oak forest and along the *Wan Gad* (river) 12 km to the village of **Wan**, 2400 m, which has a **Forest Rest House** and **GMVN Travellers' Lodge**. From Wan it is essentially wilderness travel as you make the ascent to Roopkund, first walking through thick forest to **Bedni Bugyal** (*bugyal* – meadow) which is used as summer pasture. This is at 3550 m and has good views of Trisul, Nandaghunti and the Badrinath range to the north. There are some shepherds' stone huts which you may be able to use but it is better to take a tent.

From Bedni it is a gradual 7-km climb along a well-defined path over the 4500-m **Kalwa Vinayak** to more shepherds' huts at Bhagwabasa which, at 4000 m, is the base for the final walk up to Roopkund. A stove is necessary for cooking and it can be very cold at night, but water is available about 150 m northeast and up the slope from the campsite. From here, it is two to three hours up to **Roopkund**. Immediately after the monsoon the views can disappear in cloud by 1000, so it is best to leave early. In the final steep part the ground can be icy. Roopkund Lake itself is small and unimpressive, but from the 4900-m ridge approximately 50 m above Roopkund there is a magnificent view of the west face of Trisul rising over 3500 m from the floor of the intervening hanging valley to the summit. Return to Gwaldam by the same route or via **Ali Bugyal** and village Didina which bypasses Wan.

## Curzon Trail

The Curzon Trail is an incomparably beautiful trek. However, rapid ascent follows equally steep descent from one valley to the next, and at no point does the trek get close to the high snow-covered peaks. It was the route followed by Tilman and Shipton on their way to the Rishi Gorge and by other mountaineers en route to the peaks on the Indo-Tibetan border. The crossing of the Kuari Pass is a fitting conclusion to a trek that takes in three lesser passes and five major rivers – the Pindar, Kaliganga, Nandakini, Birehiganga and Dhauliganga. The trail was named after Lord Curzon, a keen trekker, and the path may have been specially improved for him. After 1947 it was officially renamed the 'Nehru Trail'. Take camping equipment. Some stopping off places have no suitable accommodation.

This trek begins at **Joshimath** via Auli, or at **Gwaldam** and ends at **Tapovan** in the Dhauliganga Valley on the Joshimath–Niti Pass road. It crosses the **Kuari Pass** (4268 m), one of the finest vantage points in the Himalaya.

From Gwaldam proceed to **Wan** as in the previous trek. Then, go over the Kokinkhal Pass to **Kanol** (2900 m) through thick mixed forest for 10 km to **Sutol**, at 2100 m, in the Nandakini Valley. There is a good campsite by the river. The next two stages follow the Nandakini downstream 10 km to Padergaon, 2500 m, via Ala. The trail to Tapovan leads up over the rhododendron forest-clad **Ramni Pass** (3100 m) with a good view of the Kuari Pass. The trail southwest of Ramni goes to the nearby road head at **Ghat**, from where you can also start the trek. (There is a road between Sutol and Ghat). To reach Tapovan from Ramni is a good three days' walk, down through lush forest to cross the Birehiganga River by an impressive suspension bridge, up around the horseshoe-shaped hanging valley around Pana Village, over an intervening spur and into the forested tributary valley of the Kuari nallah. There is no settlement in this area; *bharal* (mountain goats) and the rarely seen Himalayan black bear inhabit the rich forest. Waterfalls tumble down over steep crags. There is a camp and a cave (about one hour) before the Kuari Pass at **Dhakwani** (3200 m).

Leave early to get the full effect of sunrise over the peaks on the Indo-Tibetan border. Some of the peaks seen are Kamet, Badrinath (7040 m), Dunagiri (7066 m) and Changabang (6863 m). There is a wonderful wooded campsite with marvellous views about 300 m below the pass. From here one trail leads along a scenic ridge to Auli, where you can finish with a cable car ride to Joshimath, while another drops down over 2000 m to **Tapovan** and the Joshimath–Niti road. There is a hot sulphur spring (90°C) here and a bus service to **Joshimath**. Allow 10 days for the trek.

## Nanda Devi East Base Camp and Milam Glacier Trek

Much of this area was only reopened to trekkers in 1993 after more than 30 years of seclusion. The Milam Valley, incised by the 36-km-long Gori Ganga Gorge, was part of the old trade route between Kumaon and Tibet, only interrupted by the Indian-Chinese War of 1962. Milam, which once had 500 households, many occupied by wealthy traders and surrounded by barley and potato fields, has been reduced to a handful of occupied cottages. The trek is moderate, with some sustained steady walking but no really steep gradients or altitude problems. The route is through some of the remotest regions of the Himalaya with spectacular scenery and rich wildlife.

**Day 1** From **Munsiari**, a 10-hour drive from Almora, takes you down to Selapani where the trail up the Milam Valley begins. **Lilam** (1800 m) is an easy 7-km walk (2½ hours) where the tiny **Rest House** offers a convenient halt or camping ground for the first night. See page 127 for details about Munsiari.

**Day 2** (14 km; seven hours) From Lilam the trail enters the spectacular 25-km-long gorge. Etched into the cliff face above the Gori Ganga the hillsides above are covered in dense bamboo thickets and mixed rainforest. After the junction of the Ralam and Gori Ganga rivers the track climbs to a tea shop at Radgari, then goes on to a small **Rest House** at **Bugdiar** (2700 m). A memorial commemorates villagers and army personnel lost in the avalanche of 1989. Only a few houses remain on the edge of a wasteland.

**Day 3** (16 km; six hours) The valley opens up after climbing quite steeply to a huge overhanging cliff, which shelters a local deity. The route enters progressively drier terrain, but there are two waterfalls of about 100 m, one opposite a tea shop at Mapang. The track climbs to **Rilkote** (3200 m).

**Day 4** (13 km; six hours) Passing deserted villages in the now almost arid landscape the track goes through the large village of **Burphu**, backed by the Burphu Peak (6300 m). Nanda Devi East comes into view before reaching **Ganghar** village (3300 m) where only three of the former 60 families remain. Some of the houses have beautiful carved wooden door and window frames; the carefully walled fields below are deserted.

**Day 5** (7 km; three hours) A steep narrow track leads into the **Pachhu Valley**, dominated by the northeast face of Nanda Devi East, 3800 m above the Pachhu Glacier. Dwarf rhododendron and birch, with anemones and primulas below, line the first section of the track before it emerges into alpine meadows below the debris of the glacier itself. **Tom Longstaff** came through this valley in his unsuccessful attempt to climb Nanda Devi East in 1905 before trying the parallel valley to the south of Pachhu via what is now known as Longstaff's Col. There is a campsite (3900 m), 3 km from the base of Nanda Devi East, with both the col and the summit clearly visible in good weather.

**Day 6** Side treks are possible up to the Pachhu Glacier and along its edge to the glacial lake **Nanda Kund**.

**Day 7** (17 km; six hours) Returning via Ghanghar at Burfu, the track crosses the Gori Ganga on a wooden bridge then climbs to the former staging post of **Milam** (3300 m).

**Day 8** Another 'excursion' (10 km; eight hours) is possible from Milam to the **Milam Glacier** (4100 m). There are superb views of the clean ice uncovered by debris from the track which runs along the left bank of the Milam Glacier. Three tributary glaciers join the main Milam Glacier.

**Day 9** (13 km; five hours) The track runs along the left bank of the river via Tola village to the base of the 4750 m Brijganga Pass, outside **Sumdu** village (3400 m).

**Day 10** (12 km; seven hours) Superb views characterize this steady climb to the top of the pass. The razor sharp Panchchulis dominate the south while the twin peaks of Nanda Devi are straight ahead. **Ralam** village is a steep drop below the pass (3700 m).

**Day 11** (10 km; six hours) This can be a rest day or a day trek up to the **Shankalpa Glacier** along the watershed between the rarely visited Ralam and Darma valleys.

**Day 12-14** (six hours each day) The trek runs steadily down through the thickly forested Ralam Valley, passing Marjhali, Bhujani, Buria, Sarpa and Besani villages.

**Day 15** (11 km; four hours) Return from Lilam to Munsiari via a number of villages.

### Darma Valley Trek

The easternmost of the Kumaon valleys, the Darma Valley is now also open to trekkers but you need permission. Separated from western Nepal by the Kaliganga River and with Tibet to the north, the valley is one of the least explored in the Himalaya. From the roadhead at **Dharchula** (on the India/Nepal border) it is possible to trek for four or five days up to Sipu and also to spend time exploring the numerous side valleys. Buses are available from Pithoragarh, see page 127, and Almora up to Dharchula from where it is often possible to get local transport for a further 32 km up to **Sobala**. Then it is a three- to four-day trek up to Sipu, the northernmost point allowed under present regulations.

# Nainital and around

*Kumaon's hill stations offer access to some relatively unexplored sections of the Himalaya. Nainital itself is a congested Indian holiday town set around a steadily diminishing lake, albeit in the midst of some excellent birdwatching territory. Further northeast, the lush hillsides around Almora have inspired some of India's greatest mystics, and now provide a venue for some interesting projects in sustainable tourism. ➤➤ For listings, see pages 128-133.*

**Nainital** → *For listings, see pages 128-133. Colour map 1, C5. Phone code: 05942. Population: 50,000. Altitude: 1938 m. See map, page 124.*

Much of Nainital's historic appeal has waned with the influx of mass tourism. Its villas, bungalows and fine houses are swamped with Indian holidaymakers in the summer season, and although it holds some attractive walks and only a few foreign tourists, congestion and pollution is taking its toll, particularly on the fragile ecosystem of the lake. It can be very cold in winter, and depressions sometimes bring cloud and rain obscuring the views of the mountains. Many now prefer to break the journey to Almora from Corbett or Rishikesh at Ranikhet instead.

### Arriving in Nainital

**Getting there** The nearest railway station is 1¾ hours away at Kathgodam, linked to Nainital by frequent buses. The climb from Kathgodam to Nainital is dramatic, rising 1300 m over 30 km. The road follows the valley of the Balaya stream then winds up the hillsides through forests and small villages. After the long drive the town around the *ta* (lake) appears suddenly; the land south and on the plains side falls away quite steeply so you only see the lake when you are at its edge. Buses from Delhi and the surrounding hill stations use the Tallital Bus Stand at the southern end of the lake, while some buses from Ramnagar (for Corbett National Park) use the Mallital Bus Stand at the northern end.

**Getting around** The Mall, pedestrianized at peak times, is the hub of Nainital's life. You can hire a cycle-rickshaw if the walk feels too much, or take a taxi for travelling further afield. ▸▸ *See Transport, page 132.*

**Tourist information** KMVN Information Centre Head Office ① *Oak Park House, T05942-236356.* **KMVN Information** ① *Parvat Tours; at Secretariat, T05942-231436.* **Tourist Bungalow** ① *T05942-235400.*

## Background
In 1839 the small hamlet of Nainital was 'discovered' by a Mr P Barron, a sugar manufacturer from Saharanpur. He was so impressed by the 1500-m-long and 500-m-wide lake that he returned with a sailing boat a year later, carried up in sections from the plains. In due course Nainital became the summer capital of the then United Provinces. An old legend of Siva and Sati, see page 411, associates the place as where Sati's eyes fell (hence *naini*). The *tal* (lake) is surrounded by seven hills, the Sapta-Shring. On 18 September 1880 disaster struck the town. At the north end of the lake, known now as Mallital (the southern part is Tallital) stood the **Victoria Hotel**. In two days nearly 1000 mm of rain fell leading to a landslip which crushed some outhouses, burying several people. The cliff overhanging the hotel collapsed, burying the soldiers and civilians engaged in rescue work and making it impossible to save the 150 buried. Later the area was levelled, became known as The Flats, and was used for public meetings and impromptu games of football and cricket. Today it is more a bus park in the tourist season, though sports tournaments are held here in June, August and December.

## Places in Nainital
There is little of architectural interest other than the colonial-style villas overlooking the lake (walking is the major attraction of this town). The **Church of St John in the Wilderness** (1846), one of the earliest buildings, is beyond Mallital, below the Nainital Club. The most distinctive building is **Government House** (1899, now the Secretariat) which was designed in stone by FW Stephens who was also responsible for VT (now CST) and Churchgate Stations in Mumbai. Early in the season it is pleasant to walk round (the Lower Mall is pedestrianized) or take a boat across the lake; remember it can still be very cold in March.

 **Naina (Cheena) Peak** (2610 m) is a 5-km walk from the lake. From the top, there are stunning views of the Himalaya including Nanda Devi (7816 m) and the mountains on the Tibetan border. In season there is a '**cable car**' (ropeway) ① *0900-1700, winter 1000-1600, Rs 15 return,* which runs from the Mallital end of the lake to Snow View (2270 m), another good vantage point for viewing the snow-capped peaks. It is also possible to make the 2-km steep climb up to the viewpoint from the north end of the lake, passing the small Tibetan *gompa* which has fluttering prayer flags marking it.

 **Hanumangarh** with a small temple off Haldwani Road, and the **Observatory** ① *3 km from the lake, Mon-Sat 1400-1600 and 1930-2100,* further along the path, have lookouts for watching the sun set over the plains. The opposite side has only a few cottages and much higher up near the ridge are two private boys' schools – Sherwood College and St Joseph's. The atmospheric **British Cemetery** with its crumbling graves is about 3 km southeast of town. Take the minor road at the south end of the lake (not the Rampur Road); on the right side, the remains of the entrance gate are just visible behind some trees.

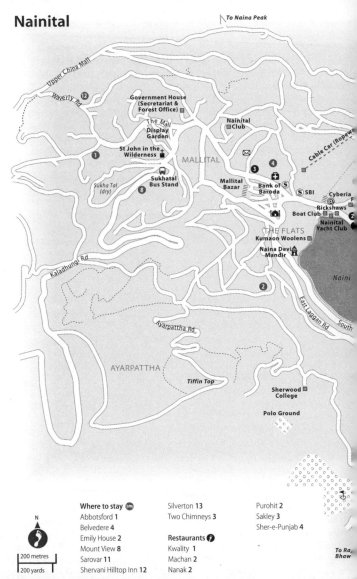

# Nainital

To Naina Peak

Upper China Mall

Waverly Rd

Government House
(Secretariat &
Forest Office)

The Mall
Display
Garden

St John in the
Wilderness

Nainital
Club

Cable Car (Ropewa

MALLITAL

Sukha Tal
(dry)

Sukhatal
Bus Stand

Mallital
Bazar

Bank of
Baroda

SBI

Cyberia
F

Rickshaws

Boat Club

Nainital
Yacht Club

THE FLATS

Kumaon Woolens

Naina Devi
Mandir

Naini

Kaladhungi Rd

East Laggan Rd

South

Ayarpattha Rd

AYARPATTHA

Tiffin Top

Sherwood
College

Polo Ground

N

200 metres
200 yards

To Ra
Bhaw

**Where to stay**
Abbotsford 1
Belvedere 4
Emily House 2
Mount View 8
Sarovar 11
Shervani Hilltop Inn 12

Silverton 13
Two Chimneys 3

**Restaurants**
Kwality 1
Machan 2
Nanak 2

Purohit 2
Sakley 3
Sher-e-Punjab 4

## Excursions from Nainital

**Sat Tal**, 24 km away, has seven lakes including the jade green Garud Tal, the olive green Rama Tal and Sita Tal. **Naukuchiyatal**, 26 km away, is a lake with nine corners, hence the name. It is beautifully unspoilt and quiet paddling round the lake allows you to see lots of birds; boats for hire. Tour buses stop around 1630.

**Pangot**, 15 km from Nainital via Kilbury, is in ideal birding territory where over 580 species have been recorded. **Jeolikote**, a small hamlet on the main road up from Ranpur, 18 km south of Nainital, is known for its health centre and butterflies, honey and mushrooms. It offers a peaceful weekend retreat.

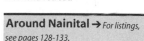

## Around Nainital → *For listings, see pages 128-133.*

### Almora and around → *Phone code: 05962.*
*Colour map 1, C5. Population: 32,500.*
*Altitude: 1646 m. 66 km northeast of Nainital.*

Almora is a charming bustling hill town occupying a picturesque horseshoe-shaped ridge. The Mall runs about 100 m below the ridge line, while the pedestrianized historic bazar above is jostling and colourful. For information contact: **KMVN** ⓘ *Holiday Home, 2 km west of the bus stop*, or **Almora Tourism** ⓘ *opposite GPO, T05962-230180, 1000-1700.*

The town was founded in 1560 by the Chand Dynasty who ruled over most of Kumaon, which comprises the present districts of Nainital, Almora and Pithoragarh. Overrun by the Gurkhas in 1798, it was heavily bombed by the British as they tried to expel them in the Gurkha Wars of 1814-1815. Traces of an old Chand fort, stone-paved roads, wooden houses with beautifully carved façades and homes decorated with traditional murals, reflect its heritage. Today an important market town and administrative centre, it is also regarded as the cultural capital of the area. It richly rewards exploring.

Swami Vivekenanda came to Almora and gained enlightenment in a small cave at

**Kasar Devi** on Kalimatiya Hill, 7 km northeast of town. This is a tranquil mountain hamlet with stunning views, visited by everyone from Cat Stevens to DH Lawrence, and was dubbed '**Crank's Ridge**' after Timothy Leary streaked here in the 1960s. Another vantage point for sunrise and sunset is **Bright End Corner**, 2.5 km southwest of Mall Road, near All India Radio. The stone **Udyotchandesvar Temple**, above Mall Road, houses Kumaon's presiding deity, Nanda Devi, whose festival is in August/ September. Almora's Tamta artisans still use traditional methods to work with copper. Copper metallurgy was used here as early as the second century BC and is associated with the Kuninda Dynasty who traded in copper articles. The hand-beaten copper pots are 'silver plated' in the traditional way, *kalhai*.

**Jageswar**, 34 km northeast, lies beside a brook in a dappled clearing in the nape of a serene cedar wooded gorge. It is famous for the 164 ornamented temples built by the Chand rajas and also holds one of the 12 *jyotirlingas*. The scores of temples here, shaded by the trees' canopy, and in nearby Gandeswar are very fine examples of early medieval hill temple architecture but are rarely visited by outsiders. Some elegant examples of vernacular architecture lie in the village. The temple dedicated to Jogeswar with finely carved pillars has a small museum; 6 km before Jageswar, a roadside sign points to stone-age **cave paintings**, about 50 m off the road. Though several paintings were damaged by storage of cement bags during bridge-building work nearby, many can be seen and are worth the short stop. Once the capital of the Chand rajas, **Binsar** has a bird sanctuary sited at 2410 m with panoramic mountain views. It is 28 km away.

### Kausani → *Colour map 1, C5. Altitude: 1892 m. 50 km north of Almora.*
Kausani sits on a narrow ridge among pine forests with wonderfully wide views of the **Nanda Devi** group of mountains stretching over 300 km along the horizon; the view is particularly stunning at sunrise. Modern Kausani has a strong military presence, so be careful with your camera. You may trek from here to Bageswar, Gwaldam and the Pindari Glacier. In 1929 **Mahatma Gandhi** spent 12 days at what is now Anashakti Ashram.

### Baijnath and Garur → *Colour map 1, C5. 17 km northwest of Kausani.*
From Kausani, the road descends to Garur and Baijnath. The small town of **Baijnath** on the banks of the Gomti River has distinctively carved 12th-and 13th-century Katyuri temples. They are now mostly ruined, but its houses have intricately carved wooden doors and windows. The main 10th-century temple houses a beautiful image of Parvati. Siva and Parvati are believed to have married at the confluence of the Gomti and Garur Ganga. The Katyur Dynasty, which ruled the valley for 500 years, took their name from Siva and Parvati's mythical son, Karttikeya. **Garur** has plenty of buses and taxis northwards. Just north of Garur a road runs to Gwaldam, see Roopkund Trek, page 119, and another east to Bageshwar.

### Dunagiri → *Altitude: 2400 m.*
Dunagiri is a small village 65 km north of Almora en route to the pilgrimage sites of the Char Dam. It is steeped in spiritual legend and has been the home of many yogis and sages including Mahavatar Babaji (there is an account of a meeting between Babaji and Lahiri Mahashaya in a cave at Dunagiri in *Autobiography of a Yogi* ) and Neemkaroli Baba who was the guide for US teacher Ram Dass (formerly Harvard professor Dr Richard Alpert and co-conspirator of Timothy Leary) in the 1960s. There is a powerful Shakti temple here - Dunagiri Devi. See box, opposite, for more on the myths and legends of the area.

## Preserving India's plant heritage

The Dunagiri Foundation for Himalayan Herbal Research and Yogic Studies aims to preserve endangered species of ayurvedic and medicinal plants – the heritage of these sacred mountains. The mountain of Dunagiri is part of the Ramayana legend and is where Hanuman goes to scoop up medicines to save the dying warrior Lakshman. "Dunagiri Mountain or Dhronagiri as it is called by some, is the source of the herbs that restore life", says Prashanti de Jager, one of the founders of the **Dunagiri Foundation**. "Dhrona in this case likely refers to a 'container of Soma,' Soma being the nectar of immortality. Giri means mountain, and hence Dhronagiri can be seen as the mountain of Soma, of the deepest healing and empowering possible from herbs." The foundation are focusing on planting these medicinal high altitude plants, educating the locals about their uses and staving off the damage of illegal harvesting. It is possible to volunteer with the foundation and plans are afoot to create a research centre and yoga facility here. For more information check out www.dunagiri.org.

**Bageshwar and the Saryu Valley** → *Altitude: 960 m. 90 km north of Almora, 23 km east of Baijnath.*

**Bageshwar**, meaning Siva as 'Lord of Eloquent Speech', stands at the confluence of the Gomti and Saryu rivers. It is Kumaon's most important pilgrimage centre and has several temples, the most important of which is the 17th-century Bhagnath temple, overlooking the confluence. From Bageshwar a jeep road runs northwards along the Saryu, through beautiful wooded gorges where lammergeiers and griffon vultures soar overhead, to Talai. This is an alternative trailhead for treks to the **Pindari Glacier** (see page 117), and also gives access to a string of beautiful villages perched on mountainsides among terraced fields and rhododendron forests: Supi, Basham and Khal Jhuni. This area has virtually no tourist infrastructure, but is being developed by the communities in association with Village Ways (see page 131).

**Munsiari** → *Altitude: 2300 m. 207 km from Almora.*

This is a quiet hill town overlooked by the majestic five peaks of **Panchchuli** which, in legend, served as the five *chulis* (stoves) used to cook the last meal of the five Pandava brothers before they ascended to heaven. Munsiari is a base for treks into the Milam, Ralam and Namik glaciers, and towards Panchchuli. It is also the start of an easy trek (three to four days) via Namik to Dwali in the Pindar Valley.

**Pithoragarh** → *Colour map 1, C5.*

Sitting in a small valley with some fine temples built by the Chands, it is overlooked by a hill fort, 7 km away, dating from times when the town was at the crossroads of trade routes. The district, separated from Almora in 1962, borders Nepal and Tibet and has a number of high peaks such as Nanda Devi East (7434 m) and West (7816 m), and offers trekking to many glaciers including **Milam**, **Namik**, **Ralam** and **Panchchuli**. See page 121 (no permit needed). There are good views from **Chandak Hill** (1890 m), 7 km away. It is on the Pilgrim road to **Mount Kailash** and **Mansarovar Lake**. The Mount Kailash trek (Indian nationals only) starts from Askot (The only way to go to Mount Kailash if you are a foreigner is from the Chinese side). The place is known for its fine gold and silver jewellery and bowls carved out of *sal* wood.

*For hotel and restaurant price codes and other relevant information, see pages 22-26.*

## ● Where to stay

The regional tourist office, **Kumaon Mandal Vikas Nigam**, T05942-231436, www.kmvn. gov.in, has rest houses throughout the state, including: Bhimtal; Ramnagar; Almora; Ranikhet; Jageshwar; Binsar, Munsyari; Dharchula; Kausani; Pindari Glacier route; and Kashipur. The office also runs budget treks to Pindari, Panchachuli, Adi Kailash (from Rs 3000 for a 1-week trek).

### Nainital *p122, map p124*
Peak rates (given here) can be high. Off-season discounts of up to 60% are usual but may mean inadequate heating.
**$$$$ Shervani Hilltop Inn**, Waverly Rd, T05942-233800, www.shervanihotels.com. 21 rooms in old royal home, some in cottages, there is also a new block but in keeping with heritage style of hotel, peaceful, lovely garden, free jeep to centre.
**$$$$-$$$ Abbotsford**, Prasada Bhawan, T05942-236188, www.abbotsford.in. Just 4 rooms in the stunning former summer mansion for the Agra and Oudh's ruler. A classic mountain house with tinned roof and pinewood flooring and art deco interiors. Library with antiquarian books.
**$$$$-$$$ Belvedere** (WelcomHeritage), above Bank of Baroda, Mallital, T05942-237434, www.welcomheritagehotels.com. 19 large, comfortable rooms (good-value family suite) with lake views, in former raja's summer palace, a colonial building with pleasant garden, restaurant, well located, quiet, friendly owners, helpful staff.
**$$$ Emily House**, Ayarpatta Slopes, T022-6150 6363 (contact through Nivalink, www.nivalink.com). Pretty house in a peaceful location, it's close to Jim Corbett's summer house. Simply decorated with home-cooked food and friendly atmosphere.

**$$$ Two Chimneys**, House No 1, Chinkuwa, Village Gethia, T05942-224541, www.two chimneysgethia.com. With one careful British lady owner back in the 1890s, this thoughtfully renovated property has bags of history and myth. Simple but beautiful rooms, lovely pool, you can even stay in the goat shed. Perfect place to read Tarun J Tejpal's *Alchemy of Desire* which was inspired by this house and its stories. Also lovely for birdwatching. Recommended.
**$$$-$$ Rewa Retreat**, Ramgarh Rd, Bhowali, T(0)9411-199490, www. rewa retreat.com. Friendly place with spacious airy rooms. There is an art gallery with local Kumaon *aiparn* folk art.
**$$ Silverton**, Sher-ka-Danda, 2.5 km to centre, T05942-235549, www.hotelsilverton. com. 27 rooms in 'chalets', some with good views, peaceful, vegetarian restaurant.
**$$-$ Sarovar**, near Tallital Bus Stand, T05942-235570. Good value, with 30 rooms, 8-bed dorms, hot water.
**$ Mount View** (KMVN), near Sukhatal Bus Stand, T05942-235400, www.kmvn.org. Good value, 42 small, grubby rooms with bath, some with TV, restaurant, gardens.

### Around Nainital *p125*
**$$$$ The Cottage**, nestled on the hillside, Jeolikot, T05942-224013, www.thecottage jeolikot.com. Swiss-chalet style, with 6 beautiful spacious rooms with good valley views, great walks to be had, delicious meals included. Highly recommended.
**$$$ Jungle Lore Birding Lodge**, Pangot, T01126-923283 (thru Asian Adventures Delhi), www.pangot.com. Comfortable cottages and huts with baths, 2 tents with shared facilities, meals included (from home-grown produce), library, naturalist guides. Over 200 species of bird on property. Recommended.
**$$ Lake Side**, Naukuchiyatal, T05942-247138, www.kmvn.org. Well maintained and attractive. 12 rooms and dorm (Rs 100).

**$$-$ KMVN Rest Houses**, www.kmvn.org.
Good-value outside May to mid-Jul.

## Almora *p125*

Most hotels give off-season discount of 50%.
**$$-$ Holiday Home** (KMVN), 2 km
southwest of bus stand, T05962-230250,
www.kmvn. gov.in. 14 simple cottages
and 18 rooms with hot bath, dorm (Rs 60),
restaurant, garden, good mountain views.
**$$-$ Konark**, just east of bus stand on
Mall Rd, T05962-231217. Good views,
13 clean rooms, TV, hot water in mornings.
**$$-$ Savoy**, up hill opposite GPO, near
Uttarakhand Tourism, T(0)9411-327415.
17 good-sized but basic rooms, some with
hot bath, restaurant, pleasant terrace and
quiet garden.
**$ Shyam**, east and uphill from bus stand
on LR Shah Rd, T05962-235467, www hotel
shyam.com. 18 small but clean rooms, good
terrace views.

## Around Almora

**$$$ Kalmatia Sangam**, Kalimat Estate,
T05962-251176, www.kalmatia-sangam.com.
10 cottages with stunning mountain views
spread across hillside on the approach to
Kesar Devi. Some cottages' beds are on a
mezzanine from where you can see Nanda
Devi. Cottages are named after local birds,
such as the Himalaya magpie and the cuckoo.
The construction and day-to-day running of
the cottages is environmentally friendly.
**$$$-$$ Deodars Guest House**, Papparsalli
village (4 km uphill from Almora), T05962-
233025, rwheeler@rediffmail.com. Just 3
rooms in a charming 150-year-old former
missionary's residence, stunning views
across the mountains set off by carefully
tended flower gardens. Stuffed leopards,
tigers and bears adorn the characterful
interiors. Shared sitting room has a TV,
stacks of books. Recommended.
**$$$-$$ Mohan's Binsar Retreat**, Kasar Devi
Binsar Rd, T05962-251215, www.mohans
binsarretreat.com. Characterful place with
amazing views, close to the bird sanctuary.

**$$-$ Nanda Devi** (KMVN), in the heart
of the sanctuary, Binsar, T05962-251110.
Only filtered rainwater, electricity from
solar batteries for few hours each evening.
**$$-$ Tourist Rest House** (KMVN), Binsar,
T05962-280176. On a thickly wooded spur
near Nanda Devi, 1920s with antique cutlery
and table linen lists still hanging on the walls.
The furniture and decor are evocative of the
Raj, and the caretaker may occasionally be
persuaded to open the house for a viewing.
**$ Tara**, Papersallie Village, T05962-231036.
Guesthouse, simple restaurant and shop, each
run by one of 3 brothers. Rooms come with
valley views, tiled bathrooms and solar showers.

## Jageswar

**$ Jageshwar Jungle Lodge**, near Jataganga,
T(0)9818-069440, www.jageshwarjungle
lodge.com. Airy rooms with pretty balconies,
nice grounds, with a pleasant 25-min walk
to the Jageshwar temples.
**$ Tara**, T05962-263068, mesutara@hotmail.
com. A cottage set in a garden with 6 simple
rooms on the hillside above the tourist office
bungalow, overlooking the temple.

## Kausani *p126*

**$$$-$$ Kausani Best Inn**, View Point
Kausani Estate, T05962-258310, www.
kausanibestinn.com. Great views and
long verandas at this small hotel with
8 rooms. Good Kumaoni home-cooked
food. No lie-ins though, the staff insist
that you see the spectacular sunrise!
**$$-$ Uttarakhand**, 5-min walk from bus
stand, T05962-258012, www.uttarakhand
kausani. com. Clean and spacious rooms
in a freshly upgraded hotel.
**$ Trishul** (KMVN), 2 km from town, T05962-
258006, www.kmvn.gov.in. 12 deluxe rooms
plus 12 separate cottages, food available
with a few hours' notice. Superb views and
compass on the lawn to spot the peaks.

## Baijnath *p126*

**$ Tourist Bungalow**, T05963-250101, and
Inspection House.

### Dunagiri *p126*

**$$$ Dunagiri Nature Retreat**, Dunagiri Village, 2 hrs from Kausani, T(0)9810-267719, www.dunagiri.com. With 360-degree views and at 2400 m, you can literally feel on top of the world at this beautiful retreat space. You can walk to the Sukhdevi temple from here – Sukhdev Muni was the son of Ved-Vyasa, a great Rishi (seer) and author of the *Mahabharata*. This whole area is steeped in the legends of the Vedas. Simple rooms, friendly atmosphere and organic vegetables available. Recommended.

### Bageshwar and the Saryu Valley *p127*

**$$$$ 360 Leti**, in the village of Leti, near Sharma village, 2 hrs north of Bageshwar, T0124-456 3899, www.shaktihimalaya.com. 4 understated but exquisitely deluxe cottages on a 2700-m plateau at the very brink of the Himalaya in the Ramganga Valley. Solar electricity, en suites, private sit outs, Indian, Tibetan and continental food, guided tours, yoga and meditation by appointment, but the main prize are the glorious views of sky and mountains. Absolutely unique.

**$$ Wayfarer Retreat**, Vijaypur, 13 km before Chaukori, T022-6150 6363, book via www.nivalink.com. Cottages surrounded by forest, nighttime campfires and good home-cooked food.

**$ Bagnath**. 20 rooms, trekking equipment for hire, restaurant.

**$ Gomati**, Pindari Rd, 2-min walk from bus stand, T05963-220071. Smart, newly refurbished rooms, some with views over mango orchards and river. Good room service meals and obliging staff.

### Munsiari *p127*

**$$$ Wayfarer Munsiyari**, 1 km beyond town, T011-4760 3625, www.wayfarer adventures.com. Comfortable Swiss tents, toilets, electricity, phone, forest walks, treks, trout fishing, jeeps, professionally run.

**$ Tourist Rest House**, main road just before the town, T05961-222339. Comfortable,

welcome hot showers, good value; also 2 other cheap lodges.

### Pithoragarh *p127*

**$ Ulka Devi** (KMVN), T05964-225434. Has a restaurant. Others near the bus station are very basic.

## 🍴 Restaurants

### Nainital *p122, map p124*

**$$ Kwality**, on the lake. Western and good Indian. Ideally located.

**$$ Machan**, The Mall. Good Indian/Chinese and pizzas.

**$ Kumaon Farm Products**, towards Ropeway. Good for vegetarian snacks.

**$ Nanak**. Vegetarian Western fast food.

**$ Purohit**, The Mall, opposite Kwality. Recommended for *thalis*.

**$ Sher-e-Punjab**, Mallital Bazar. Tasty, North Indian. Halfway to Tallital, with one serving very good local Kumaon dishes.

### Almora *p125*

Plenty of choice along the busy Mall Rd.

**$$ Glory**, good North Indian, but a bit pricey.

**$ Dolma's Place**, Papersallie village near Kasar Devi. Fluffy pancakes, good Tibetan, lemon ginger tea, spring rolls.

**$ Madras Café**, beyond the bus stand. Good Indian meals and snacks.

**$ Mohan's**, Binsar Rd, Kasar Devi, T05962-251215, mohan_rayal72@hotmail.com. Popular backpacker hangout with excellent pizza, internet and confectionery and travel services. Also has 4 rooms down the hill side with kitchenettes.

### Kausani *p126*

**$$-$ Hill Queen**, above Uttarakhand Tourist Lodge. Serves reasonably priced meals.

## 🎉 Festivals

### Almora *p125*

**Sep-Oct** Dasara is celebrated with colourful Ramlila pageants. Also **Kumaon Festival of Arts**

## O Shopping

**Almora** *p125*
**Almora Kithab Ghar**, The Mall. Has a good selection of books.
**Anokhe Lal Hari Kishan Karkhana**, Bazar Almora, T05962-230158. Traditional copper ware manufacturer.
**Ashok Traders**, LR Shah Rd. Sells local copper articles.
**Panchachuli Women Weavers Cooperative**, T05962-232310, www.panchachuli.com. 10-year-old self-sufficient artisan cooperative turning high-quality raw materials into beautiful pashmina, lambswool, merino and sheepwool stoles, fabrics, scarves and tweeds. Expensive but stunning.

## O What to do

**Nainital** *p122, map p124*
**Boating**
**Boat Club**, Mallital, T05942-235153. Sail on the lake or try out a pedal boat.

### Fishing
Permits for the lake from Executive Officer, Nagar Palika. For other lakes, contact the Fisheries Officer in Bhimtal.

### Horse riding
There is a horse stand in Bara Pathar. Various treks: Snow View; Tiffin Top; Naina (Chinna) Peak (2½-3 hrs; can leave at 0500 to see sunrise from the top, but dress warmly); Naina Devi; horses are generally fit and well cared for. You can no longer ride through the town itself. You can phone Nainital Tourism for more info T05942-237476.

### Mountaineering and trekking
Equipment can be hired from **Nainital Mountaineering Club**, T05942-222051, and **KMVN**, Tourist Office, Mallital, T05942-236356. The club organizes rock climbing at Barapathar, 3 km away.

### Tour operators
**Parvat Tours & Information** (KMVN), Dandi House, Tallital, near rickshaw stand, T05942-235656, among others on the Mall. Day tours: Sat tal; Ranikhet; Mukteshwar (with the Veterinary Research Centre); Kaladhungi. 2-day trips: Kausani; Ranikhet/Almora; Corbett.
**Shakti Experience**, T01244-563899, www.shaktihimalaya.com. Educated guides steer you through the pristine mountain terrain between villages in the Kumaon. Food is immaculate and cooked by local villagers. Accommodation is with local families, in rooms that are adapted to an elegantly understated high standard. A highly recommended way to immerse yourself in rural India.

**Almora** *p125*
**High Adventure**, Mall Rd, opposite the Post Office, T(0)9012-354501. Organizes treks, cave tours, bus tickets.
**Village Ways**, Khali Estate, Ayapani, Almora, T(0)8108-14999 (in the UK T01223-750049), www.villageways.com. This award-winning community-based enterprise runs walking tours of 9-12 days through the Binsar Wildlife Sanctuary, staying in specially constructed guesthouses managed by locals. The tours take in beautiful scenery and provide an interesting insight into village life, while bolstering economic opportunities for the villagers.

**Bageshwar and the Saryu Valley** *p127*
**Village Ways** (see above for contact details). In a similar vein to the company's tours in Binsar, but here the walking is through wilder country around Supi village, with the high Himalaya almost at your fingertips. Nights in cosy village guesthouses are combined with a campout on alpine meadows at 3000 m, with exhilarating sunrise views of the Nanda Devi range. Guiding, accommodation and food are all of a high standard.

**Munsiari** *p127*
Nanda Devi Mountaineering Institution
is in the SBI Building. In the main bazar
is **Panchuli Trekking** and **Nanda Devi
Trekking**, the former run by an elderly
Milam tribal villager who has vast and
accurate knowledge of the area.

## Transport

**Nainital** *p122, map p124*
Wherever possible, avoid night driving.
The hill roads can be dangerous. Flat,
straight stretches are rare, road lighting
does not exist and villagers frequently drive
their animals along them or graze them at
the curbside. During the monsoon (Jun-
Sep) landslides are fairly common. Usually
these are cleared promptly but in the case
of severe slips requiring days to clear, bus
passengers are transferred.

On the Mall Rd there is an access toll
of Rs 50. Access is barred, May, Jun, Oct:
heavy vehicles, 0800-1130, 1430-2230;
light vehicles, 1800-2200; Nov-Apr: all
vehicles, 1800-2000.
**Air** The nearest airport is Pantnagar (71 km)
on the plains; No flights at time of writing.
**Bus** Roadways, Tallital, for major inter-city
services, T05942-235518, 0930-1200, 1230-
1700; DTC, Hotel Ashok, Tallital, T35180.
Kumaon Motor Owners' Union (KMOU),
bus stand near tourist office, Sukhatal,
Mallital, T05942-235451; used by private
operators. Regular services to **Almora**
(66 km, 3 hrs); **Dehra Dun** (390 km); **Delhi**
(322 km), a/c night coach, 2100 (8-9 hrs),
or via Haldwani. **Haridwar** (390 km, 8 hrs);
**Kausani** (120 km, 5 hrs); **Ranikhet** (60 km,
3 hrs) and **Ramnagar** for **Corbett** (66 km,
3½ hrs plus 3½ hrs).
**Rickshaw** Cycle-rickshaw and *dandi*
Rs 5-10 along The Mall.
**Ropeway** Cable car/gondola, T05942-
235772, from 'Poplars', Mallital (near GB Pant
Statue) to Snow View, summer 0800-1730
in theory, but usually opens at 1000, winter

1000-1630, return fare Rs 15, advance
booking recommended in season, tickets
valid for a 1-hr halt at the top. Some claim
its anchorage is weak.
**Taxi** From **Parvat Tours** (see Tour operators).
**Train** All India computerized reservation
office, Tallital Bus Stand, T05942-235518.
Mon-Fri, 0900-1200, 1400-1700, Sat, 0900-
1200. The nearest railhead is **Kathgodam**
(35 km), taxi, Rs 850 (peak season), bus Rs 30.
**Delhi** (OD): *Ranikhet Exp 15014*, 2040, 7 hrs.
Towards **Dehradun** and **Haridwar** (OD):
*Dehradun-Kathgodam Exp 14321*, 1940, 9 hrs.
**Kolkata** (H) via **Lucknow** and **Gorakhpur**,
*Howrah Bagh Exp 13020*, 2155, 40 hrs
(Lucknow 8 hrs, Gorakhpur 15 hrs).

**Almora** *p125*
**Bus** Connect Almora with **Kathgodam**
(90 km, 3 hrs) for rail links, and with **Nainital**
(3 hrs) and **Ranikhet** (2½ hrs). Hourly buses
to **Kausani** (3 hrs). For the **Nepal border**,
take a bus from the Dhara Naula bus stand
(4 km from town centre) to Champawat,
and change there for Banbassa.
**Jeep** Share jeeps to **Ranikhet**, Rs 70;
**Kathgodam**, Rs 120. For **Nainital**, take
**Haldwani** jeep as far as **Bhowali**, then
bus or jeep to Nainital.

**Kausani** *p126*
**Bus** From **Almora** and **Ranikhet**
(2½-3½ hrs). **Joshimath** is a tough
but spectacular 10-hr journey.

**Bageshwar and the Saryu Valley** *p127*
Buses and share jeeps to **Almora**. To reach
the far end of the Saryu Valley, take jeeps
bound for Kapkot, and change there for
Song or Munar.

**Munsiari** *p127*
**Bus** From Almora, change at Thal; from
**Haldwani** or **Nainital**, take a bus to
Pithoragarh and change. To **Almora** (11 hrs)
and **Pithoragarh** (8 hrs), 0500 and another
for Pithoragarh in the afternoon.

**Nainital** *p122, map p124*
**Medical services** Ambulance: T05942-235022. BD Pande Govt Hospital, Mallital, T05942-235012. **Post** Mallital. Branch at Tallital. **Useful contacts** Fire: T05942-235626. **Police**: T05942-235424 (Mallital), T05942-235525 (Tallital).

**Almora** *p125*
**Medical services** District Hospital, Chowk Bazar, T05962-230322.

# Corbett National Park

*The journey from Delhi to one of the finest wildlife parks in India offers excellent views of the almost flat, fertile and densely populated Ganga-Yamuna doab, one of the most prosperous agricultural regions of North India. Corbett is India's first national park and one of its few successfully managed tiger reserves. As well as rich and varied wildlife and birdlife it is also extremely picturesque with magnificent sub-montane and riverain views.* ▶▶ *For listings, see pages 137-138.*

### Arriving in Corbett National Park → *Colour map 1, C5. Phone code: 05945.*
*Altitude: 400-1200 m.*

### Entry fees
ⓘ *Corbett Tiger Reserve Reception Centre, T05947-251489, www.corbett nationalpark.in.*
Current fees and opening hours are available from the website. At **Dhikala Gate**: foreigners Rs 1000, Indians Rs 200, valid for three days (two nights); each additional day, Rs 450, Indians Rs 100. At **Bijrani**, **Sonanadi**, **Jhirna** and **Doumunda** gates: Rs 450, Indians Rs 100 per visit (four hours). Entrance permits are not transferable between gates (eg a morning visit to Bijrani and a night halt at Dhikala will require separate payment). **Vehicle fees**: Dhikala Rs 1500 per car/jeep, Indians Rs 500 (covers overnight stay). Bijrani, Sonanadi, Jhirna and Doumunda: Rs 500 per car/jeep, Indians Rs 250.

### Access
The main gate at Dhangarhi (for Dhikala) is approximately 16 km north of Ramnagar on the Ranikhet road. Only visitors who are staying overnight may enter Dhikala. Day visits are allowed at the Amdanda and Laldhang gates for Bijrani and Jhirna respectively. There are also entry gates for the Sonanadi Wildlife Sanctuary, which borders Corbett to the north and forms part of the larger tiger reserve, at Sonanadi and Doumunda. A limit of 30 vehicles per day at each entrance is applied, half of which can be booked in advance – try to reserve at the time of booking your accommodation, with several months' notice. Prior reservation to enter is recommended for day visits, although not always necessary at dawn, when half the entry is determined on a first-come-first-served basis. This can mean queuing for hours in the dark in Ramnagar, being shuffled from one office to another, and still not getting in – you may be refused entry when the quota is filled. Travel agents cannot help as they are not allowed to apply for permits. A reservation at the Bijrani or Dhela **Forest Rest Houses** does not entitle visitors to enter by the Dhangari Gate. From 1 March until the monsoon all roads around Dhikala, except the main approach road, are closed between 1100 and 1500 when visitors are not allowed to move about the forest. Most of the park is closed 30 June to 15 October; the Dhikala section is closed 15 June to 15 November.

## Viewing

**Elephant rides** are available from Dhikala, Khinanauli, Bijrani, Gairal and Jhirna. Each elephant can carry four people. This is the best way to see the jungle and the wildlife. Morning and evening, two hours, Rs 1000, Indians Rs 300 from government, more with private operators; book at Dhikala or Bijrani reception (whichever is relevant). Book as early as possible on arrival since these rides are very popular. **Cars** and **jeeps** may drive round part of the park. A seat in a **cantor** (large open-topped truck) costs Rs 1500 for foreigners, Rs 620 Indians for a full-day tour (0800-1800). Apart from the immediate area within the complex at Dhikala, **don't go walking in the park**. Tiger and elephant attacks are not unknown. The two watch towers are good vantage points for spotting wildlife. Night driving is not allowed in the park.

# Corbett National Park

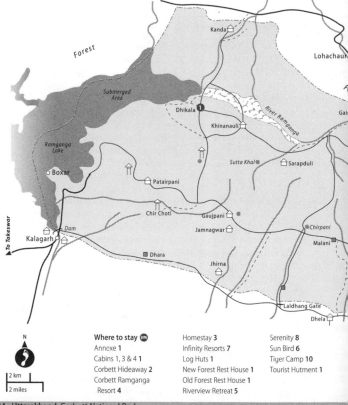

**N**

2 km
2 miles

**Where to stay** 
Annexe **1**
Cabins 1, 3 & 4 **1**
Corbett Hideaway **2**
Corbett Ramganga
  Resort **4**

Homestay **3**
Infinity Resorts **7**
Log Huts **1**
New Forest Rest House **1**
Old Forest Rest House **1**
Riverview Retreat **5**

Serenity **8**
Sun Bird **6**
Tiger Camp **10**
Tourist Hutment **1**

## Climate

Rainfall is heavier in the higher hills, on average the valley receives 1550 mm, the bulk from July to mid-September. Summer days are hot but the nights quite pleasant. Winter nights can get very cold and there is often a frost and freezing fog in the low-lying tracts. Birdwatching is best between December and February. Summer is the best time for seeing the larger mammals, which become bolder in leaving the forest cover to come to the river and water holes; early summer is best for scenic charm and floral interest.

## Wildlife and vegetation

### Wildlife

The park has always been noted for its tigers; there are now over 150 but they are not easily spotted. About 10% of visitors see one – usually entering at the Bijrani Gate. There are leopards too but they are seldom seen. Sambar, chital, para (hog deer) and muntjac (barking deer) are the main prey of the big cats and their population fluctuates around 20,000. Some, like the chital, are highly gregarious whilst the large sambar, visually very impressive with its antlers, is usually solitary. The two commonly seen monkeys of North India are the rhesus (a macaque – reddish face and brownish body) and the common langur (black face and silvery coat). Elephants are now permanent inhabitants since the Ramganga Dam has flooded their old trekking routes. There are a few hundred of them and they are seen quite often. Other animals include porcupine and wild boar (often seen around Dhikala – some can be quite dangerous, attacking unsuspecting visitors who have food with them). In total there are more than 50 species of mammal alone, though the dam appears to have caused significant losses. The last swamp deer was seen in March 1978, and the loss of habitat has been keenly felt by the cheetal, hog deer and porcupine, all of which appear to be declining.

There are 26 species of reptile and seven of amphibian. In certain stretches of the river and in the Ramganga Lake are the common mugger crocodile: notices prohibiting swimming warn "Survivors will be prosecuted"! The fish-eating gharial can also be found, as can soft-shelled tortoises, otters and river fish. The python is quite common.

The birdlife is especially impressive with over 600 species including a wide range of water birds, birds of prey such as the crested serpent eagle, harriers, Pallas' fishing eagle, osprey, buzzards and vultures. Woodland birds include: Indian and great pied hornbills, parakeets, laughing thrushes, babblers and cuckoos. Doves, bee-eaters, rollers, bulbuls, warblers, finches, robins and chats are to be seen in the open scrub from the viewing towers. The rarer ibisbill is one of the main attractions for serious twitchers.

## Vegetation
There are 110 species of trees, 51 species of shrubs, three species of bamboos and 27 species of climbers. The valley floor is covered with tall elephant grass (*Nall* in the local terminology), lantana bushes and patches of *sal* and *sheesham* (*Dalbergia sissoo*) forest, whilst the enclosing hills on both sides are completely forest covered, with *sal*, *bakli*, *khair*, *jhingan*, *tendu*, *pula* and *sain*. *Charas* grows wild in the fields. Nullahs and ravines running deep into the forests are dry for much of the year, but there are swift torrents during the monsoon. These hold brakes of bamboo and thick scrub growth.

---

## Around the park → *For listings, see pages 137-138.*

### Ramnagar → *Colour map 1, C5.*
Ramnagar, with a railway station, 134 km from Moradabad, is 18 km from the park boundary and 50 km from **Dhikala**. It is a noisy town with the Project Tiger Office for Corbett reservations, and provides a night halt. They will receive faxes and hold them.

### Kaladhungi
At Kaladhungi visit **Jim Corbett's house** ① *Rs 10*, now a small museum. The area is an extension of the Tiger Reserve with equally good wildlife but minus the restrictions, and is also excellent for birdwatching. If you turn up the road opposite and continue up into the hills, travelling along a delightful, metalled road that winds its way up the hillsides through *chir* pine forest and the occasional village, you'll see impressive views of the plains. You enter Nainital at the north end of the lake.

### Ranikhet → *Colour map 1, C5. Phone code: 05966.*
Rani Padmadevi, the queen of Raja Sudhardev is believed to have chosen the site of this scenic place, hence Ranikhet (Queen's Field). In 1869 the land was bought from local villagers and the British established a summer rest and recreation settlement for their troops, made it a cantonment town and developed it as a quiet hill station. Set along a 1800-m-high ridge, Ranikhet sprawls out through the surrounding forest without having a proper centre. This is one of its attractions and there are many enjoyable walks. The views from the ridge are magnificent and the twin peaks of Nanda Devi (at a height of 7816 m and 7434 m) can be clearly seen. **Uttarakhand Tourist Office** ① *The Mall, T05966-220227, 1000-1700*. At **Upat**, 6 km away, there is Kali temple.

## ◉ Corbett National Park listings

*For hotel and restaurant price codes and other relevant information, see pages 22-26.*

## ◉ Where to stay

**Corbett National Park** *p133, map p134*
Corbett is hugely popular, and it's essential to book your accommodation as far ahead as possible – up to 2 months in high season. If you are travelling to the park without reserved accommodation, you must go to Ramnagar first to make a booking. Dhikala is the park centre and has accommodation. Remember to get a clearance card from Dhikala from the office here before leaving in the morning.

### Within the park
Reservations for all accommodation, except the Annexe at Dhikala, can be booked at the **Corbett Tiger Reserve Reception Centre** in Ramnagar, T05947-251489. Office open daily 0830-1300, 1500-1700. For the Annexe, book through **Uttarakhand Tourism**, Indraprakash Bldg, Barakhamba Rd, Delhi, T011-2371 2246, www.kmvn.gov.in. Foreigners pay 2-3 times the price of Indians, and prices are raised frequently. Entry permits and vehicle charges are payable at the respective gate.

For information on the various rest houses, see www.corbettnationalpark.in and follow links to 'Permits and Reservations'. Rates range from Rs 400 per night for a dorm bed in Dhikala's Log Hut to Rs 5000 for a room in the **Old Forest Rest House**.

### Outside the park
**$$$$ Infinity Resorts**, 8 km north of Ramnagar, T(0)9650-193662, www.infinity resorts.com. Established by the **Corbett Foundation**, who have done pioneering work in compensating farmers for lost livestock to prevent revenge killings of big cats. 24 rooms, pool, lawns, mango orchards, good food, old world feel, charming staff. Don't miss the Jim Corbett documentary.

Elephant safaris and excellent birdlife. Highly recommended.
**$$$$ Riverview Retreat**, on the periphery of the park, T05947-284135, www.corbett hideaway.com. 1.2 ha of luxury tented accommodation actually inside the tiger sanctuary. The jungle cacophony is incredibly atmospheric, and staying a number of nights overlooking the stunning Ramganga river plain gets you a ringside seat to the park's wildlife. They also have the lovely **Corbett Hideaway** with lovely cottages.
**$$$$-$$$ Corbett Ramganga Resort** (WelcomHeritage), Jhamaria, 17 km from Dhangarhi, T(0)9310-510582, www.ramganga.com. 10 well-appointed rooms in cottages, 8 Swiss cottage tents, safe spring water, river rafting, riding, climbing, gliding, fishing, excellent pool and picturesque position on river edge.
**$$$ Tiger Camp**, Dhikuli, T05974-287901. Book through **Asian Adventures**, www.tiger-camp.com. 20 cottages in Kumaoni Village style but modern interiors, rooms with fan and bath electricity (plus generator), good food, beautiful garden, jeep, hiking, friendly owner, lovely atmosphere. Recommended.
**$$$-$$ Serenity**, close to Infinity Resorts, T05974-244415, www.serenitycorbett.com. A good option with nice airy rooms and restaurant on-site.
**$$-$ Sunbird Guest House**, Dhikuli, T05947-284226, www.corbettsunbird guesthouse.com. Best of the budget options, clean and friendly place with a/c and non a/c options.
**$ Homestay**, Nature Shop, Dhikuli, close to Infinity. Look for the **Nature Shop** sign (there are a few) and behind the shop are 2 lovely rooms. Basic but full of charm. Friendly family and home-cooked food.

### Ramnagar *p136*
**$ Govind**, 100 m down the road. Simple rooms, good pancakes!

**Kaladhungi** *p136*
**$$$ Camp Corbett**, 25 km east of Corbett, T05942-242126, www.campcorbett.net. Cottages and tents, wonderful meals, an outstanding resort run by the hospitable Anand family, relaxing and totally hassle free, pick-up from Haldwani station arranged. They also have **Mountain Quail Lodge** in Pangot, 1½ hrs from Corbett surrounded by oak and rhododendron forests.

**Ranikhet** *p136*
**$$-$ Moon**, Sadar Bazar, T05966-220382. 14 clean rooms plus 2 'honeymoon' cottages.
**$$-$ Parwati Inn**, above bus stand, T05966-220325. Good choice from 32 large rooms, restaurant, friendly staff, credit cards accepted, best in the town itself. You can choose from Himalaya or garden view.
**$ Kalika**, upper cantonment, T05966-220893, www.kmvn.gov.in. Pleasant rooms with bath, restaurant (mostly Indian), attractive location, good views.
**$ Tourist Rest House**, Chilianaula, 7 km west, T05966-220588, www.kmvn.gov.in. New unit next to the temple complex, rooms, dorm, stunning mountain views.

## ⚙ What to do

**Corbett National Park** *p133, map p134*
KMVN runs 3-day tours from Delhi departing every Fri in season, around Rs 11000 for foreigners, Rs 9000 Indians, taxes extra.
Reservations: 1st floor, Indraprastha Building, Barakhamba Rd, New Delhi, T011-2371 2246, www.kmvn.gov.in, or from **Uttar Pradesh Tourist Office**, Chandralok Building, 36 Janpath, New Delhi, T011-2332 2251.

**Reception Centre** in Ramnagar runs day tours to Dhikala – the only access to this part of the park wihout reserved accommodation.
**Tigerland Safaris**, T05947-284173, www.tigerlandsafaris.com. Well-organized safaris, professional service. Recommended.

## ⊖ Transport

**Corbett National Park** *p133, map p134*
**Air** Althought there is Phoolbagh airport at Pantnagar (130 km) there were no scheduled flights at time of writing.
**Bus** The **Delhi–Dhikala** road (260 km) passes through Moradabad (turn left after Moradabad, towards Kashipur and Ramnagar), 5½-6 hrs – strewn with bus/lorry/car crashes. Frequent buses from Ramnagar **Delhi**, **Dehra Dun**, **Moradabad**, **Nainital** and **Ranikhet** (if coming from Dhikala wait outside Dhangarhi gate, no need to return to Ramnagar). Bus to **Dhikala**, 1530, not reliable; return leaves 1000 from Dhikala after elephant ride.
**Jeep** Becoming very expensive. Expect to pay Rs 1800-2500 for a day. Hire from near Ramnagar park office. Petrol vehicles are cheaper (up to Rs 2000 per day) and quieter. You also pay Rs 50 admission for the driver.
**Train** Nearest station is at Ramnagar (50 km), for **Moradabad** and Delhi. **To Delhi** (**OD**): *Ramnagar Delhi Link Exp* 25036, 0950, 5½ hrs; *Corbett Park Link Exp 25014*, 2200, 6 hrs. **From Delhi** (**OD**): *Uttarakhand Sampark Kranti Exp 15035*, 1600, 4½ hrs; *Ranikhet Exp 15013*, 2235, 6¼ hrs.

# Contents

## At a glance

◉ **Getting around** Buses or cars are the only way to get around most of this mountainous state; Kalka–Shimla narrow-gauge train and the Kangra Valley Railway.
◔ **Time required** 2-3 days each for Shimla and Manali; many people spend weeks in Dharamshala.
☀ **Weather** The hills are a mercifully cool retreat in Apr and May.
✗ **When not to go** Monsoon rains can bring landslides and closed roads.

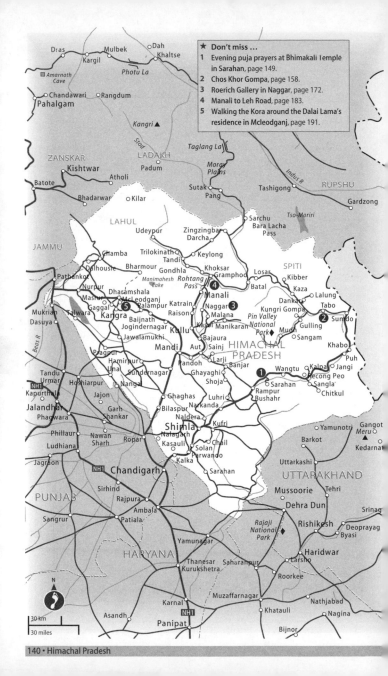

★ **Don't miss ...**
1. Evening puja prayers at Bhimakali Temple in Sarahan, page 149.
2. Chos Khor Gompa, page 158.
3. Roerich Gallery in Naggar, page 172.
4. Manali to Leh Road, page 183.
5. Walking the Kora around the Dalai Lama's residence in Mcleodganj, page 191.

Himachal Pradesh is defined more than anything by the mighty Himalaya, towering over its northern periphery with implacable dominance, both feared and revered by the state's sparse population. The mountains have long attracted nature lovers, climbers and trekkers, while in recent years a number of more adrenalin-inducing sports have also come to prominence. Manali has become a centre for adventurous activities: from heli-skiing to rafting, mountain biking to paragliding and horse riding, there's a huge range on offer. The arrival of the Tibetans after the Chinese invasion of Tibet in 1959 has added attractions of an altogether more mellow manner. McLeodganj (Dharamshala), home to His Holiness the Dalai Lama, has become a mecca for those after more spiritual pursuits; many come to follow courses in Buddhism meditation, yoga, or to learn about the Tibetan cause.

Some of the state's finest mountain views can be seen from Dalhousie, a popular hill station during the Raj and today a quaint if anachronistic reminder of how the British used to build their homes. Himachal's other Raj relic, and its capital city, Shimla, is part quaint English village, part traffic, touts and mayhem. Arriving via the 'toy train' from Kalka is by far the best way and the scenery is almost painfully picturesque. Although most people come to Himachal to see the mountains, the plains also have much to offer. Kangra Valley is especially pretty, with charming villages connected by quiet, windy roads. Those in search of more rugged adventures should head for Kinnaur, Spiti and Lahaul, accessible only in the summer when the snow melts on the higher passes, meaning they can be crossed by road, giving access to the barren but spectacular scenery beyond. This area also forms the start of the incomparable Manali–Leh road, the highway from Himachal to Ladakh and one of the world's best road trips.

## The land

**Geography** Himachal Pradesh (Himalayan Province) is wholly mountainous, with peaks rising to over 6700 m. The **Dhaula Dhar** range runs from the northwest to the Kullu Valley. The **Pir Panjal** is further north and parallel to it. High, remote, arid and starkly beautiful, Lahaul and Spiti are sparsely populated. They contrast strongly with the well-wooded lushness of those areas to the south of the Himalayan axis.

**Climate** At lower altitudes the summers can be very hot and humid whereas the higher mountains are permanently under snow. In Shimla, the Kangra Valley, Chamba and the Kullu Valley, the monsoon arrives in mid-June and lasts until mid-September, giving periods of very heavy rain; in the Kullu Valley there can be sudden downpours in March and early April. To the north, Lahaul and Spiti are beyond the influence of the monsoon, and consequently share the high-altitude desert climatic characteristics of Ladakh.

## History

Originally the region was inhabited by a tribe called the Dasas who were later assimilated by the Aryans. From the 10th-century parts were occupied by the Muslims. Kangra, for example, submitted to Mahmud of Ghazni and later became a Mughal province. The Gurkhas of Nepal invaded Himachal in the early 19th century and incorporated it into their kingdom as did the Sikhs some years later. The British finally took over the princely states in the middle of the 19th century.

## Culture

**Religion** Although the statistics suggest that Himachal is one of the most Hindu states in India, its culture reflects the strong influence of Buddhism, notably in the border regions with Tibet and in the hill stations where many Tibetan refugees have made their homes. In the villages many of the festivals are shared by Hindus and Buddhists alike. There are also small minorities of Sikhs, Muslims and Christians.

**People** Hill tribes such as the Gaddis, Gujars, Kinnaurs, Lahaulis and Pangwalas have all been assimilated into the dominant Hindu culture though the caste system is simpler and less rigid than elsewhere. The tribal peoples in Lahaul and Spiti follow a form of Buddhism while Kinnauris mix Buddhism with Hinduism in their rituals. Their folklore has the common theme of heroism and legends of love. *Natti*, the attractive folk dance of the high hills, is widely performed.

**Language** The dominant local language is Pahari, a Hindi dialect derived from Sanskrit and Prakrit but largely unintelligible to plains dwellers. Hindi is the medium for instruction in schools and is widely spoken.

**Handicrafts** Handicrafts include woodcarving, spinning wool, leather tanning, pottery and bamboo crafts. Wool products are the most abundant and it is a common sight in the hills to see men spinning wool by hand as they watch over their flocks or as they are walking along. Good-quality shawls made from the fine hair from pashmina goats particularly in Kullu, are highly sought after. *Namdas* (rugs) and rich pile carpets in Tibetan designs are also produced. Buddhist *thangkas*, silverware and chunky tribal silver jewellery are popular with tourists and are sold in bazars.

## Modern Himachal Pradesh

Himachal Pradesh was granted full statehood in 1970. There are 68 seats in the State Assembly, but as one of India's smallest states Himachal Pradesh elects four members of the Lok Sabha and three representatives to the Rajya Sabha. Since 1966 Shimla has been the state capital. Dharamshala (McLeodganj) has been the home of His Holiness the Dalai Lama and the Tibetan government in exile since 1959, following the Chinese takeover of Tibet. With the long-term closure of routes through Kashmir, Himachal Pradesh has seen a sharp rise in tourism, and is the main land route to Ladakh. The new strategically important tunnel under the Rohtang Pass is scheduled for completion in 2016.

**Current political developments** Even though Himachal is relatively close to Delhi, it still has the feel of a political backwater. News from the state rarely makes the national newspapers and, while the contest for representation in the Lok Sabha and in the Assembly is intense, the two-horse race between Congress and the BJP rarely attracts much attention. The Congress party gained power in March 2003 under Chief Minister Shri Virbhadra Singh, his third appointment to the post after earlier tenures covering much of the 1980s and 1990s, but the BJP won three of the four Lok Sabha seats in 2009. In the 2012 elections, Congress secured an absolute majority.

# Southern Himachal

*Southern Himachal offers an intriguing mix of experiences. Shimla's colonial past, with its Little England architecture and anachronistic air, seems to be fighting for survival amidst the modern-day bustle of Himachal's capital city. The area around Shimla offers stunning views of the foothills of the Himalaya and plenty of attractive places to stay nestled amongst the cool pine forests. This area is also the gateway to the altogether more rugged landscapes of Kinnaur, a world far less affected by the advance of time.* ▶ *For listings, see pages 150-154. For trekking, see page 210.*

## Shimla → *For listings, see pages 150-154. Colour map 1, B3. Phone code: 0177. Population: 150,000. Altitude: 2213 m.*

Once a charming hill station and the summer capital of the British, an air of decay hangs over many of Shimla's Raj buildings, strung out for 3 km along a ridge. Below them a maze of narrow streets, bazars and shabby 'local' houses with corrugated-iron roofs cling to the hillside. Some find it delightfully quaint and less spoilt than other hill stations. There are some lovely walks with magnificent pines and cedars.

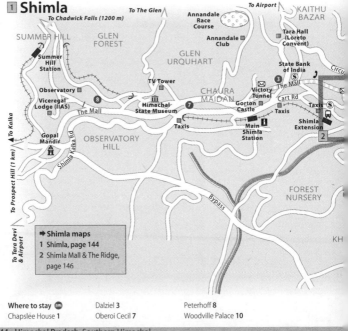

**1 Shimla**

To Chadwick Falls (1200 m)
To The Glen
To Airport
KAITHU BAZAR
Annandale Race Course
SUMMER HILL
GLEN FOREST
Annandale Club
Tara Hall (Loreto Convent)
GLEN URQUHART
Summer Hill Station
State Bank of India
Observatory
TV Tower
CHAURA MAIDAN
The Mall
Viceregal Lodge (IIAS)
The Mall
Himachal State Museum
Victory Tunnel
Gorton Castle
Cart Rd
Taxis
Taxis
Shimla Extension
To Kalka
Shimla Kalka Rd
Gopal Mandir
OBSERVATORY HILL
Taxis
Main Shimla Station
To Prospect Hill (1 km)
Bypass
FOREST NURSERY
To Tara Devi & Airport
KH

**➤ Shimla maps**
1 Shimla, page 144
2 Shimla Mall & The Ridge, page 146

**Where to stay**
Chapslee House **1**
Dalziel **3**
Oberoi Cecil **7**
Peterhoff **8**
Woodville Palace **10**

## Arriving in Shimla

**Getting there** Despite the romance of the narrow-gauge railway from Kalka, see page 147, most arrive in Shimla by bus or taxi as it is so much quicker. The bus stand and the station are on Cart Road, where porters and hotel touts jostle to take your luggage up the steep hill – possibly the best few rupees you will ever spend. If you are staying on the western side of town it is worth getting off the bus at the railway station. Buses from the east, including Rampur and Kinnaur, stop at the Rivoli Bus Stand. Shimla (Jabbarhatti) airport has a coach (Rs 50) in season, and taxis (Rs 400-500) for transfer.

**Getting around** The Mall can only be seen on foot; it takes about half an hour to walk from the Viceroy's Lodge to Christ Church. The main traffic artery is Cart Road, which continues past the station to the main bus stand, taxi rank and the two-stage lift which goes to The Mall above. The Victory Tunnel cuts through from Cart Road to the north side of the hill. ▸ *See Transport, page 153.*

**Tourist offices** Himachal Pradesh Tourism Development Corportation (HPTDC) ① *The Mall, T0177-265 2561, www.hptdc.nic.in, 0900-1800, in season 0900-1900; also at Cart Rd, near Victory Tunnel, T0177-265 4589, 1000-1700,* is very informative and helpful.

**Climate** October and November are very pleasant, with warm days and cool nights. December-February is cold and there are snowfalls. March and April are changeable; storms are not infrequent and the air can feel very chilly. Avoid May-June, the height of the Indian tourist season prior to the monsoon.

## Places in Shimla

Shimla is strung out on a long crescent-shaped ridge that connects a number of hilltops from which there are good views of the snow-capped peaks to the north: Jakhu (2453 m), Prospect Hill (2176 m), Observatory Hill (2148 m), Elysium Hill (2255 m) and Summer Hill (2103 m). For the British, the only way of beating the hot weather on the plains in May and June was to move to hill stations, which they endowed with mock-Tudor houses, churches, clubs, parks with bandstands of English county towns, and a main street invariably called The Mall.

**Christ Church** (1844), on the open area of The Ridge, dominates the eastern end of town. Consecrated in 1857, a clock and porch were added later. The original chancel window, designed by Lockwood Kipling, Rudyard's father, is no longer there. The mock tudor **library** building (circa 1910) is next door. The Mall joins The Ridge at Kipling's **'Scandal Point'**, where today groups gather to exchange gossip. Originally the name referred to the stir caused by the supposed 'elopement' of a lady from the Viceregal Lodge and a dashing Patiala prince after they arranged a rendezvous here.

The **Gaiety Theatre** (1887) and the **Town Hall** (circa 1910) are reminiscent of the 'arts and crafts' style, as well as the timbered **General Post Office** (1886). Beyond, to the west, is the **Grand Hotel**. Further down you pass the sinister-looking **Gorton Castle**, designed by Sir Samuel Swinton Jacob, which was once the Civil Secretariat. A road to the left leads to the railway station, while one to the right goes to Annandale, the racecourse and cricket ground. The Mall leads to the rebuilt **Cecil Hotel**. On Observatory Hill, the **Viceregal Lodge** (1888) is the most splendid of Shimla's surviving Raj-era buildings, built for Lord Dufferin in the Elizabethan style. Now the **Rashtrapati Niwas** ① *1000-1630, Rs 10 including a brief tour*, it stands in large grounds with good views of the mountains. Reminders of its British origins include a gatehouse, a chapel and the meticulously polished brass fire hydrants imported from Manchester. Inside, you can visit the main reception rooms and the library which are lined from floor to ceiling with impressive teak panelling. It is a long up the hill walk from the gate. It is now the Indian Institute of Advanced Study and there is a café on-site.

**Himachal State Museum** ① *near Chaura Maidan, Tue-Sun 1000-1330, 1400-1700, free*, is a 30-minute walk west from the GPO along The Mall; then it's a short climb from the Harsha Hotel. Small, with a good sculpture collection and miniatures from the Kangra School, it also houses contemporary art including work by Nicholas Roerich, costumes, jewellery, bronzes and textiles (everything is well labelled).

## ② Shimla Mall & The Ridge

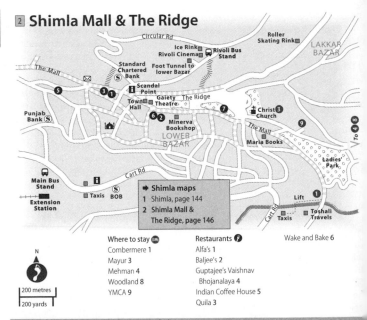

**Where to stay** 🛏
Combermere 1
Mayur 3
Mehman 4
Woodland 8
YMCA 9

**Restaurants** 🍴
Alfa's 1
Baljee's 2
Guptajee's Vaishnav
   Bhojanalaya 4
Indian Coffee House 5
Quila 3

Wake and Bake 6

## Walks

**Jakhu Temple** on a hill with excellent views (2455 m), dedicated to Hanuman the monkey god, is 2 km from Christ Church. Walking sticks (handy for warding off monkeys, which can be vicious – keep all food out of sight) are available at *chai* shops at the start of the ascent. **The Glen** (1830 m), to the northwest, is a 4-km walk from the centre past the **Cecil Hotel**. **Summer Hill** (1983 m), a pleasant 'suburb' 5 km from town, is a stop on the Shimla-Kalka railway. **Chadwick Falls** (1586 m), 3 km further, drops 67 m during the monsoon season.

    **Prospect Hill** (2175 m) is 5 km from The Ridge and a 20-minute walk from Boileauganj to the west. **Tara Devi** (1851 m), with a hilltop temple, 11 km southwest from the railway station, can also be reached by car or train.

## Around Shimla → *For listings, see pages 150-154. Colour map 1, B3.*

## Kufri

About 16 km from Shimla, at 2500 m, Kufri hosts a winter sports festival in January which includes the **National Snow Statue Competition**. Don't expect European or American resort standards though. There are some attractions around and about the town. At **Danes Folly** (2550 m), 5 km away, is a government-run orchard. A 10-minute walk uphill takes you to a mini zoo of Himalayan wildlife. **Mahasu Peak** (bus, Rs 15) 20 minutes from a path behind the Kufri Resort cottages, offers fabulous mountain views on a clear day and there is a small but interesting temple at the start of the walk. The best time to visit is in January and February.

## Chharabra

Chharabra is an enjoyable 3-km forest walk down from Kufri. The Wildflower Hall which once stood here was the residence of **Lord Kitchener**, commander-in-chief of the Indian Army. The original building was replaced; its successor was converted into a hotel which burnt down in 1993. **Oberoi** has opened a new luxury hotel (see Where to stay, page 151).

## Naldera

Off the Hindusthan-Tibet road, 26 km north of Shimla, Naldera has a nine-hole golf course, possibly the oldest in India and one of the highest in the world, and the beautiful Mahung temple. The colourful **Sipi Fair** in June attracts handicraft-sellers from surrounding villages.

## Chail

In a superb forest setting with fine snow views, 45 km southeast of Shimla (2½ hours by bus), off the NH22, Chail was once the Maharaja of Patiala's summer capital. Built across three hills, it claims to have the country's highest cricket ground at 2444 m, a 2-km walk from the bus stand. The old palace on Rajgarh Hill has been converted to a hotel while the old residency, Snow View, and a Sikh temple stand on the other hills. The **Chail Sanctuary**, once a private hunting reserve, is popular with birders and has a Cheer pheasant-breeding programme. It is an idyllic spot until the weekend when day-trippers descend on the tiny resort.

## Kalka

Kalka is the terminus for the narrow-gauge railway from Shimla. The Kalka-Shimla line (0.76 m), completed in 1903, runs 97 km from Kalka in the foothills to Shimla at over 2000 m. The magnificent journey takes just over five hours. The steepest gradient is 1:33; there are 107 tunnels covering 8 km and 969 bridges over 3 km. Take snacks or order a meal in advance at Kalka or Shimla station.

## Nalagarh

The area around Nalagarh was once ruled by the Chandela Rajputs. The fort has wonderful views above an estate of forests and orchards and is built on five levels around manicured grassy courts. Originally built in the 15th century; the **Diwan-i-Khas** (1618) is now the Banquet Hall. The present raja has opened his home to guests. You can request the **Nalagarh Fort** hotel pickup from Ropar (20 km) or Kalka (40 km).

## Old Hindustan Tibet Road → *For listings, see pages 150-154. Colour map 1, B3/4.*

The Old Hindustan Tibet road runs east from Shimla to the Tibetan border through a landscape of lush tropical valleys, snow-clad peaks and precipitous gorges. Connecting a string of prosperous-looking farms, villages and towns, it passes through terraced slopes covered with orchards before entering the high-altitude deserts of Spiti. As the narrow road winds even deeper towards the Tibetan border its unprotected sides plunge hundreds of metres to the roaring monsoon-swollen River Sutlej below, grasping at huge boulders brought down by thundering landslides into the gloomy gorges. By bus or jeep this road is not for the faint-hearted. The road may be severely damaged in the rains.

### Arriving at the Old Hindustan Tibet Road

**Inner Line Permits**, which are needed for travel close to the Tibetan border (essentially the area between Kaza and Jangi), are easy enough to get. Permits are issued free to individuals for seven days from the date of issue (easily renewable for three days at Kaza or Recong Peo). Take your passport, two copies of the details and Indian visa pages, and three passport photos and complete the form from the **Sub-Divisional Magistrate's office** (SDM) in **Shimla** ⓘ *T0177-265 5988*; **Recong Peo** ⓘ *T01786-222452*; or **Kaza** ⓘ *T01906-222212*, where you need the additional 'No Objection' certificate from the chief of police (a mere formality of a stamp and signature). In Recong Peo, the whole process takes about an hour, which may include *chai* or breakfast with the SDM. Permits are also available (in theory) from the **Resident Comissioner of Himachal Pradesh** ⓘ *Himachal Bhavan, 27 Sikandra Rd, New Delhi, T011-2371 6574*, and other magistrates offices. In Shimla, travel agents charge Rs 150. Permits are checked at Jangi if coming from Shimla and at Sumdo coming from Spiti. Carry about 10 photocopies as some checkpoints demand to keep one. Rules regarding overnight stays have been relaxed considerably; it is now possible to sleep in Puh and Nako. Accommodation is limited to simple rest houses, lodges or tents. In some places enterprising local families are opening their modest homes to paying guests. Local village shops often stock canned food and bottled water. It is virtually impossible to get foreign exchange in this area.

### Narkanda

The small market town at 2700 m occupies a superb position. The town offers a base from which to ski but the skiing does not compare with that found in Western resorts. Enquire at the Marketing Office in Shimla for skiing in winter and the seven-day beginners' course.

### Nirath

The road drops sharply through woodland interspersed with apple orchards from Narkanda down to Kingel from where it zig-zags down to Sainj. The seasonal route is best by 4WD though buses cover this route very carefully. Some 5 km beyond Sainj there are superb views both across the valley, and of a wall of eroded outwash deposits at least 50 m thick

The main road passes through Nirath where there is a **Surya Temple** believed to date from the eighth century which still has some fine carving preserved on the outer walls and has carved wooden panels within. At an altitude of 800-900 m the Sutlej Valley towards Rampur has a subtropical summer climate, with mango trees and bananas replacing apples.

## Rampur Bushahr

This is one of Himachal's most important market towns. **Padam Palace** (1920s), opposite the bus stand, once the residence of the raja, has interesting carved wooden panels and wall murals, but is difficult to enter. **Sat Narain Temple** in the main bazar (1926) has a beautiful but decaying façade. **Lavi Fair** (November) draws large crowds of colourful hill people who bring their produce – handicrafts, carpets, rugs, fruit and nuts and animals – to the special market. There are sporting competitions in the day, and dancing and making music around bonfires after dark.

## Rampur to Sarahan

From Rampur the highway enters one of the most exciting (and geologically active) stretches of road in the region. During the rains, the Sutlej River is a surging torrent of muddy water, dropping over 450 m in under 30 km and passing through gorges and deeply incised valleys. Although an ancient trade route, the road is comparatively recent and is constantly being upgraded particularly in connection with the Nathpa-Jhakhri HEP scheme, with a 28-km-long tunnel from **Nathpa**, near Wangtu, to **Jhakhri**, about 10 km beyond Rampur. When completed this will be one of the largest Hydel schemes in the world. The blasting both for the shafts and for road widening has further destabilized the already landslide-prone hillsides and during the rains the road may be blocked. Blockages are usually cleared within hours, though travelling times are wholly unpredictable. You also need a strong stomach, both for the main road and for diversions, especially up the Baspa Valley to Sangla. Some 9 km west of Jeori the river passes through a dramatic gorge. On the north side of the river isolated tiny pockets of cultivated land cling to the hillside. **Jeori** is the junction for Sarahan, 21 km south, an hour away. There are several provisions stores to pick up the basics here since Sarahan has very limited supplies.

## Sarahan → *For listings, see pages 150-154. Colour map 1, B4. Phone code: 01782. Population: 1200. Altitude: 2165 m.*

An important market for traders of neighbouring regions, Sarahan is an attractive town, surrounded by high peaks, with a pheasant-breeding centre nearby (see below). The bazar is interesting: friendly villagers greet travellers, shops sell flowers, bright red and gold scarves and other offerings for worshippers among local produce, fancy goods, clothes and jewellery. It is also a stop on the trekkers' route.

Sarahan was the old capital of the local Rampur Bushahr rulers and has a palace complex containing the strikingly carved wood-bonded **Bhimakali Temple** (rebuilt circa 1927), in a mixture of Hindu and Buddhist styles. The two temples stand on a slope among apple and apricot orchards behind the bazar. The Bhimakali is dedicated to Durga as the destroyer of the *asuras* (demons) and has a Brahmin priest in attendance. Plan for an early-morning visit to the temple to see morning prayers; evening prayers are around 1900. Leave shoes and leather objects with the attendant and wear the saffron cap offered to you before entering. You may only photograph the outside of the temples. It is worth climbing around the back of the complex for a picturesque view.

According to some sources the ancient temple on the right (closed for safety reasons) is many centuries olde. Built in traditional timber-bonded style it has whitewashed dry stone and rubble masonry alternating with horizontal deodar or spruce beams to withstand earthquakes. The upper floors have balconies and windows with superb ornamental woodcarving; the silver repoussée-work doors are also impressive. The first floor has a 200-year-old gold image of goddess Bhimkali which is actively worshipped only during the **Dasara festival** when animals and birds are sacrificed in the courtyard, while on the second floor daily early-morning *puja* is carried out to a second image. The sacrificial altar and the old well are in the courtyard with three other shrines. The palace of the Rampur rajas behind the temple has a drawing room with ornate furniture and a painted ceiling the caretaker may let you in.

**Pheasant Breeding Centre** ① *summer 0830-1830, winter 0930-1630, free*, on a hill, a 1-km strenuous walk from the main road, on a wooded trail, has Monal, Khalij, Western Tragopan and other varieties in cages.

A pilgrimage route encircles **Shrikhand Mahadev peak** (5227 m), which takes pilgrims seven days to go round. On a clear day you get fantastic panoramic views of the snow covered peaks.

## ◉ Southern Himachal listings

*For hotel and restaurant price codes and other relevant information, see pages 22-26.*

## ● Where to stay

**Shimla** *p144, maps p144 and p146*
Prices soar May-Jun when modest rooms can be difficult to find especially after midday, so book ahead. Some places close off-season; those that remain open may offer discounts of 30-50%. From the railway or bus station it is a stiff climb up to hotels on or near the Ridge. Porters are available (Rs 20 per heavy bag).
**$$$$ Chapslee House**, Lakkar Bazar, T0177-280 2542, www.chapslee.com. 6 suites only, charming, full of bygone-era character, large grounds, exquisite interior, good views, excellent meals (disappointing *thali* though) and excellent service, if you can get in.
**$$$$ Oberoi Cecil**, Chaura Maidan (quiet end of The Mall), T0177-280 4848, www.oberoihotels.com. 79 sumptuous rooms, colonial grandeur on the edge of town, with superb views, beautifully renovated, stylishly furnished, good restaurant, special ultra-modern pool, full-board. Recommended.
**$$$$-$$$ Woodville Palace** (Heritage), Raj Bhavan Rd, The Mall, T0177-262 4038, www.woodvillepalacehotel.com. 30 rooms (variable), some good suites with period furniture (freezing in winter), dining hall worth visiting for eclectic mixture of portraits, weapons and hunting trophies (non-residents on advance notice), owned by the Raja of Jubbal's family and featured in *Jewel in the Crown*. Good views, spacious, large grounds, one of the quietest.
**$$$ Combermere**, 2 entrances, next to the lift at top and bottom, T0177-265 1246, www.hotelcombermere.com. Good central location, 40 decent rooms (including penthouses) on 6 levels (partly served by lift), well located, friendly, efficient, very helpful, pleasant terrace café and bar, game room, central heating/a/c, super deluxe rooms worth spending a little extra on.
**$$$-$$ Peterhoff** (HPTDC), Chaura Maidan near All India Radio, T0177-265 2538, www.hptdc.nic.in. 35 sombre but spacious rooms in very quiet location with beautiful lawn terrace and friendly, helpful staff.
**$$ Aapo Aap Homestay**, Panthaghati Bazaar, Sargheen Chowk, 10 km outside Shimla, T(0)8091-208353, www.aapoaapshimla.com. In a beautiful location outside of Shimla with stunning views, this homestay has

3 lovely guest rooms. There is also Wi-Fi and a meditation room.

**$$ Dalziel**, The Mall, above station, T0177-645 1306, www.dalzielhotel.com. 30 clean enough, comfy, creaky valley-facing rooms with bath (hot water) in heritage building, Indian meals, prices depend on size of TV.

**$$-$ Mayur**, above Christ Church, T0177-265 2393, www.hotelmayur.com. 30 rooms in 1970s style, some with mountain views, some with tub, good restaurant but check bill, modern and clean, great central location.

**$$-$ Mehman**, above Christ Church, T0177-281 3692. Modern with 21 rooms (some with mirrored ceilings), plumbing suspect, very clean, great views from the front, very helpful staff.

**$$-$ Woodland**, Daisy Bank, The Ridge, T0177-281 1002, www.hotelwoodland himla.com. 21 rooms, some wood-panelled, some with great views, all with bath, cleanliness varies, avoid noisy downstairs rooms near reception, friendly, room service, safe luggage storage, off-season bargain.

**$$-$ YMCA**, The Ridge, above Christ Church, T0177-265 2375. 40 rooms in annexe (best with bath), clean linen, hot water in mornings, clean bathrooms on 2nd floor, avoid west side near noisy cinema, mediocre meals (breakfast included), quiet, relaxed, popular but very efficient/institutionalized, gym and billiards.

**Kufri** *p147*

**$$$ Kufri Holiday Resort**, T0177-264 341, www.kufriholidayresort.com. 30 rooms and 8 modern cottages (2-3 bedrooms), limited hot water, cold in winter, but attractive design and setting with flower-filled gardens, outstanding views from cottages above and good walks.

**Chharabra** *p147*

**$$$ Wildflower Hall**, T0177-264 8585, www.oberoihotels.com. Standing on the grounds of the former residence of Lord Kitchener, retains period exterior but has been completely refurbished inside. 87 sumptuous

rooms, beautifully decorated, mountain views, good restaurants and lovely gardens surrounded by deodar forest with beautifully peaceful walks, plus extensive spa, yoga classes under pine trees, Ayurvedic treatments.

**Naldera** *p147*

**$$$$ The Chalets Naldehra**, Durgapur Village, T0177-274 7715, www.chalets naldehra.com. 14 alpine-style pine chalets plus restaurant and a wide range of outdoor activities including world's highest golf course.

**$$$ Koti Resort**, T0177-274 0177, www.kotiresort. net. 40 modern, if slightly spartan rooms in beautifully located hotel surrounded by deodar forest, friendly manager, very relaxing.

**$$ Golf Glade** (HPTDC), T0177-274 7739, www.hptdc.nic.in. 5 simple rooms, plus 7 log huts (2 bedrooms), restaurant, bar, golfing requirements including clubs and instructors.

**$$-$ Mitwa Cottage**, near Koti Resort, T0177-201 2279. Sweet little homestay with kitchens and balconies. Lovely food as well and plenty of nature walks around. Recommended.

**Chail** *p147*

**$$$$-$$$ Tarika's Jungle Retreat**, Chail, T01792-248684, www.tarikasjungle retreat.com. 35 well-appointed 'suite' cottages with lots of wood panelling. Geodesic glass reception. Popular family resort.

**$$$$-$$$ Toshali Royal View Resort**, Shilon Bagh (5 km outside Chail), T(0)9350-916051, www.toshaliroyalview.com. 77 modern rooms in this huge alpine-style lodge, great views from dining terrace, friendly staff.

**$$$-$$ Chail Palace**, T01792-248141, www.hptdc. nic.in. 19 rooms and 3 suites in old stone-built mansion; avoid basement rooms 21, 22, 23, dark, dingy wooden chalets but others OK, billiards, tennis, orchards, well-maintained lawns and gardens, slightly institutional feel, interesting museum.

**$ Himneel**, T01792-248141, www.hptdc.nic.
in. 16 rooms, modest but full of character.
Kailash restaurant serves good-value
breakfasts and lunches.

## Kalka p147

If using your own transport, there are many
hotels, guesthouses and *dhabas* along the
Kalka–Shimla road. Kasauli is an attractive
hill resort with a distinctly English feel, 16 km
off the main road with a few hotels, notably:
**$$$$ Baikunth**, Village Chabbal, near Kasauli,
T(0)98571 66230, www.baikunth.com.
Red brick building in the hills. Lovely
airy, sunny rooms with all mod cons.
Recommended for its spa.
**$$$$-$$$ Kasauli Resorts**, T01792-273651,
www.hotelkasauliresort.net. 33 luxurious
rooms in a modern, upmarket development
in the hills, extra clean, gym, mountain views.
**$$$ Alasia**, T01792-272008. 13 rooms in
hugely atmospheric Raj-era hotel, remarkably
authentic English cuisine, impeccable staff.
**$ Railway Retiring Rooms**. Good for early-
morning departures. Reserve ahead at Kalka
or Shimla.

## Nalagarh p148

**$$$ Nalagarh Fort**, T01795-223179,
www.nalagarh.com. 15 comfortable rooms
(some suites), with modern baths, traditional
furniture, good food (buffets only), small
pool, tennis, rural surroundings, plenty of
atmosphere. Recommended. Book ahead.

## Narkanda p148

**$$$$ Banjara Orchard Retreat**, Thanedar
Village, 15 km from Narkanda (80 km from
Shimla), T(0)9418-077180, www.banjara
camps.com. 6 double rooms, 2 suites and
2 lovely log cabins, set in apple orchards
with stunning views down the Sutlej Valley.
Evenings round the fire under the stars,
trekking and excellent food. Recommended.
**$$$$ Tethy's Narkanda Resort**, T01782-
242641. Comfortable rooms and some
swiss cottage tents with stunning views.
They organize snow skiing, hiking, mountain

biking, river rafting, horse riding.
Meals are included.
**$$$-$$ The Hatu** (HPTDC), T01782-
242430. Typical government fare,
but with great views.

## Rampur Bushahr p149

**$$ Bushehar Regency**, 2 km short
of Rampur on NH22, T01782-234103.
20 rooms, some a/c, well positioned.
Restaurant, huge lawn, bar nearby.
**$ Bhagwati**, below bus stand near river,
T01782-233117, www.hotelbhagwati
ramputbsr.com. Friendly hotel, 24 clean
rooms with bath (hot water), TV, restaurant.

## Sarahan p149

**$$-$ Srikhand** (HPTDC), T01782-274234,
www.hptdc.nic.in. Superb hilltop site,
overlooking the Sutlej Valley, Srikhand peak
and beyond. 19 rooms with bath and hot
water (3 large with balcony, 8 smaller with
views, 4 in annexe cheaper), dorm (Rs 75),
2-bedroom royal cottage, restaurant but
limited menu. Very close to stunning temple.
**$ Bhimakali Temple**. You can stay in
the temple itself – very basic rooms with
clean bathrooms and shared balconies,
highly atmospheric.
**$ Sagarika**, near Police Assistance, T01782-
274491. 6 rooms with Western toilets on
1st floor, 8 others with Indian toilets, family-
run, home-cooked meals.

## 🍴 Restaurants

**Shimla** *p144, maps p144 and p146*
Below The Mall, towards Lower Bazar, good
cheap *dhabas* sell snacks (eg *tikki channa*).
**$$$ Woodville Palace** (see Where to stay).
Attractive dining room full of antiquities,
good buffet.
**$$ Alfa's**, The Mall. Modern interior, range
of continental dishes in addition to good
*thalis*, courteous service.
**$$ Baljees**, 26 The Mall, opposite Town Hall.
Good snacks, justifiably packed, cakes and
sweets available from takeaway counter.

**$$ Café Sol** (Hotel Combermere).
Airy glass building with decent Western and Indian foods.

**$$ Qilaa**, The Mall, below Syndicate Bank.
Serving up Indian, Chinese and Lebanese food, Qilaa is a relaxed affair with low seating and billowing fabrics.

**$$ Wake & Bake**, The Mall. Up some rickety stairs, you will find good coffee, baked goods and international food – cute place. There is internet café below.

**$ Guptajee's Vaishnav Bhojanalaya**,
62 Middle Bazar. 1st-class Indian vegetarian fare including tasty stuffed tomatoes, great *thali*. Recommended.

**$ Indian Coffee House**, The Mall.
International. South Indian snacks, excellent coffee, some Western dishes, old-world feel, uniformed waiters, spartan and dim. Recommended.

**$ Sagar Ratna**, 6/1 The Mall, upstairs, T0177-280 0526. Good vegetarian South Indian food, *dosas*, *idlis*, good value.

## ✸ Festivals

**Shimla** *p144, maps p144 and p146*
**May-Jun** Summer Festival includes cultural programmes from Himachal and neighbouring states, and art and handicrafts exhibitions.
**25 Dec** An ice skating carnival is held on Christmas Day.

## ☯ What to do

**Shimla and around** *p144, maps p144 and p146*
**Golf**
There is a 9-hole course in Naldera. Casual members: green fee and equipment, about Rs 100, see page 147.

**Ice skating**
Skating rink: below Rivoli, winter only, Rs 50 to skate all day to loud Indian film hits.

## Skiing
Early Jan to mid-Mar. Ski courses at Narkanda (64 km) organized by **HPTDC**, 7- and 15-day courses, Jan-Mar, Rs 1700-3000; see page 148.

## Tour operators
**Band Box**, 9 The Mall, T01772-658157, bboxhv@satyam.net.in. Jeep safaris round Kinnaur and Spiti (around Rs 2500 per day), helpful advice, safe drivers and guides who clearly love the mountains. Recommended.
**Hi-Lander**, 62 The Mall, T(0)9816-007799, www.hilandertravels.com. Adventure tours and treks, hotel and transport bookings.
**HPTDC**'s various tours during the season are well run, usually 1000-1700. All start from Rivoli, enquire when booking for other pickup points. Return drop at Lift or Victory Tunnel. 2 tours visit Kufri, Chini Bungalow and Nature Park; 1 returns to Shimla via Fagu, Naldehra and Mashobra, the other by Chail and Kairighat. A further tour visits Fagu, Theog, Matiana and Narkanda. Book in advance at HPTDC office on The Mall.

## ☉ Transport

**Shimla** *p144, maps p144 and p146*
**Air** Shimla (Jabbarhatti) airport (23 km from town) had flights with Kingfisher until their demise, at the time of writing no other airline was operating flights.
**Local bus** From Cart Rd. Lift: 2-stage lift from the Taxi Stand on Cart Rd and near Hotel Samrat on The Mall, takes passengers to and from The Mall, 0800-2200. Porters at bus stand and upper lift station will ask anything from Rs 10 to Rs 50 per bag; lower prices mean hotel commission.
**Long distance bus** From main bus stand, Cart Rd, T01772-806587. Buy tickets from counter before boarding bus (signs in Hindi so ask for help) some long-distance buses can be reserved in advance: HPTDC coaches during the season are good value and reliable. **Kalka**, 3 hrs quicker than train but requires strong stomach; **Chandigarh**, 4 hrs **Dehra Dun**, 9 hrs;

Delhi, 10-12 hrs; overnight to **Dharamshala**, 10 hrs. **Manali**, departs outside the 'Tunnel', 8-10 hrs, tickets from main bus stand. HPTDC deluxe buses between Shimla and **Delhi** in the summer, 9 hrs.

From Rivoli Bus Stand (Lakkar Bazar) T01772-811259: frequent buses to **Kufri**, **Rampur**, hourly from 0530, 8 hrs, and **Chitkul**, 2 daily; **Jeori** for **Sarahan** (8 hrs). **Car hire** HPTDC (see page 145), has a/c cars. Shimla Taxis, T(0)9418-082385, www. shimlataxis.in, have a wide range of cars. **Taxi** Local taxis have fixed fares and run from near the lift on Cart Rd, T01772-657645. Long-distance taxis run from Union Stands near the lift, T01772-805164, and by the main bus stand on Cart Rd. **Chandigarh**, Rs 2500; **Kalka** (90 km), Rs 1600; **Mussoorie**, Rs 5500, 8 hrs, including stops; **Rekong-Peo**, around Rs 7000 (11 hrs).

**Train** Enquiry T131. Computerized reservations at main station (T01772-652915), 1000-1330, 1400-1700, Sun 1000-1400, and by tourist office on The Mall. The newer extension station, where some trains start and terminate, is just below the main bus stand. Travel to/ from Shimla involves a change of gauge to the slow and cramped but extremely picturesque 'toy train' at Kalka. To reach Shimla from **Delhi** in a day by train, catch the *Himalayan Queen* or *Shatabdi Exp 12011* leaving New Delhi station at 0740 to arrive in Kalka by 1200 (see Kalka, below). In the reverse direction, the 1030 train from Shimla has you in Kalka at 1600 in time to board the Delhi-bound *Himalayan Queen 14096*. Book tickets for the toy train in advance; the 'Ticket Extension Booth' on Kalka station sells out by 1200 when the *Shatabdi* arrives, and the train often arrives on the Kalka platform already full of locals who board it while it waits in the siding. Worth paying Rs 150-170 plus reservation fee of Rs 20 to guarantee a seat on 1st class. **Kalka to Shimla**: *Kalka Shimla Passenger 52457*, 0400, 5½ hrs; *Shivalik Exp Deluxe 52451*, 0530, 4¾ hrs (has bigger windows and comfy seats); *Kalka Shimla Express 52453*, 0600, 5 hrs; *Himalayan Queen 52455*, 1210, 5 hrs. Extra

trains in season (1 May-15 Jul; 15 Sep-30 Oct; 15 Dec-1 Jan): You can book a special train carriage which can be attached to regular trains with elegant furnishings and big windows which accommodates 8 people through IRCTC Chandigarh. **Shimla to Kalka**: *Himalayan Queen*, 1030, 5½ hrs; *Shivalik Exp Deluxe 52452*, 1740, 4¾ hrs.

### Kalka *p147*
**Bus or taxi** Easily reached from **Shimla**, by bus or taxi (Rs 1600), and from **Chandigarh** by taxi (Rs 500).
**Train** **Kalka to Delhi**: *Shatabdi Exp 12006*, 0615, 4 hrs; *Shatabdi Exp 12012*, 1745, 4 hrs; *Himalayan Queen 14096*, ND, 1650, 5½ hrs; *Kalka Mail 12312*, OD, 2345, 6¾ hrs; day trains are better. All via Chandigarh, 45 mins. **Delhi to Kalka**: *Himalayan Queen 14095*, DSR, 0600, 5¼ hrs; *Shatabdi Exp 12011*, ND, 0740 (4 hrs); *Howrah Kalka Mail 12311*, OD, 2215 (7½ hrs).

### Rampur Bushahr *p149*
**Bus** Buses are often late and overcrowded. To **Chandigarh**, **Delhi**; **Mandi** (9 hrs); **Recong Peo** (5 hrs) and **Puh**; **Sarahan** (2-3 hrs), better to change at Jeori; **Shimla**, several (5-6 hrs); **Tapri** (and Kalpa) 0545 (3¼ hrs), change at Karchham for Sangla and Chitkul.

### Sarahan *p149*
**Bus** Daily buses between **Shimla** (Rivoli Bus Stand) and **Jeori** on the Highway (6 hrs) quicker by car. Local buses between Jeori and the army cantonment below Sarahan.

## ⊙ Directory

**Shimla** *p144, maps p144 and p146*
**Medical services** Tara Hospital, The Ridge, T0177-280 3785; Dr Puri, Mehghana Complex, The Mall, T0177-280 1936, speaks fluent English, is efficient, and very reasonable. **Post** GPO, The Mall, T0177-265 2518. Open Sun 1000-1600. **Poste Restante**: Counter 10 (separate entrance), chaotic, 0800-1700, Sun 1000-1600. **CTO** nearby. **Useful contacts** Police: T0177-265 2860.

# Kinnaur and Spiti

*The regions of Kinnaur and Spiti lie in the rainshadow of the outer Himalayan ranges. The climate in Spiti is much drier than in the Kullu Valley and is similar to that of Ladakh. The temperatures are more extreme both in summer and winter and most of the landscape is barren and bleak. The wind can be bitingly cold even when the sun is hot. The annual rainfall is very low so cultivation is restricted to the ribbons of land that fringe rivers with irrigation potential. The crops include potatoes, wheat, barley and millet. The people are of Mongol origin and almost everyone follows a Tibetan form of Buddhism.*

*Kinnaur and Spiti can be seen by following a circular route, first along the Old Hindustan Tibet Road by the Sutlej River, then crossing into the wild Spiti Valley, which has the evocative Tibetan Buddhist sites of Tabo and Kaza set against the backdrop of a rugged mountain landscape. The road continues round to the Rohtang Pass and Manali, or on up to Ladakh. It's also worth making a side trip up the Baspa Valley via Sangla to Chitkul for its views and landscapes, villages, pagodas and culture.* ▸▸ *For listings, see pages 164-167.*

## Kinnaur and around ▸▸ *For listings, see pages 164-167. Colour map 1, B3.*

Most Kinnauri Buddhist temples only accept visitors at around 0700 and 1900. You must wear a hat and a special belt available locally. ▸▸ *For trekking, see page 210.*

## Along the Sutlej

An exciting mountain road runs through cliffside cuttings along the left bank of the Sutlej – frequently blocked by rockfalls and landslides during the monsoons. At **Choling** the Sutlej roars through a narrow gorge, and at **Wangtu** the road re-crosses the river where vehicle details are checked. Immediately after crossing the Wangtu bridge a narrow side road goes to **Kafnoo village** (2427 m), in the Bhabha Valley (a camping site and the start for an attractive 10-day trek to the Pin Valley). From Wangtu the road route runs to **Tapri** (1870 m) and **Karchham** (1899 m) both of which have hot springs. Here the Baspa River joins the Sutlej from the south. A hair-raising excursion by a precipitous winding rough road leads 16 km up the Baspa Valley to Sangla; buses take approximately 1½ hours.

## Baspa Valley

The valley carries the marks of a succession of glacial events which have shaped it, although the glaciers which formed the valley have now retreated to the high slopes above Chitkul at over 4500 m. Recently the valley has been terribly scarred by the Baspa Hydroelectric Project, with blasting, dust and truck logjams commonplace, but persevere and carry on up the valley and the rewards are worth it. All villages in Baspa are characterized by exaggerated steeply sloping slate roofs, rich wood carving and elaborate pagoda temples. Although Kinner Kailash (sacred to Hindus and Buddhists) is not visible from here, the valley is on the circumambulating **Parikrama/Kora** route which encircles the massif. Fields of the pink coloured *ogla*, a small flower seed grown specifically in the Baspa Valley for grinding into grain, add a beautiful colouring in the season.

**Sangla**, at 2680 m, is built on the massive buttress of a terminal moraine which marks a major glacial advance of about 50,000 years ago. The Baspa River has cut a deep trench on its south flank. Immediately above is the flat valley floor, formed on the dry bed of a lake which was once dammed behind the moraine. The village has excellent carving and is full of character. No foreign exchange is available but there are telephone facilities. Sangla is famous for its apples, while a **saffron farm** just north of the village is claimed to be better than that at Pampore in Kashmir.

The old seven-storey **Killa** (Fort) ① *0800-0900, 1800-1900*, where the Kinnaur rajas were once crowned, is 1 km north of new Sangla just before the road enters the village. It was occupied by the local rulers for centuries. It now has a temple to Kamakshi where the idol is from Guwahati, Assam, see page 361.

**Barseri**, 8 km from Sangla, is situated on an outwash cone which has engulfed part of the Baspa's valley floor. This well-kept 'green village' is happy to show visitors its solar heaters, *chakkis* (water mills) and water-driven prayer wheels. The Buddha Mandir, with *Shakyamuni* and other images and a large prayer wheel, is beautiful inside. Villagers weave shawls and do woodcarving.

# Kinnaur & Spiti

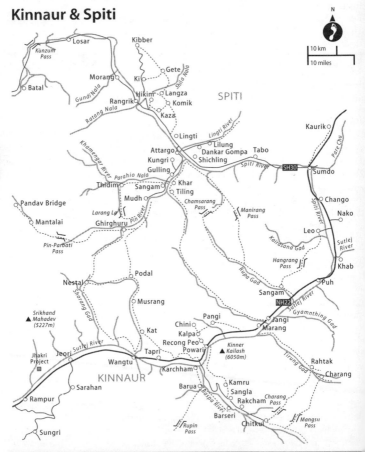

The beautifully carved pagoda-style Rakcham temple is dedicated to Shamshir Debta, Devi and Naga, combining Buddhist and Hindu deities. The ibex horns on the roof are ancient male fertility symbols. There is also a pre-Buddhist, animist Bon cho shrine and a Siva temple.

**Chitkul**, some 18 km from Barseri, at an altitude of 3450 m, is the furthest point foreigners can travel without special permits. With its typical houses, Buddhist temple and a small tower, it is worth the trip. The Kagyupa (Oral Transmission School), has a highly valued, old image of the Shakyamuni Buddha. There are four directional kings on either side of the door as well as a Wheel of Life. You can walk along the Baspa River which has paths on both sides. The rough path along the tributary starting at the bridge across the river, below the bus stand, is very steep in places with loose stones. Do not attempt alone. A shop sells a few provisions.

## Recong Peo to the Spiti River

**Recong Peo**, also called 'Peo', at 2290 m, is the District HQ and a busy little market town. The Sub-Divisional Magistrate's office in a three-storey building below the bus stand deals with Inner Line Permits (see page 148). A short walk above the town takes you to the Kalachakra Temple with a large Buddha statue outside and good views of Kinner Kailash. A shop here sells provisions, medicines and has a telephone, but there's nowhere to change money.

**Kothi village**, reached by a path from the Kalachakra Temple, has ancient Hindu temples associated with the Pandavas. One has a tank of sacred fish, 30 minutes' walk from the bazar.

**Kalpa** (Chini), 12 km from Recong Peo at 2960 m, is reached after a stiff climb. It has an interesting temple complex and Budh mandir and is surrounded by apple, *bemi* (wild apricot) and plum orchards and chilgoza pine forests, with striking views across to Kinner Kailash (6050 m).

A high road from Kalpa/Recong Peo with little traffic passes through Chilgoza pine forests, north to the hamlet of **Pangi**, 10 km away. Pangi is surrounded by apple orchards. The colourful Sheshri Nag temple at the top of the village has an inscription in a strange script above the entrance and standing stones in the courtyard. Apart from two Buddhist temples, the carved pagoda temple to Sheshri's mother encloses a huge boulder representing the Devi. The road then goes over bare and rugged hills beyond to **Morang** which has impressive monasteries with wood carvings and sculptures.

Inner Line Permits are checked at **Jangi**. From here the road goes to Puh, a steep climb with hairpin bends.

**Spiti** → *For listings, see pages 164-167. Colour map 1, B4. For trekking information, see page 210.*

The bridge at **Khab**, 11 km beyond Puh, marks the confluence of the Sutlej and Spiti rivers. The entry into the Spiti Valley at Khab is a rare example of crossing from the Himalaya to the Trans-Himalaya without going over a major pass. The Sutlej now disappears east towards the Tibet border, while the road follows the Spiti. Major deforestation of the mountain slopes has resulted in sections of the road being washed away. The new road, a remarkable feat of engineering, hairpins up to the village of **Nako**, with some basic guesthouses, and rejoins the river at Chango.

**Sumdo**, the last village of Kinnaur, has a border police checkpost and a tea shop, and is the starting point of State Highway 30, which passes through an arid valley with small patches of cultivation of peas and barley near the snow melt streams. It is 31 km from Sumdo to Tabo.

## Tabo → *Colour map 1, B4. Altitude: 3050 m.*

At the crossroads of two ancient trade routes, Tabo was one of the great centres of Buddhist learning and culture. Founded in 996, the **Chos Khor Gompa** (see below) is the oldest living Buddhist establishment in this part of the world. Today, the small town is rapidly being modernized with paved streets and electric lights. Government offices have appeared alongside traditional mud homes and the local shops stock basic provisions for trekkers. There is a post office.

**Chos Khor Gompa** Founded in AD 996 as a scholastic institution, the monastery's original layout was planned as a *mandala* centred around a **Du khang** (Assembly Hall). The deodar wood used was imported from Kullu, Kinnaur, Chamba and Kashmir while the lack of quality structural stone resulted in the extensive use of earth, strengthened with gypsum for the high walls. Today the *gompa* houses 60 *lamas* and has a good collection of scriptures, *thangkas* and art pieces. It is most important and has an immense sense of the spiritual. Carry a torch. No photography allowed.

Many of the **colourful murals** come close to the pure Indian style identified with Ajanta. The technique required the surface to be coated with several thin layers of lime and yak-skin glue and burnished vigorously to provide the 'ground' which was then smoothed and freshened with animal fat and butter. Natural vegetable dyes and powdered stone colours were mixed with *dzo* milk and yak urine for painting. The early Indian style murals used a profusion of reds and yellows with little stress on landscaping, the area around the principal figures being filled with small divinities. These images wear seraphic smiles and have half-shut dreamy eyes denoting introspective meditation. The later 17th-century paintings illustrate the Central Tibetan/Chinese art form where ultramarine takes over from the earlier dominance of reds and yellows, and landscapes become lively and vivid with the appearance of cliffs, swirling clouds, stylized flames, flora and fauna. Here the twists and turns of the limbs and the flowing elaborate drapery show great fluency. This is one of the few *gompas* in the Tibetan Buddhist-influenced areas of Ladakh, Lahaul and Spiti where the highly structured art of painting the complex Tibetan religious iconography is taught. What appears outwardly as a free art form is taught on lined paper where each shape and form is closely measured.

**Nine Temples Tsuglhakhang** (academy) The 'resplendent' central *Mahavairochana* – a composite of four figures, each facing a cardinal direction, represents the unity of all Buddhas. On the walls inside are stucco figures of different Buddhas and Bodhisattvas. The floral ceiling decorations are in the Ajanta style.

**Dri Tsang khang** (Inner Sanctum) and **Kora** (Circumambulatory Path) At the centre of the 'mandala', the five *Dhyani* Buddhas escorted here by four Bodhisattvas, emerge from the darkness lit by a shaft of sunlight.

Masks, weapons and ritual costumes are stored in the **Gon Khang** which is closed to visitors. **Zhalma** (Picture Hall) has a 17th-century entrance temple where the murals are recent and in pure Tibetan style.

**Dromton Lhakhang Chenpo** (17th century) Dominated by Medicine Buddhas. The ceiling, in high Tibetan style, is exceptional, depicting *nagas*, titans, peacocks and parrots amongst rainbows.

**Ser Khang** (Golden Temple) The walls were believed to have been coated with a layer of gold dust as thick as a yak's skin for painting the numerous larger-than-life figures. They were renewed in the 16th and 17th centuries.

**Chamba Chenpo La Khang** Dedicated to the Maitreya (Future) Buddha, this temple has a 6-m-high seated statue. The murals of the eight Buddhas may be some of the earliest in Tabo.

**Buddhist caves** To the north, the small natural caves above the road were an integral part of the monastic complex. **Pho Gompa**, the only surviving, with early murals showing pure Indian influence, has been restored. These post-Ajantan paintings, however, are already fading. On open ground to the east, on both sides of a dyke, there are pre-Buddhist rock carvings on metamorphosed igneous rocks showing ibex, swastikas, *yonis*, horses, panthers and human figures.

## Dankar

Once the capital of Spiti, Dankar is a tiny village. The early 16th-century fort/monastery **Dankar Gompa** (3890 m), which once served as a jail, stands on an impressive overhang, perched on crumbling towers. Today it has more than 160 *lamas* in residence. The 'highest temple' has a collection of Bhotia Buddhist scriptures, a four-in-one *Dhyani Buddha* and interesting murals of Medicine Buddhas and protector deities. The *gompa* is a very steep two-hour climb from a point 2 km away, beyond Shichling on the main road. The 4WD road from the SH30, about 1 km west of Shichling, winds up 8 km to Dankar (a two-hour walk) and is easier. A beautiful large pond at just under 4100 m is reached by a 2.5-km track.

## Lalung Gompa

Lalung Gompa, known for its carved wood panelling, is off the SH30, 22 km from Kaza, reached by 8-km narrow, drivable track. From Dankar Gompa this is a two-hour trek. Carry plenty of water as there are no streams and it can get very hot.

## Pin Valley

About 5 km from Dankar is a sign for the Pin Valley National Park which is on the other side of the river. The Pin River joins the Spiti at Attargo. Above Attargo, 10 km along the Pin Valley, is the **Kungri Gompa** (circa 1330), which though not old is in an established monastic site with old carved wooden sculptures and is commonly understood to be a Bon monastery still practising elements of the pre-Buddhist Bon religion. The trek from the Bhabha Valley ends at the road head at Kungri, see page 212. One bus a day departs from Kaza at 1200, goes along the Pin Valley as far as Mikkim and turns straight back at 1400, not allowing enough time to visit the *gompa*. You therefore face a long walk unless you can hitch a lift on a passing tractor, truck or yak.

At the confluence of the Pin River and one of its tributaries, 1 km from Mikkim, **Sangam** can be reached by car over a new iron bridge, or more adventurously by a pulley system with a person-sized bucket, 750 m west of the bus stop along the river. It requires a reasonable degree of fitness to negotiate, especially if crossing alone. The local greeting is *joolay, joolay*!

**Pin Valley National Park** is described as the "land of ibex and snow leopard" and was created to conserve the flora and fauna of the cold desert. It adjoins the Great Himalayan National Park (southwest), and Rupi Bhabha Sanctuary (south) with the Bara Shigri Glacier forming its north boundary. The park covers 675 sq km with a buffer zone of 1150 sq km mainly to its east where there are villages, and varies in altitude from 3600 m to 6630 m.

The wildlife includes Siberian ibex, snow leopard, red fox, pika, weasels, lammergeier, Himalayan griffon, golden eagle, Chakor partridge, Himalayan snow cock and a variety of rose finches. The Siberian ibex can be sighted at high altitudes, beyond Hikim and Thango village. From July to September the young ibex kids need protection and so the females move up to the higher pastures near cliffs while the adult males concentrate on feeding lower down. The 60-km-long Lingti Valley is famous for its fossils.

## Kaza
Kaza, at 3600 m, is 13 km from Lingti village and is the main town of the Spiti Valley. Old Kaza has village homes while New Kaza sports government offices. It is a busy bus terminus with plenty of hotels and homestays, a small market, a basic health centre and jeeps for hire. Inner Line Permits are issued by the **SDM's office** ① *T01906-222202, 1030-1700 – closed 2nd Sat of each month*. Tourist facilities are open May to October. For an exceptional insight into the area, check out www.spitiecosphere.com with a focus on conservation.

There is an attractive one-day circular trek from here to **Hikim** and **Komik** villages visiting the monastery midway. **Hikim Gompa** (early 14th century), modelled on a Chinese castle, was built under Mongol patronage. ▶▶ *For trekking in Himachal, see page 210.*

## Kibber-Gete Wildlife Sanctuary
One of the world's highest wildlife sanctuaries, covering an area of 98 sq km, Kibber-Gete has **Mount Gya** (6754 m) to the north and **Kamelong** (5867 m) to the south. On the drive from Kibber to Tashigang, you may spot musk deer and bharal sheep but to see larger mammals (bear, wolf and the rare snow leopard) you would need to trek. Also to be seen are Himalayan birds of prey as well as snowcock and other high-altitude birds. Buses from Kaza take about an hour.

## Tashigang
Tashigang, 18 km away, is one of the highest villages in the world connected by road. **Ki Monastery** on the way is the largest in Spiti and houses 300 *lamas*. Although it has suffered from wars, fires and earthquakes it still has a good collection of *thangkas* and *kangyurs* (scriptures). Although no permit is needed, the monks have instituted their private 'entrance fee' system which, by all accounts, appears quite flexible and linked to the visitor's perceived ability to pay. There are a few cheap guesthouses and camping is possible. If you cannot stay take a bus up and walk down via the Ki Monastery, 11 km from Kaza.

## To Lahaul
**Losar**, at 4079 m, is the last village in Spiti, reached after driving through fields growing peas and cabbage among poplars, willows and apple orchards. There is a rest house and guesthouse and a couple of cafés serving Tibetan/Spitian food.

The road continues up for 18 km to the **Kunzum La** (Pass) at 4551 m. It means 'meeting place for ibex' and gives access to Lahaul and good views of some of the highest peaks of the Chandrabhaga group that lies immediately opposite the Kunzum La to the west. To the southeast is the Karcha Peak (6271 m). The pass has an ancient *chorten* marker. The temple to **Gyephang**, the presiding deity, is circumambulated by those crossing the pass; the giver of any offering in cash which sticks to the stone image receives special blessing.

The road descends through 19 hairpin curves to reach the rock strewn valley of the River Chandra at **Batal**, where a tea shop serves noodles and sells biscuits and bottled water. It continues to **Chhota Dhara** and **Chhatru**, with rest houses and eateries, and then

**Gramphoo** joining the Manali–Keylong–Leh highway around three hours after leaving the pass. From Gramphoo to Manali is 62 km.

## Shimla to the Kullu Valley → *For listings, see pages 164-167.*

### Bilaspur and Bhakra-Nangal Dam → *Colour map 1, B3.*
**Bilaspur** used to be the centre of a district in which the tribal Daora peoples panned in the silts of the Beas and Sutlej for gold. Their main source, the Seer Khud, has now been flooded by the Bhakra Nangal Lake and they have shifted their area of search upstream. For a bite to eat visit the **Lake View Café**.

The dam on the River Sutlej is one of the highest dams in the world at 225 m and was built as part of the Indus Waters Treaty between India and Pakistan (1960). The Treaty allocated the water of the rivers Sutlej, Beas and Ravi to India. The dam provides electricity for Punjab, Haryana and Delhi. It is also the source for the Rajasthan Canal project, which takes water over 1500 km south to the Thar Desert. There is accommodation should you wish to stay.

### Una to Mandi
Having passed through Una, along the main bus route, **Ghanahatti**, 18 km further on, has the adequate **Monal Restaurant**. There are some magnificent views, sometimes across intensively cultivated land, sometimes through plantations of chilgoza, khir and other species. In **Shalaghat**, further on, accommodation is available. The road descends into a deep valley before climbing again to the small market town of **Bhararighat**. A jeep can take over two hours for this part of the journey. In **Brahmpukar** the road to Beri and Mandi is a very attractive country lane. The more heavily used though still quiet road to the main Bilaspur–Manali road joins it at **Ghaghas**. During the monsoons landslides on the NH21 may cause long delays. Carry plenty of water and some food. The tree-lined and attractive approach to **Sundernagar** from the south gives some indication of the town's rapid growth and prosperity.

### Mandi (Sahor) → *Colour map 1, B3. Phone code: 01905. Population: 26,900. Altitude: 760 m.*
Founded by a Rajput prince in circa 1520, Mandi is held sacred by both Hindus and Buddhists. The old town with the main (Indira) bazar is huddled on the left bank of the Beas at the southern end of the Kullu Valley, just below its junction with the River Uhl. The Beas bridge – claimed to be the world's longest non-pillar bridge – is across Sukheti Khad at the east end of town. The main bus station is across the river, just above the open sports ground. It is worth stopping a night in this quaint town with 81 temples, a 17th-century palace and a colourful bazar. **Tourist information** ⓘ *T01905-225036.*

**Triloknath Temple** (1520), on the riverbank, built in the Nagari style with a tiled roof, has a life-size three-faced Siva image (Lord of Three Worlds), riding a bull with Parvati on his lap. It is at the centre of a group of 13th- to 16th-century sculpted stone shrines. The Kali Devi statue which emphasizes the natural shape of the stone, illustrates the ancient Himalayan practice of stone worship.

**Panchavaktra Temple**, at the confluence of the Beas and a tributary with views of the Trilokinath, has a five-faced image (*Panchanana*) of Siva. The image is unusually conceived like a temple *shikhara* on an altar plinth. Note the interesting frieze of yogis on a small temple alongside.

**Bhutnath Temple** (circa 1520) by the river in the town centre is the focus at **Sivaratri fair** (see page 166). The modern shrines nearby are brightly painted.

In lower Sumkhetar, west of the main bazar, is the 16th-century **Ardhanarishvara Temple** where the Siva image is a composite male/female form combining the passive Siva (right) and the activating energy of Parvati (left). Although the *mandapa* is ruined, the carvings on the *shikhara* tower and above the inner sanctum door are particularly fine.

From the old suspension bridge on the Dharamshala road, if you follow a narrow lane up into the main market you will see the slate roof over a deep spring which is the **Mata Kuan Rani Temple**, dedicated to the 'Princess of the Well'. The story of this Princess of Sahor (Mandi) and her consort **Padmasambhava**, who introduced Mahayana Buddhism in Tibet, describes how the angry king condemned the two to die in a fire which raged for seven days and when the smoke cleared a lake appeared with a lotus – Rewalsar or *Tso Pema* (Tibetan 'Lotus Lake').

## Around Mandi
The small dark **Rewalsar Lake**, 24 km southeast, with its floating reed islands, is a popular pilgrimage centre. The colourful Tibetan Buddhist monastery was founded in the 14th century, though the pagoda-like structure is late 19th century. The Gurudwara commemorates Guru Gobind Singh's stay here. Start early for the hilltop temples by the transmission tower as it is a steep and hot climb. The **Sisu fair** is held in February/March. There are many buses to the lake from Mandi Bus Stand, one hour; you can also board them below the palace in Indira Bazar.

At **Prashar**, a three-tiered pagoda Rishi temple sits beside a sacred lake in a basin surrounded by high mountains with fantastic views of the Pir Panjal range. The rich woodcarvings here suggest a date earlier than the Manali Dhungri Temple (1553), which is not as fine. No smoking, alcohol or leather items are allowed near the temple or lake. There are basic pilgrim rest houses. A forest rest house is 1 km west of temple. To reach the temple, follow a steep trail from Kandi, 10 km north of Mandi, through the forest of rhododendron, oak, deodar and kail (three hours). After arriving at a group of large shepherd huts the trail to the left goes to the temple, the right to the forest rest house.

You can walk to **Aut**, see below, from Prashar in six to seven hours. A level trail east crosses a col in under a kilometre. Take the good path down to the right side of the *nullah* (valley) and cross the stream on a clear path. Climb a little and then follow a broad path on the left bank to the road. Turn right and down to **Peon village** in the *Chir nullah* and continue to Aut.

## Tirthan Valley and Jalori Pass
From Mandi the NH21 runs east then south along the left bank of the Beas, much diminished in size by the dam at **Pandoh**, 19 km from Mandi, from which water is channelled to the Sutlej. The dam site is on a spectacular meander of the Beas (photography strictly prohibited). The NH21 crosses over the dam to the right bank of the Beas then follows the superb **Larji Gorge**, in which the Beas now forms a lake for a large part of the way upstream to Aut. A large hydroelectric project is being constructed along this stretch. At **Aut** (pronounced 'out') there is trout fishing (season March to October, best in March and April); permits are issued by the Fishery Office in Largi, Rs 100 per day. The main bazar road has a few cheap hotels and eating places. It is also a good place to stop and stock up with trekking supplies such as dried apricots and nuts.

From Aut, a road branches off across the Beas into the **Tirthan Valley** climbing through beautiful wooded scenery up to the Jalori Pass. Allow at least 1½ hours by jeep to **Sojha**, 42 km from Mandi, and another 30 minutes to Jalori. Contact tourist office in Kullu for trekking routes. One suggested trek is Banjar–Laisa–Paldi–Dhaugi/Banogi–Sainj, total 30 km, two days.

**Banjar**, with attractive wood-fronted shops lining the narrow street, has the best examples in the area of timber-bonded Himalayan architecture in the fort-like rectangular temple of **Murlidhar** (Krishna). Halfway to **Chaini**, 3 km away, the large **Shring Rishi Temple** to the deified local sage is very colourful with beautiful wooden balconies and an impressive 45-m-tall tower which was damaged in the last earthquake. The entrance, 7 m above ground, is reached by climbing a notched tree trunk. Such free-standing temple towers found in eastern Tibet were sometimes used for defence and incorporated into Thakur's castles in the western Himalaya. The fortified villages here even have farmhouses like towers.

From Banjar the road climbs increasingly steeply to **Jibhi**, 9 km away, where there are sleeping options and trekking. Two kilometres beyond is **Ghayaghi**, also with accommodation. A few kilometres on is **Sojha**, a Rajput village in the heart of the forest, which offers a base for treks in the Great Himalayan National Park.

Finally you reach the **Jalori Pass** (altitude: 3350 m), open only in good weather from mid-April, which links Inner and Outer Seraj and is 76 km from Kullu. You may wish to take the bus up to the pass and walk down, or even camp a night at the pass. Check road conditions before travelling. A ruined fort, **Raghupur Garh**, sits high to the west of the pass and from the meadows there are fantastic views, especially of the Pir Panjal range. Take the path straight from the first hairpin after the pass and head upwards for 30-40 minutes. The road is suitable for 4WD vehicles. There is a very pleasant, gradual walk, 5 km east, through woodland (one hour), starting at the path to the right of the temple. It is easy to follow. **Sereuil Sar** (Pure Water) is where local women worship Burhi Nagini Devi, the snake goddess, and walk around the lake pouring a line of *ghee*. It is claimed that the lake is kept perpetually clear of leaves by a pair of resident birds. *Dhabas* provide simple refreshments and one has two very basic cheap rooms at the pass.

**Great Himalayan National Park and Tirthan Sanctuary** ① *foreigners Rs 200 per day, Indians Rs 50, students half price, video Rs 300/150*, lies southeast of Kullu town in the Seraj Forest Division, an area bounded by mountain ridges (except to the west) and watered by the upper reaches of the rivers Jiwa, Sainj and Tirthan. The hills are covered in part by dense forest of blue pine, deciduous broadleaved and fir trees and also shrubs and grassland; thickets of bamboo make it impenetrable in places. Attractive species of iris, frittilaria, gagea and primula are found in the high-altitude meadows. Wildlife include the panther, Himalayan black bear, brown bear, tahr, musk deer, red fox, goral and bharal. The rich birdlife includes six species of pheasant. The park is 60,561 ha with an altitude of 1500-5800 m and the sanctuary covers 6825 ha; its headquarters are in Shamshi. Access is easiest from April to June and September to October. Check it out at www. greathimalayannationalpark.com. **Goshiani** is the base for treks into the park. The first 3 km along the river are fairly gentle before the track rises to harder rocky terrain; there are plenty of opportunity to see birds and butterflies. The trout farm here sells fresh fish at Rs 150 per kg. Fishing permits, Rs 100, are obtainable from the Fisheries Department.

*For hotel and restaurant price codes and other relevant information, see pages 22-26.*

### ⊙ Where to stay

**Baspa Valley** *p155*

**$$$$ Banjara Camps**, Barseri, 8 km beyond Sangla, T01786-242536, www.banjara camps.com. Superb riverside site with impressive mountains looming above you. 18 twin-bed rooms and some 4-bed deluxe tents, delicious meals included, hot water bottles in the bed, friendly staff, mountain biking, trekking, Lahaul, Spiti, Ladakh tours. Buses stop 2 km from the site, where road drops down to right, car park at foot of hill is 500-m walk from camp (horn will summon porters). Highly recommended.

**$$ Hotel River Rupin View**, Rakcham Village, 12 km from Sangla, T(0)9999-989548. Pretty little place well off the beaten track, set in garden with basic rooms.

**$$ Kinner Camp**, Barseri, T(0)9769-375993, www.kinnerkamps.com. Small tents with beds/sleeping bags, shared baths, birdwatching, trekking, jeep safaris, meals, caféteria, superb location.

**$ Amar Guest House**, Chitkul. Clean double rooms (Rs 100), hot water, friendly family atmosphere. Recommended.

**$ Hotel Apple Pie**, Sangla, T07186-226304. Run by a veteran mountaineer.

**$ Mount Kailash**, Sangla, T01786-242527. 8 clean, pleasant rooms (hot shower), 4-bed dorm, too.

**$ Negi Cottage**, Sangla, T(0)9418-904161. 3 rooms with bath, all brightly coloured inside and out so has more character than most.

**$ PWD Rest House**, Chitkul. 4 rooms, lawns, attractive.

**$ Shruti Guest House**, www.shrutiguest house.com, Sangla, near market. Comfortable, clean rooms with TV and attached bath. Friendly welcome and good home-cooked food as well as mighty Himalaya views.

**Recong Peo to the Spiti River** *p157*

**$$$-$$ Inner Tukpa** between Kalpa and Recong Peo, T01786-223077, www.inner tukpahotel.com. Nestled in the woods between Kalpa and Recong Peo, There are spacious rooms here and even more spacious views.

**$$ Monk Resort** Roshi Rd, 1.5 km from Kalpa, T(0)9816-737004, www.kinnaur geotourism.com. 4 spacious swiss cottage tents, huts and airy rooms available in pretty surroundings. Recommended.

**$$-$ Aucktong Guest House ('Aunties')**, near Circuit House, 1 km north on Pangi road, Kalpa, T01786-226019. Pleasant, 6 clean spacious rooms, large windows, restaurant, very friendly ("arrived for one night and stayed a week!").

**$$-$ Kinner Kailash Cottage** (HPTDC), Kalpa, T01786-226159, www.hptdc.nic.in. May-Nov. Commanding position, 5 rooms (bath tub Rs 1100), limited menu, camping.

**$$-$ Kinner Villa**, 4 km outside Kalpa, T01786-226006, circuits@vsnl.net.in. 20 rooms with bath, attractively located, seasonal tents and a 6-bed dorm.

**$ Forest Rest House**, Chini, 2 km from Kalpa. Caretaker can prepare meals, modern building, camping overnight (with permission) in school grounds 1600-1000.

**$ Shivling View**, near bus stand, Recong Peo, T01786-222421. Good view of Shivling peak. OK but better to stay up near Kalpa.

**Tabo** *p158*

Guesthouses in the village allow camping. There is a good list of homestays throughout Tabo and Spiti on www.spitiecosphere.com and www.himachaltourism.gov.in.

**$$$ Dewachen Retreat**, Tabo T(0)9459-566689, www.dewachenretreats.com. Large comfortable cosy rooms, hot water and great views. They have another property in Rangrik, Kaza.

**$$-$ Millennium Monastery Guest House** run by monks in monastery complex,

13 colourful rooms, shared dirty toilets, hot water on request, meals.

**$ Tanzin**, near monastery. Tibetan food, friendly, family-run, best in village.

### Dankar *p159*

**$** The *gompa* has 2 rooms; only 1 has a bed.
**$ Dolma Guest House**. 8 perfectly fine rooms.

### Pin Valley *p159*

**$ Norzang Guest House**. Rooms for Rs 100.
**$ PWD Rest House**.

### Kaza *p160*

Kaza is ideal for camping and there are great opportunities for homestay in this area, contact the fantastic **Spiti Ecosphere** (T09418-860099) for more information – see What to do.

**$$$ Kaza Retreat**, T(0)9418-718123, www.banjaracamps.com. 11 clean, modern rooms with attached bathrooms. You can expect high standards here, good food and relaxing atmosphere, with stunning views a bonus. Recommended.

**$$ Monk Resorts**, Shego, 6 km from Kaza, T(0)9816-737004, www.kinaurgeotourism.com. 8 spacious Swiss cottage tents in pretty location surrounded by flowers. They have other camps in Nako and Kalpa.

**$$-$ Sakya's Abode**, T01906-222254. 10 rooms in a fine-looking building with a wide range of rooms and a cheap dorm (Rs 80). It offers a friendly welcome and delicious home-cooked food.

**$$-$ Snow Lion Guest House**, T01906-222525. 8 large, comfortable rooms with great home-cooked food and majestic views.

**$ Kumphen Guest House**. Simple rooms, good service and delicious Tibetan food right inside the Monastery compound.

**$ Mahabuddha Guest House**. Basic but large room, shared bath, very clean, meals.

### Una to Mandi *p161*

**$$$-$$ Raj Mahal**, lane to right of palace, Indira Bazar, T01905-222401, www.rajmahalpalace.com. Former 'palace' has character

but in need of attention. 14 rooms, including atmospheric deluxe rooms with bath (sharpened sword in one might be mistaken for a towel rail). Rooms in palace are charismatic, in the other block they are quite dull, but cheap. Restaurant, bar, garden temple. Recommended. Although be persistent – they don't always answer phone.

**$$$-$$ Visco Resorts**, 2 km south of Mandi, T01905-225057, www.viscoresorts.com. 18 large rooms (some for 4) in modern resort, by the river, good cheap vegetarian restaurant, extremely well run.

**$ Mehman**, Shalaghat. Occupies an extraordinarily bold setting. Restaurant.

**$ Relax Inn**, Sundernagar, on Mandi side of town, T01907-262409. Modern, clean.

### Mandi *p161*

**$$ Hotel Regent Palms**, near Kargil Park, close to Raj Mahal, T01905-222777. Bright new hotel with all the mod cons and nice decor.

**$$ Munish Resorts**, on hillside 2 km above New Beas Bridge, T01905-235035, www.munishresorts.com. 15 clean rooms with bath, restaurant, lovely views, colourful garden with tempting fruit, friendly family.

**$ Evening Plaza**, Indira Bazar, T01905-223318. 14 reasonable rooms, some a/c, TV, changes cash and TCs at a good rate.

**$ Hotel Lotus Lake**, Rewalsar, above the lake, T01905-240239. Run by the folks at Ziggar Monastery, this place has had a fresh lick of paint. If going to Rewalsar you can also stay by donation at the Sikh gurudwara (temple).

**$ Rewalsar Inn** (HPTDC), above the lake, T01905-240252, www.hptdc.nic.in. 12 reasonable rooms with bath, some with TV and balcony, dorm (Rs 75), good lake views.

**$ Vyas**, 5-min walk from bus stand, past sports ground, T01905-235556. 6 small rooms, 4-bed dorm (Rs 40), clean enough, quiet location overlooking Beas, good value.

**Tirthan Valley and Jalori Pass** *p162*
**$$$$-$$$ Himalayan Trout House**, below Banjar, T01903-225112, www.mountain highs.com. All-weather eco-cabins, mud hut suites and stone cottage suites. Stunning location, fine food, great hospitality. Artist's studio, gazebo with fire and library. Trekking and fishing. Little shop selling organic wares. Highly recommended.
**$$$ Sojha Retreat**, Sojha, T01903-200070, www.banjaracamps.com. 5 basic double rooms and 4 lovely suites in wooden lodge with fantastic views, good food and trekking information. You can see all the way to the mountains above Manali from here. Stunning.
**$ Dev Ganga**, 9 km from Banjar in Jibhi, T01903-227005. 8 double rooms, friendly, comfortable, with exceptional views.
**$ Doli Guest house**, Jhibi village, T01903-227034, www.kshatra.com. Nice little rooms in traditional building. Sweet little café by the river in very pretty little village. Ask about the cottages above the village with sitting rooms and woodburning stove. In tune with the local area and a growing number of backpackers, they are offering healthy retreats. Recommended.
**$ Forest Rest House**, near Sojha, spectacular and isolated just below the Jalori Pass.
**$ Fort View Home Stay**, Sojha, just by entrance to Banjara Camp, T(0)9418-626634. Traditional building with four rooms inside – shared bathroom. Atmospheric.
**$ Meena**, beyond bus stand, Banjar, T01902-222258, 4 double rooms.
**$ Raju's Place**, Goshaini, is a family-run river-facing guesthouse, 3 rooms with bath. They offer meals – great home-cooked food, treks and safaris. Access by zip wire over the river.
**$ Whispering Woods**, Jibhi village, T(0)9418-776699. Lovely views right by the river, nice little sit-outs. Basic clean rooms.

## 🍴 Restaurants

**Baspa Valley** *p155*
**$ Sonu**, Sangla. Good Tibetan and travellers' fare, *momos* and pancakes.

**Kaza** *p160*
There are several bakeries and cafés.
**$ German Bakery**, serves up the usual travellers' fare, decent bread and yak cheese.
**$ Layul**, does Chinese, Tibetan and Indian dishes, and cold beer.

**Mandi** *p161*
There are some *dhabas* by the bus terminal.
**$$ Mayfair**. Efficient and tasty North Indian food, some continental and Chinese.
**$ Café Shiraz**, HPTDC, Gandhi Chowk, near Bhutnath Temple. Snacks, bus ticketing.
**$ Gomush Tibetan Restaurant**, near *gompa* at Rewalsar Lake. Excellent *momos*.
**$ Raj Mahal**. Quiet, peaceful (interesting photos and antiques), pleasant garden, good value but limited menu and surly waiters.

## ✸ Festivals

**Mandi** *p161*
**Feb/Mar** Sivaratri Fair, a week of dance, music and drama as temple deities from surrounding hills are taken in procession with chariots and palanquins to visit the Madho Rai and Bhutnath temples.

## ⊙ What to do

**Kaza** *p160*
**Tour operators**
**Spiti Ecospheres**, www.spitiecospheres. com. Based in Kaza, this is an exceptional project with a nod towards conservation, environmental and livelihoods; also volunteering projects, unique treks and promoting organic agriculture. They have an interesting range of tours including **Spiritual Sojourns** where you spend time with the Bhuchens, a rare sect of Tibetan Buddhist theatrical artists, and **Rustic Revelations** and **Spiti Kaleidoscope** where you get real insight into the lives and culture of these Himalayan peoples. There are also several Carbon Neutral volunteering projects. Ecosphere also put in 6 solar installations in 2013 as part of its initiative to provide

reliable, green and decentralized energy to the Spiti valley. Highly recommended.

## ⊕ Transport

### Baspa Valley *p155*
### Sangla
**Bus** To **Chitkul** (often 2-3 hrs late); **Shimla** via Tapri (9 hrs); **Recong Peo**, 0630; from Tapri, 0930. 4WD recommended between Karchham and Chitkul in bad weather.

### Chitkul
**Bus** Twice daily to/from **Karchham** (0930) via **Sangla** (1100) and **Rakcham**; from **Tapri**, 0930; from **Recong Peo** 0600 (prompt).

### Recong Peo to the Spiti River *p157*
### Recong Peo
**Bus** Reserve tickets from booth shortly before departure. Bus to **Chandigarh**; **Delhi** 1030; **Kalpa**, occasional; **Kaza** (9 hrs), gets very crowded so reserve seat before 0700; **Puh**; **Rampur**, frequent (5 hrs); **Sangla/ Chitkul** (4 hrs); **Shimla**; **Tabo**, via Kaza (9-10 hrs).

### Kalpa
**Bus** To **Shimla**, 0730; **Chitkul**, 1300. To get to Peo for Kaza bus at 0730, walk down (40 mins) or arrange taxi from Peo. Travellers may not be allowed beyond Jangi without an 'Inner Line' permit. Contact SDM in Recong Peo a day ahead (see page 148).

### Tabo *p158*
**Bus** To **Chandigarh** via Kinnaur, 0900; **Kaza**, 1000.

### Kaza *p160*
**Bus** Reserve a seat at least 1 hr ahead or night before. The road via Kunzum-La and Rohtang Pass can be blocked well into Jul. New bus stand, bottom end of village. In summer: from **Manali** (201 km), 12 hrs via Rohtang Pass and Kunzum La; **Shimla** (412 km) on the route described, 2 days.

Approximate times shown: daily to **Chango**, 1400; **Kibber** 0900, **Losar** 0900; **Mikkim** (19 km from Attargo), in the Pin Valley, 1200 (2 hrs); returns 1400. Long-distance buses to **Kullu**, 0400; **Manali** (from Tabo), 0500; **Chandigarh** 0630. The last 3 are heavily used.

### Mandi *p161*
**Bus** Bus information T01905-235538. **Chandigarh** 1100 (203 km, 5 hrs). **Dharamshala** 1215, 6 hrs; **Kullu/ Manali** every 30 mins, 3 hrs (Kullu), 4 hrs (Manali); **Shimla** (5½ hrs). Book private buses in town or opposite the bus stand at least 1 day in advance; they do not originate in Mandi. **Dharamshala**, 5 hrs; **Kullu/Manali**, 2 hrs (Kullu), 3½ hrs (Manali).
**Taxi** Rs 1500 to Kullu; Rs 2200 to Manali; Rs 2000 to **Dharamshala**.
**Train** Jogindernagar (55 km), T01908-222088, is on the narrow gauge from Pathankot.

### Tirthan Valley and Jalori Pass *p162*
**Bus** From **Jibli** the bus to **Jalori** can take 1 hr. Some go via **Ghayaghi** (approximate times): **Kulla–Bagipul**, 0800; **Manali– Rampur**, 1000; **Kullu–Dalash**, 1100; **Manali–Ani**, 1100. If heading for Shimla or Kinnaur, change buses at Sainj on NH22.

Bus from **Ani** and **Khanag** to the south, runs to **Jalori Pass** and back. 4 buses daily traverse the pass in each direction when it is open (8-9 months). Bus to **Sainj**, 3½ hrs, and on to **Shimla**, 5 hrs.
**Taxi** From **Banjar** to Jalori Pass costs Rs 800 (Rs 1200 return), to **Jibhi/Ghayaghi**, Rs 300, to **Kullu**, Rs 600, to **Manali**, Rs 1200, to **Mandi** Rs 700, to **Shimla**, Rs 3000. Buses are rare.

## ⊕ Directory

### Mandi *p161*
**Medical services** Hospital, T01905-222102.
**Useful contacts** Police: T01905-235536.

# Kullu Valley

*The Kullu Valley was the gateway to Lahaul for the Central Asian trade in wool and borax. It is enclosed to the north by the Pir Panjal range, to the west by the Bara Bangahal and to the east by the Parvati range, with the Beas River running through its centre. The approach is through a narrow funnel or gorge but in the upper part it extends outwards. The name Kullu is derived from Kulantapith 'the end of the habitable world'. It is steeped in Hindu religious tradition; every stream, rock and blade of grass seemingly imbued with some religious significance. Today, the main tourist centre is Manali, a hive of adventurous activity in the summer months, a quiet and peaceful place to relax in the winter snow.* ▸▸ *For listings, see pages 176-183. For trekking, see page 210.*

**Kullu** → *For listings, see pages 176-183. Colour map 1, B3. Phone code: 01902. Population: 18,300. Altitude: 1219 m.*

Sprawling along the grassy west bank of the Beas, Kullu, the district headquarters, hosts the dramatically colourful **Dasara festival**. Less commercialized than its neighbour Manali it is known across India as the home of apple-growing and the locally woven woollen shawls. There is little to occupy you here as a tourist.

## Arriving in Kullu
**Getting there** Kullu-Manali (Bhuntar) airport, 10 km south, has flights from Delhi, Shimla and Ludhiana; transfer by bus or taxi to Manali (Rs 750), Manikaran (Rs 650). If travelling or buses from the south, alight at Dhalpur Bus Stand. ▸▸ *See Transport, page 182.*

**Getting around** The central area, including the main bus stand and Dhalpur (with ample hotels and restaurants) are close enough to cover on foot. Buses and taxis go to nearby sights.

**Tourist information** Himachal Pradesh Tourism Development Corporation (HPTDC ① *T01902-222349, near Maidan, 1000-1700*, provides maps and advice on trekking.

**Climate** Mid-September to mid-November is the best time to visit. May and June are hot but offer good trekking. March to mid-April can be cold with occasional heavy rain.

## Places in Kullu
Kullu's bulky curvilinear temples seem to have been inspired by the huge boulders that litter the riverbeds and hillsides outside town. A peculiar feature of the Nagari temples is the umbrella-shaped covering made of wood or zinc sheets placed over and around the *amalaka* stone at the top of the spire.

The **Raghunathji Temple** is the temple of the principal god of the **Dasara festival**. The shrine houses an image of Shri Raghunath (brought here from Ayodhya circa 1651 in his chariot. **Bhekhli**, a 3-km climb, has excellent views from the **Jagannathi Temple**. The copper 16th- to 17th-century mask of the Devi inside has local Gaddi tribal features. The wall painting of Durga is in traditional folk style. There are also superb views on the steep but poorly marked climb to the tiny **Vaishno Devi Temple**, 4 km north, on Kullu-Manali road.

## Off the beaten track: the Tosh Valley

One of my favourite treks is located in the Kullu Valley of Himachal Pradesh. The trek begins from the village of Tosh which is 25 km ahead of Manikaran. The Tosh is a feeder valley of the popular Parvati Valley which leads to the Pin Parvati Pass. The Tosh Nallah meets the Parbati river at Pulga coming from the North. Initially narrow, the Tosh Valley starts to open up as you go higher.

The trek follows the raging Tosh river from the village to the snout of the Tosh Glacier. Along the way you cross several beautiful meadows, run into Gaddis (the shepherd tribe of Himachal) and maybe catch a rare glimpse of the Himalayan black or brown bear. I love this trek especially for the amazing variety of bird life and some of the birds I normally see include: white-capped water red starts,

brown dippers, rose finches, bull finches, Himalayan griffons and lamagiers. On a recent trip, I also spotted the rare golden eagle which was spectacular.

The valley is also stunning for its flowers; you will catch sight of various varieties of buttercups, primulas, Himalayan balsam, irises, Himalayan blue poppies and marsh marigolds in the higher meadows.

At the head of the valley is the Tosh Glacier which is surrounded by some well-known climbing peaks: Devachan (6200 m), Papasura (6451 m), White Sail (6446 m), Angduri (6300 m) and Pinnacle (6345 m). There are also several unclimbed peaks in the area. You can even ski in the Tosh Valley in March and April.

Kaushal Desai, tour guide with Above14000ft

## Around Kullu

**Bijli Mahadev**, 11 km from Kullu at 2435 m, is connected by road most of the way with a 2-km walk up steps from the road head. The temple on a steep hill has a 20-m rod on top which is reputedly struck by *bijli* (lightning) regularly, shattering the stone *lingam* inside. The priests put the *lingam* together each time with *ghee* (clarified butter) and a grain mixture until the next strike breaks it apart again. Several buses until late afternoon from Left Bank Bus Stand, the road to Bijli is rough and the buses are in a poor state.

**Bajaura Temple**, on the banks of the Beas River, about 200 m off the NH21 at **Hat** (Hatta), is one of the oldest in the valley. The massive pyramidal structure is magnificently decorated with stone images of Vishnu, Ganesh and Mahishasuramardini (Durga as the Slayer of the Buffalo Demon, see page 413) in the outer shrines. The slender bodies, elongated faces and limbs suggest East Indian Pala influence. Floriated scrollwork decorate the exterior walls.

## Parvati Valley → *For listings, see pages 176-183. Colour map 1, B3. Phone code: 01902.*

The Parvati (Parbati) Valley runs northeast from Bhuntar. Attractive orchards and the fresh green of terraced rice cultivation line the route. Known for its hot springs at Manikaran, more recently the valley has become infamous for the droves of chillum-smoking Israelis and Europeans who decamp here in the summer months attracted by the intensive cultivation of narcotics.

Several local buses (and jeep taxis) travel daily to the valley from Kullu via Bhuntar, taking about two hours to Manikaran, which also has buses from Manali. The area is prone to landslides and flash floods – take special care. ➤➤ *See Transport, page 182. For trekking, see page 213.*

### Jari

Jari is the point where the deep Malana Nala joins the Parvati River. It is a popular resting place for trekkers but also for drug users. The guesthouses vary; a few away from the village centre have better views.

### Kasol

Kasol is the next village en route to Manikaran. The rapidly expanding village has spread on both sides of the road bridge which crosses a tributary that flows into the Parvati, not far from the village itself. About 500 m beyond the village, a narrow side road leads to the river and the location of a fine hot spring on the riverbank. Kasol is the main destination for long-stay visitors, many of whom sit in a haze of *charas* smoke by day, repeating the process by night. **Chhalal** is a 20-minute walk from Kasol. It is a quiet village where families take in guests. A couple of guesthouses have also sprung up here.

# Kullu Valley treks

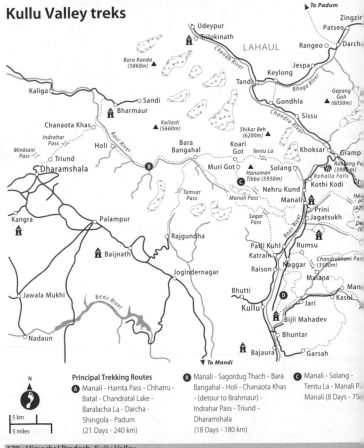

**Principal Trekking Routes**

**A** Manali - Hamta Pass - Chhatru - Batal - Chandratal Lake - Baralacha La - Darcha - Shingola - Padum (21 Days - 240 km)

**B** Manali - Sagordug Thach - Bara Bangahal - Holi - Chanaota Khas - (detour to Brahmaur) - Indrahar Pass - Triund - Dharamshala (18 Days - 180 km)

**C** Manali - Solang - Tentu La - Manali Pa Manali (8 Days - 75

## Manikaran

Manikaran, 45 km from Kullu, is at the bottom of a dark gorge with **hot sulphur springs** emerging from the rock-strewn banks of the Parvati. A local legend describes how while Parvati bathed in the river, Naga, the serpent god stole her *manikaran* (earrings). At Siva's command Naga angrily blew them back from underground causing a spring to flow. Hindu and Sikh pilgrims come to the Rama temple and the *gurdwara* and gather to cook their food by the springs, purportedly the hottest in the world. There are separate baths for men and women. Manikaran, though not attractive in itself, provides a brief halt for trekkers. Short treks go to Pulga and Khirganga beyond while a footpath (affected by landslips in places), leads to the Pin Valley in Spiti. If trekking this route, always go with a registered guide; do not attempt it alone. A road continues for 15 km to **Barseni**, which has become a popular place with long-term travellers.

Manali - Naggar - Malana -
Manikaran - Kasol - Jari - Bijli
Mahadev - Naggar - Manali.
(9 Days - 140 km)

## Pulga and Khirganga
**Pulga** is in a beautiful location with some cheap guesthouses. It is a good four-hour walk east of Manikaran. Some long-stay travellers prefer the basic airy guesthouses outside the village which offer meals.

Khirganga is along the trek which winds through the lush Parvati Valley, east of Pulga. It is known for its sacred ancient hot springs marking the place where Siva is thought to have meditated for 2000 years. There is an open bathing pool for men and an enclosed pool for women, next to the humble shrine at the source. A few tents may be hired. *Dhabas* sell vegetarian food. This is the last village in this valley.

**Kullu to Manali** → For listings, see pages 176-183. Colour map 1, B3.

The NH21 continues north along the west side of the Beas. The older road to the east of the river goes through terraced rice fields and endless apple orchards, and is rougher and more circuitous but more interesting. Sections of both roads can be washed away during the monsoon.

## Kullu to Katrain
As you wind out the centre of Kullu along the right bank you'll pass the **Sitaramata Temple** embedded in the conglomerate cliff and **Raison**, a grassy meadow favoured by trekkers. **Katrain**, in the widest part of the Kullu Valley, mid-way between Kullu

## Dasara in Kullu

The festival of Dasara celebrates Rama's victory over the demon Ravana. From their various high mountain homes about 360 gods come to Kullu, drawn in their *raths* (chariots) by villagers to pay homage to Raghunathji who is ceremoniously brought from his temple in Kullu.

The goddess Hadimba, patron deity of the Kullu Rajas, has to come before any other lesser deities, are allowed near. Her chariot is the fastest and her departure marks the end of the festivities. All converge on the Maidan on the first evening of the festival in a long procession accompanied by shrill trumpeters. Thereafter there are dances, music and a market. During the high point of the fair a buffalo is sacrificed in front of a jostling crowd. Jamlu, the village God of Malana, high up in the hills, follows an old tradition. He watches the festivities from across the river, but refuses to take part. See box, page 214.

On the last day Raghunathji's rath is taken to the riverbank where a small bonfire is lit to symbolize the burning of Ravana, before Ragunathji is returned to his temple in a wooden palanquin.

and Manali, is overlooked by **Baragarh Peak** (3325 m). There are plenty of options for an overnight stay. Across the bridge at **Patli Kuhl**, the road climbs through apple orchards to Naggar.

## Naggar → *Colour map 1, B3. Phone code: 01902.*

Naggar's (Nagar) interesting castle sits high above Katrain. Built in the early 16th century, it withstood the earthquake of 1905 and is a fine example of the timber-bonded building of West Himalaya. It was built around a courtyard with verandas, from where there are enchanting views over the valley. With a pleasant, unhurried atmosphere, it is a good place to stop a while. It is also an entry for treks to Malana, see page 214.

The **castle**, probably built by Raja Sidh Singh, was used as a royal residence and state headquarters until the 17th century when the capital was transferred to Sultanpur (see Kullu). It continued as a summer palace until the British arrived in 1846, when it was sold to Major Hay, the first assistant commissioner, who Europeanized part of it, fitting staircases fireplaces and so on. Extensive renovations have produced fine results, especially in the intricately carved woodwork. In the first courtyard are several black *barselas* (sati stones) with primitive carvings. Beyond the courtyard and overlooking the valley the **Jagti Pat Temple** houses a cracked stone slab measuring 2.5 m by 1.5 m by 2 m believed to be a piece of Deo Tibba, which represents the deity in 'the celestial seat of all the gods'. A priest visits the slab every day.

The small **museum** ① *Rs 10*, has some interesting exhibits, including examples of local *pattu* and *thippu* (women's dress and headdress) and *chola* (folk dance costumes). There are also local implements for butter and tea making, and musical instruments like the *karnal* (broad bell horn) and *singa* (long curled horn).

**Roerich Art Gallery** ① *Tue-Sun 0900-1300 (winter from 1000), 1400-1700, Rs 30*, a 2-km climb from the castle, is Nicholas Roerich's old home in a peaceful garden with excellent views. The small museum downstairs has a collection of photos and his distinctive stylized paintings of the Himalaya using striking colours. It's a beautiful collection from an inspiring family. Nicholas Roerich created the Roerich Pact in the 1930s in order to preserve cultur and the arts in the wake of WWI. It was originally signed by 21 countries.

Uruswati Institute ⓘ *uphill from the main house, Rs 15*, was set up in 1993. The **Himalayan Folk and Tribal Art Museum** is well presented, with contemporary art upstairs. One room upstairs is devoted to a charming collection of Russian traditional costumes, dolls and musical instruments.

There are a number of **temples** around the castle including the 11th-century Gauri Shankar Siva near the bazar, with some fine stone carving. Facing the castle is the Chaturbhuj to Vishnu. Higher up, the wooden Tripura Sundari with a multi-level pagoda roof in the Himachal style celebrates its fair around mid-May. Above that is the Murlidhar Krishna at Thawa, claimed as the oldest in the area which has a beautifully carved stone base. Damaged in the 1905 earthquake, it is now well restored. There are fine mountain views from here.

---

## Manali and around → *For listings, see pages 176-183. Colour map 1, B3. Phone code: 01902. Population: 30000. Altitude: 1926 m.*

Manali occupies the valley of the Beas, now much depleted by hydroelectric projects, with the once-unspoilt Old Village to the north and Vashisht up on the opposite hillside across the river. Set amidst picturesque apple orchards, Manali is packed with Pahari-speaking Kullus, Lahaulis, Nepali labourers and enterprising Tibetan refugees who have opened guesthouses, restaurants and craft shops. The town has become increasingly built-up with dozens of new hotel blocks. It is a major tourist destination for Indian holidaymakers and adventure-seeking foreigners, attracted by the culturally different hill people and the scenic treks this part of the Himalaya offers. In summer months Manali is the start of an exciting two-day road route to Leh.

### Arriving in Manali

**Getting there** Kullu-Manali (Bhuntar) airport is 50 km away with bus and taxi transfers. The bus and taxi stands are right in the centre (though many private buses stop short of the centre) within easy reach of some budget hotels – the upmarket ones are a taxi ride away. ➺ *See Transport, page 182. For trekking in the Himachal, see page 210.*

**Getting around** Manali, though hilly, is ideal for walking. For journeys outside taxi rates are high, so it is worth hiring a motorcycle to explore.

**Tourist information** HPTDC ⓘ *next to Kunzam Hotel, The Mall, T01902-252175*, is helpful.

**Climate** The best season is March-April but there is occasional heavy rain and snow in the villages. May-June and mid-September to mid-November offer better trekking.

### Places in Manali

The **Tibetan Monastery**, built by refugees, is not old but is attractive and is the centre of a small carpet-making industry. Rugs and other handicrafts are for sale. The colourful **bazar** sells Kullu shawls, caps and Tibetan souvenirs.

**Old Manali** is 3 km away, across Manalsu Nala. Once a charming village of attractive old farmsteads with wooden balconies and thick stone-tiled roofs, Old Manali is rapidly acquiring the trappings of a tourist economy: building work continues unchecked in the lower reaches of the village, as ever more guesthouses come up to thwart those seeking an escape from the crowds of modern Manali, while the arrival of the drugs and rave scene in summer extinguishes most of Old Manali's remaining charm. The main road continues through some unspoilt villages to the modern **Manu Mandir**, dedicated to Manu, the Law Giver from whom Manali took its name and who, legend tells, arrived here by boat when

# Manali

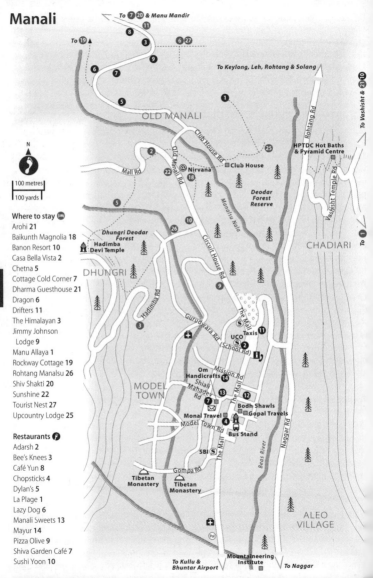

To ⑦ ⑳ & Manu Mandir

To ⑲ ▲

To ⑥

To Keylong, Leh, Rohtang & Solang

To Vashisht & ㉑ ⑩

OLD MANALI

HPTDC Hot Baths & Pyramid Centre

Club House

Deodar Forest Reserve

CHADIARI

To ①

Dhungri Deodar Forest
Hadimba Devi Temple

DHUNGRI

Manslu Nala

Gurudwara Rd (School Rd)

Taxis

UCO $

Om Handicrafts
Shiali Mahadev Rd

MODEL TOWN

Bodh Shawls

Monal Travel
Gopal Travels

Model Town Rd

Bus Stand

SBI $

Beas River

Naggar Rd

ALEO VILLAGE

Tibetan Monastery

Gompa Rd

Tibetan Monastery

Mountaineering Institute

To Kullu & Bhuntar Airport

To Naggar

**N**

100 metres
100 yards

**Where to stay** 🛏
Arohi **21**
Baikunth Magnolia **18**
Banon Resort **10**
Casa Bella Vista **2**
Chetna **5**
Cottage Cold Corner **7**
Dharma Guesthouse **21**
Dragon **6**
Drifters **11**
The Himalayan **3**
Jimmy Johnson
  Lodge **9**
Manu Allaya **1**
Rockway Cottage **19**
Rohtang Manalsu **26**
Shiv Shakti **20**
Sunshine **22**
Tourist Nest **27**
Upcountry Lodge **25**

**Restaurants** 🍴
Adarsh **2**
Bee's Knees **3**
Café Yun **8**
Chopsticks **4**
Dylan's **5**
La Plage **1**
Lazy Dog **6**
Manali Sweets **13**
Mayur **14**
Pizza Olive **9**
Shiva Garden Café **7**
Sushi Yoon **10**

fleeing from a great flood centuries ago. Aged rickshaws may not make it up the hill, so visitors might have to get off and walk.

**Vashisht** is a small hillside village that can be reached by road or a footpath, a 30- to 40-minute walk from the tourist office. Note the carvings on the houses of the wealthy farmers. Vashist Temple is very atmospheric and there are hot spring baths for men and women. The village, with its messy jumble of old village houses and newer buildings, has cheap places to stay which attract young travellers. A two-hour walk past the village up the hillside leads to a **waterfall**.

**Hadimba Devi Temple**, the Dhungri temple (1553), in a clearing among ancient deodars, is an enjoyable 2-km walk from the tourist office. Built by Maharaja Bahadur Singh, the 27-m-high pagoda temple has a three-tier roof and some fine naturalistic wood carving of animals and plants, especially around the doorway. The structure itself is relatively crude, and the pagoda is far from perfectly perpendicular. Massive deodar planks form the roof but in contrast to the scale of the structure the brass image of the goddess Hadimba inside, is tiny. A legend tells how the God Bhima fell in love with Hadimba, the sister of the demon Tandi. Bhima killed Tandi in battle and married Hadimba, whose spirituality, coupled with her marriage to a god, led to her being worshipped as a goddess. Today, she is seen as an incarnation of Kali. The small doorway, less than 1 m high, is surrounded by wood-carved panels of animals, mythical beasts, scrolls, a row of foot soldiers and deities, while inside against a natural rock is the small black image of the Devi. To the left is a natural rock shelter where legend has it that Hadimba took refuge and prayed before she was deified. The greatly enlarged footprints imprinted on a black rock are believed to be hers. Hadimba Devi plays a central part in the annual festival in May, at both Kullu and Manali. To prevent the master craftsman producing another temple to equal this elsewhere, the king ordered his right hand to be cut off. The artist is believed to have mastered the technique with his left hand and reproduced a similar work of excellence at Trilokinath (see page 186) in the Pattan Valley. Unfortunately, his new master became equally jealous and had his head cut off. It's a stunning temple, incredibly atmospheric.

A **feast and sacrifice** is held in mid-July when the image from the new temple in Old Manali is carried to the Hadimba Temple where 18 ritual blood sacrifices are performed. Sacrifices include a fish and a vegetable, and culminate with the beheading of an ox in front of a frenzied crowd. This ceremony is not for the faint-hearted. Pickpockets are known to take advantage of awestruck tourists, so take care.

## Walks

Manali is the trail-head for a number of interesting and popular treks (see below). Beyond Old Manali, the **shepherd trail**, which winds its way up and down the hillside, allows you to capture a picture of Himalayan life as well as see some superb birdlife. The path starts at some concrete steps (after The Lazy Dog lounge/bar) on the first hairpin bend along the paved road to Old Manali (or you can pick it up where the road ends and taxis turn around at the top of the hill) and continues along the cemented path, which turns into a dirt trail. Return the same way, four to five hours.

**Walk 1** This walk takes you towards Solang. In Old Manali Village take the right fork and then turn left in front of the new temple. This trail is a classic, following the right bank of the Beas River up towards the Solang Valley passing the villages of **Goshal**, **Shanag**, **Buruwa** to **Solang** (2480 m), a small ski resort with 2.5 km of runs. Solang is 14 km (five hours). You can get tea, biscuits, nuts and plates of steaming spicy noodles along the walk, and there are also places to stay (see Manali, Where to stay, page 178). To return to Manali it is a steady walk down the valley side to the main Rohtang Pass-Manali Highway where you can pick up a bus (Rs 5) or shared jeep (Rs 10).

**Walk 2** Go prepared for cold for this walk as it takes you through woodland shading you from the sun. Keeping the **Hadimba Temple** on your right follow the contour of the hill and bear right to pick up a clear pack-horse trail which heads up the steep valley. This is a steady uphill climb through woodland giving superb views of the river below, abundant Himalayan birdlife and a chance to see all manner of activity in the woods, chopping, cutting and burning. An enjoyable three- to four-hour walk.

**Walk 3** This walk takes you to the village of **Sethan** (12 km). Take a local bus to the Holiday Inn on the Naggar road. With the hotel behind you, cross the road and pass through the orchard and fields which have low mud walls all round which can be walked on. Bear east till you come to a disused track and then bear right and follow it to the once-untouched village of **Prini** which now has several five-star hotels. If you are lucky the *chai* shop will be open. Further east, the trail to Sethan village becomes somewhat indistinct, though local people are at hand to point you in the right direction. It is a superb three-hour hike up a wooded valley to Sethan (3000 m), which is well off the tourist trail.

## ⊙ Kullu Valley listings

*For hotel and restaurant price codes and other relevant information, see pages 22-26.*

## ⊜ Where to stay

**Kullu Valley** *p168*
The choice of hotels is widening, some good hotels in all ranges, though very full during Dasara. Large off-season discounts (30-50%).
**\$\$\$\$-\$\$\$ Apple Valley Resorts**, Mohal, NH21, on the Beas River, 6 km from airport, T01902-260001, www.applevalleyresorts. co.in. 36 comfortable, very well-designed modern chalets in landscaped grounds, excellent food, rafting nearby.
**\$\$\$-\$\$ Airport Inn**, next to Bhuntar airport, T01902-268286, airportinncomplex@ gmail.com. A convenient place to stay before travelling the 50 km to Manali.
**\$\$\$-\$\$ Shobla**, Dhalpur, T01902-222800, www.shoblainternational.com. 25 rooms, flashy exterior, clean, pleasant atmosphere, airy restaurant, overlooking river.
**\$\$ Gaur Niwas**, Dhalpur, close to tourist office, T01902-240555. Charming period property with 4 spacious, comfortable

rooms, beautiful balconies. Easily the most atmospheric place in town.
**\$\$-\$ Sarwari** (HPTDC), 10-min walk south of Dhalpur Bus Stand, T01902-222471. Peaceful hotel with 16 simple but comfortable rooms (10 in more spacious new wing), 8-bed dorm (Rs 75), good-value restaurant, beer, pleasant gardens, elevated with good views.
**\$ Aaditya**, Lower Dhalpur, T01902-224263. Decently furnished rooms with bath (hot shower), some with river-facing balcony.
**\$ Silver Moon** (HPTDC), perched on a hill, 2 km south of centre, T01902-222488, www.hptdc.nic.in. 6 rooms with bath and heaters, each with small sitting room in traditional style, very clean, good food, has character (enhanced because Mahatma Gandhi stayed here). Taxis Rs 50 from Kullu centre, buses stop at gate if requested – ask for the last barrier south out of Kullu.

**Jari** *p170*
**\$\$\$ The Himalayan Village**, Doonkhara, between Jari and Kasol, T01902-276266, www.thehimalayanvillage.in. Inspiring new

construction based on traditional principles, in fact builders had to be trained in how to build this old-style property with layered wood and stone. Planning to expand with more rooms and tented area but seamlessly blending into the forest. Good restaurant and spa. Recommended.

**$ Village Guest House**, 10-min walk beyond the village, follow signs, T01902-276070. One of several budget options that are springing up along the main road. This one is in the most peaceful setting and has 5 simple rooms with clean, shared hot bath and a restaurant. An excellent location on the edge of a traditional farming village, very friendly, good value.

## Kasol *p170*

**$ Alpine**, T01902-273710, www.alpine guesthouse.net. By far the best place in town right next to the river and deservedly popular. Friendly and welcoming with good clean rooms.

**$ Green Valley**, T01902-273869. Friendly place although genuinely surprised if you are not Israeli – clean basic rooms on the way into town.

**$ Panchali Holiday Home**, T01902-273895. Good range of rooms.

**$ Sasi**, new Kasol riverside, T(0)9817-009523. Cheap and cheerful place with basic rooms, often full. Good terrace by the river.

## Manikaran *p171*

There are a large number of budget guesthouses in the lower part of the village, some with baths fed by the hot springs. However, prices in season rise to unbelievable rates given that most rooms are basic at best.

**$$-$ Country Charm**, main bus stand, T01902-273703. Not really in the country, and not all that charming, but one of the smarter places in town, with 10 brand new rooms, good-value off season.

**$ Padha Family Guest House**, Manikaran bazar, near Gurudwara, T(0)9817-044874. Cheap rooms, super basic but clean with hot

shower. Downstairs separate hot bathing room. **Moon Guest House** nearby offers much the same.

**$ Parvati**, near the temple, T01902-273735. 10 simple rooms, sulphur baths, restaurant.

## Katrain and Raison *p171*

**$$$$ Neeralaya**, Raison, T0 1902-245725, www.neeralaya.com. Beautiful riverside cottages and villas made of stone and wood in the local *kathkuni* style with private kitchens and large verandas. Great local food. It's a sedate place here by the river with walk through the orchards, trout fishing possibilities and campfire suppers. Recommended.

**$$$-$$ Ramgarh Heritage Villa**, near Raison between Kullu and Manali, T(0)9816-248514, www.ramgarhheritagevillamanali. com. A farm since 1928, nicely furnished rooms with TV and Wi-Fi, but beyond the front door there are orchards of pear, pomegranate and walnut trees and great views of the mountains. You can do trips to their kiwi plantation and they can organize paragliding, river rafting, yoga and picnics.

**$ Anglers' Bungalow**, Katrain, T01902-240136. Superb views from 6 spartan rooms – although at time of writing, this was no longer run by HPTDC so details might change.

**$ Orchard Resorts**, Dobhi, 2 km south of Katrain, T01902-240160. Good off-season discount. 16 attractive wood-panelled 'cottages', with hot water, TV, heaters.

## Naggar *p172*

**$$$-$ Castle**, T01902-248316, www.hptdc. nic.in. Built in 1460, has been a hotel since 1978, 13 rooms, stylish but traditional decor and furniture, comfortable beds, fireplaces, modernized baths, best (**$$**) overlook valley, some share bath, very basic dorm (Rs 75), restaurant, good service. May-Jun add Rs 150 for vegetarian meals. Absolutely beautiful property with amazing temple.

**$ Alliance**, 200 m above castle, T01902-248263, www.allianceguesthouse.com.

Run by French ex-pat, 6 rooms, hot water, meals, clean, simple, homely, very good value. Good for families.

**$ Poonam Mountain Lodge**, close to Castle, T01902-248248, www.poonammountain.in. 6 spotless rooms, very good food. Friendly family. They also organize treks and jeep safaris and have a traditional cottage to rent.

**$ Ragini**, T01902-248185, raginihotel@ hotmail.com. 16 smart rooms with modernized baths (hot water), large windows, good views from rooftop restaurant, excellent breakfasts, Ayurvedic massage and yoga, good value, friendly.

**$ Sheetal**, T01902-248319. Overlooking valley, clean and spacious, 14 very pleasant rooms with bath, hot water (some tubs), TV, use of kitchen.

**$ Snow View**, down steps past Tripura Sundari Temple, T(0)9481-388335, snowviewhomestay@gmail.com. Weaving co-op outlet, 7 rooms and restaurant.

**Manali and around** *p173, map p174*
Hotels are often full in May and Jun so better to visit off-season when most offer discounts. Winter heating is a definite bonus.

In **Old Manali**, generally the further you walk, the greater the reward. Those above the Club House are almost out of Old Manali and are in a great location overlooking the valley but still close enough to town.

**Vashisht** village is another popular choice.

**$$$$ The Himalayan**, Hadimba Rd, T01902-250999, www.thehimalayan.com. One Manali resident described this place as a bit like Hogwarts, it's a new build echoing a Gothic castle with turrets to boot. You can expect rooms with 4-posters and fireplaces and there is a magnificent view from the Crows Nest.

**$$$$ Manu Allaya**, Sunny Side, Chadiari, overlooking Old Manali, T01902-252235, www.manuallaya.com. Formerly **Ambassador Resorts** – 53 smart, imaginative rooms, most done in a contemporary design using wood and marble, stunning views and good facilities, a definite cut above

the rest, ie an architect has been involved. Recommended.

**$$$$-$$$ Banon Resort**, The Mall, opposite Mayflower, T01902-253026, www.banonresortsmanali.com. 32 plush rooms, including 12 suites and 6 stylish stone and wooden cottages set in stunning gardens.

**$$$ Baikunth Magnolia**, Circuit House Rd, The Mall, T(0)9816-792888, www.baikunth. com. Definitely the most stylish place to stay in Manali – beautiful decor, heavy wooden doors and floors, chic 4-posters. Come in Apr to catch the magnolia tree in bloom. Great place for a romantic getaway. Highly recommended.

**$$$ Jimmy Johnson Lodge**, The Mall, T01902-253023, www.johnsonhotel.in. 12 very elegant rooms (cottages also available), great bathrooms, pretty gardens, great views, outstanding restaurant (see Restaurants, below). Recommended.

**$$$ Strawberry Garden Cottages**, below Sersai village on the Manali–Nagar road, T(0)9218-924435, www.strawberrygarden manali.com. Stunning location, 4 self-contained, cute, 2-floor cottages in a beautiful garden with great views. Friendly, helpful English owner. Recommended.

**$$ Himalayan Country House**, near Manu Temple, T01902-252294. 15 smart double rooms, plenty of marble and pine, with great views over Old Manali. Popular, specializes in trekking and motorbike safaris. Getting a bit pricey though.

**$$ Shanti Guest House**, Prini Village, 10 km south of Manali towards Naggar, T(0)9816-929704, www.highmountainstourism.org. In a cluster of little hotels in Prini, near **Club Mahindra** this is a place to feel at home. Comfy rooms, nice living rooms and open terrace, Spanish and Chilean food.

**$$-$ Dharma Guest House**, above Vashist, T01902-252354, www.hoteldharmamanali. com. Perched high on the hill above Vashist, this place has great views. Rooms are clean and comfortable. Buns of steel guaranteed climbing up there.

**$$-$ Dragon**, Old Manali, T01902-252290, www.dragontreks.com. This hardy perennial of the Old Manali scene has had a chic facelift and offers a smarter alternative in this part of town. Nice decor, lovely outdoor sitting areas, great vibe. There's a good family suite. Recommended.

**$$-$ Drifters' Inn**, Old Manali, T(0)9805-033127, www.driftersinn.in. In the heart of Old Manali, comfortable rooms with TV, free Wi-Fi and popular café downstairs.

**$$-$ Rohtang Manalsu** (HPTDC), near Circuit House, The Mall, T01902-252332, www.hptdc.nic.in. 27 large rooms, good restaurant, garden, superb views.

**$ Arohi**, Vashisht, T01902-254421, www.arohiecoadventures.com. Clean, attractive rooms, big windows facing mountains, owner good for trekking knowledge.

**$ Cottage Cold Corner**, Old Manali, T01902-252312. Strange name and certainly not the vibe, very warm and friendly welcome indeed. Basic rooms, little outdoor seating area.

**$ Didi Guest House**, Vashisht. Through the village and above the school, on the way to waterfall. 10 wood panelled bedrooms. Cheap, chilled and cheerful with yoga and excellent views up and down the valley.

**$ Rockway Cottage**, above Old Manali, the last one before the wilderness, a 10-min walk from the road, T01902-254328. Very friendly, 10 well-crafted, but simple rooms, most with woodburners, clean common bath, excellent location. Recommended.

**$ Shiv Shakti**, above Old Manali, beyond Manu Temple, T01902-254170. Fine views across valley and mountains beyond, 4 pleasant rooms and café, attached hot bath, friendly farming family. Reiki courses and treatments.

**$ Sunshine**, The Mall, next to Leela Huts, T01902-252320. Lots of character, 9 rooms in old traditional house, others in newer cottage, log fires, restaurant, lovely garden, peaceful, family atmosphere, friendly, such good value you might need them to repeat the price! Highly recommended.

**$ Tourist Nest Guest House**, near Dragon, Old Manali, T(09816-266571. Bright clean rooms with balconies – top floors still have views, whereas building in front obscures views from lower floors. There are now family rooms on a new top floor. Recommended.

**$ Upcountry Lodge**, above Club House, Old Manali, T01902-252257. Quiet location in orchards, 9 clean rooms, attached hot bath, pleasant garden.

## ❼ Restaurants

### Manikaran *p171*
**$ Gurudwara**, near the temple, Excellent meals, steam-cooked at the springs (donation only).

### Pulga *p171*
**$ Paradise Restaurant**, in the village. Great vegetarian dishes. Also has information on guides and equipment for treks up the valley and over the Pin-Parvati Pass (5300 m). If you are lucky, you may be able to persuade the watchman of the old **Forest Rest House** to let you in. The 'visitors' registration book' contains entries that date back to the 1930s and include several well-known mountaineers who have passed by.

### Naggar *p172*
There is also a *dhaba* up at the Jana waterfall recommended for trying real Himachal food – *dhal* made with sour milk, corn flour *rotis*.

**$$ Nightingale**, 200 m above bus stand. Serves trout and Italian.

**$$ Ragini**, roof terrace at hotel of the same name. Excellent for breakfast.

**$ German Bakery**, next to **Ragini**. Sweet little café offering up the usual GB fare, beautiful photography on walls.

### Manali and around *p173, map p174*
There are some great fine dining options. In **Old Manali** there are plenty of Israeli dishes and music which can range from techno to Tibetan.

**$$$ Johnson Café**, Circuit House Rd, T01902-253023. Western (varied menu). Elegant restaurant in a large garden, specializes in trout – you can have it oven-baked, curried, masalad or smoked, excellent home-made pasta, good filter coffee, delicious ice creams. Beautiful lighting, quite magical at night. Highly recommended.

**$$$ La Plage**, Old Manali, Sister restaurant of the renowned **La Plage** from Goa, this is a beautiful restaurant with divine food. You can expect delicious trout cooked with almonds, chicken in soy and sesame with wasabi mash and amazing deserts. It's a stunning location with amazing views, beautiful interiors and garden/terrace dining and great service. Highly recommended.

**$$$ The Lazy Dog**, Old Manali, on left past shops going uphill (before road swings to right). Funky interior design with excellent food, good music, filter coffee, free Wi-Fi and a lovely terrace overlooking the river.

**$$ Adarsh**, The Mall (opposite Kunzam). One of many Punjabi places, but has more style and better menu than others.

**$$ Café Yun**, opposite Drifters Inn, Old Manali. Korean café with lovely vibe serving up trout *sushi* and *sashimi*, as well as other Korean delights and plenty of veggie options. There is an amazing whole-cooked trout on the menu too.

**$$ Chopsticks**, The Mall, opposite bus stand. Tibetan, Chinese, Japanese. Good food, although some say with its growing popularity, its portions have downsized.

**$$ Mayur**, Mission Rd. Vast international menu. Excellent food, smart, efficient service, subdued decor, very pleasant with linen table cloths and candles on tables, Indian classical music, great ambience, cosy with wood-burning stove and generator.

**$$ Peace Café**, behind post office. Good Tibetan, Japanese, some Chinese. Unpretentious, pleasant, warm (wood-burning stove), friendly owner.

**$$ Sa Ba**, Nehru Park. Excellent Indian, snacks, pizzas, cakes, some outdoor seating for people-watching. Recommended.

**$$ Sushi Yoon**, Vashist. Chic little hole-in-the-wall café with just 12 seats serving up tasty sushi, delicious teas and coffees and the ultimate – green tea ice cream. Highly recommended.

**$$ Vibhuti's**, The Mall, corner of Model Town Rd, up short flight of steps. South Indian vegetarian. Delicious *masala dosas*.

**$ Bee's Knees**, Old Manali. Under the watchful eye of Avi – the man with the greatest smile, you can get big plentiful plates of Mexican food and all the usual Indian fare. Recommended.

**$ Dylan's Toasted and Roasted**, Old Manali, www.dylanscoffee.com. The best coffee this side of Delhi, if not one of the best in India, served up by the affable Raj. The cookies are legendary as is his 'Hello to the Queen' – great atmosphere. Highly recommended.

**$ Green Forest**, Dhungri village, on the forest path, past temple down towards Old Manali, just after leaving the forest. Vegetarian. Excellent breakfasts and meals.

**$ Manali Sweets**, Shiali Mahadev Rd. Excellent Indian sweets (superb *gulab jamuns*), also good *thalis*.

**$ Pizza Olive**, Old Manali. Very tasty wood-oven pizzas, great range of pastas and even tiramisu. Recommended.

## ⊛ Festivals

**Kullu** *p168*
**End Apr** Colourful 3-day **Cattle Fair** attracts villagers from the surrounding area. Numerous cultural events accompany.
**Oct-Nov** Dasara is sacred to the Goddess Durga which, elsewhere in India, tends to be overshadowed by **Diwali** which follows a few weeks later. In this part of the Himalaya it is a big social event and a get-together of the gods.

**Manali and around** *p173, map p174*
**Mid-Feb** Week-long **Winter Sports Carnival**
**May** 3-day colourful **Dhungri Forest festival** at Hadimba Devi Temple, celebrated by hill women.

## O Shopping

### Kullu *p168*
Best buys are shawls, caps, *gadmas*. The state weaving cooperative, **Bhutti Weavers Colony**, 6 km south, has retail outlets; **Bhuttico**, 1 store 2 km south of Apple Valley Resorts.

Akhara Bazar has a **Government Handicrafts Emporium, Himachal Khadi Emporium** and **Khadi Gramudyog. Charm Shilp** is good for sandals.

### Manali and around *p173, map p174*
**Crafts and local curios**
**Bhutico Bodh**, by the Hindu temple in Traders, Gulati Complex. Sikh tailors, quick, good quality, copies and originals (caps to order, ready in hours, Rs 75). There's another branch by the Hindu temple in the bazar, with good range of shawls.
**Charitable Trust Tibetan Handicrafts**, The Mall. Government shop.
**Great Hadimba Weaver's**, near Manu Temple, Old Manali. Excellent value, hand-woven, co-op produced shawls/scarves and there is a little workroom to the side where you can watch them at work. Recommended.
**Manushi**, in the market. Women's co-op producing good quality shawls, hats, socks.
**Shree-la Crafts**, near the main taxi stand. Friendly owner, good value silver jewellery. Tibetan Bazar and Tibetan Carpet Centre.

### Tailors
**Gulati Traders**, Gulati Complex. Sikh tailors, quick, good quality, copies and originals.

### Trekking equipment
**Ram Lal and Sons**, E9 Manu Market, behind bus stand. Good range of well-made products, friendly, highly recommended.

## O What to do

### Kullu *p168*
**Look East**, c/o Bajaj Autos, Manikaran Chowk, Shamshi, T01902-065771. Operator recommended for river rafting and bike hire.

### Naggar *p172*
For trekking to Malana, it is best to employ a local guide. Pawan, from the old *chai* shop in the main village, is recommended.

### Manali and around *p173, map p174*
**Body and soul**
**Spa Magnolia** at Johnson's Lodge Circuit House Rd, T(0)9816-100023. Stylish spa with pricy treatments – but a bit of a treat. Ayurvedic and Western treatments available.
**Yogena Matha Ashram**, Kanchani Koot, below Vashist, T(0)9418-240369, www.yoga inmanali.com. Swami Yogananda has a great following and offers down-to-earth spirituality with your downward dog. Recommended.

### Skiing and mountaineering
**Mountaineering and Allied Sports Institute**, 1.5 km out of town, T01902-252342. Organizes courses in mountaineering, skiing, watersports, high-altitude trekking and mountain rescue courses; 5- and 7-day ski courses, Jan-Mar. There is a hostel, an exhibition of equipment and an auditorium.

### Tour operators
**Himalayan Adventurers**, opposite tourist office, T01902-252750, www.himalayan adventurers.com. Wide range of itineraries and activities from trekking and motorbiking to ski-touring and birdwatching.
**HPTDC**, T01902-253531/252116. Daily, in season by luxury coach (or car for 5): to Nehru Kund, Rahla Falls, Marhi, Rohtang Pass, 1000-1700, Rs 200 (car Rs 1200); to Solang, Jagatsukh and Naggar; 1000-1600, Rs 190 (car Rs 1200); to Manikaran, 0900-1800, Rs 250 (car Rs 1100).
**Swagatam**, opposite **Kunzam**, The Mall, T01902-251073. Long-distance buses, trekking, rafting, very efficient.

### Trekking
Clarify details and number of trekkers involved and shop around before making any decisions.

**Above 14000ft**, log huts area, T(0)9816-544803, www.above14000.ft.com (No 679, 6th Main Rd, Vijayanagar, Bengaluru 56004). Expert, environmentally conscious adventure organizers, specializing in treks, mountain biking, climbing expeditions and mountaineering courses throughout the region. Paperless office. Highly recommended.

**Magic Mountain**, no office as such, but call Raju on T(0)9816-056934, www.magicmountainadventures.com. Manali's most experienced cycling guide, Raju also offers trekking and jeep safaris, and is honest, friendly and reliable. Highly recommended.

**Shangri-la Adventures**, Tibetan Colony, Rohtang Rd, T01902-252734, shang-adv@hotmail.com. Treks to Zanskar, Ladakh, Spiti, fishing, rafting, experienced Tibetan guides, competitive pricing for small groups, excellent service from Jigme, honest, friendly.

## ☉ Transport

### Kullu *p168*
**Air** Bhuntar Airport, T01902-265727. Air India, T1-800-180 1407, www.airindia.in.
**Bus** Most buses coming to Kullu continue to Manali. Most long-distance buses use main bus stand, **Sarvari Khad**, with a booking office. For long distance and to **Manali**, left bank bus stand across the bridge: buses for **Naggar** (every 30 mins in summer) and **Bijli Mahadev**, and several to **Manali**; HPTDC deluxe bus to **Chandigarh** (270 km), 0800, 8 hrs; **Delhi**, 512 km, 15 hrs, extra buses during season, often better than private buses, you will pay more for a/c, Volvo service is pricier; **Dharamshala**, 0800-0900, 8 hrs; **Shimla** (235 km), 0900, 8 hrs, Tickets from tourist office.

### Parvati Valley *p169*
**Bus** There are frequent buses from Bhuntar Bus Stand, outside the airport, with many connections to/from **Kullu** and **Manali**. To **Manikaran**, 2½ hrs.

### Naggar *p172*
**Bus** The bus stop is in the bazar, below the castle. Several daily between **Kullu** and **Manali** via scenic east bank route (1½ hrs). From Manali, more frequent buses to **Patli Kuhl** (6 km from Naggar, 45 mins), where you can get a local bus (half hourly in summer) or rickshaw.

### Manali and around *p173, map p174*
**Air** Flights connect **Bhuntar Airport** near Kullu T01902-265037, with **Delhi**. Transport to town: taxi to Manali, Rs 1000 **Himachal Transport** (green) bus, every 15 mins (allow 2½ hrs travel time from Manali).
**Bus** Local bus stand, T01902-252323. Various state RTCs offer direct services to major towns. **HRTC Bus Stand**, the Mall, T01902-252116, reservations 1000-1200, 1400-1600. HPTDC coaches in season (fewer in winter); deluxe have 2 seats on either side: **Harisons** and **Swagatam** (see Tour operators, above), run their own buses. **Chandigarh** 0700, 10 hrs, Rs 415; **Delhi** a/c 1830, 15 hrs, Rs 825; a/c sleeper Rs 1100; non a/c, 1700, Rs 425. **Dharamshala** 0530, 0810, Rs 210, **Keylong** 0600, 6 hrs, Rs 145. **Kullu** via **Naggar**: 2 daily, Rs 30, 1 hr; most Kullu buses go via the national highway and stop at **Patli Kuhl** (see Naggar, above). **Mandi**, Rs 112. **Rohtang Pass** 0900, day trip with photo-stops, striking scenery (take sweater/jacket), 1½ hrs at pass, Rs 120. **Shimla** (280 km), 0830, 1900, 9 hrs, Rs 415.

To **Leh** HPTDC and private coaches run ordinary and luxury buses during the season (mid-Jun to end Sep), but not always daily; usually based on demand. Seats should be reserved ahead. Front seats are best though the cab gets filled by locals wanting a 'lift'. Those joining the bus in Keylong must reserve from Manali to be certain of a seat. Rs 1600 (including tent and meals); usual overnight stop is at Sarchu where other cheaper tents may be available (some choose to sleep on the bus). The 530 km takes about 24-28 hrs on the road, so leave 0600, arrive Leh next afternoon. There are reports of some drivers getting drunk or taking 'medicines' to keep them awake, hence unsafe.

**Motorbike** The uncrowded Kullu–Manali road via Naggar is an ideal place for a test ride.

**Anu Auto Works**, halfway up the hill to Vashisht. Excellent selection; insurance and helmets provided. Mechanical support and bike safaris organized throughout the region.

**Bike Point**, Old Manali. Limited choice of bikes in good condition, mechanical support and competitive rates.

**Enfield Club**, Vashisht Rd, T(0)9418-778899. Enfields and Hondas for hire; reasonable charges, friendly, honest service.

**Local taxi** The local union is very strong, office near tourist office, T01902-254032. Fares tend to be high; from bus stand: Rs 50

for hotels (2-3 km). To Vashisht or top of Old Manali Rd, Rs 90; auto-rickshaws Rs 50.

**Long distance taxi** Dharamshala, Rs 3500; **Kaza**, Rs 6000; **Keylong**, Rs 4200; **Kullu**, Rs 700; **Mandi**, Rs 1500; **Naggar**, Rs 650; **Rohtang Pass**, Rs 1900.

**Train** Reservations at HPTDC office, T01902-251925.

## ⊕ Directory

**Manali and around** *p173, map p174*
**Medical services** Mission Hospital, T01902-252379. Men Tsee Khang Hospital, Gompa Rd, highly recommended for Tibetan herbal/ mineral treatments. Chemists: opposite NAC Market. **Post** GPO, off Model Town Rd, T01902-252324, Mon-Sat 0900-1700. Very efficient.

# Lahaul and the Manali–Leh road

*Lying between the green alpine slopes of the Kullu and Chamba valleys to the south and the dry, arid plateau of Ladakh, the mountainous arid landscapes of Lahaul manage to get enough rain during the monsoon months to allow extensive cultivation, particularly on terraces, of potatoes, green peas and hops (for beer making). Lahaul potatoes are some of the best in the country and are used as seed for propagation. These and rare herbs have brought wealth to the area. Most people follow a curious blend of both Hindu and Buddhist customs though there are a few who belong wholly to one or the other religion.* ▸▸ *For listings, see pages 188-189. For trekking, see page 210.*

### Arriving at the Lahaul and the Manali–Leh road

The whole region can be approached by road from three directions: Shimla via the Spiti Valley; Manali over the Rohtang Pass (3985 m) into Upper Lahaul; and from Zanskar and Ladakh over the Shingo La and Baralacha La (passes). The Shingo La gives access to Lahaul from Zanskar (see page 211), while the Baralacha La (4880 m) on the Leh–Manali road provides access from Ladakh. There is a trekking route from Manali to Zanskar. Streams cross the road at several places. These may be impassable during heavy rain, and those fed by snow-melt swell significantly during the day as meltwater increases, so travel in the late afternoon can be more difficult than in the early morning when the flow is at its lowest. Rockfalls are also a common hazard. ▸▸ *See Transport, page 188.*

### Background

Historically there are similarities between this region and Ladakh since in the 10th century Lahaul, Spiti and Zanskar were part of the Ladakh Kingdom. The Hindu rajas in Kullu paid tribute to Ladakh. In the 17th century Ladakh was defeated by a combined Mongol-Tibetan force. Later Lahaul was separated into Upper Lahaul which fell under the control of Kullu, and Lower Lahaul which came under the Chamba rajas. The whole region came under the Sikhs as their empire expanded, whilst under the British Lahaul and Kullu were part of the administrative area centred on Kangra.

## Manali to Leh → *For listings, see pages 188-189. Colour map 1, B3-A3.*

This stunningly beautiful road, one of the highest in the world, is currently the main route for foreigners into the region of Lahaul and on to Leh. The 530-km highway is usually open from July to September, depending on snow fall; most buses stop in mid-September. The first 52 km runs up the Kullu Valley, then climbs through the Rohtang Pass. The pass itself normally opens at the end of May and is the only way into Lahaul, pending the completion of a delayed tunnel, which is currently scheduled to open in 2016. No permits are necessary.

### Leaving Manali

From Manali the NH21 goes through the village of Palchan and then begins a sharp climb to **Kothi**, at 2530 m, set below towering cliffs. Beautiful views of coniferous hillsides and meadows unwind as the road climbs through 2800 m, conifers giving way to poplars and then banks of flowers. The 70-m-high **Rohalla Falls**, 19 km from Manali at an altitude of 3500 m, are a spectacular sight.

The landscape, covered in snow for up to eight months of the year, becomes totally devoid of trees above Marrhi, a seasonal settlement and restaurant stop, as the road climbs through a series of tight hairpins to the Rohtang Pass.

### Rohtang Pass → *Colour map 1, B3.*

From the pass you get spectacular views of precipitous cliffs, deep ravines, large glaciers and moraines. Buses stop for photos. From June until mid-October, when **Himachal Tourism** (HPTDC) runs a daily bus tour from Manali, the pass becomes the temporary home to a dozen or more noisy roadside 'cafés'.

The descent to **Gramphoo** (Gramphu), which is no more than a couple of houses at the junction of the road from Tabo and Kaza, offers superb views of the glaciated valley of the Chandra River, source of the Chenab. To the north and east rise the peaks of Lahaul, averaging around 6000 m and

**Manali To Leh**

## Motorcycling from Manali to Leh

Allow four days on the way up, to help acclimatize as the 500 km road will take you from 2000 m to 5420 m and down to 3500 m (Leh). The last petrol station is in Tandi, 7 km before Keylong. A full tank plus five to 10 litres of spare petrol will take you to Leh. Above 3500 m, you should open the air intake on your carb to compensate for the loss of power.

Apart from Keylong, there are no hotels, only a few tented camps, providing basic food and shelter from mid-June to mid-September. Some will be noisy and drafty.

The lack of toilet facilities leads to pollution near the camps (don't forget your lighter for waste paper). A tent and mini-stove plus pot, soups, tea, biscuits, muesli, will add extra comfort, allowing you to camp in the wild expanses of the Moray Plains (4700 m).

Unless you plan to sleep in the camp there, you must reach Pang before 1300 on the way up, 1500 on the way down, as the police will not allow you to proceed beyond the checkpoint after these times. The army camp in Pang has helpful officers and some medical facilities.

with the highest, Mulkila, reaching 6520 m. As the road descends towards Khoksar there is an excellent view of the Lumphu Nala coming down from the Tempo La glacier. An earlier glacial maximum is indicated by the huge terminal moraine visible halfway up the valley.

There is a police check post in **Khoksar**, at 3140 m, where you may be required to show your passport and sign a register. This can take some time if more than one bus arrives at the same time. About 8 km west of Khoksar work is in progress on the Rohtang tunnel, which will link the Solang Valley with the Chandra Valley. If you cross the bridge here you find an attractive waterfall.

### Gondhla to Keylong and the Pattan Valley

It is worth stopping here to see the 'castle' belonging to the local *thakur* (ruler), built around 1700. The seven-storey house with staircases made of wooden logs has a veranda running around the top and numerous apartments on the various floors. The fourth floor was for private prayer, while the Thakur held court from the veranda. There is much to see in this neglected, ramshackle house, particularly old weapons, statues, costumes and furniture. The 'sword of wisdom', believed to be a gift from the His Holiness the Dalai Lama, is of special interest. On close inspection you will notice thin wires have been hammered together to form the blade, a technique from Toledo, Spain. The huge rock near the Government School, which some claim to be of ancient origin, has larger-than-life figures of *Bodhisattvas* carved on it.

As the road turns north approaching **Tandi**, the Chandra rushes through a gorge, giving a superb view of the massively contorted, folded and faulted rocks of the Himalaya. Tandi itself is at the confluence of the Chandra and Bhaga rivers, forming the Chandrabhaga or Chenab. Keylong is 8 km from here, see page 187. At Tandi you can take a left turn and visit the Pattan Valley before heading to Keylong to continue on the journey.

**Pattan Valley** → *For listings, see pages 188-189. Colour map 1, A3/B3.*

The Pattan Valley has a highly distinctive agricultural system which despite its isolated situation is closely tied in to the Indian market. Pollarded willows are crowded together all around the villages, offering roofing material for the flat-roofed houses and fodder for the cattle during the six-month winter. Introduced by a British missionary in the 19th century to try and help stabilize the deeply eroded slopes, willows have become a vital part of the valley's village life, with the additional benefit of offering shade from the hot summer sun. Equally important are the three commercial crops which dominate farming: hops, potatoes and peas, all exported, while wheat and barley are the most common subsistence grain crops.

## Tandi to Trilokinath

Just out of **Tandi** after crossing the Bhaga River on the Keylong road, the Udeypur road doubles back along the right bank of the Chenab running close to but high above the river. The road passes through **Ruding**, **Shansha**, 15 km from Tandi, **Jahlma**, 6 km and **Thirot**, another 11 km on (rest house here). A bridge at **Jhooling** crosses the Chenab. Some 6 km further on, the road enters a striking gorge where a bridge crosses the river before taking the road up to **Trilokinath**, 6 km away.

## Trilokinath

Trilokinath, at 2760 m, is approached by a very attractive road which climbs up the left bank of the Chenab. The glitteringly white-painted Trilokinath temple stands at the end of the village street on top of a cliff. The **Siva temple** has been restored by Tibetan Buddhists, whose influence is far stronger than the Hindu. Tibetan prayer-flags decorate the entrance to the temple which is in the ancient wooden-pagoda style. In the courtyard is a tiny stone Nandi and a granite lingam, Saivite symbols which are dwarfed in significance by the Buddhist symbols of the sanctuary, typical prayer-wheels constantly being turned by pilgrims, and a 12th-century six-armed white marble Avalokiteshwara image (Bodhisattva) in the shrine, along with other Buddhist images. The original columns date from Lalitaditya's reign in the eighth century, but there has been considerable modernization as well as restoration, with the installation of bright electric lights including a strikingly garish and flickering *chakra* on the ceiling. Hindus and Buddhists celebrate the three-day **Pauri Festival** in August.

## Udeypur

Some 10 km from the junction with the Trilokinath road is Udeypur (Udaipur). Visited in the summer it is difficult to imagine that the area is completely isolated by sometimes over 2 m of snow during the six winter months. It is supplied by weekly helicopter flights (weather permitting). The helipad is at the entrance to the village. Trekking routes cross the valley here and further west, see page 211.

The unique **Mrikula** (Markula) **Devi temple** (AD 1028-1063) is above the bazar. The temple dedicated to Kali looks wholly unimposing from the outside with a battered-looking wood-tiled 'conical' roof and crude outside walls. However, inside are some beautiful, intricate deodar-wood carvings belonging to two periods. The façade of the shrine, the *mandapa* (hall) ceiling and the pillars supporting it are earlier than those beside the window, the architraves and two western pillars. Scenes from the *Mahabharata* and the *Ramayana* epics decorate the architraves, while the two *dvarapalas* (door guardians), which are relatively crude, are stained with the blood of sacrificed goats and rams. The wood carvings here closely resemble those of the Hadimba Temple at Manali and some believe it was the work of the same 16th-century craftsman (see page 175). The silver image of Kali (*Mahisha-shurmardini*) 1570, inside, is a strange mixture of Rajasthani and Tibetan styles (note the *lama*-like head covering), with an oddly proportioned body.

The principal town of the district of Lahaul, Keylong is set amidst fields of barley and buckwheat surrounded by brown hills and snowy peaks and was once the home of Moravian missionaries. Only traders and trekkers can negotiate the pass out of season. Keylong is an increasingly widely used stopping point for people en route to Leh or trekking in the Lahaul/Spiti area. Landslides on the Leh–Manali road can cause quite long delays and the town can be an unintended rest halt for a couple of days. It has little to offer, though the views are very attractive and there are pleasant walks.

There is a pleasant circuit of the town by road which can be done comfortably in under two hours. Tracks run down into the town centre. The **local deity** 'Kelang Wazir' is kept in Shri Nawang Dorje's home which you are welcome to visit. There is a **Tibetan Centre for Performing Arts**. A statue in the centre of Keylong commemorates the Indian nationalist **Rash Behari Bose**, born 15 May 1886 near Kolkata.

**Khardong Monastery**, 3 km away across the Chandra River up a steep tree-shaded path, is the most important in the area. It is believed to have been founded 900 years ago and was renovated in 1912. Nuns and monks enjoy equality; married *lamas* spend the summer months at home cultivating their fields and return to the monastery in winter. The monastery contains a huge barrel drum, a valuable library and collections of *thangkas*, Buddha statues, musical instruments, costumes and ancient weapons.

**Sha-Shur Monastery**, a kilometre away, was in legend reputedly founded as early as AD 17 by a Buddhist missionary from Zanskar, Lama Deva Tyatsho who was sent by the Bhutanese king. It has ancient connections with Bhutan and contains numerous wall paintings and a 4.5-m *thangka*. The annual **festival** is held in June/July.

**Tayul Monastery**, above Satingri village, has a 4-m-high statue of Padma Sambhava, wall paintings and a library containing valuable scriptures and *thangkas*. The *mani* wheel here is supposed to turn on its own marking specially auspicious occasions, the last time having been in 1986.

From Keylong the road passes through very high-altitude desert with extraordinary mountain views. **Jispa**, 21 km on at an altitude of 3200 m, has a hotel, a campsite, a few tea stalls and a mountaineering institute. **Himachal Tourism**'s concrete 'lodge' has three basic rooms with toilets and cheap camping in the yard. About 2 km beyond Jispa is **Teh** which has accommodation. There is a 300-year-old palace, built in the Tibetan style, comprising 108 rooms over four storeys – apparently the largest traditional structure in Lahaul. It is 3.5 km off the main highway (turn off at Ghemur, between Keylong and Jispa) in a village called **Kolong**, and has recently been converted into a heritage hotel. A museum has also been opened there, with some interesting exhibits depicting the traditional and ceremonial life of the local rulers, who still own the property.

All vehicles must stop for passport checks at **Darcha** checkpost where the Bhaga River is bridged. Tents appear on the grassy riverbank in the summer to provide a halt for trekkers to Zanskar. The road climbs to **Patseo** where you can get a view back of Darcha. A little further is **Zingzingbar**. Icy streams flow across the road while grey and red-brown scree reach down from the bare mountainside to the road edge. The road then goes over the **Baralacha La** (54 km; 4880 m), 107 km from Keylong, at the crossroads of Lahaul, Zanskar, Spiti and Ladakh regions before dropping to **Sarchu** (on the state border). There are a dozen or so tented camps in Sarchu, including on run by **Himachal Tourism** (**HPTDC**), mostly with two-bed tents (sometimes reported dirty), communal toilet tents, late-night Indian meal and breakfast; private bus passengers without reservations are accommodated whenever possible (Rs 150 per person); open mid-June to mid-September.

The road runs beyond Brandy Nala by the Tsarap River before negotiating 22 spectacular hairpin bends, known as the 'Gata Loops', to climb up to the **Nakli La** (4950 m) and **Lachalung La** (5065 m). It then descends past tall earth and rock pillars to **Pang**, a summer settlement in a narrow valley where you can stop for an expensive 'breakfast' (usually roti, vegetables and omelettes to order). The camp remains open beyond 15 September; an overnight stop is possible in communal tents. The 40-km-wide Moray plains (4400 m) provide a change from the slower mountain road. The road then climbs to **Taglang La** (5370 m), the highest motorable pass along this route and the second highest in the world; the altitude is likely to affect many travellers at this point. You descend slowly towards the Indus valley, passing small villages, before entering a narrow gorge with purple coloured cliffs. The road turns left to continue along the Indus basin passing **Upshi** with a sheep farm and a checkpost, and then **Thikse**, before reaching **Leh**.

## ⊚ Lahaul and the Manali–Leh road listings

*For hotel and restaurant price codes and other relevant information, see pages 22-26.*

## ⊜ Where to stay

### Udeypur *p186*
Camping is possible in an attractive site about 4 km beyond the town (permission from Forest Officer) but since there is no water supply, water has to be carried in from a spring about 300 m further up the road. Carry provisions too as there is little in the bazar.
**$ Amandeep Guest House**, T01909-222256. 7 semi deluxe rooms with limited hot water. Good *dhaba* opposite serves good Indian food.
**$ Forest Rest House**, off the road in a pleasant raised position, T01900-222235. 2 rooms with bath, very basic, bring your own sleeping bag.

### Keylong *p187*
**$$-$ Chandrabhaga** (HPTDC), T01900-222247. Open mid-Jun to mid-Oct, reserve ahead. 3 rooms with bath, 2-bed tents, dorm (Rs 150), meals to order, solar-heated pool, rates include vegetarian meals.
**$ Dekyid**, below police station, T01900-222217. 3-storey hotel, friendly, helpful

reception, decent-sized rooms with bath, quiet, excellent views over fields, good restaurant but service very slow.
**$ Gyespa**, on main road, T01900-222207. 11 basic but adequate rooms plus a good restaurant.
**$ Snowland**, above Circuit House, T01900-222219. Modest but adequate, 15 rooms with bath, friendly reception. Recommended.
**$ Tashi Deleg**, on main road through town, T01900-222450. Does well from being the first place you come to from Tandi, slightly overpriced as a result. Rooms are comfortable though, and the restaurant is one of the best in town. Also has a car park.

### Keylong to Leh *p187*
**$$ Ibex Hotel**, Jispa, T01900-233204, www.ibexhoteljispa.com. Glass and cement block, 27 comfortable rooms, dorm, impressive location. Reserve ahead.

## ⊛ Transport

### Keylong *p187*
**Bus** State and private luxury buses are most comfortable but charge more than double the 'B'-class fare. To **Manali** (6-8 hrs);

to **Leh** (18 hrs). To board deluxe buses to Leh in Keylong, reserve ahead and pay full fare from Manali (Rs 1300, plus Rs 300 for tent and meals in Sarchu).
**Jeep** To **Manali** by jeep, 4 hrs, weather permitting; **Sarchu** 6 hrs, **Leh** 14 hrs.

**ⓘ Directory**

**Keylong** *p187*
**Banks** State Bank of India, but no foreign exchange.

# Northern Himachal

*Dominated by Dharamshala, this is a region replete with some of the most breathtaking mountain views imaginable. From Dalhousie eastwards there are tantalizing glimpses of snow-capped peaks, while McLeodganj has been attracting Western travellers for decades, coming in search of peace, tranquillity, the Dalai Lama and sometimes even themselves. The Kangra Valley sees far fewer visitors, but has an unhurried charm all of its own, epitomized by Pragpur, India's first heritage village.* ⏩ *For listings, see pages 199-209. For Trekking, see page 210.*

**Dharamshala** → *For listings, see pages 199-209. Colour map 1, B3. Population: 30,774. Altitude: 1250-2000 m.*

Dharamshala has a spectacular setting along a spur of the Dhauladhar range, varying in height from 1250 m at the 'Lower Town' bazar to 1768 m at McLeodganj. It is this 'Upper' and more attractive part of town that attracts the vast majority of visitors. Although the centre of McLeodganj itself has now become somewhat overdeveloped, it is surrounded by forests, set against a backdrop of high peaks on three sides, with superb views over the Kangra Valley and Shiwaliks, and of the great granite mountains that almost overhang the town.

## Arriving in Dharamshala
**Getting there** Flights to Gaggal Airport (13 km). Lower Dharamshala is well connected by bus with towns near and far. You can travel from Shimla to the southeast or from Hoshiarpur to the southwest along the fastest route from Delhi. The nearest station on the scenic mountain railway is at Kangra, while Pathankot to the west is on the broad gauge.

**Getting around** From Dharamshala, it is almost 10 km by the bus route to McLeodganj but a shorter, steeper path (3 km) takes about 45 minutes on foot. Local jeeps use this bumpy, potholed shortcut. Compact McLeodganj itself, and its surroundings, are ideal for walking.

**Tourist information** HPTDC ⓘ *behind post office, McLeodganj, T01892-221205, Mon-Sat 1000-1700*. There are many opportunities for foreign volunteers (see box, page 191).

## Background
The hill station was established by the British between 1815 and 1847, but remained a minor town until the **Dalai Lama** settled here after Chinese invasion of Tibet in October 1959. There is an obvious Tibetan influence in McLeodganj. The Tibetan community has tended to take over the hospitality business, sometimes a cause of friction with the local population. Now many Westerners come here because they are particularly interested in Buddhism, meditation or the Tibetan cause. A visitor's attempt to use a few phrases in

Tibetan is always warmly responded to: *tashi delek* (hello, good luck), *thukje-chey* (thank you), *thukje-sik* (please), *gong-thag* (sorry), and *shoo-den-jaa-go* (goodbye).

## Places in Dharamshala

**Church of St John-in-the-Wilderness** (1860) ① *open for Sunday morning service*, with attractive stained-glass windows, is a short distance below McLeodganj. Along with other buildings in the area, it was destroyed by the earthquake of 1905 but has been rebuilt. In April 1998 thieves tried to steal the old bell, cast in London, which was installed in 1915, but could only move it 300 m. The eighth Lord Elgin, one of the few viceroys to die in office, is buried here according to his wish as it reminded him of his native Scotland.

**Namgyal Monastery** ① *0500-2100* at McLeodganj, with the Buddhist School of Dialectics, mostly attended by small groups of animated 'debating' monks, is known as 'Little Lhasa'. This *tsuglagkhang* (cathedral) opposite the Dalai Lama's residence resembles the centre of the one in Lhasa and is five minutes' walk from the main bazar.

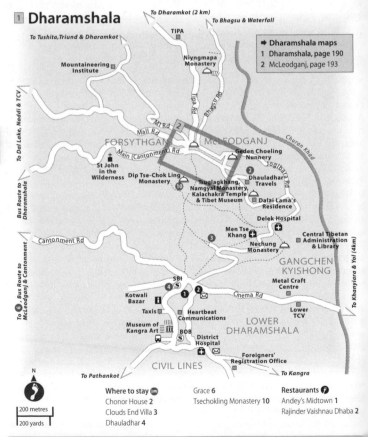

# ⬚ Dharamshala

To Dharamkot (2 km)
To Bhagsu & Waterfall
TIPA

To Tushita, Triund & Dharamkot

Niyngmapa
Monastery

➡ **Dharamshala maps**
1 Dharamshala, page 190
2 McLeodganj, page 193

Mountaineering
Institute

Tipa Rd
Bhagsu Rd

M Rd
Mall Rd 2
FORSYTHGANJ McLEODGANJ
Main (Cantonment) Rd
Churan Khad

To Dal Lake, Naddi & TCV

St John
in the
Wilderness
Dip Tse-Chok Ling
Monastery
10
Geden Choeling
Nunnery
Jogibara Rd
Dhauladhar
Travels

Tsuglagkhang,
Namgyal Monastery,
Kalachakra Temple
& Tibet Museum
Dalai Lama's
Residence

Bus Route to Dharamshala

Delek Hospital

Men Tse
Khang
5
Central Tibetan
Administration
& Library

Cantonment Rd

Nechung
Monastery

GANGCHEN
KYISHONG

To McLeodganj & Cantonment
To 6 Bus Route to

SBI
4 S
Kotwali
Bazar
Taxis i
1
2
Heartbeat
Communications

Metal Craft
Centre

Cinema Rd

Lower
TCV

To Khanyiara & Yol (4km)

Museum of
Kangra Art
BOB
S
District
Hospital
Foreigners'
Registration Office

LOWER
DHARAMSHALA

CIVIL LINES

N

To Pathankot
To Kangra

200 metres
200 yards

| Where to stay 🛏 | Grace 6 | Restaurants 🍴 |
|---|---|---|
| Chonor House 2 | Tsechokling Monastery 10 | Andey's Midtown 1 |
| Clouds End Villa 3 | | Rajinder Vaishnau Dhaba 2 |
| Dhauladhar 4 | | |

## Open your heart: volunteering in Mcleodganj

There are many opportunities for volunteer work in and around Dharamshala, from conversation to work at the hospital. Many offer a great insight into Tibetan culture and are key in empowering refugees. **Lha Charitable Trust** ① *Temple Rd, T01892-220992, www.lhasocialwork.org. Office open Mon-Sat 0900-1700, lunch 1200-1300.* Volunteers are wanted for language classes, IT and web design, healthcare, fundraising, etc. Short-term or long-term placements are possible, or you can just drop in. They also offer Tibetan cooking classes, language, meditation, homestay, etc. **Lha** means 'innate goodness'. Also look in at or check the free monthly magazine *Contact*, T(0)98161-55523,

www.contactmagazine.net (also a useful resource for restaurant information and events in McLeodganj, Buddhist-related and otherwise). English-language teachers are in high demand to teach newly arrived refugees, for short- or long-term stints. There are a couple of places for teaching and conversation near **Dokebi** restaurant including **Learning and Ideas for Tibet** (www. learningandideasfortibet.org) who have conversation classes, movie parties and talks from ex-political prisoners. You can also volunteer with **Rogpa** (www. tibetrogpa.org ) who provide free childcare for Tibetan people trying to juggle jobs and education – they run a lovely café on the Jogibara road too.

It contains large gilded bronzes of the Buddha, Avalokitesvara and Padmasambhava. To the left of the Tsuglagkhang is the **Kalachakra Temple** with very good modern murals of *mandalas*, protectors of the Dharma, and Buddhist masters of different lineages of Tibetan Buddhism, with the central image of Shakyamuni. Sand *mandalas* (which can be viewed on completion), are constructed throughout the year, accompanied by ceremonies. The temple is very important as the practice of Kalachakra Tantra is instrumental in bringing about world peace and harmony. Within the monastery complex is the **Tibetan Museum** ① *Tue-Sun 0900-1700, Rs 5*, with an interesting collection of documents and photographs detailing Tibetan history, the Chinese occupation of Tibet and visions of the future for the country. It is an essential visit for those interested in the Tibetan cause. It is traditional to walk the Kora in Mcleodganj, which is a ritual circuit of the Temple complex and the Dalai Lama's residence with stunning views of the mountains and numerous prayer wheels and prayer flags along the way. It is a very beautiful walk, a sacred path which is done clockwise around the complex and finishes by the Namgyal Temple entrance. The kora in Mcleodganj replicates the ancient Lingkhor path around the Potala Palace in Lhasa.

The **Dalai Lama** ① *www.dalailama.com*, usually leads the prayers on special occasions – 10 days for **Monlam Chenmo** following **Losar**, **Saga Dawa** (May) and his own birthday (6 July). If you wish to have an audience with him, you need to sign up in advance at the security Office (go upstairs) by **Hotel Tibet**. On the day, arrive early with your passport. Cameras, bags and rucksacks are not permitted. His Holiness is a Head of State and the incarnation of Avalokitesvara, the Bodhisattva of Love and Great Compassion; show respect by dressing appropriately (no shorts, sleeveless tops, dirty or torn clothes); monks may 'monitor' visitors. **Tsechokling Monastery**, in a wooded valley 300 m below McLeodganj (down rather slippery steps), can be seen from above. The little golden-roofed monastery was built between 1984-1986; the monks are known for their skill in crafting *tormas* (butter sculptures) and sand *mandalas*, which decorate the prayer hall (see Where to stay, page 200). Further down the 3-km steep but motorable road to Dharamshala is the Nechung Monastery in **Gangchen Kyishong** with the **Central Tibetan Administration** (**CTA**), which began work in 1988.

**Norbulingka Institute** ①*T01892-246402, www.norbulingka.org*, is becoming a major centre for Buddhist teaching and practical work. Named after the summer residence of the Seventh Dalai Lama built in 1754, it was set up to ensure the survival of Tibetan Buddhism's cultural heritage. Up to 100 students and 300 Tibetan employees are engaged in a variety of crafts in wood, metal, silk and metal, *thangka* painting (some excellent) and Tibetan language. The temple has a 4.5-m-high gilded statue of the Buddha and over 1000 painted images. There is a small **museum** of traditional 'dolls' made by monks and a **Tibetan Library** with a good range of books and magazines. You can attend lectures and classes on Tibetan culture and language and Buddhism or attend two **meditation** classes, free but a donation is appreciated.

**Museum of Kangra Art** ①*Main Rd, Tue-Sun 1000-1330, 1400-1700, free, allow 30 mins*, near the bus stand in Lower Dharamshala, includes regional jewellery, paintings, carvings, a reminder of the rich local heritage contrasted with the celebrated Tibetan presence. Copies of Roerich paintings will be of interest to those not planning to visit Naggar.

Lhamo Tso who runs **Lhamo's Croissant**, recommends tuning into the heart of Mcleodganj and the Tibetan people by "walking the Kora (outer-circumnambulation of the temple and palace) and buying the *Essence of the Heart Sutra* at **The Namgyal Bookshop** by the temple. It is a commentary by His Holiness the Dalai Lama on one of the Buddha's main teachings. It is a book that can transform your life."

## Around McLeodganj

**Bhagsu**, an easy 2-km stroll east, or Rs 40 auto-rickshaw ride, has a temple to Bhagsunath (Siva). The mountain stream here feeds a small pool for pilgrims, while there is an attractive waterfall 1 km beyond. Unfortunately this has resulted in it becoming very touristy, with increasing building activity and an influx of noisy day-trippers. The hill leading up the valley towards Dharamkot is known as Upper Bhagsu, and is lined with little shops, restaurants and guesthouses. It is a relaxing place with great views, and so attracts many backpackers for long stays here. Outside the rainy season lovely walks are possible.

**Dharamkot**, 3 km away (from McLeodganj by auto Rs 80, or on foot from Bhagsu), has very fine views and you can continue on towards the snowline. Villagers' homes and guesthouses are dotted up the hillside, accessible via pathways, and there is even a Chabbad House for the numerous Israeli tourists. In September, a fair is held at **Dal Lake** (1837 m), 3 km from McLeodganj Bus Stand; it is a pleasant walk but the 'lake', no more than a small pond, is disappointing.

**Naddi Gaon**, 1.5 km further uphill from the bridge by Dal Lake (buses from Dharamshala 0800-1900), has really superb views of the Dhauladhar Range. **Kareri Lake** is further on. The TCV (Tibetan Childrens' Village) nearby educates and trains children in traditional handicrafts. Big hotels are rapidly appearing next to the traditional Naddi village. Most enjoy excellent views.

It is an 8-km trek to **Triund**, 2827 m, at the foot of the Dhauladhar where there is a **Forest Lodge** on a hill top. Some trekkers pitch tents, whilst others make use of caves or shepherds' huts. Take provisions and warm sleeping gear if planning to stay overnight. It is well worth the effort. A further 5 km, one-hour walk, brings you to **Ilaka**.

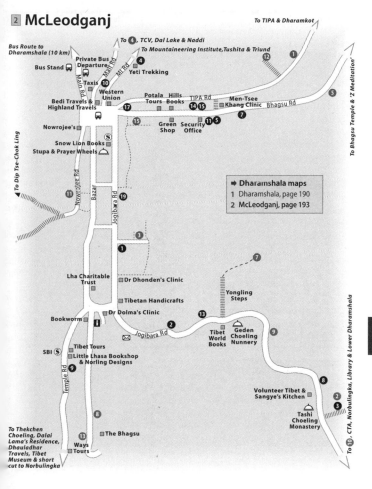

# 2 McLeodganj

To TIPA & Dharamkot

Bus Route to Dharamshala (10 km)

To ④, TCV, Dal Lake & Naddi
To Mountaineering Institute, Tushita & Triund

Private Bus Departure
Bus Stand

Main Rd
Mt Rd

Yeti Trekking

Taxis

Western Union

Bedi Travels & Highland Travels

Potala Hills
Tours Books

Men-Tsee
Khang Clinic

Bhagsu Rd

TIPA Rd

To Bhagsu Temple & 'Z Meditation'

Nowrojee's

Green Shop
Security Office

To Dip Tse-Chok Ling

Snow Lion Books

Stupa & Prayer Wheels

Bazar

Jogibara Rd

➡ Dharamshala maps
1 Dharamshala, page 190
2 McLeodganj, page 193

Lha Charitable Trust

Dr Dhonden's Clinic

Tibetan Handicrafts

Yongling Steps

Dr Dolma's Clinic

Bookworm

Jogibara Rd

Tibet World Books

Geden Choeling Nunnery

Tibet Tours

SBI

Little Lhasa Bookshop & Norling Designs

Temple Rd

Volunteer Tibet & Sangye's Kitchen

Tashi Choeling Monastery

To Thekchen Choeling, Dalai Lama's Residence, Dhauladhar Travels, Tibet Museum & short cut to Norbulingka

The Bhagsu

Ways Tours

To ⑩, CTA, Norbulingka, Library & Lower Dharamshala

50 metres
50 yards

**Where to stay** 🛏
Annex **8**
Drepung Loseling **3**
Glenmoor Cottages **4**
Green **5**
Ladies Venture **9**
McLeod Ganj Homestay **1**
Norling Guest House **10**
Om & Namgyal Café **11**
Paljor Gakyil **12**
Pawan House **2**
Pema Thang **13**

Sidharth House **7**
Tibet **15**

**Restaurants** 🍴
Carpe Diem **2**
Common Ground Café **4**
Dokebi Seven Hills **3**
Gakyi **1**
German Bakery **10**
Jimmy's Italian Kitchen **19**
Kunga's/Nick's Italian Kitchen **7**

Lhamo's Croissant **5**
Lhasa **17**
Lung-Ta **8**
Moonlight & Sunrise **14**
Moonpeak Espresso & Thali **9**
Rangzen **11**
Rogpa Café **13**
Tara Café **15**

The Kangra Valley, between the Dhauladhar and the Shiwalik foothills, starts near Mandi and runs northwest to Pathankot. It is named after the town of Kangra but now the largest and main centre is Dharamshala. Chamba State, to its north, occupies part of the Ravi River Valley and some of the Chenab Valley.

## Background

In 1620 Shah Jahan captured Kangra fort for his father Jahangir, and Kangra became a Mughal province. Many of the court artists fled to neighbouring Chamba and Kullu as the Rajas submitted to Mughal rule. When Mughal power weakened, the 16-year-old **Sansar Chand Katoch II** (1775-1823) recaptured the fort and the rajas reasserted their independence. Under his powerful leadership, Kangra sought to extend its boundaries into the Chamba and Kullu Valleys but this was forestalled by the powerful Gurkhas from Nepal. With the rise of the Sikh empire, the valley was occupied until the Treaty of Amritsar. Then under the British, Dharamshala was made the administrative capital of the region which led to the decline of Kangra.

The **Kangra School of Painting** originated by virtue of Raja Goverdhan Singh (1744-1773) of Guler, who gave shelter to many artists who had fled from the Mughals, and during the mid-18th century a new style of miniature painting developed. Based on Mughal miniature style, the subject matter derived from Radha/Krishna legends, the rajas and gods being depicted in a local setting. Under Sansar Chand II the region prospered and the Kangra School flourished. Kangra fort, where he held court for nearly 25 years, was adorned with paintings and attracted art lovers from great distances. The 1905 earthquake damaged many of these buildings though you can still see some miniature wall paintings.

## Kangra → *Colour map 1, B3. Phone code: 01892. Altitude: 615 m.*

Kangra, 18 km south of Dharamshala, was once the second most important kingdom in the West Himalaya after Kashmir. Kangra town, the capital, was also known as Bhawan or Nagarkot. It overlooks the Banganga River and claims to have existed since the Vedic period with historical reference in Alexander's war records.

**Kangra Fort** ① *foreigners US$2, Indians Rs 5, auto-rickshaw Rs 150 return, taxi Rs 250* stands on a steep rock dominating the valley. A narrow path leads from the ticket office up steps to the fort, which was once protected by several gates (now reconstructed) and had the palace of the Katoch kings at the top. Just inside the complex is a small museum displaying Hindu and Jain stone statues, while further up the hill is an old Jain temple (still in use) and the ruins of a temple with exquisite carvings on its rear outer wall. At the very top, the remains of Sansar Chand's palace offer commanding views. The fort is worth the effort for these views alone. At its foot is a large modern Jain temple which has pilgrim accommodation (worth considering if you get stuck). There is also an overgrown British cemetery just next to the fort entrance.

**Brajesvari Devi Temple**, in Kangra Town, achieved a reputation for gold, pearl and diamonds and attracted many Muslim invaders from the 11th century, including Mahmud of Ghazni, the Tughlaqs and the Lodis, who periodically plundered its treasure and destroyed the idols. In the intervening years the temple was rebuilt and refurbished several times but in the great earthquake of 1905 both the temple and the fort were badly damaged. The Devi received unusual offerings from devotees. According to Abul Fazal, the pilgrims "cut out their tongues which grew again in the course of two or three days and sometimes in a few hours"! The present temple in which the deity sits under a silver dome with silver *chhatras* (umbrellas) was built in 1920 and stands behind the crowded, colourful bazar. The State Government maintains the temple; the priests are expected to receive gifts in kind only. The area is busy, atmospheric and rather dirty, with mostly pilgrim-oriented stalls. Above these is **St Paul's Church** and a Christian community. Along the river between Old Kangra (where the main road meets the turning to the fort) and Kangra Mandir is a pleasant trail, mostly following long-disused roads past ruined houses and temples which evidence a once sizeable town. Kangra's bus stand is 1.5 km north of the temple.

## Masrur → *Colour map 1, B3. 34 km southwest of Dharamshala. Altitude: 800 m.*

A sandstone ridge to the northeast of the village has 15, ninth- to 10th-century *sikhara* temples excavated out of solid rock. They are badly eroded and partly ruined. Even in this state they have been compared with the larger rock-cut temples at Ellora in Maharashtra and at Mamallapuram south of Chennai. Their ridge-top position commands a superb view over the surrounding fertile countryside, but few of the original *shikharas* stand, and some of the most beautifully carved panels are now in the State Museum, Shimla. There are buses from Kangra.

## Jawalamukhi → *Colour map 1, B3.*

This is one of the most popular Hindu pilgrimage sites in Himachal and is recognized as one of 51 *Shakti pitha*. The **Devi temple**, tended by the followers of Gorakhnath, is set against a cliff and from a fissure comes a natural inflammable gas which accounts for the blue 'Eternal Flame'. Natural springs feed the two small pools of water; one appears to boil, the other with the flame flaring above the surface contains surprisingly cold water. Emperor Akbar's gift of gold leaf covers the dome. In March/April there are colourful celebrations during the **Shakti Festival**; another in mid-October. There is accommodation here, and buses to/from Kangra.

## Pragpur → *Colour map 1, B3.*

Pragpur, across the River Beas, 20 km southwest of Jawalamukhi, is a medieval 'heritage village' with cobbled streets and slate-roofed houses. The fine 'Judges Court' (1918) nearby has been carefully restored using traditional techniques. A three- to four-day stay is recommended here and it is advisable to reserve ahead.

## Stops along the Kangra Valley Railway

**Jogindernagar** is the terminus of the beautiful journey by narrow-gauge rail (enquiries Kangra, T01892-252279) from Pathankot via Kangra. The hydro-power scheme here and at nearby Bassi channels water from the River Uhl. Paragliding and hang-gliding is possible at Billing (33 km), reached via Bir (19 km, see below).

   **Baijnath**'s temples are old by hill standards, dating from at least 1204. Note the Lakshmi/Vishnu figure and the graceful balcony window on the north wall. The **Vaidyanatha Temple** (originally circa 800), which contains one of 12 *jyotirlingas*, stands by the roadside on the Mandi-Palampur road, within a vast rectangular enclosure. Originally known as **Kirangama**, its name was changed after the temple was dedicated to **Siva** in his form as the Lord of Physicians. It is a good example of the Nagari style; the walls have the characteristic niches enshrining images of Chamunda, Surya and Karttikeya and the *sikhara* tower is topped with an *amalaka* and pot. A life-size stone Nandi stands at the entrance. There is a bus to and from Mandi taking 3½ hours.

**Palampur**, 16 km from Baijnath, 40 km from Dharamshala (via Yol), is a pleasant little town for walking, with beautiful snow views, surrounded by old British tea plantations, thriving on horticulture. It is a popular stop with trekkers; see page 214. The Neugal Khad, a 300-m-wide chasm through which the Bandla flows is very impressive when the river swells during the monsoons. It holds a record for rainfall in the area.

**Bir**, 30 km east of Palampur, has a fast-growing reputation as one of the best paragliding locations in the world. Bordered by tea gardens and low hills, it also has four Buddhist monasteries worth visiting. Most prominent among these are Choling. You can also pick up fine Tibetan handicrafts from Bir, which has a large Tibetan colony. The village of Billing is 14 km up sharp, hair-raising hairpins and has the hilltop from where paragliders launch. Although unsuitable for beginners, there are courses available for intermediate fliers and a few residential pilots with tandem rigs. One excellent company based in Bir is **Touching Cloud Base**, www.touchingcloudbase.comwww.touchingcloudbase.com. They offer great instruction and tandem flights.

**Andretta** is an attractive village 13 km from Palampur. It is associated with **Norah Richards**, a follower of Mahatma Gandhi, who popularized rural theatre, and with the artist **Sardar Sobha Singh** who revived the Kangra School of painting. His paintings are big, brightly coloured, ultra-realistic and often devotional, incorporating Sikh, Christian and Hindu images. There is an art gallery dedicated to his work and memory; prints, books and soft drinks are sold in the shop. The **Andretta Pottery** (signposted from the main road), is charming. It is run by an artist couple (Indian/English), who combine village pottery with 'slipware'. The Sikh partner is the son of Gurcharan Singh (of Delhi Blue Pottery fame) and is furthering the tradition of studio pottery; works are for sale.

---

## Chamba Valley → *For listings, see pages 199-209. Colour map 1, B2.*

## Dalhousie → *Population: 7400. Altitude: 2030 m.*
**Himachal Tourism** ① *Near bus stand, T01899-242225, 1000-1700, helpful for transport information, but opening hours can be irregular out of season.*

Dalhousie, named after the governor-general (1848-1856), was developed on land purchased by the British in 1853 from the Raja of Chamba. It sprawls out over five hills just east of the Ravi River. By 1867 it was a sanatorium and reached its zenith in the 1920s and 1930s as a cheaper alternative to Shimla, and the most convenient hill station for residents of Lahore. Rabindranath Tagore wrote his first poem in Dalhousie as a boy and Subhash Chandra Bose came secretly to plan his strategies during the Second World War. Its popularity declined after 1947 and it became a quiet hill station with old colonial bungalows, now almost hidden among thick pine forests interspersed with oak, deodar and rhododendron. Its spectacular mountain views mean that it remains a popular bolt hole for tourists from the plains, but its importance today is mainly due to the number of good schools and the presence of the army.

The three Malls laid out for level walks are around Moti Tibba, Potreyn Hill and Upper Bakrota. The last, the finest, is about 330 m above **Gandhi Chowk** around which the town centres. From there two rounds of the Mall lead to Subhash Chowk. The sizeable Tibetan community make and sell handicrafts, woollens, jackets, cardigans and rugs. Their paintings and rock carvings in low relief can be seen along Garam Sarak Mall. Echoes of the colonial past include five functioning churches: diminutive **St John's** (1863) on Gandhi Chowk is open for Sunday service (0930 summer, 1000 winter) and the large Catholic church of St Francis (1894) on Subhash Chowk is often open to visitors. The nostalgic

**Dalhousie Club** (1895) displays old Raj-era photos and has preserved the original billiards table. The library contains bizarre English fiction and biographies, but sadly beer is not available in the bar.

Just over 2 km from Gandhi Chowk is the **Martyr's Memorial** at Panchpulla (five bridges), which commemorates Ajit Singh, a supporter of Subhash Bose and the Indian National Army during the Second World War. There are several small waterfalls in the vicinity, and on the way you can see the **Satdhara** (seven springs), said to contain mica and medicinal properties. **Subhash Baoli** (1.5 km from Gandhi Square), is another spring. It is an easy climb and offers good views of the snows. Half a kilometre away **Jhandri Ghat**, the old palace of Chamba rulers, is set among tall pine trees. For a longer walk try the Bakrota Round (5 km), which gives good views of the mountains and takes you through the Tibetan settlement.

### Kalatope and Khajjiar

**Kalatope Wildlife Sanctuary**, 9 km from Dalhousie, with good mountain views, is a level walk through a forest sanctuary with accommodation in a pretty forest resthouse bungalow (permission required from the DFO, Wildlife, Chamba, dfocha-hp@nic.in). There are good walking routes in the area, and wildlife includes black bears, leopards and serows. **Khajjiar**, 22 km further along the motorable road, is a long, wide glade ringed by cedars with a small lake and a floating island. Locals call it 'Mini Switzerland'. You can explore both areas in a pleasant three-day walk, alternatively a 30-km path through dense deodar forest leads from Khajjiar to Chamba. Buses to Khajjiar from Dalhousie take one hour.

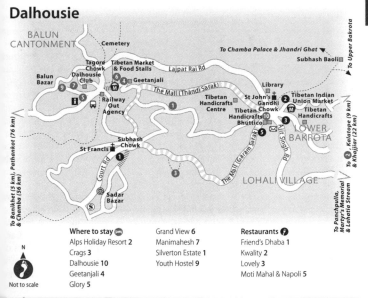

# Dalhousie

BALUN CANTONMENT

Cemetery

To Chamba Palace & Jhandri Ghat

Subhash Baoli

To Upper Bakrota

Tagore Chowk

Tibetan Market & Food Stalls

Lajpat Rai Rd

Balun Bazar

Dalhousie Club

Geetanjali

The Mall (Thandi Sarak)

Library

Tibetan Handicrafts Centre

St John's

Tibetan Indian Union Market

Railway Out Agency

Gandhi Chowk

Tibetan Chowk

Tibetan Handicrafts

Tibetan Handicrafts

Bhuttico

LOWER BAKROTA

To Banikhet (5 km), Pathankot (76 km) & Chamba (56 km)

Subhash Chowk

St Francis

Court Rd

The Mall (Garam Sarak)

Ajit Singh Rd

LOHALI VILLAGE

To Kalatope (9 km) & Khajjiar (22 km)

Sadar Bazar

To Panchpulla, Martyr's Memorial & Lohatia Stream

N

Not to scale

| Where to stay | | Restaurants |
|---|---|---|
| Alps Holiday Resort 2 | Grand View 6 | Friend's Dhaba 1 |
| Crags 3 | Manimahesh 7 | Kwality 2 |
| Dalhousie 10 | Silverton Estate 1 | Lovely 3 |
| Geetanjali 4 | Youth Hostel 9 | Moti Mahal & Napoli 5 |
| Glory 5 | | |

**Chamba** → *Colour map 1, B2. Population: 20,000. Altitude: 996 m.*

Picturesque Chamba is on the south bank of the Iravati (Ravi), its stone houses clinging to the hillside. Some see the medieval town as having an almost Italian feel, surrounded by lush forests and with its Chaugan (or grassy meadow) in the centre. Although that's stretching it a little and recent developments have somewhat diminished its appeal, the warmer climes, unusual temples and mellow ambiance remain most attractive. Most hotels, temples and palaces are within walking distance of the bus stand.

The **Tourist Office** ① *T01899-224002, Mon-Sat 1000-1630*, is in the **Hotel Iravati** complex (see Where to stay, page 203).

Founded in the 10th century, Chamba State was on an important trade route from Lahaul to Kashmir and was known as the 'Middle Kingdom'. Though Mughal suzerainty was accepted by the local rajas, the kingdom remained autonomous but it came under Sikh rule from 1810-1846. Its relative isolation led to the nurturing of the arts – painting, temple sculpture, handicrafts and unique 'rumal'. These pieces of silk/cotton with fine embroidery imitate miniature paintings; the reverse is as good as the front.

The **Chaugan**, once almost a kilometre long, is the central hub of the town but sadly over the last three decades, shops have encroached into the open space. There are several ancient Pahari temples in the town with attractive curvilinear stone towers. Follow the steep and winding road through the market to the **Lakshmi Narayana Temple Complex** (ninth to 11th centuries) containing six *sikhara* temples with deep wooden eaves, several smaller shrines and a tank. Three are dedicated to Vishnu and three to Siva, with some of the brass images inlaid with copper and silver. The **Hari Rai Temple**, next to the Chaugan (14th century), contains a fine 11th-century life-sized bronze Chaturmurti (four-armed Vishnu), rarely visible as it is usually 'dressed'; carved on the outer wall are Tantric couples. Close to the Aroma Hotel is the **Champavati Temple**, with carved wooden pillars, named after the daughter of Raja Sahil Varma who moved the capital here from Bharmour in 920 AD at her request. Others of note in the town centre are the Bansigopal, Sita Ram and Radha Krishna temples.

The 10th-century wooden **Chamunda Devi Temple**, 500 m uphill via steep steps from the bus stand, has some interesting wood carvings on its eaves and a square sanctum decked with bells. A further 500 m along the road to Saho is the elegantly slender **Bajreshwar Temple** with an octagonal roof, adjoined by a small, square unadorned temple.

The eye-catching **Akhand Chandi**, the Chamba Maharajas' palace, beyond the Lakshmi Narayan complex, is now a college. The old **Rang Mahal** (Painted Palace) in the Surara Mohalla was built by Raja Umed Singh in the mid-18th century. A prisoner of the Mughals for 16 years, he was influenced by their architectural style. The wall paintings in one room are splendid. The theme is usually religious, Krishna stories being particularly popular. Some of these were removed, together with carvings and manuscripts, to the Bhuri Singh Museum after a fire. The building now houses a sub-post office and a handicrafts workshop.

**Bhuri Singh Museum** ① *Museum Rd, Mon-Sat 1000-1700, Rs 100*, is a three-storey building (top floor currently closed) housing a heritage collection including some excellent *rumals*, carvings and fine examples of Chamba, Kangra and Basholi schools of miniature paintings. Archaeological finds include the remarkable 'fountain slabs' that adorned the spouts of village water sources. Dating from the 10th-18th centuries and hewn from local stone, these were memorials erected to the deceased; they are unique in Indian art. There are also many old photographs showing Chamba in its heyday. Opposite the museum is the finely built **St Andrew's Church**, belonging to the Church of Scotland and completed in 1905.

**Bharmour** → *Colour map 1, B2. Altitude: 2130 m.*

Capital of the princely state of Chamba for over 400 years, the tiny town of Bharmour is surrounded by high ranges and is snow-covered for six months of the year. It's 65 km from Chamba along a gruelling but incredibly scenic road, beset by landslides. Bharmour's ancient temples and its proximity to Manimahesh Lake and Manimahesh Kailash peak (5656 m) make it hallowed place, while alpine pastures in the region are home to Gaddi tribespeople (see below). The stone-built villages with slate-roofed houses adjoining Bharmour, and the snowy peaks all round, make it a beautiful spot.

The famous **Chaurasi** temple square has 84 shrines within, of varying architectural styles, built between the seventh-10th centuries. The towering *sikhara* of **Manimahesh (Shiv) Temple** dominates the complex. Giant deodars flank the entrance, which is guarded by a life-size Nandi bull in polished brass; devotees whisper a wish in his ear and crawl under him for good health (a tight squeeze for some). The sanctum of the delicate **Lakshna Devi temple** (c 700 AD) houses a metre-high idol of the goddess cast in bronze. The wooden exterior, particularly the door jambs, is beautifully carved; a marvellous pair of un-eroded lions flank the door to the inner shrine.

**Manimahesh**, 34 km distant, has a lake in which pilgrims bathe during the Yatra (August-September) and worship at the lakeside temple. Shiva resides on the holy mountain of the same name. Helicopter flights go from the helipad above the Chaurasi complex in Bharmour to Gaurikund during the Yatra, return journey Rs 7000 (www.simmsamm airways.com). For information on trekking to Manimahesh, see page 215.

Bharmour is the centre of the **Gaddis**, shepherds who move their flocks of sheep and goats, numbering from a couple of hundred to a thousand, from lower pastures at around 1500 m during winter to higher slopes at over 3500 m, after snow-melt. They are usually only found in the Dhauladhar range which separates Kangra from Chamba. Some believe that these herdsmen first arrived in this part of Himachal in the 10th century though some moved from the area around Lahore (Pakistan) in the 18th century, during the Mughal period. Their religious belief combines animism with the worship of Siva; Bharmour's distinctive Manimahesh Temple is their principal centre of worship. In the winter the Gaddis can be seen round Kangra, Mandi and Bilaspur and in the small villages between Baijnath and Palampur. The men traditionally wear a *chola* (a loose white woollen garment), tied at the waist with a black wool rope and a white embroidered cap.

## Northern Himachal listings

*For hotel and restaurant price codes and other relevant information, see pages 22-26.*

### Where to stay

**Dharamshala** *p189, maps p190 and p193*
Most visitors stay in McLeodganj (see below). With the new IPL cricket ground in Dharamshala, more 3-star and upmarket hotels are under construction in the area.
**$$$-$$$ White Haven Tea Estate**, below Dharamshala, T01892-226162, www.hotelwhitehaven.in. Charming working colonial tea estate set in 2.8 ha of beautiful gardens. 8 sumptuous rooms with creaking floorboards, log fires, lots of wood panelling and period antiques, exceptional service and tons of history. Recommended.
**$$$ Clouds End Villa**, north of Dharamshala, steep approach off Naoroji Rd, T01892-222109, www.cloudsendvilla.com. 7 rooms and 1 bungalow in Raja of Lambagraon's bungalow (Raj period), not luxurious but very clean, annexe has excellent valley views, authentic local cuisine (everything home-made), tours, peaceful, very friendly, excellent service.

**$$$ Grace Hotel**, 558 Old Chari Rd, Kotwali Bazar, T01892-223265, www.welcom heritagegracehotel.com. 14 comfortable suites in a 200-year-old wooden manor, formerly the residence of India's first Chief Justice. Pleasantly situated slightly out of town, a good place to relax and admire the views. This is a stunning place with beautiful artefacts. There is a meditation room and do try the delicious Himachali food, it's exquisite with subtle spicing and yoghurt.

**$$$-$$ Blossoms Village**, Sidhpur, near Dharamshala, T(0)9816-561213, www. blossomsvillage.com. 19 lovely rooms including cottages and suites. Stylishly decorated using local timber. New spa in 2013, with treatments and well-being therapies. Lovely rooftop bar and restaurant.

**$$$-$$ Chonor House**, Thekchen Choeling Rd, T01892-221006, www.norbulingka.org. 11 very comfortable, stylish rooms furnished in Tibetan style (murals of lost monasteries and mythical beasts), good restaurant, clean, well managed, popular with foreign diplomats, beautiful garden, a quiet and lovely place. Book ahead. Accepts credit cards. Highly recommended.

**$$ Dhauladhar** (HPTDC), Kotwali Bazar, T01892-224926, www.hptdc.nic.in. Several categories of room, all clean and large, 2 suites (**$$$**), cheaper in annexe, sombre restaurant, bar, pleasant garden, terrace for meals, friendly staff.

**$ Tsechokling Monastery**, Camel Track Rd, 300 m below McLeodganj, down 300 steps, T01892-221726. 20 clean rooms, 3 attached, some singles, hot showers, breakfast and dinner at set times, 'wonderfully peaceful'.

## McLeodganj

**$$$ Glenmoor Cottages**, off Mall Rd, T01892-221010, www.glenmoorcottages. com. Very peaceful, 7 large, modern, well-equipped 'cottages' with bedroom, kitchen, veranda, secluded old colonial house surrounded by forest, good valley views, great walks from doorstep.

**$$$-$$ Norling Guest House**, Norbulingka Institute, Gangchen Kyishong, T01892-246406, normail@norbulingka.org. Clean, comfortable rooms, in modern facilities in a Tibetan-style house. Café accepts Master/Visa cards. Beautiful setting inside the Norbulingka Institute, so surrounded by art and meditative peace.

**$$ Annex Hotel**, Hotel Surya Rd, T01892-221002, 0941-8020814, www.annexhotel.in. A short walk from the bus stand, all the rooms in this clean hotel have a balcony and are reached by the free Wi-Fi. Lounge and library, plus rooftop restaurant is excellent and has majestic sunset views.

**$$ Pema Thang**, opposite Hotel Bhagsu, T01892-221871, www.pemathang.net. 15 rooms with a bit more character than the average, good views from private balconies (better from upper floors), wooden floors, quiet, friendly, hot water and Wi-Fi works in rooms, nice rooftop restaurant with good pizza and pasta. Yoga hall at the rear (see What to do).

**$$-$ McLeod Ganj Homestay**, Flourishing Flora, close to TIPA Gate, Dharamkot Rd, T(0)9736-083878, www.mcleodganj homestay.net. With 3 lovely rooms and 1 hillside hut, this is a short walk up the TIPA road towards Dharmkot and has a lovely family vibe. All the rooms have a little touch of Tibet, there's great Indian home-cooked food with as much organic as possible and cookery lessons with Nisha. Sometimes there is roast chicken on an open fire. Recommended.

**$$-$ Tibet**, Bhagsu Rd, T01892-221587, hoteltibetdasa@yahoo.com. 20 well-maintained rooms with bath and TV, those on roadside can be noisy, good restaurant, cosy bar, accepts credit cards.

**$ Drepung Loseling**, Jogibara Rd, T01892-221087. Friendly hotel, 17 clean, well-maintained rooms with bath (some with hot water), dorm (Rs 90), terrace. Profits to Loseling Moanstery in Karnataka.

**$ Green Hotel**, Bhagsu Rd, T01892-221200, www.greenhotel.biz. Popular with backpackers, 30 variable rooms (avoid ground floor ones near the noisy courtyard), restaurant with comfy sofas, good internet.

**$ Ladies Venture**, Jogibara Rd, T01892-221559, www.ipcardesign.com/ladies venture. Peaceful hotel with dorm and 13 clean rooms, cheapest with shared bath, standard rooms have bath and TV, while top category are huge with seating areas. Trees rather obscure any mountain views, however. Very clean, respectable and popular (in part due to the helpful staff) and a good place to meet people. As they say, it's "just a name" and every body and soul is welcome. Small restaurant (good Chinese and Western food), terrace, often full so book ahead.

**$ Om**, western edge of bazar, T01892-221322, (0)9857-632037. Friendly hotel with 18 clean rooms, the en suite ones are excellent value with fresh paint and consistent hot water, while cheap room share baths (but shower is excellent), great views at sunset from patio terrace and rooftop. Free Wi-Fi. The excellent **Namgyal** restaurant which used to be at the Temple has moved here, so expect the best pizza in northern India.

**$ Paljor Gakyil**, TIPA Rd, up steps, T01892-221343. 14 clean rooms with bath (hot shower), dorm (Rs 25), excellent views, charming owners speak French and German, best of nearby bunch.

**$ Pawan House**, next to Dokebi, Jogibara Rd, T01892-220069, www.pawanhouse.com. Good views across the valley. Nice spacious clean rooms – good vibe. Recommended.

**$ Shambhala Guest House**, at Prayer Wheels, Jogibara Rd. Cosy family run place. Small rooms but nicely decorated, lots of warm blankets, hot shower, TV.

**$ Sidharth House**, bottom of Yongling school Steps off Jogibara Rd, T(0)8679-991907, www.sidharthhouse.in. Great guest house with conscious eco-vibe who established the 'Clean McLeodganj Project' and they have bins for compost as well as encouraging recycling. Much needed. Highly recommended.

### Around McLeodganj p192

**$$$ Eagles Nest**, Upper Dharamkot, T(0)9218-402822, www.hoteleaglesnest. com. 8 lovely themed rooms and suites in a beautiful old colonial house set in 20 ha of forest. Perched on top of the hill with spectacular views over Kangra and Kullu valleys. All inclusive, with excellent food and plenty of activities. Price includes all meals, horse-riding and guides for trekking. Recommended.

**$$-$ Hotel High Land**, Bhagsu Main Drag, T01892-220501. Big rooms with a bit of a view, TV.

**$$-$ Udechee Huts**, Naddi Gaon, T01892-221781, www.udecheehuts.com. Blending in with local style, 10 pleasantly furnished circular huts with bath (hot water), restaurant plus dining terrace, well kept, friendly hosts.

**$ 9 Chimes**, Upper Bhagsu, near Tree House, T(0)9736-130284, www.9chimes.com. 8 spacious rooms with balconies and nice views and one apartment. Recommended.

**$ DK House**, Upper Bhagsu, T01892-220671. 14 comfortable, spacious and clean rooms with big terrace and **Evergreen Restaurant** attached. Friendly family.

**$ Om Tara**, Lower Dharamkot, T(0)981-687949, www.houseomtara.com. Keeping their eye on the environment and with friendly service, this is a popular little guest house among fruit trees. There are big verandas to enjoy the views. Recommended.

**$ Pink House**, between Dharamkot and Bhagsu, T(0)9805-642060. Excellent value place with great views. Really peaceful and run by president of local women's group – she is quite right-on.

**$ Sapna House**, Upper Bhagsu, just above Unity Pizza, T01892-221594. Perennial favourite of the area – friendly family run place with pleasant rooms and garden.

**$ Shiv Shakti Guest House**, off Dharamkot Rd, T(0)9418-247776. Run by friendly father and son, 18 basic rooms with attached bath plus a stand alone, well-equipped cottage available too.

**$ Trimurthi Garden Café**, above Unity Pizza, Bhagsu, T(0)9816-869144. Favourite haunt with simple rooms, café and numerous workshops and yoga classes.

**$ ZKL Guesthouse**, above Bhagsu Rd, 500 m before Bhagsu itself, T01892-221581, www.zkl-monastery.com. 12 very basic but clean rooms in this charming monastery, Buddhist teachings and a café in the summer, outstanding value.

### Kangra p194

Most hotels on the busy main road are noisy, even at night.

**$$$$ Raas Kangra**, 20 km from Kangra aiport. Opening winter 2014 from the team behind the stunning **Raas** in Jodhpur. Boutique hotel with 41 suites all featuring balconies for panoramic views. It will bring innovative design together with natural beauty.

**$ Dilraj Guest House**, near Tehsil Chowk (taxi stand), T01892-265362. Friendly family house with 5 simple rooms, meals available. Recommended.

**$ Jannat**, Chamunda Rd, T01892-265479. 5 rooms, restaurant, TV, hot water, closest to Kangra Mandir railway station.

### Pragpur p195

**$$$ Judge's Court** (Heritage), set in a large orchard, T01970-245035, www.judgescourt. com. 10 tastefully decorated rooms in a fine mansion, 1 in an annexe, 1 large private modernized suite with veranda overlooking the Dhauladhar in a separate building. Family hospitality, home-grown vegetables and fruit, fresh river fish, authentic Himachali meals (Rs 350-550), tours of Kangra Fort and other sights included (a ride on a part of the narrow-gauge mountain railway is possible) friendly, efficient management. Pragpur very pretty village with lovely atmosphere. Recommended.

### Stops along the Kangra Valley Railway p195

**$$$ Taragarh Palace**, Al-hilal, 11 km southeast of Palampur, T01894-242034,

www.taragarh.com. 26 rooms in 1930s summer resort, period furniture and tasteful decor in public spaces, tennis, pool, lovely meandering gardens and mango orchards, luxury Swiss tents in summer. Decent service, but food a bit hit and miss.

**$$ Colonel's Resort**, 1 km out of Bir on the Billing road, T(0)9805-534220, www.colonelsresort.com. 8 doubles, 2 singles (simple, comfortable rooms) and 2 cottages, tents in garden (seasonal). Set in pear orchards and working tea plantation, with sublime views down the valley and behind into Dhauladhar mountains. Good food (breakfast and dinner included), warm hospitality, superb value. Popular with paragliders, plus good hiking in the area. 30% discount off-season.

**$$ Darang Tea Estate**, 10 km from Palampur, T(0)9418-012565, www.darang teaestate.com. 2 cottages and 1 room in the main house. Family run homestay in beautiful working tea estate. Exceptional food and warm hospitality. Recommended.

**$$ The Tea-Bud** (HPTDC), 2 km from bus stand, Palampur, T01894-231298, www. hptdc.nic.in. Beautiful setting, 31 rooms, deluxe category are in a newer block, older rooms are totally acceptable, hot water, restaurant, pleasant lawn, clean and quiet, good service, ayurvedic treatments available.

**$ Standard**, Baijnath, behind bus station, T01894-263714. 5 fairly clean and surprisingly tidy rooms with bath and hot water.

**$ Uhl** (HPTDC), near Power House, on hill outside Jogindernagar, T01908-222002, www.hptdc.nic.in. Unpretentious, clean and peaceful hotel, 16 rooms with bath, best upstairs with balcony, restaurant.

### Dalhousie p196, map p197

Some hotels look neglected and run-down, because the cost of maintaining the Raj-built structures is prohibitive. Most have good mountain views and massive discounts out of season.

**$$$ Grand View**, near bus stand, T10899-240760, www.grandviewdalhousie.in.

53 spacious, well-equipped rooms (5 price categories) in the best-preserved of Dalhousie's many Raj-era hotels. The views from the terrace are stunning, while the restaurant and lounge bar (awaiting license at the time of research!) are quintessentially British. Gym and sauna and off-season package deals are worth checking out. Recommended.

**$$$-$$ Silverton Estate Guest House**, near Circuit House, the Mall, T01899-240674, www.heritagehotels.com/silverton. Old colonial building in large grounds, 5 rooms with dressing rooms, TV, closed off season.

**$$ Alps Holiday Resort**, Khajjiar Rd, Bakrota Hills, T01899-240781, www.alpsresort.in. 19 smart rooms in old-fashioned retreat, with lovely large lawns, fine views of the Pir Panjal, 2-km climb.

**$$ Manimahesh** (HPTDC), near bus stand, I01899-242793, www.hptdc.nic.in. The 18 carpeted rooms are rather faded in this typical tourist department hotel, cheap restaurant, bar with sofas, good mountain views.

**$$-$ Hotel Dalhousie**, Gandhi Square, T(0)9815-550958. Period building with large terrace which lower rooms share; however, better quality rooms are on the upper level. All are very spacious. Friendly management, huge discounts off-season.

**$ Crags**, off the Mall, T01899-242124. The 100 steps separating this place from the Mall are the only disadvantage to this excellent budget choice. The rooms are dated but very clean with attached bath (hot water) and a bell to ring for service. Cheap and delicious meals, good views cast down the valley from the huge (if not particularly attractive) terrace, very friendly, the elderly owner is pretty stylish and used to catering to foreign travellers. A separate cottage is a more recent addition for a slightly higher price.

**Geetanjali** (HPTDC), Thandi Sarak, steep -min climb from bus stand, T01899-242155. 0 huge rooms with bath (reliable hot ater), towels and clean sheets provided –

but expect mildew-scented air as it's a very run-down colonial building.

**$ Glory**, near bus stand, T01899-242533. 4 rooms with bath in this seriously cheap option.

**$ Youth Hostel**, behind Manimahesh, T01899-242189, www.youthhostel dalhousie.org. Well-maintained, modern building with double rooms (Rs 300) and single sex dorms (Rs 150). Internet, free Wi-Fi and dining hall. Gets busy with groups – book ahead.

### Kalatope and Khajjiar *p197*

**$$$-$$ Mini Swiss**, Khajjiar, T(0)9810-229464, www.miniswiss.in. Comfortable, very clean rooms in a 5-storey building with great views, good restaurant and bar, pool table and ping-pong.

**$$ Devdar** (HPTDC), Khajjiar, T01899-236333, www.hptdc.nic.in. Clean rooms (doubles and suites), dorm (Rs 150) and a nice cottage (Rs 3000), simple restaurant, horse riding, beautiful setting. Free Wi-Fi.

### Chamba *p198*

During Manimahesh Yatra in Sep hotels are often full.

**$$ Hotel City Heart**, near Champavati Temple, opp. Chowgan, T01899-222032, www. hotelcityheartchamba.com. Large rather ugly hotel, but modern a/c rooms. Lowest category, on ground floor at rear, are windowless; however, deluxe and super deluxe are spacious with wood floors, big bathrooms and smart furniture. Bar is lacking in atmosphere, but restaurant is busy and serves good Indian food. Massive discounts off-season

**$$ Iravati** (HPTDC), Court Rd, near bus stand, T01899-222671. Friendly management, 19 variable rooms with bath and hot water. Regular rooms start at Rs 1500, spacious, nicely tiled, clean and overlook the Chaugan. The higher up the building, the better the views and the higher the prices. Decent restaurant.

**$$-$ Aroma Palace**, near Rang Palace, Court Lane, T01899-225577, www.hotel aromapalacechamba.com. Rooms range from economy to sumptuous honeymoon suite, all spotless, plus there's a restaurant and airy terrace. Breakfast included and discounts possible.

**$$-$ Chourasi**, Chourasi Rd, T01895-225615. Bright red structure on the road up to the temple. The cheaper basement rooms only have views of rubbish, and the top rooms are a bit overpriced at Rs 2000. Best deal are the Rs 1000 on the mid-levels. The restaurant has good food.

**$$-$ Himalayan Orchard Huts**, 10 km out of town, book through **Mani Manesh Travels** next to Lakshmi Narayana Temple, www.himalayanlap.com. Idyllic location (20 mins' walk from nearest road, rooms in guesthouse set in delightful garden with a spring-water pool, beautiful views from large terraces with hammocks, clean shared shower and toilets, or pitch a tent in the garden, superb home cooking (great all-inclusive deal), very friendly family. Recommended. Also own **Ridgemore Cottage**, a trekkers' hut atop a ridge, 4 hrs' walk from Orchard Hut.

**$$-$ White House**, near Post Office and Gandhi Gate, Main Bazaar, T01899-224111, rafeevwhitehouse@gmail.com. This red-roofed hotel on the edge of the road looks down onto the Ravi River. A range of room categories, all clean, bright and modern with pictures on walls, plus the **Copper Chimney Restaurant** (see Restaurants, page 206) make it a convenient choice.

**$ Akhand Chandi**, College Rd, Dogra Bazar, 1 km from bus stand, T01899-222371. Attractive stone building with 10 rooms, attached bath and TV, restaurant.

**$ Chamba Guesthouse**, Gopal Nivas, near Gandhi Gate, by the Chaugan, T01899-222564, (0)9805-282372. Simple lodgings with wooden floors and charm, this budget hotel almost hangs over the Ravi River affording amazing views from the balcony. Popular choice, try to book ahead. Bharmour

**$ Him Kailash Homestay**, near the bus stop, T01895-225100. Simple, friendly place with clean freshly painted rooms enjoying good

valley views. Cheapest rooms (Rs 500) don't have TV or geyser, or indeed curtains; much larger rooms with proper amenities cost Rs1000. Not much English spoken.

## 🍴 Restaurants

**Dharamshala** *p189, maps p190 and p193*
Most memorable food is in McLeodganj.
**$$-$ Andey's Midtown**, Kotwali Bazar. Indian and Chinese, some continental, best in town.
**$ Rajinder Vaishnau Dhaba**, Kotwali Bazar. Very simple sit-down *dhaba* serving Punjabi basics and thalis, tasty and busy.

### McLeodganj
Enterprising Tibetans in the upper town offer good traveller favourites for those tired of curries; some serve beer. Try *thukpa* (Tibetan soups), noodle dishes, steamed or fried *momos* and *shabakleb*. Save plastic waste (and money) by refilling your bottles with safe filtered, boiled water at the eco-friendly **Green shop** on Bhagsu Rd, Rs 5 per litre; also recycle used batteries.
**$$ Café Illiterati Books and Coffee**, LHS Jogiwara Rd, near Usho Institute. This trendy mellow café has slate floors and wonderful views, full bookshelves on Buddhism, society or literature and coffee-table tomes, exciting menu (eg chilli ginger red-bean burger) including good salads.
**$$ Carpe Diem**, past Post Office, Jogibara Rd. Nepali-run joint with excellent Indian, Thai and continental flavours. Good vibe, nice rooftop, beer under the table and open mic nights. Recommended.
**$$ Dokebi Seven Hills**, near Lung Ta, Jogibara Rd. Wonderful cosy restaurant with delicious range of vegetarian food including spicy hotpot-style soups, spicy kimchi and kimbap (Korean sushi). Upstairs there is lovely airy room with floor seating. Great fresh juices and smoky green tea. Highly recommended.
**$$ Jimmy's Italian Kitchen**, near prayer wheels, Jogibara Rd. Tibetan-run with

excellent food and views and a rooftop terrace. Live music most weekends; there was even a contestant from **American Idol** once!
**$$ Kunga's/Nick's Italian Kitchen**, Bhagsu Rd. Good vegetarian food, Italian including excellent pumpkin ravioli, plus quiches, pies, cakes, etc, but some small portions. With a huge terrace, deservedly popular, recommended.
**$$ Namgyal**, at Om Hotel, western end of bazaar. Open 1000-2200. Cosy and welcoming venue with amazing pizzas like roquefort and walnut or smoked cheese and spinach – best in the area. Good salads and Tibetan dishes too. Highly recommended.
**$ Common Ground Café**, Tushita Rd, above bus stand, Aldan Plaza, www.commongroundsproject.org. Serving up a Chinese-Tibetan food fusion, their menu underpins their ethos to foster shared understanding and respect between Chinese and Tibetans. It's a lovely place with great teas and desserts too.
**$ Gakyi**, Jogibara Rd. Tibetan. Also excellent porridge, fruit muesli. Lovely lady owner.
**$ Hotel Tibet**, behind old bus stand (see Where to stay). Good Tibetan/Japanese restaurant and take-out bakery.
**$ Lhamo's Croissant**, Bhagsu Rd. Beautiful café with furniture from **Norbulingka** offering tip top cappuccino, healthy salads, monumental club sandwiches, home-made soups and outrageously good cakes and tarts all served up by the eponymous Lhamo. They show films about the Tibetan cause every evening. Free Wi-Fi. Highly recommended.
**$ Lhasa**, on 1st floor opposite **Hotel Tibet**. Tucked away, very mellow interior serving good Tibetan dishes, well worth a visit.
**$ Lung-Ta**, Jogibara Rd. Mon-Sat 1200-2030. Classy Japanese vegetarian restaurant, not for profit, daily set menu or à la carte, good breads and cakes, sushi on Tue and Fri. Try the *okononiyak* (Japanese veg omelette). Great value and very popular. Little shop on-site too. Highly recommended.
**$ Pema Thang** (see Where to stay). Good vegetarian buffet brunch on Sun 1000-1400,

plus normal menu featuring great pasta, salads and pizza.
**$ Snow Lion**, near prayer wheels, T01892-221289. Offers good Tibetan and Western meals, excellent cakes.

### Cafés and snacks
**German Bakery**, Mirza Ismail Rd, steep road to Dharamkot. Open till 0100.
Best bread, brown rice.
**Moonlight** and **Sunrise**, opposite Tibetan Welfare Office, Bhagsu Rd. Small *chai* shops adjacent to each other with basic food. Excellent for meeting other travellers, especially in the evenings when overspill occupies benches opposite.
**Moonpeak**, Temple Rd, www.moonpeak.org. Very atmospheric café where people spill out onto outside tables to enjoy great cappuccinos, sandwiches and fantastic cakes. The first of the many coffee shops. Shows photography and art exhibitions. Free Wi-Fi.
**Moonpeak Thali** next door has some Himachali dishes.
**Rangzen** (Freedom), Bhagsu Rd.
Good health food, cakes.
**Rogpa**, Jogibara Rd. Tiny little café serving up lovely cakes and tasty coffee – all for charity. There's a little shop and second-hand stuff too. Recommended.
**Tara Café**, Bhagsu Rd.
Huge pancakes, friendly.
**Tenyang**, Temple Rd. Delicious coffee and cakes. Recommended.

### Around McLeodganj *p192*
**$$ Unity**, Upper Bhagsu, on path to Dharamkot. English owner creates amazing food, well presented and now a larger restaurant so more opportunity for wood oven pizzas.
**$ Family Pizzeria**, between Upper Bhagsu and Dharamkot. Excellent pizzas, French pastries, quiches and desserts, friendly staff and cider.
**$ Sansu's**, Upper Bhagsu. Renowned for its epic 'fruit-muesli-curd' – the best on the hillside.

**$ Singh Corner**, Bhagsu. Ah Bhagsu cake straight from the fridge – the original and best chocolate, caramel, biscuit combo – beware of imitators!
**$ Wa Blu**, Upper Bhagsu. Climb the steps for tempting Japanese food, miso soups and juices.

### Kangra *p194*
**$ Chicken Corner**, Dharamshala Rd, near the main bazar. An eccentric though fairly clean little hut does chicken dinners.

### Dalhousie *p196, map p197*
**$$ Kwality**, Gandhi Chowk. Good Indian and Chinese if a bit pricey. Nice place with TV.
**$$ Moti Mahal**, Gandhi Chowk. Closed off season. Good North Indian and tandoor.
**$$ Napoli**, near Gandhi Chowk. Similar to Kwality, serving pizza, Indian and Chinese, meat and veg dishes. Very friendly and comfortable. Large portions.
**$ Friend's Dhaba**, Subhash Chowk. Good, unpretentious Punjabi, *paneer burji* to die for.
**$ Lovely**, near Gandhi Chowk. Funky mirrored interiors, tasty North Indian.

### Chamba *p198*
There are a number of atmospheric little *dhabas* in the alleys through Dogra Market.
**$$-$ Copper Chimney**, 5th floor, White House Hotel (see Where to stay, page 204). Not at all pricey for good tandori, and veg/non-veg Indian and Chinese food. Comfy a/c indoor section or 4 intimate tables on the roof terrace. A long slog up the stairs, however.
**$ Jagaan**, 1st floor, Museum Rd. Reasonable selection, relatively calm, serves *chamba madhra* (Rs 90), a rich stew of kidney beans, ghee and curd that is a local speciality.
**$ Ravi View Café**, next to Chaugan. Reasonable snacks and Indian veg food plus beer (strong, Rs 110), this HPTDC-run circular hut even has outside tables with killer views overlooking the river.

## ☻ Entertainment

**Dharamshala** *p189, maps p190 and p193*
See *Contact*, a free, monthly publication. With everyone travelling with laptops now, there is only 1 film-club on the strip now on Jogibara Rd with a programme of Western films at a rather pricey Rs 150. **Lhamos Croissant**shows documentaries on Tibet. There are open mics at **Carpe Diem**. Indian classical music and Tibetan traditional music often at Yongling School.
**One Nest**, Lower Dharamkot. Regular live music in the evenings (Indian Classical and Western nomads), contact dance and free dance sessions.
**Tibetan Institute of Performing Arts (TIPA)**, www.tibetanarts.org, McLeodganj, stages occasional music and dance performances; details at Tourist Office.

## ☻ Festivals

### Chamba *p198*
**Apr** **Suhi Mela**, lasts 3 days, commemorates a Rani who consented to be buried alive in a dry stream bed in order that it could flow and provide the town with water. Women and children in traditional dress carry images of her to a temple on the hill, accompanied by songs sung in her praise. Men are strictly prohibited from participating.
**Jul-Aug** **Gaddis** and **Gujjars** take part in many cultural events to mark the start of harvesting. **Minjar** is a 7-day harvest festival when people offer thanks to Varuna the rain god. Decorated horses and banners are taken out in procession through the streets to mark its start. Sri Raghuvira is followed by other images of gods in palanquins and the festival ends at the River Irawati where people float *minjars* (tassels of corn and coconut).

## ☻ Shopping

**Dharamshala** *p189, maps p190 and p193*
It is pleasantly relaxed to shop here, although competition and prices have

increased in recent years. Many items on sale have been imported from the Tibetan market in New Delhi. McLeodganj Bazar is good for Tibetan handicrafts (carpets, metalware, jewellery, jackets, handknitted cardigans, gloves); special market on Sun.
**Bookworm**, near Surya Resort, has a good selection of paperbacks, some second-hand. Recommended.
**Dolls 4 Tibet** is an initiative bringing together Tibetan refugees and local Indian women, making beautiful dolls together. 'We see our Doll Makers grow in confidence and their sense of self worth. Their eyes and smiles say it all when a doll they've finished is admired. The skills they learn are empowering, the money they take home spells a new-found independence and their social interactions across our diverse community benefits not only our team but the wider society.' You can buy them at The Green Shop and Common Ground Café.
**Doritsang Tibetan Culture Centre**, Temple Rd, near SBBI. Great range of books, CDs, clothes and Tibetan bits and pieces.
**Green Shop**, Bhagsu Rd. Sells recycled and handmade goods including cards and paper. Also sells filtered drinking water for half the price of bottled water.
**Jewel of Tibet**, opposite prayer wheels. Best selection of singing bowls, jewellery and Tibetan arts. Maybe not the cheapest, but certainly the best value.
**Norbulingka Shop**, Temple Rd, close to Moonpeak. Well-crafted bags, cushion covers and clothes from **Norbulingka** – preserving Tibetan cultural arts.
**Rogpa**, Jogibara Rd. Charity based shop selling great gifts, notebooks, cards, bags and wallets. And second hand clothes.
**Tibet Book World**, Jogibara Rd, near Yongling School steps. Best bookshop in town – great range.
**Tibetan Children's Villages (TCVs)**, Main office on Temple Rd and workshops at various locations around town. Fabrics and jewellery at fixed prices.

**Tibetan Handicrafts Centre**, Jogibara Rd, near the tourist office. Ask at the office for permission to watch artisans working on carpets, *thangkas*, etc, reasonable prices.

### Dalhousie *p196, map p197*
**Bhuttico**, The Mall (Garam Sarak), www.bhutticoshawls.com. Mon-Sat 0900-1930. Fixed price shop, with branches nationwide, selling top quality Kullu shawls, socks and pullas (slippers with grass soles) that incorporate traditional designs.

### Chamba *p198*
**Handicrafts Centre**, Rang Mahal. Rumal embroidery and leather goods.

## ○ What to do

### Dharamshala *p189, maps p190 and p193*
**Body and soul**
See also **Tibetan Library**, page 192.
**Buddha Hall**, Main Rd, Bhagsu, T01892-221749. Yoga, meditation and healing courses.
**Dr Gonpo Kyi Acupuncture**, T(0)9857-119800. Attentive and reliable healer working with acupuncture, massage and Tibetan medicine.
**Himachal Vipassana Centre**, Dhamma Sikhara, next to Tushita, T(0)9218-414051, www.sikhara.dhamma.org. 10-day retreat, meditation in silence, donations only, reserve in advance, information and registration Mon-Sat 1600-1700.
**Himalayan Iyengar Yoga Centre**, Dharamkot, www.hiyogacentre.com. Offers 5-day course in Hatha yoga, starting every Thu at 0830. Information and registration Mon 1330. Now has retreat centre too.
**Tushita Meditation Centre**, Dharamkot village 2 km north of McLeodganj, T(0)8988-160988, www.tushita.info. Quiet location, offers individual and group meditation; 10-day 'Introduction to Buddhism' including lectures and meditation (residential courses get fully

subscribed), enquiries Mon-Sat 0930-1130, 1230-1600, also drop-in guided meditation Mon-Sat 0915-1015 throughout the year, movies relevant to Buddhist interests Mon and Fri 1400, simple accommodation on site.
**Z Meditation**, Kandi village, T(0)9418-036956, www.zmeditation.com. Interesting course including yoga and meditation. Retreats offered in silence with separate discussion sessions, 5 days (Mon 1600-Sat 1100), includes a 'humble' breakfast; highly recommended for beginners, run by friendly couple in peaceful location with beautiful views.

### Tibetan cookery
**Lhamo's Kitchen** Next to Green Shop, Bhagsu Rd T(0)9816-468719. Runs 3 courses (soups, bread, *momos*), 1100-1300, 1700-1900, Rs 200 each. Friendly, fun, eat what you cook.

### Tour operators
**Dhauladhar Travels**, Temple Rd, McLeodganj, T01892-221158, dhauladhar@hotmail.com. Agents for Indian Airlines.
**HPTDC** luxury coach in season: Dharamshala to McLeodganj, Kangra Temple and Fort, Jawalamukhi, 1000-1900, Rs 200; Dharamshala to McLeodganj, Bhagsunath, Dal Lake, Talnu, Tapovan, Chamunda, 1000-1700, Rs 200. Tickets from HPTDC Marketing Office, near SBI, Kotwali Bazar in Dharamshala, T018920-224928.
**Skyways Travels**, just off main square, Temple Rd, T(0)9857-400001. Reliable travel agent who is a mine of knowledge and even has paypal. Can make travelling in India a whole lot easier. Also for tours to Jammu and Kashmir, Rajasthan; trekking, camping and paragliding locally.
**Summit Adventures**, main square, Bhagsu Nag, McLeodganj, T01892-221679, www.summit-adventures.net. Specialist in trekking and climbing, also cultural trips and a yoga trekking tour.
**Ways Tours & Travels**, Temple Rd, T01892-221355, waystour@vsnl.net. Most reliable,

Mr Gupta is very experienced, and provides professional service.

### Trekking
Best season Apr-Jun and Sep-Oct. Rates upwards of Rs 1400 per person per day. See Summit Adventures above.
**Highpoint Adventures**, Kareri Lodge, T01892-220931, www.trek.123himachal.com. Organize treks for smaller groups and a range of tours.
**Mountaineering Institute**, Mirza Ismail Rd, T01892-221787. Invaluable advice on routes, equipment, accommodation, campsites, etc. Equipment and porters can be hired for groups of 8 or more, reasonable charges. The deputy director (SR Saini) has described many routes in *Treks and Passes of Dhauladhar and Pir Pinjal* (Rs 150) although the scale of maps can be misleading. Consult the author for detailed guidance. Mon-Sat 1000-1700.

## ⊖ Transport

**Dharamshala** *p189, maps p190 and p193*
It is dangerous to drive at night in the hills. The roads are not lit and the risks of running off the edge are great.
**Air** Nearest airport is at Gaggal, T01892-232374, 13 km (taxi Rs 650). To/from **Delhi** with Spicejet, www.spicejet.com. 1 service each daily.
**Local bus** Buses and share jeeps between Dharamshala and McLeodganj, 10 km, 30 mins, Rs 10/ Rs 25.
**Long-distance bus** Most originate in Dharamshala, T01892-224903, but some super and semi-deluxe buses leave from below the taxi stand in McLeodganj. HRTC enquiries, T01892-221750. HPTDC run luxury coaches in season. **Delhi** (Kashmir Gate, 521 km), semi-deluxe coach departs McLeodganj 1700, 14 hrs; deluxe coach 1830, 1945; super deluxe coach, 1900 (Volvo). Prices vary – deluxe coach is around Rs 880 and some of the private companies charge Rs 1200. Avoid **Bedi Travels** with

bad suspension. From Delhi at same times. 1930 arrives Lower Dharamshala 1000, recommended for best morning views of the foothills (stops en route). **Dalhousie** and **Chamba**, 0730, 0830, 1730, Rs180, 8 hrs; **Manali**, 1700, Rs 400, 8 hrs; luxury coach 2030, Rs 650, **Pathankot**, from Mcleod 1000, 1100, 1320, 1450, 1600, Rs150. HRTC buses to **Baijnath**, 2½ hrs; **Chandigarh** (248 km), 9 hrs, via Una (overnight stop possible); also deluxe buses to **Dehra Dun**, 1420 and 2000, Rs 410 and **Shimla**, 6000, 0820 and 2130 (from Dharamshala). **Kangra**, 50 mins, Rs 14; **Kullu** (214 km) 10 hrs; **Manali** (253 km) 11 hrs; best to travel by day (0800), fabulous views but bus gets overcrowded; avoid sitting by door where people start to sit on your lap! Always keep baggage with you; **Pathankot** (90 km), several 1000-1600, 4 hrs, connection for **Amritsar**, 3 hrs; **Shimla** (317 km, via Hamirpur/Bilaspur), 10 hrs.

**Private bus service** Dalhousie, 0740, 6 hrs, Rs 250; **Delhi** (Connaught Pl), 1800, 1830, 11 hrs, Rs 600-900. **Dehra Dun**, 1900, 13 hrs, Rs 650; **Kullu** 2100, 8 hrs, Rs 550; **Manali**, 0900, 2030, 9 hrs, Rs 550; **Rishikesh** 1930, 13 hrs. Several private agents, see Sky Travels.

**Local taxi** Shared by 4, pick up shuttle taxi at Kotwali Bazar on its way down before it turns around at the bus stand, as it is usually full when it passes the taxi stand.

**Long-distance taxi** Can be hired from near the bus stands, T01892-221205. Between Dharamshala and McLeodganj, Rs 150; to Pathankot around Rs 1500-2000 depending on size of vehicle.

**Train** Nearest broad-gauge railhead is at Pathankot. Booking office at bus stand, below tourist office, 1000-1100. For narrow gauge, see below.

### Kangra p194
**Air** Gaggal Airport, see Dharamshala, above.
**Bus** To **Dharamshala**, Rs 20, under 1 hr.
**Taxi** A taxi to **Dharamshala** costs Rs 400.
**Train** Narrow-gauge Kangra Valley Railway, enquiries T01892-265026. From

**Pathankot** to **Jogindernagar** (10 hrs) or **Baijnath**, reaching Kangra after 4½ hrs: 0430, 0710, 0925, 1300, 1640, 1740, 5 hrs (often 1 hr late). **Jogindernagar to Pathankot**: 0720, 1220, reaches Kangra in 5-6 hrs; **Baijnath to Pathankot**: 0420, 0735, 1425, 1800, to Kangra in 3-4 hrs. Kangra station serves Old Kangra with the fort, near the main road, while Kangra Mandir station is near the temple, bazar and most of the hotels. During the day there are regular rickshaw shuttles between Kangra Mandir station and Tehsil Chowk.

### Dalhousie p196, map p197
**Air** The nearest airport is at Gaggal, see Dharamshala, above.
**Bus** Dalhousie is on NH1A. **Amritsar**, 0600, 0945, 7 hrs; **Delhi**, 1830, 12 hrs; To **Chamba** 4 buses daily, 2 go via Khajjiar, 2½ hrs; **Dharamshala** 0715, 1115, 1400, 7 hrs; **Jammu**, 1000, 7 hrs; **Pathankot** first bus 0530, 1-2 buses per hr until 1630, 3½ hrs (change in Pathankot for frequent services to main towns/cities); **Shimla**, 1245, 14 hrs. Note that Banikhet village, 10 mins from Dalhousie, has many more bus options.
**Jeep/Taxi** From bus stand up to **Gandhi Chowk**, Rs 100, **Bakrota**, Rs 200.
**Train** Nearest station is at Pathankot, 2 hrs by taxi. There is a helpful Railway Out Agency close to the bus stand.

### Chamba p198
**Bus** The hectic bus stand is at the south end of the Chaugan. To **Bharmour** (3 hrs, Rs 70); **Dalhousie** (2½ hrs, Rs 50); and to **Shimla** once per day.
**Jeep** hire is relatively expensive. Special service during **Manimahesh Yatra**.
**Train** Nearest station is at Pathankot, 120 km away.

### ⊙ Directory

**Dharamshala** p189, maps p190 and p193
**Medical services** Delek Hospital, T01892-220053/223381, often foreign volunteer

doctors, good for dentistry. **District Hospital**, T01892-222133. **Men Tse Khang** (Tibetan Medical Institute) T01892-222484, Gangchen Kyishong, for Tibetan herbal medicine. **Dr Dolma's** and **Dr Dhonden's** clinics, near McLeodganj Bazar for Tibetan treatment. **Post** GPO, 1 km below tourist office on Main Rd T01892-222912, Mon-Sat 1000-1630, another in Kotwali Bazar. In McLeodganj, the post office, Jogibara Rd, has poste restante. **Hospital** Civil Hospital, T01899-242125. **Post** GPO: Gandhi Chowk. **Useful contacts** Foreigners' Registration Office: Civil Lines, beyond GPO, near petrol pump. **Police**: T01892-224893.

# Trekking in Himachal

*Himachal has something to offer every type of trekker. From short, leisurely walks through the pine forests that surround Shimla, with ample food and accommodation options meaning that nothing need be carried, to demanding treks over the high passes of Lahaul, Kinnaur and Spiti, the choice is almost as staggering as the views.* ⇥ *For listings, see pages 150-154, 164-167, 176-183 and 199-209.*

## Trekking from Shimla

From Shimla on the Hindustan–Tibet Highway, there are opportunities for short and long treks. These include **Chharabra**, 13 km beyond Shimla at 2593 m, and **Naldera**, 23 km from Shimla, which was Curzon's summer retreat, see page 147.

Still further on at **Narkanda**, 64 km from Shimla, is another trek with very good walks, especially up Hattu Peak. From Narkanda the road runs down to the Sutlej Valley and enters Kinnaur and Spiti. Foreigners are allowed into Spiti if they have a permit.

From just beyond Narkanda you can trek northwest over the **Jalori Pass** (3350 m) in the **Seraj** region. Starting from Ani village reached by bus/jeep from Luhri in the Sutlej Valley below Narkanda, you trek into the lower part of the Kullu Valley, joining the Kullu–Manali road at Aut. There is a road, accessible to jeeps, over much of this route. An alternative is to proceed 65 km from Narkanda to **Rampur** and then trek into the Kullu Valley via the **Bashleo Pass** (3600 m). There are forest rest houses en route so a tent is not essential. The pass is crossed on the third day of this five-day trek. Both treks end at **Banjar** in the Tirthan Valley from where there are buses to Kullu.

## Trekking in Lahaul, Kinnaur and Spiti

The border areas are being opened to trekkers with permits. At the same time the local tribal people are being exposed to outside influences which started with the introduction of television in these valleys. Now enterprising families open their homes to paying guests, youths offer their services as guides and muleteers and shops stock bottled drinks and canned food. However, anyone trekking in this region is advised to carry food, tents and all essentials.

### Lahaul → *Colour map 1, A3.*
Lahaul, like Zanskar and Ladakh immediately to the north, is an ideal trekking destination during the monsoon, as it is not nearly as wet as most other regions. The best time to go is from mid-June to mid-October but some passes, eg Shingo-La, Parvati Pass, may remain snow bound until mid-July or even later.

You can take a trek from **Darcha**, see page 187, up the valley over the **Shingo La** and on to **Padum**, the capital of the Zanskar region. Padum is linked with Leh. Shingo-La is over 5000 m so some acclimatization is desirable. The route is well marked.

An alternative route to Zanskar is up the Chandra valley and over **Baralacha La**. From here a trail leads over a high pass Phitsela to Phuktal, where you join the main trail coming from Darcha. Most travellers drive into Darcha; however, a fine trek past the 'Lake of the Moon' or Chandratal makes a nice and less known addition for those with a little more time. The route taken from **Manali** is over the **Hamta Pass** with good views of Deo Tibba (6001 m), weather permitting, to **Chhatru** village in the Chandra Valley. Here, there is camping in the grounds of a rest house and local families can put up visitors in very basic homes. It is four days' trek from Manali. Two days along the dirt road brings you to **Batal** (to save time you can take the bus from Manali over the Rohtang Pass). The next stage of both variations is to Chandratal.

**Chandratal** (4270 m) is 18 km from Batal. The first section up to Kunzum Pass is on the bus route. The remaining 8.5-km trail is open June-October and brings you to the beautiful clear blue-water lake, about 1 km long and 500 m wide, which lies on a glacial bowl. Carry your own tent and provisions. The lake can also be reached on a lower 14-km trail that directly runs from Batal (no regular buses from Manali). From Chandratal the route crosses several fast flowing streams before reaching the Baralacha La (usually three days). You need to be very careful and take adequate safety precautions while negotiating these stream crossings. It then goes over another pass along the same ridge as the Shingo-La, to join the main Darcha–Padum trail. From here you can continue on to **Padum** or return to Darcha in Lahaul. This second option makes for a very good circular trek.

Another possibility is to trek down the Chenab Valley and either cross the Pir Panjal by one of a number of passes into the Ravi Valley via Bahrmaur, to Chamba or carry on to Kishtwar.

Around lower Lahaul, you can trek from the district town of **Udeypur** at the base of the Miyar Nullah, the upper section of which is glaciated. To the east, high passes give access to the Bhaga valley and to the west to the Saichu Nala (Chenab tributary). The Trilokinath Temple nearby is well worth a visit, see page 186.

Trails run into the Miyar Nullah, renowned for flowers, then over the 5100-m Kang La Pass to Padum. Alternatively, you can follow the Chandrabhaga River to the scarcely visited Pangi valley with its rugged scenery, then over the 4240-m Sach Pass leading to Chamba District.

In the Pangi Valley, the Chandrabhaga flows at over 2400 m after the two rivers meet in this desolate and craggy region. The cheerful and good-looking Pangiwals keep their unique heritage alive through their singing and dancing. The Mindhal temple to Devi is their focus of worship. **Kilar** is the HQ which has a rest house and the Detnag Temple nearby. From Kilar a wide trail follows the steep slopes above the Chandrabhaga (Chenab) River to Dharwas on the Himachal/Kashmir border and then onwards to **Atholi** in the Paddar region of Kishtwar, known for its sapphire mines.

### Kinnaur → *Colour map 1, B3. See also page 155.*

Close to the Tibetan border on its east, Kinnaur has the Sutlej flowing through it. Garhwal is to the south, Spiti Valley to the north and Kullu to the west. The rugged mountains and sparse rainfall make Kinnaur resemble Lahaul. The Kinners (Kinnauris) are Hindu but the Tibetan Buddhist influence is evident in the numerous *gompas* that can be seen alongside the temples. The **Phulaich** (Festival of Flowers) takes place in September when some villagers leave for the mountains for two days and nights to collect scented blossoms, then return on the third day to celebrate with singing and dancing. Kinnaur, including the lovely side valleys of **Sangla** and **Bhabha**, is now open and permits are easily available from the District Magistrates in Shimla, Kullu or Keylong. These treks are immensely enjoyable; although there are stone huts and the occasional rest house, always carry a tent in this area.

**Baspa Valley** Starting from **Sangla** (2680 m), you can take a fairly level forest walk up to Batrseri (5 km), then along the road up to Rakcham (8 km; 3130 m) and climb gradually to reach **Chitkul** (18 km; 3450 m), passing through Mastrang. Another option is to start at **Morang**, see page 157, which has a bus from Kalpa. The trail follows the Sutlej River bank for a short distance until the Tirung Gad meets it. Here it turns southeast and after going through a narrow valley reaches **Thangi**, a village connected to Morang by road (4WD only) where mules are available for hire. The track continues along barren hills to Rahtak (camping possible), before rising steeply to Charang Pass (5266 m), then drops down following a mountain stream to Chitkul.

**Bhabha Valley** Starting from **Kafnoo** (2427 m), 22 km from Wangtu, this is another beautiful valley to trek. Permit details have to be entered and stamped at the police post 1 km before Kafnoo reservoir. They are checked at Tabo.

There is level ground at the end of the road by the reservoir suitable for camping, but it can get flooded. Local guides are available. From Kafnoo, the trail follows the right bank of the river for about 1 km before crossing to the left bank over a new bridge. From here, the trail gradually ascends to **Chokhapani**, about a five-hour walk away. The riverside trail is slippery and not recommended. The upper trail climbs past Yangpa II then through fields around Musrang hamlet. There is an adequate campsite at Chokhapani (10 km, 3000 m).

From Chokhapani to **Upper Mulling** (3470 m) is a beautiful 8 km, four hours' walk (including lunch stop), following the left bank of the Bhabha stream. Initially going through forests the track then crosses open meadows. At the far end of the meadows is an ideal camping site by the river. The trail from Mulling enters a forested section leading to a snow bridge across the stream. Cross the stream and follow the steeply rising trail to the **Kara** meadows where the Government Animal Husbandry Department has a merino sheep breeding centre. Ford the Bhabha River with care (either on horseback or by wading across with support from a fixed line), to the campsite at Pasha. This section takes three hours, so you can continue to the **Kara-Taria Pass Base**. The 5-km walk up a steep trail along the right fork of the Bhabha stream takes another four hours. Taria Base Pass (4290 m) camp is below the steep slope leading to the Pass. Camp well away from the slope as it is prone to rock falls.

**Pin Valley** There is a steep descent over scree for the first kilometre from **Taria Pass**, followed by a five-hour 15-km walk along a narrow but clear trail to the first camp in the Pin Valley. None of the apparently promising campsites on the way has a good water source. The **Bara Boulder** site has a stream and good grazing for horses.

The 11-km stretch from Bara Boulder to **Mudh** (3925 m) takes four hours. It is the highest permanently inhabited village in the Pin Valley and is surrounded by summer cultivation. Log bridges cross several streams feeding into the Pin River. There are places to stay and food is available but some villagers charge up to Rs 200-300 for a room. It is possible to camp outside the village. One campsite is on the flat plateau overlooking the river near the summer hut of the lay *lama* (before crossing the narrow foot bridge on the river), another is near the fields immediately below the village where a side stream runs below the old monastery into the Pin. It is worth visiting the old *gompas* in the village. From here you can get a ride back to Kaza.

## Spiti → *Colour map 1, B4.*

Spiti is a high-altitude desert, bare, rugged and inhospitable, with the Spiti River running from the slopes of Kunzum La (4551 m) to Sumdo (3230 m). Kunzum La offers seasonal access by road to Kullu from the valley, and it is also directly connected with Shimla via the NH22 and the SH30. Like neighbouring Lahaul, Spiti is famous for its *gompas*. Foreigners are allowed to trek in this region up to Kibber with permits.

At **Tabo**, the Buddhist monastery is one of the region's most famous, see page 158. There is a dispensary and two adequate teashops. Foreigners are now allowed to stay overnight in Tabo. There are other important *gompas* at Dankar, Ki, Kungri and Lalung. Trekkers interested in **fossils** choose a trail starting at **Kaza** and travel to **Langza** (8.5 km), which has a narrow track accessible to 4WD. The trek goes to Hikim, the Tangyut monastery, Komik (8 km) and returns to Kaza (6 km). From Kibber (4205 m) there is a 6-km track through alpine meadows to **Gete** (4520 m) which claims to be one of the highest permanent settlements in the world only reached on foot.

## Trekking in the Kullu and Parvati valleys

Treks here vary in duration and degree of difficulty. There are pleasant walks up the subsidiary valleys from Aut and Katrain with the opportunity to camp in spectacular and high locations without having to spend very long getting there. An option is to take the bus up to the Rohtang Pass, 51 km from Manali, which is spectacular and then walk down. There is a path and it only takes a few hours.

The post-monsoon period (September to mid-November) is the most reliable **season**. Longer treks with crossings of high passes can be undertaken then, before the winter snows arrive. During the monsoon (June to September) it is wet but the rain is not continuous. It may rain all day or for only an hour or two. Visibility is affected and glimpses of mountains through the clouds are more likely than broad clear panoramic views. However, many flowering plants are at their best. There is trekking in the spring, that is April to May, but the weather is more unsettled and the higher passes may still have quite a lot of snow on them. There can be very good spells of fine weather during this period and it can get quite hot in May.

You will need to take your own **equipment** since that hired out by local agencies is often inferior. Kullu now has pony unions with fixed rates for guides, porters and horses. Ask at the tourist office and the **Mountaineering Institute** for information.

### Routes
From **Manali** you can go north into **Lahaul** (see trek A on map, page 170) and **Spiti** Valleys by crossing the Rohtang (3985 m) or the Hampta Pass (4270 m). Once over the great divide of the Pir Panjal the treks are briefly described – see Trekking in Lahaul, Kinnaur and Spiti, above. West of Manali there are routes into the **Chamba** and **Kangra** Valleys (see trek B on map, page 170).

The trek to Malana Valley offers an opportunity to see a relatively isolated and comparatively unspoilt hill community. From Manali you go to Naggar (28 km, which can also be reached by bus) and stay at **Rumsu** (2377 m), which is higher. The Chandrakhani Pass (3500 m) takes you into the Malana Valley at the head of which is the glacier. On the third day you can reach **Malana** (2650 m, 20 km from Naggar), which has two guesthouses. In the past you could only enter with permission from the villagers but this is no longer needed. On the fourth day you trek to **Jari** (1500 m) where you can catch a bus to Kullu. The

## The Valley of the Gods

No one knows the origin of the village of Malana. People believe that a band of renegade soldiers who deserted Alexander's army in the fourth century BC settled here (some wooden houses have soldiers carved on them); it is more probable that their antecedents were from the Indian plains. Their language, Kanashi, has no script but is linked to Tibetan. The villagers are directly involved in taking decisions on important matters affecting them, thus operating as an ancient democratic 'city state'. Language,

customs and religious practices also differ from neighbouring hill tribes, polygamy being permitted.

A charming myth is associated with Jamlu, the principal deity in the valley. Jamlu, possibly of pre-Aryan origin, was carrying a casket containing all the important deities of Hinduism and while crossing the mountains through the Chandrakhani Pass into Kullu, a strong gust of wind blew open the box and spread the deities all over the valley. Since then Malana has been known as 'The Valley of the Gods'.

road from Jari to Malana may destroy the distinct character of the community. The whole of the Malana Valley is dominated by **Deo Tibba** peak in the north.

### Parvati Valley

To extend the trek from Malana it is possible to continue to **Manikaran** and onwards to Pulga and beyond in the scenic Parvati Valley. You can also get to Manikaran by bus from Kullu, see page 168. Up to **Khirganga** the trail is fairly clear but take care since the area is prone to heavy rain and land slips. Beyond Khirganga, the trek follows the valley up-river passing the tree line to Pandav Bridge and eventually arriving at the sacred lake and shrine at **Mantalai**. Here it splits leading up and over the Pin-Parvati Pass, and down into the dry Pin Valley.

Alternatively, you can explore the lower Parvati Valley by walking to **Kasol**, and then to Jari and Naggar via the temple of Bijli Mahadev (see trek **D** on map, page 170).

### Pin Valley → *Colour map 1, B4. See also page 159.*

The difference between the Parvati and the Pin Valley is striking. Immense glaciers and bizarre moonscape rock formations here contrast with the verdant pastures and evergreen forests of the Parvati Valley behind. The trek leads down to the traditional village of **Mudh**, see page 212. The road to Mudh is still incomplete so it takes about five hours to walk to Sangam and Chatral, leading to Kinnaur and Spiti. There are buses from Chatral to Kaza, see page 160. The trek from Manikaran to Kaza with passes over 5300 m, can take 10 to 14 days. Guides and porters are necessary.

### Trekking in Kangra → *Colour map 1, B3. See also page 194.*

**Baijnath**, **Palampur** and **Dharamshala** are popular starting points. See pages 195, 196 and 189. From here you go over the **Dhaula Dhar** at passes such as the Indrahar and Minkiani (both from Dharamshala) and the Waru (from Palampur), then enter a feeder of the Upper Ravi Valley.

Midway up the valley, which lies between the Manimahesh Dhar and Dhaula Dhar range, is Bara Bangahal. From there you can go downstream to **Chamba** or upstream which offer the choice of at least three passes for crossing into the Kullu Valley. The northernmost of these is the Taintu Pass which passes Beas Kund beneath Hanuman Tibba. In the middle is the Manali Pass whilst the southernmost is Kalihani Pass. A good trip which includes the upper part of this valley is the round trip trek from Manali, see page 173.

## Trekking from Chamba → *Colour map 1, B2.*

The Chamba region receives less rain than the Kangra Valley to the south. A trek, particularly over the Pir Panjal into Lahaul is possible during the monsoon months (June to September). The ideal season, though, is just after the monsoon. There are several short and longer treks from Chamba and Bahrmaur in the Upper Ravi Valley.

To the north there are three main passes over the **Pir Panjal** into Lahaul: the Kalicho, Kugti and Chobia passes. At least five days should be allowed for crossing them as their heights are around 5000 m and acclimatization is highly desirable. All the first stages of the walks are along the Budhil River. After the first two days, the services of a guide or porters are recommended for picking the right trail. Views from the passes are very good both of the Himalaya to the north and the Chenab Valley to the south. The descent from the passes is very steep. On reaching the road you can take a bus from **Udeypur** or **Trilokinath** in the Pattan Valley, to the Kullu Valley over Rohtang Pass. Several trails cross the high passes over the Pir Panjal range to give access to the Pattan Valley of Lahaul. The semi-nomadic Gaddi shepherds regularly use these to take their flocks across to the summer grazing grounds located in the high-sided valleys of Lahaul.

**Bharmour** (1981 m), also spelt Brahmaur or Bharmaur, is 65 km from Chamba and can be reached by bus. It was the original capital Brahmapura for four centuries and has 8th-10th-century *Pahari* style temples. The best known are the Lakshminarayan group which is the centre of worship for the semi-nomadic Gaddi tribe (also see page 199). From Bharmour a three-day trek is possible to **Manimahesh Lake** (3950 m), 34 km, in the Manimahesh Kailash (5575 m), a spur running off the Pir Panjal. The **Manimahesh Yatra** begins in Chamba and ends at the lake, revered by local people as a resting place of Siva. Pilgrims arrive at the Manimahesh temple here and take a holy bath a fortnight after *Janmashtami* (September/October). The temple has a brass *Mahisasuramardini* image. During the *yatra* period buses, minibuses and taxis are laid on from Chamba to Bharmour. Many pilgrims trek the next 12 km to Hadsar although jeeps are available. From here it is a two-day climb to the lake with a night halt at Dhanchho. Himachal Tourism tents available at Bharmour and there is also a rest house, Hadsar, Dhanchho and Manimahesh; contact tourist office, Dalhousie, T01899-242736. Ponies and porters can be hired at each place. The nine-day trek starting from Chamba includes **Rakh** (20 km) on Day 1, **Bharmour** on Day 2, a rest stop there, then continuing to **Hadsar** (12 km), **Dhanchho** (7 km) and **Manimahesh** (7.5 km) with a brief halt at **Bhairon Ghati**. The return is by the same route.

## Contents

### Footprint features

### At a glance

⊖ **Getting around** Trains run as far as Jammu. Buses and jeeps go to Srinagar and on to Leh, which also has a spectacular road connection to Manali in Himachal Pradesh. Domestic flights to Srinagar and Leh.

⦿ **Time required** At least a week for the Vale of Kashmir and a house-boat stay; 8 days in Ladakh to acclimatize and visit sights – more if you want to add in a trek or the Nupra Valley.

☀ **Weather** Ladakh is best May-Oct, and drops far below freezing over winter. The snow season in Gulmarg runs Dec-Apr.

✖ **When not to go** Avoid the harsh mid-winter in Ladakh, and the Vale of Kashmir on contentious dates such as Republic Day (26 Jan).

**Jammu & Kashmir**

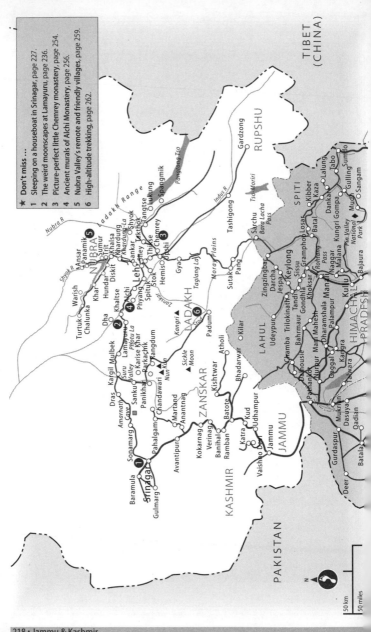

★ Don't miss ...
1  Sleeping on a houseboat in Srinagar, page 227.
2  The weird moonscapes at Lamayuru, page 236.
3  Picture-perfect little Chemrey monastery, page 254.
4  Ancient murals of Alchi Monastery, page 256.
5  Nubra Valley's remote and friendly villages, page 259.
6  High-altitude trekking, page 262.

The lakes, fertile valleys and remote, snow-covered peaks of Jammu and Kashmir have had a magnetic appeal to rulers, pilgrims and humble travellers, from the Mughals onwards.

Yet, tragically, extended and bitter political violence has put the beauty of the Vale of Kashmir either literally or psychologically out of bounds for almost 25 years. Despite the prominent marketing of houseboats, golf courses and ski resorts and the fact that Indian tourists are returning to Srinagar in large numbers, there remains an obvious military presence. While levels of violence have gone down in recent years, be aware that curfews or demonstrations might occur and be sure to check the latest travel situation with your embassy. The major pilgrimage to Amarnath is open, and conspicuously guarded by the army, but trekking elsewhere in the Vale of Kashmir should be undertaken only after careful research and with a reliable guide. However, foreigners will find themselves warmly welcomed by the Kashmiris and in Srinagar and the surrounding area there is plenty to see and do – not to mention to buy and to eat.

The state is equally famed for the magnificent realm of Ladakh and its capital, Leh, set in some of the world's most beautiful scenery. Here you can trek to your heart's content among some of the highest-altitude passes in the world, in one of India's remotest regions. The spectacular high-altitude deserts of Ladakh and Zanskar provide the setting for a hardy Buddhist culture whose villages and monasteries retain strong links with Tibet. Alchi, Hemis and Thikse are just three of the most striking of the many monasteries clinging to mountainsides.

## The land

**Geography** The largest of India's Himalayan states comprises three regions of stark geographical and cultural diversity. **Jammu**, in the southwest, is a predominantly Hindu region bordering the **Punjab**, its foothills forming the transitional zone between the plains and the mountains. To the north the Shiwalik mountains give way to the Pir Panjal, which attain heights of 5000 m. Between the Pir Panjal and the High Himalaya, at an average altitude of 1580 m, lies the largely Islamic **Vale of Kashmir**, where snow-capped peaks form a backdrop to the capital, Srinagar, and the Nagin and Dal lakes. Rising behind the Vale are the Great Himalaya which culminate in the west with Nanga Parbat (Naked Mount) at 8125 m.

To the west and north are the Buddhist mountain provinces of **Ladakh** and **Zanskar**, crossed by four mountain ranges – Great Himalaya, Zanskar, Ladakh and Karakoram – as well as by the River Indus and its tributaries the Zanskar, Shingo and Shyok. The Zanskar cuts an impressive course of 120 km before slicing through the Zanskar range in a series of impressive gorges to join the Indus at Nimmu near Leh, the capital of Ladakh. During the winter months, the frozen Zanskar provides the only access for Zanskaris into Ladakh. Combined with its two subsidiary valleys, the Stod (Doda Chu) and the Lung-Nak (Tsarap Chu or 'Valley of Darkness'), which converge below Padum, the main valley is approximately 300 km long and is ringed by mountains, so access to it is over one of the high passes. The most important are the Pensi La connecting Zanskar with the Suru Valley in the west, the Umasi La with the Chenab Valley in the south and the Shingo La with Lahul in the east. Ladakh also has the world's largest glaciers outside the polar regions, and the large and beautiful lake Pangong Tso, 150 km long and 4 km wide, at a height of over 4000 m. This makes for spectacular trekking country.

**Climate** Even in the Vale, the air in summer is fresh and at night can be quite brisk. The highest daytime temperatures in July rarely exceed 35°C but may fall as low as -11°C in winter. A short climb quickly reduces these temperatures. In Ladakh the sun cuts through the thin atmosphere, and daily and seasonal temperature variations are even wider. The rain-bearing clouds drifting in from the Arabian Sea never reach Ladakh; while Srinagar receives over 650 mm per annum, Leh has only 85 mm, much as snow. Over half Srinagar's rain comes with westerly depressions in the winter.

## Background

Ruled for many years by Scythian and then Tartar princes, **Kashmir** was captured in 1341 by Shams ud Din who spread Islam across the Vale. In 1588 the Mughal Emperor Akbar conquered Kashmir and his son Jahangir (1605-1627), captivated by the beauty of the Vale of Kashmir, planted chinar trees and constructed pleasure gardens. Later, the area fell under Sikh rule and when they were defeated by the British at the end of the first Sikh War in 1846, Jammu, the Vale of Kashmir, Ladakh, Baltistan and Gilgit were assigned to the Maharaja Gulab Singh of Jammu, who had aided the British victory. He founded a dynasty of Dogra Rajputs, descended from the Katoch branch of the lunar race of Rajputs. Thus began a period of Hindu rule over the mainly Muslim population of the Vale of Kashmir.

Rock carvings in Ladakh indicate that the region has been used for thousands of years by nomadic tribesmen who include the Mons of North India, the Dards, the Mongols and Changpa shepherds from Tibet. In Roman times Kashmir and Ladakh lay on a feeder of the great Silk Road that ran from China to the Mediterranean. By the end of the 10th century, Ladakh was controlled by the Thi Dynasty which founded a capital at Shey and built many forts. Tibetan Lamaistic Buddhism took hold at the same time and over 100 *gompas* were built. In 1533 Soyang Namgyal united the whole region up to the outskirts of Lhasa and made his capital at Leh. The Namgyal Dynasty still exists today and the Rani (Queen) of Stok was elected to the Indian Parliament. During the reigns of Senge Namgyal (circa 1570-1620) and Deldan Namgyal (circa 1620-1660) Ladakh was threatened from the south and west by the Baltis, who had enlisted the assistance of the Mughals. They were beaten back and the Namgyals extended Ladakhi power. The expansionist era came to an end when the fifth Dalai Lama of Tibet, Nawang Lobsang Gyatso (1617-1682) persuaded the Mongols, whom he had converted to Buddhism, to enter a military campaign against West Tibet and Ladakh. The Ladakhis were unable to repel the invading Mongol forces and in desperation Delegs Namgyal turned to Kashmir for help. The Mughal Governor of Kashmir sent troops to help the King of Leh regain his throne but in return he had to pay regular tribute and build a mosque. From then on the country became an extension of the Mughal empire. In 1834 Zorwar Singh, an Army General, conquered Ladakh and brought the area under the control of the Dogra Maharajah of Kashmir. The dethroned royal family received the Stok Palace where they still live today.

Zanskar became an administrative part of Ladakh under Senge Namgyal whose three sons became the rulers of Ladakh, Guge and Zanskar/Spiti. This arrangement collapsed after Ladakh's war with Tibet and the Zanskar royal house divided, one part administering Padum, the other Zangla. Under the Dogras, the rulers were reduced to puppets as the marauding army wreaked havoc on the villages, monasteries and people.

When India gained Independence from Britain, rulers of 'princely states' such as Kashmir were given the choice of whether to stay with India or join Pakistan. But Kashmir's maharajah, Hari Singh, played for time, in the hope that Kashmir could remain independent of both countries. In October 1947, Kashmir was invaded by tribesmen from Pakistan's North West Frontier Province, with the support of the Pakistani army. Singh, supported by popular leader Sheikh Abdullah, had to turn to India for help. Nehru sent in the Indian army and 18 months of fighting followed until 1949, when the state was split by a UN-monitored cease-fire line, much of which remains the de facto border between India and Pakistan today. Of the total area of the pre-Independence State, over which India continues to claim the legitimate right to govern, 78,000 sq km are currently controlled by Pakistan and a further 42,600 sq km by China. Kashmir has remained the single most important cause of conflict between India and Pakistan since 1949, while arguments for autonomy within the Kashmir Valley have periodically dominated the political agenda, erupting in 1987, when – it is widely accepted – India rigged the state elections to bring about a favourable result. Widespread unrest followed and hundreds of young men fled over the border to receive arms training in Pakistan. The militancy started in earnest in 1988 and continues today, although it is now much less overt than during the early years.

Following India's Independence and partition in 1947, Ladakh, like Kashmir, was divided. Indian and Chinese troops have been stationed on the eastern border since the Chinese invasion of Tibet in 1950-1951. From the early 1950s Chinese troops were stationed in the Aksai Chin, which India also claimed, and without Indian knowledge built a road linking Tibet with Xinjiang. This was one of the two fronts in China's war with India in 1962, which confirmed China's de facto hold on the territory. India still disputes its legality. Since the 1962 war the Indian army has maintained a very strong presence in Ladakh. The strategic requirements of better links with the rest of India were primarily responsible for Ladakh being 'opened up' to some influences from outside.

## The current political situation

The insurgency that started in the late 1980s has gone through several evolutions. Until the mid-1990s, it was overt and highly visible, with parts of Srinagar being held by the militants, openly carrying arms. Fierce counter-insurgency measures forced them underground, but the violence continued. Meanwhile, in May 1999, war broke out between Pakistan and India, in the Kargil area, lasting two months. Even after the cease fire, the two countries continued shelling each other across the border, badly affecting the Jammu border districts of Poonch and Rajouri.

The tension reached a peak in June 2002 after an attack on the Indian parliament in December 2001 – allegedly carried out by Pakistan based militants. Internationally, there were serious fears that the two countries were on the brink of nuclear war but thankfully the situation was wound down following a new agreement between India and Pakistan to try and find a peaceful solution to the problem.

On 8 October 2005 a massive 7.6 magnitude earthquake struck Kashmir, killing 73,000 people and injuring hundreds of thousands more on either side of the Line of Control. While border controls were loosened to allow families to search or grieve for loved ones, the potential longer-term benefits of international cooperation have not yet been realised. By April 2007 only 1600 people had availed of the Peace Bus (set up in 2005 to enable Kashmiris to visit their relatives on the other side of the Line of Control, and as a "confidence-building measure" between India and Pakistan), in part due to the bureaucracy involved in making the crossing. However, the Peace Bus is still operational despite frequent interruptions and suspensions to the service when tensions along the border are high.

In December 2008, state elections saw the highest voter turnout since the militancy began. The National Conference won, in a coalition with the Indian National Congress party and Omar Abdullah, aged 38, became the state's youngest ever chief minister.

Instability and the rise of the Taliban in Pakistan's North-West Frontier through 2009 along with the holding of peaceful elections for the state assembly and the Lok Sabha in Indian-held Kashmir have relegated Kashmir to the back pages, but a solution which meets with the full support of Kashmiris in both Indian and Pakistani Kashmir is still a distant prospect.

## Traditional Ladakhi dress

Ladakhis dress in *gonchas*, loose woollen robes tied at the waist with a wide coloured band. Buddhists usually wear dark red while Muslims and nomadic tribes often use undyed material. The headdress varies from the simple Balti woollen cap with a rolled brim and the traditional *gonda* (a high embroidered hat) to the snake-shaped ornate black lambskin *perak* worn by some women. Studded with turquoise and lapis lazuli these are precious enough to be handed down as heirlooms.

## Modern government

The state enjoys a special status within the Indian nation. As defined in Article 370 of the constitution, since 1956 Jammu and Kashmir has had its own constitution affirming its integrity. The central government has direct control over defence, external affairs and communications within the state and indirect influence over citizenship, Supreme Court jurisdiction and emergency powers. In normal times the state sends six representatives to the Lok Sabha and two members who are nominated by the governor to the Rajya Sabha.

In Ladakh, the local government body, the Autonomous Hill Council, was created in 1995 due to reasons of cultural uniqueness and the fact that they do not wish to be part of any separatist movement in Kashmir.

## Culture

Culturally, the people of Jammu, Kashmir and Ladakh could scarcely be more different from each other. The 12.5 million population is unevenly scattered. The Vale of Kashmir has more than half the population, whilst Ladakh is the most sparsely populated region. Jammu was traditionally the seat of Dogra power and serves a largely Hindu population whose affinities lie more with the Punjab than the Vale. Kashmir marks the northernmost advance of Islam in the Himalaya while Ladakh is aptly named 'Little Tibet'. Ethnically the Ladakhis are of Tibetan stock. Indeed, it was once a province of Tibet and was governed in secular matters by an independent prince and in spiritual affairs by the Dalai Lama. Tibetan Changpas form the bulk of the population in central and eastern Ladakh. These nomadic herdsmen can be seen living in black yak-hair tents on the mountains with their yaks, goats and sheep. They still provide the fine pashm goat wool. The Mons, nomads of Aryan stock, introduced Buddhism and established settlements in the valleys. The Droks or Dards from the Gilgit area settled along the Indus Valley and introduced irrigation; many converted to Islam 300 years ago. Most are cultivators speaking a language based on Sanskrit. The Baltis with Central Asian origins mostly live in the Kargil region. The Zanskaris are of the same stock as the Ladakhis and because of the sheer isolation of their homeland were able to preserve their Buddhist culture against the onslaughts of Mughal India. The majority of Zanskaris are Buddhist, though there are Muslim families in Padum, the capital, dating from the Dogra invasion.

Kashmiri is influenced by Sanskrit and belongs to the Dardic branch of the Indo-Aryan languages. Linguistically and physically Kashmiris are similar to the tribes around Gilgit in Pakistan. The Ladakhis physically reveal Tibetan-Mongolian and Indo-Aryan origins while their language belongs to the Tibetan-Burmese group.

# Religion

In the Vale of Kashmir, 97% of the people are **Muslim**, the majority being Sunnis, while in Jammu about 65% are **Hindu**. In Ladakh, 46% are Lamaistic **Buddhists**. Most follow Mahayana Buddhism of the Vajrayana sect with a mixture of Bon animism and Tantric practices. The Red Hat Drukpa (or Kagyupa) sect of Tibetan monastic Buddhists enjoy royal patronage. The reformist Yellow Hat sect are Gelugpa Buddhists and, like the Dalai Lama, wear a yellow headdress with their maroon robes. The more ancient Nyingmapa Buddhists have their seat in Takthok. Ladakhi *lamas* may also be physicians, teachers and astrologers; they also work in the fields, as do the *chomos* (nuns). Nearly every family has a member who chooses to become a *lama* (often the third son) or a *chomo*. The most important in the Tibetan tradition are recognized reincarnate *lamas* (Trulku), who are born to the position. The Buddhist *gompas* (monasteries) are places of worship, meditation and religious instruction and the structures, often sited on spectacular mountain ridges, add to the attraction of the landscape while remaining a central part of Ladakhi life. Ladakh also has a large number of Shi'a Muslims, mainly in Kargil District, many being immigrant Kashmiris and Dards. Their mosques and *imambaras*, influenced by Persian architecture, can be found in Leh proper and villages nearby.

The foundation of Sani in the 11th century is recognized as the first monastery in Zanskar. Phugtal and Karsha date from the same period. The sects developed alongside those in Ladakh. The Gelugpa (Yellow Hat) order was established in the 15th century and monasteries at Karsha, Lingshet and Mune belong to this. The Drukpa sect set up monasteries at Bardan and Zangla and 'occupied' that at Sani. These have links with Stakna near Leh and the Gelugpa is associated with the Lekir monastery. Traditional Ladakhi and Zanskari life, even today, comes close to Gandhi's idealized vision of life in ancient India.

# Handicrafts

Kashmir is deservedly famous for its distinctive and fine handicrafts. Many of these developed when Srinagar was a trading post on the ancient trans-Himalayan trade route. High-quality craftsmanship in India initially owed much to the patronage of the court and Kashmir was no exception. From the 15th century onwards, carpet making, shawl weaving and embroidery and decorative techniques were actively encouraged and the tradition grew to demands made at home and abroad. Since tourism has been severely affected in the Vale since 1989, Kashmiri tradesmen have sought markets in other parts of India.

Kashmir **shawls** are world renowned for their softness and warmth. The best are pashmina and shahtush, the latter being the warmest, the rarest and, consequently, the most expensive. Prized by Moghuls and maharajas they found their way to Europe and through Napoleon's Egyptian campaign, became an item of fashion in France. The craft was possibly introduced from Persia in the 15th century. Originally a fine shawl would take months to complete especially if up to 100 colours were used. The soft fleece of the pashmina goat or the fine under hairs of the Tibetan antelope were used, the former for pashmina (cashmere) shawls, the latter for shahtush. The very best were soft and warm and yet so fine that they could be drawn through a finger ring. The designs changed over the years from floral patterns in the 17th century to Paisley in the 19th century. The Mughals, especially Akbar, used them as gifts. However, with the introduction of the Jacquard loom, cheap imitations were mass produced at a fraction of the price of hand woven shawls. Kashmiri shawls thus became luxury items, their manufacture remaining an important source of employment in the Vale, but they ceased to be the major export.

Hand-knotted **carpets** were traditionally made in either pure wool or mixed with cotton or silk. However, nowadays pure wool carpets are hardly produced in the valley, the preference being for silk. The patterns tend to be the traditional, the Persian and Bukhara styles being common, though figurative designs such as The Tree of Life are becoming increasingly popular. A large carpet will take months to complete, the price depending on the density of knots and the material used, silk being by far the most expensive. The salesmen usually claim that only vegetable dyes are used and whilst this is true in some instances, more readily available and cheaper chemical dyes are commonplace. After knotting, the pile is trimmed with scissors, loose threads burnt off and the carpet washed and dried. Young boys work with a master and it is common to hear them calling out the colour changes in a chant. Child labour in carpet making across North India is increasingly widely criticized, but government attempts to insist on limiting hours of work and the provision of schooling are often ignored. Look for the rug mark awarded when no child labour is used.

**Papier mâché** boxes, trays, coasters make ideal gifts. Paper is soaked, dried in a mould, then painted and lacquered. Traditionally, natural colouring was used (lapis lazuli for blue, gold leaf for gold, charcoal for black) but this is unlikely today. The patterns can be highly intricate and the finish exquisite.

Other crafts include **crewel** work (chain stitching) on fabric, Kashmiri silver **jewellery**, silk and fine **woodcarving**, particularly on walnut wood.

# Kashmir Valley

*The beauty of the Vale of Kashmir, with its snow-dusted mountains looming in shades of purple above serene lakes and wildflower meadows, still has the power to reduce grown poets to tears. Nonetheless, the reality of military occupation pervades many aspects of daily life, with army camps, bunkers and checkposts positioned every few hundred metres along the highways and throughout the countryside. Travellers not dissuaded by the ever-present threat of violence or the official warnings to stay away can expect to encounter extremes of beauty and friendliness, not to mention hard salesmanship, in an economy that's been starved of tourist income for over 20 years.* ▸▸ *For listings, see pages 237-246.*

## Jammu → *For listings, see pages 237-246. Colour map 1, A2. Phone code: 0191. Population: 951,373.*

Jammu, the second largest city in the state, is the winter capital of government and main entry point for Kashmir by train. While it doesn't possess the charm of Srinagar, it is a pleasant enough city to spend a day in. Built in 1730 by the Dogra rulers as their capital, Jammu marks the transition between the Punjab plains and the Himalaya hills.

### Arriving in Jammu

**Getting there** The airport is within the city; a pre-paid taxi to the centre (Ragunath Bazar) costs around Rs 200. There are daily flights from Delhi and Srinagar, and twice weekly flights to Leh. The railway station is in the New Town, across the Tawi River, a few kilometres from the old hilltop town where most of the budget hotels are located. The general bus stand, where inter-state buses come in, is at the foot of the steps off the Srinagar Road in the Old Town. ▸▸ *See Transport, page 245.*

**Getting around** The frequent, cheap city bus service or an auto-rickshaw comes in handy as the two parts of the town and some sights are far apart.

**Tourist information** Jammu and Kashmir Tourist Reception Centre ①*Vir Marg, T0191-254 8172, www.jktourism.org* has brochures. **Jammu Tawi** ①*railway station, T0191-247 6078.* **JKTDC** ①*T0191-257 9554.*

**Climate** Temperatures in summer reach a maximum of 40°C, minimum 28°C. Rainfall in July and August is 310 mm, with other months measuring an average 40 mm. The best time to visit is from November to March.

## Places in Jammu

**Raghunath Temple** ①*0600-2130, inner sanctum closes 1130-1800, museum 0600-1000, cloakroom for bags/cameras,* in the old centre is one of the largest temple complexes in North India, and dates from 1857. The temple, dedicated to Lord Rama, has a series of glittering gilded spires and seven shrines. The main shrine's interior is gold-plated, while surrounding shrines contain millions of 'saligrams' (mini-lingams fixed onto slabs of stone), most of which are fossils. **Rambiresvar Temple** (1883), centrally located on the Shalimar Road, is the largest Siva temple in North India. It is dedicated to Siva and named after its founder Maharaja Ranbir Singh. The 75-m orange tower is rather unattractive, but the central 2.3-m sphatik shivling is an extraordinary crystal lingam. A fine bronze Nandi bull watches the entrance to the shrine.

About 700 m from the Rambiresvar Temple are the palace buildings of **Mubarak Mandi**. Dating from 1824, it blends Rajasthani, Mughal and baroque architectural elements. Within the dilapidated complex is the **Dogra Art Gallery** ①*Tue-Sun 1030-1630, foreigners Rs 5,* displaying royal memorabilia in the Pink Hall.

The **Amar Mahal Museum** ①*Apr-Sep 0900-1300, 1400-1800, Oct-Mar 0900-1300, 1400-1700, foreigners Rs100, Rs 150 by auto-rickshaw from the centre of town, or take a minibus,* is superbly sited on the bend of the Tawi, just off Srinagar Road , and has great views of the river. There is a maharajas' portrait gallery and 18th-century Pahari miniature paintings of *Mahabharata* scenes. The early 20th-century palace is a curiosity; its French designer gave it château-like roofs and turrets. Look through a rear window to see Hari Singh's 100 kg golden canopied throne. Other rooms show modern art; admission to the library (with a fine collection of antique books) is only for researchers. The Hari Niwas Hotel is adjacent; the lawns are a welcome spot for refreshments when it's not too hot.

Across the Tawi River lies the impressive **Bahu Fort**, thought to have a 3000-year history. The ramparts have been renovated and are now surrounded by a lush terraced garden, the Bagh-e-Bahu.

## Vaishno Devi → *For listings, see pages 237-246. Colour map 1, A2.*

The Vaishno Devi cave, 61 km north of Jammu, is one of the region's most important pilgrimage sites. As the temple draws near you hear cries of 'Jai Matadi' (Victory to the Mother Goddess). Then at the shrine entrance, pilgrims walk in batches through cold ankle-deep water to the low and narrow cave entrance to get a glimpse of the deity. Visitors joining the *yatra* find it a very moving experience.

The main pilgrimage season is March to July. The arduous climb along the 13-km track to the cave temple has been re-laid, widened and tiled, and railings provided. Anothe road from Lower Sanjichat to the Darbar brings you 2 km closer with 300 m less to climb. Ponies, *dandies* (a kind of local palanquin for carrying tourists) and porters are available from Katra at fixed rates. Auto-rickshaws and taxis can go as far as the Banganga. Yatra slips are issued free of charge by the **Yatra Registration Counter** (YRC) in the bus stand in Katra. The slip must be presented at the Banganga checkpoint within six hours (or face disciplinary action if caught). One slip can be used for up to nine people. Tea, drinks and snacks are available on the route.

Visitors should leave all leather items in a cloakroom at Vaishno Devi before entering the cave; take bottled water and waterproofs. If you are on your own or in a small group, you can usually avoid having to wait for a group if you present yourself at Gates 1 or 2, and smile.

**Katra** is an attractive town at the foot of the Trikuta Hills where visitors to the Vaishno Devi cave can stay.

---

**Srinagar** →*For listings, see pages 237-246. Colour map 1, A2. Population: 1,269,751. Altitude: 1730 m.*

Founded by Raja Pravarasen in the sixth century, ringed by mountains and alluringly wrapped around the Dal and Nagin lakes, Srinagar ('beautiful city') is divided in two by the River Jhelum. Once known as the city of seven *kadals* (bridges), there are now 12 that connect the two sides, the older ones giving their names to their adjoining neighbourhoods. It is the largest city in the state and the summer seat of government. Sadly the troubles of the past 20 years have scarred the town, leading to the desertion and neglect of many of its fine houses, buildings and Hindu temples. The famous Dal Lake has shrunk to a sixth of its former size and has become badly polluted. Older Srinagaris lament the passing of the formerly spruce city, yet even so, Srinagar is a charming city with a strong character, unique in India for its Central Asian flavour.

## Arriving in Srinagar

**Getting there** The airport is 14 km south of town; a taxi to the main tourist areas takes 30-45 minutes and costs Rs 400. Srinagar has several daily direct flights from Delhi and weekly flights from Leh. Direct buses from New Delhi take 24 hours, but this is an arduous trip. If you want to travel overland, it's more comfortable to take the train as far as Jammu (12 hours), stop for the night and then travel to the valley by jeep or bus the next day (eight to nine hours, including stops for lunch and tea). It's a stunning journey through the mountains as the bus winds its way up to the Jawahar tunnel that burrows through the Pir Panjal, the jade-green Chenab river flowing hundreds of feet below. Emerging from the tunnel on the other side, high in the hills of south Kashmir, travellers are treated to a breathtaking view of the valley spread before out before them. There are several bus stations; tourist buses from Jammu and Delhi arrive and leave from the Tourist Reception Centre, see below.

**Getting around** There are government taxi stands with fixed rates at the Tourist Reception Centre (Residency Road), Dal Gate and Nehru Park, and an abundance of auto-rickshaws. Local buses are cheap, but can be crowded and slow. The days of dusk-to-dawn curfews are over, but even so, the city shuts down relatively early; by 2100 the streets are deserted and it can be tricky to find transport. → *See Transport, page 245.*

**Tourist information** The **Tourist Reception Centre** ① *Residency Rd, close to the tourist area of Dalgate, T0194-245 2691, www.jktourism.org, open 24/7,* houses the state department of tourism, the **Jammu and Kashmir Tourism Development Corporation (JKTDC)** ① *T0194-2457927, www.jktdc.co.in,* and **Adventure Tourism** for booking accommodation and tours.

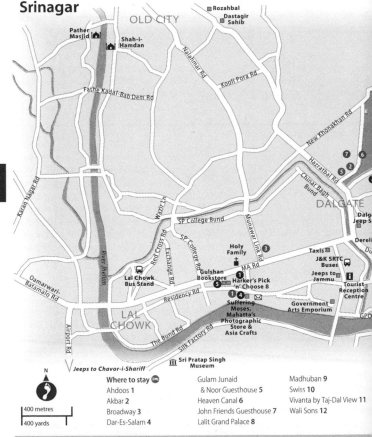

# Srinagar

**Where to stay** 🛏
Ahdoos **1**
Akbar **2**
Broadway **3**
Dar-Es-Salam **4**

Gulam Junaid
 & Noor Guesthouse **5**
Heaven Canal **6**
John Friends Guesthouse **7**
Lalit Grand Palace **8**

Madhuban **9**
Swiss **10**
Vivanta by Taj-Dal View **11**
Wali Sons **12**

Also within the complex is the **J&K State Transport Corporation** ① *T0194-245 5107* for bus tickets. You can pick up an excellent map showing both the city and the whole state at the TIC.

**Safety** At time of writing the British **Foreign and Commonwealth Office** ① *www.fco. gov.uk*, was advising against all rural travel in Jammu and Kashmir, except in Ladakh, the cities of Jammu and Srinagar, and along the Jammu-Srinagar highway. For an on-the-ground perspective, check www.greaterkashmir.com, www.kashmirtimes.com and www.freepresskashmir.com. Most travellers report no problems, but it is essential to be careful and keep informed about the situation.

Grenade attacks on army bunkers in the city used to be common, but are currently rare. However, in 2006 six Indian tourists were killed during grenade attacks on two bus loads of tourists from West Bengal. Given the tensions between Kashmir and the Indian government, Indian tourists are more likely to be directly targeted than foreigners.

Since the uprising in 2008, demonstrations, stone throwing and daytime curfews – particularly in the old city – have been increasing in frequency. The Dal and Nagin lake areas are hardly affected on such occasions – at worst, you might not be able to get transport during a *bandh* (general shutdown).

If you are in town and see the shop shutters coming down before closing time, this is generally a sign that a protest is approaching. Either beat a hasty retreat in an autorickshaw, or take shelter in a shop until the demonstrators and police have passed. Always ask how the situation is before heading to the old city (Downtown) and don't go there on Fridays, when spontaneous demonstrations following afternoon prayers are common.

### Places in Srinagar

The city falls into three parts; the commercial area (**Uptown**), the old city (**Downtown**) and the area around the lakes (**Dalgate**, the **Boulevard**, **Nehru Park**). Downtown can be reached from Uptown either directly, by driving through Dalgate or by driving all the way around Dal Lake, which takes you past the gardens of Cheshma Shahi, Nishat and the turning for the road to Shalimar. This route also takes you past the Grand Palace Hotel, the village of Brein, the Char Minar Island restaurant

estaurants ❼
afé Robusta **1**
ishna Dha ba **2**
aasa **3**
ughal Darbar & Tao Café **4**

Shakti Sweets
& Modern Sweets **5**
Shamyana **6**

and reaches Downtown via the Hazrat Bal mosque and Makhdoom Sahib. Uptown is the place for shopping, particularly Polo View and the Bund, which is a footpath that runs along the Jhelum. Residency Road and Lal Chowk are also in Uptown.

Hotels on the Boulevard are popular – particularly with Indian tourists – but tend to be huge, impersonal and overpriced. The city is famous for its houseboats and staying on one can be a very pleasant experience, but it is necessary to book carefully; if the deal sounds too good to be true, then it probably is and you will end up paying in other ways (ie by being coerced into shopping trips, from which your hosts will take a hefty commission). Don't be bullied into booking a trip by pushy, Kashmiri travel agents in New Delhi – much better to book through the **Houseboat Owners Association**. Try and find a boat with good references from other travellers, through sites such as www.tripadvisor.com. Also be aware that many boats in the Dal and Nagin lakes can only be accessed by *shikara*. While boat owners will always insist that a *shikara* will always be at your disposal, some tourists have found that this has not been the case and have found themselves marooned on boats with hosts they don't particularly like.

The Uptown area is good to stay in if you are interested in exploring the city and prefer to be away from the tourist rush. There are also some houseboats on the Jhelum River, with walk-on/walk-off access. You can hear the noise of the traffic from these boats, but there are no hawkers in this area.

Hotels around Dalgate tend to offer more budget options and can be very enjoyable. Those actually inside the lake are a good choice (Heaven Canal, Akbar) as the area is interesting with good views, but less hassle than the Boulevard.

**Old City** Srinagar's old city (known locally as Downtown) is a fascinating area to wander around with rather a Central Asian feel. Once the manufacturing and trade hub of Kashmir, each *mohalla* (neighbourhood) had its own speciality, such as carpet weaving, goldsmithery and woodcarving. It was said that you could find even the milk of a pigeon in the thriving bazars and its traders grew rich, building themselves impressive brick and wood houses, in a style that is a charming fusion of Mughal and English Tudor.

In the north of the Old City is the distinctive mound of **Hari Parbat Hill**, on which stands a fort built by Shujah Shah Durrani in 1808 (closed to the public). On the southern side of Hari Parbat, the **Makhdoom Sahib shrine** is dedicated to Hazrat Sultan and has wonderful views of the city. The actual shrine is off-limits to women and non-Muslims, but you can peek through the ornate, carved screen from outside and marvel at the fabulous array of chandeliers. In 2013, a **cable car** ①*tourists Rs 100*, up to the shrine was opened. Alternatively, you can access the steps up the hill from near the Sikh Gurdwara **Chhatti Padshahi**, by the imposing **Kathi Darwaza** (gate) in the Old City walls. This arched gateway (recently restored) was the principle entrance to the fort; a Persian inscription states that it was built by Akbar in 1597-8. In the city wall on the opposite side of fort is the Sangeen Darwaza, which is more ornate (currently being restored).

From Makhdoom Sahib take an auto-rickshaw (or walk 15 minutes) to the **Jama Masjid** (1674). The mosque is notable for the 370 wooden pillars supporting the roof, each made from a single *deodar* tree. The building forms a square around an inner courtyard, with a beautiful fountain and pool at its centre. Its four entrance archways are topped by the striking, pagoda-like roofs that are an important architectural characteristic of the valley's mosques and shrines. The mosque was where the sacred hair of the Prophet Mohammed was kept before being moved to the Hazratbal Mosque.

About 10 minutes' walk to the southeast lies the 17th-century **tomb of Naqash Band Sahib**, a sufi saint. The interior of the shrine is covered with (modern) colourful papier-mâché flower designs; there is a women's section. The ornate mosque adjacent to the shrine is meticulously maintained, and is constructed of brick and wood alternate layers. Next to the shrine lie the graves of the 'martyrs' who died in the 1931 uprising against the Dogras. They are claimed as heroes by both the state government and the separatists – one of the few things both sides agree on.

Continue further in the same direction and you will reach the **Dastagir Sahib shrine**, which houses the tomb of Abdul Qazi Geelani. A fire in 2012 almost entirely destroyed the main structure, including antique chandeliers, exquisite papier mâché and carved wood decoration. The 300-year-old, giant, handwritten Qu'ran and the holy relic of the saint were saved, as they were in a fireproof vault. The shrine is to be rebuilt according to its original structural character, and many devotees still come to pray here.

A minute's walk away is little **Rozahbal shrine**, which claims to contain the 'tomb of Jesus' (Holger Kersten's *Jesus Lived in India* recounts the legend; also see www.tombofjesus.com). The community here are sensitive about inquiring visitors: do not produce a camera, and don't be surprised if locals warn you away. Head west towards the river for the beautiful **Shah-i-Hamdan Masjid**, the site of Srinagar's first mosque, built in 1395 by Mir Sayed Ali Hamadni. The original building was destroyed by fire and the current wooden structure dates back to the 1730s. The entrance is worth seeing for its exquisite papier-mâché work and woodcarving, but non-Muslims are not allowed inside the actual shrine. However, there is a women's section at the rear which female non-Muslims can enter and you can linger by the doorway with devotees, peeping inside to see the richly painted walls and chandeliers.

Facing Shah-i-Hamdan, across the river is the limestone **Pathar Masjid** (1623), built for the Empress Nur Jahan and renamed Shahi Mosque. Further up the river, on the same side as Shah-i-Hamdan, lies the 15th-century bulbous brick **tomb of Zain-ul-Abidin's mother** ⓘ*daily 0900-1700*, which is embellished with glazed turquoise tiles. The tomb adjoins a graveyard, containing the sultan Zain-ul-Abidin's grave and those of his wives and children, enclosed by an old stone wall that has been reused from an earlier Hindu temple. The area, Zaina Kadal, is interesting to walk around – carved copperwork is still produced here and you can see the craftsmen at work. It's the best place to buy your souvenir samovar.

South of the old city and the river is the remarkable **Sri Pratap Singh Museum** (1898) ⓘ*Lal Mandi, Tue-Sun 1030-1630, foreigners Rs 50*. Kashmir's Hindu and Buddhist past stares you in the face as 1000-year-old statues of Siva, Vishnu and the Buddha, excavated from all over the valley, casually line the walls. One room houses an eclectic mix of stuffed animals, bottled snakes and birds' eggs, topped off by the dissembled skeleton of a woolly mammoth and looked down on by a collection of stags' heads, mounted on the papier-mâché walls. There are also miniature paintings, a selection of ancient manuscripts and coins, as well as weapons, musical instruments and an anthropology section. Look out for the extraordinary Amli shawl in the textiles room: an embroidered map of Srinagar, showing the Jamia mosque and the Jhelum dotted with houseboats (it took 37 years to complete). The collection will be displayed in full when the museum extends into the larger building being constructed next door.

**Dal Lake and the floating gardens** Of all the city's sights, **Dal Lake** must be its trademark. Over 6.5 km long and 4 km wide, it is divided into three parts by manmade causeways. The small islands are willow covered, while round the lake are groves of *chinar*, poplar and willow. The Mihrbahri people have lived around the lakes for centuries and are market gardeners, tending the floating beds of vegetables and flowers that they have made and cleverly shielded with weeds to make them unobtrusive. Shikaras, the gondola-like pleasure boats that ply the lake, can be hired for trips around the Dal (the official rate Rs 300 per hour, but it's possible to bargain for half that). The morning vegetable market is well worth seeing by boat, it starts around 0600 and a one-hour tour is adequate; it is in a Shi'ite area adorned with appropriate flags. If you're curious about the city, take a boat up the Jhelum as far as Shah-i-Hamdan, where you can get out for a walk. If you do this, it's worth taking a guide with you who can speak English.

Set up on a hill, behind the Boulevard (known as Takht-i-Sulaiman or 'Throne of Soloman'), is the **Shankaracharya Temple**, with great views and a good place to orientate yourself. The temple was constructed during Jahangir's reign but is said to be on the same site as a second-century BC temple built by Asoka's son. The inelegant exterior houses a large lingum, while beneath is a cave where Shankaracharya is said to have performed a *puja*. The temple is 5.5 km up a steep road from the Boulevard; walking up the road is not permitted, although hitching a ride from the security check at the bottom is possible (open 0900-1700). There is an alternative rough path starting from next to the gate of the City Forest Hotel on Durganag Road (one hour up, 30 minutes down).

Set in front of a triangle of the lake created by intersecting causeways (now demolished), with a slender bridge at the centre, lies the famous **Nishat Bagh** (Garden of Gladness) ① *Sat-Thu 0900-sunset, Rs 10*. Sandwiched between the hills and the lake, the steep terraces and central channel with fountains were laid out by Asaf Khan, Nur Jahan's brother, in 1632 (see page 393).

The **Shalimar Bagh** ① *Apr-Oct 0900-sunset, Nov-Mar 1000-sunset, Rs 10*, gardens are about 4 km away and set back from the lake. Built by Jahangir for his wife, Nur Jahan, the gardens are distinguished by a series of terraces linked by a water channel with central pavilions. These are surrounded by decorative pools, which can be crossed by stones. The uppermost pavilion has elegant black marble pillars and niches in the walls for flowers during the day and candles or lamps at night. The chinar (plane trees) have become so huge that some are falling down. **Chashma Shahi** (Royal Spring, 1632) ① *0900-sunset, Rs 10*, is a much smaller garden built around the course of a renowned spring, issuing from a miniature stone dome at the garden's summit. It is attributed to Shah Jahan though it has been altered over the centuries. Nearby are the **Botanical Gardens** ① *Sat-Thu 0800-sunset, Rs 10*. Rather wilder than the other gardens, its tucked-away location makes it popular with runners.

West (2.5 km) of Chashmi Shahi, nestling in the hills, is the smallest and sweetest of the Mughal gardens, the charmingly named **Pari Mahal** (Fairy Palace) ① *sunrise-sunset, Rs 10*. Built in the 17th century by the ill-fated prince Dara Shikoh, who was later beheaded by his brother Aurangzeb, the garden has six terraces and the best sunset views of Srinagar. The terraced gardens, backed by arched ruins, are being restored and are illuminated at night.

Close to Nagin Lake, **Hazratbal Mosque** (Majestic Place) is on the western shore of Dal Lake and commands excellent lake views. The modern mosque stands out for its white marble dome and has a special sanctity as a hair of the prophet Mohammad is preserved here. Just beyond is the **Nazim Bagh** (Garden of the Morning Breeze), one of the earliest Mughal gardens and attributed to Akbar.

At the end of the Boulevard in Nehru Park the tiny **Post Office Museum** ① *daily 1100-2000*, is unique in that it floats. You can send your mail from here.

# The most expensive spice in the world

Pampore, 11 km from Srinagar, is the centre of Kashmir's saffron industry. Saffron, a species of crocus (*Crocus sativus*), grows here in abundance, and in a few other places in the world, and is harvested by hand. Within each purple bloom, the three orange-red anthers yield pure saffron. Over 4500 blooms make one ounce (28 g) of the spice, so the price of this delicate flavouring and colouring in cooking is high (once far more valuable than gold). Its value has led the Indian government to set up a saffron research farm at Sangla in Himachal Pradesh.

The precious orange-coloured dye was used by royalty and the colour saffron was chosen by monks for their robes after the Buddha's death.

Enterprising traders have found a way to disguise dyed shreds of newspaper as saffron. You can test by rubbing a strand or two in a few drops of water on your palm: fake saffron will turn to red paste almost immediately, while the genuine article takes longer to stain and remains yellow.

**Dachigam National Park** ①*22 km east, past the Shalimar gardens. Passes available from the Tourist Reception Centre.* This national park is home to the endangered Hangul deer as well as black and brown bears, leopards, musk deer and various migratory birds. Permits and further information about the best time to see the wildlife can be obtained from the Tourist Reception Centre in Srinagar.

## Around Srinagar → *For listings, see pages 237-246.*

**Gulmarg** → *Colour map 1, A2. 56 km west of Srinagar. Altitude: 2650 m.*

India's premier winter sports resort, Gulmarg attracts a colourful mix of characters, from the off-piste powder-addict adventurers who stay for months to the coach-loads of Indian tourists. Three times host of the country's annual Winter Games, it is one of the cheapest places in the world to learn to ski, although there are only a few beginners' runs. The resort is served by three ski lifts and boasts the world's second highest **gondola** ① *daily 1000-1800, Rs 800 return*, which stops at the Kangdori mid-station before rising up to Apharwat Top (4000 m), from where you can ski the 5.2 km back to Gulmarg. Or in summertime, take the cable car up and then half-way back, and walk down the remaining distance (take a picnic). Check with **Gulmarg J&K Tourism** ① *T01954-254 439*, about opportunities for heli-skiing. The season runs from December to April (best in January-February), and equipment is available for hire for around Rs 400-500 a day. Lift passes cost Rs 700-1250. Outside the winter season, Gulmarg is a popular day trip from Srinagar, with pony rides, walks and the world's highest green golf course being the main attractions.

## Charar-i-Sharief

From Srinagar it's a scenic one-hour drive to Charar-i-Sharief (27 km), the last 10 km of road climbing through orchards and vales of willow. Spread over a series of ridges, the colourful roofs of modern houses date from a fire in 1995, when most of the town was burnt down – including the famed 700-year-old wooden **shrine and mosque** – during a battle between militants and Indian troops. The complex is now rebuilt as a grand tiered pagoda with carved walnut-wood screens. Entombed here is Sheikh Noor-u-Din Noorani, one of many names given to the great Sufi poet, seer, philospher and saint who died in

1438. He preached peace, tolerance and non-violence, and his shrine attracts thousands of visitors both Muslim and Hindu. It's possible to combine a visit to the shrine and a day-trip to Yusmarg (45 minutes away); or there's a nice J&K bungalow on the edge of town, should you get stranded.

## Yusmarg → *Colour map 1, A2. 47 km southwest of Srinagar. Altitude: 2400 m.*

Yusmarg, a rolling meadowland surrounded by conifer forests and snowy peaks, is an up-and-coming tourist spot for Indian day-trippers. Pony rides are popular, and you will probably be inundated by horsemen on arrival (a board shows official rates). Views over **Nilnag Lake** are a pleasant one-hour walk (or pony ride) through undulating forest. The walk to **Doodh Ganga** river takes 30 minutes through the meadows; you can link Doodh Ganga and Nilnag for a longer day-trek. There's a tourist reception centre and JKTDC have huts and cottages (or locals will offer you cheaper accommodation); there are a couple of very simple eateries near the jeep stop.

## Pahalgam → *Colour map 1, A2. 90 km southeast of Srinagar. Altitude: 2133 m.*

Pahalgam ('village of shepherds') is the main base for the yearly 'Amarnath Yatra' pilgrimage, which sees thousands of Hindu pilgrims climbing to a cave housing an 'ice lingam'. During the Yatra season, which runs from June to August, it gets very busy. Situated at the convergence of two dramatic river valleys, the town is surrounded by conifer forests and pastures. Central Pahalgam is packed with shawl shops, eateries and hotels; there's a striking mosque and some pleasant parks (one of which surrounds the Pahalgam Club). The pointy-roofed Mamleshwar Temple, across Kolahoi stream, is devoted to Shiva. There are many short walks you can take from Pahalgam and it is also a good base for longer treks to the Suru Valley and Kishtwar. A good day walk is the 12 km up the beautiful Lidder Valley to Aru; from there you can continue on to to Lidderwat (22 km) and Kolahoi Glacier (35 km). A wide selection of accommodation caters for all budgets; some of the best options are a couple of kilometres up the valley from the town centre.

## Sonamarg → *Colour map 1, A2. 84 km northeast of Srinagar.*

Literally meaning the 'golden valley', Sonamarg gets its name from the yellow crocus blooms that carpet the valley each spring. At an altitude of 2740 m, it's the last major town in Kashmir before the Zoji La Pass – the gateway to Ladakh. Mountains and blankets of pine trees surround the village, and Indian tourists make pony trips to nearby Thajiwas glacier. It's also a start/end point for the Amarnath Yatra (www.amarnathyatra.org). The area is highly regarded for its trekking and fishing; trout were introduced here by the British in the 19th century. Treks to high-altitude Himalayan alpine lakes, including Vishnsar (4084 m), Krishnasar (3810 m), Satsar, Gadsar, and Gangabal (3658 m), take eight days; the trekking season runs from July to October. Accommodation is available through **JKTDC** (see page 228) in the summer months and there are several hotels.

## Kargil → *Population 119,307. Altitude 2704 m.*

On the bank of the River Suru, Kargil was an important trading post on two routes, from Srinagar to Leh, and to Gilgit and the lower Indus Valley. In 1999 the Pakistan army took control briefly of the heights surrounding the town before being forced to retreat. The town is considered grim by most visitors; however, it is the main overnight stop on the Srinagar–Leh highway, and provides road access to the Zanskar Valley. With a largely

Shi'ite population, Kargil has a very different vibe to both Srinagar and Leh. Centred around the busy main bazaar are cheap internet cafés (unreliable), ATMs and plenty of hotels (see page 241). There is a **tourist office** ① *behind the bus station, T01985-232721, Mon-Sat 1000-1600.* Walking up the valley slope, perpendicular to the main bazaar, takes you past old village houses to finish at Goma Kargil (4 km) for excellent views.

## Suru Valley

The motorable road extends from Kargil south to Padum through the picturesque and relatively green Suru Valley, where willow trees dot a wide valley floor flanked by mountain ridges. The valley's population have been Muslim since the 16th century, but some ancient Buddhist monuments remain. The first (and largest) settlement is **Sankoo**, 42 km from Kargil, which has a 7-m rock-carved relief of the Maitreay Buddha and the ruins of Kartse Khar (a fort) 3 km distant. It's also a bus rest-spot and place to pick up last-minute supplies. The road continues 15 km to **Purtikchay**, a lonely spot with just a scattering of houses but with stunning views down to the **Nun-Kun** peaks. A further 10 km on is **Panikhar**, set in an attractive agricultural bowl of the valley and where a glacier and Nun-Kun frame the horizon. From Panikar you can trek (a hard day) over the Lago La to Parkachik, or take pleasant strolls around the hamlet and the neighbouring village of Te-Suru. It is also possible to cross the mountains to Pahalgam in Kashmir from here, and you should be able to find local guides and ponies to make the one-week trek. The regular bus from Kargil terminates at **Parkachik**, after which is Rangdum (see below) and the Zanskar Valley. There are J&K Tourist Bungalows at settlements along the Suru Valley (see page 241 for details).

## Zanskar → *For listings, see pages 237-246. Colour map 1, A2/3.*

Zanskar is a remote area of Ladakh contained by the Zanskar range to the north and the Himalaya to the south. It can be cut off by snow for as much as seven months each year when access is solely along the frozen Zanskar River. This isolation has helped Zanskar to preserve its cultural identity, though this is now being steadily eroded; a road is being currently being constructed to link Padum with Nimmu, on the Kargil–Leh highway. Traditional values include a strong belief in Buddhism, frugal use of resources and population control: values which for centuries have enabled Zanskaris to live in harmony with their hostile yet fragile environment. The long Zanskar Valley was 'opened' up for tourism even later than the rest of Ladakh and quickly became popular with trekkers. There is river rafting on the Zanskar River, with trips up to 11 days . For trekking, see page 263.

## Background

Zanskar became an administrative part of Ladakh under Senge Namgyal whose three sons became the rulers of Ladakh, Guge and Zanskar/Spiti. This arrangement collapsed after Ladakh's war with Tibet and the Zanskar royal house divided, one part administering Padum, the other Zangla. Under the Dogras, the rulers were reduced to puppets as the marauding army wreaked havoc on the villages, monasteries and population.

### Rangdum → *Altitude 3657 m.*

Making a convenient night's stop between Kargil and the Zanskar Valley (130 km from Kargil, halfway to Padum), Rangum sits on a plateau of wild and incredible beauty. The isolated **Rangdum Monastery** perched on a hillock is particularly striking, and two Buddhist villages surrounded by *chortens* lie nearby.

**Padum** → *Colour map 1, A3. Population 1300. No permit needed.*
About 40% of Padum, the capital of Zanskar, are Sunni Muslim. The present king of the Zanskar Valley, Punchok Dawa, who lives in his modest home in Padum, is held in high regard. The ruined old town, palace and fort are 700 m from the rather uninspiring new town, which has transport, guesthouses and internet. Access is by the jeep road over the **Pensi La** (4401 m), generally open from mid-June to mid-October with a twice weekly bus service from Leh via Kargil (highly unreliable and crammed); the alternative method is to trek in. There is accommodation available (see page 241).

## Srinagar to Leh road

The road to Leh from Srinagar must be one of the most fascinating journeys in the world as it negotiates high passes and fragile mountainsides. There are dramatic scenic and cultural changes as you go from verdant Muslim Kashmir to ascetic Buddhist Ladakh. When there is political unrest in Kashmir, the route, which runs very close to the Line of Control, may be closed to travellers. For more details about the monasteries and villages along the way, see page 254. The alternative route to Leh from Manali is equally fascinating, see page 184.

After passing through **Sonamarg** (see page 234), you reach the pass of **Zoji La** (3528 m). The pass is slippery after rains and usually closed by snow during winter months (November to April). From Zoji La the road descends to **Minamarg meadow** and **Dras** (3230 m). The winter temperatures have been known to go down to -50°C, and heavy snow and strong winds cut off the town. Dras has a spectacular setting and a scruffy centre with restaurants and shops; there's a TIC and decent enough J&K bungalows. The broad Kargil basin and its wide terraces are separated from the Mulbekh Valley by the 12-km-long **Wakha Gorge**.

From Kargil (see page 234) the road continues 30 km to **Shargol** – the cultural boundary between Muslim and Buddhist areas, with a very ambient very tiny monastery located down a side-road – and then after another 10 km reaches **Mulbek**, a pretty village with a large (9 m) ancient Maitreya Buddha relief fronted by a *gompa* on the roadside. The ruins of Mulbek Khar (fort) sit atop a stalk of cliff next to two small *gompas*, a steep climb with fabulous views. Shortly after Mulbek is its larger sister village of Wahka, then the road crosses **Namika La**, at 3720 m (known as the 'Pillar in the Sky'). There is a tourist bungalow in tiny **Haniskut**, set in a pretty river valley marred by roads and pylons, where a very ruined fort lies on the northern side of the valley. The road then climbs to **Fotu La** at 4093 m, the highest pass on the route. From here you can catch sight of the monastery at Lamayuru. The road does a series of loops to descend to the ramshackle village of **Khaltse** with a couple of garden-restaurants, shops and lodges, where it meets the milky green Indus River.

**Lamayuru**, 10 km from Khaltse, with a famous monastery and spectacular landscapes, is worth a long lunch break or overnight stop (see page 258). There is a comfortable eco-camp in **Uletokpo**, just by the highway (see page 268). From Uletokpo village a 6-km track leads to dramatic **Rizong**, with a monastery and nunnery, which sometimes accommodate visitors. **Saspol** village marks the wide valley from which you can reach **Alchi** by taking a branch road across the Indus after passing some caves. **Lekir** (see page 256) is off the main road, 8 km after Saspol.

Further along the road you catch sight of the ruins of **Basgo** before it crosses the Chargyal Thang plain with *chortens* and *mani* walls and enters **Nimmu**. The road rejoins the Indus Valley and rises to a bare plateau to give you the first glimpse of Leh, 30 km away. **Phyang** is down a side valley and finally **Spituk** is reached.

*For hotel and restaurant price codes and other relevant information, see pages 22-26.*

◉ **Where to stay**

**Jammu** *p225*

**$$$$-$$$ Hari Niwas Palace**, Palace Rd, T0191-254 3303, www.hariniwaspalace.com. 40 a/c rooms and suites in a heritage property with elegant bar and classy restaurant. Meals and drinks are also served on the immaculate lawns, with a sweeping view. The cliff-top location next to Amar Mahal is the chief attraction. The Royal Deluxe and Semi Suites are the most attractive, huge and with wonderful views from either front or back. Heated pool and health club.

**$$$ Asia Jammu-Tawi**, Nehru Market, north of town, T0191-243 5757, www.asia hotelsjammu.com. The 44 rooms are beginning to show their age a little, but this Jammu stalwart has an excellent Chinese restaurant, bar, currency exchange and a clean pool. There is also a function room, so if you need peace and quiet it's worth checking if there are any weddings going on. Close to the airport.

**$$$ Jehlum Resorts**, Bahu Plaza, T0191-247 0079, www.traveltokashmir.com. A comfortable option near the railway station with a bar, multi-cuisine restaurant, travel desk and ATM.

**$$$ KC Residency**, Vir Marg, T0191-252 0770, www.kcresidency.com. Rising from the heart of Jammu, the KC tower is a good place to stay if you have a day or so to check out the city. There are 61 good-quality a/c rooms, a currency exchange, and health club specializing in Ayurvedic massage, all extraordinarily crowned by a superb, multi-cuisine revolving restaurant.

**$ Jewel's**, Jewel Chowk, T0191-252 0801-3, www.jewelshotel.com. Located in a busy, congested area, but the 18 a/c rooms are

good value in an increasingly expensive city. There's a good fast-food restaurant and bar.

**$$-$ Tourist Reception Centre**, AKA Hotel Jammu Residency, Vir Marg, T0191-257 9554. Set back from the main road, the TRC has 173 rooms with bath ranging in price and quality arranged around well-kept gardens, price is dictated by size and views. The best accommodation is in Blocks NA and A. The restaurant has a very good reputation, in particular for its Kashmiri food, and there's a bar.

**$ Kranti Hotel**, near the railway station, T0191-247 0525. One of the better budget hotels in the railway area with 45 clean rooms with attached bath and a restaurant.

**Vaishno Devi** *p226*

**$$$ Asia Vaishnodevi**, Katra, T01991-232061, www.asiavaishnodevi.in. 37 a/c rooms, restaurant, transport to Banganga.

**$$ Ambica**, Katra, T01991-232062, www.hotelambika.com. 58 rooms, a/c, *puja* shop and health centre.

**$ Dormitories**, at the halfway point to Vaishno Devi. Simple rooms provide sheets.

**$ Prem**, Main Bazar, Katra, T01991-232014. Rooms with hot water and a fire, adequate.

**$ Tourist Bungalow**, Katra, T01991-232009. 42 basic but clean rooms.

**Srinagar** *p227, map p228*

The room costs quoted reflect peak-season prices (Mar-Aug); if you go in the winter, you can expect to get a hefty discount. Be prepared to haggle.

**$$$$ The Lalit Grand Palace**, Gupkar Rd, a few kilometres outside the city, T0194-250 1001, www.thelalit.com. This former palace was once the residence of Kashmir's last maharajah, Hari Singh. Situated on a hillside overlooking Dal Lake, it has been tastefully kitted out with antiques befitting its history, including India's largest handmade carpet. One wing houses enormous, classically styled suites, while the other has 70 recently refurbished modern rooms. The restaurant, bar and health club are open to non-guests. It's a good place to go on a summer evening for the al fresco buffet.

**$$$$ Vivanta by Taj – Dal View**, Kralsangri Hill, Brein, T0194-246 1111, www.vivantabytaj.com. All-out luxury in this sprawling elegant resort, atop a peak with sublime Dal Lake views. Rooms are chic without being over-the-top, with Kashmiri details and warm colours. 24-hr fitness suite, fantastic restaurants (speciality Sichuan), spa to open soon (check website). Gorgeous place, worth going for a meal if you can't stay here.

**$$$$-$$$ Hotel Broadway**, Maulana Azad Rd, T0194-245 9001, www.hotelbroadway. com. One of Srinagar's oldest and best-known hotels, the **Broadway**'s original 1970s interior has been well maintained. With lots of wood panelling, rooms can be a little dark. The staff are professional and polite, while the comfortable, centrally heated rooms, Wi-Fi service and city location make it popular with business travellers and journalists. It houses one of the city's few drinking spots, has an informal cinema and is attached to the city's 1st coffee shop, **Café Arabica**. Book online for discounts.

**$$$ Dar-Es-Salam**, Nandpora, Rainawari, T0194-242 7803, (0)9810-899584, www. hoteldaressalam.com. This white Art Deco ex-stately home is the only hotel on Nagin Lake, with an established garden and a sweep of lawn onto the shore overlooking houseboats. Mounted heads over the entrance set the colonial tone, while period furnishings in the 2 lounges include brass antique pots and a Raj-era tiger's head. An enclosed balcony surveys the lake. Modernized rooms (and **$$$$** suites), central heating, white duvets, new floors, meals available in the (formal) dining room.

**$$$-$$ Hotel Akbar**, Dalgate, Gate No 1, T0194-250 0507, www.hotelakbar.com. Smart, clean hotel with 36 spacious rooms arranged around a pretty lawn with rose

arbours. Attractive lobby and restaurant, some rooms have a balcony and it's a great location on the lakeside. Souvenir shop and travel desk.

**$$ Ahdoos**, Residency Rd, T0194-247 2593, www.ahdooshotel.com. A Srinagar institution, **Ahdoos** backs onto the Jhelum river and is well situated for the city's classiest handicraft and shawl shops, on and around Polo View. The deluxe rooms are huge with new TVs, the standard rooms are not much smaller and all have marble bathtubs. Back rooms have river views. It's a little old-fashioned, however, and some rooms could do with a revamp. But a good choice for those who want to get a feel of the city, rather than the more touristy area around the lake. Staff are friendly and the restaurant is renowned among locals for its Kashmiri (Wazwan) food, the chicken patties, and their tea.

**$$ Hotel Madhuban**, Gagribal Rd, T0194-245 3800, www.hotelmadhuban-kashmir.net. The **Madhuban** has bags of character, with a lot of wood going on in its homely rooms. The restaurant has an attractive veranda where guests can sit out in the summer and there is a small but well-kept garden.

**$$ Hotel Wali Sons**, Boulevard Lane No 1, T0194-250 0345, www.walisonshotel.com. A smart red-brick building, complemented by white window-frames and green roof. The 17 immaculate spacious rooms have white duvets, flatscreen TV, fan, clean carpets and huge bathrooms with modern fixtures and decor. Central location, and some public balconies overlook Shankaracharya Hill. Free use of computer, 24-hr electricity, respectful staff.

**$$-$ Hotel Heaven Canal**, Dal Gate, T0194-250 0943, sayeedyousuf@yahoo.com. A funky little place, reached via a crooked footbridge over a canal. Both upstairs and downstairs rooms front onto a shared terrace, with chairs and tables facing out over the lake – a great spot for watching the world float by over a cup of *kahwa*, out of reach of the hawkers.

**$ John Friends Guesthouse**, Pedestrian Mall Rd (opposite Ghat No.1), Dalgate, T0194-245 8342, johna_mondoo@yahoo.com. Set back from Dal Lake, along wooden walkways and gangplanks, is this family guesthouse with 9 rooms across 2 buildings. Charming flowery garden with seating, surrounded by poplars and willows, with fairy lights at night. Decent budget rooms, some with attached bathroom and TV, shared bathroom, very clean, 24-hr hot water. Fascinating snapshot into life on the lake. Free pick-up service.
**$ Swiss Hotel**, Old Gagribal Rd, T0194-2472766, www.swisshotelkashmir.com. The **Swiss** has 35 clean rooms with attached bath and running hot water (morning and evening) with greatly discounted rates to foreign tourists. The attractive red-painted old house has the best-value budget rooms in town starting at Rs 450. The annex has well-maintained rooms, prices increase as you go up to the 3rd floor where rooms with coffee-table, couch, numerous side lights are immaculate. There's a big garden. One of the few hotels with a stated environmental policy, it uses energy efficient lighting. Recommended.
**$** There's a backpacker-conscious enclave on the lake at Dalgate, where small and simple guesthouses include **Gulam Junaid** and **Noor Guesthouse**. The latter has a little garden and internet café at the front, balconies and character.

## Houseboats

Houseboats are peculiar to Srinagar and can be seen moored along the shores of Dal Lake, the quieter and distant Nagin Lake and along the busy Jhelum River. They were originally thought up by the British as a ruse to get around the law that foreigners could not buy land in the state: being in the water, the boats didn't technically count as property.

In the valley's heyday the boats were well kept and delightfully cosy; today some are still lavishly decorated with antiques and traditional Kashmiri handicrafts, but others have become distinctly shabby. Still mostly family-run, they usually include all meals and come in 5 categories: deluxe, A, B, C and D. The tariff for each category is given by the **Houseboat Owners Association**, T0194-245 0326, www.houseboatowners.org, through whom you can also make bookings.

Most tourists enjoy their houseboat holidays, however a significant number complain of being ripped off in various ways. It's better to spend extra on a boat with a good reputation than to go for a bargain that is probably too good to be true.

The following all quote **$$$-$$**, but prices are generally negotiable if you go in person.
**Athena Houseboats**, opposite **Hotel Duke**, Dal Lake, T0194-476957. One of the larger houseboat operators with voluminous boats that can comfortably sleep larger groups. Excellent service, with real integrity: discourages hawkers and tries to support only legitimate retail and onward tourism.
**Butt's Clermont Houseboats**, west side of Dal Lake, T0194-242 0325, www.butts clermonthouseboat.com. Moored by Naseem Bagh, "Garden of Breezes", shaded by chinar trees by a wall built by Emperor Akbar. Far from the densely packed south side of Dal Lake, 4 cream-painted boats feature crewelwork on fabrics, carved cedar panels, rosewood tables and a view of Hazratbal mosque. In operation since 1940, they are now on guestbook No 16. Former guests include Lord Mountbatten, George Harrison, PG Wodehouse, Ravi Shankar and Michael Palin.
**Chapri Tours and Travels**, Nagin Lake, T(0)9418-023936, www.chapritoursand travels.com. Recommended for houseboats and local tours.
**Gurkha Houseboats**, Nagin Lake, T0194-242 1001, www.nivalink.com/gurkha. The **Gurkha** group are renowned for their comfortable rooms and stylish boats on peaceful Nagin Lake. Good service and food.
**Mantana**, Dal Lake, Gate 2, T0194-250 1488, www.mantanakashmirtours.com. If you want

to experience the old-style opulence of a traditional Kashmiri houseboat, the *Mantana* is a good option. As well as the carefully preserved, sumptuous interior, there is also an ingeniously constructed floating garden. Owned and run by a reliable family.

**Marguerite**, The Bund, T0194-247 6699. A charming boat with some lovely woodcarving. The trustworthy Thulla family are great fun and as the boat is moored to riverbank, guests can come and go as they please with no need to take a *shikara*. Recommended.

**Zaffer Houseboats**, on Nagin Lake, T01954-250 0507, www.zafferhouseboats.com. Deluxe boats with a long history, walnut panelled walls, single-piece walnut tables, old writing desks, backed onto the lake which means the front terrace is delightful place to sit. Peaceful and quiet despite the *sikhara* salesmen. Excellent food, courteous staff and interesting owners.

## Gulmarg p233

As with Srinagar, prices can be negotiated in the winter months, particularly for longer stays.

**$$$$ Khyber Himalayan Resort & Spa**, T01954-254666, khyberhotels.com. Absolute luxury in a new resort with an Ayurvedic spa, gym, heated pool and amazing restaurants. Rooms are beautifully furnished with teak floors, silk carpets, walnut carving and rich Kashmiri fabrics. There are state-of-the-art bathrooms, while huge windows make the most of views. Also 4 cottages, some with own pool.

**$$$ Grand Mumtaz**, near Gondola, T9013-527195, www.grandmumtazkashmir.com. Part of a Kashmir chain with big hotels and tour packages.

**$$$ Hotel Highlands Park**, T01954-254430, www.hotelhighlandspark.com. Oozing with old-world charm, rooms and suites are decorated with Kashmiri woodcraft and rugs. Renowned for its atmosphere – the best bar in Gulmarg is here, a large yet cosy lounge, straight out of the 1930s – it's a wonderful place to unwind after a hard day on the slopes. Rooms have *bukharis* (wood stoves) to keep you warm and electric blankets are available on request. Recommended.

**$$$-$$ Nedou's Hotel**, T01954-254428, www.nedoushotel.com. The oldest hotel in Gulmarg, the **Nedous** has the same cosy colonial charm as **Highlands Park**. Its rooms and suites are comfortingly old-fashioned, with spotless bathrooms. The food isn't flash, but it's home-cooked, wholesome and delicious.

**$$ Hotel Yemberzal**, T01954-254523, www.yembarzalhotel.com. Rooms are on the small side, but at least this means they heat up quickly. Each has its own gas heater and the bathrooms have 24-hr running hot water. If you ask for the corner room, you can enjoy a panoramic view of the mountains. The restaurant is very good and the management are extremely helpful. It's a 10-min walk to the lifts, but there's a taxi stand next door if you feel lazy.

**$$-$ Green Heights**, T01954-254404. This wood-built hotel is slightly shabby, but the quirky staff more than compensate, making this a budget choice with character. The decent-sized rooms come with wood stoves and if you ask nicely, you might get a hot-water bottle. Close to the gondola.

**$$-$ JK Tourism Huts**, T(0)9419-488181. These comfortable huts come with 1-2 bedrooms, a living room and kitchen. Very good value and close to the drag-lift.

**$ Raja's**, T(0)9797-008107. Buried in the woods, **Raja's** colourful shack consists of 3 rooms with shared bath and can accommodate up to 9 people. Popular with long-stayers.

## Yusmarg p234

**$ J&KTDC Huts**, T(0)9797-292001, www.jktourism.org. Dotted around the centre of Yusmarg's meadow, connected by flagged paths, these comfortable huts are well-maintained and fresh, if simple. There are various configurations, some with pine walls, others whitewashed with pretty bedspreads, so check them all out. Basic doubles Rs 1000, 30% discount low-season.

### Pahalgam *p234*
**$$$$Pahalgam Hotel**, T01936-243252, www.pahalgamhotel.com. Upper-end Raj-era hotel dating back to 1931, 4 buildings, with 36 of 40 rooms enjoying splendid views of forested peaks across the River Lidder. Rooms are tastefully decorated, centrally heated, very spacious, some have been recently renovated but all are pleasing (18 suites). Pool in summer. Prices include all meals. Excellent shop (see page 244).
**$$-$Brown Palace**, T01936-243255, www.brownpalace.in. Another decent budget option. All rooms have attached bath with hot water, wood panelling abounds, the lounge has bark walls and a fire, 2 newer bungalows at rear.
**$$-$Himalaya House**, 3 km from the bus stand, 1 km from Laripora village, T(0)9411-9045021, gulzarhakeem@hotmail.com. A cosy hotel on the river with an enchanting island garden and a restaurant of repute. 2 rooms, all with attached bath and hot water, some with bathtub and balcony, nice crewelwork curtains and bedspreads. The comfortable lobby has a fireplace and is a good place to make friends. Free Wi-Fi. The hotel is linked to the recommended **Himalaya Fun N' Tours**, see page 244. Cheaper older rooms in house across laneway.

### Sonamarg *p234*
**$$-$Snowland**, on the edge of town. This is a good choice, well managed with cottage-style rooms. Those at the back are quieter and have great mountain views; the vegetarian restaurant is merely average.

### Kargil *p234*
Hotels are quite expensive, but bargaining is expected. On Hospital Rd, running uphill just off the Main Bazaar, there's a further cluster of budget hotels (not listed here). Restaurants all serve meat; for vegetarian food (hard to find) look for signs advertising Punjabi meals. There's a little dairy outlet selling superb lassi (Rs 20) near the J&K ATM off the Main Bazaar (it's locally famous, ask around).
**$$$-$Green Land**, signed down an alley off Main Bazaar, T01985-232324, www.hotelgreenlandkargil.com. A popular and well-kept place, it's not cheap but prices reflect the standard of the rooms. Old block doubles **$**, new block (much preferable) with a range of rooms. Open all year round.
**$$-$PC Palace**, off Main Bazaar, T01985-202189, pcpalace@live.in. Smart white building with well-appointed rooms with flatscreen TV, fawn carpets, blankets and curtains, fancy lights and good bathrooms. Slightly smaller, darker rooms are at the rear, but they are also cheaper and quieter.
**$J&K Tourist Bungalow**, T01985-232266, behind the bus station, it's a bargain, but rather worn and often booked up.
**$Tourist Marjina**, off Main Bazaar, T09419-831517. An ageing pink- and blue-painted building that is being encircled by high new hotels, making dark rooms even darker. It's a bearable budget option though, with reliable hot showers.

### Suru Valley *p235*
J&K tourist bungalows, costing from Rs150-200 per person, are found in villages along the Suru Valley. Sankoo also has plenty of shops and several *dhabas*, while the **Tourist Bungalow** in Panikhar enjoys remarkable views of Nun and Kun, but is isolated – take supplies with you. In Panikhar, the **Dak Bungalow** has 3 basic gloomy rooms and a better choice is **$Khayoul Hotel**, T(0)9469-293976, with 2 sunny rooms in a family house, decked with cheerful fabrics and plants, meals Rs 50-70.

### Padum *p236*
Places to stay are limited, but there is a choice of 4 simple lodges. There is also a **tourist complex** with basic rooms and meals; you can camp there.

**$ Ibex** has the best rooms in town, a decent restaurant and a courtyard garden.

### Mulbek *p236*

**$ Karzoo Guesthouse**, T(0)9419-880463. In an impressive old Ladakhi building, with restaurant and camping space, conveniently located for walking to the monastery; all rooms share clean bathrooms, and the family are very hospitable. There are also a couple of other simple guesthouses and a J&K Tourist Bungalow. In Wakha, the sister village 3 km on the road towards Leh, there are a few *dhabas* and shops.

## 🍴 Restaurants

### Jammu *p225*

The best eateries tend to be found in the upmarket hotels. However, there are some good snack places dotted around town, which can be fun to check out.

**$$-$ Sagar Ratna**, Hotel Premier, opposite KC Plaza, Residency Rd. Vegetarian delights, both South and North Indian plus Chinese, at reasonable prices for smart-casual surrounds (a/c), and generous portions. Loud TV.
**$$-$ Smokin' Joes Pizza**, Bahu Plaza, near the railway station. Very acceptable veg and non-veg pizza and pasta, but strictly no pork. Take away and home delivery also available.
**$ Barista**, KC Cineplex and City Square Mall. Popular Indian café chain, also sells sandwiches and cakes.

### Vaishno Devi *p226*

Excellent vegetarian food is available – curd and *paneer* (curd cheese) dishes are especially good. For non-*dhaba* food try the 2 vegetarian fast food places on the main street. Both are clean and good. No alcohol.

### Srinagar *p227, map p228*

While Kashmiris generally prefer to eat at home, being a tourist town, Srinagar has its fair share of good restaurants catering for all tastes. For a special treat, do the buffet at the Lalit Grand or a meal at the Taj Vivanta

(with killer views).There are 3 wineshops on the left side of the ground floor of the Hotel Heemal building on the Boulevard.

Traditional Kashmiri food is centred around meat, with mutton generally being the favoured flesh. The traditional 36-course banquet served at weddings is known as a *wazwan* and you will find several of its signature dishes on the menu in restaurants. *Yakhnee* is a delicious mutton stew cooked in a spiced curd sauce. *Goshtabas* and *rishtas* are meatballs made from pounded (not ground) meat, which makes a big difference in consistency. *Goshtabas* come in a curd sauce; *rishtas* in red sauce. *Roganjosh* is made with chicken or mutton and is curd based, owing its colour to red Kashmiri chilies. *Hakh* is the Kashmiri version of spinach and *nadroo* are lotuses, usually served in a *yakhnee* sauce.

**Qayaam Chowk** street, close to Dalgate, is locally known as 'the barbeque'. It's lined with small restaurants serving *sheesh* and *seekh* kebabs, accompanied by an array of delicious, home-made Kashmiri chutneys. Recommended.
**$$ Char Chinar**, Boulevard Rd, near Brein village. You'll need to take a *shikara* to get to this houseboat restaurant, moored on a tiny island in Dal Lake. Named after the 4 giant *chinar* trees that grow there, the food is average, but it's a perfect place to sit in peace with a good book on a sunny day.
**$$ Lhasa**, Boulevard Lane No 2. Daily 1200-2230. Enjoy the lovely back garden with rose bushes and well-spaced tables, each with its own awning. The central fountain is defunct, but old houses surround. The low-ceilinged vaguely Tibetan-themed indoor area has fish-tanks and is cosy on a cold night. They serve a varied menu of excellent Chinese, Tibetan, and Indian non-veg and veg food.
**$$ Mughal Darbar**, Residency Rd. Popular with middle-class locals, the cosy Mughal Darbar offers multi-cuisine fare, specializing in Kashmiri *wazwan*. It's located on the 1st floor, up the stairs.

**$$ Shamyana**, Boulevard Rd,
www.shamyana.net. Daily 1230-2230.
Consistently highly rated by locals and
popular with middle-class customers, this
restaurant serves high-quality Chinese and
Indian food (meat and veg, good tikka).
The calm front section is separated from
a 'funkier' back room by wooden lattices.
Professional service.

**$$ Tao Café**, Residency Rd. A popular
hangout with local journalists, politicians
and artists, the **Tao** serves decent Kashmiri
and Chinese food, as well as Tibetan *momos*,
fish, and various snacks. Its attractive
gardens make it a good summer spot.

**$$-$ Café Robusta**, Maulana Azad Rd, near
Polo View. Competes with nearby **Café
Arabica** (in the Broadway Hotel) to attract
Srinagar's latte lovers. Aside from pizza,
kebabs and cake, you can also sample a
*shisha* (Middle Eastern water pipe) with a
range of flavoured tobaccos on offer. Bring
your laptop and make use of the Wi-Fi.

**$ Krishna Dhaba**, Durga Nag Rd.
Closed 1600-1900. A haven for vegetarians
in a city of meat-eaters, the Krishna's
canteen environment gets the thumbs-
up from fastidious Indian tourists for its
cleanliness and delicious pure veg fare –
the best in town.

**$ Shakti Sweets** and **Modern Sweets**,
Residency Rd. If you are invited to a
Kashmiri home, a box of *burfi* will go
down well as a gift. Both serve great
snack food at rock-bottom prices, such
as *channa bhatura* and *masala dosa*,
as well as very popular chow mein.

### Gulmarg *p233*

Most hotels serve their own food but some
close their kitchens in low season. In the
bazar there is a row of *dhabas* serving a wide
variety of Indian vegetarian food including
*thalis*, *dosas* and *punjabi*. Outside seating.

**$ Sahara Hotel**, next to Yemberzal Hotel.
Well worth venturing out in the cold for. The
owner spent 15 years working as a chef in
Saudi Arabia, Japan and China, so has a wide

repertoire. If you need a break from Indian
food, the continental choice here is good,
especially the chicken champion.

**$ Lala's**, close to the JK Tourism Huts
(see Where to stay). Good, honest home-
cooked food.

### Pahalgam *p234*

**$$$-$ Trout Beat** restaurant and the
welcoming **Café Log Inn**, both at the
Pahalgam Hotel. Serve the same menu
of vegetarian meals and snacks and, of
course, fish.

**$ Nathu's Rasoi**. Open 0800-2230. You can't
miss this self-service fast-food vegetarian
restaurant near the bus stand, which serves
excellent North/South Indian and Chinese
dishes – but most famed for its South Indian,
the best in Kashmir.

## ⊛ Festivals

### Srinagar *p227, map p228*
**Apr** Tulip Festival, Indira Gandhi Memorial
Tulip Garden. First 2 weeks of April, with over
1 million blooms.

## O Shopping

### Jammu *p225*
**J&K Arts Emporium**, next to J&K Tourism,
Residency Rd. Mon-Sat 1000-2000. Good
selection, cheap.

### Srinagar *p227, map p228*
If you arrived in Srinagar without your
thermals or you're craving a bar of chocolate,
a bowl of cornflakes, marmite on toast or
just about any other Western goods, then
look no further than **Harker's Pick 'n' Choose
Supermarket** on Residency Rd, for all your
expat needs.

**Gulshan Bookstore**, a few mins' walk from
Residency Rd, towards Lal Chowk. Here you
will find all manner of books about Kashmir,
some of them extremely rare. If you are
interested in the political situation, it's an
excellent place for books on Kashmir's history.

**Mahatta's Photographic Store**, next to Suffering Moses. Mon-Sat 1030-1830. Worth stopping by for its old-world charm, its history and above all for the priceless visual memory of old Srinagar it houses. Founded in 1918, this was once the place to have your portrait taken and was patronized by the elite of the day. The walls are lined with large prints of the city, taken up in the 1930s and 1940s. They are not for sale, but they have produced a booklet, 'Srinagar Views 1934-1965' for Rs 300, and sell black and white postcards.

### Handicrafts

There are plenty of handicraft shops, particularly around Dal Lake and Dalgate, but beware of touts who are on commission. Much of what is sold is not even Kashmiri: inferior quality papier mâché products from Bihar and shawls from Amritsar have flooded the market and are bought merrily by tourists who don't know the difference. As a result, along with the troubles of the past 20 years, the valley's handicraft industry has been tragically eroded.

For a real understanding of Kashmiri craftwork and to support the local industry, call into any of the quality shops on **Polo View** or the **Bund**. The prices may seem high, but the quality and authenticity are guaranteed and shop-keepers do not usually pay commission. Shopkeepers here are rather more restrained than the average Kashmiri salesman making it a pleasant place to wander around.

**Asia Crafts**, next to Suffering Moses (see below). Very fine embroidery and genuine Kashmiri carpets, but much of its stock is now sold in New Delhi.

**Habib Asian Carpets**, Zaldagar Chowk, Downtown, T0194-247 8640. If you are serious about buying a genuine Kashmiri carpet, this is one of the few companies that has its workshop in the city.

**Heritage Woodcrafts**, on the way to Shalimar gardens. It's worth making the trip here for the carved walnut wood. Stuffed

with fine pieces including some antiques, the authenticity of the work is guaranteed by the on-site workshop.

**Kashmir Government Arts Emporium**, the Bund. Mon-Sat 1000-1800, closed for noon prayers. Large showroom of fixed-price Kasmiri goods: rugs, papier mâché, crewel-work, furniture and more. In the old British Residency, a beautifully restored building with heritage gardens (and moth-eaten tigers lurking among the wares).

**Sadiq's Handicrafts**, next to Tao Café (see Restaurants). Owned by the same family as Suffering Moses and is almost as much a museum as a shop; many of the antique treasures are not for sale and Mr Sadiq, a man passionate about art, will happily explain their history to you. Prices in both shops are fixed and there is no pressure to buy.

**Suffering Moses**, next to Mughal Darbar restaurant (see Restaurants). Famous for its exquisite papier mâché goods. The curious name was apparently awarded to the owner's father by the British, who were impressed by the amount of suffering that went into each work. Really beautiful top-quality stock; they can ship overseas.

### Pahalgam *p234*

**Almirah Books etc**, at Pahalgam Hotel. An average book selection and some tasteful souvenirs. Also sell 'Shepherd's Craft' goods – brightly decorated bags/purses, embellished with the traditional designs of the Bakkarwala nomadic shepherds (who embroider saddlebags and hats with colourful threads).

**Himalayan Products**, T(0)9419-045420, www.himalyancheese.com. Fair-trade cheesemakers, making organic Gouda and local-style Kelari, deep-fried and flavoured with chilli.

---

## ○ What to do

### Pahalgam *p234*

**Himalaya Fun N' Tours**, www.himalayafun andtours.com. 25 years' trekking experience

1- to 10-day circular treks from Pahalgam or even 21-days to Leh via Suru and Zanskar valleys (US$50 per person per day, includes all meals, equipment, ponies, guides) and can also arrange white water rafting along the Lidder River (best May-Jul).

## ⊙ Transport

### Jammu *p225*

**Air** Rambagh Airport, 6 km. Transport to town: taxis (Rs 200) and auto-rickshaws. Air India, flies to **Delhi** and **Srinagar** daily; **Leh** (Thu, Sat). Jet Konnect, to **Delhi** and **Srinagar** daily. Also Spicejet, twice daily flights to Delhi, and GoAir, www.goair.in.
**Bus** J&KSRTC, TRC, Vir Marg, T0191-257 9554 (1000-1700), general bus stand, T0191-257 7475 (0400-2000). To **Amritsar** (6 hrs) at least hourly via **Pathankot** (3 hrs); direct buses to **Srinagar** (9 hrs), **Katra** (for Vaishno Devi), and **Kishtwar**. To **Delhi** (12 hrs), hourly. **Srinagar** buses also leave from the railway station, usually 0600-0700.
**Jeep** *Sumos* to **Srinagar** leaving early morning (Rs 500, 8-9 hrs), to **Katra** from the station private jeeps cost Rs 900 (Rs 1200 a/c).
**Train** 5 km from centre; allow at least 30 mins by auto. Enquiries T0191-245 3027. Daily to **Delhi** (OD): *Jammu Tawi Mail 14034*, 1615, 14¼ hrs; *Jammu All Exp 12414*, 1815, 10½ hrs *Jat Muri Exp 18110*, 1430, 14 hrs;. **Delhi** (ND): *Jammu Tawi Indore Malwa Exp 12920*, 0900, 10½ hrs; *Duronto Exp 12266*, Mon, Wed, Sat 1920, 9 hrs. **Kolkata** daily: *Sealdah Exp 13152*, 1855, 45 hrs.

### Vaishno Devi *p226*

Buses and taxis leave from the general bus stand, Jammu (or the railway station at peak season) and go to **Katra** (48 km); Rs 30, a/c Rs 60; taxi Rs 500 for 4.

### Srinagar *p227, map p228*

**Air** Srinagar Airport, 14 km south, T0194-230 3000. Taxi to town: Rs 500. Stringent security checks on roads plus 2 hrs' check-in at airport. Tight on hand luggage but you can generally get away with a laptop. Daily flights to **Delhi** and **Mumbai** with: Air India, JetKonnect, Spicejet, GoAir. To **Leh** with Air India and JetKonnect, daily.
**Bus** Srinagar is on NH1A linked to the rest of India by 'all-weather' roads, through superb scenery. To **Jammu** (293 km), by a narrow mountain road, often full of lorries and military convoys, takes 9-10 hrs; few stops for food.

   J&KSRTC, TRC, Srinagar, T0194-245 5107. Summer 0600-1800, winter 0700-1700.

   Bus to **Kargil** (alternate days in summer), **Leh** (434 km). **Gulmarg**, daily bus at 0800 in ski season from Tourist Reception Centre, returning in the evening. Taxis charge around Rs 2000 for same-day return. Or take J&KSRTC bus to **Tangmarg**, 8 km before Gulmarg and take a *sumo* from there, Rs 20. To **Pahalgam** at 0830 (2-3 hrs).
**Jeep** Jeeps are faster than the bus and leave when full from various locations near Dalgate. To **Jammu**, 8-9 hrs, Rs 500. To **Yusmarg**, 1 hr 45 mins, at 1400. Shared jeeps to **Charar-i-Sharief**, 1 hr, leave when full from Iqbal Park, in west Srinagar.
**Train** The most nearest railhead is Jammu Tawi with coach (12 hrs) and taxi transfer (8-9 hrs). Govt TRC, 0700-1900. T0191-243 1582 for reservation of 2nd-class sleeper and a/c only. Summer 0830-1900, winter 1000-1800. Connections with several cities including **Guwahati**, **Kolkata**, **Mumbai**, **Chennai**.

### Yusmarg *p234*

**Jeep** To Batmulla bus stand, **Srinagar**, at 0800 (1 hr 45 mins). Or go via Charar-i-Sharief (last *sumo* from Yusmarg 1630).

### Kargil *p234*

**Bus** To **Leh** at 0430 (Rs 350, 7 hrs); to **Srinagar** at 2230-2300, some are deluxe (Rs 300-400, 9 hrs). Buses to the Suru Valley leave from the crossroads of Main Bazaar and Lal Chowk, to **Panikhar** daily at 0700 (Rs 70, 4 hrs; return bus at 0600, 0800 and 1100.) and to **Parkachik** at 1130 on

alternate days (5 hrs, returning at 0700). Bus booking counter T01985-232066.
**Jeep** Shared jeeps to Srinagar leave from taxi stand on Lal Chowk, connected to the bus station by an alleyway, at 0400-0600 and 1300-1500 (Rs 750, 6 hrs). Shared taxi to Leh (Rs 800, 7 hrs).

## ❶ Directory

**Jammu** *p225*
**Banks** State Bank of India, Hari Market, among several. **Medical services** Hospital: T0191-254 7637.

**Srinagar** *p227, map p228*
**Useful contacts** Ambulance: T0194-247 4591. **Fire:** T0194-247 2222. **Police:** T100. **Foreigners' Registration Office:** Supt of Police, Residency Rd. 1000-1600.

# Ladakh

*The mountains of Ladakh – literally 'many passes' – may not be as typically spectacular as some parts of the high Himalaya for, as even the valleys are at an altitude of 3500 m, the summits are only 3000 m higher. Because it is desert there is little snow on them and they look like big brown hills, dry and dusty, with clusters of willows and desert roses along the streams. Yet bright blue skies are an almost constant feature, as the monsoon rains do not reach here, and the contrast with the dramatic landscape creates a beautiful and heavenly effect. For thousands of visitors Ladakh is a completely magical place, remote and relatively unspoilt, with delightful, gentle, ungrasping people.* ▶▶ *For listings, see pages 265-274.*

**Arriving in Ladakh** → *Colour map 1, A3. Population: 280,000. Altitude: 2500-4500 m, passes 4000-6000 m, peaks up to 7500 m.*

**Getting there and around Inner Line Permits** for the Nubra Valley, Dha-Hanu, Tso-moriri and Pangong Tso cost Rs 50 per person per day (for each area; Dha-Hanu is more expensive, at Rs 300 per person for an enrolment fee card, then Rs 70 per person per day) for a maximum of seven days in each place, while trekkers in the Hemis High Altitude Park must pay Rs 25 per day. Permits are available from the District Commissioner's office in Leh (see Directory, page 274), but all trekking/travel agents can arrange them for you – a much easier option. Allow at least half a day for an agent to obtain a permit, given only for groups of two or more. Permits are not extendable, but can be post-dated. Many people opt for permits covering all restricted areas. As a matter of course you should carry your passport with you since Ladakh is a sensitive border region. It's also worth carrying multiple photocopies of your passport and permits, as some checkpoints demand a copy.

**Note** Given the darkness of many buildings even at midday it is worth taking a torch wherever you go; a must at night. ▶▶ *See Transport, page 273.*

**Climate** The temperature can drop to -30°C in Leh and Kargil and -50°C in Dras, remaining sub-zero from December to February. Yet on clear sunny days in the summer, it can be scorching hot and you can easily get sunburnt; take plenty of sun cream. Ladakh lie beyond the monsoon line so rainfall is only 50 mm annually and there are even occasional dust storms.

## Background

Until recently Ladakhi society has generally been very introverted and the economy surprisingly self-sufficient. An almost total lack of precipitation has meant that cultivation must rely on irrigation. The rivers have been harnessed but with difficulty as the deep gorges presented a problem. Altitude and topography determine the choice of crop and farming is restricted to the areas immediately around streams and rivers. Barley forms the staple food while peas are the most common vegetable and apples and apricots the most popular fruits – the latter are dried for winter sustenance, while the kernel yields oil for burning in prayer-lamps. Because of the harshness of the climate and lack of rain, the cropping season usually lasts from April to October. At lower altitudes, grape, mulberry and walnut are grown.

Livestock is precious, especially the yak which provides meat, milk for butter, hair and hide for tents, boots, ropes and dung for fuel. Goats, especially in the eastern region, produce fine *pashm* for export. Animal transport is provided by yaks, ponies, Bactrian camels and the broad-backed *hunia* sheep. The Zanskar pony is fast and strong and used for transport – and for the special game of Ladakhi polo. Travellers venturing out of Leh are likely to see villagers using traditional methods of cultivation with the help of *dzos* and donkeys and using implements that have not changed for centuries.

Cut off from the outside world for six months a year, Ladakh also developed a very distinct culture. Polyandry (where a woman has more than one husband) was common but many men became *lamas* (monks) and a few women *chomos* (nuns). Most people depended on subsistence agriculture but the harsh climate contributed to very high death rates and a stable population. That is rapidly changing. Imported goods are now widely available and more and more people are taking part in the monetary economy. Ladakh and its capital Leh have been open to tourists since 1974, and some feel there are now far too many; the pitfalls of modern society are all too evident in the mounds of plastic rubbish strewn along the roadsides. The population of Leh has increased by more than five times in the last decade, and during the summer months tourists descend in numbers that equal the local population. In winter, those who can, leave for the plains – so this is when a more traditional Leh experience can be had, if you can bear the cold and the inconvenience.

## Leh → For listings, see pages 265-274. Colour map 1, A3. Population: 147,104. Altitude: 3500 m.

Mysterious dust-covered Leh sits in a fertile side valley of the Indus, about 10 km from the river. Encircled by stark awe-inspiring mountains with the cold desert beyond, it is the nearest experience to Tibet in India. The old Palace sits precariously on the hill to the north and looms over Leh. The wide Main Bazar Street (circa 1840s), which once accommodated caravans, has a colourful vegetable market where unpushy Ladakhi women sell local produce on the street side while they knit or chat. Makeshift craft and jewellery stalls line parts of Fort Road to the east to attract summer visitors along with Kashmiri shopkeepers who have come in search of greener pastures. The Old Town, mainly to the east of the Main Street, with its maze of narrow lanes, sits on the hillside below the palace and is worth exploring.

## Arriving in Leh

**Getting there** For seven to eight months in the year Leh is cut off by snow and the sole link with the outside world is by air. Tickets are in high demand so it is essential to book well ahead (on the internet). From mid-June to the end of September (weather permitting)

# Prepare for a different lifestyle in Leh

The whitewashed sun-dried brick walls of a typical two-storey, flat-roofed Ladakhi house, often with decorative woodwork around doors and windows and a carefully nurtured garden, look inviting to a traveller after a long hard journey. Many local families have opened up their homes to provide for the increasing demand for accommodation over a very short peak season and new hotels are springing up everywhere. However, prices do not reflect the type of furniture, furnishings and plumbing you might expect elsewhere in India although on the whole the rooms are kept clean. There is usually a space for sitting out – a 'garden' with a

tree or two, some flower beds and some grass struggling to establish itself.

Electricity is limited, so expect power cuts, which are random and unpredictable. Some hotels have generators. Those without may run out of tap water but buckets are always at hand. Hot water is a luxury, available only during mornings and evenings. Plumbing allows for flush WCs in most hotels, although compost toilets are the more ecological method.

Guests are encouraged to economize on water and electricity – you will notice the low-power bulbs and scarcity of lights in rooms and public areas, so put away your reading material until sunrise.

the Manali–Leh highway opens to traffic, bringing travellers to the New Bus Stand south of town. Taxis wait at both the airport and bus stand to take you to town.

**Getting around** Many hotels are within a few minutes' walk of the Main Bazar Street around which Leh's activities are concentrated. All the places of interest in Leh itself can also be tackled on foot by most visitors though those arriving by air or from Manali are urged to acclimatize for 48 hours before exerting themselves. For visiting monasteries and spots out of town arrange a jeep or taxi, although there are some buses and hitchhiking is possible. ▶ See Transport, page 273.

**Tourist information** J&K Tourism ① *2 km south on Airport Rd, T01982-25229, www.jktourism.org; or try the more convenient office on Fort Rd, T01982-253462, 1000-1600.*

## Background

The city developed as a trading post and market, attracting a wide variety of merchants from Yarkand, Kashgar, Kashmir, Tibet and North India. Tea, salt, household articles, wood and semi-precious stones were all traded in the market. Buddhism travelled along the Silk Road and the Kashmir and Ladakh feeder, which has also seen the passage of soldiers, explorers and pilgrims, forerunners of the tourists who today contribute most to the urban economy.

## Places in Leh

Dun-coloured **Leh Palace** ① *sunrise to sunset, Rs 100*, has been described as a miniature version of Lhasa's Potala Palace. Built in the mid-16th century, the palace was partly in ruins by the 19th century. It has nine storeys, sloping buttresses and projecting wooden balconies. From the town below it is dazzling in the morning sun and ghostly at night. Built by King Singe Namgyal and still owned by the royal family, it is now unoccupied; they live in the palace at Stok. Visible damage was caused during Zorawar Singh's invasion

# 1 Leh Orientation

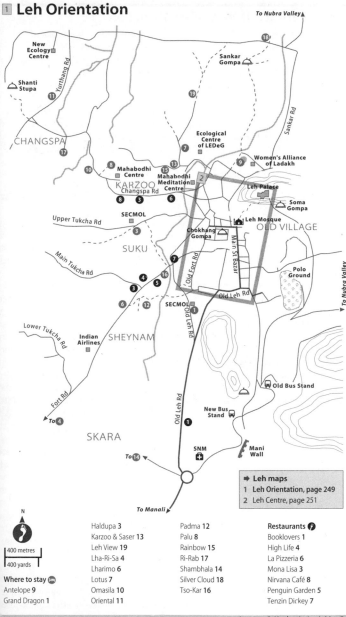

To Nubra Valley

New Ecology Centre

Yurthang Rd

Shanti Stupa

11

CHANGSPA

17

Sankar Gompa

18

19

Sankar Rd

Ecological Centre of LEDeG

7

Women's Alliance of Ladakh

9

8 Mahabodhi Centre

10

15 13

KARZOO

Changspa Rd

8 3

Mahabodhi Meditation Centre

6

2

Leh Palace

Soma Gompa

Upper Tukcha Rd

SECMOL

3

SUKU

Chokhang Gompa

Leh Mosque

OLD VILLAGE

Main St Bazar

Main Tukcha Rd

7

4 5 16

3

6 12

SECMOL

1

Old Fort Rd

Old Leh Rd

Polo Ground

To Nubra Valley

Lower Tukcha Rd

Indian Airlines

SHEYNAM

Old Leh Rd

Fort Rd

To 4

SKARA

1

To 14

Old Leh Rd

New Bus Stand

SNM

Mani Wall

Old Bus Stand

To Manali

**➡ Leh maps**
1 Leh Orientation, page 249
2 Leh Centre, page 251

N

400 metres
400 yards

**Where to stay** 🛏
Antelope **9**
Grand Dragon **1**

Haldupa **3**
Karzoo & Saser **13**
Leh View **19**
Lha-Ri-Sa **4**
Lharimo **6**
Lotus **7**
Omasila **10**
Oriental **11**

Padma **12**
Palu **8**
Rainbow **15**
Ri-Rab **17**
Shambhala **14**
Silver Cloud **18**
Tso-Kar **16**

**Restaurants** 🍴
Booklovers **1**
High Life **4**
La Pizzeria **6**
Mona Lisa **3**
Nirvana Café **8**
Penguin Garden **5**
Tenzin Dickey **7**

from Kashmir in the 1830s. The palace is under restoration, with new window and door frames fitted, and structural improvements being made – but still be wary of hazardous holes in the floor. After a steep climb some find the palace disappointing, but the views from the roof are exceptional. Like the Lhasa Potala Palace it has numerous rooms, steps and narrow passages (take a torch). The central prayer room has religious texts lining the walls, and contains dusty deities and time-worn masks. The upper levels have some painted carved wooden lintels and old murals that give a hint of past splendours. The Archaeological Survey of India is responsible for restoration and you will be able to watch work in progress.

South of the palace, the striking **Leh Mosque** in the main bazar is worth visiting – the inner section is not open to women visitors. The Sunni Muslim mosque is believed to stand on land granted by King Deldan Namgyal in the 1660s; his grandmother was the Muslim Queen of Ladakh.

The new **Central Asian Museum** is housed in a beautifully constructed building in the Tsa Soma gardens, where camel caravans used to camp. The museum explores the history of the caravan trade that for centuries linked Ladakh, until its mid-20th century isolation, with Tibet, Afghanistan, Samarkand, Kashmir and other city states. The museum is shaped like a Ladakhi fortress tower, with four floors inspired by the architecture of Ladakh, Kashmir, Tibet and Baltistan. Exhibits, including metalware, coins and masks, reveal the cultural exchange throughout the region; a garden café and museum shop are planned. A walking tour that includes the museum and visits restored buildings of the Old Town leaves from **Lala's Art Café** daily (see page 270), 1000-1300, Rs 300.

The **Chokhang Gompa** (New Monastery, 1957), off Main Bazar, was built to commemorate the 2500th anniversary of the birth of Buddha. The remains of the **Leh Gompa** houses a large golden Buddha.

The 15th-century **Tsemo Gompa** ('Red' Temple) is a strenuous walk north of the city and has a colossal two-storey-high image of Maitreya, flanked by figures of Avalokitesvara (right) and Manjusri (left). It was founded in 1430 by King Graspa Bum-Lde of the Namgyal rulers and a portrait of Tashi Namgyal hangs on the left at the entrance. Just above the *gompa* is **Tsemo Fort** ① *dawn-dusk, Rs 20*, the classic landmark above Leh which can be seen from miles around.

**Sankar Gompa** (17th-18th centuries) ① *3 km north of the centre, 0700-1000, 1700-1900, prayers at 1830 with chanting, drums and cymbals*, of the Yellow Hat Sect, is one of the few *gompas* built in the valley bottom; it's an enjoyable walk through fields from town. It houses the chief *lama* of Spituk and 20 others. The newer monks' quarters are on three sides of the courtyard with steps leading up to the *dukhang* (Assembly Hall). There are a number of gold statues, numerous wall paintings and sculptures including a large one of the 11-headed, 1000-armed *Avalokitesvara*. It's an atmospheric and beautiful enclave in the increasingly busy valley.

On Changspa Lane, across the stream from Sankar Gompa, you reach the start of the stiff climb up to the white Japanese **Shanti Stupa** (1989). This is one of a series of 'Peace Pagodas' built by the Japanese around the world. There are good views from the top where a café offers a welcome sight after the climb. There is also a road which is accessible by jeep. Below the *stupa*, the **New Ecology Centre**, has displays on 'appropriate technology', as well as a handicrafts centre, a technical workshop and an organic vegetable garden.

The **Ecological Centre of LEDeG** (Ladakh Ecological Development Group) and the **craft shop** ⓘ *T01982-253221, www.ledeg.org, Mon-Fri 100-1800*, opened in 1984 to spread awareness of Ladakhi environmental issues, encourage self-help and the use of alternative technology. It has a library of books on Ladakhi culture, Buddhism and the environment. Handicrafts are sold, and you can refill water for Rs 10.

The **Women's Alliance of Ladakh (WAL)** ⓘ *Sankar Rd, Chubi, T01982-250293, www. womanallianceladakh.org, video shown Mon-Sat 1500 (minimum 10 people)*, is an alliance of 5000 Ladakhi women, concerned with raising the status of traditional agriculture, preserving the traditionally high status of women and creating an alternative development model based on self-reliance for Ladakh. The centre has a café selling local and organic foods (see page 270), and a craft shop. They hold festivals, cultural shows, dances, etc which are advertized around Leh; it's mainly aimed at local people, but all visitors are welcome.

The **Donkey Sanctuary** ⓘ *www. donkeysanctuary.in*, opened in 2008. This charity looks after 40-60 donkeys at any one time and is well worth a visit.

West of the centre, the non-profit making **Students' Educational and Cultural Movement of Ladakh (SECMOL)** ⓘ *Karzoo, with an office on Old Leh Rd, T01982-252421, www.secmol.org*, encourages the teaching of Ladakhi history, culture and crafts.

From the radio station there are two long *mani* walls. **Rongo Tajng** is in the centre of the open plain and was built as a memorial to Queen Skalzang Dolma by her son Dalden Namgyal. It is about 500 m long

## 2 Leh centre

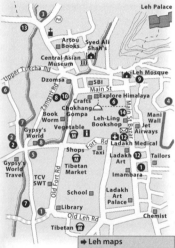

Restaurants ⑦
Amdo Food **1**
Chansa Traditional
  Ladakhi Kitchen **6**
Chopsticks **2**
Il Forno **8**
Lala's Art Café **9**
Mentokling Apple
  Garden **13**
Open Hand Espresso Bar **7**
Pumpernickel **10**
Shubh Panjabi Dhaba **14**
Tibetan Friend's Corner **12**

Not to scale

Where to stay ⊜
Alpine Villa **1**
Atisha **7**
Indus **2**
Kang-lha Chen **3**
Malpak **6**
Old Ladakh **4**
Tsomo-Ri **8**
Yak Tail **5**

and was built in 1635. The stones have been meticulously carved. The other, a 350-m wall down the hill, is believed to have been built by Tsetan Namgyal in 1785 as a memorial to his father the king.

## Southeast of Leh → For listings, see pages 265-274. Colour map 1, A3.

South and east of Leh is an amazing stretch of road with some fascinating monasteries strung along it. Many of these make good day trips from Leh, and are possible excursions by bus and hitching. If you hire a car or jeep (which is good value when shared by four), you can see many of the places below in a single day. Camera flash is usually not allowed in monasteries to reduce damage to wall paintings and *thangkas*. Carry a torch.

### Choglamsar

Choglamsar, 7 km south of Leh on the east bank of the Indus, is a green oasis with poplars and willows where there are golf links and a polo ground as well as horticultural nurseries. The road between Leh and Choglamsar is now quite built up and at times clogged with traffic. The Central Institute of Buddhist Studies is here with a specialist library. Past the Tibetan refugee camps, children's village and the arts and crafts centre, the Choglamsar Bridge crosses the Indus. The **Chochot Yugma Imambara** ① *a few minutes' walk from the bridge*, is worth a visit. Buses depart Leh hourly from 0800-1800.

### Stok

Across Choglamsar Bridge, 16 km south of Leh, is the royal palace dating from the 1840s when the King of Ladakh was deposed by the invading Dogra forces. The last king died in 1974 but his widow still lives here. His son continues the royal line and ascended to the throne in July 1993. The palace is a rambling building where only a dozen of the 80 rooms are used. The small **Palace Museum** ① *May-Oct 0900-1300 and 1400-1900, Rs 50*, with three rooms, is a showpiece for the royal *thangkas*, many 400 years old, crown jewels, dresses, coins, *peraks* (headdresses) encrusted with turquoise and lapis lazuli as well as religious objects. There's also a rather lovely café, which has superb views.

The **gompa**, a short distance away, has some ritual dance masks. **Tsechu** is in February. A three-hour walk up the valley behind Stok takes you to some extraordinary mountain scenery dominated by the 6121-m-high Stok Kangri.

There is an **archery contest** in July. There are at least three simple guesthouses in town of which the Yarsta is most comfortable. Buses to Stok leave Leh at 0730 and 1700. Taxis from the Leh central taxi stand are available at fixed rates at any time.

### Shey

① *Palace open all day; try to be there 0700-0900, 1700-1800 when prayers are chanted, Rs 20.*
Until the 16th century, Shey was the royal residence, located at an important vantage point in the Indus Valley. Kings of Leh were supposed to be born in the monastery. The royal family moved to Stok in order to escape advancing Dogra forces from Kashmir who came to exploit the trade in pashmina wool. Shey, along with Thikse, is also regarded as an auspicious place for cremation.

Most of the fort walls have fallen into disrepair but the palace and its wall paintings have now been restored. The palace *gompa* with its 17.5-m-high blue-haired Maitreya Buddha imitating the one at Tsemo Gompa, is attended by Drukpa monks from Hemis. It is made of copper and brass but splendidly gilded and studded with precious gem stones. Paintings i the main shrine have been chemically cleaned by the Archaeological Society of India. The large victory *stupa* is topped with gold. Extensive grounds covering the former lake bed to the east contain a large number of *chortens* in which cremated ashes of important monks, members of the royal family and the devout were buried. A newer temple houses another old giant Buddha statue. There are several rock carvings; particularly noteworthy is that of five *dhyani* Buddhas (circa eighth century) at the bottom of the hill. The small hotel below the *gompa* has spartan but clean rooms. It is 15 km southeast of Leh on the Indus River or can be reached along a stone path from Thikse. Hourly buses depart Leh 0800-1800.

## Thikse
① *Rs 30, hourly buses from Leh 0800-1800.*
Situated 25 km south of Leh on a crag overlooking the flood plain on the east bank of the Indus, this is one of the most imposing monasteries in Ladakh and was part of the original Gelugpa order in the 15th century. The 12-storey monastery, with typical tapering walls painted deep red, ochre and white, has 10 temples, a nunnery and 80 *lamas* in residence whose houses cling to the hillside below. The complex contains numerous *stupas*, statues, *thangkas*, wall paintings (note the fresco of the 84 Mahasiddhas, high above) swords and a large pillar engraved with the Buddha's teachings.

The new temple interior is dominated by a giant 13-m-high Buddha figure near the entrance. The principal *Dukhang* (assembly hall) at the top of the building has holes in the wall for storing religious texts and contains the guardian deities. At the very top, the Old Library has old wooden bookcases with ancient texts and statues; adjacent is the tiny *Chamsing Lhakhang*. Views from the roof are staggeringly good. The slightly creepy *Gonkhang* has Tibetan-style wall paintings. The **museum** ① *0600-1800, closed 1300-1330,* is near the entrance, and also sells souvenirs. There's a restaurant and guestrooms, below the museum. Thikse is a popular place to watch religious ceremonies, usually at 0630 or 1200. An early start by taxi makes even the first possible, or it's possible to stay overnight (see page 267). They are preceded by the playing of large standing drums and long horns similar to *alpenstock*. Masked dances are performed during special festivals.

## Stakna
Across the valley on a hill, Stakna is the earliest Drukpa monastery, built before Hemis though its decorations are not as ancient. It is also called 'Tiger's nose' because of the shape of the hill site. This small but well-kept monastery has a beautiful silver-gilt *chorten* in the assembly hall, installed around 1955, and some interesting paintings in the dark temple at the back. No need for a local guide as the *lamas* are always willing to open the doors. There are excellent views of the Indus Valley and the Zanskar range.

## Hemis
① *0800-1300, 1400-1800.*
On the west bank of the Indus, 45 km southeast of Leh, the monastery, built on a green hillside surrounded by spectacular mountain scenery, is tucked into a gorge. The **Drukpa Monastery** was founded by Stagsang Raspa during the reign of Senge Namgyal (circa 1630). It is the biggest (350 lamas) and wealthiest in Ladakh and it's a 'must', thus is busy with tourists. Pass by *chortens* and sections of *mani* walls to enter the complex through the east gate which leads into a large 40 m by 20 m courtyard. Colourful flags flutter in the breeze from posts, and the balconied walls of the buildings have colourfully painted door and window frames. On the north side are two assembly halls approached by steps.

The large three-tiered *Dukhang* to the right used for ceremonies is old and atmospheric; the smaller *Tshogskhang* (main temple) contains three silver gilt *chortens* and is covered in murals. The murals in the verandas depict guardian deities, the *kalachakra* (wheel of life) and 'Lords of the four quarters' are well preserved. A staircase alongside the *Tshogskhang* leads to a roof terrace where there are a number of shrines including a bust of the founder. The *Tsom Lakhang* (chapel) has ancient Kashmiri bronzes, a golden Buddha and a silver *chorten*. The largest of The monastery's prized possession is a heavy silk *thangka*, beautifully embroidered in bright coloured threads and pearls, which is displayed every 12 years (next 2016). The museum contains an important library of Tibetan-style books and an impressive collection of *thangkas*.

Not many people make the walk to the new golden Buddha on a nearby cliff, and there is also a pleasant 3-km walk uphill to another *gompa*. A stay in Hemis overnight enables you to attend early-morning prayers, a moving experience and recommended. Bus services make a day trip possible.

## Chemrey
Picture-perfect Chemrey is a short way off the main road, walkable from where the bus drops passengers. Perched on a little peak above encircling barley fields is **Thekchok Gompa**, home to 70 monks. A road winds to the top, but it's nicer to walk up the steep steps through traditional homesteads. The wonky prayer hall has countless murals of the Buddha, and there are three further *lhakhang* (image halls) to visit; a museum on the roof contains *thangkas* and statues. The beautiful setting and relative lack of visitors makes Chemrey a very worthwhile stop.

## Sakti and Takthok
The road continues through a sloping valley to Takthok, first passing Sakti village with the dramatic ruins of a fortress by the roadside. At ancient **Takthok Gompa** ⓘ *Rs 30*, there is a holy cave-shrine in which the sage Padmasambhava meditated in the eighth century. The walls and ceiling are papered with rupee notes and coins, numerous statues are swathed in prayer scarves, and centuries of butter lamps have left their grime. A highly colourful *dukhang* hall contains three beautiful statues. It is the only monastery in Ladakh belonging to the Nyingma sect of Buddhism; about 60 lamas reside here, and at the new *gompa* constructed nearby in 1980. It's possible to take a morning bus from Leh to Takthok and walk the 5 km back down the valley to Chemrey. Should you get stranded in Takthok, a **Tourist Bungalow** ⓘ *opposite the Gompa, T(0)9622-959513*, has four jaded but sunny rooms, some with squat toilets.

## Along the Srinagar road → *For listings, see pages 265-274. Colour map 1, A3.*

The Srinagar road out of Leh passes through a flat dusty basin mostly occupied by army encampments with mile after mile of wire fencing. The scenery is stunning and, as with the Leh–Manali Road, is punctuated with monasteries. A bus leaves Leh each afternoon for Alchi (see below), allowing access to most of the sites described in this section. A few places make for interesting and peaceful overnight stops.

## Spituk
Standing on a conical hill, some 8 km from Leh, Spituk was founded in the 11th century. The buildings themselves, including three chapels, date from the 15th century and are set in a series of tiers with courtyards and steps. The Yellow-Hat Gelugpa monks created the

precedent in Ladakh for building on mountain tops rather than valley floors. You can get good views of the countryside around.

The long 16th- to 17th-century *dukhang* (assembly hall) is the largest building and has two rows of seats along the length of the walls to a throne at the far end. Sculptures and miniature *chortens* are displayed on the altar. Spituk has a collection of ancient Jelbagh masks, icons and arms including some rescued from the Potala Palace in Lhasa.

Also 16th- to 17th-century, the **Mahakal Temple**, higher up the hill, contains a shrine of Vajrabhairava, often mistaken for the Goddess Kali. The terrifying face is only unveiled in January, during the **Gustor festival**. The Srinagar buses can drop you on the highway (four daily, 20 minutes).

## Phyang
**Phyang Gompa**, 16 km from Leh, dominates a beautiful side valley dotted with poplars, homesteads and *chortens* with a village close by. It belongs to the Red-Hat Kagyupa sect, with its 16th-century Gouon monastery built by the founder of the Namgyal Dynasty which is marked by a flagstaff at the entrance. It houses 60 lamas and hundreds of statues including some Kashmiri bronzes (circa 14th century), *thangkas* and manuscript copies of the Kangyur and Tengyur. The temple walls have colourful paintings centring on the eight emblems of happiness. The walls in the main prayer hall are covered with ancient smoke-blackened murals, and a giant rolled-up *thangka* hangs from the ceiling. The faces of the statues in the Protector's Hall have been covered. A grand new wing is being constructed, with rather gawdy paintings by the artists (many of whom come from Bhutan). Morning prayers take place 0600-0730. Phyang is the setting for a spectacular July **Tseruk festival** with masked dancing. There are three buses daily (0900, 1400 and 1630, 45 minutes; return to Leh at 0800, 1000, 1300 from the monastery, 1600 and 1730); the morning bus allows you to explore the valley and walk back to Leh, but the afternoon bus only allows a short visit. However, it is worth overnighting in Phyang as there is a pleasing guesthouse (see page 267), good walks around the traditional village and dramatic valley up to the fort, and stunning views to the pyramid-peak of Stok Kangri.

## Phyang to Nimmu
About 2 km before Nimmu the Indus enters an impressive canyon before the Zanskar joins it, a good photo opportunity. As the road bends, a lush green oasis with lines of poplars comes into view. The mud brick houses of Nimmu have grass drying on the flat rooftops to provide fodder for the winter. A dry stone *mani* wall runs along the road; beyond Nimmu the walls become 2 m wide in places with innumerable *chortens* alongside. The rocky outcrops on the hills to the right appear like a natural fortress. Nimmu serves mainly as a bus rest-stop, but there are a couple of small hotels (Nilza Guesthouse is most acceptable) and a collection of *dhabas* and shops.

## Basgo
The road, lined by *mani* walls and *chortens*, passes through Basgo Village with the ruins of a Buddhist citadel impressively sited on a spur overlooking the Indus Valley. It served as a royal residence for several periods between the 15th and 17th centuries. The **fort palace** was once considered almost impregnable having survived a three-year siege by Tibetan and Mongol armies in the 17th century.

Among the ruins two temples have survived. The higher **Maitreya Temple** (mid-16th century) built by Tashi Namgyal's son contains a very fine Maitreya statue at the rear of the hall, flanked by *bodhisattvas*. Some murals from the early period illustrating the Tibetan Buddhist style have also survived on the walls and ceiling; among the Buddhas and *bodhisattvas* filled with details of animals, birds and mermaids, appear images of Hindu divinities. The 17th-century **Serzang Temple** (gold and copper), with a carved doorway, contains another large Maitreya image whose head rises through the ceiling into a windowed box-like structure. The murals look faded and have been damaged by water. The fort is very photogenic, particularly so in the late afternoon light. The Chamba View guesthouse and restaurant is by the road, as you exit the village.

## Lekir (Likir)
Some 5.5 km from Basgo, a road on the right leads up to Lekir Monastery via a scenic route. Lower Lekir, a scattering of houses where most accommodation is found, is about 1 km off NH1 accessed by confusing unpaved tracks. You can walk from Lower Likir up to the monastery, about 5 km on the road, or via short-cuts crossing the river. The picturesque whitewashed monastery buildings rise in different levels on the hillside across the Lekir River. A huge gold-coloured Maitreya Buddha flanks the complex. Lekir was built during the reign of Lachen Gyalpo who installed 600 monks here, headed by Lhawang Chosje (circa 1088). The *gompa* was invested with a collection of fine images, *thangkas* and murals to vie with those at Alchi. The present buildings date mainly from the 18th century since the original were destroyed by fire. A path up leads to the courtyard where a board explains the origin of the name: Klu-Khyil (snake coil) refers to the *nagas* here, reflected in the shape of the hill. Lekir was converted to the Gelugpa sect in the 15th century. The head *lama*, the younger brother of the Dalai Lama, has his apartments here, which were extended in the mid-1990s.

The **dukhang** (assembly hall) contains large clay images of the Buddhas (past, present and future), *thangkas*, and Kangyur and Tengyur manuscripts, the Kangyur having been first compiled in Ladakh during Lachen Gyalpo's reign. The **Nyenes-Khang** contains beautiful murals of the 35 confessional Buddhas and 16 arahats. Wooden steps lead up to the **Gon-Khang** housing a statue of the guardian deity here, as well as *thangkas* and murals. Further steps lead to a small but very interesting **museum** ① *Rs 20, opened on request (climb to a hall above, up steep wooden stairs)*, displays *thangkas*, old religious and domestic implements, costumes, etc, which are labelled in English.

Village craftsmen produce *thangkas*, carved wooden folding seats and clay pottery. If you wish to stay overnight, the monastery has guestrooms which share bathrooms (by donation); for further accommodation options in the villages, see page 268. A bus goes to Leh at 0730 from the monastery.

## Alchi
① *0800-1300, 1400-1800, Rs 50, www.achiassociation.org*
The road enters Saspol, 8 km after the Lekir turn-off. About 2 km beyond the village, a link road with a suspension bridge over the river leads to Alchi, which is hidden from view as you approach. As the road enters the village, impressive old houses in various states of repair can be seen. It's possible to climb up the small rocky peak behind these, to a square white turret with graves around, for good views up the Indus valley and of the village. A patchwork of cultivated fields surrounds the monastery complex.

A narrow path from the car park winds past village houses, donkeys and apricot trees to lead to the **Dharma Chakra monastery**. You will be expected to buy a ticket from one of the three *lamas* on duty. The whole complex, about 100 m long and 60 m wide, is enclosed by a whitewashed mud and straw wall. Alchi's large temple complex is regarded as one of the most important Buddhist centres in Ladakh and a jewel of monastic skill. Founded in the 11th century by Rinchen Zangpo, the 'Great Translator', it was richly decorated by artists from Kashmir and Tibet. Paintings of the *mandalas*, which have deep Tantric significance, are particularly fine; some decorations are reminiscent of Byzantine art. The monastery is maintained by monks from Lekir and is no longer a place for active worship.

A path on the right past two large prayer wheels and a row of smaller ones leads to the river which attracts deer down to the opposite bank in the evenings. At the rear, small *chortens* with inscribed stones strewn around them, line the wall. It is worth walking around the exterior of the complex, and you'll get a beautiful view of the Indus River with mountains as a backdrop. For accommodation options, see Where to stay, page 268.

**The temple complex** The entrance *chortens* are worth looking in to. Each has vividly coloured paintings within, both along the interior walls as well as in the small *chorten*-like openings on the ceilings. The first and largest of these has a portrait of the founder Rinchen Zangpo (closed at the time of research).

The first temple you come to is the **Sum-stek**, the three-tier temple with a carved wooden gallery on the façade and triple arches. Inside are three giant four-armed,

# Alchi Choskor

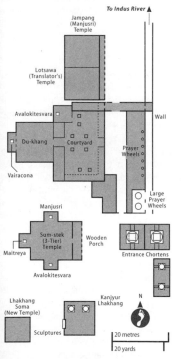

garlanded stucco figures of *Bodhisattvas*: the white *Avalokitesvara* on the left, the principal terracotta-red *Maitreya* in the centre at the back, and the ochre-yellow *Manjusri* on the right; their heads project to the upper storey which is reached by a rustic ladder (inaccessible). The remarkable features here are the brightly painted and gilded decorations on the clothing of the figures which include historical incidents, musicians, palaces and places of pilgrimage. Quite incongruous court scenes and Persian features appear on *Avalokitesvara* while the figures on *Maitreya* have Tantric connotations illustrating the very different styles of ornamentation on the three sculptures. The walls have numerous *mandalas* and inscriptions, as well as thousands of tiny Buddhas.

The oldest temple is the **dukhang**, which has a covered courtyard (originally open to the sky) with wooden pillars and painted walls; the left wall shows two rowing boats with fluttering flags, a reminder perhaps of the presence in ancient times of lakes in this desert. The brightly painted door to the *dukhang*, about 1.5 m high, and the entrance archway has some fine woodcarving. The subsidiary shrines on either side of the doorway contain

*Avalokitesvaras* and *Bodhisattvas* including a giant four-armed Maitreya figure to the extreme right. This main assembly hall, which was the principal place of worship, suffers from having very little light so visitors need a good torch. The 'shrine' holds the principal gilded *Vairocana* (Resplendent) Buddha (traditionally white, accompanied by the lion) with ornate decorations behind, flanked by four important Buddha postures among others. The walls on either side of the main hall are devoted to fine but damaged *Mandala* paintings illustrating the four principal manifestations of the *Sarvavid* (Omniscient) Buddha – *Vairocana*, *Sakyamuni* (the Preacher), *Manjusri* (Lord of Wisdom) and as *Prajna Paramita* (Perfection of Wisdom). There are interesting subsidiary panels, friezes and inscriptions. On exiting, note the terrifying figure of *Mahakala* the guardian deity above the door with miniature panels of royal and military scenes. The one portraying a drinking scene shows the royal pair sanctified with haloes with wine-cups in hand, accompanied by the prince and attendants – the detail of the clothing clearly shows Persian influence.

The **Lotsawa** (Translator's) and **Jampang** (Manjusri) *Lhakhangs* were built later and probably neglected for some time. The former contains a statue of Rinchen Zangpo along with a seated Buddha while the latter has a finely carved doorway and exterior lintels. Ask for the lights to be switched on.

**Lhakhang Soma** (New Temple) is a square hall used as a meditation centre with a *chorten* within; its walls are totally covered with *mandalas* and paintings portraying incidents from the Buddha's life and historic figures; the main figure here is the preaching Buddha. There is an interesting panel of warriors on horseback near the door. Ask for the temple to be opened if it is locked. **Kanjyur Lhakhang** in front of the Lhakhang Soma houses the scriptures.

## Lamayuru

In Lamayuru, 10 km before Khaltse, the famous monastery is perched on a crag overlooking the Indus in a striking lunar landscape between a drained lake and high mountains. Little medieval houses nestle on the steep slope beneath the monastery, and the effect is dramatically photogenic. The monastery complex, which includes a library thought to be the oldest in the region, was founded in the 11th century and belongs to the Tibetan Kagyupa sect. The present monastery dating from the 16th century was partly destroyed in the 19th. You can still see some of the murals, along with the redecorated *dukhang* (assembly hall). A small glass panel in the right hand wall of the *dukhang* protects a tiny holy cave, and there are many beautiful bronzes displayed. In a small temple, below the monastery, is an 11-headed and 1000-armed Avalokiteshvara image; the walls here are coated with murals – you will need to ask someone to get the key. Some of the upper rooms are richly furnished with carpets, Tibetan tables, statues, silver *stupas* and butter lamps. In June/July the monastery holds the famous **Yuru Kabgyat** festival, with colourful masked dancing, special prayers, and burning of sacrificial offerings. There are several guesthouses strung along the road and up the hillside (see page 269); it's also possible to camp near the stream in a willow grove. There are daily buses from Leh at 0800; buses to Leh and Kargil leave Lamayuru at around 0930, and to Chitkan at 1000.

Shortly after Lamayuru, a jeep road leaves the highway heading south down the Yapola Valley to **Wanla** which has a beautiful *gompa*, from the same era as Alchi and decorated by same artists. It has been recently restored, see www.achiassociation.org, and is adjoined on a dramatic ridge by a ruined fort. In Wanla village there are guesthouses. The next village is **Phanjila**, and further along there is a homestay in the delightful village of **Hinju**, from where the track peters out into a fantastic trekking route (see page 263).

## Nubra Valley, Nyona and Drokhpa area → *For listings, see pages 265-274.*
*Colour map 1, A4.*

These once-restricted areas are now open to visitors with an Inner Line Permit. Permits are issued in Leh to groups of two or more travelling together by jeep, for a maximum of seven days. You can get a joint permit to cover all areas. Allow a day to get a permit, which costs around Rs 250 (more if you include Dha-Hanu). A lot of ground can be covered in the period but it is best to consult a Leh-based trekking and travel agent. Always carry multiple photocopies of your passport and ILP with you, to facilitate the crossing of checkpoints.

### Nubra Valley → *Colour map 1, A3/A4.*
For an exhilarating high-altitude experience over possibly the highest motorable pass in the world, travel across the Ladakh range over the 5600-m **Khardung La**. This is along the old Silk Route to the lush green Nubra Valley up to **Panamik**, 140 km north of Leh. Camel caravans once transported Chinese goods along this route for exchanging with Indian produce. The relatively gentle climate here allows crops, fruit and nuts to grow, so some call it 'Ldumra' (orchard). There are guesthouses in villages throughout the valley, and temporary tented camps are occasionally set up by tour companies during the season, but it's still a good idea to take a sleeping bag.

It is possible to visit the Nubra-Shyok valleys over two days, but it's much preferable (and the same cost) to make the journey over three. After crossing the Khardung La, the first village is **Khardung**, 42 km later, boasting a majestic setting. The road continues down the Shyok Valley to **Deskit**, which has an old and a new (less appealing) town centre and several places to stay. On a hill above the old village is a Gelugpa sect **monastery** (the largest in Nubra) built by the Ladakhi king Sohrab Zangpo in the early 1700s. There is large statue of Tsongkhapa, and the Rimpoche of Thikse monastery south of Leh oversees this monastery also. A further 10 km past Diskit is the village of **Hunder**, probably the most popular place to overnight, with several garden-guesthouses to chose from. Highly-prized double-humped camels can occasionally be seen on the sand dunes near Hunder, allegedly descendents of the caravan-camels that used to ply the Silk Route, and it is possible to take a 15- to 30-minute camel ride (on a tame beast). Past Hunder the road continues to **Turtuk**, opened to tourists in 2010. The scenery is impressive and the tiny settlements here are culturally Balti and practise Islam.

The second biggest monastery in Nubra is near **Tiger** village along the road to Panamik in the Nubra Valley. Called the **Samtanling** *gompa*, it was founded in 1842 and belongs to the Gelugpa sect. **Panamik** has several guesthouses and reddish, sulphurous hot springs nearby. The ILP allows travel only up **Ensa Gompa**, included on some itineraries, and approached by foot for the last 30 minutes.

Should you need medical help, there is a health centre at Deskit and a dispensary at Panamik. Traffic into and out of the Nubra Valley is controlled by the army at Pulu. From Leh there are two buses per week from June to September; a few have tried by bike, which can be put on the roof of the bus for the outward journey.

### Pangong-Tso → *Colour map 1, A4.*
A popular excursion from Leh (permit required) is to the narrow 130-km-long Pangong-Tso, at 4250 m, the greater part of which lies in Tibet. The road, which is only suitable for 4WD in places, is via **Karu** on the Manali–Leh Highway, where the road east goes through **Zingral** and over the Chang La pass. Beyond are **Durbuk**, a small village with low-roofed

houses, and **Tangste**, the 'abode of Chishul warriors' with a Lotswa Temple, which is also an army base with a small bank. The rough jeep track takes you through an impressive rocky gorge which opens out to a valley which has camping by a fresh water stream in the hamlet of **Mugleb** and then on to **Lukung** and finally **Spangmik**, 153 km from Leh. On the way you will be able to see some Himalayan birds including *chikhor* (quail) which may end up in the cooking pot.

An overnight stop on the lake shore allows you to see the blue-green lake in different lights. You can walk between Lukung and Spangmik, 7 km, on the second day, passing small settlements growing barley and peas along the lake shore. You return to Leh on the third day. There are tented camps at Durbuk, Tangtse and Lukung. At Spangmik there is a wider choice of accommodation, in the form of homestays (mats on floor) or in the rather pricey Pangong Tso Resort (rooms have attached bath). Buses go from Leh at 0630 on Saturdays and Sundays, but almost everyone makes the journey by private jeep.

### Tso-Moriri → *Colour map 1, A4.*
The Rupshu area, a dry, high-altitude plateau to the east of the Leh–Manali Highway, is where the nomadic Changpas live (see page 223), in the bleak and windswept Chamathang highlands bordering Tibet. The route to the beautiful Tso-Moriri (*tso* – lake), the only nesting place of the bar-headed geese on the Indus, is open to visitors. It is 220 km from Leh; jeeps make the journey. To the south of the 27-km-long lake is the land of the Tibetan wild ass.

You can travel either via **Chhumathang**, 140 km, visiting the hot spring there or by crossing the high pass at Taglang La, leaving the Manali–Leh Highway at Debring. The route takes you past the **Tsokar** basin, 154 km, where salt cakes the edges. A campsite along the lake with access to fresh water is opposite **Thukje** village which has a *gompa* and a 'wolf-catching trap'. The road then reaches the hot sulphur springs at **Puga** before arriving at the beautiful Tso-Moriri, about four hours' drive from Tsokar. You can follow the lake bank and visit the solitary village of **Karzog**, at 4500 m, north of the lake, which also has a *gompa*. There are some rest houses and guesthouses at Chhumathang and Karzog and camping at Tsokar and Karzog as well as a tent camp at Chhumathang.

### Drokhpa area → *Colour map 1, A3.*
**Dha** and **Biama** (Bema) are two Drokhpa (aka Brokpa) villages where the so-called pure Aryan tribe speaking a distinct dialect live in a fair degree of isolation; Buddhism here is mixed with animist practices. You may reach these Indus Valley villages from **Khaltse** on the Leh–Srinagar road via the scenic villages of Dumkhar, Tirit, Skurbuchan and Hanu. There are homestays and a campsite at Biama, but Dha (3 km further) is the more popular option for overnight stays.

## Trekking in Ladakh → *Colour map 1, A3.*

Make sure your trekking guide is experienced and competent. A detailed book, although dated, is the Trailblazer guide Trekking in Ladakh which can be bought in bookshops in Leh. Some treks, eg Spituk to Hemis and Hemis High Altitude National Park, charge a fee of Rs 25 per person per day or Rs 10 for Indians. For trekking, July and August are pleasant months. Go earlier and you will be trudging through snow much of the time. September and October are also good months, though colder at night.

## Markha Valley Trek, Spituk to Hemis

Both places are in the Indus Valley, just 30 km apart. A very satisfying nine to 10 days can be undertaken by traversing the Stok range to the Markha Valley, walking up the valley and then back over the Zanskar range to Hemis. The daily walking time on this trek is five to six hours so you must be fit. Places to camp are highlighted below, but there are also basic homestays or guesthouses in the villages if you don't want to carry equipment.

There is an interesting monastery at **Spituk**, a short drive from Leh (see page 254). From Spituk proceed southwest of the Indus along a trail passing through barren countryside. After about 7 km you reach the **Zingchen Valley** and in a further five hours, the beautiful village of **Rumbak**. Camp below the settlement. You can also trek here from Stok which takes one-two days and a steep ascent of the **Namlung La** (4570 m).

From Rumbak it is a five-hour walk to **Utse** village. The camp is two hours further on at the base of the bleak **Gandha La** (4700 m), open, bare and windswept. To go over the pass takes about three hours, then the same time again to negotiate the wooded ravine to **Skiu**. Here the path meets the Markha Valley. You can make a half-day round trip from Skiu to see the impressive gorges on the Zanskar River. The stage to **Markha**, where there is an impressive fort, is a six-hour walk. The monastery, while not particularly impressive from the outside, has some superb wall paintings and *thangkas*, some dating from the 13th century. You need to take a torch.

The next destination is **Hankar** village, whose ruined fort forms an astonishing extension of the natural rock face, an extremely impressive ruin. From here the path

# Ladakh & Zanskar

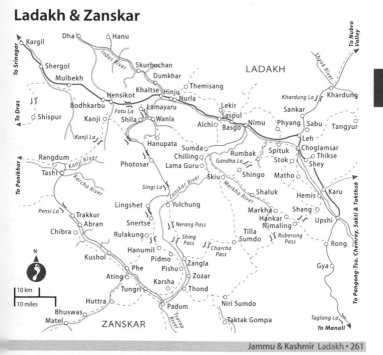

## Who might you meet along the way – birds and wildlife

The Himalayan range is the longest and the highest mountain range in the world. The sheer diversity of the topography makes it one of the best places to spot some of the rarest wildlife and birds. The forested regions offer a large variety of birds. You might see Himalayan griffons, crested serpent eagles, lamagiers, forest owlets, common flamebacks, golden orioles, scarlet minivets, rose finches, chukors, snow cocks, pigeons, Himalayan blue magpies, monals, khaleej pheasants, the critically endangered western tragopans, or black-necked cranes around Tso Kar. In fact, the flatlands around Tso Kar in Ladakh is one of my favourite places to see birds. Another great place to venture to in order to see birds and wildlife is the Great Himalayan National park, in Himachal Pradesh. The park is a habitat to 375 fauna species, which includes 31 mammals, 181 birds and 127 insects.

In my 16 odd years of trekking in the Western Himalayas the sighting that has had me the most excited is seeing a snow leopard for the first time in Rumbak valley of Ladakh in 1995. Watching a snow leopard was awe-inspiring. Once I was even offered a chanko cub, which is a Tibetan wolf. I was camped in the village of Rumtse where I met a villager from the Khanag valley who had a two- or three-month-old cub that he had found and was not sure what to do with.

My work as a trekking and climbing guide takes me to some remote parts and over the years I have seen dramatic changes in not just glaciers receding due to global warming but also extensive deforestation because of many hydro electric projects. This has affected carnivores like the snow leopard and the chanko due to the loss of prey caused by habitat destruction. A positive development is the increase in snow leopard tourism in Ladakh which has prompted the locals to stop viewing the big cat as an enemy and has opened doors to alternative income generation.

Kaushal Desai, tour guide at Above 14000ft.

climbs quite steeply to a plateau. There are good views of Nimaling Peak (6000 m) and a number of *mani* walls en route. From **Nimaling** it is a two-hour climb to **Gongmaru La** (5030 m) with views of the Stok range and the Indus Valley. The descent is arduous and involves stream crossings. There is a lovely campsite at **Shogdu** and another at **Sumda** village, 3 km further on. The final stage is down the valley to **Martselang** from where you can walk down 5 km to **Karu** village on the Leh–Manali road or take a 2-km diversion to visit **Hemis** monastery.

### Hemis High Altitude National Park

Set up in 1981, the park adjoining the monastery comprising the catchments of Markha, Rumbak and Sumda *nalas*. The reserve area has been expanded a couple of times, and now covers 4400 sq km making it the largest national park in South Asia. The rugged terrain with valleys often littered with rocks and rimmed by high peaks (some over 6000 m), supports limited alpine vegetation but contains some rare species of flora and fauna, including the ibex, Pallas' cat, *bharal* and *shapu*. It is the habitat of the endangered and elusive snow leopard, now numbering around 200 (mainly in the Rumbak area, best spotted in winter). It is hoped that the activities of local villagers, who graze livestock within the park, can be restricted to a buffer zone so that their animals can be kept safe from attack by wolves and snow leopards. Villages used to trap the leopard, but now they are reimbursed for any livestock lost to snow leopard attacks.

There are camping sites within the park, which can be reserved through the Wildlife Warden in Leh. There are also homestays, see www.himalayan-homestays.com, run in conjunction with the **Snow Leopard Conservancy India Trust (SNC-IT)** ① *www.snowleopardconservancy.org*. SNC-IT also run 10-day winter expeditions. Since most of the park lies within 'restricted' areas, you need a special permit for entry, also issued in Leh. Contact a local travel agent for advice.

## Ripchar Valley Trek

This is a shorter trek of four to five days; however, the average daily walking time is seven hours so don't think that the shortness of the trek means less effort. A guide is recommended.

The first stage involves transport from Leh (five to six hours), then an hour's walk to **Hinju** (3750 m); camp or homestay overnight at the village. Stage two continues up through the Ripchar Valley to cross the **Konze La** (4570 m), from where you will see the Zanskar River and gorge and the Stok range. Then descend to **Sumdo Chenmo**, quite a treacherous route as it involves river crossings. There is a monastery here with an impressive statue of the Buddha and some attractive wall paintings. A campsite lies just beyond the village. The next day takes you from Sumdo Chenmo to **Lanak** (4000 m), a walk of five to six hours. The final stage, about seven hours, from Lanak to **Chilling**, is over the **Dungduchan La** (4700 m) with excellent views. The path continues down the valley following a stream to Chilling. Overnight in Chilling or do the two-hour drive back to Leh. Some agents also offer the option of rafting back to Leh from Chilling along the Zanskar River.

## Trekking in Zanskar

Trekking in Zanskar is not easy. The paths are often rough and steep, the passes high and the climate extreme. Provisions, fuel and camping equipment should be bought in advance from Kishtwar, Manali or Leh. You can get necessities such as dried milk, biscuits, noodles and sugar from Padum, though supplies are scare at the beginning of the season. In Padum the Tourism Officer and Government Development Officer will be able to advise and maybe even assist in hiring horses. Porters can be hired at **Sani** village for the traverse of the **Umasi La** into Kishtwar. Horses cannot use this pass. In Padum you may be able to hire porters with whom you can cover rougher terrain. It is best to contact a trekking agent in advance. ▸▸ *See What to do, page 273.*

**Pensi La to Padum** You can trek this three-day route before the road opens (June-October) when it is free of vehicles.

**Karsha to Lamayaru** This is a demanding nine-day trek which includes seven passes, five of which are over 4500 m. The highest is the Singi La (5060 m). It is essential to be very fit before starting the trek. Each day's walking should take under six hours, but with time for rests and lunch this adds up to a full day. An extra day allows for flexibility.

The 16th-century monastery of the Tibetan Gelugpa (Yellow Hat) sect at **Karsha** is the largest and wealthiest in the Zanskar Valley and is occupied by nearly 200 monks. Karsha has an inn with dormitory beds and a vegetarian canteen.

**Padum to Leh** This is another demanding trek which also takes about 10 days. Some are through the spectacular gorges between Markha and Zangla. A local guide is recommended as this is truly a wilderness area. The trek involves walking along stream beds and in July there is still too much snow melt to allow safe crossings. Recommended only for August/September.

It is seven hours' walking from Padum to Zangla and this includes crossing the Zanskar River by a string and twig bridge that spans over 40 m. Ponies are not allowed on it and if it is windy sensible humans don't cross. You can now start your trek at Zangla as there is a motorbike route from Padum to Zangla. At **Zangla** you can see the King's Palace, which has a collection of *thangkas* painted by the king's son (who was once a monk). The third stage takes you over the **Cha Cha La** (5200 m). On the next stage river crossings are again necessary. This is time consuming and if you are travelling in mid-summer, an extra day may be called for.

You then follow the **Khurna River** to a narrow gorge that marks the ancient border between Zanskar and Ladakh, and end up below the **Rubarung La**. When you cross this you get good views of the Stok range. You then descend into the Markha Valley and from here you can reach Leh in six stages by heading west into the heart of the valley and then crossing the Ganda La to Spituk, or in three stages by crossing the Gongmaru La and descending to Martselang and nearby Hemis.

**Padum to Darcha** This is a week-long trek and starts with a walk along the Tsarap Chu to **Bardan**, which has *stupas* and interesting idols, and **Reru**. There is a now a motorable road till Mune from where the trek starts towards Darcha.

After two stages you reach **Purni** (with a couple of shops and a popular campsite), where you can stay two nights and make a side trip to the impressive 11th-century **Phugtal monastery** (a two-hour walk). On a spectacular site, it has been carved out of the mountainside round a limestone cave. Usually there are about 50 monks in attendance. From Purni you continue on to Kargiakh, the last village before the **Shingo La**. It's another day's walk to the camp below this high pass (5200 m).

The mountain scenery is stunning with 6000 m-plus peaks all around. Once over the pass you can stop at **Rumjack** where there is a campsite used by shepherds or you can continue to the confluence of the **Shingo** and the **Barai** rivers where there is now a bridge. From here the trail passes through grazing land and it is about 15 km to **Darcha**, the end of the trek. Keen trekkers can combine this with a trek from Darcha to **Manali**. The average daily walking time of the Padum-Darcha trek is six hours so you have to be very fit. There is now a motorable road from Darcha all the way to Zanskar Sumdo which is after the Shingo La Pass.

## Trekking in the Nubra and Shyok valleys
The easing of controls to visit the Nubra-Shyok valleys has made possible treks that start from points in the Indus Valley not far from Leh, cross the Ladakh Range to enter the Shyok River valley and then re-cross the Ladakh range further to the west to re-enter the Indus Valley near Phyang monastery. Ask a good local trekking agent for advice on how to get the required 'Restricted Area Permits'.

**Day 1** Drive from Leh south along the Manali road to Karu, near Hemis, where you turn left and drive about 10 km to the roadhead at the village of Sakti, just past **Takthak monastery**. Trek about 90 minutes to **Chumchar** and camp.

**Day 2** Cross the Ladakh range at the **Wari La** (4400 m) and descend to Junlez on the northern flank.

**Day 3** Walk downhill to **Tangyar** (3700 m) with a nice *gompa*.

**Days 4, 5, 6** A level walk along the **Shyok River** valley takes you to **Khalsar** from where you follow the military road west to the confluence of the Shyok and Nubra rivers at **Diskit** (see Nubra Valley, above).

**Days 7, 8, 9** Three days to gradually ascend the northern flanks of the Ladakh Range passing the hamlets of **Hunder**, **Wachan** and **Hunder Dok** to the high pastures of **Thanglasgo** (4700 m).

**Days 10, 11** Trek back over the Ladakh Range via the Lasermo La pass (5150 m) to a campsite on the southern base of the pass.

**Day 12** Camp at Phyang village about 1 km above Phyang monastery before driving back to Leh.

---

## ◉ Ladakh listings

*For hotel and restaurant price codes and other relevant information, see pages 22-26.*

### ◉ Where to stay

**Leh** *p247, maps p249 and p251*
For eco-conscious homestays in Ladakh, see www.himalayan-homestays.com.

Grand Dragon, Omasila, Oriental remain open throughout the year. There are now scores of guest houses and many traditional Ladakhi homes offer rooms during the summer. Outside the peak period expect discounts (as much as 25-50%). Those in Karzoo and Changspa (some way from the bus stand) are quieter and more rural.

There is lots of budget accommodation along Fort Rd and in the Changspa area; some are very basic and you might want to use your own sleeping bag. But generally you will find a clean simple room, without needing to book in advance.

**$$$$-$$$Grand Dragon**, Old Leh Rd, Sheynam, T01982-257786, www.thegrand dragonladakh.com. Big hotel with all mod cons, Wi-Fi and great views. Stunning dining room and a nod to eco tourism with double-glazing, under-floor heating and solar panels.

**$$$Lha-Ri-Sa**, Skara, T01982-252000, www.ladakh-lharisa.com. With a boutique vibe, they offer stylish rooms and the outside

of the building is simply beautiful. In the restaurant they serve up flavours from all over India as well as traditional Ladakhi food. Recommended, although it's on the outskirts of town.

**$$$Shambhala**, Skara, T01982-251100, www.hotelshambhala.com. Large airy rooms, excellent restaurant (often caters for German packages), breakfast included, very pleasant friendly staff and lovely owners, peaceful away from crowds, attractive garden with hammocks and fruit trees, free transport to centre.

**$$Alpine Villa**, Chulung, T01982-252354, www.alpinevilla.co.in. The modern design is rather out of keeping with Leh, but public areas are adorned with Ladakhi furniture, and door jambs and ceilings are painted with traditional motifs. 22 spacious new rooms have bedside lights, flatscreen TV and comfy beds; bathrooms are a cut above the rest, with an attempt at stylish tiling. Large public terraces have mountain views; restaurant, and lawn

**$$Antelope**, Chubi Rd, near Women's Alliance, T01982-252086, discoverladakh@ yahoo.com. Guesthouse with simple, clean rooms, some wear-and-tear, quiet, small shady garden. Great central location, well-priced, free Wi-Fi, helpful staff.

**$$Kang-lha Chen**, T01982-252144, www.hotel-klcleh.com. May-Oct. 23 simple rooms, with attached bathrooms. Recently renovated with larger dining area, lobby done in traditional style with old family furniture and carpets, restaurant, pleasant shaded inner courtyard garden and lawns with sitting area at hotel entrance, own spring, quiet and peaceful and centrally located, old fashioned but well maintained.

**$$ Leh View**, Upper Karzoo, T01982-251124, hotellehview@gmail.com. Modern building with large rooms, some with private balconies, TV, duvets, and decent bathrooms. Nice public areas with cushion seating and little Ladakhi tables, meals available, fields surround. Discounts are possible.

**$$ Lharimo**, Fort Rd, T01982-252101, lharimo@yahoo.com. Attractive central hotel with scarlet window-frames and whitewashed exterior, large comfortable rooms have traditional bamboo ceilings and inoffensive ageing wooden furniture, TV, clean tiled bathrooms. The big grassy lawn is perfect for relaxing.

**$$ Lotus**, Upper Karzoo, T01982-257265, www.lotushotel.in. 17 high-spec rooms with quality furniture, modern amenities, and a nod to traditional Ladakhi decor. 24-hr hot water, central heating and good multicuisine restaurant. Views from the flowery garden straight onto the palace.

**$$ Omasila**, Changspa, T01982-252119, www.hotelomasila.com. A series of annexes around a pleasant back lawn, plus huge terrace and ornate restaurant (garden vegetables). Rooms have TV, wooden floors, worth paying bit extra for the deluxe rooms with seating areas, all have decent tiled bathrooms. More mature clientele, heating system. Free Wi-Fi.

**$$ Tso-Kar**, Fort Rd, T01982-253071, www.lehladakhhotel.com. Very reasonably priced and well-maintained rooms, bathrooms a little old but clean, TV, and comfortable beds. Astroturf, flowers, and cane chairs and tables in the courtyard.

**$$ Yak-Tail**, Fort Rd, T01982-252118, www.hotelyaktail.com. May-Oct. One of Leh's oldest hotels, comfortable and cosy

(decent heating), some of the 30 rooms are 'houseboat style', others have balconies, some have lots of patterns. Restaurant nicely decorated with murals serves good Indian food, courtyard has been astro-turfed but swinging vines create a pleasing greenhouse effect.

**$$-$ Oriental**, below Shanti Stupa, T01982-253153, www.orientalguesthouse.com. 35 very clean rooms in traditional family home, good home cooking in the dining hall, great views across the valley, friendly, treks and travel arrangements reliable. Recommended.

**$$-$ Padma Guesthouse & Hotel**, off Fort Rd down an alley, T01982-252630, (0)9906-982171, www.padmaladakh.net. Clean, charming rooms with common bath in guesthouse in the old family home, upstairs has mountain views (rooftop restaurant), plus hotel-style rooms in newer block, beautiful and peaceful garden, Buddhist chapel/meditation room, solar panels, good library, but most known for their outstanding hospitality. Highly recommended.

**$ Atisha**, Malpak, off Fort Rd, T09906-992187, atisha_leh@rediffmail.com. Not much to look at on arrival, but simple rooms are spotless with bright paint and shiny tiled bathrooms. Prices increase as you go up from ground to third floor, rooftop terrace is lovely, and although there's not much of an aspect it feels rural and a burbling brook surrounds. Very pleasant low-key family.

**$ Haldupa**, Upper Tukcha Rd, Malpak, T01982-251374. Cheapest rooms in the old building share (smelly) bathrooms, hot buckets available, and memorable shrine is in same building. New 2-level wing is swish and there's a delightful garden with plenty of seating, organic food available.

**$ Indus**, Malpak, off Fort Rd, T01982-252502 masters_adv@yahoo.co.in. A range of rooms, all large and with clean sheets and attached bath. Basic rooms on the ground floor contain only beds, furniture is added as the price goes up. There's a central sociable yard, and food is available.

**$ Karzoo**, Karzoo Lane, T(0)9906-997015. The usual flowery garden; very cheap rooms with shared bath in an old Ladakhi house and modern clean rooms in the new annex (still waiting for the upper storey to be built), but very relaxed and helpful staff, omelette for breakfast. Recommended.

**$ Malpak**, Upper Tukcha Road, Malpak, T01982-257380, dollayleh@yahoo.co.in. Quaint 6-room guesthouse in an old building, all rooms with attached bath. Shady outdoor tables next to a luxuriant flower and vegetable garden, and a convenient yet peaceful location. Recommended budget choice.

**$ Old Ladakh**, in the Old Town, T01982-252951. 8 rooms around an inner courtyard (varying in comfort), has bags of character with red lacquered windows and doorframes, the odd cracked window, great views from top floor, pleasant atmosphere (old-school vibes).

**$ Palu Guest House**, Changspa, T(0)9419-218674, gurmatpalu@yahoomail.com. Sweet family home, very spacious rooms have clean sheets, carpets and big windows, some have private bath and TV, others share a bathroom, all have working geysers. Particularly attractive flowery garden and veg patch, with shady seating, secluded and set back from Changspa Rd.

**$ Rainbow**, Karzoo. Big clean rooms, some with wonderful views of mountains and Shanti Stupa, hot water in the morning, great hospitality, and lovely garden and restaurant. Rooms in old house share baths, or new wing has en suite. Recommended.

**$ Ri-Rab**, Changspa, T01982-253108, chhospel@hotmail.com. 18 clean simple rooms with baths in an old-fashioned building, very well-maintained, big rear garden, restaurant (own fresh garden vegetables), parking.

**$ Saser**, 500-800, Karzoo Lane, T01982-257162, nam_gyal@rediff.com. A good clean choice with large freshly painted rooms arranged around a grassy garden. Pay more for new laminate floors, cheerful bed-covers and better bathrooms. There's a generator and breakfast is available.

**$ Shanti Guest House**, below Shanti Stupa, Changspa, T01982-253084. Guesthouse with well-heated rooms, most with great views, very good food, summer/winter treks arranged with guide, free Wi-Fi, friendly Ladakhi family.

**$ Silver Cloud**, by Sankar Gompa, 15 mins' walk from centre, T01982-253128, (0)9622-175988, silvercloudpsd@hotmail.com. Ladakhi guesthouse with very clean rooms, friendly helpful family, rural homestay atmosphere, excellent food, large garden, open during the winter months. Recommended.

**$ Tsomo-Ri**, Fort Rd, T019822-252271, www.ladakhtsomori.com. 15 rooms arranged around a central whitewashed courtyard with trellises of runner beans running up the stairs. Surprisingly quiet, rooms have TV, new carpets, plain wood furniture and clean walls – and plenty of good bedding. Wicker chairs for relaxing in courtyard. Very hospitable manager. Good choice.

### Thikse *p253*

**$ Chamba**, T01982-267385, www.thiksey monastery.org. Basic chalet rooms with Indian toilets lie next to a scruffy yard, or the main building has more comfortable rooms. The garden restaurant makes for a good lunch-break after exploring the monastery.

### Hemis *p253*

Many householders take in guests. Not ideal.
**$ Tourist**, camp or sleep on the floor, own sleeping bag, Rs 100; or in the homestay Rs 150 per person. Basic tented restaurant.

### Phyang *p255*

**$ Hidden North Guesthouse**, T01982-226007, (0)9419-218055, www.hidden north.com. This attractive guesthouse, set on a hillside, has marvellous views. There are 7 unfussy clean rooms, most with views, one with private terrace, some with private bath; run by a nice Ladakhi-German couple.

Huge shared terrace and garden. Meals available. It's perched at the top end of the village, a 5-min uphill walk from the last bus stop. Treks can also be arranged by their responsible outfit.

## Lekir *p256*

The bus directly to the monastery facilitates staying in 1 of 4 options near the monastery. Or, if you are dropped off on NH1, there are half a dozen choices in Lower Likir, about 1 km on dirt tracks from NH1. Hotels all provide dinner and breakfast. Just below the monastery gate is the **Gonpa Restaurant** (0630-2030) for breakfast and reasonably priced Tibetan and Chinese food.

**$$Lhukhil**, T01982-253588, www.ladakh packages.com. Grand gateway and luxuriant garden, although outdoor seating is on patchy grass next to scary statues and dragon-wrapped pillars. 24 rooms are well-fitted out and comfortable, with towels, toiletries, and some views. Meals included.

**$Lotos Guesthouse**, T01982-227171, (0)9469-297990, opposite Hotel Lhukhil, Lower Likir. 3 clean modern rooms with mats over the floor and plenty of warm bedding, sharing a bathroom, nice front garden and fruit trees, food costs extra. Cheap and cheerful.

**$Norboo Lagams Chow Guesthouse and Camp**, Lower Likir. A bit of a building site, set at the back of a long scruffy orchard (camping possible) with small un-curtained rooms, 1 with bath (no light or toilet seat), others use traditional Ladakhi toilet in the house behind. It's cheap and dinner is served in the traditional kitchen-cum-dining room surrounded by pots of all shapes and sizes.

**$Norboo Spon Guesthouse and Camping**, Lower Likir. Signed off the road to the monastery, or 300 m walk from Lower Likir on the way to the monastery; worth the slight climb if walking. In a large Ladakhi house, roof decked with prayer flags, bright white paint and red trims, set among trees in a large garden with plenty of seating. Dining-seating area of little tables, rugs and cushions with the odd decorative mask is cosy and homely; shared balcony. Rooms upstairs have good views, wicker chairs and a very decent shared bathroom. Rs 700 double with breakfast and dinner. Charming and kind family.

**$Old Likir Guesthouse**, a 10-min walk downhill through the fields from the monastery (signed) has 3 rooms (2 upstairs are best). Very simple, in a farming family's home. Mattresses on floor and little else, but fabulous views either of the valley below or the Buddha's back and the monastery above. Rs 300 per person including breakfast and dinner.

**$A** short walk up from the monastery are **Dolker Tongol** and **Chhuma** guesthouses, both basic but with views.

## Alchi *p256*

Alchi has a several guesthouses, some are not great value, but the ones listed here are well-priced for what they offer. It is a pleasant little village with some shops, *dhabas*, hotel restaurants, and souvenir stalls, none of which are a long walk from the bus stop or the monastery.

**$$Alchi Resort**, T(0)9419-218636, www.alchiresort.tripod.com. "The first never before hut type twin roomed resort in Ladakh"! Cross over a little bridge after the unattractive main building (restaurant downstairs) to a flowery fruit-filled garden edged by whitewashed cottages in adjoining pairs; cottages at the end, around a central gazebo, enjoy more privacy. Well-appointed motel layout rooms differ slightly in configuration, all have flatscreens, laminate wood floors or carpets, plain tiled bathrooms

**$$Ule Ethnic Resort**, Uletokpo, next to the highway, 10 km past Saspol, T01982-253640 www.uleresort.com. 15 cottages and 31 posh canvas tents in a well set up eco-resort. It caters mainly to groups, but an alternative night's stop to Alchi.

**$$-$Zimskhang Holiday Home**, on the lane to the monastery, T01982-227086, www.zimskhang.com. Some pricier rooms in a large building that is more attractive outside than in, appealing public balcony upstairs, clean spacious rooms with flatscreens, bathrooms with marble basin-tops and floors, but by no means swanky. Cheap clean rooms in an older building share bathrooms and are good value, but overlook the open-air restaurant.

**$ Choskor**, 15-min walk back along the road towards Leh, T01982-227084, (0)9419-826363. Set in a lovely garden this colourful guesthouse has rooms ranging from simple doubles with shared baths, to great-value upstairs rooms with attached bath. A roof terrace has rural views, you can eat outdoors in the garden or inside the restaurant with painted motifs on the wall. You can camp for Rs 100, or they provide tented accommodation near the temple for Rs 600-700. Taxi and laundry services available, and they pride themselves on their clean sheets.

**$ Heritage Home**, right next to the monastery entrance. A very pleasant and convenient choice. Rooms are large, carpeted, freshly painted, en suite (hot water in the evening), soap and clean towel. Upstairs is more expensive, there's a decent restaurant out front with apricot trees.

## Lamayuru p258

Most guesthouses are on NH1 in the lower village, with a couple of homestays on the hill towards the monastery. They all provide food, and little **Zambala Restaurant**, on the highway opposite the Dragon Hotel, does surprisingly good chai and *aloo paratha*.

**$$-$ Fotola**, T01982-224528, 09469-048470, fotolahotellamayouru@gmail.com. 12 plain rooms, slightly set back from the road facing the rocky valley wall, with attached bath, towels provided. There's no garden as such, but a bonus is the upstairs restaurant serving a variety of Indian and Italian food.

**$ Dragon**, Lower Rd, T01982-224501, dragon_skyabu@yahoo.com. A range of spacious carpeted rooms, 4 with en suite by the garden restaurant, 8 with shared bath in the building to the rear, most are south-facing, and room 10 has attractively painted walls. Clean sheets and very reasonably priced. Restaurant serves up excellent Indian meals. Internet available (during the 3 hrs of electricity in the evenings), as is hot water.

**$ Lion's Den**, 300 m from the village centre, T01982-224542, lioondenhouse@gmail.com. Ignore the unfinished-concrete ground floor, as upstairs rooms are given warmth by colourful walls, rugs and bedding (shared bath Rs 500). Good views of the weird rock formations in the valley from the 2 corner rooms with attached bath (Rs 700). Little outdoor restaurant with checked cloths has shade or there's a Ladakhi dining room.

**$ Niranjana Hotel**, T01982-224555. Next to the monastery, this institutional-looking hotel has 20 rooms on 3 levels with excellent valley views. Rooms are plain but comfortable, they take the time to turn down the sheets. All share modern, clean communal bathrooms, hot shower in the evenings. Downstairs restaurant is good.

**$ Tharpaling**, 100 m past the village centre on main road, T01982-224516. The warm family atmosphere is what appeals most to visitors, who are made wonderfully welcome at this simple guesthouse.

## Nubra Valley p259

**$$$ Yarab Tso**, Tiger, T(0)9622-820661, www.hotelyarabtso.com. 13 carpeted rooms with private baths and attractive furnishings; in an idyllic setting with large garden, plus very good food.

**$ Olgok**, Hunder, T01980-221092. Large simple rooms are very clean in this homely guesthouse, where the owners go out of their way to be helpful. Fresh food from the quaint garden. Recommended.

**$ Snow Leopard**, Hunder, T01980-221097. Busy yet cosy place with lovely central garden and fruit trees; choice between older (cheaper) and newer rooms.

## ◉ Restaurants

**Leh** *p247, maps p249 and p251*

**$$ Chopsticks Noodle Bar**, Fort Rd.
Great East Asian, Tibetan and regional
food in a clean and attractive restaurant.
Deservedly popular and worth at least
1 visit when in Leh.

**$$ Penguin Garden**, just off Fort Rd.
Good garden café with nice atmosphere
care of Nepali owners.

**$$-$ Booklovers' Retreat**, Changspa.
Perennial favourite as cosy place for food
and hanging out. There's a roof terrace.

**$$-$ Il Forno**, Zangsti Rd. Serves up pretty
decent pizzas, pastas and there's beer too.

**$$-$ La Pizzeria**, Changspa Rd, Changspa.
Pretty authentic pizza, very pleasant
ambiance, some mattress seating,
and soft lantern light at night.

**$$-$ Mona Lisa**, Fort Rd. International
food covers all bases (pizzas, *momos*,
garlic cheese bread), particularly
recommended for tandori selection. Nice
atmosphere under lamps on the terrace.

**$$-$ Nirvana Café**. Live music after 2100.
Indoor and outdoor seating under lanterns
and fairy lights, some Sinai-style slouching
areas. Laid-back vibe and varied menu of
South Asian, Asian and lots of Italian, prices
slightly higher than average. No alcohol.

**$$-$ Open Hand Espresso Bar & Bistro**,
off Fort Rd, www.openhand.in. A chic retreat,
with loungers and seating on decking by
an active vegetable garden, chunky wood
furniture inside, great cakes, cappuccinos
and home-cooked meals, healthy smoothies
and more. Ethical shopping – clothes, silks,
cushions, gifts etc – plus Wi-Fi.

**$ Amdo Food**, Main Bazar. Tibetan.
Good fried *momos*, friendly (better than
Amdo Café opposite) but slow service.

**$ Chansa Traditional Ladakhi Kitchen**,
next to Chokhang Vihara, off Main Bazar.
A chance to try traditional Ladakhi cuisine
(vegetarian); simple indoor seating, or
outside under the shade of a parachute.
Whiteboard shows the day's dishes, such

as *sku* – a delicious chunky wholewheat
pasta and veg broth, plus limited offerings
of Chinese, Indian (great mushroom masala)
and Western food. Cheap and tasty.

**$ High Life Tibetan Restaurant**, Fort Rd.
Exceptional range of high quality Tibetan
food, plus good salads and Western dishes,
inviting indoor seating with gingham table
cloths or big outdoor area.

**$ Lala's Art Café**, off Main Bazar, Old Town.
Quaint restored Ladakhi house in the Old
Town with a roof terrace, and shrine on the
ground floor. Coffee and cakes are the order
of the day.

**$ Local Food Café**. Mon-Sat 1100-1630.
Serves good Ladakhi snacks, while
promoting traditional farming methods
threatened by the modern cash economy,
run by the Women's Alliance.

**$ Mentokling Apple Garden**, Changspa Rd,
Zangsti. Great *paratha* breakfasts, good menu
generally, with Indian and Thai dishes, lovely
garden. Free Wi-Fi with orders over Rs100.

**$ Shubh Panjabi Dhaba**, Main Bazar.
Typical Sikh-style *thalis* and cheap dishes in
a basic restaurant; half-plates available, great
lassis and good paratha breakfasts.

**$ Tenzin Dickey**, Fort Rd. Delicious *kothay*
(fried *momos*), soups, and other Tibetan/
Chinese dishes, some western food,
all veg, and the Tibetan herbal tea is
pretty good. Simple and neat little
place with checked tablecloths.

**$ Tibetan Friend's Corner**, Main St, Bazar.
Clean and cheerful, *kothay* and wide
menu of Tibetan/Chinese veg and
non-veg, thick pancakes and great
hot drinks, locally popular.

**$** Also recommended are the kebab stalls
near the mosque.

### Bakeries

Four German bakeries sell good bread
(trekking bread keeps for a week) and
excellent cakes and muesli. There are also
traditional ovens turning out delicious local
bread in the laneway next to the Museum,
behind the mosque.

## Gompas and festivals

Buddhist festivals usually take place in the bleak winter months when villagers gather together, stalls spring up around the *gompas* and colourful dance dramas and masked dances are performed in the courtyards. Musical instruments, weapons and religious objects are brought out during these dance performances. The *Kushak* (high priest) is accompanied by monks in monotonous recitation while others play large cymbals, trumpets and drums. The serious theme of victory of Good over Evil is lightened by comic interludes. A few monasteries celebrate their festivals in the summer months, for example Lamayuru, Hemis and Phyang.

**Pumpernickel**, Zangsti Rd. The original German bakery is the best and friendliest, indoor/outdoor seating, excellent apricot and apple crumble/pie, message board for trekkers.

**Alchi** *p256*
**$$-$ Zimskhang** and **Heritage** both have good drop-in restaurants, other hotels provide meals when there are guests.
**$ Golden Oriole German Bakery**, has good cake selection but doesn't always have bread; serves Chinese and Indian dishes, pizza, good place for breakfast, same menu as Zimskhang but at lower prices; terrace is a nice place to sit and watch folks pass on their way to the monastery.
There are a couple of *dhabas* near the bus stop, although the **Tibetan** has bad chowmein. **Dil Dil Restaurant**, opposite the Tibetan, is kept clean and does cheap daal, veg and rice. Most shops near bus stop also serve omelettes/daal/chai, and sell strong beer.

## Entertainment

**Leh** *p247, maps p249 and p251*
Ladakhi dancing and singing, below entrance to the palace, by Soma Gompa, 1730 (1 hr), Rs 200.

## Festivals

**Leh** *p247, maps p249 and p251*
Dates vary depending on the lunar calendar.

**Apr-May** **Buddha Purnima** marks the Buddha's birth, at full moon.
**Sep** **Ladakh Festival**. The main events are held in the Leh polo grounds with smaller events in other districts. Usually during the 1st 2 weeks in Sep, there are dances, displays of traditional costumes, handicrafts, Ladakhi plays, archery and polo matches.
**Dec** **Celebration of Losar** which originated in the 15th century to protect people before going to battle.

**Hemis** *p253*
**Jun** **Hemis Tsechu** is perhaps the biggest cultural festival in Ladakh. It commemorates the birth of **Guru Padmasambhava** who is believed to have fought local demons to protect the people. Young and old of both sexes join *lamas* in masked dance-dramas, while stalls sell handicrafts A colourful display of Ladakhi Buddhist culture, it attracts large numbers of foreign visitors.

## O Shopping

**Leh** *p247, maps p249 and p251*
Please use your own bags. Plastic bags are not allowed in the bazar as they were finding their way into streams when not piled on unsightly heaps.
In **Dzomsa** you can get water refill, dispose of batteries, get laundry done and there's organic goods available. Also at the **Ecological Shop for Organic Products** you can stock up on local produce including apricot jam, fruit and nuts in season, bottled juice.

Leh Bazar is full of shops and market stalls selling curios, clothes and knick-knacks. Tea and *chang* (local barley brew) vessels, cups, butter churns, knitted carpets with Tibetan designs, Tibetan jewellery, prayer flags, musical bowls and pashminas are all available. Prices are high especially in Kashmiri shops so bargain vigorously. It is better to buy Ladakhi jewellery and souvenirs from Ladakhis who generally ask a fairer price. There are tight restrictions on the export of anything over 100 years old. Baggage is checked at the airport partly for this reason. However, even though most items are antique-looking, they are, in fact, fresh from the backstreet workshops. If you walk down the narrow lanes, you will probably find an artisan at work from whom you can buy direct.

### Books
**Book Worm**, second-hand books, coffee table books and fiction.
**Leh-Ling Bookshop**, near the Post Office, Main Bazar. Good selection, especially on trekking in the region.

### Tailor
There are many tailors lining Nowshara Gali.

## ◑ What to do

**Leh** *p247, maps p249 and p251*
### Archery
The **Archery Stadium** is nearby where winter competitions attract large crowds; the target is a hanging white clay tablet.

### Meditation
Mahabodhi Meditation Centre Changspa Lane, off Changspa Rd. Enquire about short courses and yoga classes, www.mahabodhi-ladakh.com.

### Polo
Polo, the 'national' sport, is popular in the summer and is played in the polo ground east of the city. The local version which is

fast and rough appears to follow no rules! The **Polo Club** is the highest in the world and worth a visit.

### Tour operators
Women on their own should take special care when arranging a tour with a driver/guide.
**Eco-Adventures**, New Delhi, T011-477 2550, www.theecoadventures.com. Tailor-made and group tours.
**Explore Himalayas**, Main Bazar (opposite SBI), T01982-252727, www.explore himalayas.com. Recommended, normally excellent crew though some reports of inept guides, friendly, good to animals, environment conscious.
**K2**, Hill Top Building, Main Bazar, T01982-253980, www.k2adventureleh.com. Good rates for treks (Markha Valley), very friendly, environment conscious.
**Rimo Expeditions**, Kang-lha Chen Hotel, T01982-253348, www.rimoexpeditions.com. Insightful and informative about the local area, running a whole host of treks, as well as mountain biking, mountaineering, river rafting, cultural tours and family holidays. The best of the lot. Highly recommended.
**Shakti Experiences**, Gurgaon, Delhi, T01244-563899, www.shaktihimalaya.com. Sensitively run sustainable tours and personalized treks to remote villages 30 km from Leh in the rugged high mountains of Ladakh. Luxurious but understated.
**Yama Treks**, Leh, www.yamatreks.com. Efficient, run by the very personable Mr Rinchen Namgial; cultural tours as well as treks. Recommended.

### Whitewater rafting and kayaking
Possible on the Tsarap Chu, Indus and Zanskar rivers from mid-Jun; the upper reaches of the former (Grade IV rapids) are suitable for experienced rafters only, though the remaining stretch can be enjoyed by all. Along the Indus: Hemis to Choglamsar (easy, very scenic); Phey-Nimmu (Grade III); Nimmu-Khaltse (professional). Ensure that life jackets and wet suits are provided. Half

## To fly or not to fly

Ecological implications aside, travel by road from Srinagar gives you an advantage over flying into Leh as it enables you to acclimatize to a high-altitude plateau. The journey from Manali, however, normally involves staying overnight at very high altitudes (eg Sarchu at almost 4300 m) which can cause altitude sickness even before arrival in Leh. In addition, some people find the journey from Manali or Srinagar terrifying and very uncomfortable, although if you are able to hire a jeep or car it will give you the flexibility of stopping to see the several sights on the way. Most healthy people find that if they relax completely for two days after flying in, they acclimatize without difficulty. If you have a heart condition, consult your doctor on the advisability of going to Leh.

to full day, including transport and lunch, Rs 1000-1500.

### Trekking in Zanskar *p263*
Most agents in Leh can arrange trekking expeditions to the Zanskar Valley.
**Aquaterra Adventures**, www.aquaterra.in, have 12-day rafting trips down the Zanskar River each Aug.

## ⊖ Transport

**Leh** *p247, maps p249 and p251*
**Air** The small airport is 5 km away on Srinagar Rd. It is surrounded by hills on 3 sides and the flight over the mountain ranges is spectacular. Transport to town by taxi is around Rs 200.

Allow 2 hrs for check in. Weather conditions may deteriorate rapidly even in the summer resulting in flight cancellations (especially outside Jul and Aug) so always be prepared for a delay or to take alternative road transport out of Ladakh. Furthermore, the airlines fly quite full planes into Leh but can take fewer passengers out because of the high-altitude take-off. This adds to the difficulty of getting a flight out. **Book your tickets as soon as possible** (several months ahead for Jul and Aug).

Air India, office near Shambhala Hotel (often chaotic), T01982-252076, airport T01982-252255, flies to/from **Delhi**, also Jet Airways, T01982-250999; airport T01982-250324, Go Air, Spicejet and JetKonnect. To **Srinagar**, direct on Wed, with Air India. For **Jammu**, connections via Delhi, or direct with Air India on Fri.

**Local bus** The Bus Stand is near the cemetery. The vehicles are ramshackle but the fares are low. See under monasteries for details. Enquiries J&KSRTC, T01982-252285.
**Long distance** Leh is connected to Manali via Keylong and to Srinagar, via Kargil, by state highways. Both roads can be seriously affected by landslides, causing long delays. The Leh–Srinagar road is also often blocked by army convoys. **Himachal Tourism** runs regular Deluxe buses between Manali and Leh, 530 km, usually mid-Jun to end Sep. Book at HPTDC Office, 1st floor, Fort Rd, T(0)9622-374300, a/c Volvo, leaves alternate days at 0500 from opposite the J&K Bank, Fort Rd, overnight in Keylong (Rs 1500); J&K SRTC run ordinary/deluxe buses (Rs 585/850), gruelling journey departs 0430, booked at bus stand, stop overnight at Keylong. J&K SRTC bus **Kargil**, 230 km, 0430, 10 hrs, Rs 300, **Srinagar** 434 km, 1400, 20 hrs, Rs 92.
**Shared jeeps** or **minibuses** make the journey to **Manali** in 1 day, leaving at between 2400-0200 taking 22-24 hrs, costing about Rs 1500 per seat. Jeeps leave from the Old Bus Station, to **Srinagar** at 1700, 15 hrs (Rs 1400); to **Kargil** at 0700, 8-9 hrs (Rs 650). Book seats a day in advance, worth paying the extra for front seats.

**Warning** If you have already spent some time in the Himalaya, you may be better acclimatized, but a mild headache is common and can be treated with aspirin or paracetamol. Drink plenty of fluids on journeys.

The road to **Manali**, crossing some very high passes, is open mid-Jun or early Jul, until end Sep (depending on the weather) and takes 2 days by bus. Road conditions may be poor in places. Departure from Leh can be early (0400) with overnight stop in Keylong; next day to Manali. Alternatively, camp in Sarchu (10 hrs from Leh), or Jespa; next day 14 hrs to Manali (charge Rs 800-1200 per night in Sarchu). Roadside tents provide food en route during the tourist season; carry snacks, water and a good sleeping bag when planning to camp. Many travellers find the mountain roads extremely frightening and they are comparatively dangerous. Some are cut out of extremely unstable hillsides, usually with nothing between the road's edge and the near-vertical drop below; parts remain rough and pot-holed and during the monsoons, landslides and rivers can make it impassable for 2-3 days. It is also a long and uncomfortable journey, but there is some spectacular scenery.

**Taxi** 4WD between Leh and Manali are expensive but recommended if you want to stop en route to visit monasteries. 2-day trip, about Rs 15,000. Taxis often return empty to Manali (some visitors choose to fly out of Leh) so may agree a reduced fare for the return leg. Officially, Manali (or Srinagar) taxis are allowed to carry their passengers to and from Leh but are not permitted to do local tours, a rule fiercely monitored by the Leh Taxi Operators' Union.

**Tourist taxi and jeep** Ladakh Taxi Operators' Union, 1st floor at bus stand, T01982-252723, 0700-1900 daily, with fixed-rate fares, eg to Stok for Rs 1200. A day's taxi hire to visit nearby *gompas* can also be arranged through travel agents.

### Alchi *p256*
**Bus** One daily direct bus from **Leh** in summer, 1500, 3 hrs, returns around 0700. **Srinagar**-bound buses stop at **Saspol**; from there it is a 2.5-km walk across the bridge.

## ⊙ Directory

**Leh** *p247, maps p249 and p251*
**Banks** J&K Bank, Main Bazar, with ATM; State Bank of India, slow exchange and temperamental ATM, next to tourist office. **Medical services** SNM Hospital, T01982-252014, open 0900-1700 is well-equipped (also for advice on mountain sickness), after hours, T01982-253629. During the day, doctors have little time; better at clinics in evenings, get advice from your hotel. **Post** There is a Tourist Post Office on Main Bazar. **Useful contacts** Deputy Commisioner's Office for Inner Line Permits: T01982-252010. Take passport, copies of visa and personal details pages and 2 photos.

## Contents

### At a glance

⊝ **Getting around** An efficient metro runs north-south, ferries cross the Hooghly, taxis are cheap and buses cheaper, trams criss-cross the eastern city (very slowly) and of course there are hand-pulled rickshaws.

◑ **Time required** 3-4 days to get to grips with Kolkata.

☀ **Weather** Best during Oct-Feb, about the only time that isn't muggy.

✖ **When not to go** Extremely humid from Apr until the monsoon arrives in early Jun.

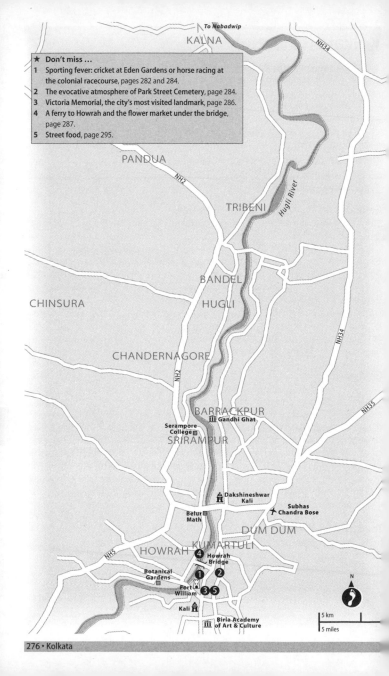

★ Don't miss ...
1 Sporting fever: cricket at Eden Gardens or horse racing at the colonial racecourse, pages 282 and 284.
2 The evocative atmosphere of Park Street Cemetery, page 284.
3 Victoria Memorial, the city's most visited landmark, page 286.
4 A ferry to Howrah and the flower market under the bridge, page 287.
5 Street food, page 295.

To Nabadwip

KALNA

NH34

PANDUA

NH2

TRIBENI

Hugli River

BANDEL

CHINSURA

HUGLI

CHANDERNAGORE

NH2

BARRACKPUR
🏛 Gandhi Ghat

NH34

Serampore College 🏛
SRIRAMPUR

NH35

🛕 Dakshineshwar Kali

Belur 🏛 Math

✈ Subhas Chandra Bose

DUM DUM

HOWRAH

NH5

KUMARTULI

④ Howrah Bridge

Botanical Gardens

① Fort William 🏛

② ③ ⑤

Kali 🛕

🏛 Birla Academy of Art & Culture

N

5 km
5 miles

# Kolkata (Calcutta)

*To Bengalis Kolkata is the proud intellectual capital of India, with an outstanding contribution to the arts, services, medicine and social reform in its past, and a rich contemporary cultural life. As the former imperial capital, Kolkata retains some of the country's most striking colonial buildings, yet at the same time it is truly an Indian city. Unique in India in retaining trams, and the only place in the world to still have hand-pulled rickshaws, you take your life in your hands each time you cross Kolkata's streets. Hugely crowded, Kolkata's Maidan, the parkland, give lungs to a city packed with some of the most densely populated slums, or bustees, anywhere in the world.➤➤ For listings, see pages 291-304.*

## Arriving in Kolkata

### Getting there

**Subhas Chandra Bose Airport** at Dum Dum serves international and domestic flights with the new 'integrated terminal' (opened 2013). Taxis to the city centre take 45-60 minutes and there is a pre-paid taxi booth before exiting the airport (to Sudder Street, the backpacker hub, costs Rs 270). There are air-conditioned buses which leave from outside Terminal 1, some of which go to Howrah and Esplanade (for Sudder Street), and cost about Rs 40. Arrival at **Howrah Train Station**, on the west bank of the Hugli, can be daunting and the taxi rank outside is often chaotic; the pre-paid taxi booth is to the right as you exit – check the price chart near the booth, note that Sudder Street is less than 5 km. Trains to/from the north use the slightly less chaotic **Sealdah Terminal** east of the centre, which also has pre-paid taxis. Long-distance buses arrive at Esplanade, 15 minutes' walk from most budget hotels.➤➤ See Transport, page 303.

### Getting around

You can cover much of Central Kolkata on foot. For the rest you need transport. You may not fancy using hand-pulled rickshaws, but they become indispensable when the streets are flooded. Buses and minibuses are often jam packed, but routes comprehensively cover the city – conductors and bystanders will help you find the correct bus. The electric trams can be slightly better outside peak periods. The Metro, though on a limited route and very crowded, is the easiest way of getting from north to south. Taxis are relatively cheap (note that the meter reading is not the true fare – they have conversion charts which work out at about double the meter) but allow plenty of time to get through very congested traffic. Despite the footpath, it is not permitted to walk across the Vidyasagar Bridge (taxi drivers expect passengers to pay the Rs 10 toll).

### Tourist information

**India Tourism** ⓘ *4 Shakespeare Sarani, T033-2282 5813, Mon-Fri 0930-1800, Sat 0900-1300,* can provide a city map and information for all India. More useful is **West Bengal Tourism Development Corporation (WBTDC)** ⓘ *BBD Bagh, T033-2248 8271, www.westbengaltourism.gov.in, Mon-Fri 1030-1630, Sat 1030-1300; also a counter at the station in Howrah.*

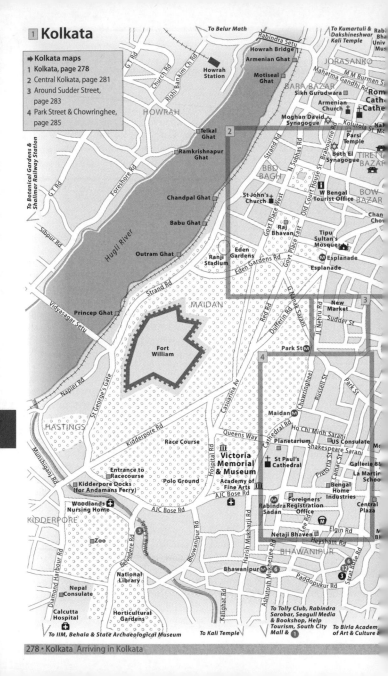

# 1 Kolkata

➡ **Kolkata maps**
1  Kolkata, page 278
2  Central Kolkata, page 281
3  Around Sudder Street, page 283
4  Park Street & Chowringhee, page 285

### Where to stay
66/2B The Guest House 7
Bodhi Tree & Art Café 1
Chrome 4
Samilton 6
Sharani Lodge 9
Taj Bengal & Chinoiserie
Restaurant 3
Tollygrange Club 2
Vedic Village 5

### Restaurants
Banana Leaf 2
Beijing 1
Bhojohori Manna 4
Bliss 11
Dolly's, The Tea Shop 8
Mainland China 5
Mirch Masala 9
Nepal Sweets 3
Rehmania & Shiraz 7
South India Club 10

### Bars & clubs
6 Ballygunge Place 12
Tripti's 6

## Background

Calcutta, as it came to be named, was founded by the remarkable English merchant trader **Job Charnock** in 1690. He was in charge of the East India Company factory (ie warehouse) in Hugli, then the centre of British trade from eastern India. Attacks from the local Muslim ruler forced him to flee – first down river to Sutanuti and then 1500 km south to Chennai. However, in 1690 he selected three villages – Kalikata, Sutanuti and Govindpur – where Armenian and Portuguese traders had already settled, leased them from Emperor Aurangzeb and returned to what became the capital of British India.

The first fort here, named after King William III (completed 1707), was on the site of the present BBD Bagh. A deep defensive moat was dug in 1742 to strengthen the fort – the Maratha ditch. The Maratha threat never materialized but the city was captured easily by the 20-year-old **Siraj-ud-Daula**, the new Nawab of Bengal, in 1756. The 146 British residents who failed to escape by the fort's river gate were imprisoned for a night in a small guard room about 6 m by 5 m with only one window – the infamous '**Black Hole of Calcutta**'. Some records suggest 64 people were imprisoned and only 23 survived.

The following year **Robert Clive** re-took the city. The new Fort William was built and in 1772 Calcutta became the capital of British administration in India with **Warren Hastings** as the first Governor of Bengal. Some of Calcutta's most impressive colonial buildings were built in the years that followed, when it became the first city of British India. It was also a time of Hindu and Muslim resurgence.

Colonial Calcutta grew as new traders, soldiers and administrators arrived, establishing their exclusive social and sports clubs. Trade in cloth, silk, lac, indigo, rice, areca nut and tobacco had originally attracted the Portuguese and British to Bengal. Later Calcutta's hinterland producing jute, iron ore, tea and coal led to large British firms setting up headquarters in the city. Calcutta prospered as the commercial and political capital of British India up to 1911, when the capital was transferred to Delhi.

## Central Kolkata → For listings, see pages 291-304.

### BBD Bagh (Dalhousie Square) and around

Many historic Raj buildings surround the square, which is quietest before 0900. Renamed Benoy Badal Dinesh (BBD) Bagh after three Bengali martyrs, the square has an artificial lake (tank) fed by natural springs that used to supply water to Kolkata's first residents. On Strand Road North is the dilapidated **Silver Mint** (1824-1831). The **Writers' Building** (1780), designed by Thomas Lyon as the trading headquarters of the East India Company, was refaced in 1880. It is now the state Government Secretariat. The classical block with 57 sets of identical windows was built like barracks inside. The white domed **General Post Office** (1866) was built on the site of the first Fort William. Around the corner, there is a quaint little **Postal Museum** ① *Mon-Sat 1100-1600, free*, which displays shabby maps, original post boxes and has a philatelic library. Facing the Hooghly (also spelt Hugli) on Strand Road is colonnaded **Metcalfe Hall** ① *Mon-Sat 1000-1700, entrance from rear*, modelled on the Palace of Winds in Athens. This was once the home of the Imperial Library, and still contains the journals of the Asiatic Society in the ground floor **library** ① *Mon-Fri 0945-1815 (allegedly)*, plus a small exhibition on the first floor including glazed tiles from Gaur and Pandua, and a gallery of bricks. Unsurprisingly, the visitors' book shows an average of two tourists per month. Elegant **St Andrew's Kirk** ① *0900-1400* (1814), like the earlier St John's Church (1787), was modelled partially on St Martin-in-the-Fields, London. **Mission Row** (now RN Mukherjee Road) is Kolkata's oldest street, and contains the **Old Mission Church** (consecrated 1770), built by the Swedish missionary Johann Kiernander. The **Great Eastern Hotel** (1841) was in Mark Twain's day "the best hotel East of the Suez", but from the 1970s it steadily declined. It is now undergoing major restoration by the Lalit group of hotels and was due to open in 2013 (though that looks unlikely from the present state of the building).

Directly south of BBD Bagh is the imposing **Raj Bhavan** (1799-1802), the residence of the Governor of West Bengal, formerly Government House. It was modelled on Kedleston Hall in Derbyshire, England (later Lord Curzon's home), and designed by Charles Wyatt, one of many Bengal engineers who based their designs on famous British buildings (entrance not permitted). The beautiful old **Town Hall** (1813) has been converted into the **Kolkata Museum** ① *Mon-Sat 1100-1800 (ticket counter closes 1700), foreigners Rs 10 (Rs 15 on Sat), bag deposit*, telling the story of the independence movement in Bengal through a panoramic, cinematic display, starring an animatronic Rabindranath Tagore. Visitors are sped through in grouped tours, however, and some of the videos drag on rather. There's a good life-size diorama of a Bengali street and some great film posters. The bright-red gothic **High Court** (1872) was modelled on the medieval cloth merchants' hall at Ypres in Flanders. It is possible to enter through Gate F: a fascinating glimpse into Bar Rooms crammed floor-to-ceiling with books, and bustling with black-robed lawyers (no cameras allowed). The **State Bank Archives and Museum** ① *11th Fl, SBI, 1 Strand Rd, open Tue-Fri 1430-1700, free*, in a recent building designed to look period, is a grand marble-floored repository of information; it also contains paintings of Raj India, furniture and memorabilia related to the early days of banking. The **Floatel** bar (see page 298), on the Hooghly, is a good place to relax after wanderings.

**Esplanade Mansions** is a stunning Art Nouveau building on Esplanade Row East, built in 1910 by Jewish millionaire David Ezra. At the other end of the street, the minarets and domes of **Tipu Sultan's Mosque**, built by Tipu's son in 1842, poke above market stalls selling stationery and little kebab restaurants. The **Ochterlony Monument** (1828),

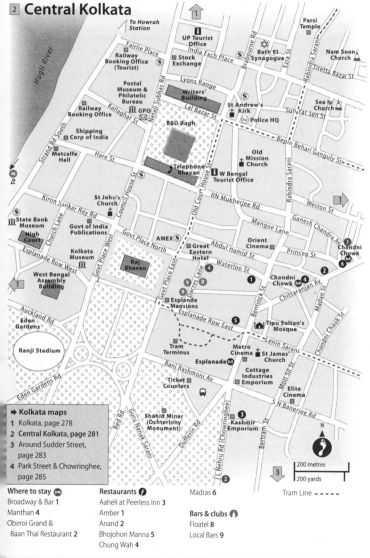

## 2 Central Kolkata

To Howrah Station

Parsi Temple

UP Tourist Office

India Exch Place

Fairlie Place

Beth El Synagogue

Nam Soon Church

Railway Booking Office (Tourist)

Stock Exchange

Lyons Range

Writers' Building

St Andrew's Kirk

Sea Ip Church

Postal Museum & Philatelic Bureau

GPO

Lal Bazar St

Police HQ

Railway Booking Office

BBD Bagh

Shipping Corp of India

Bepin Behari Ganguly St

Old Mission Church

Metcalfe Hall

Hare St

Telephone Bhavan

W Bengal Tourist Office

RN Mukherjee Rd

Kiron Sankar Roy Rd

St John's Church

Weston St

Ganesh Chandra Av

State Bank Museum

Govt of India Publications

Mangoe Lane

AMEX

Abdul Hamid St

Orient Cinema

Princep St

Chandni Chowk

High Court

Kolkata Museum

Raj Bhavan

Great Eastern Hotel

Waterloo St

Dacres Lane

Chandni Chowk

Esplanade Row West

West Bengal Assembly Building

Chittaranjan Av

Madan St

Esplanade Mansions

Esplanade Row East

Tipu Sultan's Mosque

Auckland Rd

Eden Gardens

Tram Terminus

Metro Cinema

St James Church

Lenin Sarani

Chandni Chauk St

Ranji Stadium

Rani Rashmoni Av

Esplanade

Cottage Industries Emporium

Mott St

Elite Cinema

Ticket Counters

S N Banerjee Rd

Shahid Minar (Ochterlony Monument)

Kashmir Emporium

**→ Kolkata maps**
1 Kolkata, page 278
2 Central Kolkata, page 281
3 Around Sudder Street, page 283
4 Park Street & Chowringhee, page 285

200 metres
200 yards

**Where to stay**
Broadway & Bar **1**
Manthan **4**
Oberoi Grand &
   Baan Thai Restaurant **2**

**Restaurants**
Aaheli at Peerless Inn **3**
Amber **1**
Anand **2**
Bhojohori Manna **5**
Chung Wah **4**

Madras **6**

**Bars & clubs**
Floatel **8**
Local Bars **9**

Tram Line ----

renamed Shahid Minar (Martyrs' Memorial) in 1969, was built as a memorial to Sir David Ochterlony, who led East India Company troops against the Nepalese in 1814-1816. The 46-m-tall Greek Doric column has an Egyptian base and is topped by a Turkish cupola.

**St John's Church** (1787) ① *0800-1700, Rs 10*, was built on soft subsoil that did not allow it to have a tall spire and architecturally it was thought to be 'full of blunders'. Verandas were added to the north and south in 1811 to reduce the glare of the sun. Inside the vestry are Warren Hastings's table and chair, plus Raj-era paintings and prints. *The Last Supper*, by Johann Zoffany was restored in 2010 and shows the city's residents dressed as the apostles. Job Charnock is buried in the grounds. His octagonal mausoleum, the oldest piece of masonry in the city, is of Pallavaram granite (from Madras Presidency), which is named charnockite after him. The monument built by Lord Curzon to the **Black Hole of Calcutta** was brought here from Dalhousie Square (BBD Bagh) in 1940.

**Eden Gardens** ① *daily 1200-1700*, which are situated in the northwest corner of the Maidan, were named after Lord Auckland's sisters Emily and Fanny Eden. There are pleasant walks, a lake and a small Burmese pagoda (typical of this type of Pyatthat). Laid out in 1834, part forms the **Ranji Stadium** ① *usually open for matches only, a small tip at Gate 14 gains entry on other days*, where the first cricket match was played in 1864. Revamped in 2011 for the Cricket World Cup, massive crowds are attracted for IPL and Test matches.

## Around Sudder Street

Conveniently close to Chowringhee and Esplanade, Sudder Street is the focus for Kolkata's backpackers and attracts touts, beggars and drug pushers aplenty. Beggars on Chowringhee and Park Street often belong to organized syndicates to whom they have to pay a large percentage of their 'earnings' for the privilege of working the area. Women asking for milk or rice for their baby is the most popular ploy on Sudder Street. Nearby is the vast and archaic shopping hub of **New Market**, opened in 1874 (largely rebuilt since a fire in 1985 and recently revamped), and originally called Sir Stuart Hogg Market. The clock tower outside, which strikes every 15 minutes, was imported from England. It used to be said that you could buy anything from a needle to an elephant (on order) in one of its stalls. Today it's still worth a visit; arrive early in the morning to watch it come alive (closed Sundays).

Around the corner from Sudder Street is the **Indian Museum** ① *27 Chowringhee (JL Nehru Rd), T033-2286 1679, www.indianmuseumkolkata.org, Mar-Nov Tue-Sun 1000-1700, Dec-Feb 1000-1630, foreigners Rs 150, Indians Rs 10, cameras Rs 50/100 with tripod; no bags allowed (there is a cloakroom)*, possibly Asia's largest. The Jadu Ghar (House of Magic) was founded in 1814 and has an enormous collection. The colonnaded Italianate building around a central courtyard has 36 galleries (though large sections are often closed off for restoration). Parts are poorly lit and gathering dust so it is best to be selective. Highlights include: the stone statutory with outstanding exhibits from the Harappa and Moenjodaro periods; the Cultural Anthropology room with information on India's tribes; and the excellent new Mask Gallery (hidden on the fourth floor, up the stairs past the ground floor coin collection and library). There are some lovely miniature paintings, the Egyptian room has a popular mummy and the Plant Gallery is curiously beautiful, with jars, prints and samples filling every inch of space. The animals in the Natural History Gallery have been there since 1878 while the birds are so dirty they are all uniformly black in colour. The geological collection with Siwalik fossils is mind-bogglingly huge. Allow a couple of hours.

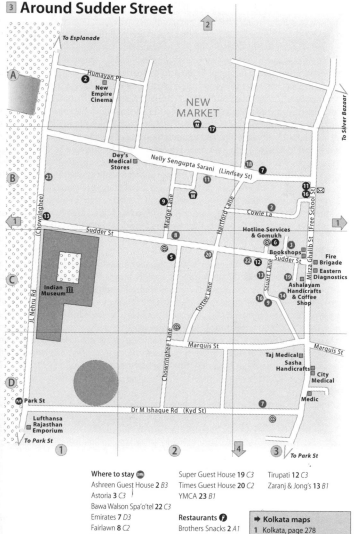

# 3 Around Sudder Street

To Esplanade

Humayan Pl

New Empire Cinema

NEW MARKET

To Silver Bazaar

Dey's Medical Stores

Nelly Sengupta Sarani (Lindsay St)

Madge Lane

Hartford Lane

Cowle La

Chowringhee

Sudder St

Hotline Services & Gomukh

Bookshops

Sudder St

Mirza Ghalib St

Free School St

Fire Brigade

Eastern Diagnostics

Ashalayam Handicrafts & Coffee Shop

Torrtee Lane

Stuart Lane

Indian Museum

JL Nehru Rd

Chowringhee Lane

Marquis St

Marquis St

Taj Medical

Sasha Handicrafts

City Medical

Medic

Park St

Dr M Ishaque Rd (Kyd St)

Lufthansa Rajasthan Emporium

To Park St

To Park St

N

100 metres
100 yards

**Where to stay** 🛏
Ashreen Guest House **2** *B3*
Astoria **3** *C3*
Bawa Walson Spa'o'tel **22** *C3*
Emirates **7** *D3*
Fairlawn **8** *C2*
Galaxy **9** *C3*
Lindsay and Blue & Beyond **11** *B2*
Maria **13** *C3*
Modern Lodge **14** *C3*
Paragon **16** *C3*
Sapphire Suites **18** *B3*

Super Guest House **19** *C3*
Times Guest House **20** *C2*
YMCA **23** *B1*

**Restaurants** 🍴
Brothers Snacks **2** *A1*
Fresh & Juicy **5** *C2*
Jimmy's **7** *B3*
Kathleen's **16** *B3*
Khalsa **9** *B2*
Nahoum **17** *B2*
NV Stores **11** *B3*
Raj's Spanish Café **6** *C3*

Tirupati **12** *C3*
Zaranj & Jong's **13** *B1*

➡ **Kolkata maps**
**1** Kolkata, page 278
**2** Central Kolkata, page 281
**3** Around Sudder Street, page 283
**4** Park Street & Chowringhee, page 285

## Park Street

**Park Street Cemetery** ① *daily 0800-1630, free, information booklet Rs 100, security guard opens gate and will expect you to sign the visitors' book,* was opened in 1767 to accommodate the large number of British who died 'serving' their country. The cemetery is a peaceful paradise and a step into history, located on the south side of one of Kolkata's busiest streets, with a maze of soaring obelisks shaded by tropical trees. The heavily inscribed decaying headstones, rotundas, pyramids and urns have been restored, and gardeners are actively trying to beautify the grounds. Several of the inscriptions make interesting reading. Death, often untimely, came from tropical diseases or other hazards such as battles, childbirth and even melancholia. More uncommonly, it was an excess of alcohol, or as for Sir Thomas D'Oyly, through "an inordinate use of the hokkah". Rose Aylmer died after eating too many pineapples! Tombs include those of Colonel Kyd, founder of the Botanical Gardens, the great oriental scholar Sir William Jones, and the fanciful mausoleum of the Irish Major-General 'Hindoo' Stuart. Across AJC Bose Road, on Karaya Road, is the smaller and far more derelict **Scottish Cemetery** ① *daily 0700-1730, free, pamphlet by donation to the caretaker,* established in 1820. The Kolkata Scottish Heritage Trust began work in 2008 to restore some of the 1600 tumbledown graves but the undergrowth is rampant and jungle prevails. It is also known as the 'dissenters' graveyard', as this was where non-Anglicans were buried. Also nearby, on AJC Bose Road, is the enormous **Lower Circular Road Cemetery** created in 1840 when Park Street Cemetery became full.

The **Asiatic Society** ① *1 Park St, T033-2229 0779, www.asiaticsocietycal.com, Mon-Fri 1000-1800, free,* the oldest institution of Oriental studies in the world, was founded in 1784 by the great Orientalist, Sir William Jones. It is a treasure house of 150,000 books and 60,000 ancient manuscripts in most Asian languages, although permission is required to see specific pieces. The museum includes an Ashokan edict, rare coins and paintings. The library is worth a visit for its dusty travelogues and titles on the history of Kolkata. The original 1804 building is to the rear; you can ask to view the impressive staircase adorned with statues and paintings. Here also is the manuscript restoration department, where staff are pleased to explain the work they undertake. Bring a passport, as the signing-in process to visit the building is (at least) a triplicate process.

## The Maidan

This area, 200 years ago, was covered in dense jungle. Often called the 'lungs of the city', it is a unique green, covering over 400 ha along Chowringhee (JL Nehru Road). Larger than New York's Central Park, it is perhaps the largest urban park in the world. In it stands Fort William and several clubhouses providing tennis, football, rugby, cricket and even crown green bowls. Thousands each day pursue a hundred different interests – from early morning yogis, model plane enthusiasts, weekend cricketers and performers earning their living, to vast political gatherings.

The massive **Fort William** was built by the British after their defeat in 1756, on the site of the village of Govindapur. Designed to be impregnable, it was roughly octagonal and large enough to house all the Europeans in the city in case of an attack. Water from the Hugli was channelled to fill the wide moat and the surrounding jungle was cleared to give a clear field of fire; this later became the Maidan. The barracks, stables, arsenal, prison and St Peter's Church are still there, but the fort now forms the Eastern Region's Military Headquarters and entry is forbidden.

At the southern end of the Maidan is **Kolkata Race Course**, run by the Royal Calcutta Turf Club. The history of racing goes back to the time of Warren Hastings and the 1820 grandstand is especially handsome.

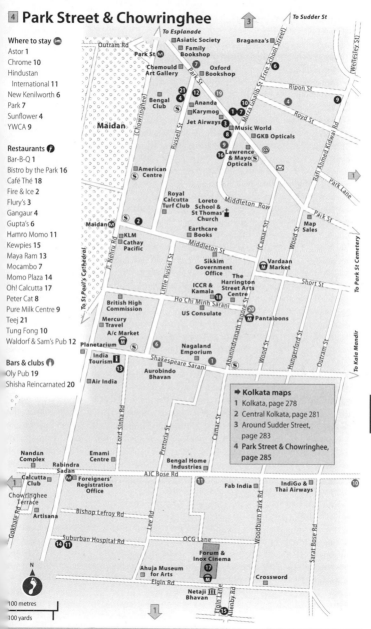

## Chowringhee and around

You can still see some of the old imposing structures with pillared verandas (designed by Italian architects as residences of prominent Englishmen), though modern high-rise buildings and a flyover have transformed the skyline of what was the ancient pilgrim route to Kalighat.

**St Paul's Cathedral** ① *0900-1200, 1500-1800, 5 services on Sun*, is the original metropolitan church of British India. Completed in 1847, its Gothic tower (dedicated in 1938) was designed to replace the earlier steeples which were destroyed by earthquakes. The cathedral has a fine altar piece, three 'Gothic' stained-glass windows, two Florentine frescoes and the great West window by Burne-Jones. The original stained-glass East window, intended for St George's Windsor, was destroyed by a cyclone in 1964 and was replaced by the present one four years later.

**Academy of Fine Arts** ① *2 Cathedral Rd, Tue-Sun 1500-2000 (ground floor galleries), 1200-1900 (museum), free*, was founded in 1933. The first floor museum has a newly restored gallery showing 33 pictures by Rabindranath Tagore, plus his writings and some personal effects. The textiles gallery and other sections have been closed for years, but may reopen soon. The ground floor galleries show changing exhibitions contemporary paintings and sculptures by Indian artists.

The **Victoria Memorial** ① *T033-2223 1889-91, www.victoriamemorial-cal.org; gardens open 0530-1815 (ticket counter closes at 1745), Rs 4; museum open Tue-Sun 1000-1700 (ticket counter closes at 1630, very crowded on Sun), foreigners Rs 150, cameras not permitted inside; son et lumière show, summer 1945, winter 1915, 45 mins, Rs 20 front seats, Rs 10 elsewhere* (1906-1921), was the brain-child of Lord Curzon. The white marble monument to Queen Victoria and the Raj, designed in Italian Renaissance/Indo-Saracenic style, stands in large, well-kept grounds with ornamental pools. A seated bronze Queen Victoria dominates the approach from the north, while a marble statue stands in the main hall where visitors sometimes leave flowers at her feet. The building is illuminated in the evening; the musical fountain is a special draw. The statues over the entrance porches (including Motherhood, Prudence and Learning), and around the central dome (of Art, Architecture, Justice, Charity) came from Italy. The impressive weather vane, a 5-m-tall bronze winged Angel of Victory weighing three tonnes, looks tiny from below. The principal gallery, covering the history of the city, is well presented and makes interesting reading. It includes some fascinating lithographs and illustrations of the city during the Raj period. The painting gallery has magnificent works by European artists in India from 1770-1835, including Zoffany, the two Daniells and Samuel Davis. Recently, the upper gallery of the Queen's Hall was reopened after more than a decade, and visitors can now walk around the inside of the rotunda again.

## North Kolkata → *For listings, see pages 291-304.*

## College Street

This is the heart of intellectual Kolkata with the **university** and several academic institutions, including the old **Sanskrit College** and the elite **Presidency College**. Europeans and Indian benefactors established the Hindu College (1817) to provide liberal education. In 1855, this became the Presidency College. A centre for 19th-century Bengali writers, artists and reformers, it spawned the early 20th-century Swadeshi Movement. The famous **Indian Coffee House** (opened in 1944), cavernous haunt of the city's intelligentsia, has tonnes of atmosphere and is always packed despite the average coffee and food. Along the pavements are interesting second-hand book stalls. The

**Ashutosh Museum of Indian Art** ① *University Centenary Building, Mon-Fri 1100-1630, closed university holidays, Rs 10,* is well maintained and worth a visit. The ground floor is packed with eastern Indian sculptures and terracotta tiles depicting figures. The first floor has colourful Bengali and Orissan folk art, faded textiles, and a hoard of paintings including 14th- to 19th-century miniatures, Kalighat paintings, Nepalese art and Tibetan *thankas*. Also look out for the model of the Senate Hall (1873-1960) which was pulled down to make way for the concrete monster of the present Centenary block, in the days before heritage buildings were accorded any value.

## Marble Palace

① *46 Muktaram Babu St, closed Mon and Thu, 1000-1600. Free pass from WBTDC (see page 277), 24 hrs ahead, or baksheesh (Rs 20 per person) to the security man at the gate and a further tip to the attendant who will accompany you around. Shoes must be removed, no photography allowed.*

Located in Chor Bagan ('Thieves' Garden'), the one-man collection of Raja Rajendra Mullick is in his ornate home (1835) with an Italianate courtyard, classical columns and Egyptian sphinxes. Family members still inhabit a portion of the house while servants' descendants live in the huts that encircle the grounds. Six sleeping marble lions and statuary grace the lawns and there is a veritable menagerie at the back of the garden. The galleries, disorganized and gathering dust, are crammed with statues, porcelain, clocks, mirrors, chandeliers and English (Reynolds), Dutch (Reubens) and Italian paintings. The pink, grey and white Italian marble floors are remarkable, as is the solid rosewood statue of Queen Victoria. Allow one hour to look round, or take a book and relax in the garden. The rambling two-floor museum has more than just curiosity appeal – it is one of Kolkata's gems.

## Howrah Bridge area

**Howrah Bridge** (Haora), or Rabindra Setu, was opened in 1943. This single-span cantilever bridge, the quintessential image of Kolkata, replaced the old pontoon (floating) bridge that first joined the city of Kolkata with Howrah and the railway station. To avoid affecting river currents and silting, the two 80-m-high piers rise from road level; the 450-m span expands by a metre on a hot day. It is the busiest bridge in the world in terms of foot passengers, with more than 3.5 million pedestrians per day (many with improbable loads on their heads). Wrestlers can be seen underneath and there is a daily **flower market** beneath the eastern end at Mullik Ghat, with piles of marigolds glowing against the mud. At night the bridge is illuminated, which makes a fine sight – if waiting for a night train at Howrah station go to the first floor waiting rooms for a good view. The pedestrian-free **Vidyasagar Setu Bridge**, further south, has eased the traffic burden slightly.

Southeast of Howrah Bridge, the gorgeously well-kept **Armenian Church** of **Holy Nazareth** (1724) is a reminder of the important trading role the small Armenian community, who mostly came from Iran, played from the 17th century. The church is open 0600-1200 on weekdays or you can ask someone to open up in order to view the beautifully maintained interior. A gravestone in the compound is inscribed with the date 1630. The 150 or so Armenians in the city still hold a service in Armenian in one of their two churches in the city every Sunday. Their college on Mirza Ghalib Street (also the birthplace of William Makepeace Thackery in 1811) has boarding pupils from Armenia who are usually orphans. To the east of the Church of Holy Nazareth is the **Roman Catholic Cathedral** (1797), built by the Portuguese. The Jewish community, mostly Sephardic, of Baghdadi origin, was also once very prominent in commerce. Their two synagogues are well maintained with stained-glass windows. The grander of the two is the church-like and cavernous **Moghan David Synagogue** (1884) ① *Canning St, daily 0900-1700*, while the nearby **Beth El Synagogue** ① *26/1 Pollock St, Sun-Fri 1000-1700*, is smaller. Just around the corner from the Moghan David Synagogue, on Brabourne Road hidden behind market stalls, is the older and derelict **Neveh Shalome Synagogue** (now inaccessible). There are only around 30-40 elderly Jews left in the city (the community numbered about 6000 before the Second World War) who continue to congregate at **Nahoum & Son's bakery** in the New Market. The Jewish Girls School in Park Street no longer has Jewish pupils, in fact the vast majority of the girls are Muslims from a nearby neighbourhood. To view the interior of the synagogues, it is necessary to get signed permission either from Nahoum's Bakery (easiest) or from the office at 1 Hartford Lane.

A few reminders that there was once a Chinatown in Kolkata remain in the form of Chinese 'churches'. Seek out the **Sea Ip Church** (1905), which has an intricately carved wooden altar and the **Nam Soon Church**, with a school at the rear. The latter is gorgeously maintained with bright paint, a huge bell and drum, and a little courtyard with trees. Both are willingly opened by the custodians. At the top of Bentinck Street, where it meets BB Ganguly Street, are several tiny old-fashioned shoe shops run by aging members of the Chinese community.

## Rabindra Bharati Museum

Trams run along Rabindra Sarani, previously known as the Chitpur Road and one of the oldest streets in the city. Rising above the street-level are the three green domes, 27 minarets and multiple archways of **Nakhoda Mosque** (1926), Kolkata's principal mosque holding 10,000 worshippers. A large brick gateway leads to **Rabindra Bharati Museum** ① *6/4 Dwarakanath Tagore Lane (red walls visible down lane opposite 263 Rabindra Sarani) Mon-Fri 1000-1700, Sat 1000-1330, Sun and holidays 1100-1400, www.museum.rbu.ac.in, about_rb*, in a peaceful enclave away from the teeming chaos of Rabindra Sarani, occupies the family home of Rabindranath Tagore, who won the Nobel Prize for Literature in 1913. It showcases Tagore's life and works, as well as the 19th-century Renaissance movement in Bengal. Be sure to explore along all the corridors, as it's easy to miss the galleries of Indian and European art, and the Japanese exhibition rooms.

## Kumartuli

South of the Dakshineshwar Temple (see below) is Kumartuli. Off Chitpur Road, the *kumar* or potters work all year, preparing clay images around cores of bamboo and straw. For generations they have been making life-size idols for the *pujas* or festivals, particularly of goddess Durga on a lion, slaying the demon. The images are usually unbaked since they are immersed in the holy river at the end of the festival. As the time of the *puja* approaches, you will see thousands of images, often very brightly painted and gaudily dressed, awaiting the final finishing touch by the master painter. There are also *shola* artists who make decorations for festivals and weddings. The potters' area of Kumartuli is being slowly rebuilt, and concrete structures are replacing the towering bamboo workshops that were so very photogenic.

## Northeast of the city centre

Just north of the Belgachia Metro station is a cluster of three Digambar Jain temples, one of the most tranquil spots in the city. The meticulously maintained and ornate **Paresnath Temple** ① *0700-1200, 1500-2000, no leather*, is dedicated to the 10th Tirthankara. Consecrated around 1867, it is richly decorated with mirrors, Victorian tiles and Venetian glass mosaics.

Difficult to find (and perhaps not worth the effort unless you are a true aficionado of Raj history) is **Clive's House** ① *off Jessore Rd in Nagarbajar, Dum Dum*. This was the country home of the first Governor-General of the East India Company and is the oldest colonial monument in Kolkata. For years, Bangladeshi immigrants lived in and around the derelict property until it was restored in 2008. The brick walls are being re-consumed by plant life and it requires some imagination to envisage its former glory.

## Belur Math and the Dakshineshwar Kali Temple

Some 16 km north of the city is **Belur Math** ① *0600-1200, 1600-1900*, the international headquarters of the **Ramakrishna Mission**, founded in 1899 by Swami Vivekananda, a disciple of the 19th-century Hindu saint Ramakrishna. He preached the unity of all religions and to symbolize this the *Math* ('monastery') synthesizes Hindu, Christian and Islamic architectural styles in a peaceful and meditative atmosphere.

On the opposite side of the river from Belur Math is the **Dakshineshwar Kali Temple** ① *0600-1200, 1500-1800, 1830-2100, no photography allowed inside*. This huge Kali temple was built in 1847 by Rani Rashmoni. The 12 smaller temples in the courtyard are dedicated to Siva and there are also temples to Radha and Krishna. Because of the Rani's low caste, no priest would serve there until Ramakrishna's elder brother agreed and was succeeded by Ramakrishna himself. Here, Ramakrishna achieved his spiritual vision of the unity of all religions. The temple is crowded with colourfully clad devotees, particularly on Sundays when there are lengthy queues, and is open to all faiths.

A boat (Rs 8) takes 20 minutes to/from Belur Math across the Hooghly. Buses from BBD Bagh go to Dunlop Intersection, from where it's a short auto ride to the temple; trains run from Sealdah to Dakshineshwar.

## South Kolkata → *For listings, see pages 291-304.*

## Netaji Museum

① *Netaji Bhavan, 38/1 Elgin Rd, Tue-Sun 1100-1430 (last entry 1615), Rs 5, no photography.*
This museum remembers the mission of Subas Chandra Bose, the leader of the INA (Indian National Army), and is in the house where he lived before he had to flee the British oppressors. On the first floor, you can view his bedroom and study (where walls are painted with the tricolours of the Congress flag), although panes of glass prevent close inspection of his possessions. A detailed video is played in the second floor rooms showing old footage and giving a detailed explanation of his life's work. Interesting is the German Room, with a photo of Netaji meeting Hitler and information on Azad Hind and the Indo-German Friendship Society.

## Kali Temple

① *Off Ashok Mukherjee Rd, 0500-1500, 1700-2200.*
This is the temple to Kali (1809), the patron goddess of Kolkata, usually seen in her bloodthirsty form garlanded with skulls. There was an older temple here, where the goddess's little toe is said to have fallen when Siva carried her charred corpse in a frenzied dance of mourning, and she was cut into pieces by Vishnu's *chakra*. Where once human sacrifices were made (up until 1835, a boy was beheaded every Friday), the lives of goats are offered daily on two wooden blocks to the south of the temple. When visiting the temple, priests will attempt to snare foreigners for the obligatory *puja*. A barrage may start as far away as 500 m from the temple. Don't be fooled in to handing over your shoes and succumbing to any priests

until you are clearly inside the temple, despite being shown 'priest ID' cards. An acceptable minimum donation is Rs 50. Books showing previous donations of Rs 3000 are doubtless faked. Having done the *puja*, you'll probably be left alone to soak up the atmosphere.

## Mother Teresa's homes

Mother Teresa, an Albanian by birth, came to India to teach as a Loreto nun in 1931. She started her Order of the Missionaries of Charity in Kalighat to serve the destitute and dying 19 years later. **Nirmal Hriday** ('Pure Heart'), near the Kali Temple, the first home for the dying, was opened in 1952. Mother Teresa died on 5 September 1997 but her work continues. You may see nuns in their white cotton saris with blue borders busy working in the many homes, clinics and orphanages in the city.

## Gariahat and Rabindra Sarobar

The southern neighbourhoods around Gariahat are more middle class and greener than Central Kolkata, but no less interesting, with plenty of good restaurants and small hotels. On Gariahat Road, the shiny white edifice of **Birla Mandir** ① *0600-1100 and 1630-2030*, pulls in a lot of devotees and it is particularly impressive when lit up at night. Taking 22 years to complete, another gift of the Birla family, it is modelled on the Lingaraj Temple at Bhubaneshwar and is covered with carvings both inside and out. No photos are permitted inside. Just north of the temple is the **CIMA Gallery** (see page 299) which is worth a look. South of the Birla Mandir, beyond the southeast corner of Gariahat Crossing, is **Gariahat Market** which specializes in fish and is a fascinating hive of activity, especially in the early morning. Running west from the crossing is Rash Behari Avenue, one of the city's liveliest streets: a 2-km stretch lined with sari stalls, *menhdi* (henna) artists, momo vendors and vegetable sellers. A couple of blocks south, housed in a modern high-rise, the **Birla Academy of Art and Culture** ① *108/109 Southern Av, T033-2466 2843, Tue-Sun 1600-2000*, concentrates on medieval and contemporary paintings and sculpture. The ground floor sculpture gallery has been recently remodelled, and displays some beautiful pieces including Buddhist and Hindu statues. It is well lit and worth visiting. The upper levels host changing art exhibitions.

The large and pleasant lake of **Rabindra Sarobar** is shaded by ancient trees and surrounded by a pathway perfect for joggers and walkers. There are several rowing clubs (the oldest dates from 1858), and Laughing Clubs meet in the mornings (around 0600) to mix yoga and group laughing. A road from the southwest corner of the lake leads to the trim little **Japanese Buddhist Temple** (1935) ① *Lake Rd*, the oldest temple of the Nichiren sect in India. Visitors are welcomed, and can join in the hypnotic prayers by beating handheld drums (at dawn and dusk). A slim congregation of ex-Ghurkhas, Nepali ladies and bemused Bengalis are drawn in. The interior is restful with an elaborate golden shrine, gaudy flowers, ornamental lanterns and origami birds which somehow come together to pleasing effect. It's possible to walk from the temple south, via Dhakuria Bridge, to the **Dakshinapan** shopping complex (handicrafts and handloom) and refresh at **Dolly's, The Tea Shop** (see page 297).

## Alipore

South of the Maidan, the elite address of Alipore is home to a couple of sights. On Belvedere Road the **National Library** was once the winter residence of the Lieutenant Governors of Bengal. Built in the Renaissance Italian style, with a double row of classical columns, it is approached through a triple arched gateway and a drive between mahogany and mange trees. The library itself, the largest in the country with over eight million books, is now mainly housed in an adjacent newer building (sadly the old building can no longer be entered). Opposite is the **zoo** ① *Fri-Wed 0900-1700, Rs 10.* Opened in 1876, the grounds house a wide variety of animal and bird life. The white tigers from Rewa and the tigon – a cross between a tiger and a lion – are the rarest animals. A reptile house and aquarium are across the road. There are restaurants and picnics are permitted, however it's often terrifyingly busy (particularly at the weekend). Nearby, on Alipore Road, the expansive **Agri Horticultural Gardens** ① *0600-1300 and 1400-1830, Rs 10,* are the most peaceful green space in the city. The Horticultural Society was started in 1820 by the Baptist missionary William Carey. Bring a book; you'll be the only visitor during the week.

## State Archaeological Museum

① *Next to Behala tram depot, 1 Satyen Roy Rd, off Diamond Harbour Rd, Behala, Wed-Sun 1000-1630 (last entry 1600), Rs 5. Shared autos run from Kalighat metro to Behala, finishing close to the museum entrance.*

This little-visited yet well-presented museum has seven galleries over two floors, housed in a modern structure adjacent to the original colonial building. Galleries are devoted to West Bengal sites, such as the Buddhist remains of Nandadirghi Vihara near Malda, and the terracotta Hindu temples in Purulia. There's a meagre selection of local stone sculpture, intricate metal work, and a selection of Bengali paintings including Kalighat Pat (mostly religious in nature, but the famous *Two Women and a Rose* is a notable secular exception), and Murshidabad-style painting.

## Botanical Gardens

① *20 km south from BBD Bagh, 0700-1700, Rs 50, avoid Sun and public holidays when it is very crowded, catch a bus from Esplanade; minibuses and CTC buses (No C-12) ply the route.*

Kolkata's Botanical Gardens, on the west bank of the Hugli, were founded in 1787 by the East India Company. The flourishing 250-year-old banyan tree, with a circumference of almost 400 m, is perhaps the largest in the world. The original trunk was destroyed by lightning in 1919 but over 2800 offshoots form an impressive sight. The avenues of Royal Cuban palms and mahogany trees are impressive and there are interesting and exotic specimens in the herbarium and collections of ferns and cactii. The gardens are peaceful and deserted during the week and make a welcome change from the city.

---

## ◉ Kolkata listings

*For hotel and restaurant price codes and other relevant information, see pages 22-26.*

### ◉ Where to stay

Watch out for the 10% luxury tax and 10% service charge in the higher price brackets. Medium price and budget hotels attracting foreigners are concentrated in the **Sudder St** area.

**Central Kolkata** *p280, map p281*
**$$$$ Oberoi Grand**, 15 Chowringhee (JL Nehru), T033-2249 2323, www.oberoi hotels.com. Atmospheric Victorian building opposite the Maidan, exquisitely restored, range of rooms and suites with giant 4-posters, all are spacious, those with balconies overlooking the raised garden and pool are charming, bathrooms a tad old-fashioned but in keeping with the colonial style, excellent Thai restaurant and 24-hr **La Terrasse** with international

cuisine, billiards in the bar, lovely pool for guests, wonderful spa. Reasonable prices available online for a standard room.

**$$ Manthan**, 3 Waterloo St, T033-2248 9577, manthanhotel@gmail.com. Only 4 rooms, spacious and well appointed, TV, a/c and pleasant furnishings. The bar/restaurant and banquet service mean it's fairly bustling. Bargaining is most certainly possible.

**$ Broadway**, 27A Ganesh Chandra Av, T033-2236 3930, www.broadwayhotel.in. Amazingly good-value hotel in a characterful building that hasn't changed much since it opened in 1937. Very clean rooms are non-a/c but airy with powerful fans, antique furniture and Bengali-red floors, towels, some with common bath, plus 24-hr checkout. Noisy on the lower levels at the front. The bar is very appealing (see Bars, page 298). Highly recommended.

### Around Sudder Street *p282, maps p283 and p285*

Kyd St has changed its name to Dr Md Ishaque Rd and Free School St is now called Mirza Ghalib St.

**$$$ Lindsay**, 8-A Lindsay St, T033-2252 2237/8, www.hotellindsay.com. Recently refurbished hotel towering over Newmarket, mainly for business travellers, Wi-Fi in rooms, good breakfast. **Blue & Beyond** rooftop restaurant/bar has panoramic city views and great food.

**$$$ Sapphire Suites**, 15 Lindsay St, T033-2252 3052-4, www.sapphiresuites.in. 29 a/c rooms in a new hotel in an attractive period building, right next to New Market. Aimed at business travellers, rooms have sleek black and white furnishings, flatscreen TVs, bathrobes, tea/coffee facilities. Breakfast included, good multi-cuisine restaurant and fitness centre. A few teething problems, however good deals available online.

**$$$-$$ Bawa Walson Spa'o'tel**, 5A Sudder St, T033-2252 1512, www.bawahotels.com. An unlikely situation for a Spa'o'tel, but the **Walson** is immaculate with Thai accents throughout. Rooms are wood and white,

swish shower rooms, free Wi-Fi, Arabic restaurant. Huge discounts possible, also when booking online.

**$$ Astoria Hotel**, 6 Sudder St, near fire station, T033-2252 2241, www.astoria.in. Offers 41 rooms of a good standard, after being recently renovated. All have a/c, hot water, and there's free Wi-Fi, it's a good standard for the price. Great top-floor room with a terrace.

**$$ Fairlawn**, 13A Sudder St, T033-2252 1510/8766, www.fairlawnhotel.com. A Calcutta institution, the old-fashioned but characterful rooms have a/c, TV, hot water, and are comfortable. Semi-formal meals at set times aren't the best, but breakfast and afternoon tea are included. The hotel and management provide a throwback to the Raj, bric-a-brac everywhere, photos cover all the communal spaces, quite a place and the garden terrace is great for a beer. Wi-Fi Rs 250 per day.

**$ Ashreen Guest House**, 2 Cowie Lane, T033-2252 0889, ashreen_guesthouse@ yahoo.com. Modern rooms with above-average facilities (for Sudder St) with TV and hot water, a suitable place to break yourself into Kolkata gently, however prices are ever escalating while standards slip. Pick-up for late night flights.

**$ Emirates**, 11/1 Dr Md Ishaque Rd (Kyd St), T033-2217 8487. Fresh, bright rooms in a building with character, some a/c, bathrooms are a bit jaded but there's a pleasant terrace.

**$ Galaxy**, 3 Stuart Lane, T033-2252 4565, hotelgalaxy@vsnl.net. 12 good tiled rooms with attached bath and TV, singles Rs 500, doubles Rs 700/900 without/with a/c, a decent choice but often full with long-stayers. Try at around 1030 just after checkout.

**$ Maria**, 5/1 Sudder St, T033-2252 0860. 24 clean, basic rooms (hard beds), some with bath, dorm, internet, TV in the 'lobby', hot water, water filter for guests' use. Popular budget place with a good atmosphere.

**$ Modern Lodge**, 1 Stuart Lane, T033-2252 4960. Very popular, 14 rooms, attached or shared bath, cheapest at ground level, prices rise as you go up to the breezy rooftop, pleasant lobby with plants but sinister 'lounge', quirky staff, no reservations so try at 1000.

**$ Paragon**, 2 Stuart Lane, T033-2252 2445. Textbook backpacker haunt with 45 rooms, some tiny and prison-like but it's clean just about (some doubles have attached bath) and mixed sex dorms (with shared/ private bath), rooftop rooms are better. Water heater to fill buckets. Open communal spaces, indifferent management.

**$ Super Guest House**, 30A Mirza Ghalib St, T033-2252 0995, super_guesthouse@ hotmail.com. This guesthouse has some of the cleanest rooms in the area for Rs 1200-1500 per double, all a/c with hot bath, tiled and simple box rooms. Be sure to ask for a room that does not suffer noise from the daily live music in **Super Pub Bar**. No single rates.

**$ Times Guest House**, 3 Sudder St, T033-2252 1796. Get a room at the front with balcony to view the action on the street below. Has character, jolly staff, very cheap singles with shared bath.

**$ YMCA**, 25 Jl Nehru Rd, T033-2249 2192, www.calcuttaymca.org. 17 rooms, some a/c, all with bath, geyser and TV, in large, rambling colonial building, clean linen, recently renovated but check room first as some are nicer than others. Helpful staff, rates include bed, tea and breakfast. The oldest YMCA in Asia.

## Park St and Chowringhee p284, map p285

**$$$$ Park**, 17 Park St, T033-2249 9000, www.theparkhotels.com. Trendy designer hotel, one of Kolkata's most reputable, good restaurants, nightclubs, health club, 24-hr café, service can be disappointing, entrance themed on underground car park. Go online for the best discounts.

**$$$$-$$$ New Kenilworth**, 1 & 2 Little Russell St, T033-2282 3939/40, www. kenilworthhotels.com. A very comfortable and attractive hotel, though overpriced at rack rates (good deals online). The foyer is all marble and chandeliers, but modern

rooms are neutrally furnished with soft lighting, flatscreen TV, minibar, nice bathrooms. The older period building contains suites and the **Big Ben** English-style pub, which has appeal as a dark den with a pool table and sports TV, plus there's a spa.

**$$$ Astor**, 15 Shakespeare Sarani, T033-2282 9957-9, www.astorkolkata.com. In a red-brick colonial building, comfortable a/c rooms with bath tubs, inferior annexe, have not retained original features, although public areas have fared better. The tiny blue-lit bar (**Cheers**, daily 1100-2300) is a nice place to be, and **Plush** lounge-bar is also fun (every night except Mon, liveliest on Wed, Fri and Sun). Breakfast included, minibar, off-season discounts, Wi-Fi (charge per 24 hrs).

**$ Sunflower Guest House**, 7 Royd St, T033-2229 9401, www.sunflowerguesthouse.com. An airy 1950s building with very clean well-maintained rooms, TV, hot water, more costly with a/c and newer bathrooms. Spacious lounge area, the numerous staff are kindly. Good location, near Sudder St but out of the backpacker scene. No single room rates.

**$ YWCA**, 1 Middleton Row, T033-2229 2494. Old colonial building with good atmosphere, airy verandas and tennis courts. Some rooms with bath (Rs 650) but doubles with shared bath have windows (Rs 350), dorm, all spotless, very friendly staff. Rates include breakfast, alcohol forbidden, a pleasant if shabby oasis in the city. A recommended alternative to Sudder St for female travellers.

## South Kolkata p289, maps p278 and p285

South Kolkata is a more salubrious area than elsewhere in the city, where quiet residential streets hide some good (mainly mid-range) guesthouses. Excellent little restaurants and vibrant markets are in plentiful supply.

**$$$$ Chrome**, 226 AJC Bose, T033-3096 3096, www.chromehotel.in. Space-age hotel with slick modern rooms dense with gadgetry, 'adrenalin' showers and trendy colour schemes. 6 categories, the 'Edge' suites being the zenith, but all are supremely comfortable. Good city-scapes from the higher levels. Minimalist **Khana Sutra** restaurant has huge set lunch/dinner North Indian menus as well as à la carte and world cuisine, rooftop bar/club **Inferno** on the 7th floor, and **Nosh** café in the lobby is good for speciality coffee and global cuisine. Swimming pool is planned. Discounts possible, especially for stays of a few days.

**$$$$ Hindusthan International**, 235/1 AJC Bose Rd, T033-2283 0505, www.hindusthan. com. Comfortable quiet rooms on 8 floors are priced right, but staff are distracting with their demands for tips. The food is nothing special although there are a couple of quite cool bars/coffee shop and **Underground** nightclub is popular, pool (non-residents Rs 500). Big discounts are possible.

**$$$ Samilton**, 35A Sarat Bose Rd, T033-3051 7700/77, www.samiltonhotel.com. Modern business-like rooms with good amenities, free Wi-Fi and hot drinks. Decent restaurant/coffeeshop. Basement nightclub and rooftop with shishas.

**$$$-$$ The Bodhi Tree**, 48/44 Swiss Park (near Rabindra Sarovar metro, exit Swiss Park), T033-2424 6534, www.bodhitree kolkata.com. Simply beautiful little boutique hotel with just 6 rooms, each uniquely furnished in a different regional style (eg rural Bengal, with mud-plastered walls), flatscreen TVs, 1 penthouse. The owners are active promoters of young artistic talent, the in-house café is a delight (see Coffee shops, page 297), dinner is available, business centre, free Wi-Fi, small library, serves alcohol. Prices are entirely reasonable for the special experience. Discounts for single women travellers/social workers. A real oasis; recommended.

**$$ 66/2B The Guest House**, 66/2B Purna Das Rd, T033-2464 6422/1, www.662bthe guesthouse.com. On a tree-lined street with some great restaurants a 2-min walk away (2 of which are owned by **66/2B**), this cheerful place is well furnished, with decent baths, all rooms have a/c, geysers and flatscreen TV. A more relaxing area to stay in. Breakfast included, as is Wi-Fi. Recently refurbished.

**$ Sharani Lodge**, 71/K Hindustan Park, T033-2463 5717, gautam_sharani@ rediffmail.com. In a quiet area, yet very close to hectic Rash Behari Av, this well-maintained and well-run lodge has an old-fashioned Indian ambiance. The a/c rooms are not worth really worth the extra money, but non-a/c are a great deal (Rs 770-880), ones with common bath also share balconies at the front, all have TV, towels and plenty of space. Use of PC (Rs 20 per hr). They have a second building, across Rash Behari, with lovely little outdoor terrace (again, the non-a/c rooms are more spacious and attractive than a/c).

**Other areas** *map p278*

**$$$$ Taj Bengal**, 34B Belvedere Rd, Alipore, T033-2223 3939, www.tajhotels.com. Opulent and modern, restaurants are plush, imaginative, intimate, with good food (ground floor Indian cheaper than 5th floor), leisurely service, unusual Bengali breakfast, **Khazana** shop is excellent (see Shopping).

**$$$$ Vedic Village**, T033-2280 2071, www.thevedicvillage.com. In Rajarhat, 20 mins from the airport on the eastern edge of the city, but a world away from the rest of Kolkata. The appeal is the clean air and rural surrounds as much as the luxuriou rooms, fabulous pool and of course the spa. Top-end villas and suites are stunning while studio rooms are not unreasonable when compared to other options in the city.

**$$$ Tollygunge Club**, 120 Deshapran Sasmal Rd, T033-2473 4539, www.thetolly gungeclub.org. On the south side of the city in 100 acres of grounds with an 18-hole golf course, swimming pool, tennis and other activities. Good bar and restaurants, one of which is open air. The place has charm and atmosphere which helps you overlook worn-out towels and casual servic ask for a renovated room, and enjoy the colonial feel. Interesting mid-range choice.

## 🍴 Restaurants

Licensed restaurants serve alcohol (some are unpleasant places to eat in since the emphasis is on drink). Be prepared for a large surcharge for live (or even recorded) music. This, plus taxes, can double the price on the menu. Many restaurants outside hotels do not accept credit cards. Special Bengali sweets are made fresh every afternoon at thousands of sweet shops (1600-1730): try *shingaras*, *kochuris* and *nimkis*.

**Central Kolkata** *p280, map p281*
**$$$ Aaheli** and **Oceanic**, at the Peerless Inn, 12 JL Nehru Rd, T033-2278 0301. Aaheli has an excellent menu of Bengali specialities, carefully selected from around the state by the chef, open from 1900. Oceanic has interesting seafood and is more pricey, open lunch and dinner. Both are comfortable with a/c and serve alcohol.
**$$$ Baan Thai**, Oberoi Grand (see Where to stay, page 291), T033-2249 2323. Excellent selection, imaginative decor, Thai-style seating on floor or chairs and tables.
**$$$-$$ Amber**, 11 Waterloo St, T033-2248 3477. Open 1100-2330. 2 floors of North Indian and continental gourmet delights (best for meat tandoori), generous helpings, fast service. **Essence** on 2nd floor fancies itself as a cocktail bar, but alcohol is served on both. There's also a functional bar on the ground floor (strictly no women). Also has a smaller restaurant on Middleton Row (T033-4000 7490), open 1200-1600 and 1900-2300.
**$$-$ Anand**, 19 Chittaranjan Av, T033-2212 9757. Open 0900-2130, Sun from 0700, closed Wed. Great South Indian food. Mammoth *dosas*, stuffed *idly*, all-vegetarian, family atmosphere and warmly decorated. Barefoot waiters are efficient. Queues at weekends.
**$$-$ Bhojohori Manna**, Esplanade. Open 1130-2130 (closed for cleaning 1630-1800). The newest branch of the Bengali chain, with budget prices for veg dishes and pricier fish items. Ticks on the whiteboard indicate availability, choice can be limited in the evenings as they sell out.

**$$-$ Chung Wah**, 13A Chittaranjan Av. Open 1100-2300. This hectic restaurant is functional and basic, with curtained-off booth seating down the sides. Hugely popular and with a large menu, it attracts a mostly male clientele, alcohol served. Recommended for the old-style atmosphere rather than the spicy Chinese food. Lone women are not encouraged.
**$ Madras Restaurant**, 25/B Chittaranjan Av, T033-2237 9764. A simpler setting than nearby **Anand** and slightly cheaper, but still has a/c. The list of *dosa* and *uttampams* is endless, plus there are a few Chinese dishes. Go between 1130-1530 for the South Indian thalis.

**Coffee shops, sweets and snacks**
**Indian Coffee House**, Albert Hall, just off College St (see page 286).

**Around Sudder Street** *p282, maps p283 and p285*
**$$$ Zaranj** and **Jong's**, 26 JL Nehru Rd. Adjacent restaurants, both tasteful, stylish, subdued decor, excellent food. Try *pudina paratha*, *murgh makhani*, tandoori fish in Zaranj, or delectable Burmese fare in Jong's.
**$$ Jimmy's**, 14D Lindsay St. Chinese. Small, a/c, good *momos*, Szechuan dishes, ice cream. Alcohol served.
**$ Fresh and Juicy**, Chowringhee Lane, T033-2286 1638. Newly renovated with a/c and 1st floor seating, good place for a sociable breakfast with reasonably authentic Indian meals and Western favourites, attracts a loyal following. Phone ahead for parcel-order.
**$ Khalsa**, 4C Madge Lane, T033-2249 0075. Excellent *lassis*, Western breakfasts, Indian mains, all super-cheap, and beyond excellent service from the utterly charming Sikh owners.
**$ NV Stores**, T033-2252 9661, and Maa Kali, 12/2 Lindsay St. Closed Sun. Stand-up street eateries making surprisingly good sandwiches (toasted are best) from any possible combination of ingredients; great *lassis* too.

**$ Raj's Spanish Café**, 7 Sudder St. Daily 0800-2200. Great Spanish nibbles, real coffee from a real machine, salads, pastries, pasta and sandwiches also good. Wi-Fi. A sociable spot. Recommended.
**$ Tirupati**, street stall next to **Hotel Maria**. A Sudder St institution; find a spot on the busy benches and enjoy enormous helpings of food from every continent. Closes out of season.

### Coffee shops, sweets and snacks

**Ashalayam**, 44 Mirza Ghalib St. Peaceful oasis run by an NGO, sells handicrafts made by street children as well as coffee and snacks.
**Kathleen's**, several branches, including 12 Mirza Ghalib St, corner of Lord Sinha Rd.
**Nahoum**, Shop F20, New Market, T033-6526 9936. Good pastries, cakes, savouries and brown bread. The original 1930s till and some fixtures still in situ.

### Kathi-rolls

**Brothers Snacks**, 1 Humayun Pl, Newmarket. Safe, tasty bet with outdoor seats. Kathi-rolls (tender kebabs wrapped in *parathas*) are hard to beat. Try mutton/chicken egg roll (if you don't want raw onions and green chillis, order *'no piaaz e mirchi'*) There are also plenty of great vegetarian options.

### Park St *p284, map p285*

Visitors craving Western fast food will find plenty of familiar names in this area.
**$$$ Bar-B-Q**, 43 Park St, T033-2229 9916. Always popular, always delicious. 3 sections serving Indian and Chinese food, bar.
**$$$ Bistro by the Park**, 2A Middleton Row, T033-2229 494. It's near the park rather than 'by' it, but this attractive contemporary place serves world cuisine (including Southeast Asian, Middle Eastern) with the main focus on Italian fare (salads, pockets, pizzas, etc). Serves alcohol.
**$$ Fire and Ice**, Kanak Building, Middleton St, T033-2288 4073, www.fireandicepizza.com. Open 1100-2330. Pizzas here are the real deal, service is excellent, and the ambience

relaxing. Decor is very much what you would expect from a pizza place at home.
**$$ Flury's**, 18 Park St. Classic Kolkata venue with hit-and-miss Western menu, but pastries and afternoon tea are winners and the bakery has brown bread. It's an institution.
**$$ Gangaur**, 2 Russell St. A wide menu of Indian delights, if you can resist the superb *thali* (1130-1530). Afterwards head next door for Bengali sweets.
**$$ Mocambo**, 25B Park St. International. A/c, pleasant lighting, highly descriptive menu. Long-standing reliable favourite.
**$$ Peter Cat**, 18A Park St (entrance on Middleton Row), T033-2229 8841. Chiefly Indian, with some international dishes. Good kebabs and sizzlers, hilarious menu of cheap cocktails, pleasant ambience but can rush you on busy weekend nights. No booking system, expect to queue outside.
**$$ Teej**, 2 Russell St, T033-2217 0730. Pure vegetarian Rajasthani delights washed down with cold beer, colourful *haveli*-esque setting.
**$$ Tung Fong**, Mirzah Ghalib St. Quality Chinese food for a reasonable price, the setting spacious and subtly Asian, white linens and Ming vases. Great Manchurian dishes, good fish and chilli garlic paneer, excellent desserts. Super-swift service.
**$$-$ Gupta's**, 53C Mirza Ghalib St, T033-2229 6541. Open 1100-2300. Excellent Indian and Chinese. More intimate and softly lit upstairs, low ceilings (beware of the fans), try fish *tikka peshwari* and *bekti tikka*, alcohol reasonably priced.
**$ Hamro Momo**, Suburban Hospital Rd (near Momo Plaza, see below). Open 1300-2100. Cheap and good Chinese and Tibetan dishes in simple eat-and-run surroundings, always packed out and there's very little space.
**$ Maya Ram**, 1 Lord Sinha Rd, T033-6515 5837. Open 1100-2300. A good place to try 'snacks' such as *paw bhaji*.
**$ Momo Plaza**, 2A Suburban Hospital Rd, T033-2287 8260. Open 1200-2200. With black half-tiling and pastel pink walls accentuated by kitsch ornaments,

which could be intentionally bohemian. Recommended for plentiful and delicious Tibetan and Chinese meals. Try the soups, chilli chicken, huge *momos* and *thukpa*.

## Coffee shops, sweets and snacks
**Café Thé**, Tagore Centre, 9A Ho Chi Min Sarani, T033-4003 5878. Daily 0900-2100. Modern, clean café serving Western/ Indian/Chinese snacks and meals, with an interesting menu of hot/cold teas.
**Pure Milk Centre**, near Rafi Ahmed Kidwai St/Ripon St corner. Good sweet 'curd' (*mishti doi*), usually sold out by lunchtime. Excellent hot *roshogollas*.

**South Kolkata** *p289, maps p278 and p285*
**$$$ Mainland China**, 3A Gurusaday Rd, T033-2283 7964; also at South City Mall, 3rd floor. Sublime Chinese. Unusual offerings, especially fish and seafood, tastefully decorated with burnished ceiling and evocative wall mural, pleasant ambience, courteous. Book ahead.
**$$$ Oh! Calcutta**, Forum Mall, 10/3 Elgin Rd, T033-2283 7161. Fantastic fish and seafood, plus many vegetarian options, this award-winning restaurant re-creates Bengali specialities.
**$$$-$$ 6 Ballygunge Place**, Ballygunge, T033-2460 3922. In a charming Raj-era bungalow, the intricate Bengali menu is as delightful as the ambiance. For more than a decade, the perfect place for a special night out. Fish dishes are a highlight.
**$$ Kewpie's**, 2 Elgin Lane (just off Elgin Rd), T033-2486 1600/9929. Tue-Sun 1200-1500, 1700-2245. Authentic Bengali home cooking at its best, add on special dishes to basic *thali*, unusual fish and vegetarian. Just a few tables in rooms inside the owners' residence, a/c, sells recipe book. Highly recommended, book in advance.
**$$ Mirch Masala**, 49/2 Gariahat Rd, Gariahat, T033-2461 8900. Lunch 1200-1500, dinner 1900-2230. This popular restaurant-bar has walls decorated with *pukkah* murals depicting Bollywood stars. Food can be a

bit heavy (mainly Indian, non-veg) but the atmosphere is lively and staff competent.
**$$-$ Bhojohori Manna**, 13 PC Sorcar Sarani (aka Ekdalia Rd); also at JD Park. Budget prices and a perfect little place to sample pure Bengali cuisine, veg and non-veg. Ticks on the wall menu indicate availability, try *echor dalna* (jackfruit curry) and *bhekti paturi* (mustard-drenched fish steamed in banana leaves). 2 people should order 4-5 different dishes to share. Much better than the newer **Bhojohori 6** outlet on Hindustan Rd nearby. Decent toilet.
**$ Banana Leaf**, 73-75 Rash Behari Av, T033-2464 1960. Open 0730-2200. Vegetarian South Indian, top-notch *dosas* and *thalis* plus superb *mini-idli* and decent southern-style coffee.
**$ Bliss**, 53 Hindustan Park, T033-2463 5962. For Chinese in a fast-food environment, **Bliss** is ideal. Portions are generous, the soups delicious, it's tiny but there's seating.
**$ South India Club**, off Rash Behari Av. Daily 0700-2130. An authentic taste of the South in a canteen environment, full meals for under Rs 5, and a good place to experiment with less commonly seen dishes such as *pongal* or *upma*. Highly recommended.

## Coffee shops, sweets and snacks
**Art Café**, at The Bodhi Tree (see Where to stay, page 294). Tue-Sat, 1400-1830. This beautiful slate-floored café is lit by green lights and decorated with Buddhas and palm trees. There's a tempting drinks menu (plus beer). Something quite out of the ordinary for Kolkata.
**Dolly's, The Tea Shop**, Dakshinapan market (just after Dhakuria Bridge). The quaintest place in the city for a variety of teas, refreshing iced-teas (try watermelon) and decent toasties. Tea-chest tables, low basket chairs, indoor and outdoor seating, even the walls are lined with old tea-crates. Dolly is a formidable lady.
**Nepal Sweets**, 16B Sarat Bose Rd. *Chandrakala*, almond *pista barfi*, mango *roshogolla*, *kheer mohan* (also savouries). Recommended.

**Other areas** *map p278*

**$$$ Chinoiserie**, Taj Bengal (see Where to stay, page 294), T033-2223 3939. Good for a splurge on excellent Chinese.

Chinese food fans also go to South Tangra Rd off EM bypass, east of the city centre. The approach is none too picturesque, past tanneries and open drains, but among the maze of lanes (in places lit by lanterns) many eateries are quite swanky.

**$$ Beijing**, 77/1A Christopher Rd, T033-2328 1001. Try garlic chicken, sweet and sour fish, chop suey, steamed fish, generous portions.

**$$ Golden Joy**, Kafulok and Sin Fa, to name but a few, offer excellent soups, jumbo prawns and honey chicken, best to go early (1200 for lunch, 2000 for dinner).

### Kathi-rolls

**Rehmania** and **Shiraz Golden Restaurant**, on opposite corners of Park St/AJC Bose Rd crossing. Muslim joints famed for their mutton rolls and kebabs.

## ⊙ Bars and clubs

### Kolkata *p277, maps p278, p281, p283, p285*
### Bars

The larger hotels have pleasant bars and upmarket restaurants serve alcohol. The top hotels are well stocked, luxurious but pricey. In Sudder St, **Fairlawn's** pleasant garden terrace is popular at dusk attracting anyone seeking a chilled beer. The clientele is quite mixed, fairy lights set the greenery glowing and it's perfect for a 1st night drink to acclimatize – but beware the below-average food and stiff charges for snacks. **Super Pub Bar**, Sudder St, is always busy and sociable, but expect gruff service and check your change. The 1st floor has live music (Hindi and Bengali singing) every night from 1600-2400. (If you need a beer after hours, **Super Chicken** next door has take-away beers tucked in the fridge and is open later than the wine-shops). The 9th-floor bar **Blue & Beyond** at the Lindsay Hotel, is a rooftop bar/restaurant with great views over New

Market and Kolkata and some excellent Indian and Chinese food (quite pricey), plus a few Western dishes. The 'ceiling' is composed of blue fairy lights, there is an indoor a/c section, but it's quite pricey. **Sam's Pub**, off Park St, is open later than most (last orders at 2330 on weekend nights) and still permits smoking in a curious indoor gazebo; football and cricket matches are shown on the flatscreen. For a sunset drink on the water, try the **Floatel**, a floating hotel on the Hooghly moored close to Babu Ghat. The simple bar is usually quiet, and has a small outdoor area, good for watching the river life.

'Local' bars, open usually from 1100-2230, often lack atmosphere or have deafening live singing; some are positively men only – there is a seedy choice down **Dacres Lane**, just north of Esplanade. Women also welcome in the **Broadway Bar** at the Broadway Hotel (last orders 2230), where marble floors, polished Art Deco seating, soft lighting, whirring fans and windows open to the street make it probably the best choice in the city. Lone women will feel comfortable as it's a busy and respectable place. The bar at the **New Empire Cinema**, between New Market and Chowringhee, is pleasant, blue-lit and efficiently staffed. **Oly Pub**, 21 Park St, is an institution: very noisy, serves steak and eggs, more airy downstairs, expect rats by the end of the night upstairs. Another classic is **Tripti's**, SP Mukerjee Rd (next to Netaji Bhavan metro), Mon-Sat 1100-2300, Sun 1100-2200. Established in 1935, Tripti's is styled like a canteen, sadly it's been tackily refurnished but 1950s flooring and shuttered windows remain, expect rowdiness and cheap booze. It's on the 1st floor up hidden steps, look for the sign; take a wander round sprawling and atmospheric **Jadu Babu Bazar** to the rear while in the area.

### Discos and nightclubs

At hotels: **Incognito** (Taj Bengal), closed Mon, understated, relaxed ambience, 30-plus crowd, good food, taped music, fussy dress codes. **Someplace Else** (Park Hotel).

Pub, live bands play loud music to the same crowd each week. **Tantra** (Park Hotel). Taped music, large floor, young crowd, no shorts or flip-flops, cover charge. Next door **Roxy** is less popular, but has free entry and is more relaxed, with slouchy sofas upstairs. **Underground** (Hindusthan International). Good live band, young crowd, good sizzlers, pool tables. The noisy dance-bar beneath **Ginger** restaurant (106 SP Mukerjee Rd, T033-2486 3052/3, near JD Park metro) accommodates same-sex couples, open 1130-2330. You can hear a variety of live music (Wed-Fri) at pub/club **The Basement** (Samilton Hotel), 35A Sarat Bose Rd, where there's also a shisha place on the rooftop. **Shisha Reincarnated**, Block D, 6th floor, 22 Camac St, T033-2281 1313, www.shisha reincarnated.com. Open 1800-2400, Wed, Fri and Sat -0200. Dark and stylish with a chilled atmosphere and low red lights, huge bar lined with spirits, and DJs every night (varying music styles) and a decent sized dancefloor. Hookahs cost Rs 300, the roof-deck is the best place to hang out.

## ⊕ Entertainment

**Kolkata** *p277, maps p278, p281, p283, p285*
The English-language dailies (*Telegraph*, *Times of India*, etc) carry a comprehensive list.

### Cinema
A/c and comfortable cinemas showing English-language films are a good escape from the heat, and many are still very cheap. Check the newspapers for timings; programmes change every Fri. **Elite**, SN Banerjee Rd, and **New Empire Cinema**, New Market St, are conveniently close to Sudder St. **Nandan Complex**, AJC Bose Rd, T033-2223 1210, shows classics and art house movies; the **Kolkata International Film Festival** is held here in Nov, an excellent event. Swish **Inox** multiplexes (www.inox movies.com) are scattered around town (Forum, City Centre); tickets for these are Rs 100-150 and can be booked by credit

card over the phone. **Fame cinema**, www.famecinemas.com, Rs 100-250, in South City Mall is open 1000-0100, ticket line T4010-5555.

### Dance, music, theatre and art
Regular performances at **Rabindra Sadan**, Cathedral Rd. **Kala Mandir**, 48 Shakespeare Sarani. **Gorky Sadan**, Gorky Terrace, near Minto Park. **Sisir Mancha**, 1/1 AJC Bose Rd. **ICCR**, 9A Ho Chi Min Sarani, has a lovely new concert hall. You can see Bengali theatre of a high standard at **Biswaroopa**, 2A Raja Raj Kissen St, and **Star Theatre**, 79/34 Bidhan Sarani. **Girish Mancha**, government theatre complex, 76/1 Bagbazar St, T033-2554 4895.

### Galleries
**Academy of Fine Arts**, Cathedral Rd (see page 286).
**Ahuja Museum for Arts**, 26 Lee Rd (Elgin Rd crossing with AJC Bose), T033-2289 4645, www.ahujaptm.com/museum. The private collection of Mr SD Ahuja contains over 1200 works of art, which are displayed here in rotation.
**Bengal Gallery, ICCR**, 9A Ho Chi Min Sarani. Has a large space showing established artists.
**Chemould Art Gallery**, 12F Park St. One of the big names in contemporary art, and worth keeping an eye on.
**CIMA Gallery**, 2nd floor, Sunny Towers, 43 Ashutosh Chowdhury Av, T033-2485 8717, www.cimaartindia.com. Tue-Sat 1100-1900, closed Sun, Mon 1500-1900. The best exhibition space in the city and the shop has a good stock in wall-hangings, metalwork, clothes, stoles, ornaments, etc.
**Experimenter**, 2/1 Hindustan Rd, Gariahat. A trendy contemporary space with great exhibitions by Indian and international artists.
**The Harrington Street Arts Centre**, 2nd Floor, 8 Ho Chi Minh Sarani. Cool white space in an old apartment, hosting quality photography and art exhibitions.
**Seagull Arts and Media Centre**, 36C SP Mukherjee Rd (just off Mukherjee on a

sidestreet), T033-2455 6492/3, www.seagull
india.com. Holds regular photography
exhibitions (see listings in the daily papers)
from 1400-2000. Also has a bookshop on
the opposite side of SP Mukherjee.
**Studio 21**, 17/L Dover Terrace (off
Ballygunge Phari), T033-2486 6735, studio21.
gallery@gmail.com. A minimalist new space
for emerging artists from all disciplines, art/
photography exhibitions change regularly.

### Performing arts

English-language productions are staged by
the British Council and theatre clubs. **Sangeet
Research Academy**, near Mahanayak Uttam
(Tollygunge) Metro station, a national centre
for training in Indian Classical music, stages
free concert on Wed evenings. **Rabindra
Bharati University**, 6/4 Dwarakanath Tagore
Lane, holds performances, particularly during
the winter, including singing, dancing and
*jatras*. *Jatra* is community theatre, highly
colourful and exaggerated both in delivery
and make-up, drawing for its subject romantic
favourites from mythology or more up to
date social, political and religious themes.

## ✹ Festivals

**Kolkata** *p277, maps p278, p281, p283, p285*
**Jan** Ganga Sagar Mela at Sagardwip,
105 km south of Kolkata, where the River
Hugli joins the sea, draws thousands of
Hindu pilgrims.
**Mar/Apr** Holi (*Dol Purnima*) spring festival.
**Jun-Jul** Ratha Yatra at Mahesh, nearby.
**Sep-Oct** Durga Puja, Bengal's celebration
of the goddess during **Dasara**. See box,
page 172.
**Oct-Nov** Diwali (*Kali Puja* in Bengal) is the
festival of lights.
**Dec** Christmas. Many churches hold special
services, including Midnight Mass, and the
New Market takes on a new look in Dec as
Barra Din (Big Day) approaches with stalls
selling trees and baubles. Other religious
festivals are observed as elsewhere in India.

## ○ Shopping

**Kolkata** *p277, maps p278, p281, p283, p285*
Most shops open Mon-Sat 1000-1730 or
later (some break for lunch). New Market
stalls, and most shops, close on Sun.

### Books

**College St**, a thicket of second-hand
pavement bookstalls along this street mainly
for students but may reveal an interesting 1st
edition for a keen collector (see page 286).
**Crossword**, Elgin Rd. Deservedly popular
chain store, with 2 floors of books, CDs,
good selection of magazines and films
and a busy coffee shop.
**Earthcare Books**, 10 Middleton St (by
Drive Inn), T033-2229 6551, www.earthcare
books.com. Excellent selection of children's
books, Indian-focussed titles, socially
conscious books, plenty of fiction, has
small photo exhibitions.
**Kolkata Book Fair**, Milan Mela Prangan,
EM Bypass, www.kolkatabookfair.net.
End of Jan for a fortnight, stalls sell
paperback fiction to antiquarian books.
**Mirza Ghalib St**. Has a string of small shops
selling new, used and photocopied versions
of current favourites. Bargaining required.
**Oxford Book Shop**, Park St. Huge selection
of English titles, postcards and films, nice
café upstairs where you can browse through
titles. Excellent for books on Kolkata, and a
children's bookshop next door.
**Seagull**, 31A SP Mukherjee Rd, T033-2476
5869/5, www.seagullindia.com. Large and
unusual stock of art-related books, coffee-
table tomes, etc.
**Starmark**, top floor, Emami Centre, 3 Lord Sinha
Rd, T033-2282 2617-9; also City Centre and
South City Mall. The best selection of fiction
in Kolkata, plus imported magazines, films.

### Clothes and accessories

**Ananda**, 13 Russell St. Fancy saris.
**Anokhi**, Shop 209, Forum Shopping Mall,
10/3 Lala Lajpat Rai Sarani, near AJC Bose Rd.
Beautiful block-print bed-linens, floaty bed-

wear, scarves, accessories, clothes and more. Made in Jaipur, mid-range prices.
**Biba**, South City Mall, Prince Anwar Shar Rd, www.bibaindia.com; also has franchises in **Pantaloons** department stores. Chic cotton print dresses, tasteful *salwar*.
**Fabindia**, 16 Hindustan Park (also branches at Woodburn Park Rd, near AJC Bose Rd, and City Centre Mall in Salt Lake). Clothes, textiles, toiletries, rugs and home furnishings from fair-trade company. Hugely successful due to their tasteful and high-quality selection. Well worth a visit.
**Gomukh**, next to **Raj's Spanish Café**, 7 Sudder St. Traveller wear, plus a range of scarves and wall-hangings, cheap and well stocked.
**Khazana**, Taj Bengal (see Where to stay, page 294). For pricey textiles, Baluchari saris, *kantha* embroidery, etc, and souvenirs.
**Ritu's Boutique**, 46A Rafi Ahmed Kidwai Rd. *Kurtas* and saris.

### Government emporia

Government emporia are mainly in the town centre and are fixed-price shops. All the Indian states are represented at **Dakshinapan**, near Dhakuria Bridge, Mon-Fri 1030-1930, Sat 1030-1400, excellent selection of handloom and handicrafts. **Central Cottage Industries**, 7 JL Nehru Rd, is convenient as is **Kashmir Art**, 12 JL Nehru Rd. **Phulkari**, Punjab Emporium, 26B Camac St. **Rajasthali**, 30E JL Nehru Rd. **Tripura**, 58 JL Nehru Rd. **UP**, 12B Lindsay St.

### Handicrafts and handloom

There are many handicraft shops around Newmarket St, selling batik prints, handloom, blockprints and embroidery, but starting prices are usually excessive so bargain hard. Shops listed below are all either fair trade-based or associated with self-help groups.
**Artisana**, 13 Chowringhee Pl (off Gokhale Rd), T033-2223 9422. Handloom and handicrafts, traditional hand-block textiles, designer jewellery, metalware and more.

**Ashalayam Handicrafts**, 1st floor, 44 Mirza Ghalib St. Products made by street children who have been trained and given shelter by the **Don Bosco Ashalayam Project**. Proceeds are split between the artisans and the trust.
**Calcutta Rescue Handicrafts**, Fairlawn Hotel. Thu 1830. Medical NGO sells great selection of cards, bags and trinkets made and embroidered by former patients.
**Kamala**, 1st floor, Tagore Centre, 9A Ho Chi Min Sarani, T033-2223 9422. Outlet shop for the Crafts Council of West Bengal; great selection of textiles, jewellery, gifts and trinkets at very reasonable prices (sourced directly from the artisans).
**Karmyog**, 12B Russell St. Gorgeous handcrafted paper products.
**Sasha**, 27 Mirza Ghalib St, T033-2252 1586, www.sashaworld.com. Attractive range of good-quality, fair trade textiles, furnishings, ceramics, metalwork, etc, but not cheap, welcome a/c.

### Jewellery

**Bepin Behari Ganguly St** (Bow Bazar) is lined with mirrored jewellers' shops; **PC Chandra**, **BB Dutt**, **B Sirkar** are well known. Also many on Rash Behari Av. **Silver market** (*Rupa bajar*) is off Mirza Ghalib St opposite Newmarket. Gold and silver prices are listed daily in the newspapers.

### Markets

**New Market**, Lindsay St, has more than 2500 shops (closed Sun). You will find mundane everyday necessities to exotic luxuries, from fragrant florists to gory meat stalls. Be prepared to deal with pestering basket-wallahs.

Kolkata has a number of bazaars, each with a character of its own. In **Bentinck St** are Muslim tailors, Chinese shoemakers plus Indian sweetmeat shops and tea stalls. **Gariahat market** early in the morning attracts a diverse clientele (businessmen, academics, cooks) who come to select choice fresh fish. In **Shyambazar** the coconut market lasts from 0500 to 0700. **Burra Bazar** is a hectic wholesale fruit market held daily. The colourful **flower market** is on Jagannath Ghat on the river bank. The old **China Bazar** no longer exists although **Tiretta Bazar** area still retains its ethnic flavour; try an exceptional Chinese breakfast from a street stall.

### Music and musical instruments
**Braganza's**, 56C Free School (Mirza Ghalib) St, T033-2252 7715. An institution; with an extensive collection.
**Music World**, 18G Park St, T033-2217 0751. Sells a wide range of all genres.
Also head to the southern end of Rabindra Sarani for musical instruments (sitars, tablas, etc).

### Tailors
Garments can be skilfully copied around New Market and on Madge Lane. Tailors will try to overcharge foreigners as a matter of course.

## ⊙ What to do

**Kolkata** *p277, maps p278, p281, p283, p285*
**Body and soul**
Look out for adverts around Sudder St for yoga classes held on hotel rooftops.
**Aurobindo Bhavan**, 8 Shakespeare Sarani, T033-2282 3057. Very informal yoga classes, women on Mon/Wed/Fri 1530-1930, men on Tue/Thu/Sat 130-1930 (Rs 200). Bring a copy of your passport and visa.

### Cricket
Occasional Test matches and One-Day Internationals and regular IPL fixtures at Eden Gardens, see page 282, 100,000 capacity; get tickets in advance.

### Golf
**Royal Calcutta Golf Club**, 18 Golf Club Rd, T033-2473 1352. Founded in 1829, the oldest golf club in the world outside the UK.
**The Tollygunge Club**, 120 Despran Sasmal Rd, T033-2473 5954. The course is on land that was once an indigo plantation.

### Horse racing
**Royal Calcutta Turf Club**, T033-2229 1104, www.rctconline.com. Racing takes place in the cool season (Nov to early Apr) and monsoon season (Jul-Oct). The Derby is in the 1st week of Jan. It's a fun, cheap day out in the public stands, better still if you can access the members enclosure to get up close to the racehorses and enjoy a drink in the bar with antlers mounted on the wall.

### Sightseeing tours
**Calcutta Walks**, www.calcuttawalks.com. Run interesting walks through the city and also do cruises on the Hooghly.
**WBTDC**, departure point is Tourism Centre, 3/2 BBD Bagh E, 1st floor, T033-2248 8271. Daily tours, 0830-1730. Tour stops at: Eden Gardens, High Court, Writers' Building, Belur Math, Dakshineswar Kali Temple, Jain Temple, Netaji Bhavan, Kolkata Panorama and Esplanade, Victoria Memorial, St Paul's Cathedral and Kali Ghat. Entry fees not included. Private tour operators also offer city tours. Approved guides from **Govt of India Tourist Office**, T033-2582 5813.

### Swimming
**Wet 'O' Wild**, at Nicco Park, HM Block, Salt Lake City. Kolkata's best waterpark with a truly enormous pool and wave machine. The **Hindustan International Hotel** pool is open to non-residents (Rs 500).

### Volunteer work
Many people come to Kolkata to work with one of the many NGOs. The following organizations accept volunteers, though it's wise to contact them in advance (except for the **Missionaries of Charity**, where you only need to attend one of the registration days).
**Don Bosco Ashalayam Project**, T033-2643 5037, www.ashalayam.org. Rehabilitates young homeless people by teaching skills.
**Hope Kolkata Foundation**, 39 Panditya Pl, T033-2474 2904, www.hopechild.org. An Irish charity focussing on the needs of disadvantaged children.

**Missionaries of Charity (Mother Teresa)**, The Mother House, 54A AJC Bose Rd, T033-2249 7115. The majority of volunteers work at one of the Mother Teresa homes. Induction/registration sessions are at 1500 on Mon, Wed and Fri in various languages.

## ⊖ Transport

**Kolkata** p277, maps p278, p281, p283, p285
Kolkata is at the eastern end of the Grand Trunk Rd (NH2). Many city centre roads become one way or change direction from 1400 to 2100 so expect tortuous detours.
**Air** Enquiries T033-2511 8787, www.calcuttaairport.com. The spacious terminals are well organized and have been recently renovated. A reservation counter for rail (same-day travel only) is found in the Arrivals hall. There are money changers by the exit of the terminal.

For transport into town, pre-paid taxis (office closes at 2200) to the city centre cost about Rs 350 (deluxe cars Rs 550-700). From the city centre to the airport costs the same or less if you bargain hard. New a/c buses leave from directly outside Arrivals, going to Howrah station (via the city centre) and Esplanade (from where it is a 15-min walk to Sudder St), taking 1 hr and costing Rs 40. They also go to Tollygunge. The old public bus is not recommended for new arrivals as it's a 400-m walk across the car park to main the road, and then changing for the nearest Metro station which is at Dum Dum; auto-rickshaws to the Metro cost about Rs 80.

**Domestic**: For schedules and prices it's best to visit a 3rd-party booking site such as www.yatra.com or www.makemy trip.com. Airlines include: **Air India**, 50 Chowringhee Rd, T033-2282 2356, airport T033-2248 2354. **Jet Airways**, 18D Park St, T033-3989 3333, airport T033-2511 9894. **IndiGo**, Crescent Tower, 229 AJC Bose Rd, T033-4003 6208, www.goindigo.com; and **Spicejet**, T1800-180 3333, www.spicejet.com.

**Bicycle** Bike hire is not easy; ask at your hotel if a staff bike is free. Spares are sold along Bentinck St, north of Chowringhee.
**Bus Local**: State transport services run throughout the city and suburbs from 0500-2030; usually overcrowded after 0830, but very cheap (minimum Rs 5 on the big blue-yellow buses, which are noteworthy for their artwork) and a good way to get around. Maroon minibuses (little more expensive, minimum Rs 6) cover major routes. Newer a/c buses are becoming commonplace.

**Long distance**: An extensive hub and spoke bus operation from Kolkata allows cheap travel within West Bengal and beyond, but long bus journeys in this region are gruelling as roads are generally terrible, and are a last resort when trains are full. The tourist office, 3/2 BBD Bagh, has timetables. Advance bookings at computerized office of **Calcutta State Transport Corp (CSTC)**, Esplanade, T033-2248 1916.
**Ferry Local**: to cross the Hugli, between Howrah station and Babu Ghat, Rs 5, except Sun. During festivals a ferry goes from Babu Ghat to Belur Math, 1 hr.
**Metro** The Metro is usually clean, efficient and punctual. The recently extended Metro line runs for 25 km from Dum Dum in the north to Kavi Subhash in the south from 0700-2145, Sun 1400-2145, every 7-12 mins; fare Rs 4-14. Note that Tollygunge has been renamed 'Mahanayak Uttam Kumar' on station signs, but is still commonly referred to as Tollygunge. There are women-only sections interspersed throughout the train. A further 5 metro lines are planned for the future.
**Rickshaw** Hand-pulled rickshaws are used by locals along the narrow congested lanes. Auto-rickshaws operate outside the city centre, especially as shuttle service to/ from Metro stations along set routes. Auto-rickshaws from Sealdah station to Sudder St cost about Rs 70.
**Taxi** Car hire with driver: **Gainwell**, 8 Ho Chi Minh Sarani, T033-2454 5010; **Mercury**, 46 JL Nehru Rd, T033-2244 8377. Tourist taxis from **India Tourism** and **WBTDC** offices.

Local taxis are yellow. Ambassadors: insist on the meter, then use conversion chart to calculate correct fare.

**Train** Kolkata is served by 2 main railway stations, **Howrah** and **Sealdah**. Howrah station has a separate complex for platforms 18-21. Enquiries, Howrah, T033-2638 7412/3542, 'New' Complex, T033-2660 2217, Sealdah, T033-2350 3535. Reservation, T138 (computerized). Foreign tourist quota is sold at both stations until 1400, at which point tickets go on general sale. Railway reservations, Fairlie Place, BBD Bagh; 1000-1300, 1330-1700, Sun 1000-1400 (best to go early), tourists are automatically told to go to the Foreign Tourist Counter to get Foreign Tourist Quota. It takes 10-30 mins. You will need to show your passport and complete a reservation form. Payment in rupees is accepted; you can also pay in US dollars, sterling or euros, but expect a poor exchange rate.

Trains listed depart from Howrah (**H**), unless marked '(**S**)' for Sealdah. **Agra Fort**: *Jodhpur Exp 12307*, 2320, 20 hrs; (**S**) *Sealdah Ajmer Exp 12987*, 2320, 19 hrs, *Howrah Mumbai Mail 12321*, 2200 (**Gaya**, 7½ hrs). **New Delhi**: *Rajdhani Exp 12301*, 1655 (except Sun), 17 hrs; *Rajdhani Exp 12305*, 1405 (Sun), 20 hrs.

**New Jalpaiguri** (**NJP**): (**S**) *Kanchenjunga Exp 15657*, 0635, 11½ hrs; *Shatabdi Exp 12041*, 1415, 8 hrs; (**S**) *Darjeeling Mail 12343*, 2205, 10 hrs; *Kamrup Exp 15959*, 1735, 12½ hrs.

**Tram** Kolkata is the only Indian city to run a tram network. 0430-2300. 2nd-class carriage Rs 4, front '1st class' Rs 4.50, but no discernible difference. Many trams originate at **Esplanade depot** and it's a great way to see the city – ride route 1 to Belgachia through the heart of North Kolkata's heritage, or route 36 to Kidderpore through the Maidan. Route 26 from the **Gariahat depot** in the south all the way to Howrah, via Sealdah and College St. Services run from 0430-2230, with a restricted service at the weekends.

## ⓘ Directory

**Kolkata** *p277, maps p278, p281, p283, p285*
**Banks** There are 24-hr ATMs all over the city centre. Money changers proliferate on Sudder St. **Cultural centres and libraries** British Council, Information Centre, L&T Chambers, 16 Camac St, T033-2282 5370. Mon-Sat 1100-1900. Good for UK newspapers, reference books. **French Association**, 217 AJC Bose Rd, T033-2281 5198. **Goethe Institut**, Max Mueller Bhavan, 8 Pramathesh Barua Sarani, T033-2486 6398, www.goethe.de/kolkata. Mon-Fri 0930-1730, Sat 1500-1700. **Internet** You will need your passport to register the first time you visit an internet café. Many across the city; lots in Sudder St area with Skype, printing, etc; standard charge is Rs 20 per hr. On Sudder St, very helpful and with good equipment are **Hotline Services**, daily 0830-2200. In the city centre, **E-Shan Digital Services**, 13B CR Av, T033-2225 5716, fast connection but no Skype, Rs 25 per hr, Mon-Sat 0900-2100. **Medical services** Apollo Gleneagles Hospital, 5B Canel Circular Rd, T033-2320 3040. Wockhardt Medical Centre, 2/7 Sarat Bose Rd, T033-2475 4320, www.wockhardt hospitals.net, reliable diagnostic centre. **Woodlands Hospital**, 8B Alipore Rd, T033-2456 7076-9. There are many chemists around Lindsay St and Newmarket. **Angel**, 151 Park St (24-hr). **Dey's**, 6/2B Lindsay St. **Moonlight**, 180 SP Mukherjee Rd (24-hr).

# Contents

## At a glance

⊙ **Getting around** Bagdogra airport for quick access to the hills, then jeeps are the most frequent and fastest way to travel.
◔ **Time required** A week for a good taste of the highlands, plus a week for a trek around Darjeeling.
☼ **Weather** Best in Oct-Nov and Mar-May, although skies can be very clear in Dec-Jan if you can take the cold.
✘ **When not to go** During Bengali holidays if you want any peace, as Kolkata evacuates en masse to the hills.

★ Don't miss ...
1 Eat, drink and be merry; Darjeeling has that holiday feel, page 307.
2 The intense nostalgia of a steam train, page 311.
3 Singalila trek, 160 km into the Himalaya, page 312.
4 Low-key Kurseong for tea estates, views and walking, page 315.
5 Atmospheric hotels for every budget in Kalimpong, page 316.

# West Bengal Hills

*The Himalayan foothills of northern West Bengal contain a wealth of trekking opportunities and hill stations in stunning locations including the region's prime tourist destination, Darjeeling. The old colonial summer retreat is surrounded by spectacular views and still draws plenty of visitors to enjoy cooler climes and a good cuppa. The area also holds one of the Indian one-horned rhino's last safe havens in the Jaldapara Wildlife Sanctuary.*

*Tensions often flare in the region over demands for a separate Gorkha (ethnic Nepali) state to be carved out of West Bengal. Protests result in strikes (bandhs) and road closures and occasional violence, though these are never directed at foreigners. Check the latest situation before travelling.* ▸▸ *For listings, see pages 318-329.*

## Siliguri → *For listings, see pages 318-329.*

Surrounded by tea plantations, **Siliguri** is a largely unattractive transport hub with busy main roads lined with shops, a couple of good markets and one of the largest stupas in India (30 m) at **Salugara Monastery**, 5 km away. The narrow-gauge diesel train to Darjeeling (supposedly taking seven hours but in reality taking much longer) was suspended at the time of writing. Siliguri is an essential stopping-off point for travel into the hills. Bagdogra airport is nearby, with connections to Kolkata and Guwahati, and there are several comfortable hotels should you get stuck overnight.

Useful tourist information is available from **WBTDC** ① *1st floor, 4 Hill Cart Rd, T0353-251 7561, www.westbengaltourism.gov.in, Mon-Fri 1000-1730, also at NJP Station and airport.* On the opposite side of Hill Cart Rd, the **Darjeeling Gorkha Hill Council (DGHC)** ① *T0353-251 1974/9, Mon-Fri 0900-1700, Sat-Sun 0900-1300,* tourism office has little information but takes bookings for its lodges in North Bengal.

## Darjeeling → *For listings, see pages 318-329.*

For tens of thousands of visitors from Kolkata and the steamy plains, Darjeeling is a place to escape the summer heat. Built on a crescent-shaped ridge the town is surrounded by hills, which are thickly covered with coniferous forests and terraced tea gardens. The idyllic setting, the exhilarating air outside town, and stunning views of the Kangchenjunga range (when you can see through the clouds) attract plenty of trekkers too. Nevertheless, Darjeeling's modern reality is a crowded, noisy and, in places, shockingly dirty and polluted town. Between June and September the monsoons bring heavy downpours, sometimes causing landslides, but the air clears after mid-September. Winter evenings are cold enough to demand log fires and lots of warm clothing.

### Arriving in Darjeeling

**Getting there Bagdogra**, near Siliguri, is Darjeeling's nearest airport. Trains connect New Jalpaiguri (NJP) with Kolkata and other major cities. The diesel 'toy train' runs from Siliguri/NJP in season and is picturesque but very slow (the service was suspended at the time of research, due to a landslide). Most people reach Darjeeling by jeep and arrive at the motor stand in the lower town, though some go to **Clubside** on The Mall, which is more convenient for most accommodation. ▸▸ *See Transport, page 327.*

**Getting around** Most of Darjeeling's roads slope quite gently so it is easy to walk around the town. The lower and upper roads are linked by a series of connecting roads and steep steps. For sights away from the centre you need to hire a taxi. Be prepared for seasonal water shortages and frequent power cuts. After dark a torch is essential.

**Tourist information** WBTDC ① *Bellevue Hotel, 1st floor, 1 Nehru Rd, T0354-225 4102, 1000-1700, off-season 1030-1600,* not much information available. **DGHC** ① *Maple Tourist Lodge, Old Kutchery Rd (below Natural History Museum), T0354-225 5351, Mon-Sat 1030-1600 (closed 2nd and 4th Sat in month),* relocated, since the old office on the Mall was burnt down in 2011. There's also a **DGHC kiosk** ① *Clubside, daily 1000-1600.*

## Background

Darjeeling means region of the *dorje* (thunderbolt) and its official but rarely used spelling is Darjiling. The surrounding area once belonged to Sikkim, although parts were annexed from time to time by the Bhutanese and Nepalese. The East India Company returned the territory's sovereignty to the Rajas of Sikkim, which led to the British obtaining permission to gain the site of the hill station called Darjeeling in 1835, in return for an annual payment. It was practically uninhabited and thickly forested but soon grew into a popular health resort after a road and several houses were built and tea growing was introduced. The Bengal government escaped from the Kolkata heat to take up its official summer residence here. The upper reaches were originally occupied by the Europeans, who built houses with commanding views. Down the hillside on terraces sprawled the humbler huts and bazars of the Indian town.

## Places in Darjeeling

In the pedestrianized centre of town, on the ridge, **Chowrasta** is the natural heart of Darjeeling and particularly atmospheric at dawn and dusk. The **Mahakal Mandir** atop **Observatory Hill**, sacred to Siva, is a pleasant walk though the views of the mountains are obscured by tall trees. Sacred to both Hindus and Buddhists, the temple is active and colourful, with prayer flags tied to every tree and pole in the vicinity. Beware of the monkeys as they bite. Further along Jawahar Road West is **Shrubbery (Nightingale) Park**, a pleasant detour if still too early to visit the zoo. Views to the north are excellent from the renovated park, and evening cultural shows take place here (information from the **DGHC** tourist office).

**Padmaja Naidu Himalayan Zoological Park** ① *daily 0830-1630 (summer), 0830-1600 (winter) except Thu, Rs 100,* houses high-altitude wildlife including Himalayan black bears, Siberian tigers, Tibetan wolves and plenty of red pandas, as well as deer, a multitude of birds and the gorgeously marked rare clouded leopard. There are large enclosures over a section of the hillside, though at feeding time and during wet weather they retreat into their small cement enclosures giving the impression that they are restricted to their cells. There is a reasonably successful snow leopard breeding programme, with over 40 births since 1983, and it is the only Asian zoo to have successfully introduced red pandas into the wild. Entrance fees to the zoo also include the **Himalayan Mountaineering Institute** ① *T0354-227 0158, no photography, entrance is through the zoo on Jawahar Rd West.* Previously headed by the late Tenzing Norgay who shared the first climb of Everest in 1953, the Institute has trained up many a mountaineer and runs training courses during dry months of the year (see page 326). Within the complex, the **Everest Museum** traces the history of attempted climbs from 1857 and the **Mountaineering Museum** displays old equipment including that used on the historic Tenzing-Hillary climb.

The decaying **Natural History Museum** ⓘ *Bishop Eric Benjamin Rd, 0900-1630, Rs 10,* was set up in 1903 has a large collection of fauna of the region and a certain charm; the basement has a curious diorama and specimen jars. The **Tibetan Refugee Self-help Centre** ⓘ *T0354-225 5938, thondup@cal.vsnl.net.in, Mon-Sat 0800-1700, closes for lunch,*

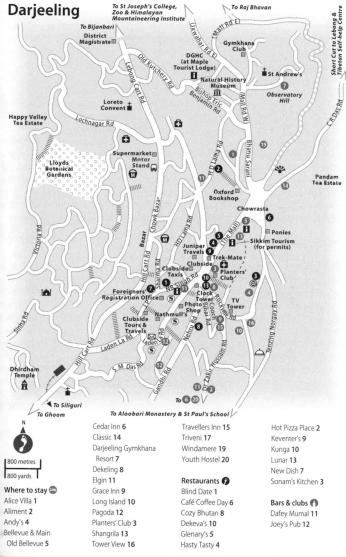

# Darjeeling

To St Joseph's College, Zoo & Himalayan Mountaineering Institute

To Bijanbari

District Magistrate

To Raj Bhavan

Gymkhana Club

DGHC (at Maple Tourist Lodge)

Natural History Museum

St Andrew's

Observatory Hill

Short Cut to Lebong & Tibetan Self-help Centre

Lebong Cart Rd

Old Kutchery Rd

Bishop Eric Benjamin Rd

Loreto Convent

Happy Valley Tea Estate

Lochnagar Rd

Lloyds Botanical Gardens

Supermarket Motor Stand

Bhanu Sarani

Pandam Tea Estate

Victoria Rd

Chow Bazar

Bazar

Hill Cart Rd

Oxford Bookshop

Chowrasta

Ponies

Sikkim Tourism (for permits)

Juniper Travels

Trek-Mate

Clubside Taxis

Clubside

Planters' Club

Foreigners' Registration Office

Clock Tower

Photo Shop

TV Tower

Nathmull's

Clubside Tours & Travels

Laden La Rd

Dhirdham Temple

To Ghoom

To Siliguri

S. M. Das Rd

Gandhi Rd

To Aloobari Monastery & St Paul's School

N

800 metres

800 yards

**Where to stay** 🏠
Alice Villa 1
Aliment 2
Andy's 4
Bellevue & Main
  Old Bellevue 5

Cedar Inn 6
Classic 14
Darjeeling Gymkhana
  Resort 7
Dekeling 8
Elgin 11
Grace Inn 9
Long Island 10
Pagoda 12
Planters' Club 3
Shangrila 13
Tower View 16

Travellers Inn 15
Triveni 17
Windamere 19
Youth Hostel 20

**Restaurants** 🍴
Blind Date 1
Café Coffee Day 6
Cozy Bhutan 8
Dekeva's 10
Glenary's 5
Hasty Tasty 4

Hot Pizza Place 2
Keventer's 9
Kunga 10
Lunar 13
New Dish 7
Sonam's Kitchen 3

**Bars & clubs** 🍸
Dafey Mumal 11
Joey's Pub 12

# Darjeeling tea gardens

An ancient Chinese legend suggests that 'tay', or tea, originated in India, although tea was known to have been grown in China around 2700 BC. It is a species of Camellia (*Camellia thea*). After 1833, when its monopoly on importing tea from China was abolished, the East India Company made attempts to grow tea in Assam using wild chai plants found growing there. Tea plants were later introduced to Darjelling and the Nilgiri hills, in the south. Today India is the largest producer of tea in the world. Assam grows over half and Darjeeling about a quarter of the nation's output. Once drunk only by the tribal people, it has now become India's national drink.

The orthodox method of tea processing produces the aromatic lighter coloured liquor of the Golden Flowery Orange Pekoe in its most superior grade. The fresh leaves are dried by fans on withering troughs to reduce the moisture content and then rolled and pressed to express the juices which coat the leaves. These are left to ferment in a controlled environment to produce the desired aroma. Finally the leaves are dried by passing them through a heated drying chamber and then graded – the unbroken being the best quality, down to the fannings and dust. The more common crushing, tearing, curling (CTC) method produces tea which gives a much darker liquor.

Most of Darjeeling's tea is sold through auction houses, the largest centre being in Kolkata. Tea tasting and blending are skills that have developed over a long period of time and are highly prized. The industry provides vital employment in the hill areas and is an assured foreign exchange earner.

with its temple, school and hospital is north of town. From Chowrasta, take the lane to the right towards the viewpoint, and then walk down for about 30 minutes (ask around). After the Chinese invasion, thousands of Tibetan refugees settled in Darjeeling (many having accompanied the Dalai Lama) and the rehabilitation centre was set up in 1959 to enable them to continue to practise their skills and provide a sales outlet. You can watch them at work (carpet weaving, spinning, dyeing, woodwork, etc) during the season, when it is well worth a visit. The shop sells fabulous woollen carpets (orders taken and posted), textiles, curios and jewellery, though not cheap to buy.

On the way to the refugee centre is the lovely **Bhutia Bustee Monastery**, which was built on Observatory Hill in 1765 but was moved to its present position in 1861. Someone will show you around and point out gold-flecked murals that have been gorgeously restored. South of town, the **Aloobari Monastery**, on Tenzing Norgay Road, is open to visitors. Tibetan and Sikkimese handicrafts made by the monks are for sale.

Near the market are **Lloyd Botanical Gardens** ① *Mon-Sat 0600-1700*. These were laid out in 1878 on land given by Mr W Lloyd, owner of the Lloyd's Bank. They have a modest collection of Himalayan and Alpine flora including banks of azaleas and rhododendron, magnolias, a good hothouse (with over 50 species of orchid) and a herbarium. It a pleasant and quiet spot. **Victoria Falls**, which is only impressive in the monsoon, provides added interest to a three-hour nature trail. There are several tea gardens close to Darjeeling, but not all welcome visitors. One that does is the **Pattabong Estate** on the road towards Sikkim.

## Around Darjeeling

ⓘ *Roads can get washed away during the monsoon and may remain in poor condition till Oct.*

At **Ghoom** (**Ghum**), altitude 2257 m, is the important **Yiga Choeling Gompa**, a Yellow Hat Buddhist Monastery. Built in 1875 by a Mongolian monk, it houses famous Buddhist scriptures (beautifully displayed) in an interior the colour of the surrounding forests. The austere monastery is a nice walk, at the end of Ghoom's main market street. Also worth visiting is the **Sakyaguru Monastery**, closer to the Darjeeling road, which has 95 monks. It is highly recommended to make the 11-km (45-minute) journey to Ghoom from Darjeeling by **steam train**, ending up at the highest railway station in India. The little **Railway Museum** ⓘ *Rs 20, daily 1000-1300 and 1400-1600, ticket from station and staff will unlock the gate*, outlines the history of the Darjeeling Himalayan Railway and has some interesting old photos. A few spruced-up carriages offer a tourist-only ride in summer with a photo stop at **Batasia** (departing 1040, returning 1200, and again at 1320, returning 1440; but check times at the station or www.dhr.in, Rs 240); bookings must be made 90 days in advance, although it is possible to buy spare seats on the day from agents who have private counters set up at Darjeeling station. Alternatively, take the passenger steam train at 1015 (first class Rs 144; second class Rs 5), which goes to Kurseong via Ghoom, or the diesel train at 0915 (first class Rs 144; second class Rs 27), and return on foot or by jeep. All pass through **Batasia Loop**, 5 km from Darjeeling on the way to Ghoom, which allows the narrow-gauge rail to do a figure-of-eight loop. There's a war memorial here in a pleasant park with good mountain views.

The disused **Lebong Race Course**, 8 km from Darjeeling, was once the smallest and highest in the world and makes a pleasant walk, heading down from Chowrasta. It was started as a parade ground in 1885, and there is now talk of it becoming a race course once more.

If the weather is clear, it is worth rising at 0400 to make the hour's journey for a breathtaking view of the sunrise on Kangchenjunga at **Tiger Hill** ⓘ *shared jeep from Darjeeling Rs 80-100 return, just go to Clubside motor stand at 0430 to pick one up.* Mount Everest (8846 m), 225 km away, is visible on a good day. The mass of jeeps and the crowds at sunrise disappear by mid-morning; it's a nice walk back from Tiger Hill (about two hours, 11 km) via Ghoom and the **Japanese Peace Pagoda**, where drumming between 1630-1900 is worth seeing.

## Trekking around Darjeeling → *For listings, see pages 318-329.*

The trekking routes around Darjeeling are well established, having been popular for over 100 years. Walks lead in stages along safe tracks and through wooded hills up to altitudes of 3660 m. Trails pass through untouched nature filled with rhododendrons, magnolias, orchids and wild flowers, together with forests, meadows and small villages, with a stunning backdrop of mountains stretching from Mount Everest to the Bhutan hills, including the third highest mountain in the world, **Kanchenjunga**. The best trekking seasons are April to May, when the magnolias and rhododendrons are in full bloom, and October to November when air clarity is best. In spring there may be the occasional shower. In autumn the air is dry and the visibility excellent. In winter the lower altitude trails that link Rimbick with Jhepi (18 km) can be very attractive for birdwatchers. There is an extensive network of varied trails that link the hillside towns and villages. Agents in Darjeeling can organize four- to seven-day treks, providing guide, equipment and accommodation (see page 326), though it is perfectly possible to go it alone.

In a bid to provide employment for local youth, the **West Bengal Forest and Wildlife Department** is strongly encouraging visitors to take a guide/porter when entering the Singalila National Park. If you haven't arranged a trek through an agent in Darjeeling, local guides can be hired in Manebhanjang for Rs 300-500 per day (although paying more secures someone who speaks good English and has a better knowledge of local flora and fauna); porters are Rs 200-250. Entry fees for the park are also paid at the checkpoint in Manebhanjang (foreigners Rs 200, still camera Rs 50, video camera Rs 100).

## Singalila trek

The 160-km Singalila trek starts from the small border town of **Manebhanjang**, 26 km from Darjeeling. The journey to and from Darjeeling can be done by shared or private jeep in one hour. Walking north to Sandakphu (rather than starting in Sandakphu and heading south) means you are always walking towards the most stunning views. Other possible starting points are: **Dhotrey** (a further hour by jeep, north of Manebhanjang which cuts out a large chunk of the steep ascent to Tonglu; or **Rimbick**, going via Gurdum to Sandakphu. If you have not arranged for transport to meet you at a particular point there it is entirely possible to travel back to Darjeeling from any roadhead by jeep, with services at least once daily, often three to four times daily.

**Note** Singalila is not an easy trek, several parts are very steep and tough. Even up to May, temperatures at night are freezing and it is essential to take plenty of warm clothes.

There are plenty of government Trekkers' Huts and private lodges of varying standards and prices (on an organized trek these will have been booked for you) at Tonglu, Sandakphu, Phalut, Gorkhey, Molley, Rammam, Rimbick, Siri Khola and other villages. Although room is usually available, it's wise to book in advance during May/June and October when trails can be very busy. Any trekking agent in Darjeeling can arrange bookings for a small fee. Private lodges, such as **Sherpa Lodge** in Rimbick and Rammam, and other trailside lodges in Meghma, Jaubari and Kalpokhri, are generally friendly, flexible and provide reasonable basic accommodation. Some places can prepare yak curry on request, and be sure to sample hot *chhang*, the local millet brew, served in a wooden keg and sipped through a bamboo straw.

The entire area is a birdwatcher's paradise with more than 600 species including oriole, minivets, flycatchers, finches, sunbirds, thrushes, piculets, falconets and Hoodson's Imperial pigeons. The mixed rhododendron, oak and conifer forests are particularly well preserved

**Day 1 To Tonglu (or Tumling)** 1 km beyond Manebhanjang town you reach a rough stone paved track leading sharply up to the left. Tonglu (3030 m) is 11 km from this point if you follow the jeep track, slightly less if you take the frequent but very steep short cut. Alternatively, head for Tumling, just the other side of the peak of the hill from Tonglu (you take the alternative road from Meghma and rejoin the main route 1 km after Tumling. There is a Trekkers' Hut at **Tonglu** with 24 beds and a fine view of the Kanchenjunga range. From here you can also see the plains of North Bengal and some valleys of Nepal in the distance. Closer to hand are the snow-fed rivers, the Teesta in the east and Koshi in the west. You can also sleep in **Tumling** where **Shikhar Lodge** has simple basic and clean rooms, run by a local teacher's friendly family, "fabulous supper and breakfast" plus a lovely garden. There are tea shops at **Chitre** and at **Meghma**, which has an interesting monastery noted for its large collection of Buddhist statues; (108, according to locals). Ask at the tea house opposite to get in.

**Day 2 To Jaubari and Gairibans** A level walk along the ridge takes you past the long 'mani' wall to the Nepalese village of Jaubari; no visa is needed and good accommodation is available should you wish to spend a night in Nepal. After Jaubari the trail turns sharply to the right back into Indian territory and down through bamboo and rhododendron forests to the village of Gairibans in a forest clearing. You could carry on all the way to Sandakphu, a long day's hiking.

**Day 3 To Sandakphu** It is 14 km uphill to Sandakphu, with a lunch break in Kalpokhri with its attractive attractive 'black' lake surrounded by fir trees, about midway. Even in winter the lake never freezes. The last 3 km from Bhikebhanjang (tea shop) to Sandakphu are particularly steep; this section takes more than an hour but the views from the Singalila Ridge make it all worthwhile. **Sandakphu**, a small collection of lodges and government buildings located at 3636 m, is the highest point in West Bengal and the finest viewpoint on the trek (the prime destination for most visitors). Located 57 km from Darjeeling, it is accessible by jeep (the same narrow bumpy track used by trekkers), which is how many Indian tourists make the journey during the season. Sandakphu offers fantastic views, including the eastern face of Everest (8846 m, 140 km away as the crow flies), Kanchenjunga (8586 m), Chomolhari (the highest peak in Bhutan), Lluhe and Makchu (the fourth and fifth highest peaks in the world, respectively) and numerous peaks such as Pandim that lie in Sikkim. A five-minute walk past the towering Sherpa lodge brings you to three hillocks on the left side of the path; the middle one of these is the very highest point at 3636 m.

# Darjeeling treks

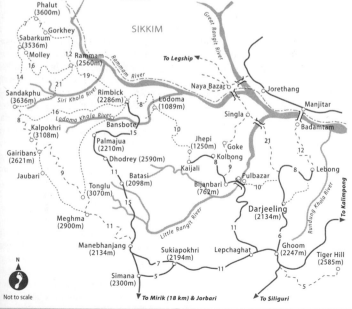

There is a Trekkers' Hut and several lodges, each with a dining area, toilets and cookhouse. These vary widely in standards and price, some costing up to Rs 500 per person with attached bathroom; it's worth seeing a few. The drive back to Manebhanjang by pre-arranged 4WD can take four hours along the very rough track, if you finish the trek here.

**Day 4 Sandakphu to Phalut** Phalut, 22 km from Sandakphu along an undulating jeepable track, is at the junction of Nepal, Sikkim and West Bengal. It offers even closer views of Kanchenjunga. It is best to avoid trekking here in May and June and mid-September to 25 October when large numbers of college trekking teams from West Bengal descend on the area. From Phalut it's possible to get a jeep back the way you came, via Sandakphu. Alternatively you can walk south for 4 km back towards **Bhikebhanjang** and then take a 16-km-long trail through fine forests of the Singalila National Park down to **Rimbick**.

**Day 5 Phalut to Rimbick** From Phalut, it takes around four hours to reach **Gorkhey**, which has accommodation, and it's a further 3 km to the village of **Samanden**, hidden in a hanging valley. From Samanden, it is a 6-km walk to **Rammam** where there is a clean, comfortable **Sherpa Lodge** in a tiny garden, recommended for friendly service and good food. Alternatively, the Trekkers' Hut is a 100-m climb (in the direction of Molley) before Rammam village. From Rammam it is a 1½-hour walk down to a couple of private lodges and a Trekkers Hut at **Siri Khola** and a further 1½ hours to Rimbick. Again, this area has a wealth of birdlife. From Rimbick there are around three jeeps a day to take you back to Darjeeling (Rs 100, four hours).

Although Gorkhey, Phalut, Rammam and Rimbick lie just south of the border with Sikkim, entering Sikkim is not permitted on this route, though agents say this may change in future; ask in Darjeeling about the current situation.

## Sabarkum via Ramman to Molley or Bijanbari

An alternative quieter trail links Sabarkum (7 km before Phalut on the main Sandakphu–Phalut trail) with Rammam, with a possible overnight halting stay at the Trekkers' Hut in **Molley**. (Note: the manager of Molley Trekkers' Hut is often to be found at the Forest Office in Sabarkum; look for him on the way through in order to secure a room). Those with five days to spare can return by the **Rammam–Rimbick–Jhepi–Bijanbari** route (153 km). From Rammam you can cross by a suspension bridge over the Siri Khola River and follow the path up the valley, which leads to Dentam in Sikkim. This less well-trodden valley has rich birdlife (particularly kingfishers), and excellent views of undisturbed forest. From **Bijanbari** (762 m) it is possible to return to Darjeeling, 36 km away by jeep, or climb a further 2 km to Pulbazar and then return to Darjeeling, 16 km away. Those wishing only to go to Rimbick can get a jeep from there, or may return to Manebhanjang via Palmajua and Batasi (80 km).

---

## Mirik → *For listings, see pages 318-329.*

The small low-key hill station of **Mirik**, at an altitude of 1600 m, has forests of japonica, orange orchards and tea gardens all within easy walking distance. Its restful ambience, dramatic views and homely accommodation make it an appealing stop for a couple of days' relaxation or for good day-trekking. The focal point is **Sumendu Lake** encircled by a 3.5-km cobbled promenade that makes a pleasant stroll, and which offers boating and pony rides. **Krishnannagar**, south of the lake, is the main tourist centre while older Miri

Bazar, north of the lake, has a more local vibe. To orientate yourself and plan treks, pick up an excellent map from the **Ratnagiri Hotel** in Krishnanagar.

Towering **Bokar Gompa**, a 15-minute uphill walk from the main road in Krishnanagar, is definitely worth visiting (daily chanting at 0530 and 1500). If you continue walking from the monastery, past old Mirik Church and some pretty houses, you reach **Rametay Dara** (Mirik's highest point at 1695 m) with a series of viewpoints across the hills to the plains. Equally impressive are the views to Nepal from the look-out tower at **Kawlay Dara** (east of Mirik), considered best at sunrise but worthwhile at any time. Near here, the tea gardens of the **Thurbo Tea Estate** roll over perfect hillocks and encompass the little **Mahadev Tar Temple** where the mark of Siva's footprint and trident imprint the rocks. Visits to the Thurbo factory can be arranged, ask your hotel for help. Another excellent walk (four to five hours) goes from the Don Bosco Church (open 0900-1000, 1400-1600) down a new road and stone paths to the *bustee* (village) and tea gardens of **Marma Tea Estate**. From here forest trails and tracks can be followed up and down past orange orchards, squash canes and colourful houses to Mirik Bustee and on to Mirik Bazar. Jeeps ply this route should you become weary; from Marma to Mirik Bazar costs Rs 25. You can even trek to Kurseong (five to six hours) starting from Marma, going down to the Balasan River to cross a large bridge, and up the winding road on the other side. Or, less ambitiously, take a jeep 6 km up the Darjeeling road and walk back past the rolling Thurbo Tea Estate and little villages of flower-laden cottages.

## Kurseong → *For listings, see pages 318-329.*

Kurseong (1450 m) or 'Place of the White Orchid' east of Mirik, is a small town worthy of a couple of nights' pause on the way to/from Darjeeling. Surrounded by tea gardens and orange orchards (through which there is pleasant walking to be done), locals will sincerely tell you that they call Kurseong 'paradise'.

There are no grand sights in the town, but it is an interesting hike up to the ridge, via St Mary's hamlet (north of the market along Hill Cart Road). Shortcuts past quaint houses and the eerie Forestry College lead up to **St Mary's Well** and **Grotto**, which has fine views and a shrine with candles. Tracks through a young forest reach imposing Dow Hill School, established 1904, and either continue up and over the ridge to tiny Chetri Bustee, or bear right to the little **Forest Museum** at Dow Hill. Head back down via scenically located **Ani Gompa**, housing a small community of nuns belonging to the Red Hat sect, and past pretty cottages. It's around a five-hour walk with stops; ask locals for directions, but double any time frame they give to destinations. Useful sketch maps can be provided by **Cochrane Place** (see Where to stay, page 321), where it is also possible to arrange guided hikes tailored to match walkers' interests and stamina. In the town itself there's the narrow and crowded *chowk* market to explore, while a half-hour walk from the railway station brings you to **Eagle's Crag** (shadowed by the TV tower), an awesome vantage point in clear weather.

The **Makaibari Tea Estate**, 4 km from town, makes an interesting excursion. Dating from 1859 it is India's oldest tea garden, responsibly managed by charismatic Rajah Banerjee who has done much to support the community and initiate environmental and organic development on the estate. The highest price ever fetched at a tea auction was for Makaibari leaves when Rs 18,000 was paid for a kilogram in 2003. Nearby **Ambootia Tea Estate** also conducts factory visits, and from here there's a walk to an ancient Siva temple amid massive Rudraksh and Banyan trees. Kurseong is famed for its plethora of boarding schools. At **Tung** nearby, the St Alphonsus Social and Agricultural Centre, run by a Canadian Jesuit, is working with the local community through education, housing, agricultural, forestry and marketing projects. They welcome volunteers; contact **SASAC** ⓘ *Tung, Darjeeling, West Bengal, T0354-234 2059, sasac@satyam.net.in*. The steam train to Darjeeling leaves every afternoon, supposedly at 1500.

## Kalimpong → For listings, see pages 318-329.

Set in beautiful wooded mountain scenery with an unhurried air about it, Kalimpong was a meeting point of the once 'Three Closed Lands' on the trade route to Tibet, Bhutan and Nepal. Away from the crowded and scruffy centre near the motor stand, the town becomes more spaced out as mountain roads wind up the hillsides leading to monasteries, mission schools and orchid nurseries. Some say that the name is derived from *pong* (stronghold) of *kalon* (king's minister), or from *kalibong*, a plant fibre.

From Darjeeling, the 51-km journey (2½ hours) is through beautiful scenery. The road winds down through tea estates and then descends to 250 m at Tista where it crosses the river on a 'new' concrete bridge. 'Lovers' Meet' and 'View Point' give superb views of the Rangit and Tista rivers.

### Arriving in Kalimpong
**Getting there** Bagdogra is the nearest airport and New Jalpaiguri the nearest railhead. Buses and shared jeeps arrive from there at the Bazar Motor Stand in about 2½ hours. ▶▶ *See Transport, page 327.*

**Getting around** The centre is compact enough to be seen comfortably on foot. The surroundings are ideal for walking, though some may prefer transport to visit nearby sights.

**Tourist information** DGHC ⓘ *DB Giri Rd, Mon-Sat 0930-1700, Sun-1230*, tourist office can advise on walking routes and rafting. Also see www.kalimpong.org.

### Places in Kalimpong
The traditional **market** at 10th Mile has a great atmosphere. The *haat* here every Wednesday and Saturday draws villagers who come to sell fruit, unfamiliar vegetables, traditional medicines, woollen cloth, yarn and much more. It is remarkably clean and laid back, a delight to explore. Unusual merchandise includes: curly young fern tops, bamboo shoots, dried mushrooms, fragrant spices, musk, *chaang* paraphernalia, large chunks of brown soap, and tiny chickens in baskets alongside gaudy posters.

There are a number of monasteries in and around Kalimpong; the oldest of which, **Thongsa Gompa Bhutanese Monastery** (1692), 10th Mile, has been renovated. The colourful **Tharpa Cheoling Monastery** (1922) has a library of Tibetan manuscripts and *thangkas*. Further north, is the **Tibetan Monastery** (Yellow Hat) at Tirpai. The **Pedong Bhutanese Monastery** (1837) near the old Bhutanese Damsang Fort at Algara (15 km away) holds ceremonial dances every February.

As well as monasteries, there are a couple of old churches worth popping into. The **Macfarlane Church** is close to the town centre, visible from the main street, and built in the Scottish style. **St Theresa's** was built by the Jesuits and resembles a Buddhist *gompa*; it is 2.5 km from the centre in 9th Mile. Another Scottish church is found at **Dr Graham's Home** on Deolo Hill, www.drgrahamshomes.org. The school was started by the missionary

Doctor John Anderson Graham in 1900 when he admitted six Anglo-Indian children. Now there are about 1000 pupils; visitors are welcome to the school as well as the dairy, poultry and bakery projects.

There are two handmade **paper factories** in town, both are small-scale enterprises employing around four people. You can buy their products and watch the paper-making process. **Gangjong Paper Factory** is a short walk from the centre of town, while **Himalayan Handmade Paper Industry** is a good place to stop off if walking from Tharpa Chelong Monastery back to Kalimpong (both open Monday-Saturday 1000-1600).

Kalimpong excels in producing orchids, amaryllis, roses, cacti, dahlias and gladioli. **Nurseries** include **Ganesh Mani Pradhan** on 12th Mile; **Universal** on 8th Mile; **Shanti Kunj** on BL Dikshit Road; and **Himalayan** on East Main Road.

# Kalimpong

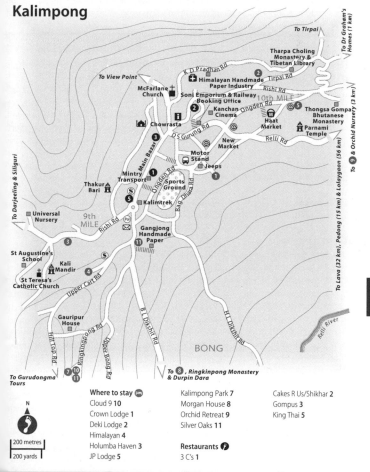

**Where to stay** 🛏️
Cloud 9 **10**
Crown Lodge **1**
Deki Lodge **2**
Himalayan **4**
Holumba Haven **3**
JP Lodge **5**

Kalimpong Park **7**
Morgan House **8**
Orchid Retreat **9**
Silver Oaks **11**

**Restaurants** 🍴
3 C's **1**

Cakes R Us/Shikhar **2**
Gompus **3**
King Thai **5**

## Walks

There are pleasant hikes along the Tista Road through rice fields to **Chitray Falls** (9 km), a three-hour walk to **Bhalu Khop**, and a 1½-hour downhill walk from the motor stand to the Relli River. You can picnic on the river beaches at Tista Bazar and Kalijhora.

Further afield, scenic two- to three-hour treks are possible from **Lava** (32 km east, monastery and weekly market on Tuesday), and **Kaffer** (**Lolaygaon**) (southeast, 56 km by road via Lava), which has spectacular views of Kangchendzonga. Lava especially is a popular destination for Bengali tourists in the school holidays. Rhododendrons flower in April around this region. Both villages are accessible by public jeep/bus from Kalimpong and have reasonably priced private and government accommodation (bookable at the Forest Dept at WBTDC office in Siliguri, see www.wbtdc.com); walking between the two is a lovely trek of about 10 km. There are other pleasant trails in the vicinity, and generally the walking is fairly level without too many ups and downs.

## West Bengal Hills listings

*For hotel and restaurant price codes and other relevant information, see pages 22-26.*

### ⬤ Where to stay

#### Siliguri *p307*

Hill Cart Rd is officially Tenzing Norgay Rd.
**$$$-$$ Cindrella**, Sevoke Rd, '3rd mile' (out of town), T0353-254 7136, www.cindrellahotels.com. Comfortable a/c rooms, decent pool, competent vegetarian restaurant, internet, car hire, pick-up from airport, breakfast included. Drinks in the bar or on the roof terrace.
**$$$-$$ Sinclairs**, Pradhan Nagar, T0353-251 2440, www.sinclairshotels.com. Architecturally curious from the outside, a/c rooms are comfortable with flatscreen TVs although getting a bit worn. The restaurant and O2 bar are stylish with good food, small pool is disappointing, attentive and warm service. Breakfast included.
**$$-$ Conclave**, Hill Cart Rd (opposite SNT bus stand), T0353-251 6144, www.hotel conclave.in. A newish hotel with good-quality rooms starting at Rs 950 per double, a/c, satellite TV, licensed bar, **Eminent** restaurant serving quality Indian/European food, intermittent internet, parking.
**$$-$ Yatri Hotel**, Hill Cart Rd (opposite main bus stand), T0353-251 4707, www.yatrihotel.in. Basic but clean rooms

with bath, some a/c, restaurant serves good food. The dim and cosy bar next door is a friendly place to have an icy beer (Rs 100-120) or watch some sport.
**$ Anjali Lodge**, Nabin Sen Rd (next to the Gurudwara), off Sevoke Rd, T0353-252 2964. Institutional building, bright white paint throughout, large rooms with concrete floors have clean sheets, towels, soap, TV, cheaper without a/c (doubles Rs 800/500), some have balcony or there is spacious public balcony. Suspicious staff soon warm up. A good choice.
**$ Mainak Tourist Lodge** (WBTDC), Hill Cart Rd (opposite main bus stand), T0353-251 2859, www.westbengaltourism.gov.in. Large and open 1970s-style hotel, 38 comfortable rooms (check a few, they vary), 14 a/c, and some **$$** suites. Set back from the road in dusty gardens, with restaurant and bar, helpful staff. Be sure not to overlap with a wedding party; call ahead.
**$ The Tiara**, Sevoke Rd (opposite the Gurudwara), T0353-243 6024, thetiarahotel@ hotmail.com. A 'boutique' hotel where ethnic mixes with kitsch (particularly in the lobby which has a plastic grotto, trees and fish pond). Top-floor rooms each styled with traditional designs and decor of NE Indian States. Public areas are clean and shiny, and the non-a/c rooms great value for a decent standard. Good restaurant (see Tera, page 323).

**Darjeeling** *p307, map p309*

Most hotels are within 2 km of the station and motor stand, a stiff walk uphill. Some top-end hotels include all meals and most offer discounts off season (Jul-Sep, Dec-Feb). Some charge extra for Christmas and New Year. Prices listed are for high season. There is a chronic water shortage, and you may find budget hotels ration their water supply.

**$$$$ Glenburn Tea Estate**, T(0)9830-070213, www.glenburnteaestate.com. Located over an hour from Darjeeling, in a beautiful tea garden. Lots of activities and good walking nearby; gorgeously restored main bungalow and equally attractive newer bungalow, each with 4 unique suites. Dinners are candlelit, public lounges charming, and the hospitality warm yet refined.

**$$$$ Windamere**, Observatory Hill, T0354-225 4041/2, www.windamerehotel.com. Enviable location, good views when clear, a true relic of the Raj. Spacious rooms and cottages (no phone or TV in some), beware those with dated bathrooms (limited hot water), terraces, chintzy and cluttered with memorabilia, coal fires (can be smoky), hotties in bed, pre-war piano favourites accompany tea. Lounge/bar is a characterful place for a drink, outside guests welcome for high tea (disappointing) or beer (Rs 180). Full-board only.

**$$$$-$$$ Cedar Inn**, Dr Zakir Hussain Rd, T0354-225 4446, www.cedarinndarjeeling.com. Slightly out of town, but with great views and free shuttle service to town throughout the day. Family friendly, health club, sauna, lovely garden with wrought iron furniture. Wood-panelled rooms are stylish and thoughtfully laid out (bathrooms a bit 1980s), fireplaces in some, public areas filled with enormous plants, bar and restaurant are welcoming and informal. Extension in same style as the original building, essential to book in advance.

**$$$-$$$ The Elgin**, HD Lama Rd, T0354-225 7226, www.elginhotels.com. Beautifully renovated 120-year-old colonial hotel, rooms are full of atmosphere with polished

floors, fireplaces, nooks and crannies while being plush and well-appointed, marble bathrooms. Photos, brass fittings and carpets give warmth to public spaces, lounge and bar area pleasantly like a country sitting room, tiered garden is small and flower-filled but looks onto a high fence. Annoyingly, there is no option but to take a package including all meals, and high tea is grossly overpriced for outside guests.

**$$$ Darjeeling Gymkhana Resort**, next to Gymkhana Club, T0354-225 4391, www.darjeelinggymkhanaresort.in. Wood-panelled rooms (all with fireplaces) are large and modern yet warm and welcoming. Nice location on Observatory Hill, club on doorstep for sports/activities. Particularly suited to families (4-bed rooms). Indian restaurant good, but its position in the central foyer means staff chatter can be irritating when you're in your room.

**$$ Bellevue**, Chowrasta, T0354-225 4075, www.bellevuehotel-darjeeling.com. Wide range of rooms with bath and geysers, some large, bright and airy (eg rooms 35, 49), some with fireplaces or stoves, all have loads of character with old wooden fittings. Genuinely friendly management. Very centrally located, and the small rooftop has unparalleled K'junga view.

**$$ Classic Guesthouse**, CR Das Rd (below Chowrasta), T0354-225 7025, www.classic guesthouse.in. A small and quiet guesthouse with a cute lawn, stunning views from the private balcony of each of the 4 large rooms. Plenty of furniture, heaters in winter, carpets, TV, decent big bathrooms. Rooms aren't stylish but they're very comfortable and the manager is nice.

**$$ Planters' Club**, The Mall, T0354-225 4348. Aka the 'Darjeeling Club', this wooden building dates from 1868 and oozes history from the curved veranda and creaking balconies. New decor in VIP rooms is actually unattractive, a better choice are the 'super' doubles which are dated but have a Raj ambience; huge fireplaces, white-painted furniture, bathrooms feel Victorian. Nice staff and a good place for an evening tipple (residents only).

**$$ Shangrila**, 5 Nehru Rd, T0354-225 4149, www.hotelshangriladarjeeling.com. A small and characterful hotel in a good spot near Chowrasta. Large rooms, tastefully renovated, subtly lit, flatscreen TVs, some with good views from the window seating. Swish new bathrooms, all double beds (no twins, 20% discount for single), 3 rooms have Victorian fireplaces. Excellent restaurant (see page 323).

**$$ Travellers Inn**, Dr Zakir Hussein Rd, T0354-225 8497. Very respectable rooms in a modern hotel, hot water, good views from the restaurant with booths, and a sweet indoor 'garden room' that catches any rays of sun.

**$$-$ Dekeling Resort**, 51 Gandhi Rd (The Mall), T0354-225 4159, www.dekeling.com. Homely rooms are noticeably warm, most have private bath (24-hr hot water), delightful lounge areas with stoves. Range of room tariffs, some attic front rooms with views, 2 doubles with shared bath are a bargain (No 11 is best). Good restaurant, brilliant hosts, reserve ahead (1 month in advance in high season). Noisy when jeeps depart at 0400 for Tiger Hill with lots of hooting.

**$$-$ Main Olde Bellevue Hotel**, Chowrasta, T0354-225 4178, www.darjeelinghotel.co.uk. Rooms with character in the Heritage bungalow on the hill are atmospheric although not high-spec, clear aspect from the picnic tables in the charming garden. Doubles in a newer front building are overpriced for shabby carpets and unrenovated bathrooms.

**$ Alice Villa**, 41 HD Lama Rd, below DGHC tourist office, Chowrasta, T0354-225 4181, hotelalicevilla@yahoo.com. Large clean rooms (fireplace in some, bucket of coal costs extra) in an old bungalow are simple, with colonial charm, and fairly priced. Bathrooms newly tiled in pastel shades and soft furnishings in the covered terrace are bad taste. The modern wing at the rear is not so appealing. Checkout 1200.

**$ Aliment**, 40 Zakir Hussain Rd, T0354-225 5068, alimentweb@sify.com. Clean rooms vary in size and cheerfulness, pay more for TV and 24-hr hot shower (otherwise hot water for 2 hrs each evening), cheap singles and triples (hot buckets Rs 10) average food in social restaurant (cheap beer), internet, packed with travellers, good atmosphere, excellent library.

**$ Andy's**, 102 Zakir Hussain Rd, T0354-225 3125, T(0)9434-166968, www.andysguest house.biz. Airy twin-bed rooms are notable for their cleanliness, some have hot shower (hot water on the night of arrival, and in the mornings) or hot buckets provided. Storage for trekkers, friendly and very honest atmosphere if slightly institutional. Discount for single travellers. Often full, ring ahead. No food.

**$ Grace Inn**, 8/B Cooch Bihar Rd, near TV Tower, T0354-225 8106, T(0)9832-615082, thegraceinn@sify.com. Some large, well-furnished rooms with hot water, the best are at the back (with views), subtly lit restaurant with ambitious menu, cheerful staff. Worth stopping by on the way to backpacker places, as massive discounts are sometimes available.

**$ Long Island**, Rockville Dham, Dr Zakir Hussein Rd, near TV tower, T0354-225 2043, pritaya19@yahoo.com. Attractive exterior, clean basic rooms, some with private shower (hot water 0800-2000) or share communal bathroom. Appealingly quaint restaurant, quiet location, internet, great views from rooftop and upper rooms. Run by friendly Nepali family. Recommended, single room rates, try to book ahead.

**$ Pagoda**, 1 Upper Beechwood Rd, T0354-225 3498. Clean but basic rooms with period furniture in a characterful building, some with bath (limited free bucket hot water), peaceful good value. Rooms at front better, though no much view from shared balcony. Away from the main backpacker scene and an easier walk from transport links. Very friendly, small library.

**$ Tower View**, Rockville Dham, down the back of TV Tower, T0354-225 4452. Pleasant, clean rooms, some with toilet but sharing bathrooms with hot bucket, more expensive with 24-hr hot water, wood stove and dusty book collection in the homely restaurant (which is a very popular place to eat, with a nice back terrace if the weather permits). Also a yoga-meditation retreat at **Nagri Farm Tea Estate**, 1 hr south from Darjeeling (www.artofliving.org).

**$ Triveni**, 85 Dr Zakir Hussain Rd, T(0)9932-673511, T(0)9932-345607. Basic box rooms with bath and hot bucket (Rs 10). Pleasant and low-key management, **Triveni** collects the overspill from the **Aliment** across the road. Good for solo travellers (some rooms share bath), 3-bed dorm, cheap doubles.

**$ Youth Hostel**, Dr Zakir Hussain Rd, T0354-225 2290. Mainly cheap dorm beds, superb position on top of the ridge, no restaurant, trekking information available.

### Trekking around Darjeeling *p311*
There is a large Trekkers' Hut at Galribans with about 20 beds.

**$$ Karmi Farm**, Bijanbari, www.karmifarm.com. A haven of rural peace at Kolbong, which you may choose to use as a base, north of Bijanbari (access via Kaijali, 4WDs stop 20 mins' walk away, or it's 2-3 hrs by pony from Pulbazar). 4 doubles with bath, simple but spotless, superb food, US$25 includes food/porters.

**$ Teacher's Lodge**, Jaubari. Excellent value.

### Mirik *p314*
The vast majority of accommodation is found in Krishnanagar on the south side of the lake, although there are also 3 hotels in Mirik Bazar on the north side.

**$$ Jagjeet**, Krishnanagar, T0354-224 3231, www.jagjeethotel.com. The cheapest rooms are comfortable but smell musty. Recommended to pay the extra for super deluxe (larger, wood-panelled, much more tasteful). Luxury rooms have contemporary settings and decor. Very good restaurant and bar.

**$-$ Ratnagiri**, Krishnanagar, T0354-224 3243, T(0)9641-041965, www.hotelratnagiri.com. A range of bright spotless

rooms, some with great views, and a cute garden for breakfast. Decent discounts negotiable for single travellers. The 2 split-level wooden cabins with working fireplaces are lovely. Excellent choice.

**$ Boudi**, Main Rd, Mirik Bazar, T(0)9932-483476 (ask for Nitai). You could choose to stay in friendly bustling Mirik Bazar (and be the only foreign tourist in the village). The back rooms have stupendous balcony views to Kanchenjunga and are a bargain. Bright paint, laminate floors, TV, hot water in the morning only, restaurant downstairs. Ask for clean sheets if it's low season – as chances are dust will have collected.

**$ Hotel Payal-cum-bar**, Main Rd, Mirik Bazar, T(0)9734-977541. Should the **Boudi** be full, the **Payal** has cheap singles with hot bucket, and more spacious rooms with geyser, all have TV. The restaurant-cum-bar is well stocked and staff sweet.

**$ Lodge Ashirvad**, Krishnanagar, T0354-224 3272, T(0)9832-439582. The best budget option with clean bright rooms, new paint and half-panelling, pay more for geyser or Rs 10 per hot bucket. Single Rs 200, doubles Rs 350/450. Rooftop with monastery views and run by a lovely family. Food available during high season. Recommended.

**$ Tourist Lodge**, 5 mins uphill from the lake, T0354-224 3371, T(0)9775-900101. Huge wood-panelled rooms, slightly more expensive for suites with balconies (excellent views), standard rooms have carpets (No 102 is best), newly tiled bathrooms, no single room rates, ignore the faded exterior.

### Kurseong *p315*
**$$-$ Cochrane Place**, 132 Pankhabari Rd, Fatak (2 km from Kurseong on the road to Mirik), T0354-233 0703, www.imperialchai.com. Rebuilt and recreated colonial home with deluxe rooms crammed with antiques and atmosphere, the personal touch of the owner in evidence throughout. Passion fruits grow by balconies, the tiered garden is delightful (organic veg), spa/yoga/meditation and 'stick' massage

are reasonably priced, superlative meals and tea menu (see page 324). Views of Kanchenjunga from some rooms. Newer annex is cheaper and simpler, still very comfortable with a chalet air. Dorm beds for backpackers. Lovely walking through tea gardens and villages nearby. Management are informative and interesting. Wheelchair access. Highly recommended.

**$$-$ Tourist Lodge**, Hill Cart Rd (1 km from station), T0354-234 4409. Gloomy corridors but some lovely wooden rooms (check a couple), good views, 24-hr hot water, heaters in winter, snack bar, decent bar and restaurant. Car hire. Recommended.

**$ Kurseong Palace**, 11 Hill Cart Rd, T0354-234 5409, kurseong_palace@yahoo.com. Acceptable rooms with TV and carpets, hot water, nice staff.

**$ Makaibari Homestays**, Makaibari, T033-2287 8560, www.makaibari.com. Villagers from the tea community provide all meals and a unique experience in their family homes, US$25 per day per couple, including all meals, Western toilets.

### Kalimpong p316, map p317

Hotels offer discounts during winter and monsoon.

**$$$ Silver Oaks**, Main Rd, T03552-255296, www.elginhotels.com. Beautiful rooms of a high standard have a Raj feel, some with fabulous views, buffet restaurant and rather formal bar, gorgeous terraced garden with views from the numerous seating areas.

**$$ Himalayan Hotel**, Upper Cart Rd, 10-min walk from town centre, T03552-255248, www.himalayanhotel.biz. The original stone-built characterful family home of the McDonalds has 8 rooms with traditional furnishings, wooden floors, working fireplaces, no TV, lovely common verandas. 2 well-designed cottages to the rear both have 4 rooms with TV, more modern, trellises and flowers in abundance. Mountain views from the attractive lawn, the restaurant has atmosphere (set menu), comfortable bar with TV, helpful

management. One of the oldest hotels in the area (since 1924). Charming.

**$$ Kalimpong Park**, Ringkingpong Rd, T03552-255304, www.kalimpongpark hotel.com. Raj atmosphere aplenty in the 4 good-sized, airy rooms in the Maharaja of Dinajpur's old 2-storeyed house, plus 20 rooms in newer building at rear. Both have new bathrooms and wooden floors; request a front room as back ones are decidedly gloomy. The **$$$** suites are not significantly better, soulless multi-cuisine restaurant but the pleasing bar (see Bars and clubs, page 325), large lawn and peaceful location are a big plus. It's a stiff walk from town. Car rental available, Wi-Fi.

**$$ Orchid Retreat**, Ganesh Villa, long walk from town (4 km from the market), T03552-274517, www.theorchidretreat.com. In an interesting orchid nursery, 6 rooms in traditional thatched cottages (built with local materials) and 4 in a duplex building, hot water (no TV or phone), home-cooked meals, lovely terrace garden with special palm collection, personal attention, peaceful. No walk-ins, must book in advance. Bring your own alcohol.

**$$-$ Holumba Haven**, 1 km before the motor stand, 9th Mile, T03552-256936, T(0)9332-414999, www.holumba.com. This charming place has 8 cottages (you will struggle to choose between them) spread through a nursery garden, amongst trees and with spacious lawns. Rooms are delightfully decorated, spotless and comfortable (no TVs), with piping hot water and real character. The owners have created a homestay atmosphere and are really friendly and informative. Singles start from Rs 700, doubles are Rs 950-2000, there are also triple rooms. Highly recommended.

**$$-$ JP Lodge**, RC Mintry Rd, T03552-257457, www.jplodge.com. Clean and simple rooms, charming staff, designated meditation space in a wood-panelled garret (also just a good place to hang out). Rates have increased too much though, and there are no single rates. See the website for details of their homestay, 20 km away in Munsong village.

**$$-$ Morgan House** (Kalimpong Tourist Lodge), Singamari, Durpin Dara Hill, 3 km from centre, T03552-255384. Beautiful location and a Raj-era building, 7 rooms with bath (good views from upstairs) but run-down and ill-managed, restaurant, bar, gardens.

**$ Cloud 9**, Ringkingpong Rd, T03552-259554, T(0)98932-039634. Clean respectable rooms though worn carpets, much better at front with balcony views, restaurant is average. Its proximity to the **Kalimpong Park Hotel** and the cosy Tibetan-styled TV lounge are the big plus points.

**$ Crown Lodge**, off Bag Dhara Rd, near Motor Stand, T03552-255846, T(0)9832-334575. 21 clean well-maintained rooms with hot water (Indian toilets), TV, generator, friendly and helpful, old-style kind of place. Doubles at the back with much light are spacious.

**$ Deki Lodge**, Tirpai Rd, 10 mins uphill from Motor Stand, T03552-255095, www.kalimpong.org/dekilodge/index.html. Very well-maintained rooms aimed at various budgets, nice terrace restaurant and outdoor seating area, kind and knowledgeable staff, a place with character. Recommended.

## 🍴 Restaurants

### Siliguri *p307*

**$$ Havelli**, SS Market Complex, Hill Cart Rd, T0353-253 5013. Open 1100-2230. Subtly lit, beige walls and wood sculptures prevail, more intimate than most. Multi-cuisine is high standard and the choices endless, including Continental. Family atmosphere.

**$$-$ Khana Khazana**, Hill Cart Rd. Open 0700-2230. Pleasant outdoor terrace plus indoor seating (fans), generous portions, South Indian is decent or there's a choice of tandoori, rolls, Chinese, veg/non-veg, but *lassis* and shakes are average. Clean family atmosphere.

**$$-$ Rasoi**, Ganeshayan Building (2nd floor), beside Sky Star Building, Sevoke Rd, T(0)99758-802071. Open 1030-2230. Pure veg food in a modern spacious environment, great for kebabs and South Indian (40 kinds of *dosa*), interesting *dhals*, plus some Chinese options.

**$$-$ Tera**, at The Tiara Hotel, 1st floor, Sevoke Rd, T0353-243 6024. An orderly restaurant with pleasing decor, tables with cloths and flowers, but a dominant TV screen. Mainly Indian cuisine, some Western breakfast choices, alcohol served.

**$ Jain Jaika Bhojnalaya**, Shikha Deep Building (3rd floor), Sevoke Rd. Opens 0800-1530, 1830-2130. Look for their red-and white sign down a tiny alley (there's a lift). Sunny orange walls and a chequered floor, pure veg food, best as a breakfast option (excellent *paratha* and veg – other items on menu generally unavailable).

### Darjeeling *p307, map p309*

Hotels with restaurants will usually serve non-residents. Several have bars.

**$$$-$$ New Elgin**, see The Elgin Hotel. Formal dining room with some character, OK meals, very pleasant service. Come for a slice of history rather than the food. Afternoon tea is overpriced, better to just have a drink and enjoy the surroundings.

**$$ Glenary's**, Nehru Rd (The Mall), T0354-225 7554, glens_getaways@sancharnet.in. Tearoom with excellent confectionery and pastries, friendly, 1st-class breakfast, Kalimpong cheese and wholemeal bread sold. Licensed restaurant upstairs is pricier but lively and with a good atmosphere, bar downstairs has local band on Sat (supposedly 1900-2200 but often finishes early). Speedy internet café.

**$$ Shangrila**, see Where to stay, page 320. Darjeeling's most chic dining experience, contemporary decor mixed with tasteful Tibetan artefacts, and a wide menu of delicious multi-cuisine food plus bar. Gracious service, open later than most. Recommended.

**$$-$ Café Coffee Day**, Chowrasta. A good spot to watch the world go by with a decent coffee, plus great views from the terrace.
**$$-$ Lunar**, 51 Gandhi Rd, T0354-225 4194. Open from 0730. Thoroughly delicious pure veg Indian dishes, and some decent sandwiches, pizzas and Chinese. Modern and informal, family environment, big windows for the view. *Lassis* are fragrant and creamy, service competent and kindly.
**$ Blind Date**, top floor, Fancy Market, NB Singh Rd, T0354-225 5404. Open 0930-1900. Warm and friendly place always packed with locals, cheap Tibetan and Chinese mains, divine soups and clean kitchen in open view, more limited choice for vegetarians.
**$ Cozy Bhutan**, Gandhi Rd. Open 0930-1930. Bhutanese cuisine consists of lots of beef and pork, plus a few interesting veg options, mix of mild or spicy. Friendly and charismatic elderly lady in charge. Lowest ceilings in Darjeeling, darkened cubby holes are rather gloomy.
**$ Dekeva's, Dekling Hotel**, 52 Gandhi Rd, Clubside. Nice little place with Tibetan specialities, plus Chinese and Continental, cosy, very popular.
**$ Hasty Tasty**, Nehru Rd. Good pure vegetarian fast food, Indian, Chinese, pizzas and sandwiches, popular *thalis* aren't very spicy. Canteen-style service, cheap.
**$ Hot Pizza Place**, HD Lama Rd. Genuinely great pizza plus other Western-friendly meals and snacks, one big table holds all-comers. Folks rave about it.
**$ Keventer's**, Nehru Rd, Clubside. This Darjeeling classic has a rooftop, serving snacks, with fabulous views.
**$ Kunga**, Gandhi Rd. Open 0830-2030. Cheerful unpretentious Tibetan joint, with great *momos*, also pizzas and huge backpacker-friendly breakfasts. But it's the range of fantastic soups that are most memorable. Has toilets.
**$ New Dish**, JP Sharma Rd. Open 0800-1930. Adventurous menu, mainly Chinese (cheap), excellent chicken entrées, friendly staff. Scruffy aquamarine mirrored walls, serves beer.

**$ Sonam's Kitchen**, Dr Zakir Hussein Rd. Open for breakfast, lunch and dinner (but not in between), Sonam has built up a loyal following for her home-cooking. Menu is limited, service can take a while, but the French toast is a must. Coffee will blow your head off.

### Mirik *p314*
The restaurant at the **Jagjeet** hotel is excellent with a varied menu; there are extremely cheap *dhabas* near the bus stand offering passable noodle and other dishes. Meals in **Mirik Bazar** are half the price of Krishnanagar (**Boudi Hotel** has great veg *momos*).
**$ Blue Lagoon**, behind PWD Rest House, near the lake, Krishnanagar. Open 0600-2130. Good Indian and Chinese veg and non-veg, served in a pleasant 'hut' with checked tablecloths and windows all around
**$ Hills Restaurant**, near the jeep stand, Main Rd, Krishnanagar. Open from 0700 but closes early. Popular little place, with some Indian dishes alongside Tibetan and Chinese, delicious *thupka*.
**$ Lakeside Restaurant**, near the boat shed. Pure vegetarian food in a simple little eatery, with a couple of tables outside on the edge of the lake.
**$ Samden**, next to Jagjeet Hotel, Main Rd, Krishnanagar. Open 0700-2030 (later than most). Great Tibetan food, spicy chai, monks for dining companions. At the time of writing the restaurant was being rebuilt, and was operating from a basement down a side alley.

### Kurseong *p315*
**$$ Chai Country**, at Cochrane Place (see Where to stay, page 321). A meal at **Cochrane** is not to be missed when in Kurseong. Food is gourmet and inventive, best are the Anglo-Indian dishes with a twist (*dhal* with mint, oyster mushrooms smoked with tea) otherwise African curry, veggie shepherd's pie and more; puddings are exquisite (baked mango). No liquor license.

**$ Abhinandan Fast Food Corner**, Naya Bazar (on way to Eagle's Crag). Open 0900-2030. Cubby hole, with lampshades made of fishing basket traps and character, good veg rolls, *thukpa*, *momos*.

**$ Gorkha Bhancha Ghar**, at the railway, opposite the platform. Open 0700-1900. This specialist *bhancha ghar* (kitchen) serves up cheap and excellent Nepali food in clean surroundings.

**$ Hill Top**, 11 TN Rd, T(0)9933-129177. Good for Chinese and Tibetan in a cosy restaurant-cum-bar that makes a nod to Chinese decor. Cheap beer.

**Kalimpong** *p316, map p317*
Most restaurants shut at 2000. Little restaurants behind the jeep stand dish out delicious *momos* and noodle soups at rock-bottom prices. Be sure to try some Kalimpong cheese, which has been produced since the days of the Swiss Jesuits, available from **Lark's Provisions** (and very cheap).

**$$ Gompus**. Open 1000-2100. Largely meat-based menu, good for Tibetan and Chinese, very popular and a nice environment, alcohol served.

**$$ King Thai**, 3rd floor, Maa Supermarket, T(0)8670-235007. Open from 0900-2130 (but sometimes till 0200 at weekends). Excellent food (more Chinese than Thai, despite the name) attracting a real mix of people. Warmly decorated and professional staff, alcohol served. Live music every night.

**$$-$ 3C's** (formerly **Glenary's**), Main Rd. Hangout for local youth, with mainly Western food, breakfast items, great pastries and average coffee. Best for the buzzy vibe rather than the food.

**$ Cakes R Us**, past DGTC on DB Giri Rd. Café-style offerings.

**$ Shikhar**, next to **Cakes R Us**. Open 0700-1930. Dirt cheap and all vegetarian, limited menu of *momos*, chow, huge bowls of *thukpa* and lassis in a busy basement.

**$ Vegetarian Snacketeria**, Main Rd, opposite Main Bazar. Tasty South and North Indian plus a wide choice of drinks.

## 🍸 Bars and entertainment

**Darjeeling** *p307, map p309*
English-language films show at the **Inox** cinema in Rink Mall. Seats from Rs 90-140.

There are several great options for a *chota peg* in Raj-era surroundings. Sadly the **Planters' Club** bar (see Where to stay, page 319), among the moth-eaten animal trophies, is only open to residents, but the **Windamere** (see Where to stay, page 319) compensates with a cosy lounge-feel among knik-knaks, or the **Gymkhana Club** for billiards, worn leather seats, and bags of atmosphere. **Joey's Pub**, though housed in an unlikely looking heritage cottage, gathers a rowdy crowd every night for drinks in a true pub ambiance. Surprisingly good typical British bar snacks, very social, open 0930-2300. **Dafey Mumal**, Laden La Rd, has a decent bar upstairs (strong beer only).

**Kalimpong** *p316, map p317*
The nicest place for a drink is the bar at the **Kalimpong Park Hotel**, which has a cosy lounge attached and green cane furniture on the small terrace, open until 2100 (beer Rs 130). Also pleasant, though not very pub-like, is the **Himalayan Hotel**.

## ✺ Festivals

**Darjeeling** *p307, map p309*
**Apr/May** Buddha Purnima/Jayanti celebrates the birth of the Buddha in the monasteries.

## 🛍 Shopping

**Darjeeling** *p307, map p309*
The markets by the motor stand are colourful and worth visiting.

### Books
**Greenland**, Laden La Rd, up some steps near entrance to **Prestige Hotel**. Book swap.
**Oxford Bookshop**, Chowrasta. Good stock especially local interest, one of West Bengal's best bookshops.

### Handicrafts

Local handicrafts sold widely include Buddhist *tankhas* (hand-painted scrolls surrounded by Chinese brocade), good woodcarving, carpets, hand-woven cloth, jewellery, copper, brass and white metal religious curios such as prayer wheels, bowls and statues. Chowrasta shops are closed on Sun, Chowk Bazar and Middle Bazar on Thu. **Dorjee**, Laden La Rd. **Eastern Arts**, Chowrasta. **H Mullick**, curios from Chowrasta, a cut above the rest. **Nepal Curios**, Laden La Rd. **Tibetan Refugee Self-help Centre** (see page 309), hand-woven carpets in bold designs and colours (from US$360 including packaging, at least 6-month waiting list).

### Tea

**Nathmull's**, Laden La Rd (above GPO) and at Rink Mall, nathmulls@goldentips tea.com. An institution, vast selection (Rs 140-10,000 per kg), avoid fancy packs, knowledgeable owner.

### Kalimpong *p316, map p317*
### Handicrafts

Tibetan and Nepalese handicrafts and woven fabrics are particularly good. There is an abundance of shops on RC Mintry Rd. **Gangjong**, Primtam Rd (ask at Silver Oaks Hotel for directions). Interesting paper factory. **Soni Emporium**, near Motor Stand, Mani Link Rd. Specializes in Himalayan handicrafts.

### ⏾ What to do

### Siliguri and Jaldapara *p307*
### Tour operators

**Help Tourism** (Association of Conservation & Tourism), 143 Hill Cart Rd, 1st floor, T0353-253 5893, www.helptourism.com. Recommended for eastern Himalaya and arranging homestays in villages around the tea gardens.

### Darjeeling *p307, map p309*
### Clubs

**Planters' Club**, The Mall, T0354-225 4348, the old Darjeeling Club, a relic of the Raj, membership (Rs 50 per day for hotel residents only), allows use of pleasant colonial restaurant (buffet meals cost extra), bar, billiards, a bit run down but log fires, warm and friendly.

### Mountaineering

**Himalayan Mountaineering Institute**, in the zoo compound, T0354-225 4087, www. himalayanmountaineeringinstitute.com. Office open Mon-Sat 1000-1300. Runs mountaineering training courses, from 'adventure' level (15-day, US$250, Nov-Dec and Apr-May), through basic (28-day, Mar-May and Sep-Nov) to advanced (28-day, Mar, May and Sep).

### Riding

Pony rides are popular starting at Chowrasta (Rs 100 per hr); also possible to do a scenic half-day ride to Ghoom – agree price in writing.

### River rafting

On the Tista, a range of trips from 1½ hrs to 2-day camps with fishing (Rs 2500 for 6 or more, transport extra), contact **DGHC** (see below).

### Tour operators

**Clubside Tours & Travels**, JP Sharma Rd, T0354-225 5123, www.clubside.in. Hotel booking, tours, treks, good jeep hire, air tickets for all domestic carriers.
**DGHC** (see page 308), runs a variety of tours leaving from the tourist office, including to Mirik, Tiger Hill, Darjeeling town and surrounding areas. Price lists are available at the office.
**Darjeeling Transport Corp**, 30 Laden La Rd. Maruti vans, jeeps, Land Rovers and a few *sumos* are available. Prices vary according to the season so negotiate rates.
**Meghma Tours & Travels**, 51 Gandhi Rd, T0354-228 9073, meghmatourstravels@ yahoo.co.in. A variety of day tours as well as trips into Sikkim.

# Border crossing: India–Nepal

**Kakarbhitta**, the Nepalese border town, about one hour from Siliguri, has only basic accommodation if you get stuck. The border is open 24 hours. Visas cost US$30 paid in exact cash (there are money-changers at the border, but rates are very bad), and you'll need two passport photos. From the border, a few buses depart around 0300-0600 arriving the same evening in Kathmandu (595 km, 15-16 hours), or night buses leave between 1500-1800; the journey can be very tiring. From Kakarbhitta it is also possible to fly (seasonal) from Bhadrapur (3 km away from Kakarbhitta) to Kathmandu (one hour). Alternatively, get a taxi to Biratnagar in Nepal (150 km) from where there are more reliable flights.

## Trekking agents

**Himalayan Travels**, 18 Gandhi Rd, T0354-225 2254, kkgurung@cal.vsnl. net.in. Long established, good for Sikkim and Singalila treks, tours to Bhutan (need 3-5 days' notice, US$180-240 per day depending on group size).
**Samsara Travel**, T0354-225 6370, www.samsaratourstravelsandtreks.com.
**Trek-Mate**, Singalila Arcade, Nehru Rd, T0354-225 6611, chagpori@satyam.net.in. Well-equipped, English-speaking guides, excellent service, recommended.

**Kalimpong** *p316, map p317*
**Gurudongma Tours & Travels**, T03552-225204, www.gurudongma.com. High-quality, personalized treks, priced accordingly. Recommended.
**Mintry Transport**, Main Rd. Jet Airways and Air India agent.

## ☺ Transport

### Siliguri *p307*

Try to arrive at **Siliguri** or **NJP** in daylight (before 1900). Rickshaw drivers can be quite aggressive at NJP.
**Air** Bagdogra Airport, 13 km away, has daily flights to **Kolkata**, **Guwahati** and **Delhi** with Air India, SpiceJet, GoAir and JetKonnect. Also daily flights to **Chennai**. Helicopter daily in fine weather to **Gangtok**, depending on demand. Taxis to Darjeeling (Rs 1300), Gangtok (Rs 1700),

Kalimpong (Rs 1150), Siliguri (Rs 330) and NJP (Rs 400).
**Bus** Siliguri is on NH31, well connected with Darjeeling (80 km), Gangtok (114 km) and Kalimpong (54 km) and served by buses from WB, Assam, Bihar, Sikkim and Bhutan.
Tenzing Norgay Central Bus Terminus (CBT) is on Hill Cart Rd, next to Siliguri Junction Railway Station. There are also many private operators just outside the CBT offering similar services. The WBSTC's overnight Rocket bus to **Kolkata** departs 1800, 1900 and 2000 from Hill Cart Rd, 12 hrs, Rs 215, but it's a tortuous journey on terrible roads. For greater comfort on a Volvo bus try **Gupta Tour & Travels**, T0353-645 4077, departing at 2000. Ticket counter 13 in the CBT for buses to Assam: **Guwahati** at 1700, 12 hrs, Rs 250; **Tezpur** at 1400, 16 hrs, Rs 330. SNT Bus Station, is opposite CBT: **Gangtok**, buses leave regularly between 0730-1330, Rs 90-110, 5 hrs; deluxe private buses from CBT (separate ticket window), Rs 100.
To **Bhutan** Bhutan Government buses, tickets from Counter 14 at CBT, 0700-1200. To **Phuntsholing**: buses at 0720, 1200, 1400, 1500, Rs 75, 3-4 hrs. NBSTC buses run at 0700 and 1200, Rs 75.
To **Nepal** To **Kathmandu** buses (or more conveniently taxi or jeep, every 15 mins or so from opposite CBT) to **Panitanki** on the border (35 km, 1 hr); transfer to **Kakarbhitta** by cycle-rickshaw. Also through tickets from private bus companies. See also box, above.

**Jeep** Shared jeeps are the best way to get to and around the hills, as they leave more frequently and are faster than buses, and only a little more expensive. **Kalimpong**, from Sevoke Rd stand, 2½ hrs, Rs 90; **Gangtok**, Sevoke Rd or outside CBT on Hill Cart Rd, 3½-4 hrs, Rs 140; **Darjeeling**, from Hill Cart Rd, 3 hrs, Rs 100; **Kurseong**, from Hill Cart Rd (near Conclave Hotel), 1½ hrs, Rs 60; **Mirik**, from Hill Cart Rd, opposite CBT, 2 hrs, Rs 60; and from the same place to **Jorethang**, 3½ hrs, Rs 120 (you need to have an ILP in advance to cross this border). Jeeps also leave from outside NJP direct for Darjeeling, Kalimpong and Gangtok, at a slightly higher price and with some waiting while drivers tout for customers.

**Train** Railway Enquiry at NJP, T0353-256 1555. **Siliguri Junction** and **NJP**, 5 km away, have tourist information. There are buses, tempos (Rs 15), cycle-rickshaws (Rs 60) and taxis (Rs 150) between the 2. NJP has good connections to other major destinations in India. For long-distance rail journeys from NJP, first buy tickets at Siliguri (computerized Reservations, Bidhan Rd near Stadium), 1000-1300, 1330-1700 (to avoid the queue go to Chief Reservations Officer at side of building), then go to NJP station for train.

To **Darjeeling**, the *Toy Train* leaves from NJP, calling at Siliguri Junction on its way.

Daily diesel service leaves at 0915, 7½ hrs (0930, 7 hrs from Siliguri, though in reality the journey is usually 9 hrs). Services are often disrupted by landslides during the rains (at the time of writing the service was suspended while the track was being fixed), though the upper section from Kurseong (accessible by bus/jeep) continues to run; check beforehand.

Steam trains run daily from Siliguri to **Sukna**, 0855 (from Siliguri Town at 08:45, 35 mins, from Siliguri Jn at 0855, 25 mins).

Several daily from NJP to **Kolkata** (**S**) including the following: *Darjeeling Mail 12344*, 2000, 10 hrs; *Uttar Bangla Exp 13148*, 1740, 11½ hrs. **Kolkata** (**H**): *Kamrup Exp 15960*, 1645, 12¾ hrs; *Kanchenjunga Exp*

*15658*, 0755, 11½ hrs. **Delhi** (**ANVT**): *NE Exp 12505*, 1715, 26 hrs; (**New Delhi**) *Rajdhani Exp 12423*, 1315, 21 hrs. From **Kolkata** (**S**) to Siliguri: *Darjeeling Mail 12343*, 2205, 10 hrs, connects with the *Toy Train* from NJP.

## Darjeeling *p307, map p309*

**Air** The nearest airport is Bagdogra (90 km), see Siliguri, above. Transfer by car takes 3 hrs. **Air India**, Bellevue Hotel, Chowrasta, T0354-225 4230. Mon-Sat 1000-1700, Sun 1000-1300.

**Bus** Minibuses go from the main transport stand to nearby villages including **Mirik** at 0825, 0900 and 0925 (Rs 40), via **Sukhia** and **Pashupati Fatak** (on the Nepalese border).

**Jeep** Shared jeep is the quickest and most convenient way of getting around the mountains. Jeeps leave regularly to local destinations, and if you pick a jeep that is already over half full, you won't be waiting long before you set off. During the high season it is well advised to book a day in advance (particularly to reserve seat No 1). To **Siliguri** from 0600-1630 (2-2½ hrs, Rs 100); to **Gangtok** from 0700-1500 (4-5 hrs, Rs 150); to **Mirik** (2 hrs, Rs 60); to **Kalimpong** from 0700-1600 (2½ hrs, Rs 80-90); to **Jorethang** frorn 0800-1500 (Sikkim permit not available at this border, 2 hrs, Rs 90-100), change at Jorethang for **Pelling**. The journeys to Kalimpong and Mirik are particularly stunning, along narrow ridges planted with tea bushes and past wooden villages teetering on precipices.

**Motorbike** Enfields and other models can be rented from **Adventures Unlimited**, based in the internet café, 0830-2000, opposite Cyber Planet on Zakir Hussein Rd. Around Rs 350 per day.

**Taxi** Easily available in the lower part of town.

**Train** Diesel service to **New Jalpaiguri** (**NJP**) at 0915, 7½ hrs, 88 km away. However, at the time of research the train was not running due to a landslide between Mahanadi and Gayabari (which has taken over 2 years to fix, so far). A passenger train runs to **Kurseong** (Rs 27/144) via **Ghoom** (Rs 10/111) daily at 1015, taking 3 hrs and returning at 1500. Darjeeling station also has some old steam engines. A narrow-gauge steam tourist train to **Ghoom** (**Ghum**) with a photo stop at Batasia Loop, departs 1040, 1320 and 1600 taking 1¼ hrs (the morning train is always packed, but the 1600 only runs if there is enough demand), Rs 240 1st-class only (see page 311). The ticket office at the station is open Mon-Sat 0800-1700, Sun 0800-1400, lunch 1200-1230.

**Mirik** *p314*
From Krishnanagar, jeeps to **Darjeeling** between 0900-1430 (2 hrs, Rs 60); to **Siliguri** every 30 mins from 0700-1530 (2 hrs, Rs 60); to **Kurseong** at 1500 (2 hrs, Rs 60); to **Kalimpong** at 0600 (4-5 hrs, Rs 140). Also jeeps to the above destinations from Mirik Bazar, departing between 0600-1000. You can go to **Sandakphu** from Mirik, change jeep at **Sukhia**.
**Train** Mirik Out Agency, Main Rd, Krishnanagar, can book train tickets to/from NJP.

**Kurseong** *p315*
**Bus and jeep** 51 km from Siliguri, off the main Darjeeling road, or via Pankhabari. Buses and jeeps to **Siliguri**, 1½ hrs and **Darjeeling**, 1 hr, leave from near the railway station; for **Mirik** jeeps leave from Pankhabari Rd.
**Train** Diesel service to **Darjeeling**, 3½ hrs.

**Kalimpong** *p316, map p317*
**Air** Nearest airport is at Bagdogra, 80 km, 2½-3 hrs, Rs 1300 private car (see Siliguri, above); seat in shared jeep Rs 110 to Bagdogra (then an auto for last couple of kilometres to airport). Flight bookings from **Mintry Transport**.
**Bus** Buses use the Motor Stand. Frequent to **Siliguri**, from 0530-1700 (2½ hrs, Rs 65); **Lava** (2 hrs, Rs 35) and **Kaffer** (3 hrs, Rs 60) at 0800; to **Karkabitta** at 0530 and 1345 93 hrs, Rs 80); to **Gangtok** at 0730 (3½ hrs, Rs 70).

**Jeep** Shared jeeps depart 0630-1500, depending on demand; much quicker than buses. To **Darjeeling**, 2 hrs, Rs 80-90; **Siliguri** Rs 70/Rs 50; **Gangtok** Rs 120.
**Train** The nearest mainline railhead is New Jalpaiguri (NJP), 67 km. Tickets from **Rly Out Agency**, next to Soni Emporium, Motor Stand. Computerized bookings and a small tourist quota for trains departing to NJP.

## Directory

**Siliguri** *p307*
**Banks** Several ATMs on Hill Cart and Sevoke roads; there's a convenient Axis Bank cashpoint opposite the CBT by Hotel Heritage. **Hospital** Hospital, T0353-252 1920; North Bengal Clinic, T0353-242 0441. **Post** GPO, Hospital Rd, Mon-Sat 0700-1900, Sun 1000-1400.

**Darjeeling** *p307, map p309*
**Banks** There are many ATMs all over town. **Couriers** FedEx at Global Express, Robertson Rd, T0354-225 8706. Mon-Fri 0900-1700, Sat 0900-1300.
**Internet** Glenary's, the Mall, speedy connection, Rs 30 per hr. **Hospitals** Planters' Hospital, Nehru Rd, T0354-225 4327. Sadar Hospital, T0354-225 4218. Mariam Nursing Home, below Gymkhana Club, T0354-225 4328, has been recommended for its medical facilities. **Post** GPO, Laden La Rd.

**Mirik** *p314*
**Banks** 2 ATMs on Main Rd, Krishnanagar.
**Internet** There are 3 internet cafés in Krishnanagar, best is Prashant IT Solutions with fast connection, Skype and printing, Rs 30 per hr, daily 0930-2000.

**Kurseong** *p315*
**Banks** SBI, has ATM, opposite station and another 500 m down Pankhabari Rd.
**Internet** Cyber Planet, in Unique Sweet Market, open 1000-2030, Rs 25 per hr.

**Kalimpong** *p316, map p317*
**Banks** Several ATMs in town.
Emporium, Mani Link Rd, accepts Visa
and Mastercard. **Medical services/
post** There is a hospital and a post
office near the police station.

# Contents

## Footprint features

## At a glance

⊖ **Getting around** Shared jeeps are cheap, fast and much more frequent than buses. The nearest airport is Bagdogra in West Bengal.

◔ **Time required** 2 days in and around Gangtok, 2 days for Yumthang Valley, minimum 4-5 days for West Sikkim.

☼ **Weather** Clear and warm in Sep, chilly Oct-Feb, warm and dry but often foggy from Mar until the start of the monsoon in late May/Jun. Best in Sep and Oct.

✕ **When not to go** The monsoon can cause havoc with road transport.

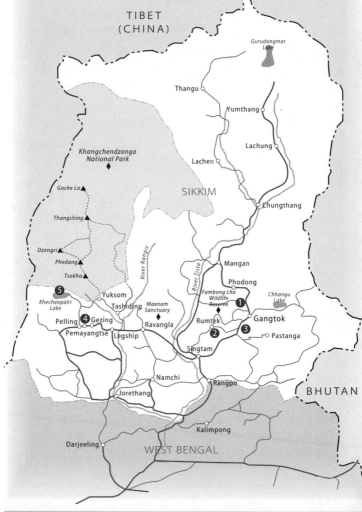

N

10 km
10 miles

★ Don't miss ...
1 Tashi Viewpoint over the Kangchendzonga range, page 338.
2 Rumtek Monastery, page 338.
3 Saramsa Gardens, page 339.
4 An overnight stay and early-morning walk at Pemayangtse Monastery, page 346.
5 Trek to Khecheopalri Lake, page 346.

TIBET (CHINA)

Gurudongmar Lake

Thangu

Yumthang

Lachung

Khangchendzonga National Park

Lachen

SIKKIM

Goche La

Chungthang

Thangshing

Dzongri

Phedang

Tsokha

Mangan

Khecheopalri Lake

Yuksom

Phodong

Tashiding

Maenam Sanctuary

Fambong Lho Wildlife Reserve

Chhangu Lake

Pelling

Gezing

Ravangla

Rumtek

Gangtok

Pemayangtse

Legship

Singtam

Pastanga

Namchi

Rangpo

BHUTAN

Jorethang

Kalimpong

Darjeeling

WEST BENGAL

Khangchendzonga, the third highest mountain in the world, dominates the skyline of Sikkim. The state is renowned as much for its wonderful wildlife and rich variety of plants and flowers as for its ethnically varied population. Sikkim's original inhabitants, the Lepchas, call the region Nye-mae-el, meaning 'Paradise'. To the later Bhutias it is Beymul Denjong, or the 'Hidden Valley of Rice'. The name Sikkim itself is commonly attributed to the Tsong word Su-khim, meaning 'New' or 'Happy House'. The monasteries of Rumtek and Pemayangtse are just two among a wealth of fascinating centres of Buddhism in the state.

Sikkim is an orchid-lovers' paradise, with 660 species found at altitudes as high as 3000 m. Organic farming and ecotourism are officially enshrined in government policy, and although trekking is less developed than in other parts of the Himalaya, the state now attracts ramblers in serious numbers to make the trek to Gocha La.

From Gangtok, it's easy to organize a jeep tour to the far-flung wilds of North Sikkim to explore the Yumthang and Tsopta valleys. You can stay a couple of days in Gangtok, with a day-trip to Rumtek, then move on to Pelling and Yuksom, visiting Pemayangtse Monastery and Khecheopalri Lake, before continuing to Kalimpong or Darjeeling in West Bengal. Road journeys within Sikkim are very scenic, but numerous hairpin bends and unsealed sections can also make them extremely slow, so expect to travel at 10-40 kph. Conditions deteriorate considerably during the monsoon, which can sometimes make travel impossible.

## The land

**Geography** Sikkim nestles between the peaks of the eastern Himalaya, stretching only 112 km from south to north and 64 km from east to west. This small area contains a vast range of landscapes and habitats, from subtropical river valleys to snow-covered peaks. Despite comprising just 0.2% of India's landmass, Sikkim accounts for an astounding 26% of its biodiversity. The state encompasses the upper valley of the Tista River, a tributary of the Brahmaputra, the watershed of which forms the borders with Tibet and Nepal. In the east lies the Chumbi Valley, a tongue of Tibetan land separating Sikkim from Bhutan that gives the state its strategic and political sensitivity. The Sikkimese believe Khangchendzonga (known as Kanchenjunga in West Bengal, or the 'Five Treasures of the Great Snows'), at 8586 m, to be the repository of minerals, grains, salt, weapons and holy scriptures. On its west is the massive 31-km-long Zemu Glacier.

**Climate** In the lower valleys Sikkim's climate is subtropical. Above 1000 m, it is temperate, while the higher mountain tops are permanently under snow. Sikkim is one of the Himalaya's wettest regions, with most rain falling between mid-May and September.

## History

From the 13th century Tibetans, like the Namgyal clan, immigrated to Sikkim. In 1642 Phuntsog Namgyal (1604-1670) became the Chogyal (king). With a social system based on Tibetan Lamaistic Buddhism, the land was split into 12 *dzongs* (fortified districts).

In the 18th century Sikkim lost land to Nepal, Bhutan and the British. When the Gurkhas of Nepal launched a campaign into Tibet and were defeated by the Chinese in 1791-1792, Sikkim won back its northern territories. The narrow Chumbi Valley, which separates Sikkim from Bhutan, remained with Tibet. When the British defeated Nepal in 1815, the southern part of the country was given back to Sikkim. However, in the next conflict with Nepal, Darjeeling was handed over to the British in return for their assistance. In 1848 the Terai region at the foot of the mountains was annexed by the British.

Nepalis migrated into Sikkim from the beginning of the 19th century, eventually becoming more numerous than the local inhabitants. This led to internal conflict also involving the British and the Tibetans. The British won the ensuing battles and declared Sikkim a Protectorate in 1890. The state was controlled by a British Political Officer who effectively stripped the *Gyalpos* of executive power. It was many years before the Sikkimese regained control.

## Culture

**Ethnic groups** The Naong, Chang and Mon are believed to have inhabited Sikkim in prehistoric times. Each ethnic group has an impressive repertoire of folk songs and dance. The **Lepchas**, who call themselves Rongpas and claim to be the original inhabitants of Sikkim, may have come from Tibet well before the eighth century and brought Lamaist Buddhism, which is still practised. They are now regarded as the indigenous peoples. They are deeply religious, peace loving and typically shy but cheerful. The government has reserved the Dzongu area in North and Central Sikkim for Lepchas, who now make up less than 10% of the population. For a long time, the Lepchas' main contact with the outside world was the market-place at Mangan, where they bartered oranges and cardamom. Their alphabet was only devised in the 18th century by the king.

# Permits

Free **Inner Line Permits (ILPs)** are issued to foreigners to enter Sikkim for up to 30 days, with a possible extension of a further 30 days. You can contact an Indian mission abroad when applying for an Indian visa (enclosing two extra photos), but it's easier to apply in India at any FRO (Foreigners' Registration Office) or the Sikkim Tourism Office in New Delhi, Kolkata, Siliguri or Darjeeling (check www.sikkim.gov.in for office details). The easiest place of all to get an ILP is at the Sikkim Tourist Office in Darjeeling (Main Old Bellevue Hotel, opposite Glenaries, Nehru Road, Monday-Saturday 1000-1600) where the processing time is 10 minutes; take one copy of your passport and visa, and one passport photo. The FRO in Darjeeling also issue ILPs but the process is longer and more complicated.

The checkpoint at Rangpo, on the border with West Bengal, issues a 30-day permit for foreigners on entering Sikkim; processing time is 10 minutes. If you wish to enter via Jorethang (for quicker access to West Sikkim) you need to arrange your ILP in advance. ILPs are extendable at the FRO in Gangtok (Yangthang Building, Kazi Road, Gangtok, T03592-203041, open daily 1000-1600) or by the Superintendent of Police in Namchi (south) and Geyzing (west). On exiting Sikkim, it is not permitted to return for three months.

Certain areas in north and west Sikkim (Chungthang, Yumthang, Lachen, Chhangu, Dzongri) have been opened to groups of two to 20 travellers, on condition that travel is with a registered agency. The required Restricted Areas Permits (RAP) can be arranged by most local travel agents and are valid for five days; apply with photocopies of your passport (Indian visa and personal details pages), ILP and two photos.

The **Magar**, a minority group, are renowned as warriors and were involved in the coronation of Phuntsog Namgyal, the first Chogyal of Sikkim in 1642.

The **Bhotias** (meaning 'of Bhot/Tibet') or Bhutias entered Sikkim in the 13th century from Kham in Tibet. Many adapted to sedentary farming from pastoral nomadism and displaced the Lepchas. Some, however, retained their older lifestyle, and combined animal husbandry with trading over the Trans-Himalayan passes: Nathula (4392 m), Jelepla (4388 m), Donkiala (5520 m) and Kongrala (4809 m). Over the years the Bhutias have come into increased contact with the Lepcha and intermarried with them. Nearly every Bhutia family has one member who becomes a monk. Monasteries remain the repositories of Bhutia culture and festivals here are the principal social events. However, those who have visited Ladakh or Zanskar may find them architecturally and artistically a little disappointing. The Bhutias are famous for their weaving and are also skilled woodcarvers.

The **Newars** entered Sikkim in large numbers from Nepal in the 19th century. Skilled in metal and woodwork, they were granted the right by the Chogyal to mine copper and mint the Sikkimese coinage. Other Nepali groups followed. With high-altitude farming skills, they settled new lands and built houses directly on the ground unlike the Lepcha custom of building on stilts. The Newars were followed by the Chettris and other Nepali clans who introduced Hinduism, which became more popular as their numbers swelled.

**Religion** In Sikkim, as in Nepal, Hinduism and Buddhism have interacted and amalgamated so Himalayan Hinduism includes a pantheon of Buddhist *bodhisattvas* as well as Hindu deities. The animist tradition also retains a belief in evil spirits.

Buddhist **prayer flags** flutter in the breeze everywhere. The different types, such as wind, luck and victory, are printed with texts and symbols on coloured pieces of cloth and are tied to bamboo poles or trees. **Prayer wheels** carrying inscriptions (which should be turned clockwise) vary in size from small hand-held ones to vast drums which are installed by a monastery or *stupa*. Whitewashed masonry **chortens** (*stupas*) usually commemorate the Buddha or Bodhisattva, the structure symbolizing the elements (earth, water, fire, air, ether). The eight **lucky signs** appear as parasol, pot or vase, conch shell, banner, two fishes, lotus, knot of eternity and the wheel of law (Dharma Chakra). Bowls of **water** (Thing Duen Tsar) are offered in prayer from left to right during Buddhist worship. The gift of water from one who is free from greed and meanness is offered to quench thirsty spirits and to wash the feet, and represents flower (or welcome), incense, lamp, perfume and food.

**Festivals** Since the 22 major festivals are dictated by the agricultural cycle and the Hindu Buddhist calendar, it is best to check dates with the Gangtok tourist office.

**Jan/Feb** Bumchu meaning 'sacred pot' is a 1-day festival at the monastery in Tashiding. The sacred pot is opened once a year and the water level within forecasts the prosperity of Sikkim in the coming year.
**Feb/Mar** Losar (Tibetan New Year) is celebrated for about a week at Tashiding. It is preceded by Lama dances in Rumtek.
**Apr/May** Buddha Purnima/Jayanti is the most sacred day in the Buddhist calendar, falling on the full moon of the lunar month of Vaishaaka. 'Buddha's birthday' is also the day he gained enlightenment and attained Nirvana.
**Jun** Saga Dawn, a Buddhist festival with huge religious processions round Gangtok.
**Rumtek Chaams Dance festival** is held in commemoration of the 8 manifestations of Guru Padmasambhava, who established Buddhism in Tibet.
**Aug/Sep** Pang Lhabsol commemorates the consecration of Khangchendzonga as Sikkim's guardian deity; the Lepchas believe that the mountain is their birthplace.

The masked warrior dance is especially spectacular; warriors wear traditional armour of helmets, swords and shields. Celebrations are held in Pemayangtse.
**Sep/Oct Dasain** is one of the most important Nepali festivals. It coincides with **Dasara** in North India, see page 172. On the 1st day barley seeds are planted in prayer rooms, invocations are made to Durga, and on the 8th day buffalo and goats are ritually sacrificed.
**Dec** Diwali (the Festival of Lights).
**Kagyat Dances** performed by monks (especially at Enchey), with religious music and chanting, enact themes from Buddhist mythology and end with the burning of effigies made of flour, wood and paper. This symbolizes the exorcism of evil spirits and the ushering in of prosperity for the coming year. **Losoog** (Namsoong for Lepchas at Gangtok) is the Sikkimese New Year, also called **Sonam Losar**. Farmers celebrate their harvest and beginning of their new cropping calendar.

## Modern Sikkim

In 1950, Sikkim became a Protectorate of India. In 1973 there were growing demand for accession to India by the local population, consisting mainly of Nepalis, and Sikkim was formally made an associate state. The Gyalpos lost their power as a result of the new democratic constitution and Sikkim became the 22nd state in the Union in 1975. Although there is no separatist movement, India's takeover and the abolition of the monarchy, supported by many of Nepali origin, is still resented by many Sikkimese who don't regard themselves as Indians. The state enjoys special tax and other privileges, partly because its highly sensitive geopolitical location on the disputed border with China. In the 2009 general election the Sikkim Democratic Front (SDF), a party confined to Sikkim, won all 32 seats in the State Assembly.

# Gangtok and around

*Gangtok ('High Hill'), the capital of Sikkim, sits on a ridge overlooking the Ranipul River. The setting is spectacular with fine views of the Khangchendzonga range, but the town has lost some of its quaint charm with the mushrooming of concrete buildings along the national highway and the main road. The crowded Mahatma Gandhi Marg and the colourful bazars below it are where all the town's commercial activity is concentrated. Away from here, there are many serene areas and quiet alleys that remain virtually untouched.* ▸▸ *For listings, see pages 340-344.*

## Arriving in Gangtok → *Colour map 4, A2. Population: 98,658. Altitude: 1547 m.*

**Getting there** There is a small airport near Gangtok linked to Bagdogra Airport (see page 327), 124 km away, by a regular helicopter service. Most visitors arrive from North Bengal by the attractive road following the Tista (NH31A), which is accessible all year except in very wet weather (mid-June to September) when there may be landslips. Permits and passports are checked at Rangpo where 30-day permits (extendable in Gangtok or district headquarters, see box, page 335) are available (copies of passport and visa, and two photos required). SNT buses terminate at the Paljor Stadium Road stand, while jeeps from Siliguri/Bagdogra stop at Nam Nang jeep stand south of Gangtok, connected to the centre by a 10-minute ride in a shared minibus taxi. Jeeps for West Sikkim use the main jeep stand on NH31A just below the tourist office, while jeeps for destinations north leave from another stand near Vajra cinema (five-minute taxi ride north of centre). ▸▸ *See Transport, page 343.*

**Getting around** The busy hub around MG Marg, pedestrianized in the evening, is a 5-minute walk from end to end. Away from the bazars, the town is pleasant for walking around (see Rajesh Verma's *Sikkim: A Guide and Handbook*, Rs 140). For excursions further afield you'll need to hire a jeep or taxi; rates are fixed and displayed on the back window.

**Tourist information** Sikkim ⓘ *MG Marg, Gangtok Bazar, T03592-221634, www.sikkimtourism.gov.in, daily 0800-2000.* Apply for permits here.

## Places in Gangtok

At the north end of town the **Government Institute of Cottage Industries** ⓘ *Mon-Sat 0900-1230 and 1330-1530, closed 2nd Sat of month*, produces a wide range of local handicrafts, including wool carpets, jackets, dolls, handmade paper, carved and painted wooden tables. Items are of high quality (and prices) but there's no parcel service for sending packages home.

**Enchey Monastery** is 3 km northeast of the main bazar. It's a pleasant walk that takes you past the small **flower garden** at Whitehall (orchids on show March-April). Originally built by the eighth Chogyal in the 1840s, the present building dates from 1909. Religious dances are held in August and December.

The **Palace of the Chogyal** is only open once a year in the last week of December for the **Pang Lhabsol Festival**. Below this is the **Tsuklakhang** or Royal Chapel, standing on a high ridge where royal marriages and coronations took place. This is the major place of worship and has a large and impressive collection of scriptures. The interior houses Buddha images and is lavishly decorated with woodcarving and murals. Visitors are welcome during Tibetan New Year but may not be permitted at other times; photography is prohibited.

Moving south along the road you pass the **Secretariat** complex on your left. Beyond this is the **Deer Park**, loosely modelled on the famous one at Sarnath, with a statue of the Buddha. From here a **ropeway** ① *0930-1700, Rs 50 one way,* descends the hill to Deorali Bazar, near which is the unique **Namgyal Institute of Tibetology** ① *Mon-Sat 1000-1600,* established in 1958 to promote research into Tibet and Mahayana Buddhism. The library maintains a large and important Buddhist collection with many fine *thangkas*, icons and art treasures on display. To the south, surrounded by 108 prayer wheels, the gold-topped **Do-drul** Chorten contains relics and a complete set of holy texts. Nearby is a monastery for young lamas with large statues of the Buddha and Guru Padmasambhava.

**Tashi Viewpoint** via Enchey Monastery is 9 km away. Go early to watch the sun rise over the Khangchendzonga range. **Hanuman Tok**, a hill with a small temple, 8 km away, is another viewpoint.

## Around Gangtok

**Rumtek Monastery** → *Colour map 4, A2. 24 km southwest of Gangtok. Altitude: 1550 m. www.rumtek.org.*

Standing in one of the attractive lower valleys with fluttering prayer flags, the monastery is the headquarters of the Kagyu ('Black Hat') order of Tibetan Lamaistic Buddhism. The monks fled Tibet after the Chinese invasion, bringing with them whatever statues, *thangkas* and scriptures they could carry. At the invitation of the Chogyal they settled in Rumtek. The new monastery was built in the 1960s in the traditional style as a faithful copy of the Kagyu headquarters in Chhofuk, Tibet, with typical monastic paintings and intricate woodwork. The **Dharma Chakra Centre** houses the unique golden reliquary of the 16th Gyalwa Karmapa, who died in 1981.

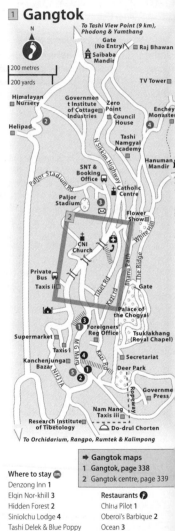

**1 Gangtok**

To Tashi View Point (9 km),
Phodong & Yumthang

To Orchidarium, Rangpo, Rumtek & Kalimpong

➡ Gangtok maps
1 Gangtok, page 338
2 Gangtok centre, page 339

Where to stay ⬤
Denzong Inn 1
Elgin Nor-khill 3
Hidden Forest 2
Siniolchu Lodge 4
Tashi Delek & Blue Poppy
Restaurant 5

Restaurants ⑦
China Pilot 1
Oberoi's Barbique 2
Ocean 3
Taste of Tibet 4

Visitors are dropped at the gate at the bottom of a gentle uphill path; passports may be checked. A 20-minute walk past local houses and curio shops leads to the monastery. Outside, you may see pairs of monks chanting prayers in their quarters or catch some younger ones playing football in the field. The main hall is impressive but lacks Pemayangtse's atmosphere. Visitors are welcome but are asked not to disturb the monks during prayers (0400, 1800, except Sunday). In the adjacent building you can watch the wood-block printing of texts on handmade paper. The peace is broken when hordes of tourists arrive.

## Fambong Lho Wildlife Reserve

① 25 km from Gangtok across the Ranipool Valley, Rs 5.

A little beyond Rumtek, this reserve has serene jungle walks in the hills, with waterfalls, mountain views, orchids and wildlife (marten, fox, red panda, boar; even wolf and sloth bear). You are free to go on your own (though this is not advisable on some stretches) and can climb or walk for one to six days. There are log huts at Golitar and Tumin with cheap beds.

## Saramsa Gardens → 14 km south of Gangtok.

The gardens contain more than 500 indigenous species in what is more like a botanical garden with large orchidariums. The best season is March to early May; you may be disappointed at other times. The road to Saramsa forks east off the NH31A a few kilometres south of **Tadong**, which has a couple of places with rooms and refreshments including the fairly modern **Tashi Tadong** and the **Daragaon**.

### 2 Gangtok centre

➡ **Gangtok maps**
1 Gangtok, page 338
2 Gangtok centre, page 339

Footbridge
CNI
Footbridge
Footbridge
Private Bus Stand
Taxis ii
HDFC ATM
Thakurbari Temple & Dharamsala
Taxis iii
Bank of Sikkim

Church Rd
Paljor Stadium Rd
NH31A
Bhanu Path
Tibet Rd
Kazi Rd
NH31A
MG Marg

N
100 metres
100 yards

**Where to stay**
Chumbi Residency 1
Chakpa 2
Mintokling Guest House 3
Modern Central Lodge 4
Mount Jopuno 5
Netuk House 6
Sonam Delek 7
Sunny Guest House 8
Tibet & Snow Lion Restaurant 9

**Restaurants**
Masala 1
Rasoi/Blue Sheep 2

### Kyongnosla Alpine Sanctuary

→ Altitude: 3200-4100 m. Permit required (see box, page 335).

Located 31 km from Gangtok on the Nathula highway, which until 1962 was the main route for mule trains trading between Gangtok and Lhasa in Tibet, the sanctuary extends from the '15th Mile' check post to the ridges bordering Rongchu and Chhangu Lake. Among the junipers and silver firs the sanctuary harbours some rare ground orchids and rhododendrons and numerous medicinal plants including the *Panax pseudo-ginseng*. The best time to visit is April-August and October-November. The Himalayan marmot has been reintroduced here. Other mammals include goral, serow, red panda, Himalayan black bear, Tibetan fox and yellow-throated martens, together with very colourful pheasants.

Two easy treks lead to the Shiv Gufa (1 km from the road), where you can crawl into a tiny cave on your hands and knees to see a small Siva image and several tridents embedded in the soft floor, and to Kheding (4 km), while longer and more difficult ones to Simulakha, Namnang Lakha and Nakcho are very scenic. Trekkers with permits for Chhangu may return from Nakcho via the lake.

### Chhangu (Tsomgo) Lake → 36 km from Gangtok. Altitude: 3774 m.

The holy Chhangu Lake lies 5 km further along the precipitous Nathula road. Completely frozen in mid-winter, it's best to visit March-May and September to mid-December. There are excellent views of Khangchendzonga from the nearby ridge and superb sunsets, but the lake area is overcrowded and spoilt by snack kiosks and loud Hindi music. You can walk around the 1-km-long lake in about an hour. Permits are needed (apply with photo and passport a day ahead) or there are organized tours. If you go independently, allow six hours for the return trip; a jeep/minivan costs about Rs 800-1000.

## ⊙ Gangtok and around listings

*For hotel and restaurant price codes and other relevant information, see pages 22-26.*

## ● Where to stay

**Gangtok** *p337, maps p338 and p339*
Heating is essential in winter. Some budget hotels charge extra for heaters. Dogs bark all night so take some ear plugs. Discounts are available Jul-Aug and Dec-Jan.
**$$$$ Elgin Nor-khill**, T03592-205637, www.elginhotels.com. Beautiful rooms in an old palace, meals included, spacious public rooms, good views and gardens, curio shop, once excellent but standards are slipping a little.
**$$$ Chumbi Residency**, Tibet Rd, T03592-206618/9, www.thechumbiresidency.com. Modern hotel decked out with traditional Tibetan furniture, plenty of marble, good rooms with old fashioned but perfectly adequate bathrooms, clean and quiet, dynamic manager. Good restaurant (see Restaurants, page 342).
**$$$-$ Sonam Delek**, Tibet Rd, T03592-202566, www.hotelsonamdelek.com. Balconied rooms with bath, best choice for views of the mountains, pleasant restaurant (great local food), terrace garden, some **$$$** suites.

**$$ Hidden Forest**, 2 km from centre in Middle Sichey, T03592-205197, www.hidden forestretreat.org. 12 spacious, timber-floored rooms in the home of a forest officer and his family, set in a 3-acre nursery full of orchids and medicinal plants, with paths leading into the surrounding forest, homegrown organic food served in cosy dining room, a unique choice. Recommended.
**$$ Mintokling Guest House**, Bhanu Path, T03592-204226, www.mintokling.com. 12 prettily decorated rooms with bath, timber-floored on 2nd storey or carpets on ground/1st, among working veg gardens, flowers, lawns and prayer flags, good restaurant, charming Sikkimese owner. Recommended, book in advance through the website as often full.
**$$ Netuk House**, Tibet Rd, T03592-222374, www.heritagehotelsofindia.com. 12 comfortable rooms built and decorated in the Himalayan style in an extension to a traditional family home, varying layouts so check a few, only 2 with double rather than twin beds. Excellent Sikkimese food (extra Rs 1000 per day for all meals), quiet location, mountain views from the huge shared terrace, friendly, excellent service. Significant discounts possible at quiet times, otherwise it is overpriced albeit charming. Down a side lane, sign obscured by foliage.

**$$ Tashi Delek**, MG Marg, T03592-204156-8, www.hoteltashidelek.com. 46 rooms and some suites (better on top floors) with lots of clutter and attractive *objets d'art*, excellent restaurant (see Restaurants, page 342), bar, exchange, airlines counter, terrace garden with enthralling views, friendly service. Pricey but recommended, it's a Gangtok institution.

**$$-$ Denzong Inn**, near Kanchenjunga Bazar, T03592-202692, denzonginn@ rediffmail.com. Set in an interesting complex with faint Chinese-mafia feel, 24 rooms and good if slightly threadbare suites (**$$**). Some rooms on the terrace come with proper green baize card tables, and Chinese restaurant isn't bad.

**$$-$ Mount Jopuno** (Sikkim Tourism), PS Rd, T03592 203502. Out of 12 rooms, 4 de luxe, good restaurant and service, eager young staff (at Institute of Hotel Management).

**$$-$ Tibet** (Dalai Lama Trust), PS Rd, T03592-202523, www.hoteltibetgangtok. com. 34 rooms, good views from those at rear, restaurant, bar, exchange, Tibetan books and crafts for sale, very pleasant and peaceful (but some critical reports).

**$ Kanchen Residency**, Tibet Rd, T(0)9232-513781, kanchenresidency@indiatimes.com. Great mountain views from front-facing large rooms, carpets, new bathrooms though some damp patches appearing. Cheaper side rooms, also older and shabbier, some rooms have squat toilets. Discounts possible.

**$ Lhakpa**, Tibet Rd, T03592-223002. Cheap rooms, some with bath, even cheaper dorm, restaurant (excellent Chinese), views.

**$ Modern Central Lodge**, MG Marg, T03592-204670, www.modern-hospitality. com. Simple, clean and colourful rooms with bath, best in front on upper floors, a bit noisy, great lounge packed with books on Sikkim, basic but good restaurant, good jeep tours (long-established, using high standard accommodation), very friendly and helpful.

**$ Siniolchu Lodge**, near Enchey Monastery, T03592-202074. Good views, 24 rooms on

3 floors up a hillside, some with bath and heating, restaurant, bar, tours.

**$ Sunny Guest House**, by jeep stand on NH31A, T(0)8533-287109. Pleasantly old-school rooms with bath, TV, carpets, super K'dzonga views from top floor, forgettable room service. Handy location means now walking up hills with luggage.

**$ Travel Lodge**, Tibet Rd, T03592-203858, travellodge.gangtok@gmail.com. Decent modern hotel, with rooms at the front that are spacious and light. Can get a good deal on smaller side rooms, a good step up from backpacker places but at budget prices. All have reliable geysers and TV; affable staff.

### Rumtek Monastery p338

**$$$ Bamboo Retreat**, Sajong Village, T0353-220 2049, www.bambooretreat. in. Gorgeous views of the mountains, set on the edge of paddy fields, with 10 large comfortable bedrooms in different colour themes. The Swiss owner has created a wonderful retreat, with meditation, massage, creative workshops, and a library to relax guests. Organic food is delicious, panoramic views from the restaurant, half-board. Recommended.

**$$$ Martam Village Resort**, Gangkha, Upper Martam, 5 km from the monastery, T03592-203314, www.sikkim-martam-resort. com. Overlooking the valley and a short day-trek from Phamnongla Wildlife Sanctuary, 14 pleasant, traditional-style thatched cottages with large picture windows, good Sikkimese meals included in the price. Recommended.

**$ Sungay**, near monastery gate. Basic rooms in old guest house, cleanish shared toilet, friendly.

### Kyongnosla Alpine Sanctuary p339

**$ Log Huts**, 2 rooms in each at Kyongnosla and Lamnang Lakha. You must apply for a permit (Rs 5) to Chief Wildlife Warden, Sikkim Forest Dept, Deorali, Sikkim 737102, to enter the sanctuary.

## 🍴 Restaurants

**Gangtok** *p337, maps p338 and p339*
Lightly spiced Sikkimese meat and
vegetable dishes are usually eaten
with noodles or rice. *Churpi* is a local
yak milk curd cheese.
**$$ Blue Poppy**, Tashi Delek (see Where to
stay). International. Good meals at Rs 450
(Sikkimese recommended, order in advance)
though the restaurant itself is soulless.
**$$ Snow Lion**, in Hotel Tibet (see Where
to stay). Good Tibetan and Sikkimese in
elaborately decorated room, but service
can be glacial and vegetarian meals may
come with flecks of meat.
**$$ Tangerine**, in Chumbi Residency (see
Where to stay). Down in the bowels of the
hotel, this appealing split-level restaurant
has a mix of Thai cushions and standard
seating, and a nice little terrace for drinks.
Sikkim dishes are good (seasonal availability)
and there is a diverse menu of Indian,
Chinese, continental plus some Thai mains.
**$$-$ Masala**, MG Marg under Karma Hotel,
T03592-20484, www.masalatherestaurant.
in. Open 0800-2230. Funkily decorated and
fastidiously clean, serving pure vegetarian
Indian (paneer is their strength) and
Chinese. Intimate and cosy, serves alcohol.
**$$-$ Taste of Tibet**, MG Marg. The better
of 2 similarly named places, serving
excellent Tibetan soups and noodles to
an accompaniment of whatever internet
radio channel happens to be tuned in.
**$ Baker's Café**, branches dotted around
town (including MG Marg). Reliable for
pastries and authentic brown bread.
**$ China Palate**, Star Cinema Building,
MG Rd. Open 1030-2030. Excellent value
Chinese in a laid-back place with a bar.
**$ Famous Roll Corner**, New Market, Lal
Bazar Bridge, T(0)97759-52175. Delicious,
fast and famous rolls are spicy or not,
depending on your choice of sauce.
**$ Marwari & Gujarati Thali** (Jain Restaurant),
Tibet Rd. Open 0700-2100. Utterly delicious

thalis, endlessly refilled, and very cheap.
Plus surprisingly good *momos* and
competent staff.
**$ Rasoi** (aka **Blue Sheep**), MG Marg (by the
Tourist Office). Opens at 0830. Wonderful
South Indian breakfast items and a broad
spectrum of multicuisine, served in an airy,
clean, smart family restaurant. Creamy thick
lassis and juices are particularly notable, gets
very busy at night.

## 🍸 Bars and clubs

**Gangtok** *p337, maps p338 and p339*
Bars in most restaurants serve local spirits
distilled at Rangpo: brandy, rum, whiskey
and liqueurs. *Chhang* is the unofficial
national drink. A bamboo mug (*thungba*) is
filled with fermented millet through which
boiled water is allowed to percolate; the
drink is sipped through a bamboo straw. You
can enjoy this mildly intoxicating pleasant
drink for over an hour simply by adding hot
water. More conventional alcoholic drinks are
available at Gangtok's numerous wine shops.
**Café Live & Loud**, Sonam Gyatso Marg,
Tibet Rd. Continental café-style ambience
on the balconies overlooking the street,
and fun live music at weekends. A great
spot to hang out.
    The terrace at the hotel **Tashi Delek** has
exceptional views and is recommended for
a sunset beer.

## 🛍 Shopping

**Gangtok** *p337, maps p338 and p339*
**Handicrafts**
Traditional crafts include carpets, *thangkas*,
traditional jewellery, shirts, boots and fur
caps and woodcarvings.
**Charitrust Handicrafts**, Tibet Hotel.
Modest collection, good quality, books
on Tibet.
**Handcrafts Centre**, Zero Point. Mon-Sat
0930-1230, 1300-1530. Artisans can be
seen at work.

## Markets

Lal Bazar (haat on Sun, closed Thu) is an interesting walk down the steps off MG Marg. It winds up at Kanchenjunga Shopping Plaza, an uninspiring concrete edifice, but selling some unusual local fruit and vegetables and yak's milk cheese fresh and dried (skewered on string).

## ⊛ Festivals

**Rumtek Monastery** *p338*
**Feb** Special colourful **Losar** dances are held 2 days before the Tibetan New Year (check date). Arrive 3 days earlier to see rehearsals without masks, *pujas* and ceremonies are held during this period.
**Jun** The important **Rumtekchaam** is performed on the 10th day of the 5th month of the Tibetan calendar; masked dancers present 8 manifestations of the Guru Rimpoche. Tours in Jul-Aug from Gangtok.

## ⊙ What to do

**Gangtok** *p337, maps p338 and p339*
**Mountaineering**
**Himalayan Mountaineering Institute**, based in Darjeeling, see page 326.

**River rafting**
Rafting trips are arranged by the **Department of Tourism**, and private travel agents, on the Tista River (from Dikchu or Singtam, 1-hr drive from Gangtok) and the Rangit River from Melli Bazar, 4 km from Tista Bridge, which has a **Wayside Inn** for refreshments, or shi). 1-day trips cost US$50, 2-day US$80, some Grade II-III rapids. A 2-hr ride is ideal for the beginner; wonderful scenery.

**Tour operators**
Jeep tours of Gangtok are arranged from the Tourist Information Centre, T03592-221634, open daily 0800-2000.
To support ecologically responsible tourism, contact **Ecotourism and Conservation Society of Sikkim (ECOSS)**,

T03592-232789, www.sikkimhomestay.com, for homestays and tours. All agents help to arrange Restricted Area Permits for trekkers.
**Adarsh Tours & Travels**, Treks and Expeditions, 17 Tse-ka Commercial Complex, 31A National Highway Rd, near Old Private Taxi Stand, T03592-205053, www.adarshtours.com. Experienced in adventure travel for over 15 years, arranges trekking and mountaineering expeditions (to remote peeks), rafting, safaris plus travel-booking services and escorted tours in India and adjacent countries.
**Modern Treks & Tours**, MG Marg, T03592-204670, www.modern-hospitality.com. Quality tour operator, good for North Sikkim where their accommodation is the best on offer.
**Yuksom Tours and Treks**, Borong House (above Telephone Exchange), T03592-226822, www.yuksom-tours.com. Professional, well-equipped treks at the higher end of the market with great food.

## ⊙ Transport

**Gangtok** *p337, maps p338 and p339*
**Air** The nearest airport is Bagdogra (124 km away), see page 327. **Air India**, above Green Hotel, MG Marg, T03592-223354, www.airindia.com, 1000-1300, 1400-1600; **Jet Airways**, MG Marg, T03592-223556, www.jetairways.com. A new airport is being constructed 14 km from Gangtok, at Pakyong, due to be operational by the end of 2014.
  To get to Gangtok: taxi Rs 1600, 4-5 hrs; or get bus/shared taxi to Siliguri and change to jeep for Gangtok (Rs 150, 4½ hrs).
**Bus** SNT (Sikkim Nationalized Transport) Bus Stand, NH31A. Private buses from **West Point Taxi Stand**, NH31A, T03592-202858. Some only operate in the high season. Buy tickets 24 hrs in advance; hotels can help. Journeys cost between Rs 8-130. To **Rumtek**, 1600 1 hr; **Namchi**, 0730 (4½ hrs); **Namok, Phodong, Chungthang, Mangan**, 0700 (return 1500); **Pelling** via

**Gezing**, 0700 (5 hrs); **Jorethang**, 0700.
North Bengal service to **Kalimpong**,
75 km, 0715 (4-4½ hrs); to **Siliguri** (5 hrs),
0630-1330 (4½-5 hrs).

**Taxi/jeep** Shared taxis (Rs 12) run along
NH31A, stopping at marked taxi stops.
Charter taxis charge fixed, relatively high
rates around town. Rates for sightseeing
negotiable; around Rs 1700 per day for
travel outside Sikkim, Rs 1400 within Sikkim.
Tourist office has a list of official rates.

Jeeps provide a quicker and more
frequent service than bus. There are several
jeep stands in the city. Most useful to
travellers is the main private bus and jeep
stand on NH31A, office hours 0600-1800,
T03592-2203 862. Advisable to book a day
in advance. For South Sikkim: to **Ravangla**,
0700, 0745, 1230 and 1430, 3 hrs, Rs 80;
several to **Namchi**, between 0700-1500,
3 hrs, Rs 90; and **Jorethang**, every 30 mins
between 0630-1600, 3 hrs, Rs 100. To West
Sikkim: **Gezing**, 0700, 1200, 1230 and 1300,
4 hrs, Rs 120; **Pelling**, 0700, 1230 and 1300,
4½ hrs, Rs 150; **Yuksom**, 0700 and 1300,
5½ hrs, Rs 150, via **Tashiding**, 4 hrs, Rs 130.
Lal Bazar jeep stand is the hub for East
Sikkim: **Rumtek**, Rs 35; Nam Nang Jeep
Stand, Rs 10 taxi ride south from MG Marg
(for North Bengal). North Jeep Stand: for
Mangan, Rs 100. Share jeeps leave on a fixed
schedule, most departing early morning;
much quicker and more frequent than buses
to most destinations.

**Train** Nearest mainline railhead is NJP.
Computerized Bookings, SNT Compound,
0800-1400 (till 1100 on Sun).

**Rumtek Monastery** *p338*
**Bus** From **Gangtok** about 1600 (1 hr) along
a steep narrow road, returns about 0800.
**Jeep** Shared jeep: Rs 50 each;
last return to Gangtok 1300.
**Rumtek** to **Pemayangtse**, 4 hrs.
**Taxi** Taxi from Gangtok, Rs 500
(return Rs 800, 1½-hr wait).

## ❶ Directory

**Gangtok** *p337, maps p338 and p339*
**Banks** Several ATMs on MG Marg,
including UTI, HDFC. **Internet** Several
on Tibet Rd and MG Marg, Rs 30 per hr.
**Medical services** STNM Hospital,
Stadium Rd, opposite Hotel Mayur, T03592-
222944. **Post** GPO, Stadium Rd, Mon-Fri
0900-1700, Sun 1000-1400, has reliable
parcel service.

# South and West Sikkim

*This enchanting region contains the essence of Sikkim: plunging rice terraces, thundering rivers, Buddhist monasteries etched against the sky, and the ever-brooding presence of Mount Khangchendzonga.* ›› *For listings, see pages 347-350.*

## Jorethang

For travellers, the market town of Jorethang on the Sikkimese border is chiefly a transport hub for destinations in south/west Sikkim and West Bengal. Darjeeling is just 30 km away, but to enter Sikkim via Jorethang (bypassing Gangtok altogether) it is necessary to obtain permission in advance as the border post does not issue permits. There is not much to see in the grid-pattern town itself; a stroll east along the riverbed from the suspension bridge brings you to a colourful hybrid temple with shady pagodas, and the market is a good place to stock up on food supplies. Near the bridge is the SNT bus station, opposite which is a **tourist information centre** ① *daily 0830-2000*, where keen staff proffer a couple of brochures. The three jeep stands, plus hotels and bars, are in the street behind and beyond the tourist office. There's an ATM machine (State Bank of India) on Street 1, opposite the Walk In Hotel.

## Ravangla and Maenam Sanctuary → *Altitude: 2155-3260 m.*

**Ravangla** (Rabongla), 65 km southwest of Gangtok, is a small village whose timber-fronted main street retains a strong frontier flavour and serves as the gateway to one of Sikkim's best day hikes. The 12-km trek through the sanctuary to **Maenam Peak** (3260 m), which dominates the town, takes about three hours. The sanctuary harbours red panda, civet, blood pheasant and black eagle, and is most beautiful when the magnolia and rhododendron are in bloom in April-May. **Bhaledunga**, another 30-minute hike along the ridge, on the steep cliff edge above the Tista, juts out in the shape of a cockerel's head.

Towering above it on the 'wish-fulfilling hill' of Samdruptse is a 45-m statue of Guru Padmasambhava, the patron saint of Sikkim who spread Buddhism to Tibet in the ninth century. Resplendent in copper and a coat of bronze paint, the **statue** ① *0700-1700, free*, can be seen from Darjeeling, around 40 km away. A ropeway from Namchi is planned; otherwise take a taxi, Rs 350 return. Not to be outdone, a 33-m statue of Siva has risen on another hill at Solophok outside Namchi, which was completed in 2011.

The administrative headquarters of West Sikkim, **Gezing** (Gayzing, Gyalshing), 105 km west of Gangtok, is at the crossroads of bus routes and has a busy market with food stalls, shops, a few hotels (none recommended) but little else to detain visitors.

## Tashiding

Some 40 km north of Gezing is the gold-topped **Tashiding monastery**, built in 1716, which stands on a conical hill between the Rathong and Rangit rivers on a spot consecrated by Guru Rimpoche. The most sacred *chorten* in Sikkim is here, even the sight of it brings blessing and washes away sins. It contains relics of the Buddha, and stands in a field of many *stupas* surrounded by *mani* walls. You will see numerous stones with high-class carvings of *mantras* around the monastery, made on site by a prolific artisan. Following the track beyond the *stupa* field brings you to a small cemetery where cremations are performed, and continuing down (beware of leeches) is an area designated for 'burial of dissenters' who are left in wooden boxes while their clothes and possessions are thrown down the hillside.

The main *gompa* has been refurbished and all the frescos repainted; these particularly fine murals are intricate and expansive, with Tantric motifs. Pilgrims attend the **Bumchu Festival** in February/March to drink water from the sacred pot which has never run dry for over 300 years. Below the monastery is the small **Tshchu Phur Cave** where Guru Rinpoche meditated; follow the trail on the left of the main steps to the monastery until you see a small building, opposite which is a painting on the rocks. Carry a torch if you plan to crawl into the cave.

## Pelling → *2 km from the monastery and 9 km by road from Gezing.*

Pelling sits on a ridge with good views of the mountains. The rather bleak little town has three areas linked by a winding road, Upper and Middle with views and hotels, and Lower Pelling with banks and other services. Upper Pelling is expanding rapidly with new hotels springing up to accommodate honeymooners from Kolkata, and makes the most convenient base for visits to Pemayangtse. You can also visit the **Sanga Choelling Monastery** (circa 1697), possibly the oldest in Sikkim, which has some colourful mural paintings. The hilltop monastery is about 3 km along a fairly steep track through thick woods (about 30 minutes). The area is excellent for walking. The Sikkim Tourist Centre ① *Upper Pelling, near Garuda, T03595-250855*, is helpful.

## Pemayangtse → *112 km west of Gangtok. Altitude: 2085 m.*

A full-day trip by car from Gangtok, along a very scenic road, Pemayangste (Perfect Sublime Lotus) was built during the reign of the third Chogyal Chador Namgyal in 1705. It is about 7 km from Gezing, above the main road to Pelling.

The awe-inspiring **monastery** ① *0700-1600, Rs 10, good guided tours, 0700-1000 and 1400-1600 (if closed, ask for key), no photography inside* is Sikkim's second oldest. For many, the monastery is the highlight of their visit to Sikkim; it certainly has an aura about it. Take an early morning walk to the rear of the monastery to see a breathtaking sunrise in perfect peace. The walls and ceiling of the large *Dukhang* (prayer hall) have numerous *thangkas* and wall paintings, and there is an exceptional collection of religious artworks including an exquisite wooden sculpture on the top floor depicting the heavenly palace of Guru Rimpoche, the *Santhokpalri*, which was believed to have been revealed in a dream. The old stone and wood buildings to the side are the monks' quarters. According to tradition the monks have been recruited from Sikkim's leading families as this is the headquarters of the Nyingmapa sect. Annual *chaam* dances are held in late February and in September.

The **Denjong Padma Choeling Academy** (DPCA), set up to educate needy children, runs several projects, such as crafts and dairy, and welcomes volunteers, who can also learn about Buddhism and local culture. The meditation centre offers courses and can accommodate visitors for a small charge and volunteers for free at the new hostel (see below); a rewarding experience. Volunteer teachers can spend up to six weeks during March-December.

**Rabdanste**, the ruined palace of the 17th- to 18th-century capital of Sikkim, is along the Gezing-bound track from the monastery, 3 km from Pelling. From the main road, turn left just before the white sign 'Gezing 6 km', cross the archery field and turn right behind the hill (road branches off just below Pemanyangtse). Follow the narrow rocky track for 500 m to reach the palace.

## Khecheopalri Lake and Yuksom

A road west of the Pelling–Yuksom road leads to this tranquil lake where the clear water reflect the surrounding densely wooded slopes of the hills with a monastery above

Lepchas believe that birds remove any leaf that floats down. Prayer flags flutter around the lake and it is particularly moving when leaflamps are floated with special prayers at dusk. The sanctity of the lake may be attributed to its shape in the form of a foot (symbolizing the Buddha's footprint), which can be seen from the surrounding hills. The lake itself is not visually astonishing, but walks in the surrounding hills are rewarding and a night or two can easily be spent here. There are staggering views from the tiny hamlet by the *gompa* on the ridge (accessed by the footpath in the car park, just ask for the *gompa*) where homestays are available. You can trek from Pelling to Yuksom via the lake (without a permit) in two days, a beautiful journey. Or, after spending a night near the lake, put your bags on a public jeep to either Yuksum or Pelling (to be dropped off at a hotel) and make a one-day trek to catch them up; locals will advise you on the way.

Delightfully scenic little **Yuksom** (Yuksam), 42 km north from Pelling by jeepable road, is where the first Chogyal was crowned in 1641, thus establishing the kingdom of Sikkim. The wooden altar and stone throne stand beside Nabrugang *chorten*, with lovely wall paintings and an enormous prayer wheel, in a beautifully peaceful pine forest. During **Buddha Purnima** (the Buddha's birthday) in late April and May, women from the local community gather mid-morning to sing and pray in a low-key yet moving ceremony. Below Nabrugang, past pretty houses, **Kathok Lake** is a small green pool though the reflection of the prayer flags that surround it are photogenic, and the monastery of the same name nearby is worth the short uphill walk.

Although most people are in Yuksom because it is the starting point for the Gocha La trek, the village makes a quiet and relaxing base for a few days' stay, with several day walks leading out from the centre. It's a 45-minute climb to the attractive **hermit's retreat** at **Dhubdi** (circa 1700) above the village. A rewarding three-hour hike leads to **Hongri Monastery**, about halfway to Tashiding, mainly following a stone trail. Descending the path between the Yangri Gang and Panathang hotels, it is 45 minutes to a wooden bridge over the Phamrong Khola which has deliciously icy pools (accessed from the other side). The trail continues to Tsong village, with a sweet homestay in the first cottage in Lower Tsong (Rs 150 per night, three beds, contact Tara Chetri T(0)9775-816745) and onwards up the steep hill to the plain stone-slab monastery. It's a perfect picnic spot, with stone tables among the mossy *chortens* and glorious views. From here, it is another three to four hours' walk to Tashiding.

## South and West Sikkim listings

*For hotel and restaurant price codes and other relevant information, see pages 22-26.*

## Where to stay

### Jorethang p345
**Hotel Janta**, near tourist information, 03595-276104. Basic place but fills up fast, only 7 rooms, dorm beds and single-person discounts. Restaurant is cosy, with good *thukpa* and *momos*, well-stocked bar.
**Hotel Namgyal**, near SNT bus station, 03595-276852. Best choice in town with

simple rooms (doubles only), typically slab-floored with walls painted split colours. Fans, TVs, hot water in garish bathrooms. Best at the back, where they have windows as well as balconies. Decent restaurant and cheap beer.

### Ravangla p345
**$$ Bon Farmhouse**, Kewzing village, 8 km towards Legship, T09547-667799, www.sikkimbonfarmhouse.com. Beautiful setting in a quiet Bhutia village, practising responsible tourism, 5 rooms and cottages

have Sikkimese decor and modern amenities. Set in a tea garden, with a small organic farm, birdwatching, trekking to the Maenam and Tendong hills, and tours available, as well as herbal stone baths.

**$$-$ Mt Narsing Village Resort**, 15th Mile (bookable through **Yuksom Tours and Treks**, see page 343). 2 rooms in a bungalow situated in a delightfully flower-filled garden, with incredible views over the terraced valley slopes to a monastery. Also tent accommodation and an isolated annex, 1 km from the main road, which is more luxurious. Quaint rooms are carpeted, homely, with simple bamboo furniture and modern bathrooms (geysers). Good meals are served in the open-sided restaurant.

**$ Melody**, Ralang Rd, T03595-260817. Basic but charming rooms with wooden floors, clean, friendly.

### Tashiding p345

**$ Blue Bird**, main market, 50 m uphill from jeep stand, T03595-243248. Very basic old-school rooms, single/double/dorm, all share a bath (hot water if there is electricity), run by a kind Bengali family. Restaurant below is by far the best place to eat.

**$ Dhakkar Tashiding Lodge**, 200 m down from jeep stand, T03595-243249. Large concrete rooms with great views from the back, 3 or 4 beds, best of the shared bathrooms in town.

**$ Mt Siniolchu**, main market (50 m beyond Blue Bird), T03595-243211. Friendly, 5 clean rooms including 3 big ones on the upper floor, shared bath, hot water.

**$ Yatri Niwas**, by monastery gate (250 m south of jeep stand), T(0)9832-623654. 4 rooms are tasteful and comfortable (pay more for wood walls and parquet floors), dorm beds. Pleasant gardens.

### Pelling p346

Power and water cuts can last 4 hrs or more and dogs often bark all night. Several **$** in Upper Pelling, with excellent views if you can overlook the often dubious cleanliness.

Best is **Kabur**, T03595-258504, with a terrace restaurant and internet. With over 70 places to choose from, and hotel building going on unchecked, the following are recommended.

**$$$-$$ Norbu Ghang Resort**, Main Rd, Upper Pelling, T03595-250566, www.norbu ghanghotels.com. Cottage rooms with a pretty garden, better views from those away from road, views from the terrace are superb. Restaurant and bar. The **Norbu Ghang Retreat and Spa**, opened 2012, is adjacent (meals inclusive).

**$$-$ Sikkim Tourist Centre**, Upper Pelling, near Jeep Stand, T03595-258556. Simple rooms, some with views, cheaper on roadside, rooftop restaurant (cooking excellent but service limited; only snacks after 1400), tours.

**$ Garuda**, Upper Pelling, near bus stop, T03595-258319. Variety of rooms with bath in a popular lodge, hot water (heaters Rs 100-150), dorm, restaurant (breakfast on rooftop, mountain views), internet, backpackers' favourite.

**$ Haven**, Khecheopalri Rd, Middle Pelling, T03595-258238. Clean doubles with hot running water.

**$ Sisters Family Guest House**, near Garuda, T03595-250569. 8 simple clean rooms, shared bath (bucket hot water). Friendly, great food.

### Pemayangtse p346

**$$$$ Elgin Mount Pandim**, 15-min walk below monastery, T03593-250756, www.elginhotels.com. Sparkling bright rooms, some with beautiful mountain views, in freshly renovated and upmarket building that once belonged to the Sikkimese royal family. Large grounds, breakfast included.

### Khecheopalri Lake p346

A couple of families take in guests at homestays in the small village on the ridge (25 mins' walk up the hill, left up the path by the car park near the lake). Highly recommended for a relaxing interlude with stunning mountain views.

**$ Pilgrims' Lodge**, on the edge of the lake. Enterprising Mr Tenang provides Sikkimese porridge and millet bread (and much more), and leads short circular hikes.

**$ Trekkers Hut**, 400 m before the lake on the left. Simple rooms and friendly staff provide food, information and a bonfire at night.

**Yuksom** *p347*
**$$$ Yuksum Residency**, Main Rd, T03595-241277, www.yuksumresidency.com. Huge construction rather out of keeping with the village, white marble predominates and terrace lit-up at night. Rooms are massive and well appointed (especially the suite with parquet flooring), furnishings high quality rather than rustic, flatscreen TVs, lots of light and some good views. Giftshop has some nice jewellery, restaurant a bit stiff.

**$$ Tashigang**, T03595-241202, hoteltashigang@rediffmail.com. Intimate rooms with lovely views (some with balcony), wooden floors, striped bedspreads and simple tasteful furnishings. Ageing in a good way. Marble and tile bathrooms, some suites, everything clean and polished. Own vegetable patch and restaurant (see below), peaceful garden. Very welcoming and staff are on the ball.

**$ Dragon**, Main Rd, T03595-241290, T(0)9733-244759. Friendly and sociable guesthouse with clean small rooms (shared bath, hot water unreliable). Nice outdoor area, and good for a snug beer/meal in the family kitchen.

**$ Hotel Pemathang**, Main Rd, T03595-241221, T(0)9002-090180, kinzongbhutia@yahoo.com. Chic reception with lavish flowers, but most rooms big and blank, carpeted, paint already getting shabby. However, the 2 back doubles with balconies and view of Kabur peak are nice, others share a balcony.

**$ Hotel Yangrigang**, Main Rd, T03595-241217, yan13jan@yahoo.com. The main backpacker hub, with an acceptable restaurant and internet facilities as well as good standard rooms (doubles Rs 400-500)

mostly with twin beds, bigger and better views upstairs (Rs 700-800), geysers and comfy beds. Manager is informative and pleasant. Treks easily arranged.

**$ Pemalingpa Cottage**, just below Tashigang Hotel. Lovely little homestay, basic, only 2 rooms one of which is delightfully rustic and sunny. Outside toilet, hot buckets provided, family make every effort to make guests welcome. Highly recommended.

## 🍴 Restaurants

**Pelling** *p346*
Don't miss local *chhang* brewed in the area.
**$$-$ Alpine**, Khecheopalri Rd (below Garuda, see Where to stay). Chinese, Kashmiri especially good. Yellow, wooden cottage run by friendly Ladakhi lady.
**$ Mock-Too**, Upper Pelling opposite **Sikkim Tourist Centre** (see What to do, below). Excellent fresh snacks including *momos*, paratha and samosas.

**Yuksom** *p347*
A 2000 curfew is imposed by the police in Yuksom, when all activities move indoors – get your food order in early.
**$$-$ Tashigang** (see Where to stay, above). Cheery hotel restaurant is unpretentious, with delicious Sikkimese specialities (seasonal) such as nettle soup and wild fern curry. Other more typically Indian dishes also available. Ingredients come from their vegetable garden or surrounding countryside. Recommended.
**$ Gupta's**, on the main street, attracts travellers to its social outdoor seating area, and does surprisingly good quesadillas and pizza, as well as *thali* (no refills) and yak's cheese *momos*. Next door, **Yak** is of a similar ilk and with friendlier owners.

## 🚌 Transport

Buses can be crowded, especially during **Pujas** and **Diwali**. Quicker, more convenient jeeps run to/from Gangtok and between all main towns in the west, often leaving early morning; check locally for current times. If no jeep is going directly to your destination, it may be best to go to Gezing, Jorethang or Namchi, which have frequent services in all directions. Direct jeeps leave from all three towns for **Siliguri**, 4-5 hrs, and **Darjeeling**, 2-3 hrs.

## Jorethang p345

The SNT bus stand has services to: **Siliguri**, 0930; **Gangtok**, 1230; **Rangpo**, 1230; **Namchi**, 0830, 1200 and 1600; **Soreng**, 1400; **Pelling**, 1500; **Ravangla**, 1200; **Teesta**, 0930.

There are 3 jeep stands in Jorethang, close together on the south side of town near the Tourism Office. The main stand serves: **Siliguri**, departures between 0700-1600, Rs 90, 2½ hrs; **Gangtok**, from 0700-1600, Rs 100, 3 hrs; **Karkabita** (for Nepal), 0730, 0830, 0930 and 1330, 4 hrs, Rs 130; **Kalimpong**, 0900-1430, 1½ hrs and **Gezing**, regular service, 2 hrs. The block slightly uphill behind the main stand has jeeps for: **Tashiding**, 1½ hrs, Rs 70 and **Yuksom**, 3 hrs, Rs 90, from 1200-1500. Closer to the Tourism Office, jeeps for: **Darjeeling**, from 0800-1530, 2 hrs and **Namchi**, 0600-1100, 45 mins.

## Tashiding p345

Several jeeps from **Gezing** via **Legship**, and from **Yuksom** (early morning). To **Jorethang**, 0700 & 0800, 1½ hrs, Rs 70; **Gangtok**, 0630 and 0700, 3½ hrs, via **Ravangla**, 1½ hrs, Rs 50; **Yuksom**, 1100 and 1300, 1 hr, Rs 50; **Gezing**, 1½ hrs, 0730, Rs 60. Tashiding is a day's trek from **Pemayangtse** or **Yuksom** (allow 7 hrs).

## Pemayangtse p346

From **Gezing**: bus or shared jeep to monastery, 1000-1430, Rs 20. From **Pelling**, taxi Rs 70 one way, easy walk back.

## Pelling p346

To **Gezing** reasonably frequent jeeps or walk along steep downhill track, 1-2 hrs. To **Khecheopalri Lake**: last bus at 1400, or you can walk 5 hrs (part very steep; last 3 hrs follows road, with short cuts). Buses and shared jeeps to **Yuksom** (until 1500, 3 hrs), **Damthang, Gangtok** (4 hrs); **Darjeeling** via Jorethang, tickets from stand opposite Hotel Garuda, Rs 180. **Siliguri**: SNT bus 0700; tickets sold at provision store next to **Hotel Pelling** where bus starts, and stops uphill at jeep stand near **Garuda** hotel.

## Khecheopalri Lake p346

From **Pelling**: jeep share, 1½ hrs; to **Tashiding** (3 options): 1) 0700 bus to Gezing, then jeep. 2) Bus to Yuksom 1500 (irregular) from 'junction', 10 km from lake, overnight in Yuksom, then bus at 0700 (or jeep) to Tashiding, 1 hr. 3) Hitch a lift on the Pelling to Tashiding jeep, which passes the 'junction'at about 1400 (try sitting on top of jeep to enjoy the beautiful scenery).

## Yuksom p347

Shared jeeps leave from near Gupta's restaurant, buy ticket a day ahead in season. To **Pelling**, 0630, 2½ hrs, Rs 60; **Gezing**, 0630, 3 hrs, Rs 60; **Jorethang**, 0630, 3½ hrs, Rs 90 via **Tashiding**, 1 hr, Rs 60; **Gangtok**, 0630 and 1300, 5 hrs, Rs 160; **Pelling**, 0630, 2½ hrs, Rs 60. To reach **Khecheopalri Lake**, private hire only.

# North Sikkim

*You'll need to join an organized tour to explore the outposts of the Yumthang and Tsopta valleys, where traditional Lepcha and Bhotia villages huddle beneath mountains that rear steeply towards Tibet. The scenery is spectacular, though the road well travelled – particularly by Indian tourists. Expect to be restricted in your movements and spend long days in a jeep. May to July is the best time to see primula and other alpine flowers in bloom in the high-altitude meadows.* ▶▶ *For listings, see page 353.*

## Phodong → *Colour map 4, A2.*

The renovated early 18th-century monastery of Phodong is 1.5 km above the north Sikkim Highway, about 2 km before Phodong village. The track is accessible by jeep, and tours to North Sikkim usually include a visit to the monastery on the way back down to Gangtok. Otherwise, it is a pleasant walk up to the *gompa* where friendly monks show you around; there are especially beautiful frescoes and wall paintings. A further hike of 2 km takes you to picturesque **Labrang** monastery of the Nyingmapa sect, unique in that it retains its original structure undamaged by time or fire. Below the track nearby is the ruined palace of **Tumlong**, the capital of Sikkim for most of the 19th century.

## Phodong to Chumthang

In addition to several police checkpoints, the road beyond Phodong passes through some mildly attractive villages, fluffy forested slopes, and past dramatic waterfalls on the way to bustling **Mangan**, the district headquarters, and then **Singhik**. In both places there are perfectly acceptable lodges with good views and a friendly welcome to the rare independent traveller who stops here (though Mangan has more opportunities for decent eating and transport connections). Beyond Singhik, permits are required for foreign tourists which travel agents arrange in Gangtok, along with vehicle, driver and accommodation, as part of a tour. The road and the Tista River part ways at Chumthang, dominated by a hydroelectric project, with one track leading northeast to the Yumthang Valley and the other northwest to Tsopta Valley.

## Yumthang Valley → *Colour map 4, A2. 135 km north of Gangtok.*

**Lachung** sits among spectacular mountain scenery at 2400 m and acts as a gateway to the increasingly popular Yumthang Valley. Still run on the traditional democratic Dzomsa system, the village is a stronghold of Bhotia culture, though the daily influx of tourists from Gangtok and the rapid construction of lodges to accommodate them has begun to take its toll. Hotels, most over three storeys high, have started to dominate the series of small villages which make up Lachung. The central point is Faka Bazar by the suspension bridge, worth crossing to visit pretty **Lachung Monastery** (open mornings/evenings only) up the opposite hillside in Sharchog village; shortcuts past patches of cultivation and neat pastel-hued homes reach the monastery in about 30 minutes. The paintings of demons and the Wheel of Life in the porch are particularly dramatic, and a path behind the *gompa* climbs up for gorgeous views back down the valley.

The road north to Yumthang passes through the **Shingba Rhododendron Sanctuary**, which has 24 of the 40 rhododendron species found in Sikkim, along with attractive aconites, gentians, poppies, saxifrages, potentillas and primulas. May-July is the best time to see these and other high-altitude alpine flowers growing in the wild.

The valley slopes of **Yumthang**, the 'Valley of the Flowers', are surrounded by imposing snow-clad mountains. Glaciers flow down slopes forested with fir towards the milky turquoise water of Lachung River and, in summertime, the valley floor is indeed carpeted with purple primulas. This is the official end-point for foreigners, and a place where all jeep tours stop for a photo opportunity. A few minutes' walk from the refreshments stalls on the main road are unappealing sulphur hot springs; from here a stone path leads into a lovely hour's walk through the rhododendron forests. It is (unofficially) possible, and usually offered (for an additional charge), to continue for a further hour along the rough road to Samdong (Tibetan, meaning 'bridge'). It is a dramatic drive with views above the pink rocky riverbed and pale khaki-coloured valley walls, to a closer encounter with snowy peaks. Indians tourists can carry on further to Zero Point, but the final halting point for foreigners is signalled by impromptu noodle and liquor stands.

## Tsopta Valley

The Bhotia village of **Lachen**, 122 km from Gangtok, is the chief overnight stop when visiting the stark landscape of the Tsopta (Chopta) Valley. Lachen straggles along one edge of the road along the steep river valley, surrounded by thick alpine forests. The 2000-strong population are known as Lachenpas, and traditionally were yak-herders. An unmetalled road follows the river from Lachen, up the mountainside past ponies, yaks and rhododendron cover to the more interesting village of Thangu 30 km north, where accommodation is also available. On the edge of **Thangu** (altitude 4260 m) potato, cabbage and spinach are cultivated from the arid land, men and women sharing the workload in the fields. Traditional sturdy wooden dwellings and dry stone walls demarcate the land and the scent of smouldering pine prevails. The wide river valley beyond the village has spectacular views towards the mountains and Tibet. It is a seasonal grazing ground for yaks, here grow Jatamasi plants which is used to make incense. Foreign tourists spend a couple of hours wandering the valley floor, covered in wild flowers in summer, while Indian tourists can continue up to Gurudongmar Lake (foreigners need a special permit from the Home Affairs Office in Delhi for this, which is not guaranteed).

Thangu is the starting point for the gruelling trek to **Green Lake** (altitude 5120 m) which takes around 14 days in total. Special permits are necessary that require at least six weeks to arrange – they are expensive, as is the entire venture as all supplies and equipment have be carried. The high cost means that tourist numbers are few. Much of the trek goes through thick spruce and fir forests, as well as the huge variety of rhododendron species for which the region is famed.

## North Sikkim listings

*For hotel and restaurant price codes and other relevant information, see pages 22-26.*

## ⬤ Where to stay

**Phodong** *p351*
**$ Yak and Yeti**, T03595-260884. Quiet and clean. Some rooms with toilet, hot water in buckets, but meals are pricey. Recommended.

### Yumthang Valley *p351*
### Lachung
The tour agents determine where you stay in North Sikkim. Try to specify a certain hotel if you don't wish to leave it up to chance, and the cost will be built into the tour accordingly. Particularly nice options are listed below, in descending order of price and comfortableness, but all hotels are of a higher standard than budget travellers will be accustomed to.
**Golden Fish**, Main Rd, Singring, T03592-214852, www.hotelgoldenfishitgo.com. This very clean and warm option has friendly, relaxed and efficient staff. Excellent food is prepared and high standards maintained. Some new suites with TVs. Can book a package through the website.
**Season House**, up the hill, Singring, T(0)9434-449042. Quaint rooms in the old log cabin or brand new ones in the chalet, excellent bathrooms. Quietly efficient staff and good food. At the highest point on the

road, save for the Rimpoche's residence next door, so fabulous views from the terrace.
**Sela Inn**, Faka Bazar, T03592-214808. Older and shabbier, this well-established welcoming place has an atmospheric restaurant and is closer to any 'action' in town.
**Sonam In Lodge**, Main Rd, Singring, T03592-214830. Run by a charming family who speak little English, cosy simple rooms in an old-style wooden building are Rs 300, hot buckets provided.
**Taagsing Retreat** (aka Modern Residency), Singring, www.modernresidency.com. Lachung's most comfortable accommodation is a striking bottle-green pagoda on the southern edge of the village. The 22 Sikkimese-styled rooms are arranged on several levels, with balconies and great views. Pure veg restaurant serves buffet meals, plus there's a meditation hall, bar, library and little museum. Staff are lovely. Tours booked through **Modern Treks & Tours**, Gangtok (see page 343).

## ⬤ Transport

**Phodong** *p351*
From Gangtok, take a bus to the start of the jeep track, 0800 (2 hrs), Rs 35; return bus, 1500. Jeeps travel up to **Labrang** monastery. Jeeps to **Mangan** leave in the early morning and it is advisable to book at least 2 days in advance.

# Trekking in Sikkim

*Trekking is the biggest draw of Sikkim for many foreign tourists, and no previous experience is necessary as most treks are at 2000-3800 m. The trail to Dzongri (three to four days) or on to Gocha La (eight to nine days) is the most popular and climbs to nearly 5000 m, but there are plenty of day trails on clear paths that are less physically taxing. An added attraction is that* dzos *(a cross between a cow and a yak) can carry your gear instead of porters, though they are slower. The trekking routes also pass through villages that give an insight into the tribal people's lifestyle. With this area coming under threat from pollution by rubbish left by trekkers, be sure to choose a trekking agency that enforces good environmental practices; ECOSS in Gangtok (see page 343) can point you in the right direction.* ▸▸ *For listings, see pages 340-344, 347-350 and 353.*

## Ins and outs

**Best time to visit** March to late May and October to early December. April is best for flowers. **Leeches** can be a problem in the wet season below 2000 m.

**Permits** Foreigners must be in a group of at least two before applying for a trekking permit. Approved trekking agents can assist with applications. Areas open to foreigners include the Khangchendzonga Biosphere Reserve near Yuksom (15-day permits can be arranged in a morning from Gangtok or Yuksom), the Lachung and Yumthang valleys in North Sikkim (five-day permits take 24 hours processing time from Gangtok) and Chhangu in East Sikkim (one day).

**Maps and guidebooks** *Sikkim: A Guide and Handbook*, by **Rajesh Verma**, updated annually, introduces the state and has descriptions of treks, with trekking profiles. The **U 502** sheets for Sikkim are *NG 45-3* and *NG 45-4*. PP Karan published a map at the scale of 1:150,000 in 1969 (US$3, available from the Program Director of Geography, George Mason University, Fairfax, VA 22030, US). A very detailed map is *Sikkim Himalaya* (Swiss Alpine Club) – Huber 1:50,000, £16.

## Khangchendzonga National Park

ⓘ *Most people arrange their trek in Gangtok/Darjeeling; US$40-60 per person per day, depending on service. There's a growing trend for agents to tag on extra group members (picked up in Yuksom) who get a greatly discounted price. While this works well for some parties, it can leave a sour taste for those who are funding the majority of the trip.*

The park offers trekking routes through picturesque terraced fields of barley, past fruit orchards to lush green forests of pines, oak, chestnut, rhododendrons, giant magnolias, then to high passes crossing fast mountain streams and rugged terrain. Animals in the park include Himalayan brown bear, black bear, the endangered musk deer, flying squirrel, Tibetan antelope, wild ass and Himalayan wild goat. The red panda lives mostly on treetops at 3000-4000 m. There are about 600 species of bird.

The Khangchendzonga trek falls within the national park, from which all forms of industry and agriculture have been officially banished. The park office in **Yuksom**, about 100 m below the trekkers' huts, has interesting exhibits and helpful staff.

The classic trekking route goes from **Yuksom to Gocha La** (variously spelt Goecha La and Gochela). This eight- to nine-day trek includes some magnificent scenery around

Khangchendzonga, and there are excellent views as you travel up the Ratong Chu River to the amphitheatre of peaks at the head of the valley. These include Kokthang (6150 m), Ratong (6683 m), Kabru Dome (6604 m), Forked Peak (6116 m) and the pyramid of Pandim (6720 m) past which the trail runs.

Trekkers' huts (**$**), in picturesque places at Yuksom, Tsokha and Dzongri, are fairly clean with basic toilets. Bring sleeping bags; meals are cooked by a caretaker.

**Day 1 Yuksom to Tsokha** An eight-hour climb to the growing village of Tsokha, settled by Tibetan refugees. The first half of the climb passes through dense semi-tropical forests and across the Prek Chu on a suspension bridge. A steep climb of two hours leads first to **Bakhim** (2740 m), which has a tea stall, a forest bungalow and good views. The track goes through silver fir and magnolia to Tsokha (2950 m), the last village on the trek. Trekkers' hut and campsite at Tsokha.

**Day 2 Tsokha to Dzongri** Mixed temperate forests give way to rhododendron. **Phedang** is less than three hours up the track. Pandim, Narsingh and Joponu peaks are clearly visible, and a further hour's climb takes the track above the rhododendrons to a ridge. A gentle descent leads to Dzongri (4030 m, 8 km from Bakhim). There is a trekkers' hut and campsite. Dzongri attracts pilgrims to its *chortens* holding Buddhist relics. From exposed and windswept hillsides nearby are good panoramic views of the surrounding mountains and of spectacular sunrises or sunsets on Khangchendzonga.

**Sikkim treks**

**Day 3 Dzongri to Thangshing** A trail through dwarf rhododendron and juniper climbs the ridge for 5 km. Pandim is immediately ahead. A steep drop descends to the Prek Chu again, crossed by a bridge, followed by a gentle climb to Thangshing (3900 m). The southern ridge of Khangchendzonga is ahead. There is a trekkers' hut and campsite.

**Day 4 Thangshing to Samity Lake** The track leads through juniper scrub to a steeper section up a lateral moraine, followed by the drop down to the glacial and holy Samity Lake. The surrounding moraines give superb views of Khangchendzonga and other major peaks. You can't camp at the lake; a new campsite is 1 km away at Lammuney.

**Day 5 To Zemathang and Gocha La and return** The climb up to Zemathang (4800 m) and Gocha La (4900 m) gives views up to the sheer face of the eastern wall of Khangchendzonga. It is a vigorous walk to reach the pass, but equally impressive views can be gained from nearby slopes. Sometimes guides stop before the official 'Gocha La' viewpoint, be wary of this and ask the advice of other trekkers that you meet on the way. Much of the walk is on rough moraine.

**Day 6 Samity Lake to Thangshing** Return to Thangshing. This is only a two-hour walk, so it is possible to take it gently and make a diversion to the former yak grazing grounds of Lam Pokhari Lake (3900 m) above Thangshing. The area is rich in medicinal plants, and you may see some rare high-altitude birds and blue sheep.

**Days 7 and 8 Thangshing to Tsokha** The return route can be made by a lower track, avoiding Dzongri. Dense rhododendrons flank the right bank of the Prek Chu, rich in birdlife. Day 7 ends in Tsokha village. The next morning you retrace your steps to Yuksom.

## Other treks in Sikkim

It's possible to trek from town to town, if you're prepared to do some road walking and ask villagers to show you short cuts. One of the best circuits, for up to seven days but also enjoyable in smaller sections, begins from Pelling or Pemayangtse, descending through terraced fields to the Rimbi Khola river, then climbing up to Khecheopalri Lake. From here you can easily reach Yuksom in a day, then continue on to Tashiding, and either return to Pemayangtse or climb eastwards towards Kewzing and Ravangla.

# Contents

# Assam & Arunachal Pradesh

## At a glance

⊟ **Getting around** Jeeps are the best (often the only) form of transport and advance planning is required to secure a seat. The nearest functioning airport is in Guwahati.

● **Time required** A week for central Arunachal, at least 4 days for the western part, and factor in a couple of days in Assam.

☾ **Weather** Wet and humid on the lowlands, chilly in the highlands almost all year round.

✕ **When not to go** Nov-Mar can be painfully cold in western Arunachal.

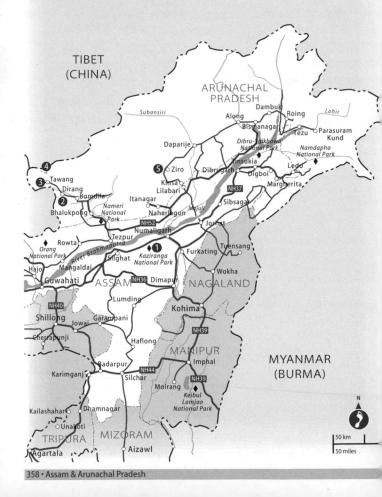

★ **Don't miss …**
1 One-horned rhinos in Kaziranga National Park, page 363.
2 Picturesque Monpa homesteads in old Dirang village, page 375.
3 Breakfast with the monks at Tawang Monastery, page 376.
4 The silent high-altitude lakes north of Tawang, page 377.
5 Tribal life in the Ziro Valley, page 378.

TIBET
(CHINA)

ARUNACHAL
PRADESH

*Subansiri*

Dambuk

Along

Bismanagar

Roing

*Lohit*

Tezu

Parasuram
Kund

Daparije

*Dibru-Saikhowa*
*National Park*

*Namdapha*
*National Park*

⑤ ○ Ziro

Tinsukia

Dibrugarh

Digboi

Ledo

Khisa ○

Lilabari

Itanagar

*Majuli*

Sibsagar

Margherita

③ Tawang

Dirang

Bomdila

Naharlagun

NH37

Bhalukpong

*Nameri*
*National Park*

Jorhat

④

Rowta

Tezpur

Numaligarh

NH52

Tuensang

*Orang*
*National Park*

Silghat

*Kaziranga*
*National Park*

Furkating

Hajo

Mangaldai

*River Brahmaputra*

① ○ ○

Wokha

Guwahati

ASSAM

NH36

Dimapur

NAGALAND

MYANMAR
(BURMA)

NH40

Lumding

Shillong

Jowai

Garampani

Kohima

Cherrapunji

Haflong

NH39

Badarpur

MANIPUR

Karimganj

NH44

Silchar

Imphal

Moirang

NH39

Kailashahar

Dhamnagar

*Keibul*
*Lamjao*
*National Park*

Unakoti ○

TRIPURA

MIZORAM

N

Agartala

Aizawl

50 km

50 miles

The northeast states of India remain a true frontier region, connected to the rest of the country by a narrow 20-km-wide strip of land – aptly coined the 'chicken neck' by locals. The entry point is the city of Guwahati, on the banks of the mighty Brahmaputra, where the scenic lowlands of Assam begin.

The state has several national parks and is a wonderful place to spot wildlife, especially as – compared to elsewhere in India – tourists are few and far between.

Arunachal Pradesh, northeast India's largest and most remote state, has only relatively recently opened its doors to visitors. Permits, organized in advance, are still required before you can cross the border from the scenic lowlands of Assam to meet the foothills of the Himalaya. Independent travel in these parts is only for the committed, as public transport connections almost always leave just once a day (usually at about at 0500) and involve gruelling jeep rides along pot-holed roads.

One of the most linguistically diverse regions in Asia, there are at least 30 distinct languages spoken within Arunachal's borders, in addition to countless dialects and sub-dialects. The plains and plateau of central Arunachal are home to fascinating unique tribal cultures, where animist religions still prevail.

# Assam

**Background** → *Population: 31.1 million. Area: 78,438 sq km.*

*The lush valley of the Brahmaputra, one of the world's great rivers, provides the setting for Assam's culturally rich and diverse communities. Although it is tea that has put the state on the world map, the fertile river valley is home to generations of rice farmers, and tribal populations continue to have a significant presence. A highlight of any visit is Kaziranga National Park, where the population of Asian one-horned rhinos has been steadily increasing over recent years meaning that sightings are virtually guaranteed.* ▸▸ *For listings, see pages 365-372.*

## The land

**Geography** Assam stretches nearly 800 km from east to west, the length of the broad floor of the Brahmaputra Valley. The Himalaya to the north and the Shillong Plateau to the south can be clearly seen. The state is dominated by the unpredictable Brahmaputra, constantly changing course to create new sandbanks, and encasing Majuli, the largest riverine island on earth.

**Climate** Unless you really want to see rain, avoid the monsoon. Assam is in one of the wettest monsoon belts in the world. Even the central Brahmaputra Valley, protected by the rain shadow of the Shillong Plateau, has over 1600 mm of annual rainfall. The rest of the Assam Valley has up to 3200 mm a year, mostly between May and September. Although summer temperatures are high, from December to February it can be cold, especially at night.

## History

The Ahoms, a Shan ruling tribe, arrived in the area in the early 13th century, deposed the ruler and established the kingdom of Assam with its capital in Sibsagar. They later intermixed with Aryan stock and also with existing indigenous peoples (Morans, Chutiyas, and most converted to Hinduism. The Mughals made several attempts to invade without success, but the Burmese finally invaded Assam at the end of the 18th century and held it almost continuously until it was ceded to the East India Company in 1826. The British administered it in name until 1947 though many areas were beyond their effective control.

## People

More than 85% of the people continue to live in rural areas. The ethnic origin of the Assamese varies from Mongoloid tribes to those of directly Indian stock. There has been a steady flow of Muslim settlers from Bengal since the late 19th century. The predominant language is Assamese, similar to Bengali although harder to pronounce. In Assamese, 'how are you?' is *'Apni kene koya?'* and 'good' is *'bahal'*.

## Modern Assam

The Assam Valley is in a strategically sensitive corridor for India, lying close to the Chinese frontier. Its sensitivity has been increased by the tension between local Assamese and immigrant groups. The state has suffered a long-running low-intensity conflict and in late 2006 and early 2007 a number of bombings occurred in the capital Guwahati. In 2012 ethnic violence erupted between the indigenous Bodo community and Muslims in the west of the state, also sparking off riots in other parts of India. The most troubled area is still the beautiful Cachar Hills in the south, and it is not recommended to visit this region. Seek advice from your consulate and local tour agencies before travelling.

## Guwahati → *For listings, see pages 365-372. Colour map 4, B4.*

Despite its commanding position on the south bank of the mighty Brahmaputra, it is easy to forget that Guwahati is a riverside town, the waterside having little impact on people's lives. The main entrance point for visitors to the northeastern, the city retains a relaxed and friendly atmosphere. Paltan Bazar, where most visitors arrive, is very busy and crowded as are the narrower streets and markets of Fancy Bazar to the west.

### Arriving in Guwahati → *Population: over 1 million.*

**Getting there** LBG International Airport (23 km) has flights from Kolkata, Delhi, Bagdogra and airports throughout the Northeast, plus flights from Bangkok and Bhutan. Assam State Transport (ASTC) runs an air-conditioned coach to the city for Rs 100 (ticket office near Arrivals); pre-paid taxis cost Rs 400 or shared taxis Rs 120. The railway station is in the central Paltan Bazar, while long distance private buses arrive at the ISBT (Interstate Bus Terminal), 8 km from the centre, connected to the city centre by canter (Rs 10). ▶▶ *See Transport, page 371.*

**Getting around** It is easy to walk around the two main commercial areas of Paltan and Pan (pronounced *Paan*) Bazars, which have most of the hotels and restaurants. Citybuses or (red) canters are cheap and very efficient around the city (conductors call out the stops), whereas auto-rickshaws need hard bargaining. Political incidents in the city mean there is a visible military presence. Carry a torch when walking at night; large holes in the pavement lie in wait to plunge unwary travellers straight down into the sewers.

**Tourist information** Information booths at the airport, with useful maps; also a counter for Assam at the railway station. **Assam Tourism** ① *Tourist Lodge, Station Rd, T0361-254 7102, www.assamtourism.org, daily 1000-1630.* **Assam Tourism Development Corporation (ASTDC)** ① *AK Azad Rd, Paryatan Bhawan, T0361-263 3654.*

## Background

Guwahati, on the site of the ancient capital of a succession of local chieftains, was once known as Pragjyotishpur ('City of Astrology'). The **Navagrah** ('nine planets') **Temple** on a hill here was the ancient centre of astronomy and astrology. It was also a centre of learning and a place of Hindu pilgrimage. In the seventh century, Hiuen Tsang described its beautiful mountains, forests and wildlife. Today it is the business capital while **Dispur**, the 'Capital Area', is just to the south.

## Places in Guwahati

The 10th-century **Janardhan Temple**, on the bank of the Brahmaputra, was rebuilt in the 17th century and has been modernised since. The Buddha image here uniquely blends Hindu and Buddhist features. The **Umananda** (Siva) **Temple** ① *Peacock Island in the Brahmaputra, reached by 10-min ferry ride, Rs 10, 0930-1630,* was built by an Ahom king in 1594, in the belief that Uma, Siva's consort, had stayed there. Enter the candlelit rear shrine with other pilgrims to receive a blessing. The wooded island can be circled by the footpath and gives pleasant views of the banks. **Assam State Museum** ① *Tue-Sun 1000-1630 (Mar-Sep), 1000-1545 (Oct-Feb), ticket counter closes 1300-1330, closed 2nd and 4th Sat of the month,*

*Rs 5*, has an extensive and beautiful sculpture collection, and covers epigraphy and textiles in recently refurbished galleries. It is also informative on the neighbouring cultures, with sections on village life, crafts and ethnography – a reconstruction of a mud-brick thatched house can be explored. **Srimanta Sankaradeva Kalakshetra** ① *Panjabari, on road to Narangi, Tue-Sun 0800-2200, Rs 10, bus No 8*, is a cultural complex set up to serve as a centre for Assamese dance, drama, music, fine arts and literature ('a theme park of Assamese life'). It features a museum, theatre, artists' village and heritage park. **Assam State Zoo and Botanical Gardens** ① *off Zoo Rd, 6 km southwest of the city, Rs 50, cameras Rs 70*, is a cheap way to get up close to one-horned rhinos, snow leopards, tigers and snakes for those who don't want to take their chances at Kaziranga or other national parks.

## Around Guwahati

**Kamakhya Temple**, 7 km west, is believed to be an old Khasi sacrificial site on Nilachal Hill. A centre for Tantric Hinduism and Sakti worship, rebuilt in 1665 after the 10th-century temple was destroyed by a Brahmin convert to Islam. It typifies Assamese temple architecture with its distinctive beehive-shape *sikhara* (spire), the nymph motifs and the long turtleback hall. The dark sanctum contains the creative part of the goddess which is said to have fallen here, and pilgrims enter to touch the wet *yoni* of Kamakhya (Sakti). Apart from the carved stone symbol of Sakti's genitals, there are (unusually) no other images of the goddess inside the sanctum. Western visitors are allowed into the sanctum but should be prepared for the highly charged atmosphere and to walk barefoot on a floor awash with the sacrificial blood of a goat. No Bengali would leave Assam without visiting this temple, hence queues can be immense (a donation to the priests of Rs 500 will grant instant access, or go at dawn to be first in line). ▶▶ *See Festivals, page 369.*

Further up the hill is a smaller temple and a viewpoint with panoramic views of the Brahmaputra. It can be visited by bus from MG Road (towards Adabari Bus Stand); ask to be dropped near Kamakhya. From here take a canter (red minibus) from AT Road to the temple or walk up the steep and slippery rocky path at the back of the hill. An intense and memorable outing.

**North Guwahati** is a sleepy town across Saraighat Bridge, which can be reached by public ferry from Sukreswar Ghat (Rs 5). The **Digheswari Temple** is worth a visit where the hazy little village is pleasant for a wander; ask the priests about the rare golden langurs that live here.

## Around Guwahati

**Hajo**, a friendly and peaceful town, 34 km across the river, produces bell-metal work and is sacred to three religions. **Hayagriba Madhab Hindu temple** is said to contain a Buddhist relic. Some believe this is where the Buddha attained Nirvana. Its hilltop location is more spectacular than the temple itself. The main street behind the tank stocked with fish leads to an old **Ganesh temple** after 2 km; a friendly priest might allow you in. Hajo is also sacred to Muslims; the **Pao Mecca Mosque**, 3 km further, built by Pir Ghiasuddin Aulia is supposed to have a *pao* (quarter) of the sanctity of Mecca. Take a bus from Adabar Bus Stand, which drops you off at the Hindu temple (one hour, last return at 1600 but very crowded; you may have to travel on the roof).

The small village of **Sualkuchi**, on the north bank of the Brahmaputra, is famous for silk production from non mulberry leaf-fed worms, hence its unique natural colour. Every household is involved with weaving of *muga*, *endi* or *pat* silk; prices are 30% cheaper than in Guwahati. Take the ferry from Guwahati or a bus from Hajo (20 minutes).

Kaziranga was declared a game sanctuary in 1916 to save the Indian greater one-horned rhino and became a national park in 1974. It is now a World Heritage Site. In a beautiful setting on the banks of the Brahmaputra, and with the Karbi Anglong Hills to the south, the 430-sq-km park combines elephant grass mixed with thorny rattan cane, areas of semi-evergreen forest and shallow swamps.

## Arriving in Kaziranga National Park

ⓘ *Park roads open 0730-1100, 1400-1630. Foreigners Rs 250. Camera fees change regularly: currently Rs 50, video, Rs 500. There's a 25% discount on fees after 3 consecutive days. The park is closed 30 Apr-1 Nov each year, during monsoons.*

Guwahati is 215 km from Kohora, the main entry point to Kaziranga on the NH37. The best months to visit are November, and February-March before it gets too hot (December and January are best for birds, but is also peak tourist season). Summer maximum 35°C, minimum 18°C; Winter maximum 24°C, minimum 7°C. Annual rainfall 2300 mm, heavy in summer. Wear cotton clothing but take a jacket.▶▶ *See Transport, page 371.*

Entry into the park is by private vehicle, hired jeep or trained elephants. Although elephants cover less ground than motor vehicles, they can get a lot closer to the wildlife, particularly rhinos and buffalo. **Elephant rides** ⓘ *book the night before through the Forest Range Officer, foreigners Rs 1000, Indians Rs 120, plus jeep transfer from town, Rs 150,* carry four people and get mixed reports; the consensus seems to be that they are less enjoyable when demand is heavy. The viewing posts just inside the park may offer quieter viewing. **Jeeps** for five or six people can be hired from the **Department of Tourism** in Kaziranga or private agents. Government jeeps cost Rs 700 (Rs 120 per person in a shared vehicle) for three hours; private ones Rs 1000-1200 for 50 km or 2½ hours. A car or jeep must be accompanied by a Forest Department Guard (Rs 50), who can give directions as well as spot wildlife. Cars and jeeps pay a road toll, Rs 150.

## Places in Kaziranga National Park

The **rhino** population is over 2000 here and they are guaranteed to be seen in the marshes and grasslands. Despite Kaziranga's status as a national park, poachers still manage to kill the animal for its horn, which is used in Chinese and Tibetan medicine. The park also has over 1000 wild buffalo, sambar, swamp deer (over 500), hog deer, wild pig, hoolock gibbon, elephant (1246 in 2004), python and tiger (89 at last count in 2000), the only predator of the one-horned rhino. There is a rich variety of shallow-water fowl including egrets, pond herons, river terns, black-necked stork, fishing eagles and adjutant storks, pelicans and the rare Bengal florican. There are otters and dolphins in the river.

There are four road routes for visiting the park: the **Central Range** (Kohora, Daflang, Foliomari) is the most visited as it is full of big mammals; the **Western Range** (Baguri, Monabeel, Bimoli, Kanchanjuri) has the highest rhinoceros density but tall elephant grass makes visibility difficult; the **Eastern Range** (Agortoli, Sohola, Rangamatia) has good possibilities for seeing wildlife, but at a distance; the **Burhapahar Range**, furthest west, only became accessible relatively recently and is jeep safaris here are more expensive. Keep receipts as fees are valid for several trips in one day.

## Sibsagar and Dibrugarh

District headquarters of the largest tea and oil producing area in the Northeast, **Sibsagar** was the Ahom capital for two centuries. The Ahoms arrived from southern China in 1228 and set up their first capital at Charaideo, 28 km from present-day Sibsagar, in 1253. Initially they were Buddhists, though Hinduism came to prevail. Daupadi (the Ahom King's wife) built the huge tank in the centre of town and the three temples on its bank in 1734. The central tower of the Siva Dol is one of the tallest in India, while the interior has an inverted lingum. It is a fascinating place to witness **Sivaratri** (celebrated in early March). On the east bank there is a small Buddhist Temple and a birdwatching tower, while on the west bank is the square red-brick **Tai Museum** ⓘ *Fri-Wed 1000-1600, Rs 5*. Ahom artefacts are displayed, including two wooden dragons found at Charaideo, brass pots and plates, silks, combs, basketry, ancient manuscripts and two *dolas* with wooden basins in which the women sat to be carried around.

All the sites around Sibsagar are open sunrise-sunset and charge foreigners a Rs 100 entrance fee. The **Joysagar Tank** at **Rangpur**, 5 km away, and the three temples on its bank date from 1697. The main Joydol (Vishnu temple) sits in pretty gardens; its exterior still has the original decorative terracotta tiles. The Shivadol and Devidol temples are less impressive, but free to enter. **Talatal Ghar**, 4 km from Sibsager, is a large two-storey palace which is being restored. Nearby, the two-storied oval **Rang Ghar** was the royal sports pavilion where elephant fights and games took place – said to be the oldest amphitheatre in Asia. Take a Tata Magic from AT or BG Rd (Rs 10, 20 minutes) to Joysagar, from where you can walk back in the direction of Sibsagar to visit Talatal Ghar and Rang Ghar (1.5 km away).

Much of the town of **Dibrugarh**, 80 km north of Sibsagar, was destroyed during the 1950 earthquake, only a few old buildings remain on the main streets. The new town on the Brahmaputra is surrounded by tea estates, where a couple of delightful old tea-planters bungalows are available for guests to soak up some Raj nostalgia. Dibrugarh is a convenient stop when setting off for (or returning from) central Arunachal Pradesh as transport connections are good and hotels are comfortable. Boats leave daily from Dibrugarh for Pasighat in Arunachal, see page 371.

## Tezpur and around → *For listings, see pages 365-372. Colour map 4, A4.*

**Tezpur**, on the north bank of the Brahmaputra, 180 km northeast of Guwahati, is the site of Assam's first tea plantations. The **Tourist Lodge** ⓘ *Jenkins Rd, T03712-221016, Mon-Sa 1000-1615; closed every 2nd and 4th Sat of the month*, has a brochure and can sketch out a map of town. The town's ancient origins can be seen at **Da Parbatia**, 5 km west, which has the entrance gate of an early Gupta-style temple. In Tezpur's centre, **Chitralekha Udyan** (Cole Park) ⓘ *Rs 10, camera Rs 20, boat Rs 10, 0900-2000*, was created after an earthquake revealed ancient remains and is now a pleasant park around a lake that is lit up at night; some of the slabs of friezes and sculpture unearthed are on display outside the **museum** ⓘ *at the Dak Bungalow, near the Tourist Lodge*. The **Station Club**, opposite the District Commissioner's office, is one of Assam's oldest planters' clubs dating from 1875, with period furniture and a bar worthy of a drink if you can find a member to invite you. Otherwise they are happy to let you look around, although only the card tables, billards and tennis courts remain. A nice spot for sunset is **Agrigarh** ⓘ *Rs 10, 0800-1930*, a 1-km stroll past Ganesh Ghat, with hilltop views over the Brahmaputra and the town. Climb the lookout tower to catch the breeze and be on the same level as circling birds of prey. Possibly the largest Siva linga in India is found inside **Mahabhairab Mandir**, a Rs 10 rickshaw ride from the centre, which has a nightly *puja* at around 1830.

An interesting excursion is to take a Guwahati-bound bus, get off at the bridge over the Brahmaputra, then negotiate with a boatman to take you to the river's confluence with the Bhoreli for some river **dolphin watching**. Some hotels, **Luit**, for example, offer such trips. It involves a 30-minute rickshaw ride, Rs 150, followed by boat hire, around Rs 1000.

**Nameri National Park** ① *35 km north of Tezpur, on the Arunachal border, entry and camera fees are similar to Kaziranga*, is on the river Jia Bhoroli and covers 210 sq km. It is home to tigers (26 in 2006), elephants, Indian bison, barking and hog deer, Himalayan black bears as well as 300 bird species, including the shy and endangered white-winged wood ducks. Flora includes evergreens, bamboo and some open grassland. Buses/*sumos* travelling between Tezpur and Tawang can drop travellers off at Hatigate on the main road. From here, it is 2.5 km down a track to the **Eco Camp** (see Where to stay, page 368), a wonderful overnight stop and good place to arrange visits to the park. There are no roads; you can trek within the park with a forest guide after taking a boat across the river. The Eco-Camp can also organize catch-and-release angling and low-level rafting excursions. The best time (climatically) to visit is October-April, and the best chance of animal sightings are December-March.

**Bhalukpong**, 20 km west of Nameri, is on the Assam-Arunachal border en route to Tawang. This nondescript village is surrounded by the forests of **Pakhui Game Sanctuary**, a mass of ferns, moss and orchids, with a hot spring, orchid garden and good fishing. You can camp (take your own tent) on the picturesque bank of the River Jia Bhoreli or stay in the government tourist cottages overlooking the river. Jeeps and buses from Tezpur all pass through Bhalukpong en route to Tawang.

## ◉ Assam listings

*For hotel and restaurant price codes and other relevant information, see pages 22-26.*

## ◒ Where to stay

**Guwahati** *p361*
There are some budget hotels at Sadullah and M Nehru Rd crossing; those in Paltan Bazar are often full by the afternoon. Most medium-priced hotels have some a/c rooms and a restaurant.
**\$\$ Brahmaputra Ashok**, MG Rd, T0361-760 2281, www.hotelbrahmaputraashok.com. Standard rooms are old style but with wooden floors and decent shower rooms (riverside ones with nice views), central a/c, TV, bamboo and cane furniture, restaurant, travel agency, Wi-Fi. The **Kaziranga** bar, with its zebra print furniture, is fun and there's Silver Streak disco on Sat nights.
**\$\$ Dynasty**, SS Rd, T0361-251 6021, www.dynastyhotel.in. 76 comfortable rooms and suites, this is Guwahati's top hotel and even has a spa. Rooms are tastefully designed and modern, public areas quiet and refined, excellent restaurants serve Indian and Chinese food (see page 369). Gym, breakfast included, efficient staff.
**\$\$ Baruah Bhavan**, T(0)9954-024165, www.heritagehomeassam.com. An Assamese mansion over 100 years old with 6 luxurious rooms, modern amenities and a charming roof terrace. Home-cooking (Assamese, Indian, Chinese, reasonably priced), breakfast included, internet, transport can be arranged. A short walk from the riverside. Recommended.
**\$\$ Nova**, SS Rd, Fancy Bazar, T0361-251 1464, www.novahotel.in. Standard rooms are a bit fusty with dated bathrooms and no a/c (double a/c, much brighter), but the vibe and public areas are nice. Delicious if utilitarian **Natraj** restaurant (Indian, Chinese) has slow service (room service quicker), yet

pleasant, friendly and helpful. Location is spot on for the action in the bazar.

**$$-$ City Palace**, opposite ASTC bus stand, Paltan Bazar, T0361-263 5848/9, www.city palacehotel.com. The lobby with white leather sofas and Astroturf on the walls sets the tone, a range of rooms/suites with a/c, the non-a/c budget rooms are good, clean, and the location couldn't be handier for transport.

**$ Broadview Lodge**, Pan Bazar (by Overbridge Point), T0361-251 2811. Central location, rooms have clean bedding, powerful fans, TV and decent bathrooms (check a couple, layout varies), it's nothing special but suitably priced for what you get.

**$ Centre Point**, opposite Hotel Nandan, GS Rd, Paltan Bazar, T0361-273 9632. Clean small rooms in a functional and respectable guest house, all with TV and decent bathrooms with hot water, some with a/c, helpful staff are a big plus point. Set back from the main road so not too noisy. Single room rates.

**$ Orchid**, B Barua Rd, opposite stadium, Ulubari, T0361-252 3471. The best value single rooms in town, clean, well-furnished and bright, pay more for a/c. Not right in the thick of things but 10-min walk to Paltan Bazar. The cheerfully decorated Magnolia restaurant is excellent, bar open till 2200.

**$ Prashaanti Tourist Lodge** (Assam Tourism), Station Rd, close to railway station, T0361-254 4475, astdcorpn@sancarnet.in. Decent sized rooms with nets, bathroom and balcony, clean sheets and TV. Good restaurant and upstairs bar, tourist information (1000-1700). Great value for non-a/c doubles but single rooms cost almost as much. Book in advance, they are often full.

**$ Suradevi**, MLN Rd, Panbazar, T0361-254 5050. Basic but totally bearable rooms are cheap and noisy, better at the rear, with attached bath, pay more for TV. Decent food in the restaurant. Dorm beds Rs 150.

## Kaziranga National Park *p363*
New lodges are springing up around Kaziranga as quickly as the elephant grass.

The government-run **Tourist Complex**, 1 km south of the main gate in Kohora village, has perfectly adequate options, while a few other places stand out for their eco-awareness and tastefulness. Good discounts are available off-season – but the park itself is closed.

**$$$$ Diphlu River Lodge**, 15 km west of Kohora, T0361-260 2223, www.diphlu riverlodge.com. Utterly chic luxury with a rustic slant, 12 Mishing-style huts, connected by bamboo walkway, surround rice paddies with a prime location on the edge of the national park. Rooms are furnished in a colonial theme from natural materials, bathrooms are inspired, 2 verandas for lounging, and the staff all faultless. Once inside the peaceful enclave everything is included in the price (apart from alcohol) – limitless visits to Kaziranga, walks with naturalists, picnics, meals, visits to Mishing villages. Come here for peace and serenity.

**$$ Jupuri Ghar**, Kaziranga Tourist Complex, Kohora, T(0)9435-196377, jupuri@gmail.com. Peaceful setting on a slope above tea garden and paddies, these new thatched cottages have cane furniture and woven walls, a/c and terraces onto the garden. Pleasant open restaurant, attractive tribal decorations, BYO until they get a license. Also bookable through **Network Travels**, see page 370.

**$$ Wild Grass**, 1.5 km from NH37, 5.5 km from Kohora, ask for Kaziranga IB Bus Stop, 400 m north of resort, T03776-262085, T(0)9954-416945, www.oldassam.com. Unpretentious and relaxing, with a lovely location, 18 spotless rooms in 2 lofty chalets, wooden floors, cane furniture, can get very cold in winter. Great meals (Rs 450 for 2 people) and service, beautiful walks through forests and tea plantations, excellent guided tours, pickup from Guwahati for groups, cultural shows in the evenings by the campfire of Assamese dancing. Half price May-Oct.

**$ Aranya Tourist Lodge**, Tourist Complex, T03776-262429. White paint and marble predominate the 24 large rooms with bath (hot water) and good balcony. A/c costs extra, simple garden, **Rhino Restaurant**, bar (slow service).

**$ Bonani**, Tourist Complex, T03776-262423. 5 breezy white rooms with fans, nets, wicker furniture and large bathrooms (geysers) are good value. Much nicer on the upper level.

**$ Bonashree**, Tourist Complex, T03776-262423. Cheaper still, 9 rooms, a large veranda lends some old-world charm, pleasant garden, but often full. Hot buckets available.

**$ Dhansree Resort**, Kohora, T03776-262501. A variety of rooms and cottages with brick-red exteriors and thatch, fans and geysers. Incongruous water features and use of paint mar the pleasant garden, but nicely located among tea trees.

**$ Kunjaban Dormitory**, Tourist Complex, T03776-262423. Linen optional (Rs 25), 2- or 3-bed rooms. Safe and secure, but no hot buckets.

### Sibsagar *p364*

**$$ Brahmaputra**, BG Rd, T03772-222200. Endless corridors lead to pleasing deluxe double/single rooms with a/c, TV, hot water, new furniture and white paint. Also some better-value singles have fans and lots of space. Kaveri restaurant serves good food, the elevator works, staff are helpful. Gentle bargaining can achieve a significant reduction in price. An annoying 2 km from the centre of town, however.

**$$ Shiva Palace**, AT Rd, T03772-225204, www.nivalink.com/shivapalace. Good restaurant and 'trendy' bar, rooms are Western-style with mod cons. Cheaper rooms getting slightly scuffed, however. Less than 1 km from Shivadol.

**$-$ Siddhartha**, BG Rd, T03772-222276, 7safari@rediffmail.com. 29 rooms, those with a/c homely and new, while non-a/c a bit faded with dirty paintwork, but both have TV and hot running water. Smart public areas and modern restaurant (open from 0630), pleasant bar. Nearly 1 km out of town centre.

**Tourist Lodge**, near Siva Dol, T03772-222394. On the southwest corner of the tank, clean and newly tiled/painted rooms with attached bath are a real bargain (double with a/c and, non-a/c single/double with fan and hot bucket). Front garden, restaurant, quiet location. Only 9 rooms so often full, call in advance. Tourist office in same building (Mon-Sat 1000-1600, closed 2nd and 4th Sat in month).

### Dibrugarh *p364*

**$$$ Chowkidinghee Chang Bungalow** (aka Jalannagar South Bungalow), off Mancotta Rd, 1.5 km from Dibrugarh. A truly charming indulgence in colonial history, this managers' bungalow on the edge of a tea estate has gloriously period rooms opening out onto enormous screened verandas with white cane furniture. Built on stilts to avoid floods and wild animals. Shiny wood floors throughout, there's a Victorian fireplace in the sitting-cum-dining room, both bedrooms are en suite and have dressing rooms. An additional room downstairs is not nearly as attractive. The proximity of the road is the only thing to gripe about. Bring your own alcohol.

**$$$-$$ Mancotta Chang Bungalow**, off Mancotta Rd, Milan Nagar, 5 km from Dibrugarh. Another heritage planter's bungalow on stilts exudes the same ambiance but is larger, with 2 fabulous colonial bedrooms on the upper level, 2 modern rooms downstairs (walk through the patio doors in the morning to enjoy the garden) and a separate bungalow with a post-war feel that sleeps 2 singles. In the upstairs rooms chintzy curtains, brass fittings, Seypoy prints and plenty of tumblers and brandy glasses make drinks on the veranda more attractive than the satellite TV. Bathrooms have enamel claw-footed tubs. Horse riding, tea tours and more are arranged by **Purvi Discovery** who also take the bookings (see What to do, page 370).

**$$ Hotel Natraj**, HS Rd, T0373-232 7275, www.hotelnatraj.net. Recently remodelled, this modern hotel has tiled rooms with comfortable beds, tonal furnishings and excellent bathrooms. 24-hr hot water, a/c, TV. Zaffran restaurant is quite chic with Oriental/Indian food, Sonali restaurant is less formal and has delicious food, there's a soulless bar (with special deals, open till 2200). Breakfast included.

**$$-$ Indsurya**, RKB Path, Dibrugarh, T0373-232 6322, www.hotelindsurya.com. A short walk from the station, the grim frontage of the Indsurya hides great-value rooms which are clean and comfy. The attractive lobby sports an impressive wooden rhino and plenty of wicker furniture. It's often full so call ahead.

**$ Asha Lodge**, AT Rd (at intersection with HS Rd), T0373-232 0053. As basic as it gets, rooms are grim but the cheapest around. The dusty wooden veranda is good for watching the street-life below.

**$ Hotel Devika**, Puja Ghat, off AT Rd, T0373-232 5956, www.hoteldevika.com. Rooms at the front are best with Western toilets and good light (others lack windows), TV, fans, very clean. Corridors are marble and the building has some character. Discounts available, staff obliging, food available. Hot water is by the bucket in cheaper rooms; a few downstairs rooms have shared baths (but they are reluctant to announce these). Also some **$$** executive rooms.

### Tezpur and around *p364*

**$$$$ Wild Mahseer**, Addabarie Tea Estate, near Balipara, T(0)9435-197650, www.wildmahseer.com. In a world of its own, this pristine heritage bungalow sits among 9 ha of gardens and trees on the edge of a working tea garden. Rooms are luxurious yet homely with huge beds and bathrooms in modern colonial style, and every inch taken care of. Absorbing library, tea-tasting café and 3 (cheaper) bungalows in the grounds. Delicious Anglo-Indian food, warm and entertaining hosts.

**$$ Eco Camp**, Nameri National Park, Sonitpur, T(0)9854-019932, www.nivalink.com/nameriecocamp or contact **Network Travels**, see page 370. Thatched-cottage

tents with twin bamboo beds, bathrooms with hot water, brightly furnished with local fabrics, set among jungle trees around a grassy lawn. 6 bunk beds in the bamboo dorm, wash block, sunny little restaurant. A friendly and special place, worth spending a couple of nights. Highly recommended.

**$$-$ Centre Point**, Main Rd (opposite the police station), Tezpur, T03712-232359, hotelcentrepoint.tezpur@gmail.com. Spanking new hotel with fresh linen and plumped up pillows, plain but pleasing decor and TVs. Cheaper rooms have hot water by the bucket, staff are eager to please and **Tiffin Restaurant** is good. Recommended, if you can deal with false windows and bad acoustics.

**$$-$ Luit**, Ranu Singh Rd, 200 m from bus stand, Tezpur, T03712-222083, hotel_luit@ rediffmail. com. Set back from the main road, this retro hotel has large but average rooms in new wing, some a/c and some bargain-basic rooms in the old wing, restaurant, bar.

**$ Basant**, Main Rd, Tezpur, T03712-230831, T(0)9401-278499. Good, clean paintwork and sheets, well-maintained rooms all with TV, recommended to phone ahead. Singles are small but totally acceptable. Soulless restaurant on the top floor.

**$ Tourist Lodge**, Jenkins Rd (opposite Chitralekha Udyan), Tezpur, T03712-221016. Budget non-a/c rooms and newly refurbed a/c for a higher price. All twin bed with attached bath. Book ahead, there are only 10 rooms. Cheap simple restaurant.

**$ Tourist Lodge**, Bhalukpong, T03782-234037. 10 raised cottages with octagonal bedrooms, or 4 airy rooms sharing a terrace (good value) look out across the Jia Bhoroli River to Nameri and Pakhuya parks. Work is underway to turn the watch-tower into a restaurant. Can arrange local transport to visit Nameri. (The private guesthouse **Kunki Resort** next door is not nearly as appealing, but it's there if the lodge is full.)

## Restaurants

### Guwahati *p361*

Assamese *thalis* including rice, fish and vegetable curry, often cooked with mustard, are milder than elsewhere in India. Try vegetarian *kharoli* (mashed mustard seeds) with *omita khar* (papaya cooked with burnt 'bark' of the banana plant). Larger hotels serve continental food and have bars.

**$$$ Mainland China**, 4th floor, Dona Planet, GS Rd, T0361 246 6222. Daily 1200-1530, 1900-2300. Fabulous Chinese food in tip-top surrounds, from the famous nationwide chain.

**$$$ Tandoor**, Dynasty Hotel (see Where to stay). Daily 1130-1430, 1830-2230. Marvellous Indian veg and non-veg delicacies, served from traditional metalware, pleasing decor, perfect for a treat, alcohol served. Mains between Rs 350-700. The hotel also has continental and Chinese restaurants, and a rooftop bar/restaurant open Oct-Mar from 1900-2300.

**$$-$ Beatrix**, MC Rd, T0361-266 7563. Mon-Sat 1030-2200, Sun from 1600. Good quality family restaurant (a/c upstairs), cartoon decor and clean surrounds. Varied menu, with some interesting dishes, lone diners with appreciate the 'mini-meals' (which are still very generous). Recommended.

**$ Breeze**, NCB Rd, Pan Bazar, T0361-273 1444. Daily 1100-2130. Huge chicken *momos*, good soups and other Chinese and Indian dishes. The coloured lanterns give a cosy feel and it's popular with couples. Next door is **Sun Flower** restaurant, which has more choice for vegetarians.

**$ New Zealand Natural**, MC Rd. Open 1000-2300. Great ice creams and sorbets, and coffee is reasonably priced. Outdoor terrace or a/c inside.

### Sibsagar *p364*

**$$ Sky Chef**, at Shiva Palace hotel (see page 367). Open 1000-2200. The glitziest place in town has excellent tandoori dishes, as well as other Indian/Chinese dishes and a pleasing environment.

**$ Hotel Priya**, AT Rd (on junction with Hospital Rd). Seriously cheap and good Assamese thalis, veg/fish/chicken, open from 0530.

**$** The little outdoor tea-shop under the birdwatching tower by the tank does excellent *chapatti/subji* throughout the day and is a good place to while away time.

### Dibrugarh *p364*

**$$ Garden Treat**, beside the flyover, Mancotta Rd, T0373-232 4140. Open 1100-2100. Despite the proximity of the flyover this garden haven is lovely for eating great-value fish with mustard, under a sun umbrella. There are several continental dishes alongside the Indian and Chinese. Has an old-world charm though the building is actually modern.

**$ Swagat Family Restaurant**, HS Rd (at the junction with AT Rd). Staggering numbers of staff milling around despite it always being busy. Rudimentary downstairs room is good for breakfast (opens at 0630), dosas and snacks while the yellow and blue restaurant upstairs is more sedate for lunch and dinner, serving Chinese and North Indian food which can take a while to prepare. Pure veg.

### Tezpur *p364*

**$$-$ Chinese Villa**, NC Rd, T03712-232726. Magnificent *momos* and a whole host of other delicacies in a high-rise block that also incorporates an Indian restaurant on the upper level and excellent south Indian snacks and *lassis* on the ground floor.

## Festivals

### Guwahati *p361*

**Jan** Magh Bihu and; **Mid-Apr** Rongali Bihu, are week-long festivities celebrated with singing, dancing and much enthusiasm. **Mid-Jun** Ambubachi marks the end of Mother Earth's menstrual cycle with a fair at Kamakhya Temple.
**Sep** The Manasa Festival honours the Snake goddess. You can watch devotees

dancing and entering into trances from galleries on the hillside.

**26-28 Dec** The Assam Tea Festival is celebrated with events in various places.

## O Shopping

### Guwahati *p361*
### Silk and handicrafts
*Muga, pat* and *endi* silks, hats, bamboo and cane baskets, flutes, drums and pipes are typical of the area. **Assam Govt Emporium**, GNB Rd, Ambari, for silks, bamboo, wood, brass and ceramics; **Assam Co-op Silk House**, HB Rd, Pan Bazar, for pure silk items; **Artfed**, opp Emporium, for knick-knacks, bags, handloom, metalware and more, Mon-Sat 1000-2000; **Purbashree**, GNB Rd. Traditional crafts. For high-quality, tastefully selected goods go to **Konyak**, 47 MG Rd, Uzan Bazar Riverside, for silks, cushions, saris, and the adjacent franchise of **FabIndia** with clothing, home furnishings, etc (both are open daily 1000-2000).

### Dibrugarh *p364*
**Art Fed**, just off Mancotta Rd, Thanachorali. Mon-Sat 1000-1900. Attractive *Muga* silks shawls, *Jhapi* wall decorations, and silk saris/ half saris with golden Assamese thread designs.

## O What to do

### Guwahati *p361*
**Assam Bengal Navigation**, 1st floor, Mandovi Apartments, GNB Rd, Ambari, Guwahati, T0361-260 2223, www.assam bengalnavigation.com. Sister concern to **Jungle Travels** (see below) runs 4-,7-, 10- and 14-day cruises along the Brahmaputra aboard the charming *RV Charaidew* and *RV Sukapha*, both with 12 en suite cabins, nostalgic saloon bar and quintessential sundeck; *Sukapha* also has a small Ayurvedic spa. Land excursions visit the national parks, villages, historical sites and provide opportunities to barbecue on the islands of

the mighty river. Cruises along the Hooghly for 7-days between Kolkata and Jangipur stop at little-visited sites and are especially atmospheric. The company also runs **Diphlu River Lodge**, a luxurious resort in Kaziranga National Park (see Where to stay).
**Jungle Travels India**, 1st floor, Mandovi Apartments, GNB Rd, Ambari, Guwahati, T0361-260 2223, www.jungletravelsindia. com. Wildlife, heritage, tribal, tea, and other tours around Assam, Arunachal and Sikkim. Top-notch service from experienced and friendly staff.
**Network Travels**, 17 Paltan Bazar, GS Rd, T0361-273 9630, www.networktravels india.net. Imaginative tours including river cruises, good for airline ticketing and buses, efficient and reliable. Recommended.
**Wild Grass**, Krishna Nagar, Chandmari (near Assam Engineering Institute), T0361213 2817, T(0)9435-048403, www. oldassam.com. Very helpful, knowledgeable, efficient. Highly recommended for good value wildlife, tribal tours and Arunachal (can get a permit in 5 days), free travel advice on phone (Nov-Apr).

### Dibrugarh *p364*
**Purvi Discovery**, T0373-230 1120, www. purviweb.com, www.assamteatourism.com. Tours around the Northeast states with very professional service and attention to detail. Experienced in tours around Arunachal. Managers of the Chowkidinghee and Mancotta Chang bunglows – a great base for the horse riding, kayaking, tea tours or cookery classes on offer. The un-signed office is located in the lane behind the Radha Krishna temple, Medical College area, Rs 50 in a cycle rickshaw from Dibrugarh centre.

### Tezpur and around *p364*
**Assam Anglers' Association**, T03712-220004, assamangling@yahoo.com, operates a strict 'catch-record-release' system to conserve the golden mahseer. **Eco Camp**, Potasali, T03714-244246. Organizes whitewater rafting, nature

watching and mahseer fishing on the Bhoreli. Reasonable rates.

## ⊙ Transport

**Guwahati** *p361*
**Air** Flights daily to **Kolkata**, 1 to **Delhi**, **Bagdogra** and other northeastern states.

The helicopter service run by Pawan Hans to Naharlagun and Tawang in Arunachal Pradesh was suspended at the time of writing.

**Long distance** Private coach tickets are sold by operators in Paltan Bazar, such as **Network Travels**, GS Rd, T0361-213 4819, reservations 0400-2100, **Blue Hill**, T0361-260 7145, and others, with morning and night buses to all the Northeast states. The buses leave from the ISBT, connected by shuttle buses run by the private operators. To: **Itanagar** (10 hrs); **Kohora** (for **Kaziranga**) (3½ hrs); **Dibrugarh** (9 hrs); **North Lakimpur** (10 hrs); **Pasighat** (16 hrs); **Siliguri** (12 hrs); **Tezpur** every 30 mins (3½ hrs).

ASTC bus stand, Paltan Bazar, T(0)9957-563033. Left luggage, Rs 10 per day. Ticket office open 0500-2000. ASTC buses are a bit slower and marginally less expensive than the private buses, but are modern. There are shuttle buses to the ISBT. ASTC also run a bus to **Along/Aalo** in Arunchal Pradesh at 1600 (Mon/Fri only, 14 hrs).
**Sumo** Jeeps can be reserved (private) for long journeys (such as to Tawang) from a counter in the ASTC compound.
**Train** Station has tourist information, left luggage (Rs 10, trunks and suitcases only), on showing ticket. Enquiries: T1316133, T0361-254 0330. Reservations: 100 m north of the station on Station Rd, T0361-254 1799, 0800-1330, 1400-2000; Foreign Tourists, Counter 3, where patience is needed. To **Kolkata** (**H**): *Kamrup Exp 15960*, 0750, 23; *Saraighat Exp 12346*, 1245, 17 hrs (via **New Jalpaiguri**, 6½ hrs); *Kanchenjunga Exp 15658* (**S**), 2230, 21 hrs (via **New Jalpaiguri**, 9 hrs);. To **New Delhi** (**ND**): *Rajdhani Exp 12423/ 12435*, 0705/0555, 27/32 hrs; *North East Exp*

*12505* (**ANVT**), 0945, 34 hrs. To **Dibrugarh** via Dimapur: *Rajdhani Exp 12436*, 1945 (Mon, Fri), 10¾ hrs; *Brahmaputra Mail 14056*, 1445, 13 hrs; *Kamrup Exp 15959*, 1600, 13½ hrs.

**Kaziranga National Park** *p363*
**Bus/car** Best to ask Wild Grass if they have a vehicle going from Guwahati, or confirm timings of private buses. ASTC buses between Guwahati and Jorhat via **Kohora** stopping at **Nagaon** (30 mins, where you can stop overnight); departs 0900, 1000, 1100, 1230, 5-6 hrs. Private buses: **Green Valley** (office behind bus station) coaches depart Guwahati for Tinsukia and Digboi, 0700 and 0730; lunch stop at **Wild Grass Resorts**, after 4 hrs. **Guwahati**: a/c bus from Dibrugarh stops at resort for lunch; leaves at 1330.
**Train** Furkating (75 km) has the nearest station with trains from **Guwahati** and **Dibrugarh**.

**Sibsagar** *p364*
Nearest railway station: Simaluguri (20 km), connected by frequent buses. Regular ASTC buses to **Guwahati** 5 in morning from 0700-0930, 5 in evening from 1830-2130 (9 hrs) plus private buses from AT Rd at 0715 and 1930. To **Dibrugarh** from 0530-1630 (2 hrs).

**Dibrugarh** *p364*
**Air** The airport is 16 km from town. Flights to **Kolkata**, and **Delhi** daily. Also flights to **Guwahati**.
**Bus** Private Bus Stand on AT Rd/RKB Path services to **Guwahati** at 1930, 2030 and 2130, **Tezpur** at 2000 (6 hrs), **Itanagar/Naharlagun** at 1800 (12 hrs) via **North Lakimpur**. ASTC Bus Stand is on Mancotta Rd, Chowkidinghee, with buses to **Guwahati**, they often go and pick up more passengers from AT Rd (in front of the Asha Hotel) before leaving town.
**Ferry** To **Pasighat** in Arunachal Pradesh. Tickets for the jeep-ferry-jeep (Rs 200) can be bought in advance from the Kusum Hotel, Talkie House Rd, T0373-232 0143,

and it is recommended to do so for ease of travel. Departure from the hotel at 0730, boat leaves at 0815. You land at Sonarighat (3 hrs) from where a jeep continues to Pasighat. There are later boats (1015, 1115, 1230 and 1330) if you wish to negotiate your own way to the ferry ghat.

**Train** To **Guwahati** (continuing to **New Delhi**, 38 hrs): *Rajdhani Exp 12423*, 2045, 10 hrs *Kamrup Exp 15960*, 1825, 13 hrs (continues to **NJP** and **Kolkata** (**H**) in further 24 hrs).

**Tezpur and around** *p364*
**Air** Salonibari Airport to the north of Tezpur is currently not operational.
**Bus/taxi** Frequent buses to/from **Guwahati** 0500-1330 (4½-5 hrs); **Kaziranga** from 0600 until 1400 (2 hrs). Daily to **Dibrugarh**, 0615-1230, luxury at 0800 (7 hrs) via **Jorhat**; **Itanagar** at 1000 and 1215 (4½ hrs); **Tawang** (14 hrs). To **Nameri**, take a Bomdila-bound bus/*sumo* and get off at Hatigate, from where its 2.5 km to the Eco-camp.
**Sumos** ASTC, T(0)9435-080318, T(0)9864-182449, and several private companies with offices near the bus stand run *sumos* to **Tawang** and destinations in between, leaving at 0530, 12-14 hrs, pickup from hotel.
**Train** The train station is 1 km past the main bus stand at Jhaj Ghat. Irregular services to **Guwahati** take 10 hrs, much better to take a bus. Trains also run from Rangapara to North Lakimpur, via Tezpur.

## ❶ Directory

**Guwahati** *p361*
**Banks** United Bank of India, HB Rd, Pan Bazar. ATM, plus many other ATMs around the centre. **Internet** There is a cluster internet cafés on Earl Rd, by the junction with GNB Rd, charging Rs 20 per hr.
**Medical services** Down Town Hospital, GS Rd, Dispur, T0361-233 6906/233 1003, by far the best.

**Kaziranga National Park** *p363*
**Bank** State Bank of India, ATM, 400 m east of the Tourist Complex gate.
**Internet** Pharmacy to the right of the gate to the Tourist Complex has 1 computer.

**Dibrugarh** *p364*
**Bank** State Bank of India, ATM at the Railway Station. **Internet** Cyber @ Generation Next, HS Rd. Fast connection, staff speak English, daily 0800-2200.

**Tezpur** *p364*
**Banks** United Bank of India and Federal Bank, Main Rd, both have ATMs.
**Internet** Animit Cyber Café, Gopal Agarwalla Complex, Main Rd, has new computers, daily 0930-2030.

# Arunachal Pradesh

## Background

### The land

On the Northeast frontier of India, Arunachal Pradesh is India's least densely populated state with less than 20 people per sq km. It stretches from the foothills of the eastern Himalaya to their permanently snow-capped peaks to the north. The Brahmaputra, known here as the Siang River, enters the state from China and flows through a deeply cut valley. Stretching from the Himalaya to the steamy plains of the Brahmaputra Valley, Arunachal Pradesh has an extraordinary range of forests from the alpine to the subtropical – from rhododendrons to orchids, reeds and bamboo. It is an orchid lover's paradise with over 550 species identified.

### Climate

Bomdila (2500 m) and Tawang (3500 m), are exceptionally cold between October and March, with temperatures in Tawang dropping as low as -12°C. However, clear skies are most likely October to December, also when many flowers are in bloom.

### History

The entire region had remained isolated since 1873 when the British stopped free movement. After 1947 Arunachal became part of the North East Frontier Agency (NEFA). Its strategic significance was demonstrated by the Chinese invasion in 1962, and the Indian government subsequently broke up the Agency giving statehood to all the territories surrounding Assam. Arunachal became the 24th state in 1987, though China continues to argue that, until the international border between it and India are agreed, some of the territory remains disputed. Having long borders with China and Myanmar, it is a truly frontier state. The state was opened to tourists in 1995 with the first foreigners being given permission to trek in 1998. Congress won both Lok Sabha seats in 2009.

### Culture

The Arunachali people are the state's greatest attraction. Even in the capital, Itanagar, you might see Nishi warriors wearing hornbill feathers in their caps, carrying bearskin bags and their knives in monkey-skin scabbards.

The tribal people are very diverse and speak over 60 different dialects. Most have an oral tradition of recording their historic and cultural past by memorizing verses handed down through generations. Some Buddhist tribes have, however, maintained written records, largely recording their religious history. Some tribes worship Donyi and Polo, the Sun and Moon gods.

# Permits for visiting Arunachal Pradesh

Local travel agents are the most efficient means of arranging a permit to Arunachal Pradesh, saving you from much bureaucratic hassle. They can obtain permits within a few days, and even supply by fax or email, with a commission charge of around Rs 1000. This is especially worthwhile for Arunachal Pradesh, as agents can now obtain permits for individual travellers, at a cost of around US$100 plus commission, valid up to 30 days (see listings for tour operators who can help). Itanagar, Ziro, Along, Pasighat, Miao, Namdapha, Tipi and Bhalukpong,

Bomdila, Dirand, Mechuka and Tawang are all open to tourists.

In Kolkata Restricted Area Permits (RAPs) are issued at the Foreigners Regional Registration Officer (FRRO), 237A AJC Bose Road, T033-2283 7034, Monday-Friday 1000-1730 but come between 1100-1400; ask for the Officer in Charge. At the FRRO, it is necessary to apply as a group of four. It can take one to two days for permits to be issued, though if you are lucky it can be the same day. The cost is at the discretion of the FRRO (usually US$200 for four people).

## Itanagar-Naharlagun → *For listings, see pages 379-384. Colour map 4, B3.*

Itanagar, the new capital, and Naharlagun, the old town 10 km away, together provide the capital's administrative offices. Itanagar, sited between two hills, has the governor's residence on one and a new Buddhist temple on the other, with shops, bazar, traditional huts and more recent earthquake-proof wooden-framed buildings in between. The capital has been identified as Mayapur, the 11th-century capital of the Jitari Dynasty.

### Arriving in Itanagar and Naharlagun → *Phone code: 0360. Population: 61,900.*
**Getting there and around** Most visitors arrive via Tezpur in Assam, from where there are jeeps or buses to Itanagar. Visitors arriving through North Lakhimpur in Assam take two hours by bus (or one and a half by jeep) to Itanagar, calling at Naharlagun Bus Station before climbing up along a scenic road to the capital. There are also direct buses from Guwahati and Shillong. Frequent transport runs between Itanagar and Naharlagun from 0600 until 2000. Cycle-rickshaws available only in Naharlagun. There are airports in Tezpur and Lilabari, but neither was serving commercial flights at the time of writing. The helicopter service between Naharlagun-Guwahati-Tawang is also currently suspended.
▶▶ *See Transport, page 383.*

**Tourist information** Arunachal Pradesh Tourism ① *Directorate of Tourism, H Sector T0360-221 4745, www.arunachaltourism.com, 400 m along a steep side road starting by Nirvachan Bhavan, near Ganga Market, Mon-Fri 1000-1630*, has some colourful pamphlets but little practical advice.

### Places in Itanagar and Naharlagun
The yellow-roofed and beautifully decorated **Buddhist temple** stands in well-kept gardens on a hilltop with good views. There is an evening puja at around 1630 each day. Below the Gompa, the **Jawaharlal Nehru State Museum** ① *Sun-Thu 0930-1600, Rs 75*, has been recently renovated and displays dioramas of tribal people and related artefacts on the ground floor. Upstairs includes a spectacular jewellery collection (look for the Ido-Mishmi

priest's belt decorated with fangs and cymbals), many carvings of figures (including animals), an impressive Thangka Gallery and archaeological finds from Malinthan, Ita Fort and Vijaynagar. Across the main road, the tiny **Archaeological Museum and Park** ⓘ *Mon-Fri, Rs 2*, has scant brick remains of the **Ita Fort** western gate, and is a five-minute visit. The Ita Fort (14th-15th century) is believed to have been built by King Ramachandra. The **Gyaker Sinyi** (Ganga Sekhi Lake), 6 km, is reached by a rough road through forests of bamboo and tree ferns. On reaching the foot of the hill, walk across a bamboo bridge, up steps cut on the hillside to reach a ridge overlooking the forest lake (water levels have been sinking in recent years). There is also a small **zoo** nearby, in Chimpu. In Naharlagun, the **Polo Park** is a garden on top of a ridge with interesting botanical specimens including a cane thicket, which looks like palm.

## Western Arunachal Pradesh → *For listings, see pages 379-384. Colour map 4, B2.*

The whole journey, from Tezpur in Assam to Tawang, is spectacular, passing waterfalls, terraced paddy fields, alpine forests and mountain streams. The road north crosses the border at **Bhalukpong** (see page 365) and continues towards Bomdila passing through low wooded slopes for about 60 km. On the bank of the Bhoreli River in the upper plains is **Tipi**, with the Orchid Research Centre and a glasshouse with 500 species of orchids. From there the road rises sharply to reach Bomdila.

### Arriving in Western Arunachal Pradesh
For those not travelling with a hired jeep, there are **ASTC** buses or **Tatasumo** services between Tezpur and Tawang (in winter, buses make it only as far as Dirang). As these leave very early in the morning (0500) you will probably need to spend a night in **Tezpur**, Assam (see Where to stay, page 379). *Sumos* are far preferable to the bus, though more expensive: they are significantly quicker and can negotiate the narrow, terrifying roads far better. To make the journey in one go means a gruelling 12-14 hours: better to do this coming back rather than going up. If breaking the journey at Bomdila or Dirang, try to book onward *sumo* tickets in advance and ask for 'number 1 seat' for best views and comfort. Coming back down from Tawang, the best seats are reserved days in advance so again do some forward planning. Check travel conditions locally (Sela Pass is frequently closed by snow) and, if in a private vehicle, don't travel after dark as visibility on the narrow mountain roads can be very poor at night.

### Bomdila → *Altitude: 2530 m.*
On a clear day, Bomdila has marvellous views of the snow-capped mountains. There's a craft centre, apple and cherry orchards, three Buddhist *gompas* and a museum. Transport links are good, there is internet connection and hotels are generally more comfortable than those in Dirang, but it is a sprawling rather unattractive place. Buses leave from the bus stand in the lower part of town and *sumos* from the main bazar, 2 km up the hill and therefore more convenient for hotels. **Himalayan Holiday** in the market has some basic tourist information.

### Dirang
About an hour's drive after Bomdila, the road cuts through the miniature village of Old Dirang and continues another 5 km to larger (newer) Dirang, which has a few guesthouses and simple places to eat. It is a more appealing stop than Bomdila when breaking the journey to Tawang, though make sure you book an onward ticket in advance. A day can

easily be spent walking to tiny peaceful villages nearby. The obvious attraction is the old village, huddled around the confluence of two rivers, where a population of some 1200 Monpa tribespeople inhabit traditional stone dwellings with slatted wooden upper levels and woven roofs. One of the morning *sumos* to Bomdila can drop you off at the ancient three-storey **Khatsikpa Gompa** atop a small ridge, from where it's a steep walk past stupas and *mani* walls down to the village. Here, women walk along knitting, men carrry woven *shingrong* baskets from head-straps and kids run around with babies tied on their backs. Across the main bridge, a sign points the way to the plain stacked stones of **Dirang Dzong** (generally locked), one of several *dzongs* in the district from where Tibetan officials collected taxes. An hour or so is sufficient to explore the pathways of the village, and then it's an easy walk back to New Dirang following the road along the river, criss-crossing a couple of bridges on the way.

From the central crossroads in New Dirang, the turning signed to the Yak Research Centre leads into a 2-km uphill tramp to lovely **Yewang** village. The tracks forks but both lead to the village: the new track to the right is quicker, but it's nice to turn left and walk through the first cluster of homes surrounded by terracing and agriculture before reaching the beautiful *gompa* at the highest point of Yewang. The forested foothills begin in earnest from here, while the village trickles down the hillside below among fields of yellow mustard flowers, pink peas, millet, cabbage or corn – depending on the season.

## To Tawang

After passing through the pretty Dirang Valley shrouded in pine woods, the route snakes past lonely army camps and teetering villages to the **Sela Pass** which at 4215 m presents a far starker view. The successor to Lama Guru Rimpoche has been found in a village nearby. Stop a while here above the clouds, along one of the highest motorable roads in the world, with views of a high-altitude lake and graphite peaks streaked with snow. **Jaswantpur**, 13 km from the pass, has the *samadhi* to the brave Jawan (soldier) Jaswant Singh, which commemorates how he, his fiancé and her friend valiantly held up the advancing Chinese army in 1962 for three days before laying down their lives. Drivers along this road, many of them ex-army personnel, stop to pay their respects at the poignant memorial.

The road then descends alongside a river before emerging on the edge of Tawang Valley, where the folded foothills are of an unimaginable scale, plunging and twisting towards Tibet. Numerous tiny hamlets and golden *gompas* speckle the near-vertical slopes opposite the improbably large village of **Jang**, 42 km before Tawang. Houses here are chequerboard Assamese-style or Monpa cubes, and many older Monpa wear a densely woven black yak-wool skullcap, the tentacles of which channel rainwater away from the wearer's face. After crossing the river, the old village of **Lhou** is especially atmospheric (worth a visit if using private transport) before the final 18 km to Tawang township.

### Tawang → *Phone code: 03794. Population: 4600.*

Although set in breathtakingly dramatic scenery at 3500 m, the town of Tawang itself is not immediately attractive. The prayer wheels in the Old Market square, overlooked by a mini *gompa* and flower-laden balconies, have charm and two Tibetan-style gates are beautifully maintained. Most people are here to see the **monastery**, birthplace of the sixth Dalai Lama, and the second largest Buddhist monastery in the world (after Lhasa). Dating originally from 1681, it houses around 450 *lamas* belonging to the Gelugpa (Reformed) Sect of Mahayana Buddhist monks. Buddhism arrived in the area with Padmasambhava in the eighth century but the local Monpas were converted to the Tantric Buddhist cult only after the establishment of the monastery here by Merag Lama in the 17th century. During renovations in the 1990s, the main building was completely rebuilt. The lofty prayer hall, containing a 5.5-m-high golden Buddha heaped with silky prayer scarves, sees monks gather at 0500 and again at 0715 for worship (observers welcome) after which the young trainees go to the monastic school next door. It generally takes 15-20 years for the *lamas* to complete their doctorates in Buddhist philosophy, though the current Dalai Lama was just 25 when he finished. The **museum** ① *open on request, Rs 20, cameras Rs 20* contains a wealth of treasures, including 700-year-old sculptures, numerous *thangkas* and priceless manuscripts. These, and other precious objects left in storage, are soon to be properly displayed in a new two-storey building.

Exiting via the south gate of the monastery complex takes you down a grassy ridge, strung with small *chortens* and *mani* walls, for some excellent views. Visible on a ridge northeast from the monastery is the **Gyamgong Ani Gompa**, home to some three dozen nuns who are studying there, a 1½-hour walk down and up a steep ravine (advisable only in dry weather).

## Lake District

Just above Tawang beyond the monastery is the **Lake District**, an exceptionally beautiful area with many high-altitude lakes, including the tranquil Sangeshar Lake where a dance sequence from the film *Koyla* was shot. After a fork and an army outpost, the road continues towards **Klemta**, just a few kilometres from the Indian border. There are a few scattered monasteries and a shrine to all faiths at the spot where Guru Nanak rested as he trekked into Tibet, over 500 years ago. **Ptso**, 25 km from Tawang, has a small cabin by a lake which is used by the military. To explore this area you'll have to hire a jeep and guide, carry snacks and drinks, and be prepared for steep, treacherous mountain roads. It is all worth it for the breathtaking mountain scenery.

## Gorsam Chorten

This immense *chorten* (stupa) is 105 km from Tawang, near Jimithang, where there are some simple places to stay. The setting is amazing, and the road little travelled by foreigners. A few public *sumos* run to the village each week, taking two to three hours; book ahead with an agent in Tawang, or hire a vehicle.

## Central Arunachal Pradesh → *For listings, see pages 379-384.*

Most visitors come to Central Arunachal to observe the fascinating tribal cultures that still predominate in the hills and valleys. It is also possible to do serious whitewater rafting on the Subansiri River, a journey of eight days, with the help of a specialist tour operator (see page 383). The Gerukamukh Dam at the southern point, due to be finished in 2014, threatens the ecosystem upstream and will probably put an end to these rafting expeditions.

## Arriving in Central Arunachal Pradesh

**Getting there and around** A loop can be made through the main settlements, using public transport or as part of a tour. Starting from Itanagar, the loop takes you from Ziro to Pasighat, or if you enter from Assam (via Dibrugarh) it loops from Pasighat to Ziro. Public transport connections work best when starting from Pasighat, although most tourists opt to hire a vehicle/go with a tour.

**Ziro Valley** → *Colour map 4, A5. Altitude: 1475 m. Population 25,000*
**Ziro** lies in a picturesque level valley of the Apatani plateau, surrounded by pine-covered hills. The settlement of Old Ziro has a small string of shops (closed on Mondays), the helipad and a government guesthouse scenically located on a hill; however, the majority of travellers stay in the commercial centre of Hapoli, 7 km to the southwest, where most jeeps arrive/depart. The **Apatani** tribals, who live in small densely populated villages clustered between the two towns, have evolved a sophisticated system of irrigated paddy cultivation which is interesting and picturesque to behold. The main tourist "attraction", however, are the Apatanis themselves. The older women wear curious bamboo nose-plugs and facial tattoos, whilst the men are more low-key with the occasional knot of hair above the forehead. Interaction with locals is problematic as the women are (unsurprisingly) shy and wary of camera-wielding foreigners and, unless you are with a sympathetic guide, it is invasive and inappropriate to attempt photographs. That said, you are free to wander around the villages and paddy fields on your own, and people are friendly and welcoming.

Villages typically consist of rows of triangular-roofed houses surrounded by high bamboo-stake fences; often there is a wicker altar (*karung agyang*) adorned with eggs at the front, and pigs and chickens living beneath. Families live in nuclear groups, hence the small size and lack of space between the huts. About 80% of villagers still practice the **Donyi Polo** religion, although Christians from Mizoram, Nagaland and Kerala have made significant conversions in the past few years. Note the *Lapung* (raised platforms, used during the *Murung* festival in January/February) and *Babo* (huge bamboo poles erected during the Myoko festival, which rotates through the villages on a three-yearly cycle each March).

To sample village life, a good day's walk starts in Old Ziro (autos run between Hapoli and Old Ziro, Rs 10) from where the village of **Hija** is signed on the western edge of town. From Hija, continue through **Dutta**, **Nenchalyang** and **Bamin**, which run into one another, before crossing the main road and following paddy-paths to **Hong**, which is allegedly the biggest tribal village in Asia. From Hong, tracks lead back (in the direction of Old Ziro, parallel to the main road) to **Biiri** (where there is a good restaurant, see listings) from where it is a short walk to **Hari**. From Hari, it is 1 km back to the main road to pick up an autorickshaw, or those with energy can continue on rural paths to Tajang, Kallung and Bulla villages.

**Hapoli** is where hotels, restaurants and transport are found; note that the bazar (where tribal women come to sell traditional foodstuffs) shuts on Sundays. The excellent **District Museum** ⓘ *Mon-Fri 0930-1600, T03788-224278, entrance free*, has an extensive collection of tribal artefacts from all over Arunachal in wonderful wooden cabinets. Of note among the jewellery collection are the biggest ear plugs imaginable; also intriguing are the penis covers crafted from brass and wood, the range of pipes, and exquisite basketry. A small selection of books is for sale and interesting photos adorn the walls. The **Emporium Crafts Centre** ⓘ *T03783-224123, Mon-Fri 0900-1600 (closed lunch)*, is worth visiting; if you are lucky you will see items being made in the workshops, while the shop sells the products. An attraction for Hindu pilgrims is the **Siva Linga** near Sibe village, 4 km, signed off the road between Hapoli and Ziro on the left-hand side.

To get right off the beaten track, enquire about visiting **Talle Valley Wildlife Sanctuary**, about 30 km from Hapoli, accessed via Pange where there is a Forest Range Office and a camp.

## Daporijo to Pasighat
**Daporijo**, a necessary overnight stop on the route from Ziro to Along/Aalo, is a rough-and-ready place of chiefly shanty-style buildings with a bustling centre. Lying in a river basin

surrounded by wooded hills, with suspension bridges crossing the Subansiri, it has a scenic setting – but travelling to surrounding villages is near impossible without your own transport.

The small town of **Along/Aalo** (altitude 700 m) is set in a picturesque landscape scattered with Adi villages that are relatively easy to access. In the town centre, the **District Museum** ⓘ *next to the Circuit House, Mon-Fri 0900-1200, 1300-1600, entrance free,* has several well-labelled rooms representing Arunachal's tribes. There are Buddhist items from the Monpa and Memba communities including painted masks, as well as woven hats (ornamented with hornbill skulls) and haversacks, clothing, statues and more.

A very enjoyable excursion from Along is to **Paya**; take an auto (Rs 200, 7 km) to Pobdi (itself a quaintly thatched village), then cross a wire bridge to unspoilt Paya, which is strung up the hillside and has a little shop for refreshments. Continue alongside the River Yomgo for 2 km, past bamboo boats, jhum (slash and burn) cultivation and friendly farmers to Ruyu, where a new metal bridge spans the river to Kabu (the original bamboo bridge is now derelict, though picturesque). You can continue for a further 6 km on the same side and cross the river at the main bridge near Along, or cross here to Kabu from where it is a 4 km walk back to Along (or hitch a lift).

Visits to the Buddhist village of **Mechuka** near the border with Tibet, where there is a monastery and high altitude lake, are possible from Along. There is a Circuit House should you wish to make the intrepid journey. This route has only recently opened up to tourists.

**Pasighat** (altitude 155 m), the oldest town in Arunachal at 100 years, is home of the Adi tribe though tribal culture is fairly invisible. Lying on the banks of the Siang River, it is a low-level bustling market town. From here, it is relatively easy to reach Dibrugarh in Assam via jeep-ferry-jeep (see Transport, page 384).

## ⊛ Arunachal Pradesh listings

*For hotel and restaurant price codes and other relevant information, see pages 22-26.*

## ⊛ Where to stay

### Itanagar-Naharlagun *p374*
Try to reserve rooms in advance. Some hotels seriously hike their prices Sep-Jan.
**$$ Donyi-Polo Ashok**, Sector C, Itanagar, T0360-221 2626/7, www.theashokgroup. com. Itanagar's most comfortable hotel, in a hilltop building with attractive gardens, all 20 rooms and 2 suites have views, a/c, heaters, fridge, hot water, and are homely despite being old-fashioned and a bit musty. The restaurant is OK and there is a very well-stocked bar. It's a 1 km uphill walk from the main road.
**$$ Hotel Dawnland**, Ganga Market, T0360-2299 1756. Modern edifice, lit up at night, with plush rooms that suit the price, all

mod cons (for this part of the world). Fancy restaurant, and bar has appeal.
**$$-$ Blue Pine**, Ganga Market, T0360-211 4196. Categorically the best value for money in Itanagar, with rooms that have been refurbished relatively recently, clean, marble floors, those at the front are best (bigger windows, although noisy), reliable hot water, and an excellent restaurant.

### Bomdila *p375*
**$$$-$ Siphiyang Phong**, T03782-222286, www.hotelsiphiyangphong.com. Pleasant and a good deal for the standard rooms, rather overpriced for the high-end executive rooms, but all rooms have hot water and TV. Restaurant is cheery with checked tablecloths and plenty of bamboo panelling. Travel desk (T03782-223676) is useful.
**$$-$ Tourist Lodge**, **Elysium** and **La** are other options in town.

## Dirang p375

**$$ Heritage Pemaling**, 1.5 km out of the village, T03780-242615. Standard/deluxe rooms are frumpy but clean with decent tiled bathrooms, the only real difference being valley views from the deluxe. Suites are much more attractive in a chintz-and-wicker way, with large bathroom and balcony. There's a bit of a garden; restaurant for residents only.

**$$-$ Awoo Diwang Resort**, Bushthang, T03780-242036/03794-202122, www.awooresort.com. Standard rooms are simple, clean and functional; others have faux-wood-panelled walls giving a more cosy feel. Multicuisine restaurant and generator back-up for the inevitable power cuts. Comfortable choice.

**$ Dirang Tourist Lodge**, next to Heritage Pemaling, T03780-242175. Spacious clean rooms, attached bath with geyser, and great views down over the river and Dirang. Only 4 rooms so booking very much necessary, same price for single or double. Meals provided, but advance warning needed.

**$ Dreamland**, Main Rd, T03780-242296. 3 simple twin rooms in a family home (sharing their very basic, yet clean, bathroom), potted plants aplenty, plenty of bedding provided although beds are hard. Beer in the little restaurant is appealing, but avoid the food. Hot buckets available for a small fee.

**$ Moon**, Main Rd, T03780-242438. Upstairs 4-bed room has a decent bathroom with geyser, but others share a smelly common bath (hot bucket available). Rooms have clean sheets and paintwork, hard beds, and nothing more.

## Tawang p376

Apart from dormitory beds (men only), single travellers to Tawang will have to pay the price of a double room. There are plenty of cheap lodges (not listed here) clustered around the Old Market area, where *sumos* terminate.

**$$ Dolma Khangsar Guesthouse**, Gompa Rd (near the monastery). A 20- to 30-min walk from the town centre, but good food is available and a homestay atmosphere is the main attraction for most guests. Rooms are a good size, and have a cosy feel, and there for hikes to Ani Gompa and easy access to the monastery.

**$$ Tawang Inn**, Nehru Market, T03794-224096/222172. The highest-spec rooms in town, particularly in terms of bathrooms. Carpets, attractive furnishings, thick pillows, TV, heaters, lots of wood and cane, and the all-important generator. 6 suites. Ask for a room with a view.

**$$ Tenzin Guest House**, 6 km from Tawang village by road, or a 45-min hike up footpaths (as is the monastery, directly above), T03794-200095/222893. A modern concrete house with 4 spotless rooms upstairs, a bit overpriced, but certainly comfortable. The setting is peaceful and attractive.

**$$-$ Tourist Hut**, Nehru Market, T03794-222739, T(0)9436-051291. The best value in Tawang, 7 rooms with heaters, towels, laminate floors, and plenty of colourfully clashing patterns and blankets – preferable on the 1st floor. A range of prices, pay more for TV or front-facing view, kind management willing to negotiate. Recommended.

**$ Nefa**, Nefa Complex, Nehru Market, T03794-222419. Double rooms are gloomy and old-fashioned while the staff are young and jolly. Men can stay in the 4-bed dorm.

**$ Tourist Lodge**, 200 m (signed) from jeep stand in the Old Market, T03794-222359. A lodge with 20 well-furnished but poorly maintained rooms, but they do have heaters and hot water. Contact the Deputy Commissioner to make reservations.

## Ziro p378

If you have your own transport, then there are some unique homestays on offer in the villages around the Ziro Valley.

**$$-$ Ziro Valley Resort**, Biiri village, 3 km from Old Ziro, T(0)985-691 0173, tagetabin@gmail.com. Very pleasing chalet rooms with modern if simple amenities, brand new and spacious, duvets, TV, best on the 1st floor with terraces. Also cheaper, simpler rooms next to the restaurant, less stylish but also have geysers. A great choice if you don't have to depend on public transport (1 km off the main road, before Hari village, sign-posted) and the villages around Ziro are an easy walk away. Worth going for a meal even if you aren't staying (see Restaurants, page 382).

**$ Blue Pine**, Pai Gate, Hapoli, T03788-224812. Most people's 1st choice for good reason, although other places are closer to town. Cosy rooms have wood panelling, TV, hot water, but dirty floors. Standard doubles, which they will be reluctant to tell you about, deluxe are larger with more character. No single room rates, but room 304 is a dorm with 2 beds (Rs 250), sharing common bathroom. Pleasant restaurant area though food is merely OK; laundry service. They were extending at the time of research, with 10 more rooms being added.

**$ Circuit House**, Hapoli, reservations through Deputy Commissioner's Office, T03788-224255. Excellent value, on a hill with views, worth the effort of contacting the DC. 6 rooms in the new block have tiled floors, TV, fresh paint, heaters, hot water request the VIP room, it is the same price as standard rooms, a steal at Rs 330). 3 rooms in the original bungalow. Food available.

**$ Government Guesthouse**, Old Ziro, T(0)8575-202663. Perched on top of a hill, with amazing views of the valley and the villages enclosed within it; 6 double rooms with bath Rs 250, nets, cheerful patterns but musty smells. Essential to phone ahead for permission to stay.

**$ Hotel Valley View**, Hapoli, T03788-225398. Institutional corridors lead to acceptable rooms with heaters and TV. Good choice for single travellers (attached bath, room 213 is best), also has doubles with shared bath for those on a budget, pay more for rooms with hot water. Extensive menu in the not unattractive restaurant.

**$ Pine Ridge**, MG Rd, Hapoli, T03788-224725. You could get lost in this maze of

a place, particularly as the lights never seem to be switched on in the corridors. It's good central location, but rooms are musty at the cheaper end. They come with TV and hot water. Restaurant is gloomy and deserted.

### Siiro

Two charming homestays in the village of Siiro are involving the community in tourist development and are the perfect place to experience local culture. Contact them direct, or through **Future Generations NGO**, T(0)9436-059165, www.future.org.

**$$-$ Ngunu Ziro**, T03788-225809, T(0)9436-047891, punyochada@gmail.com, about 5 km from Hapoli, has 3 cheerful rooms (2 share a bathroom) surrounded by a bamboo grove. Nicest on the upper floor among the eaves, hot water, meals available. Camping trips and treks to the Wildlife Sanctuary can be arranged.

To stay even deeper in the valley, next to paddies and streams (6 km from Hapoli), friendly **Hibu Tatu**, T03788-225808, T(0)9436-224834, has 2 chalets in his market garden of apple trees and veggies, simple concrete affairs with a front veranda, hot buckets, very clean, rooms have 2 big beds, B&B, all meals can be provided.

### Daporijo p378

**$ Circuit House**, on hill above town, T03792-223250. It's a steal at Rs 330 for clean sheets, mossie nets, fans, plenty of space and excellent views. Food is good and bed-tea available, as are hot buckets. It is a 10-min uphill slog from town, however, and permission is required from the DCs office in order to stay; however, on our visit, a telephone call made by staff to the EAC sufficed.

**$ Hotel Sanatu**, T03792-223531. 7 grim rooms with TV, fan, water by hot bucket in the scary bathrooms, dirty sheets. However, the very pleasant manager also has some decent rooms at a higher price in the KK Palace Hotel – but it's across the river.

## Daporijio to Pasighat p378
### Along/Aalo

**$$-$ Hotel Aagaam**, Yubo Complex, Nehru Chowk, T03783-223640/(0)9402-471774. More expensive than the **Holiday Cottage** for rooms with less appeal, but they do have geysers. Deluxe and suite rooms also available, newly renovated. There is a musty 3-bed dorm. On the main road.

**$ Circuit House**, opposite SBI, Main Rd, T03783-222232. An absolute bargain, 13 clean simple rooms, new block at the rear. On a small hill with views from the grounds. Often full, but try your luck.

**$ Holiday Cottage**, near General Hospital, T03783-222463/(0)943-6090511. On a quiet street, rooms with a bit of character and it's good value. Standard rooms have mossie nets and fans, 2 deluxe rooms have more light, space and sofas. Hot buckets available, restaurant is good.

The **Hotel Anachal Bhawan**, near the Police Station, is do-able if other places are full, though it costs more for worse rooms.

### Pasighat p379

**$$ Hotel Aane**, MG Rd, T0368-222 7777/3333. The best hotel in town, all rooms are newly and bluely painted, with fans, shiny floors, balcony, geyser and clean furnishings. A couple can easily fit in the single rooms with double beds, 2 suites are not worth the extra money. Restaurant pleasant, and roof terrace opens in the season.

**$ Hotel Oman**, Oman Complex, Main Market, T0368-222 4464. Absolutely the best budget choice, rooms have attached bath, decent furniture, clean sheets, new mossie nets, towels, TV. Singles start at Rs 400, deluxe doubles are Rs 850 (but couples can squeeze into the single rooms with 'family bed'). Food available.

The **Hotel Siang** close to the *sumo* counters is fine, should the Oman be full, though it is more costly for less appealing rooms.

## Restaurants

### Dirang p375

**$ Dipak Sweets & Snacks**, Main Rd. Open 0600-1900. Excellent *chola* with samosa or *puris* in the morning. One of few places open after noon on Thu.

**$ Hotel Raj**, Main Rd. Open 0600-1800. Good *dal baht* and *thukpa* for rock-bottom prices.

**$ Hotel Samaroh**, Main Rd. Cheap and busy rice meals/chow mein/greasy rolls are tasty. Veg and non-veg.

### Tawang p376

In Nehru Market, a small bakery sells substantial muffins and pastries.

**$$-$ Hotel Tawang View**, Nehru Market, T03794-223009. Open 0830-2100. Probably the best restaurant in town, with a huge vegetarian and non-vegetarian menu, most of which is actually available (unlike other places). Indian dishes particularly recommended. Red walls, coloured bulbs, plastic flowers, and the occasional drunk local.

**$ Dragon Restaurant**, Old Market, T03794-224475. Open 0700-2030. Delicious Chinese and Tibetan staples take a while to prepare and meat is rarely available, quite cosy surrounds with fairy lights. Look for the Chinese lanterns outside.

### Ziro p378

**$ Tribal Food Plaza**, MG Rd, Hapoli, T03788 225322. Mon-Sat 0800-1830. Indigenous cuisine is meat-oriented, also some Chinese Indian, soups, fish and Nagaland dishes. Colourful walls and lighting, view over the street as it is the 1st floor.

**$ Ziro Valley Resort**, Biiri village, T(0)985-691 0173. Open 0630-2130. A popular place with locals, excellent Indian/Chinese dishes, dining is either in the main restaurant or 3 little huts in the grounds. Alcohol available (cheap beer). It's well placed to take a break when walking around the valley villages. They also have lodgings (see page 380).

The restaurant at the **$ Hotel Valley View** as a varied menu, better for vegetarians aan others. The **$$ Blue Pine** hotel is a leasant place to sit and relax, though he food is not very memorable. There are everal cheap eateries on MG Rd.

**aporijo** *p378*
he food at the Circuit House is good, for esidents; nothing in town is outstanding hough the **$ Sanatu** hotel is a safe bet nd there are several other cheap options.

**aporijio to Pasighat** *p378*
**long/Aalo**
he restaurants at the **$ Aagaam**, T03783-22838, and Holiday Cottage hotels do ood meals and are the best places in town o dine; both have a few tribal dishes in the menu. **$ CT Restaurant**, below the **Aagaam**, bes tasty Chinese/Tibetan fare (no menu).

**asighat** *p379*
**Shangrila**, opposite Main Market. pen 0730-1930. Excellent and always usy, *thukpa*, chowmein, meat *momos*, l come with delicious soup. Half-plates e very generous and very cheap.

**Festivals**

**eb/Mar Losar** is celebrated for 8-15 days western Arunachal.
**ct Tawang Festival** known as the uddha Mahatsova in previous incarnations, he festival is a great fun with a blend of ultural programmes, fashion shows, music, aditional cuisine, bars, and tribal dances. ver 3 days.

**Shopping**

**anagar-Naharlagun** *p374*
he cotton textiles available here are plourful and are beautifully patterned. ou can also get wooden masks and figures, ane belts, haversacks and caps. **Government ales Emporium** on MG Marg in Itanagar

(opposite the Donyi-Polo Hotel) has a decent selection; Mon-Fri 0930-1000, Sat -1200.

## ⏱ What to do

**Itanagar-Naharlagun** *p374*
**Arunachal Travels**, Itanagar, agents for Air India.
**Gibbon Travels**, MLA Cottage Rd, E Sector, Itanagar, T0360-229 1181, T(0)9436-044069, www.gibbontravels.com. Helpful Komkar organizes tours throughout the northeast and can arrange permits for independent travellers to Arunachal quickly and efficiently (and at a significantly cheaper cost than other agents).
**Help Tourism**, www.helptourism.com. Known for their sustainable tourism initiatives.
**Himalayan Holidays**, APST Rd, Ganga, Itanagar, T0360-221 8534.

**Bomdila** *p375*
**Himalayan Holidays**, ABC Buildings, Main Market, T03782-222017. Useful for booking *sumo* tickets in advance.

**Tawang** *p376*
**Arunachal Tourism**, at the Tourist Lodge, Old Market, T03794-222359. Has a couple of interesting pamphlets.
**Himalayan Holidays**, Old Market, T03794-223151, T(0)94362-48216. Open 0500-1930. Organizes tours and jeep hire, good for booking advance *sumo* tickets back to Tezpur.
**Tribal Discovery** (same office as Himalayan), Old Market, T03794-223151. Reasonable prices on tours to tribal villages, the monastery, nunneries, etc. Vehicle hire (including petrol) for a day at the Lakes is around Rs 3000.

## 🚍 Transport

**Itanagar-Naharlagun** *p374*
**Air** There are airports atLilabari and Tezpur in Assam; however, at the time of writing, no commercial flights were operating. Likewise, the **helipad** at Naharlagun, which used to

connect with **Guwahati** and **Tawang**, is not currently operating.

**Bus** APST from Naharlagun Bus Station. **Guwahati** (381 km, 8 hr); **North Lakhimpur**; **Bomdila** (Mon, Thu, 12 hrs). Blue Hills overnight coach to **Guwahati** (11½ hrs). Enquiries: T0360-224 4221.

**Taxi** Naharlagun/Itanagar, Rs 200 plus fuel; Rs 30 (shared taxi).

**Train** The nearest railhead is Harmuti station, 23 km from Naharlagun. Railway Out Agency, Naharlagun bus station, T0360-224 4209.

### Bomdila, Dirang and Tawang *p375*

**Bus** ASTC buses run between Tezpur and Tawang when weather conditions permit; if there is too much snow they terminate at Dirang. The narrow and twisting road means *sumos* are recommended over the bus. **Tezpur–Tawang** (12-14 hrs, depart 0530); **Tezpur–Bomdila** (5½ hrs); **Bomdila–Dirang** (1½ hrs); **Bomdila–Tawang** (6-7 hrs, 0530); **Dirang–Tawang** (6½ hrs, 0830). *Sumos* pick up from hotels in all towns.

Use the contacts below to book seats in advance. In Tezpur: **ASTC Sumo Service**, T(0)9435-080318, T(0)9864-182449. In Bomdila: **Gourab**, T(0)9436-236055, or **Himalayan Holidays**, T03782-222017. In Dirang: **Dream Destination**, T03780-242737, **Dirang Valley Tours**, T03780-242560, or **Himalayan Holidays**, T03780-242464. In Tawang: **Himalayan Holidays**, T03794-223151, or **Pine Ridge**, T03794-222306.

### Ziro *p378*

**Sumo** Getting from Ziro to Daporijo by *sumo* is tricky, as you have to join a *sumo* coming from Itanagar, at around 1100, and take any free seats available (usually the rear seats; be warned, the road is particularly windy and bumpy on this stretch). To **Itanagar**, at 0530.

### Daporijo *p378*

**Bus** APST bus (T03792-223107) to **Itanagar**, to **Ziro** on Tue at 0700, to **Along** except Mon (9 hrs, Rs 160).

**Sumo** *Sumo* counters/departures are in the bazar area, about 200 m from the Sanat hotel. To **Ziro** at 0600 (5 hrs), to **Itanagar** at 0500 (12 hrs). For reservations try Arunacha Yatayat, T03792-223679. **Note** There are no public *sumos* to Along, so it is the bus or a hired *sumo* for Rs 5500.

### Daporijio to Pasighat *p378* Along/Aalo

**Bus** APST (T03783-222475) bus to **Itanagar** at 0600 and 1600 (except Mon, 12 hrs), to **Guwahati** at 1000 (Mon/Thu only, 14 hrs), to **Daporijo** at 0700 (except Mon, 9 hrs). **Note** There are no public *sumos* along the route to Daporijo, so it is either the bus or a hired *sumo* (see below). To **Mechukha** at 0615 (except Fri, 12 hrs).

**Sumo** It is necessary to report to the *sumo* counter 30 mins before departure. To **Pasighat** at 1100 (4½-5 hrs); to **Itanaga** at 0530 (9 hrs). *Sumos* to **Daporijo** are by reserve only, Rs 5500.

### Pasighat *p379*

**Bus** The APST bus stand is 1.5 km from the centre, Rs 50 in an auto.

**Sumo** It is necessary to report to the *sumo* counter 30 mins before departure. To **Along** at 0600 (4½-5 hrs); to **Itanagar** at 0600 (5 hrs). ASTC bus to **Guwahati** leaves from the *sumo* stand at 1130 (17-18 hrs).

**Ferry** Winger-ferry-*sumo* tickets to **Dibrugarh** (via Jonai) in Assam are sold by Otto Tours, T(0)986-209 3159 (at the *sumo* stand) departing 0600 (5 hrs).

## ❶ Directory

### Itanagar-Naharlagun *p374*
**Banks/post** There are ATMs and post offices. **Medical services** RK Mission Hospital, T0360-221 8780/2263.

### Tawang *p376*
**Banks** SBI, near the Old Market has ATM. **Internet** There are a couple of internet

...afés in town, open till around 1730 in winter, 2000 in summer.

**Ziro** *p378*
**Banks** SBI with ATM near the bazar.
**Internet** Rivi's, in the alley below the Pine Ridge hotel, Mon-Sat 0900-1900.

**Daporijo** *p378*
**Internet** B4U, fast connection, Tue-Sun 0700-1900.

**Daporijio to Pasighat** *p378*
**Along/Aalo**
**Banks** SBI with ATM on main road.
**Internet** Internet Café, opposite APST bus stand.

**Pasighat** *p379*
**Internet** Cyber Zone, Banskota Rd, off MG Rd (near Hotel Aane), open till 1830.

# Contents

Background

# History of the Indian Himalaya

The settlement history of the Indian Himalaya reflects a range of influences. Migrants from Mongolia and Central Asia to the north gave a distinctive ethnic character to many of the Himalayan peoples, and Southeast Asian tribal groups had a strong influence on ethnic character in the east. Yet the dominant influences have largely been from the Indian plains to the south, notably in the spread of the major religions practised in the mountain regions.

The first village communities in South Asia grew up on the arid western fringes of the Indus Plains 10,000 years ago. Over the following generations successive waves of settlers – sometimes bringing goods for trade, sometimes armies to conquer territory and sometimes nothing more than domesticated animals and families in search of land and peace – moved across the Indus and into India. They left an indelible mark on the landscape and culture of all the countries of modern South Asia.

## The first settlers

A site at Mehrgarh, where the Indus Plains meet the dry Baluchistan Hills in modern Pakistan, has revealed evidence of agricultural settlement as early as 8500 BC. By 3500 BC agriculture had spread throughout the Indus Plains and in the thousand years following there were independent settled villages well to the east of the Indus. Between 3000 BC and 2500 BC many new settlements sprang up in the heartland of what became the Indus Valley civilization.

Most cultural, religious and political developments during that period owed more to local development than to external influence, although India had extensive contact with other regions, notably with Mesopotamia. At its height the Indus Valley civilization covered as great an area as Egypt or Mesopotamia. However, the culture that developed was distinctively South Asian. Speculation continues to surround the nature of the language, which is still untranslated.

## India from 2000 BC to the Mauryas

In about 2000 BC Moenjo Daro, widely presumed to be the capital of the Indus Valley Civilization, became deserted and within the next 250 years the entire Indus Valley civilization disintegrated. The causes remain uncertain: the violent arrival of new waves of Aryan immigrants (a theory no one now accepts), increasing desertification of the already semi-arid landscape, a shift in the course of the Indus and internal political decay have each been suggested as instrumental in its downfall. Whatever the causes, some features of Indus Valley culture were carried on by succeeding generations.

Probably from about 1500 BC northern India entered the Vedic period. Aryan settlers moved southeast towards the Ganga Valley. Classes of rulers *(rajas)* and priests *(brahmins)* began to emerge. Grouped into tribes, conflict was common. In one battle of this period a confederacy of tribes known as the Bharatas defeated another grouping of 10 tribes. They gave their name to the region to the east of the Indus which is the official name for India today – Bharat.

The centre of population and of culture shifted east from the banks of the Indus to the land between the Rivers Yamuna and Ganga, the *doab* (pronounced *doe-ahb*, literally 'two waters'). This region became the heart of emerging Aryan culture, which, from 1500 BC onwards, laid the literary and religious foundations of what ultimately became Hinduism, spreading to embrace the whole of India.

**The Vedas** The first fruit of this development was the Rig Veda, the first of four Vedas, composed, collected and passed on orally by Brahmin priests. While some scholars date the oral origins as early as the beginning of the second millennium BC, the date of 1300 BC to about 1000 BC still seems more probable. In the later Vedic period, from about 1000 BC to 600 BC, the Sama, Yajur and Artha Vedas show that the Indo-Aryans developed a clear sense of the Ganga-Yamuna *doab* as 'their' territory.

From the sixth to the third centuries BC the region from the foothills of the Himalaya across the Ganga plains to the edge of the Peninsula was governed under a variety of kingdoms or Mahajanapadhas – 'great states'. Trade gave rise to the birth of towns in the Ganga plains themselves, many of which have remained occupied to the present. Varanasi (Benaras) is perhaps the most famous example, but a trade route was established that ran from Taxila (20 km from modern Islamabad in Pakistan) to Rajgir 1500 km away in what is now Bihar. It was into these kingdoms of the Himalayan foothills and north plains that Mahavir, founder of Jainism, and the Buddha, were born.

## The Mauryas

Within a year of the retreat of Alexander the Great from the Indus in 326 BC, **Chandragupta Maurya** established the first indigenous empire to exercise control over much of the subcontinent.

The centre of political power had shifted east into wetter, more densely forested but also more fertile regions. The Mauryans had their base in the region known as Magadh (now Bihar) and their capital at Pataliputra, near modern Patna. Their power was based on massive military force and a highly efficient, centralized administration.

The greatest of the Mauryan emperors, **Asoka** took power in 272 BC. He inherited a full-blown empire, but extended it further by defeating the Kalingans in modern Orissa, before turning his back on war and preaching the virtues of pacifism. Asoka's empire stretched from Afghanistan to Assam and from the Himalaya to Mysore.

The state maintained itself by raising revenue from taxation – on everything, from agriculture to gambling and prostitution. Asoka decreed that 'no waste land should be occupied and not a tree cut down' without permission because all were potential sources of revenue for the state. The *sudras* (lowest of Hindu castes) were used as free labour for clearing forest and cultivating new land.

Asoka (described on the edicts as 'the Beloved of the Gods, of Gracious Countenance') left a series of inscriptions on pillars and rocks across the subcontinent. Over most of India these inscriptions were written in *Prakrit*, using the *Brahmi* script, although in the northwest they were in Greek using the *Kharoshti* script. They were unintelligible for over 2000 years after the decline of the empire until James Prinsep deciphered the Brahmi script in 1837. Through the edicts Asoka urged all people to follow the code of *dhamma* or *dharma* – translated by the Indian historian Romila Thapar as 'morality, piety, virtue and social order'. He established a special force of *dhamma* officers to try to enforce the code, which encouraged toleration, non-violence, respect for priests and those in authority, and for human dignity.

However, within 50 years of Asoka's death in 232 BC the Mauryan Empire had disintegrated and with it the whole structure and spirit of its government.

## A period of fragmentation: 185 BC to AD 300

Beyond the Mauryan Empire other kingdoms survived in South India. The Satavahanas dominated the central Deccan for over 300 years from about 50 BC. Further south in what is now Tamil Nadu, the early kingdoms of the Cholas and the Pandiyas gave a glimpse

of both power and cultural development that was to flower over 1000 years later. In t
centuries following the break-up of the Mauryan Empire these kingdoms were in t
forefront of developing overseas trade, especially with Greece and Rome. Internal tra
also flourished and Indians carried goods to China and Southeast Asia.

## The classical period – the Gupta Empire: AD 319-467

Although the political power of Chandra Gupta and his successors never approach
that of his unrelated namesake nearly 650 years before him, the Gupta Empire which w
established with his coronation in AD 319 produced developments in every field of Indi
culture. Its influence has been felt profoundly across South Asia to the present.

Geographically the Guptas originated in the same Magadhan region that had given ri
to the Mauryan Empire. Extending their power by strategic marriage alliances, Chand
Gupta's empire of Magadh was extended by his son, Samudra Gupta, who took power
AD 335, across North India. He also marched as far south as Kanchipuram in modern Tar
Nadu, but the heartland of the Gupta Empire remained the plains of the Ganga.

Chandra Gupta II reigned for 39 years from AD 376 and was a great patron of the art

Wealth generated from trade with Southeast Asia, Arabia and China was distribut
to the arts on an unprecedented scale. Some went to religious foundations, such as t
Buddhist monastery at Ajanta, which produced some of its finest murals during the Gup
period. But Hindu institutions also benefited and some of the most important featur
of modern Hinduism date from this time. The sacrifices of Vedic worship were given
in favour of personal devotional worship, known as *bhakti*. Tantrism, both in its Buddh
and Hindu forms, with its emphasis on the female life force and worship of the Moth
Goddess, developed. The focus of worship was towards a personalized and monothei
deity, represented in the form of either Siva or Vishnu. The myths of Vishnu's incarnatio
arose in this period.

The **Brahmins**, the priestly caste who were in the key position to mediate chan
refocused earlier literature to give shape to the emerging religious philosophy. In th
hands the *Mahabharata* and the *Ramayana* were transformed from secular epics
religious stories. The excellence of contemporary sculpture both reflected and contribut
to an increase in image worship and the growing role of temples as centres of devotion

## The spread of Islamic power – the Delhi Sultanate

From about AD 1000 the external attacks which inflicted most damage on Rajput wea
and power came increasingly from the Arabs and Turks. Mahmud of Ghazni raided t
Punjab virtually every year between 1000 and 1026, attracted both by the agricultu
surpluses and the enormous wealth in cash, golden images and jewellery of North Indi
temples, which drew him back every year. He died in 1030, to the Hindus just anoth
*mlechchha* ('impure' or sullied one), as had been the Huns and the Sakas before him, so
to be forgotten. Such raids were never taken seriously as a long-term threat by kin
further east and as the Rajputs often feuded among themselves the northwest plai
became an attractive prey.

Muslim political power was heralded by the raids of Mu'izzu'd Din and his defeat
massive Rajput forces at the Second Battle of Tarain in 1192. Mu'izzu'd Din left his depu
Qutb u'd Din Aibak, to hold the territorial gains from his base at Indraprastha. Mu'izzu'd D
made further successful raids in the 1190s, inflicting crushing defeats on Hindu oppone
from Gwalior to Benaras. The foundations were then laid for the first extended period
such power, which came under the Delhi sultans.

**Qutb u'd Din Aibak** took Lahore in 1206, although it was his lieutenant **Iltutmish** who ally established control from Delhi in 1211. Qutb u'd Din Aibak consolidated Muslim ominion by an even-handed policy of conciliation and patronage. In Delhi he converted e old Hindu stronghold of Qila Rai Pithora into his Muslim capital and began several agnificent building projects, including the Quwwat-ul-Islam mosque and the Qutb Minar, victory tower. Iltutmish was a Turkish slave – a *Mamluk* – and the Sultanate continued to ok west for its leadership and inspiration. However, the possibility of continuing control om outside India was destroyed by the crushing raids of **Genghis Khan** through Central sia and from 1222 Iltutmish ruled from Delhi completely independently of outside thority. He annexed Sind in 1228 and all the territory east to Bengal by 1230.

A succession of dynasties followed, drawing on refugees from Genghis Khan's raids and om still further to the west to strengthen the leadership. In 1290 the first dynasty was cceeded by the Khaljis, which in turn gave way to the Tughluqs in 1320. **Mohammad bin ughluq** (ruled 1324-1351) was described by the Moorish traveller Ibn Batuta as 'a man ho above all others is fond of making presents and shedding blood'. Despite its periodic utality, this period marked a turning point in Muslim government in India, as Turkish amluks gave way to government by Indian Muslims and their Hindu allies. The Delhi ltans were open to local influences and employed Hindus in their administration. In the id-14th century their capital, Delhi, was one of the leading cities of the contemporary orld but in 1398 their control came to an abrupt end with the arrival of the Mongol Timur.

**Timur's** limp caused him to be called Timur-i-leng (Timur the Lame, known to the est as Tamburlaine). This self-styled 'Scourge of God' was illiterate, a devout Muslim, an utstanding chess player and a patron of the arts. Five years before his arrival in India he ad taken Baghdad and three years before that he had ravaged Russia, devastating land nd pillaging villages. India had not been in such danger from Mongols since Genghis nan had arrived on the same stretch of the Indus 200 years before.

After Timur, it took nearly 50 years for the Delhi Kingdom to become more than a local eadquarters. The revival was slow and fitful. The last Tughluqs were succeeded by an ndistinguished line of Sayyids, who began as Timur's deputies and were essentially ghan soldier/administrators. They later called themselves sultans and Lodi kings (1451- 26) and moved their capital to Agra. Nominally they controlled an area from Punjab to har but they were, in fact, in the hands of a group of factious nobles.

## he Mughal Empire

North India it is the impact of the Mughal rule that is most strikingly evident today. e descendants of conquerors, with the blood of both Timur and Genghis Khan in their ins, they came to dominate Indian politics, from Babur's victory near Delhi in 1526 Aurangzeb's death in 1707. Their legacy was not only some of the most magnificent chitecture in the world, but a profound impact on the culture, society and future politics South Asia.

**abur** Founder of the Mughal Dynasty, Babur ('the tiger') was born in Russian Turkestan 15 February 1483, the fifth direct descendant on the male side of Timur and 13th on the male side from Genghis Khan. He established the Mughal Empire by leading his cavalry d artillery forces to a stupendous victory over the combined armies of Ibrahim Lodi, last ler of the Delhi Sultanate and the Hindu Raja of Gwalior, at **Panipat**, 80 km north of Delhi, 1526. When he died four years later, the empire was still far from secured, but he had not ly laid the foundations of political and military power, he had also begun to establish courtly traditions of poetry, literature and art, which became the hallmark of subsequen**t** Mughal rulers.

Babur, used to Persian gardens and cool Afghan hills, was unimpressed by what he sa**w** of India. In his autobiography he wrote: "Hindustan is a country that has few pleasure**s** to recommend it. The people are not handsome. They have no idea of the charms **o**f friendly society, of frankly mixing together, or of familiar intercourse. They have no geni**us** no comprehension of mind, no politeness of manner, no kindness or fellow-feeling, n**o** ingenuity or mechanical invention in planning or executing their handicraft works, no sk**i**l or knowledge in design or architecture; they have no horses, no good flesh, no grapes **o**r musk melons, no good fruits, no ice or cold water, no good food or bread in their baza**r,** no baths or colleges, no candles, no torches, not a candlestick".

**Humayun** The strength of Babur's senior nobles posed a problem for Humayun, h**is** successor. Almost immediately after Babur's death in 1531 Humayun was forced to retre**at** from Delhi through Sindh with his pregnant wife. His son Akbar, who was to become th**e** greatest of the Mughal emperors, was born at Umarkot in Sindh, modern Pakistan, durin**g** this period of exile, on 23 November 1542.

**Akbar** Akbar was only 13 when he took the throne in 1556. The next 44 years were one **of** the most remarkable periods of South Asian history, paralleled by the Elizabethan peri**od** in England, where Queen Elizabeth I ruled from 1558 to 1603. Although Akbar inherit**ed** the throne, it was he who really created the Mughal Empire and gave it many of i**ts** distinguishing features.

Through his marriage to a Hindu princess he ensured that Hindus were given honoure**d** positions in government, as well as respect for their religious beliefs and practices. H**e** sustained a passionate interest in art and literature, matched by a determination to crea**te** monuments to his empire's political power and he laid the foundations for an artistic an**d** architectural tradition that developed a totally distinctive Indian style. This emerged fro**m** the separate elements of Iranian and Indian traditions by a constant process of blendin**g** and originality of which Akbar was the chief patron.

But these achievements were only possible because of his political and military gift**s.** From 1556 until his 18th birthday in 1560, Akbar was served by a prince regent, Baira**m** Khan. However, already at the age of 15 he had conquered Ajmer and large areas of Centr**al** India. Chittor and Ranthambore fell to him in 1567-1568, bringing most of what is no**w** Rajasthan under his control. This opened the door south to Gujarat.

Afghans continued to cause his empire difficulties, including Daud Karrani, wh**o** declared independence in East India in 1574. That threat to Mughal power was final**ly** crushed with Karrani's death in 1576. Bengal was far from the last of Akbar's conquests. H**e** brought Kabul back under Mughal control in the 1580s and established a presence fro**m** Kashmir, Sindh and Baluchistan in the north and west, to the Godavari River on the bord**er** of modern Andhra Pradesh in the south.

Akbar deliberately widened his power base by incorporating Rajput princes into th**e** administrative structure and giving them extensive rights in the revenue from land. H**e** abolished the hated tax on non-Muslims (*jizya*) – ultimately reinstated by his strict**ly** orthodox great-grandson Aurangzeb – and ceased levying taxes on Hindus who went o**n** pilgrimage. He also ended the practice of forcible conversion to Islam.

**Artistic treasures** abound from Akbar's court – paintings, jewellery, weapons – ofte**n** bringing together material and skills from across the known world. Akbar's eclecticism ha**d**

a political purpose, for he was trying to build a focus of loyalty beyond that of caste, social group, region or religion. Like Roman emperors before him, he deliberately cultivated a new religion in which the emperor himself attained divinity, hoping thereby to give the empire a legitimacy that would last. While his religion disappeared with his death, the legitimacy of the Mughals survived another 200 years, long after their real power had almost disappeared.

**Jahangir**  Akbar died of a stomach illness in 1605. He was succeeded by his son, Prince Salim, who inherited the throne as Emperor Jahangir ('world seizer'). He added little to the territory of the empire, consolidating the Mughals' hold on the Himalayan foothills and parts of central India but restricting his innovative energies to pushing back frontiers of art rather than of land. He commissioned works of art and literature, many of which directly recorded life in the Mughal court. Hunting scenes were not just romanticized accounts of rural life, but conveyed the real dangers of hunting lions or tigers; implements, furniture, tools and weapons were made with lavish care and often exquisite design.

From early youth Jahangir had shown an artistic temperament, but he also became addicted to alcohol and then to opium. In his autobiography, he wrote: "I had not drunk until I was 18, except in the time of my infancy two or three times my mother and wet nurses gave it by way of infantile remedy, mixed with water and rose water to take away a cough ... years later a gunner said that if I would take a glass of wine it would drive away the feeling of being tired and heavy ... After that I took to drinking wine ... until wine made from grapes ceased to intoxicate me and I took to drinking arrack (local spirits). By degrees my potions rose to 20 cups of doubly distilled spirits, 14 during the daytime and the remainder at night".

**Nur Jahan**  Jahangir's favourite wife, Nur Jahan, brought her own artistic gifts. Born the daughter of an Iranian nobleman, she had been brought to the Mughal court along with her family as a child and moved to Bengal as the wife of Sher Afgan. She made rapid progress after her first husband's accidental death in 1607, which caused her to move from Bengal to be a lady-in-waiting to one of Akbar's widows.

At the Mughal court in 1611, when she was 34, she met Jahangir. Mutually enraptured, they were married in May. Jahangir gave her the title Nur Mahal ('Light of the Palace'), soon increased to Nur Jahan ('Light of the World'). She was strikingly beautiful and had an astonishing reputation for physical skill and intellectual wit. She was a crack shot with a gun, highly artistic, determined yet philanthropic. Throughout her life Jahangir was so captivated by her that he flouted Muslim convention by minting coins bearing her image.

By 1622 Nur Jahan effectively controlled the empire. She commissioned and supervised the building in Agra of one of the Mughal world's most beautiful buildings, the **I'timad ud-Daula** ('Pillar of government'), as a tomb for her father and mother. Her father, **Ghiyas Beg**, had risen to become one of Jahangir's most trusted advisers and Nur Jahan was determined to ensure that their memory was honoured. She was less successful in her wish to deny the succession, after Jahangir's death at the age of 58, to Prince Khurram. Acceding to the throne in 1628, he took the title of Shah Jahan ('Ruler of the World') and in the next 30 years his reign represented the height of Mughal power.

**Shah Jahan**  The Mughal Empire was under attack in the Deccan and the northwest when Shah Jahan became Emperor. He tried to re-establish and extend Mughal authority in both regions by a combination of military campaigns and skilled diplomacy. Akbar's craftsmen had already carved outstandingly beautiful *jalis* (pierced screens) for the tomb of Salim Chishti in Fatehpur Sikri, but Shah Jahan developed the form further. Undoubtedly the finest tribute to these skills is found in the Taj Mahal, the tribute to his beloved wife Mumtaz Mahal, who died giving birth to her fourteenth child in 1631.

**Aurangzeb** The need to expand the area under Mughal control was felt even more strongly by Aurangzeb ('The jewel in the throne'), than by his predecessors. He had shown his intellectual gifts in his grandfather Jahangir's court when held hostage to guarantee Shah Jahan's good behaviour, learning Arabic, Persian, Turkish and Hindi. When he seized power at the age of 40, he needed all his political and military skills to hold on to an unwieldy empire that was in permanent danger of collapse from its own size.

Aurangzeb realized that the resources of the territory he inherited from Shah Jahan were not enough. One response was to push south, while maintaining his hold on the east and north. Initially he maintained his alliances with the Rajputs in the west, which had been a crucial element in Mughal strategy. In 1678 he claimed absolute rights over Jodhpur and went to war with the Rajput clans, at the same time embarking on a policy of outright Islamization. However, for the remaining 39 years of his reign he was forced to struggle continuously to sustain his power.

### The East India Company and the rise of British power

The British were unique among the foreign rulers of India in coming by sea rather than through the northwest and in coming first for trade rather than for military conquest. The ports that they established – Madras, Bombay and Calcutta – became completely new centres of political, economic and social activity. Before them, Indian empires had controlled their territories from the land. The British dictated the emerging shape of the economy by controlling sea-borne trade. From the middle of the 19th century railways transformed the economic and political structure of South Asia and it was those three centres of British political control, along with the late addition of Delhi, which became the foci of economic development and political change.

### The East India Company in Madras and Bengal

In its first 90 years of contact with South Asia after the Company set up its first trading post at **Masulipatnam**, on the east coast of India, it had depended almost entirely on trade for its profits. However, in 1701, only 11 years after a British settlement was first established at Calcutta, the Company was given rights to land revenue in Bengal.

The Company was accepted and sometimes welcomed, partly because it offered to bolster the inadequate revenues of the Mughals by exchanging silver bullion for the cloth it bought. However, in the south the Company moved further towards consolidating its political base. Wars between South India's regional factions gave the Company the chance to extend its influence by making alliances and offering support to some of these factions in their struggles, which were complicated by the extension to Indian soil of the European contest for power between the French and the British.

**Robert Clive** The British established control over both Bengal and Southeast India in the middle of the 17th century. Robert Clive, in alliance with a collection of disaffected Hindu landowners and Muslim soldiers, defeated the new Nawab of Bengal, the 20-year-old Sirajud-Daula and his French allies in June 1757 at **Plassey** (Palashi), about 100 km north of Calcutta.

**Hastings and Cornwallis** The essential features of British control were mapped out in the next quarter of a century through the work of **Warren Hastings**, Governor-General from 1774 until 1785, and **Lord Cornwallis**, who succeeded and remained in charge until 1793. Cornwallis was responsible for putting Europeans in charge of all the higher levels of revenue collection and administration and for introducing government by the rule of law, making even government officers subject to the courts.

## The decline of Muslim power

The extension of East India Company power in the Mughal periphery of India's south and east took place against a background of the rising power of Sivaji and his Marathas.

**Sivaji and the Marathas** Sivaji was the son of a Hindu who had served as a small-scale chief in the Muslim-ruled state of Bijapur. The weakness of Bijapur encouraged Sivaji to extend his father's area of control and he led a rebellion. The Bijapur general Afzal Khan, sent to put it down, agreed to meet Sivaji in private to reach a settlement. In an act that is still remembered by both Muslims and Marathas, Sivaji embraced him with steel claws attached to his fingers and tore him apart. It was the start of a campaign that took Maratha power as far south as Madurai and to the doors of Delhi and Calcutta.

Although Sivaji himself died in 1680, Aurangzeb never fully came to terms with the rising power of the Marathas, though he did end their ambitions to form an empire of their own. While the Maratha confederacy was able to threaten Delhi within 50 years of Aurangzeb's death, by the early 19th century it had dissolved into five independent states, with whom the British ultimately dealt separately.

Nor was Aurangzeb able to create any wide sense of identity with the Mughals as a legitimate popular power. Instead, under the influence of Sunni Muslim theologians, he retreated into insistence on Islamic purity. He imposed Islamic *sharia* law, promoted only Muslims to positions of power and authority, tried to replace Hindu administrators and revenue collectors with Muslims and reimposed the *jizya* tax on all non-Muslims. By the time of his death in 1707 the empire no longer had either the broadness of spirit or the physical means to survive.

**Bahadur Shah** The decline was postponed briefly by the five-year reign of Aurangzeb's son. Sixty-three when he acceded to the throne, Bahadur Shah restored some of its faded fortunes. He made agreements with the Marathas and the Rajputs and defeated the Sikhs in Punjab before taking the last Sikh guru into his service. Nine emperors succeeded Aurangzeb between his death and the exile of the last Mughal ruler in 1858. It was no accident that it was in that year that the British ended the rule of its East India Company and decreed India to be its Indian Empire.

Mohammad Shah remained in his capital of Delhi, resigning himself to enjoying what Carey Welch has called "the conventional triad of joys: the wine was excellent, as were the women and for him the song was especially rewarding". The idyll was rudely shattered by the invasion of **Nadir Shah** in 1739, an Iranian marauder who slaughtered thousands in Delhi and stole priceless Mughal treasures, including the Peacock Throne.

## The East India Company's push for power

**Alliances** In the century and a half that followed the death of Aurangzeb, the British East India Company extended its economic and political influence into the heart of India. As the Mughal Empire lost its power India fell into many smaller states. The Company undertook to protect the rulers of several of these states from external attack by stationing British troops in their territory. In exchange for this service the rulers paid subsidies to the Company. The British extended their territory through the 18th century as successive regional powers were annexed and brought under direct Company rule.

Progress to direct British control was uneven and often opposed. The Sikhs in Punjab, the Marathas in the west and the Mysore sultans in the south, fiercely contested British advances. **Haidar Ali** and **Tipu Sultan**, who had built a wealthy kingdom in the Mysore region, resisted attempts to incorporate them. Tipu was finally killed in 1799 at the battle of Srirangapatnam, an island fort in the Kaveri River just north of Mysore, where Arthur Wellesley, later the Duke of Wellington, began to make his military reputation.

The Marathas were not defeated until the 1816-1818 war. Even then the defeat owed as much to internal fighting as to the power of the British-led army. Only the northwest of the subcontinent remained beyond British control until well into the 19th century. Thus in 1799 **Ranjit Singh** was able to set up a Sikh state in Punjab, surviving until the late 1830s despite the extension of British control over much of the rest of India.

In 1818 India's economy was in ruins and its political structures destroyed. Irrigation and road systems had fallen into decay and gangs terrorized the countryside. Thugs and dacoits controlled much of the rural areas in Central India and often robbed and murdered even on town outskirts. The stability of the Mughal period had long since passed. From 1818 to 1857 there was a succession of local and uncoordinated revolts in different parts of India. Some were bought off, some put down by military force.

## A period of reforms

While existing political systems were collapsing, the first half of the 1800s was also a time of radical social change in territories governed by the East India Company. **Lord William Bentinck** became governor-general at a time when England was undergoing major reform. In 1828 he banned the burning of widows on the funeral pyres of their husbands (**sati**) and then moved to suppress **thuggee** (the ritual murder and robbery carried out in the name of the goddess Kali). But his most far-reaching change was to introduce education in English.

From the late 1830s massive new engineering projects began to be taken up; first canals then railways. The innovations stimulated change and change contributed to the growing unease with the British presence. The development of the telegraph, railways and new roads, three universities and the extension of massive new canal irrigation projects in North India seemed to threaten traditional society, a risk increased by the annexation of Indian states to bring them under direct British rule. The most important of these was Oudh.

## The Rebellion

Out of the growing discontent and widespread economic difficulties came the Rebellion or 'Mutiny' of 10 May 1857 by East India Company troops in Meerut, 70 km northeast of Delhi. They reached Delhi the next day, where **Bahadur Shah**, the last Mughal Emperor, sided with the mutineers. Troops in Lucknow joined the rebellion and for three months Lucknow and other cities in the north were under siege. Appalling scenes of butchery and reprisals marked the struggle, only put down by troops from outside.

## The Period of Empire

The 1857 Rebellion marked the end not only of the Mughal Empire but also of the East India Company, for the British government in London took overall control in 1858. Yet within 30 years a movement for self-government had begun and there were the first signs

## Mahatma Gandhi

Mohandas Karamchand Ghandi, a Westernized, English-educated lawyer, had lived outside India from his youth to middle age. He preached the general acceptance of some of the doctrines he had grown to respect in his childhood, which stemmed from deep Indian traditions – notably ahimsa, or non-violence. On his return the Bengali Nobel Laureate poet, Rabindranath Tagore, had dubbed him 'Mahatma' – 'Great Soul'. From 1921 he gave up his Western style of dress and adopted the hand-spun dhoti worn by poor Indian villagers.

Yet, he was also fiercely critical of many aspects of traditional Hindu society. He preached against the discrimination of the caste system which still dominated life for the overwhelming majority of Hindus. Often despised by the British in India, his death at the hands of an extreme Hindu chauvinist in January 1948 was a final testimony to the ambiguity of his achievements: successful in contributing so much to achieving India's Independence, yet failing to resolve some of the bitter communal legacies which he gave his life to overcome.

of a demand among the new Western-educated elite that political rights be awarded to match the sense of Indian national identity.

**Indian National Congress** Established in 1885, this was the first all-India political institution and was to become the key vehicle of demands for independence. However, the educated Muslim elite of what is now Uttar Pradesh saw a threat to Muslim rights, power and identity in the emergence of democratic institutions that gave Hindus, with their built-in natural majority, significant advantages. Sir Sayyid Ahmad Khan, who had founded a Muslim University at Aligarh in 1877, advised Muslims against joining the Congress, seeing it as a vehicle for Hindu, and especially Bengali, nationalism.

**The Muslim League** The educated Muslim community of North India remained deeply suspicious of the Congress, making up less than 8% of those attending its conferences between 1900-1920. Muslims from UP created the All-India Muslim League in 1906. However, the demands of the Muslim League were not always opposed to those of the Congress. In 1916 it concluded the Lucknow Pact with the Congress, in which the Congress won Muslim support for self-government, in exchange for the recognition that there would be separate constituencies for Muslims. The nature of the future independent India was still far from clear, however. The British conceded the principle of self-government in 1918, but they already fell far short of heightened Indian expectations.

**Mahatma Gandhi** Into a tense atmosphere Mohandas Karamchand Gandhi returned to India in 1915 after 20 years practising as a lawyer in South Africa. He arrived as the government of India was being given new powers by the British parliament to try political cases without a jury and to give provincial governments the right to imprison politicians without trial. In opposition to this legislation Gandhi proposed to call a *hartal*, when all activity would cease for a day – a form of protest still in widespread use. Such protests took place across India, often accompanied by riots.

On 13 April 1919 a huge gathering took place in the enclosed space of Jallianwala Bagh in Amritsar. It had been prohibited by the government and General Dyer ordered troops to fire on the people without warning, killing 379 and injuring at least a further 1200. This marked the turning point in relations with Britain and began the rise of Gandhi to the key position of leadership in the struggle for complete independence.

**The thrust for Independence** Through the 1920s Gandhi developed concepts and political programmes that were to become the hallmark of India's Independence struggle. Ultimately political Independence was to be achieved not by violent rebellion but by *satyagraha* – a 'truth force' which implied a willingness to suffer through non-violent resistance to injustice.

In 1930 the Congress declared that 26 January would be Independence Day – still celebrated as Republic Day in India today. Mohammad Iqbal, the leader of the Muslim League, took the opportunity of his address to the League in the same year to suggest the formation of a Muslim state within an Indian Federation. Also in 1930 a Muslim student in Cambridge, **Chaudhuri Rahmat Ali**, coined a name for the new Muslim state. **PAKISTAN**, composed of the letters 'P' for Punjab, 'A' for Afghania, 'K' for Kashmir, 'S' for Sindh, with the suffix *'stan'*, Persian for 'country'. The idea still had little real shape however and waited on developments of the late 1930s and 1940s to bear fruit.

By the end of the Second World War the positions of the Muslim League, now under the leadership of **Mohammad Ali Jinnah** and the Congress led by **Jawaharlal Nehru**, were irreconcilable. While major questions of the definition of separate territories for a Muslim and a non-Muslim state remained to be answered, it was clear to General Wavell, the British viceroy through the last years of the war, that there was no alternative but to accept that independence would have to be given on the basis of separate states.

## Independence and Partition

One of the main difficulties for the Muslims was that they made up only a fifth of the total population and were scattered throughout India. It was therefore impossible to define a simple territorial division that would provide a separate state to satisfy Jinnah's 'Two-Nation Theory'. On 20 February 1947, the British Labour Government announced its decision to replace Lord Wavell as viceroy with Lord Mountbatten, who was to oversee the transfer of power to new independent governments. It set a deadline of June 1948 for British withdrawal. The announcement of a firm date made the Indian politicians even less willing to compromise and the resulting division satisfied no one.

Independence arrived on 15 August for India and 14 August for Pakistan because Indian astrologers deemed the 15th to be the most auspicious moment. Several key Princely States had still not decided firmly to which country they would accede. Kashmir was the most important of these, with results that have lasted to the present day.

# Modern Indian Himalaya

India, with an estimated 1.24 billion people in 2012, is the second most populated country in the world after China. Although the birth rate has fallen steadily over the last 40 years, initially death rates fell faster and the rate of population increase has continued to be 1.4% – or 28 million – a year. Today, over 377 million (31%) people live in towns and cities.

## Politics and institutions

When India became independent on 15 August 1947 it faced three immediate crises. Partition left it with a bitter struggle between Muslims on one side and Hindus and Sikhs on the other which threatened to tear the new country into pieces at birth. An estimated 13 million people migrated between the two new countries of India and Pakistan.

In the years since Independence, striking political achievements have been made. With the two-year exception of 1975-1977, when Mrs Gandhi imposed a state of emergency under which all political activity was banned, India has sustained a democratic system in the face of tremendous pressures. The general elections of May 2004 saw the Congress Party return as the largest single party. They managed to forge alliances with some of the smaller parties and thus formed the new United Progressive Alliance (UPA) government under the prime ministership not of the Congress Party's leader, Sonia Gandhi, but of ex-finance minister, Manmohan Singh. The elections in 2009 saw Manmohan Singh re-elected as prime minister, and the next general elections will be held in 2014.

### The constitution

Establishing itself as a sovereign democratic republic, the Indian parliament accepted Nehru's advocacy of a secular constitution. The president is formally vested with all executive powers exercised under the authority of the prime minister.

Parliament has a lower house (the Lok Sabha – House of the People) and an upper house (the Rajya Sabha – Council of States). The former is made up of directly elected representatives from the 543 parliamentary constituencies (plus two nominated members from the Anglo-Indian community), the latter of a mixture of members elected by an electoral college and of nominated members.

India's federal constitution devolves certain powers to elected state assemblies. Each state has a governor who acts as its official head. Many states also have two chambers, the upper generally called the Rajya Sabha and the lower (often called the Vidhan Sabha) being of directly elected representatives. In practice many of the state assemblies have had a totally different political complexion from that of the Lok Sabha. Regional parties have played a far more prominent role, though in many states central government has effectively dictated both the leadership and policy of state assemblies.

**States and Union Territories** Union territories are administered by the president "acting to such an extent as he thinks fit". In practice union territories have varying forms of self-government. The 69th amendment to the constitution in 1991 provided for a legislative assembly and council of ministers for Delhi. The assemblies of union territories have more restricted powers of legislation than full states.

One of the key features of India's constitution is its secular principle. Some see the commitment to a secular constitution as having been under increasing challenge from the Hindu nationalism of the Bharatiya Janata Party, the BJP.

**The civil service** India continued to use the small but highly professional administrative service inherited from the British period. Renamed the Indian Administrative Service (IAS), it continues to exercise remarkable influence across the country. The administration of many aspects of central and regional government is in the hands of this elite body, whose members act largely by the constitutional rules that bind them as servants of the state. Many Indians accept the continuing efficiency and high calibre of the top-ranking officers in the administration while believing that the bureaucratic system as a whole has been overtaken by widespread corruption.

**The police** India's police service numbers nearly one million. While the top ranks of the Indian Police Service are comparable to the IAS, lower levels are extremely poorly trained and very low paid. In addition to the domestic police force there are special groups: the Border Security Force, Central Reserve Police and others. They may be armed with modern weapons and are called in for special duties.

**The armed forces** Unlike its immediate neighbours Pakistan and Bangladesh, India has never had military rule. It has more than one million men in the army, one of the largest armed forces in the world. Although they have remained out of politics the army has been used increasingly frequently to put down civil unrest, especially in Kashmir.

**Political parties** The Congress won overall majorities in seven of the 10 general elections held before the 1996 election, although in no election did they obtain more than 50% of the popular vote.

Political activity outside the Congress can seem bewilderingly complex. There are no genuinely national parties. The only alternative governments to the Congress have been formed by coalitions of regional and ideologically based parties. Parties of the left – Communist and Socialist – have never broken out of their narrow regional bases. The **Communist Party of India** split into two factions in 1964, with the Communist Party of India (Marxist) ultimately taking power in West Bengal and Kerala.

At the right of the political spectrum, the **Bharatiya Janata Party (BJP)** developed a powerful campaign focusing on reviving Hindu identity against the minorities, and became the single most powerful party across northern India in the 1990s.

**Recent developments** The 2009 elections saw the **UPA** led by the Indian National Congress form the new government. This meant Manmohan Singh became the first prime minister since Nehru to be re-elected after completing a full five-year term. In West Bengal, which had been led by a democratically elected Communist government for over 30 years, the tide turned in 2011 and the Trinamool Congress won. Mamata Banerjee was sworn in as the first Chief Minister. Assam and Arunachal also carried a UPA majority in 2009, while Sikkim saw a win by the Sikkim Democratic Front. The next general elections are likely to be held in May 2014.

# Indian Himalayan culture

## Language

The graffiti written on the walls of any Indian city bear witness to the number of major languages spoken across the country, many with their own distinct scripts. In all the states of North and West India an Indo-Aryan language – the easternmost group of the Indo-European family – is predominant. Sir William Jones, the great 19th-century scholar, discovered the close links between Sanskrit (the basis of nearly all North Indian languages) German and Greek. He showed that they must all have originated in the common heartland of Central Asia, being carried west, south and east by the nomadic tribes who shaped so much of the subsequent history of both Europe and Asia.

**Sanskrit** As the pastoralists from Central Asia moved into South Asia from 2000 BC onwards, the Indo-Aryan languages they spoke were gradually modified. Sanskrit developed from this process, emerging as the dominant classical language of India by the sixth century BC, when it was classified in the grammar of **Panini**. It remained the language of the educated until about AD 1000, though it had ceased to be in common use several centuries earlier.

**Hindi and Urdu** The Muslims brought Persian into South Asia as the language of the rulers, where it became the language of the numerically tiny but politically powerful elite. The most striking example of Muslim influence on the earlier Indo-European languages is that of the two most important languages of India and Pakistan, Hindi and Urdu respectively. Most of the other modern North Indian languages were not written until the 16th century or after. Hindi developed into the language of the heartland of Hindu culture, stretching from Punjab to Bihar and from the foothills of the Himalaya to the marchlands of central India.

**Bengali** At the east end of the Ganga plains Hindi gives way to Bengali (Bangla), the language today of over 50 million people in India, as well as more than 115 million in Bangladesh. Linguistically it is close to both Assamese and Oriya.

**The Dravidian languages** The other major language family of South Asia today, Dravidian, has been in India since before the arrival of the Indo-Aryans. Four of South Asia's major living languages belong to this family group – Tamil, Telugu, Kannada and Malayalam, spoken in Tamil Nadu (and northern Sri Lanka), Andhra Pradesh, Karnataka and Kerala respectively.

## Scripts

It is impossible to spend even a short time in India or the other countries of South Asia without coming across several of the different scripts that are used. The earliest ancestor of scripts in use today was **Brahmi**, in which Asoka's famous inscriptions were written in the third century BC. Written from left to right, a separate symbol represented each different sound.

**Devanagari** For around 1000 years the major script of northern India has been the Nagari or Devanagari, which means literally the script of the 'city of the gods'. Hindi, Nepali and

Marathi join Sanskrit in their use of Devanagari. The Muslim rulers developed a right to left script based on Persian and Arabic.

**Numerals** Many of the Indian alphabets have their own notation for numerals. This is not without irony, for what in the western world are called 'Arabic' numerals are in fact of Indian origin. In some parts of South Asia local numerical symbols are still in use, but by and large you will find that the Arabic number symbols familiar in Europe and the West are common.

## Architecture

Over the 4000 years since the Indus Valley Civilization flourished, art and architecture have developed with a remarkable continuity through successive regional and religious influences and styles. The Buddhist art and architecture of the third century BC left few remains, but the stylistic influence on early Hindu architecture was profound. From the sixth century AD the first Hindu religious buildings to have survived into the modern period were constructed in South and East India.

### Hindu temple buildings

The principles of religious building were laid down by priests in the *Sastras*. Every aspect of Hindu, Jain and Buddhist religious building is identified with conceptions of the structure of the universe. This applies as much to the process of building – the timing of which must be undertaken at astrologically propitious times – as to the formal layout of the buildings. The cardinal directions of north, south, east and west are the basic fix on which buildings are planned. Indian temples were nearly always built according to philosophical understandings of the universe. This cosmology, of an infinite number of universes, isolated from each other in space, proceeds by imagining various possibilities as to its nature. Its centre is seen as dominated by **Mount Meru** which keeps earth and heaven apart. The concept of *separation* is crucial to Hindu thought and social practice. Continents, rivers and oceans occupy concentric rings around the mountain, while the stars encircle the mountain in another plane. Humans live on the continent of **Jambudvipa**, characterized by the rose apple tree (*jambu*).

**Mandalas** The Sastras show plans of this cosmology, organized in concentric rings and entered at the cardinal points. This type of diagram was known as a **mandala**. Such a geometric scheme could be subdivided into almost limitless small compartments, each of which could be designated as having special properties or be devoted to a particular deity; the centre of the mandala would be the seat of the major god. Mandalas provided the ground rules for the building of stupas and temples across India and gave the key to the symbolic meaning attached to every aspect of religious buildings.

**Temple design** The focal point of the temple, its sanctuary, was the home of the presiding deity, the 'womb-chamber' (*garbhagriha*). A series of doorways, in large temples leading through a succession of buildings, allowed the worshipper to move towards the final encounter with the deity to obtain *darshan* – a sight of the god. Both Buddhist and Hindu worship encourage the worshipper to walk clockwise around the shrine, performing *pradakshina*.

The elevations are symbolic representations of the home of the gods. The names of mountain peaks such as Kailasa are commonly used for the most prominent of the towers.

In North and East Indian temples the tallest of these towers rises above the *garbagriha* itself, symbolizing the meeting of earth and heaven in the person of the enshrined deity. The basic structure is usually richly embellished with sculpture. When first built this would usually have been plastered and painted and often covered in gems. In contrast to the extraordinary profusion of colour and life on the outside, the interior is dark and cramped but here, it is believed, lies the true centre of divine power.

## Muslim religious architecture

Although the Muslims adapted many Hindu features, they also brought totally new forms. Their most outstanding contribution, dominating the architecture of many North Indian cities, are the mosques and tomb complexes (*dargah*). The use of brickwork was widespread and they brought with them from Persia the principle of constructing the true arch. Muslim architects succeeded in producing a variety of domed structures, often incorporating distinctively Hindu features such as the surmounting finial. By the end of the great period of Muslim building in 1707, the Muslims had added magnificent forts and palaces to their religious structures, a statement of power as well as of aesthetic taste.

## European buildings

Nearly two centuries of architectural stagnation and decline followed the demise of Mughal power. The Portuguese built a series of remarkable churches in Goa that owed nothing to local traditions and everything to Baroque developments in Europe. Not until the end of the Victorian period, when British imperial ambitions were at their height, did the British colonial impact on public rather than domestic architecture begin to be felt. Fierce arguments divided British architects as to the merits of indigenous design. The ultimate plan for New Delhi was carried out by men who had little time for Hindu architecture and believed themselves to be on a civilizing mission. Others at the end of the 19th century wanted to recapture and enhance a tradition for which they had great respect. They have left a series of buildings, both in formerly British-ruled territory and in the Princely States, illustrating this concern through what became known as the Indo-Saracenic style.

In the immediate aftermath of the colonial period, independent India set about trying to establish a break from the immediately imperial past, but was uncertain how to achieve it. In the event foreign architects were commissioned for major developments, such as Le Corbusier's design for Chandigarh and Louis Kahn's buildings in Dhaka and Ahmadabad.

## Music, dance and film

### Music

Indian music can trace its origins to the metrical hymns and chants of the Vedas, in which the production of sound according to strict rules was thought to be vital to the continuing order of the universe. Through more than 3000 years of development, India's musical tradition has been handed on almost entirely by ear. The chants of the **Rig Veda** developed into songs in the **Sama Veda** and music found expression in every sphere of life, reflecting the cycle of seasons and the rhythm of work.

Over the centuries the original three notes, which were sung strictly in descending order, were extended to five and then seven and developed to allow freedom to move up and down the scale. The scale increased to 12 with the addition of flats and sharps and finally to 22 with the further subdivision of semitones. Books of musical rules go back at least as far as the third century AD. Classical music was totally intertwined with dance and drama, an interweaving reflected in the term *sangita*.

At some point after the Muslim influence made itself felt in the north, North and South Indian styles diverged, to become Carnatic (Karnatak) music in the south and Hindustani music in the north. However, they still share important common features: *svara* (pitch), *raga* (the melodic structure) and *tala* or *talam* (metre).

**Hindustani music** probably originated in the Delhi Sultanate during the 13th century, when the most widely known of North Indian musical instruments, the *sitar*, was believed to have been invented. **Amir Khusrau** is also believed to have invented the small drums, the *tabla*. Hindustani music is held to have reached its peak under Tansen, a court musician of Akbar. The other important northern instruments are the stringed *sarod*, the reed instrument *shahnai* and the wooden flute. Most Hindustani compositions have devotional texts, though they encompass a great emotional and thematic range. A common classical form of vocal performance is the *dhrupad*, a four-part composition.

The essential structure of a melody is known as a **raga**. The music is improvised by the performer within certain rules and although theoretically thousands of ragas are possible, only around a 100 are commonly performed. Ragas have become associated with particular moods and specific times of the day. Music festivals often include all-night sessions to allow performers a wider choice of repertoire.

## Dance

The rules for classical dance were laid down in the Natya Sastra in the second century BC, which is still one of the bases for modern dance forms. The most common sources for Indian dance are the epics, but there are three essential aspects of the dance itself, *nritta* (pure dance), *nrittya* (emotional expression) and *natya* (drama). The religious influence in dance was exemplified by the tradition of temple dancers, *devadasis* – girls and women who were dedicated to the deity in major temples. In South and East India there were thousands of *devadasis* associated with temple worship, though the practice fell into widespread disrepute and was banned in independent India. Various dance forms (for example Manipuri, Bharat Natyam, Kathakali, Mohinyattam) developed in different parts of the country. India is also rich in folk dance traditions, which are widely performed during festivals.

## Film

Filmgoers around the world are taking greater note of Indian cinema, both home-grown and that produced and directed by Indians abroad. Not all fall into the category of a Bollywood '*masala*' movie' or 'curry western' churned out by the Mumbai film industry but many offer an insight into what draws millions to watch diverse versions of Indian life on the silver screen. A few titles, both all-time favourites as well as more recent releases, include: *The Apu Trilogy, Mother India; Titash Ekti Nadir Naam; Sholay; Bombay; Kuch Kuch Hota Hai; Lagaan; Kabhie Khushi Kabhie Gham; Monsoon Wedding; The Guru; The Warrior; Slumdog Millionaire, Choker Bali; Nayagan (The Leader); Junoon.*

# Indian Himalayan religion

It is impossible to write briefly about religion in India without greatly oversimplifying. Over 80% of Indians are Hindu, but there are significant minorities. Muslims number about 138 million and there are over 24 million Christians, 19 million Sikhs, nearly 8 million Buddhists and a number of other religious groups. One of the most persistent features of Indian religious and social life is the caste system. This has undergone substantial changes since Independence, especially in towns and cities, but most people in India are still clearly identified as a member of a particular caste group. The government has introduced measures to help the backward, or 'scheduled' castes, though this has produced a political backlash.

## Hinduism

It has always been easier to define Hinduism by what it is not than by what it is. Indeed, the name 'Hindu' was given by foreigners to the peoples of the subcontinent who did not profess the other major faiths, such as Muslims or Christians. While some aspects of modern Hinduism can be traced back more than 4000 years before that, other features are recent.

### Key ideas

According to the great Indian philosopher and former president of India, S Radhakrishnan, religion for the Hindu "is not an idea but a power, not an intellectual proposition but a life conviction. Religion is consciousness of ultimate reality, not a theory about God." There is no Hindu organization, like a church, with the authority to define belief or establish official practice. Not all Hindu groups believe in a single supreme god. In view of these characteristics, many authorities argue that it is misleading to think of Hinduism as a religion at all. Be that as it may, the evidence of the living importance of Hinduism is visible across India. Hindu philosophy and practice has also touched many of those who belong to other religious traditions, particularly in terms of social institutions such as caste, and in post-Independence India religious identity has become an increasingly politicized feature of national life.

**Darshan** One of Hinduism's recurring themes is 'vision', 'sight' or 'view' – *darshan*. Applied to the different philosophical systems themselves, such as *yoga* or *vedanta*, *darshan* is also used to describe the sight of the deity that worshippers hope to gain when they visit a temple or shrine, or the insight gained from a *guru* (teacher). Equally it may apply to the religious insight gained through meditation or prayer.

**The four human goals** Many Hindus also accept that there are four major human goals; material prosperity (*artha*), the satisfaction of desires (*kama*) and performing the duties laid down according to your position in life (*dharma*). Beyond those is the goal of achieving liberation from the endless cycle of rebirths into which everyone is locked (*moksha*). It is to the search for liberation that the major schools of Indian philosophy have devoted most attention. Together with *dharma*, it is basic to Hindu thought.

The *Mahabharata* lists 10 embodiments of *dharma*: good name, truth, self-control, cleanness of mind and body, simplicity, endurance, resoluteness of character, giving and sharing, austerities and continence. In *dharmic* thinking these are inseparable from five

## Karma – an eye to the future

According to the doctrine of karma, every person, animal or god has a being or 'self' which has existed without beginning. Every action, except those that are done without any consideration of the results, leaves an indelible mark on that self, carried forward into the next life.

The overall character of the imprint on each self determines three features of the next life: the nature of the next birth (animal, human or god), the kind of family the self will be born into if human and the length of the next life. Finally, it controls the good or bad experiences that the self will experience. However, it does not imply a fatalistic belief that the nature of action in this life is unimportant. Rather, it suggests that the path followed by the individual in the present life is vital to the nature of its next life and ultimately to the chance of gaining release from this world.

patterns of behaviour: non-violence, an attitude of equality, peace and tranquillity, lack of aggression and cruelty, and absence of envy. *Dharma*, an essentially secular concept, represents the order inherent in human life.

**Karma** The idea of *karma*, 'the effect of former actions', is central to achieving liberation. As C Rajagopalachari put it: "Every act has its appointed effect, whether the act be thought, word or deed. The cause holds the effect, so to say, in its womb. If we reflect deeply and objectively, the entire world will be found to obey unalterable laws. That is the doctrine of karma." See also box, above.

**Rebirth** The belief in the transmigration of souls (*samsara*) in a never-ending cycle of rebirth has been Hinduism's most distinctive and important contribution to Indian culture. The earliest reference is in one of the *Upanishads*, around the seventh century BC, at about the same time as the doctrine of *karma* made its first appearance.

**Ahimsa** AL Basham pointed out that belief in transmigration must have encouraged a further distinctive doctrine, that of non-violence or non-injury – *ahimsa*. The belief in rebirth meant that all living things and creatures of the spirit – people, devils, gods, animals, even worms – possessed the same essential soul. One inscription threatens that anyone who interferes with the rights of Brahmins to land given to them by the king will "suffer rebirth for 80,000 years as a worm in dung". Belief in the cycle of rebirth was essential to give such a threat any weight!

### Schools of philosophy

It is common now to talk of six major schools of Hindu philosophy: *Nyaya, Vaisheshika, Sankhya, Yoga, Purvamimansa* and *Vedanta*.

**Yoga** Yoga can be traced back to at least the third century AD. It seeks a synthesis of the spirit, the soul and the flesh and is concerned with systems of meditation and self-denial that lead to the realization of the Divine within oneself and can ultimately release one from the cycle of rebirth.

**Vedanta** These are literally the final parts of the Vedic literature, the *Upanishads*. The most important of all is the *Bhagavad-Gita*, which is a part of the epic the *Mahabharata*. There are many interpretations of these basic texts. Three are given here.

**Advaita Vedanta** holds that there is no division between the cosmic force or principle, *Brahman*, and the individual self, *atman* (also referred to as 'soul'). The fact that we appear to see different and separate individuals is simply a result of ignorance. This is termed *maya* (illusion), but Vedanta philosophy does not suggest that the world in which we live is an illusion. *Jnana* (knowledge) is held as the key to understanding the full and real unity of self and Brahman. **Shankaracharya**, born at Kalady in modern Kerala, in the seventh century AD, is the best known Advaitin Hindu philosopher. He argued that there was no individual self or soul separate from the creative force of the universe, or Brahman, and that it was impossible to achieve liberation (*moksha*), through meditation and devotional worship, which he saw as signs of remaining on a lower level and of being unprepared for true liberation.

The 11th- to 12th-century philosopher, **Ramanuja**, expounded the opposing ideas of **Vishishtad-vaita**. He transformed the idea of the cosmic principle from an impersonal force to a personal God and viewed both the self and the world as real but only as part of the whole. In contrast to Shankaracharya's view, Ramanuja saw *bhakti* (devotion) as of central importance to achieving liberation and service to God as the highest goal of life.

**Dvaita Vedanta** was developed by the 14th-century philosopher, Madhva. He believed that Brahman, the self and the world are completely distinct. Worship of God is a key means of achieving liberation.

## Worship

**Puja** For most Hindus today, worship ('performing puja') is an integral part of their faith. The great majority of Hindu homes will have a shrine to one of the gods of the Hindu pantheon. Individuals and families will often visit shrines or temples and on special occasions will travel long distances to particularly holy places.

Acts of devotion are often aimed at the granting of favours and the meeting of urgent needs for this life – good health, finding a suitable wife or husband, the birth of a son, or good fortune. Puja involves making an offering to God and *darshan* (having a view of the deity). Hindu worship is generally, though not always, an act performed by individuals. Thus Hindu temples may be little more than a shrine on a river bank or in the middle of the street, tended by a priest and visited at special times when a *darshan* of the resident god can be obtained. When it has been consecrated, the image, if exactly made, becomes the channel for the godhead to work through.

**Holy places** Certain rivers and towns are particularly sacred to Hindus. Thus there are seven holy rivers – the Ganga, Yamuna, Indus and mythical Sarasvati in the north and the Narmada, Godavari and Kaveri in the Peninsula. There are also seven holy places – Haridwar, Mathura, Ayodhya and Varanasi in the north, Ujjain, Dwarka and Kanchipuram to the south. In addition to these seven holy places there are four holy abodes: Badrinath, Puri and Ramesvaram, with Dwarka in modern Gujarat having the unique distinction of being both a holy abode and a holy place.

**Rituals and festivals** The temple rituals often follow through the cycle of day and night, as well as yearly lifecycles. The priests may wake the deity from sleep, bathe, clothe and feed it. Worshippers will be invited to share in this process by bringing offerings of clothes

## Hindu deities

| Deity | Association | Relationship |
|---|---|---|
| **Brahma** | Creator | One of Trinity |
| **Sarasvati** | Education and culture, 'the word' | Wife of Brahma |
| **Siva** | Creator/destroyer | One of Trinity |
| **Bhairava** | Fierce aspect of Siva | |
| **Parvati** (Uma) | Benevolent aspect of female divine power | Consort of Siva, mother of Ganesh |
| **Kali** | The energy that destroys evil | Consort of Siva |
| **Durga** | In fighting attitude | Consort of Siva |
| **Ganesh/ Ganapati** | God of good beginnings, clearer of obstacles | Son of Siva |
| **Skanda** | God of War/bringer of disease (Karttikkeya, Murugan, Subrahmanya) | Son of Siva and Ganga |
| **Vishnu** | Preserver | One of Trinity |
| **Prithvi/ Bhudevi** | Goddess of earth | Wife of Vishnu |
| **Lakshmi** | Goddess of wealth | Wife of Vishnu |
| **Agni** | God of fire | |
| **Indra** | Rain, lightning and thunder | |
| **Ravana** | King of the demons | |

and food. Gifts of money will usually be made and in some temples a charge is levied for taking up positions in front of the deity in order to obtain a *darshan*.

Every temple has its special festivals. At festival times you can see villagers walking in small groups, brightly dressed and often high spirited, sometimes as far as 80-100 km.

### Hindu deities

Today three gods are widely seen as all-powerful: Brahma, Vishnu and Siva. While Brahma is regarded as the ultimate source of Creation, Siva also has a creative role alongside his function as Destroyer. Vishnu in contrast is seen as the Preserver or protector of the universe. Vishnu and Siva are widely represented and have come to be seen as the most powerful and important. Their followers are referred to as Vaishnavite and Shaivites, and numerically they form the two largest sects in India.

**Brahma** Popularly Brahma is interpreted as the Creator. In the literal sense the name 'Brahma' is the masculine and personalized form of the neuter word 'Brahman'.

In the early Vedic writing, Brahman represented the universal and impersonal principle that governed the universe. Gradually, as Vedic philosophy moved towards a monotheistic interpretation of the universe and its origins, this impersonal power was increasingly

| Attributes | Vehicle |
|---|---|
| 4 heads, 4 arms, upper left holds water pot and rosary or sacrificial spoon, sacred thread across left shoulder | Hamsa – goose/swan |
| Two or more arms, *vina*, lotus, plam leaves, rosary | Hamsa |
| Linga; As Rudra: matted hair, 3 eyes, drum, fire, deer, trident; As Nataraja: Lord of the Dance | Nandi – bull |
| Trident, sword, noose, naked, snakes, garland of skulls, dishevelled hair, carrying destructive weapons | Dog |
| 2 arms when shown with Siva, 4 when on her own, blue lily in right hand, left hand hangs down | Lion |
| Trident, noose, human skulls, sword, shield, black colour | Lion |
| 4 arms, conch, disc, bow, arrow, bell, sword, shield | Lion or tiger |
| Goad, noose, broken tusk, fruits | Rat/mouse/shrew |
| 6 heads, 12 arms, spear, arrow, sword, discus, noose, cock, bow, shield, conch and plough | Peacock |
| 4 arms, high crown, discus and conch in upper arms, club and sword (or lotus) in lower | Garuda – mythical eagle |
| Right hand in *abhaya* gesture, left holds pomegranate, left leg on treasure pot | |
| Seated/standing on red lotus, 4 hands, lotuses, vessel, fruit | Lotus |
| Sacred thread, axe, wood, bellows, torch, sacrificial spoon | 2-headed ram |
| Bow, thunderbolt, lances | |
| 10 heads, 20 arms, bow and arrow | |

personalized. In the *Upanishads*, Brahman was seen as a universal and elemental creative spirit. Brahma, described in early myths as having been born from a golden egg and then to have created the earth, assumed the identity of the earlier Vedic deity Prajapati and became identified as the Creator.

By the fourth and fifth centuries AD, the height of the classical period of Hinduism, Brahma was seen as one of the trinity of gods – *Trimurti* – in which Vishnu, Siva and Brahma represented three forms of the unmanifested supreme being. It is from Brahma that Hindu cosmology takes its structure. The basic cycle through which the whole cosmos passes is described as one day in the life of Brahma – the *kalpa*. It equals 4,320 million years, with an equally long night. One year of Brahma's life – a cosmic year – lasts 360 days and nights. The universe is expected to last for 100 years of Brahma's life: he is currently believed to be 51 years old.

By the sixth century AD Brahma worship had effectively ceased (before the great period of temple building), which accounts for the fact that there are remarkably few temples dedicated to Brahma. Nonetheless, images of Brahma are found in most Hindu temples. Characteristically he is shown with four faces, a fifth having been destroyed by the fire from Siva's third eye. He usually holds a copy of the Vedas, a sceptre and a water jug or a bow. He is accompanied by the goose, symbolizing knowledge.

# The story of Rama

Under Brahmin influence, Rama was transformed from the human prince of the early versions into the divine figure of the final story. Rama, the 'jewel of the solar kings', became deified as an incarnation of Vishnu. The story tells how Rama was banished from his father's kingdom. In a journey with his wife, Sita, and helper and friend, Hanuman (the monkey-faced god depicted in many Indian temples, shrines and posters), Rama fought the king **Ravana**, changed in late versions into a demon. Rama's rescue of Sita was interpreted as the Aryan triumph over the barbarians. The epic is seen as South Asia's first literary poem and is recited in all Hindu communities.

Ravana, demon king of Lanka

**Sarasvati** Seen by some Hindus as the 'active power' of Brahma, popularly thought of as his consort, Sarasvati has survived into the modern Hindu world as a far more important figure than Brahma himself. In popular worship Sarasvati is the goddess of education and learning, worshipped in schools and colleges with gifts of fruit, flowers and incense. She represents 'the word' itself, which began to be deified as part of the process of the writing of the Vedas, which ascribed magical power to words. The development of her identity represented the rebirth of the concept of the Mother Goddess, which had been strong in the Indus Valley Civilization over 1000 years before and may have been continued in popular ideas through the worship of female spirits.

In addition to her role as Brahma's wife, Sarasvati is also variously seen as the wife of Vishnu and Manu or as Daksha's daughter, among other interpretations. Normally white, riding on a swan and carrying a book, she is often shown playing a *vina*. She may have many arms and heads, representing her role as patron of all the sciences and arts.

**Vishnu** Vishnu is seen as the god with the human face. From the second century a new and passionate devotional worship of Vishnu's incarnation as Krishna developed in the South. By AD 1000 Vaishnavism had spread across South India and it became closely associated with the devotional form of Hinduism preached by **Ramanuja**, whose followers spread the worship of Vishnu and his 10 successive incarnations in animal and human form. For Vaishnavites God took these different forms in order to save the world from impending disaster.

**Rama and Krishna** By far the most influential incarnations of Vishnu are those in which he was believed to take recognizable human form, especially as Rama (twice) and Krishna. As the Prince of Ayodhya, history and myth blend, for Rama was probably a chief who lived in the eighth or seventh century BC. Although Rama is now seen as an earlier incarnation of Vishnu than Krishna, he came to be regarded as divine very late, probably after the Muslim invasions of the 12th century AD. Rama (or Ram, pronounced to rhyme with *calm*) is powerful figure in contemporary India. His supposed birthplace at Ayodhya became the focus of fierce disputes between Hindus and Muslims in the early 1990s, which continue today. Krishna is worshipped extremely widely as perhaps the most human of the gods. His advice on the battlefield in the *Mahabharata* is one of the major sources of guidance for the rules of daily living for many Hindus today.

**Lakshmi** Commonly represented as Vishnu's wife, Lakshmi is widely worshipped as the goddess of wealth. Lakshmi is popularly shown in her own right as standing on a lotus flower, although eight forms of Lakshmi are recognized.

**Hanuman** The *Ramayana* tells how Hanuman, Rama's faithful servant, went across India and finally into the demon Ravana's forest home of Lanka at the head of his monkey army in search of the abducted Sita. He used his powers to jump the sea channel separating India from Sri Lanka and managed after a series of heroic and magical feats to find and rescue his master's wife. Whatever form he is shown in, he remains almost instantly recognizable, with a monkey's head.

**Siva** Siva is interpreted as both Creator and Destroyer, the power through whom the universe evolves. He lives on Mount Kailasa with his wife **Parvati** (also known as **Uma, Sati, Kali** and **Durga**) and two sons, the elephant-headed Ganesh and the six-headed Karttikeya. In sculptural representations Siva is normally accompanied by his 'vehicle', the bull Nandi (or Nandin).

Siva is also represented in Shaivite temples throughout India by the *linga*, literally meaning 'sign' or 'mark', but referring in this context to the sign of gender or phallus. On the one hand a symbol of energy, fertility and potency, as Siva's symbol it also represents the yogic power of sexual abstinence and penance. The *linga* is now the most important symbol of the cult of Siva. O'Flaherty suggests that the worship of the *linga* of Siva can be traced back to the pre-Vedic societies of the Indus Valley Civilization (circa 2000 BC), but that it first appears in Hindu iconography in the second century BC. From that time a wide variety of myths appeared to explain the origin of *linga* worship.

**Siva's alternative names** Although Siva is not seen as having a series of rebirths, like Vishnu, he nonetheless appears in very many forms, representing different aspects of his varied powers. Some of the more common are:

**Chandrasekhara** – the moon (*chandra*) symbolizes the powers of creation and destruction.

**Mahadeva** – the representation of Siva as the god of supreme power, which came relatively late into Hindu thought, shown as the *linga* in combination with the *yoni*, or female genitalia.

**Nataraja** – the Lord of the Cosmic Dance. The story is based on a legend in which Siva and Vishnu went to the forest to overcome 10,000 heretics. In their anger the heretics attacked Siva first by sending a tiger, then a snake and thirdly a fierce black dwarf with a club. Siva killed the tiger, tamed the snake and wore it like a garland and then put his foot on the dwarf and performed a dance of such power that the dwarf and the heretics acknowledged Siva as the Lord.

**Rudra** – Siva's early prototype, who may date back to the Indus Valley Civilization.

**Virabhadra** – Siva created Virabhadra to avenge himself on his wife Sati's father, Daksha, who had insulted Siva by not inviting him to a special sacrifice. Sati attended the ceremony against Siva's wishes and when she heard her father grossly abusing Siva she committed suicide by jumping into the sacrificial fire. This act gave rise to the term *sati* (*suttee*, a word

## Auspicious signs

Some of Hinduism's sacred symbols are thought to have originated in the Aryan religion of the Vedic period.

**Om** The Primordial sound of the universe, 'Om' (or more correctly the three-in-one 'Aum') is the supreme syllable. It is the opening, and sometimes closing, chant for Hindu prayers. Some attribute its three constituents to the Hindu triad of Brahma, Vishnu and Siva. It is believed to be the cosmic sound of Creation, which encompasses all states from wakefulness to deep sleep and, though it is the essence of all sound, it is outside our hearing.

**Svastika** Representing the sun and its energy, the svastika usually appears on doors or walls of temples, in red, the colour associated with good fortune and luck. The term, derived from the Sanskrit *svasti*, is repeated in Hindu chants. The arms of the symbol point in the cardinal directions, which may reflect the ancient practice of lighting fire sticks in the four directions. When the svastika appears to rotate clockwise it symbolizes the positive creative energy of the sun; the anti-clockwise svastika, symbolizing the autumn/ winter sun, is considered to be unlucky.

**Six-pointed star** The intersecting triangles in the 'Star of David' symbol represent spirit and matter held in balance. A central dot signifies a particle of divinity. The star is incorporated as a decorative element in some Muslim buildings such as Humayun's Tomb in Delhi.

**Lotus** The *padma* or *kamal* flower with its many petals appears not only in art and architecture but also in association with gods and goddesses. Some deities are seen holding one, others are portrayed seated or standing on the flower, or, as with Padmanabha, it appears from Vishnu's navel. The lotus represents purity, peace and beauty, a symbolism shared by Buddhists and Jains: as in nature, it stands away from and above the impure, murky water from which it emerges. In architecture, the lotus motif occurs frequently.

Om     Svastika     Six-pointed star     Lotus

that simply means a good or virtuous woman). Recorded in the *Vedas*, the self-immolation of a woman on her husband's funeral pyre probably did not become accepted practice until the early centuries BC. Even then it was mainly restricted to those of the Kshatriya caste.

**Nandi** – Siva's vehicle, the bull, is one of the most widespread of sacred symbols of the ancient world and may represent a link with Rudra, who was sometimes represented as a bull in pre-Hindu India. Strength and virility are his key attributes and pilgrims to Siva temples will often touch the Nandi's testicles on their way into the shrine.

**Ganesh** One of Hinduism's most popular gods, Ganesh is seen as the great clearer of obstacles. Shown at gateways and on door lintels with his elephant head and pot belly, his image is revered. Meetings, functions and special family gatherings will often start with prayers to Ganesh and any new venture, from the opening of a building to inaugurating a company, will not be deemed complete without a Ganesh puja.

**Shakti, the Mother Goddess**  Shakti is a female divinity often worshipped in the form of Siva's wife Durga or Kali. As Durga she agreed to do battle with Mahish, an *asura* (demon) who threatened to dethrone the gods. Many sculptures and paintings illustrate the story in which, during the terrifying struggle that ensued, the demon changed into a buffalo, an elephant and a giant with 1000 arms. **Durga**, clutching weapons in each of her 10 hands, eventually emerged victorious. As Kali ('black') the goddess takes on her most fearsome form and character. Fighting with the chief of the demons, she was forced to use every weapon in her armoury, but every drop of blood that she drew became 1000 new giants just as strong as he. The only way she could win was by drinking the blood of all her enemies. Having succeeded she was so elated that her dance of triumph threatened the earth. Ignoring the pleas of the gods to stop, she even threw her husband Siva to the ground and trampled over him, until she realized to her shame what she had done. Kali is always shown with a sword in one hand, the severed head of the giant in another, two corpses for earrings and a necklace of human skulls. She is often shown standing with one foot on the body and the other on the leg of Siva.

The worship of female goddesses developed into the widely practised form of devotional worship called Tantrism. Goddesses such as Kali became the focus of worship that often involved practices that flew in the face of wider Hindu moral and legal codes. Animal and even human sacrifices and ritual sexual intercourse were part of Tantric belief and practice, the evidence for which may still be seen in the art and sculpture of some major temples. Tantric practice affected both Hinduism and Buddhism from the eighth century AD; its influence is shown vividly in the sculptures of Khajuraho and Konark and in the distinctive Hindu and Buddhist practices of the Kathmandu Valley in Nepal.

**Skanda**  The god of war, Skanda (known as Murugan in Tamil Nadu and by other regional names) became known as the son of Siva and Parvati. One legend suggests that he was conceived by the goddess Ganga from Siva's seed.

**Gods of the warrior caste**  Modern Hinduism has brought into its pantheon over many generations gods who were worshipped by the earlier pre-Hindu Aryan civilizations. The most important is **Indra**, often shown as the god of rain, thunder and lightning. To the early Aryans, Indra destroyed demons in battle, the most important being his victory over Vritra, 'the Obstructor'. By this victory Indra released waters from the clouds, allowing the earth to become fertile. To the early Vedic writers the clouds of the southwest monsoon were seen as hostile, determined to keep their precious treasure of water to themselves and only releasing it when forced to by a greater power. Indra, carrying a bow in one hand, a thunderbolt in another and lances in the others and riding on his vehicle Airavata, the elephant, is thus the Lord of Heaven.

**Mitra** and **Varuna** have the power of both gods and demons. Their role is to sustain order, Mitra taking responsibility for friendship and Varuna for oaths; as they have to keep watch for 24 hours a day Mitra has become the god of the day, or the sun, Varuna the god of the moon.

**Agni**, the god of fire, is a god whose origins lie with the priestly caste rather than with the Kshatriyas, or warriors. He was seen in the Vedas as being born from the rubbing together of two pieces of dead wood. Riding on a ram, wearing a sacred thread, he is often shown with flames leaping from his mouth, for he is the god of ritual fire.

The juice of the *soma* plant, the nectar of the gods guaranteeing eternal life, **Soma** is also a deity taking many forms. Born from the churning of the cosmic ocean of milk, in later stories Soma was identified with the moon. The golden-haired and golden-skinned god **Savitri** is an intermediary with the great power to forgive sin and as king of heaven he gives the gods their immortality. **Surya**, the god of the sun, fittingly of overpowering splendour, is often described as being dark red, sitting on a red lotus or riding a chariot pulled by the seven horses of the dawn (representing the days of the week). **Ush**, sometimes referred to as Surya's wife, is the goddess of the dawn, daughter of heaven and sister of the night. She rides in a chariot drawn by cows or horses.

**Devas and asuras** In Hindu popular mythology the world is also populated by innumerable gods (*devas*) and demons (*asuras*), with a somewhat uncertain dividing line between them. Both have great power and moral character and there are frequent conflicts between them.

The multiple-hooded cobra head often seen in sculptures represents the fabulous snake gods the **Nagas**, though they may often be shown in other forms, even human. In South India it is particularly common to find statues of divine Nagas being worshipped. They are usually placed on uncultivated ground under trees in the hope and belief, as Masson-Oursel puts it, that "if the snakes have their own domain left to them they are more likely to spare human beings". The Nagas and their wives, the **Naginis**, are often the agents of death in mythical stories.

## Hindu society
**Dharma** *Dharma* is seen as the most important of the objectives of individual and social life. But what were the obligations imposed by *dharma*? Hindu law givers, such as those who compiled the code of Manu (AD 100-300), laid down rules of family conduct and social obligations related to the institutions of caste and *jati*, which were beginning to take shape at the same time.

**Caste** Although the word 'caste' was coined by the Portuguese in the 15th century All the main features of the system emerged at the end of the Vedic period. Two terms varna and jati – are used in India itself and have come to be used interchangeably and confusingly with 'caste'.

**Varna**, which literally means 'colour', had a fourfold division. By 600 BC this had become a standard means of classifying the population. The fair-skinned Aryans distinguished themselves from the darker-skinned earlier inhabitants. The priestly *varna*, the Brahmin were seen as coming from the mouth of Brahma; the Kshatriyas were warriors, coming from Brahma's arms; the Vaishyas, a trading community, came from Brahma's thighs and the Sudras, classified as agriculturalists, from his feet. Relegated beyond the pale of civilized Hindu society were the untouchables or outcastes, who were left with the jobs that were regarded as impure, usually associated with dealing with the dead (human or animal) or with excrement.

Many Brahmins and Rajputs are conscious of their *varna* status, but the great majority of Indians do not put themselves into one of the four *varna* categories, but into a *jati* group. There are thousands of different *jatis* across the country. None of the groups regard themselves as equal in status to any other, but all are part of local or regional hierarchies. These are not organized in any institutional sense and traditionally there was o formal record of caste status. While individuals found it impossible to change caste or to move up the social scale, groups would sometimes try to gain recognition as higher caste by adopting practices of the Brahmins such as becoming vegetarians. Many used to be identified with particular activities, and occupations used to be hereditary. Caste membership is decided by birth. Although you can be evicted from your caste by your fellow members, usually for disobedience to caste rules such as over marriage, you cannot join another caste and technically you become an outcaste.

Right up until Independence in 1947 such punishment was a drastic penalty for disobeying one's dharmic duty. In many areas all avenues into normal life could be blocked, families would disregard outcaste members and it could even be impossible for the outcaste to continue to work.

Gandhi spearheaded his campaign for independence from British colonial rule with a powerful campaign to abolish the disabilities imposed by the caste system. Coining the term *Harijan* (meaning 'person of God'), which he gave to all former outcastes, Gandhi demanded that discrimination on the grounds of caste be outlawed. Lists – or 'schedules' – of backward castes were drawn up during the early part of this century in order to provide positive help to such groups. The term itself has now been widely rejected by many former outcastes as paternalistic and as implying an adherence to Hindu beliefs (Hari being a Hindu deity) which some explicitly reject and today the use of the secular term '**dalits**' – the 'oppressed' – has been adopted in its place. There are several websites devoted to dalit issues, including www.dalits.org.

**Marriage**, which is still generally arranged by members of all religious communities, continues to be dictated almost entirely by caste and clan rules. Even in cities, where traditional means of arranging marriages have often broken down and where many people resort to advertising for marriage partners in the columns of the Sunday newspapers, caste is frequently stated as a requirement. Marriage is mainly seen as an alliance between two families. Great efforts are made to match caste, social status and economic position, although rules vary from region to region. In some groups marriage between first cousins is common, while among others marriage between any branch of the same clan is strictly prohibited.

## Hindu reform movements

In the 19th-century English education and European literature and modern scientific thought, alongside the religious ideas of Christian missionaries, all became powerful influences on the newly emerging Western-educated Hindu opinion. That opinion was challenged to re-examine inherited Hindu beliefs and practice.

Some reform movements have had regional importance. Two of these originated, like the **Brahmo Samaj**, in Bengal. The **Ramakrishna Mission** was named after a temple priest in the Kali temple in Calcutta, Ramakrishna (1834-1886), who was a great mystic, preaching the basic doctrine that "all religions are true". He believed that the best religion for any individual was that into which he or she was born. One of his followers, **Vivekananda**, became the founder of the Ramakrishna Mission, which has been an important vehicle of social and religious reform, notably in Bengal.

**Aurobindo Ghose** (1872-1950) links the great reformers from the 19th century with the post-Independence period. Educated in English – and for 14 years in England itself – he developed the idea of India as 'the Mother', a concept linked with the pre-Hindu idea of Shakti, or the Mother Goddess. For him 'nationalism was religion'. After imprisonment in 1908 he retired to Pondicherry, where his ashram became a focus of an Indian and international movement.

**The Hindu calendar** While for its secular life India follows the Gregorian calendar, for Hindus, much of religious and personal life follows the Hindu calendar. This is based on the lunar cycle of 29 days, but the clever bit comes in the way it is synchronized with the 365 day Gregorian solar calendar of the west by the addition of an 'extra month' (*adhik maas*) every 2½ to three years.

Hindus follow two distinct eras. The *Vikrama Samvat* which began in 57 BC (and is followed in Goa), and the *Salivahan Saka* which dates from AD 78 and has been the official Indian calendar since 1957. The *Saka* year starts on 22 March and has the same length as the Gregorian calendar. In most of South India, the New Year is celebrated in the first month, *Chaitra* (corresponding to March-April). In North India it is celebrated in the second month of *Vaisakh*.

The year itself is divided into two, the first six solar months being when the sun 'moves' north, known as the *Makar Sankranti* (which is marked by special festivals), and the second half when it moves south, the *Karka Sankranti*. The first begins in January and the second in June. The 29-day lunar month with its 'dark' (*Krishna*) and 'bright' (*Shukla*) halves based on the new (*Amavasya*) and full moons (*Purnima*), are named after the 12 constellations and total a 354-day year. The day itself is divided into eight *praharas* of three hours each and the year into six seasons: *Vasant* (spring), *Grishha* (summer), *Varsha* (rains), *Shara* (early autumn), *Hemanta* (late autumn), *Shishir* (winter).

## Islam

Even after partition in 1947 over 40 million Muslims remained in India and today there are around 138 million. Islamic contact with India was first made around AD 636 and then by the navies of the Arab Mohammad al Qasim in AD 710-712. These conquerors of Sind made very few converts, although they did have to develop a legal recognition for the status of non-Muslims in a Muslim-ruled state. From the creation of the Delhi Sultanate in 1206, by Turkish rather than Arab power, Islam became a permanent living religion in India.

The victory of the Turkish ruler of Ghazni over the Rajputs in AD 1192 established a 500-year period of Muslim power in India. By AD 1200 the Turkish sultans had annexed Bihar in the east, in the process wiping out the last traces of Buddhism with the massacre of a Buddhist monastic order, sacked Varanasi and captured Gwalior. Within 30 years Bengal had been added to the Turkish Empire and by AD 1311 a new Turkish dynasty, the Khaljis, had extended the power of the Delhi Sultanate to the doors of Madurai.

The early Muslim rulers looked to the Turkish ruling class and to the Arab caliphs for their legitimacy and to the Turkish elite for their cultural authority. From the middle of the 13th century, when the Mongols crushed the Arab caliphate, the Delhi sultans were left on their own to exercise Islamic authority in India. From then onwards the main external influences were from Persia. Small numbers of migrants, mainly the skilled and the educated, continued to flow into the Indian courts. Periodically their numbers were augmented by refugees from Mongol repression in the regions to India's northwest as the Delhi Sultanate provided a refuge for craftsmen and artists.

**Muslim populations** Muslims became a majority of the South Asian population only in the plains of the Indus and West Punjab and in parts of Bengal. Elsewhere they formed important minorities, notably in the towns of the central heartland such as Lucknow. The concentration at the east and west ends of the Ganga Valley reflected the policies pursued by successive Muslim rulers of colonizing forested and previously uncultivated land. In the

## The five pillars of Islam

In addition to the belief that there is one God and that Muhammad is his prophet, there are four requirements imposed on Muslims. Daily prayers are prescribed at daybreak, noon, afternoon, sunset and nightfall. Muslims must give alms to the poor. They must observe a strict fast during Ramadan (no eating or drinking from sunrise to sunset). Last, they should attempt the pilgrimage to the Ka'aba in Mecca, known as the Hajj. Those who have done so are entitled to the prefix Hajji before their name.

Islamic rules differ from Hindu practice in several other aspects of daily life. Muslims are strictly forbidden to drink alcohol (though some suggest that this prohibition is restricted to the use of fermented grape juice, that is wine, it is commonly accepted to apply to all alcohol). Eating pork, or any meat from an animal not killed by draining its blood while alive, is also prohibited. Meat prepared in the appropriate way is called *halal*. Finally, usury (charging interest on loans) and games of chance are forbidden.

---

central plains there was already a densely populated Hindu region, where little attempt was made to achieve converts.

The **Mughals** wanted to expand their territory and their economic base. To pursue this they made enormous grants of land to those who had served the empire and, particularly in Bengal, new land was brought into cultivation. At the same time, shrines were established to Sufi saints who attracted peasant farmers. The mosques built in East Bengal were the centres of devotional worship where saints were venerated. By the 18th century many Muslims had joined the **Sunni** sect of Islam. The characteristics of Islamic practice in both these regions continues to reflect this background.

In some areas Muslim society shared many of the characteristic features of the Hindu society from which the majority of them came. Many of the Muslim migrants from Iran or Turkey, the elite **Ashraf** communities, continued to identify with the Islamic elites from which they traced their descent. They held high military and civil posts in imperial service. In sharp contrast, many of the non-Ashraf Muslim communities in the towns and cities were organized in social groups very much like the *jatis* of their neighbouring Hindu communities. While the elites followed Islamic practices close to those based on the Qur'an as interpreted by scholars, the poorer, less literate communities followed devotional and pietistic forms of Islam.

**Muslim beliefs** The beliefs of Islam (which means 'submission to God') could apparently scarcely be more different from those of Hinduism. Islam, often described as having "five pillars" of faith (see box, above) has a fundamental creed: "There is no God but God; and Muhammad is the Prophet of God" (*"La Illaha illa 'llah Muhammad Rasulu 'llah"*). One book, the Qur'an, is the supreme authority on Islamic teaching and faith. Islam preaches the belief in bodily resurrection after death and in the reality of heaven and hell.

The idea of heaven as paradise is pre-Islamic. Alexander the Great is believed to have brought the word 'paradise' into Greek from Persia, where it was used to describe the walled Persian gardens that were found even three centuries before the birth of Christ. For Muslims, paradise is believed to be filled with sensuous delights and pleasures, while hell is a place of eternal terror and torture, which is the certain fate of all who deny the unity of God.

Islam has no priesthood. The authority of Imams derives from social custom and from their authority to interpret the scriptures, rather than from a defined status within the Islamic community. Islam also prohibits any distinction on the basis of race or colour, and most Muslims believe it is wrong to represent the human figure. It is often thought, inaccurately, that this ban stems from the Qur'an itself. In fact it probably has its origins in the belief of Muhammad that images were likely to be turned into idols.

**Muslim sects** During the first century after Muhammad's death Islam split in to two sects which were divided on political and religious grounds, the Shi'is and Sunnis. The religious basis for the division lay in the interpretation of verses in the Qur'an and of traditional sayings of Muhammad, the *Hadis*. Both sects venerate the Qur'an but have different *Hadis*. They also have different views as to Muhammad's successor.

The **Sunnis** – always the majority in South Asia – believe that Muhammad did not appoint a successor and that Abu Bak'r, Omar and Othman were the first three caliphs (or vice-regents) after Muhammad's death. Ali, whom the Sunnis count as the fourth caliph, is regarded as the first legitimate caliph by the Shi'is, who consider Abu Bak'r and Omar to be usurpers. While the Sunnis believe in the principle of election of caliphs, Shi'is believe that although Muhammad is the last prophet there is a continuing need for intermediaries between God and man. Such intermediaries are termed Imams and they base both their law and religious practice on the teaching of the Imams.

Akbar, the most eclectic of Mughal emperors, went as far as banning activities like cow slaughter, which were offensive to Hindus, and celebrated Hindu festivals in court. In contrast, the later Mughal emperor, Aurangzeb, pursued a far more hostile approach to Hinduism, trying to point up the distinctiveness of Islam and denying the validity of Hindu religious beliefs. That attitude generally became stronger in the 20th century, related to the growing sense of the Muslims' minority position within South Asia and the fear of being subjected to Hindu rule.

**The Islamic calendar** The calendar begins on 16 July 622 AD, the date of the Prophet's migration from Mecca to Medina, the Hijra, hence AH (Anno Hejirae). *Murray's Handbook for Travellers in India* gave a wonderfully precise method of calculating the current date in the Christian year from the AH date: "To correlate the Hijra year with the Christian year, express the former in years and decimals of a year, multiply by .970225, add 621.54 and the total will correspond exactly with the Christian year."

The Muslim year is divided into 12 lunar months, totalling 354 or 355 days, hence Islamic festivals usually move 11 days earlier each year according to the solar (Gregorian) calendar. The first month of the year is *Moharram,* followed by *Safar, Rabi-ul-Awwal, Rabi-ul-Sani, Jumada-ul-Awwal, Jumada-ul-Sani, Rajab, Shaban, Ramadan, Shawwal, Ziquad* and *Zilhaj.*

## Buddhism

India was the home of Buddhism, which had its roots in the early Hinduism, or Brahmanism, of its time. Today it is practised only on the margins of the subcontinent, from Ladakh, Nepal and Bhutan in the north to Sri Lanka in the south, where it is the religion of the majority Sinhalese community. Most are very recent converts, the last adherents of the early schools of Buddhism having been killed or converted by the Muslim invaders of the 13th century. However, India's Buddhist significance is now mainly as the home for

## The Buddha's Four Noble Truths

The Buddha preached Four Noble Truths: that life is painful; that suffering is caused by ignorance and desire; that beyond the suffering of life there is a state which cannot be described but which he termed nirvana; and that *nirvana* can be reached by following an eightfold path.

The concept of *nirvana* is often understood in the west in an entirely negative sense -- that of 'non-being'. The word has the rough meaning of 'blow out', meaning to blow out the fires of greed, lust and desire. In a more positive sense it has been described by one Buddhist scholar as "the state of absolute illumination, supreme bliss, infinite love and compassion, unshakable serenity and unrestricted spiritual freedom". The essential elements of the eightfold path are the perfection of wisdom, morality and meditation.

the extraordinarily beautiful artistic and architectural remnants of what was for several centuries the region's dominant religion.

India has sites of great significance for Buddhists around the world. Some say that the Buddha himself spoke of the four places his followers should visit. **Lumbini**, the Buddha's birthplace, is in the Nepali foothills, near the present border with India. **Bodh Gaya**, where he attained what Buddhists term his 'supreme enlightenment', is about 80 km south of the modern Indian city of Patna; the deer park at **Sarnath**, where he preached his first sermon and set in motion the Wheel of the Law, is just outside Varanasi; and **Kushinagara**, where he died at the age of 80, is 50 km east of Gorakhpur. There were four other sacred places of pilgrimage – **Rajgir**, where he tamed a wild elephant; **Vaishali**, where a monkey offered him honey; **Sravasti**, associated with his great miracle; and **Sankasya**, where he descended from heaven. The eight significant events associated with the holy places are repeatedly represented in Buddhist art.

In addition there are remarkable monuments, sculptures and works of art, from Gandhara in modern Pakistan to Sanchi and Ajanta in central India, where it is still possible to see the vivid evidence of the flowering of Buddhist culture in South Asia. In Sri Lanka, Bhutan and Nepal the traditions remain alive.

**The Buddha's life** Siddharta Gautama, who came to be given the title of the Buddha – the Enlightened One – was born a prince into the warrior caste in about 563 BC. He was married at the age of 16 and his wife had a son. When he reached the age of 29 he left home and wandered as a beggar and ascetic. After about six years he spent some time in Bodh Gaya. Sitting under the Bo tree, meditating, he was tempted by the demon Mara with all the desires of the world. Resisting these temptations, he received enlightenment.

The next landmark was the preaching of his first sermon on 'The Foundation of Righteousness' in the deer park near Benares. By the time he died the Buddha had established a small band of monks and nuns known as the *Sangha* and had followers across North India. His body was cremated and the ashes, regarded as precious relics, were divided among the peoples to whom he had preached. Some have been discovered as far west as Peshawar, in Pakistan and at Piprawa, close to his birthplace.

**After the Buddha's death** From the Buddha's death, or *parinirvana*, to the destruction of Nalanda (its last stronghold in India) in AD 1197, Buddhism in India went through three phases. These are often referred to as Hinayana, Mahayana and Vajrayana, though they were not mutually exclusive, being followed simultaneously in different regions.

**Hinayana** The Hinayana or Lesser Way insists on a monastic way of life as the only path to the personal goal of *nirvana* (see box, page 419), achieved through an austere life. Divided into many schools, the only surviving Hinayana tradition is the **Theravada Buddhism**, which was taken to Sri Lanka by the Emperor Asoka's son Mahinda, where it became the state religion, and subsequently spread to southeast Asia as practised in Thailand, Myanmar (Burma), Cambodia and Laos today. Suffering, sorrow and dissatisfaction are the nature of ordinary life and can only be eliminated by giving up desire. In turn, desire is a result of the misplaced belief in the reality of individual existence. Theravada Buddhism taught that there is no soul and ultimately no God. *Nirvana* is a state of rest beyond the universe, once found never lost.

**Mahayana** In contrast to the Hinayana schools, the followers of the Mahayana school (the Great Way) believed in the possibility of salvation for all. They practised a far more devotional form of meditation and new figures came to play a prominent part in their beliefs and their worship – the **bodhisattvas**, saints who were predestined to reach the state of enlightenment through thousands of rebirths. They aspired to Buddhahood, however, not for their own sake but for the sake of all living things. The Buddha is believed to have passed through numerous existences in preparation for his final mission. Mahayana Buddhism became dominant over most of South Asia and its influence is evidenced in Buddhist art from Gandhara in north Pakistan to Ajanta in Central India and Sigiriya in Sri Lanka.

**Vajrayana** A new branch of Buddhism, Vajrayana, or the Vehicle of the Thunderbolt, appeared that began to lay stress on secret magical rituals and cults of female divinities. This new 'Diamond Way' adopted the practice of magic, yoga and meditation. It became associated with secret ceremonies, chanting of mystical 'mantras' and taking part in orgiastic rituals in the cause of spiritual gain in order to help others. The ideal of Vajrayana Buddhists is to be "so fully in harmony with the cosmos as to be able to manipulate the cosmic forces within and outside himself". It had developed in the north of India by the seventh century AD, matching the parallel growth of Hindu Tantrism. The magical power associated with Vajrayana requires instruction from a teacher or *lama*, hence the Tibetan form is sometimes referred to as 'Lamaistic'.

**Buddhist beliefs** Buddhism is based on the Buddha's own preaching. However, when he died none of those teachings had been written down. He developed his beliefs in reaction to the Brahmanism of his time, rejecting several of the doctrines of Vedic religion that were widely held in his lifetime: the Vedic gods, scriptures and priesthood and all social distinctions based on caste. However, he did accept the belief in the cyclical nature of life and that the nature of an individual's existence is determined by a natural process of reward and punishment for deeds in previous lives – the Hindu doctrine of *karma* (see page 406). In the Buddha's view, though, there is no eternal soul. He denied the identification of the self with the everchanging mind-body (here, some see parallels in the Advaita Vedanta philosophy of self-*Brahman* in Hinduism). In Buddhism, *anatta* (no-self), overcame the egoistical self, given to attachment and selfishness.

Following the Buddha's death a succession of councils was called to try and reach agreement on doctrine. The first three were held within 140 years of the Buddha's death, the fourth being held at Pataliputra (modern Patna) during the reign of the Emperor Asoka (272-232 BC), who had recently been converted to Buddhism. Under his reign Buddhism spread throughout South Asia and opened the routes through Northwest India for Buddhism to travel into China, where it had become a force by the first century AD.

**Buddhism's decline** The decline of Buddhism in India probably stemmed as much from the growing similarity in the practices of Hinduism and Buddhism as from direct attacks. Mahayana Buddhism, with its reverence for *bodhisattvas* and its devotional character, was increasingly difficult to distinguish from the revivalist Hinduism characteristic of several parts of North India from the seventh to the 12th centuries AD. The Muslim conquest dealt the final death blow, as it was accompanied by the large-scale slaughter of monks as well as the destruction of monasteries. Without their institutional support, Buddhism faded away.

## Jainism

Like Buddhism, Jainism started as a reform movement of the Brahmanic religious beliefs of the sixth century BC. Its founder was a widely revered saint and ascetic, Vardhamma, who became known as **Mahavir** – 'great hero'. Mahavir was born in the same border region of India and Nepal as the Buddha, just 50 km north of modern Patna, probably in 599 BC. His family, also royal, were followers of an ascetic saint, Parsvanatha, who according to Jain tradition had lived 200 years previously.

Mahavir's life story is embellished with legends, but there is no doubt that he left his royal home for a life of the strict ascetic. He is believed to have received enlightenment after 12 years of rigorous hardship, penance and meditation. Afterwards he travelled and preached for 30 years, stopping only in the rainy season. He died aged 72 in 527 BC. His death was commemorated by a special lamp festival in the region of Bihar, which Jains claim is the basis of the now-common Hindu festival of lights, Diwali.

Unlike Buddhism, Jainism never spread beyond India, but it has survived continuously into modern India, with four million adherents. In part this may be because Jain beliefs have much in common with puritanical forms of Hinduism and are greatly respected and admired. Some Jain ideas, such as vegetarianism and reverence for all life, are widely recognized by Hindus as highly commendable. The value Jains place on non-violence has contributed to their importance in business, as they regard nearly all occupations except banking and commerce as violent.

**Jain beliefs** Jains (from the word *jina*, literally meaning 'descendants of conquerors') believe that there are two fundamental principles, the living (*jiva*) and the non-living (*ajiva*). The essence of Jain belief is that all life is sacred and that every living entity, even the smallest insect, has within it an indestructible and immortal soul. Jains developed the view of *ahimsa* – often translated as 'non-violence', but better perhaps as 'non-harming'. *Ahimsa* was the basis for the entire scheme of Jain values and ethics and alternative codes of practice were defined for householders and for ascetics.

**The five vows** may be taken both by monks and by lay people: not to harm any living beings (Jains must practise strict vegetarianism – and even some vegetables, such as potatoes and onions, are believed to have microscopic souls); to speak the truth; not to steal; to give up sexual relations and practice complete chastity; to give up all possessions – for the Digambara sect that includes clothes.

Celibacy is necessary to combat physical desire. Jains also regard the manner of dying as extremely important. Although suicide is deeply opposed, vows of fasting to death voluntarily may be regarded as earning merit in the proper context. Mahavir himself is believed to have died of self-starvation. The essence of all the rules is to avoid intentional injury, which is the worst of all sins. Like Hindus, the Jains believe in *karma*.

Jains have two main sects, whose origins can be traced back to the fourth century BC. The more numerous **Svetambaras** – the 'white clad' – concentrated more in eastern and western India, separated from the **Digambaras** – or 'sky-clad'– who often go naked. The Digambaras may well have been forced to move south by drought and famine in the northern region of the Deccan and they are now concentrated in the south of India.

Unlike Buddhists, Jains accept the idea of God, but not as a creator of the universe. They see him in the lives of the 24 **tirthankaras** (prophets, or literally 'makers of fords' – a reference to their role in building crossing points for the spiritual journey over the river of life), or leaders of Jainism, whose lives are recounted in the Kalpsutra – the third century BC book of ritual for the Svetambaras. Mahavir is regarded as the last of these great spiritual leaders. Much Jain art details stories from these accounts and the *tirthankaras* play a similar role for Jains as the *bodhisattvas* do for Mahayana Buddhists. The first and most revered of the *tirthankaras*, Adinatha, also known as Rishabnath, is widely represented in Jain temples.

## Sikhism

**Guru Nanak**, the founder of the religion, was born just west of Lahore and grew up in what is now the Pakistani town of Sultanpur. His followers, the Sikhs (derived from the Sanskrit word for 'disciples'), form perhaps one of India's most recognizable groups. Beards and turbans give them a very distinctive presence and although they represent less than 2% of the population they are both politically and economically significant.

**Sikh beliefs** The first Guru accepted the ideas of *samsara* – the cycle of rebirths – and *karma* (see page 406), from Hinduism. However, Sikhism is unequivocal in its belief in the oneness of God, rejecting idolatry and any worship of objects or images. Guru Nanak believed that God is One, formless, eternal and beyond description.

Guru Nanak also fiercely opposed discrimination on the grounds of caste. He saw God as present everywhere, visible to anyone who cared to look, and as essentially full of grace and compassion. Some of Guru Nanak's teachings are close to the ideas of the Benaras mystic **Kabir**, who, in common with the Muslim mystic Sufis, believed in mystical union with God. Kabir's belief in the nature of God was matched by his view that humanity was deliberately blind and unwilling to recognize God's nature. He transformed the Hindu concept of *maya* into the belief that the values commonly held by the world were an illusion.

Guru Nanak preached that salvation depended on accepting the nature of God. If people recognized the true harmony of the divine order (*hookam*) they would be saved. Rejecting the prevailing Hindu belief that such harmony could be achieved by ascetic practices, he emphasized three actions: meditating on and repeating God's name (*naam*), 'giving', or charity (*daan*) and bathing (*isnaan*).

Many of the features now associated with Sikhism can be attributed to **Guru Gobind Singh**, who on 15 April 1699 started the new brotherhood called the *Khalsa* (meaning 'the pure', from the Persian word *khales*), an inner core of the faithful, accepted by baptism (*amrit*). The 'five ks' date from this period: *kesh* (uncut hair), the most important, followed by *kangha* (comb, usually of wood), *kirpan* (dagger or short sword), *kara* (steel bangle) and *kachh* (similar to 'boxer' shorts). The dagger and the shorts reflect military influence.

In addition to the compulsory 'five ks', the new code prohibited smoking, eating *halal* meat and sexual intercourse with Muslim women. These date from the 18th century, when the Sikhs were often in conflict with the Muslims. Other strict prohibitions include: idolatry, caste discrimination, hypocrisy and pilgrimage to Hindu sacred places. The Khalsa also explicitly forbade the seclusion of women, one of the common practices of Islam. It was only under the warrior king Ranjit Singh (1799-1838) that the idea of the Guru's presence in meetings of the Sikh community (the *Panth*) gave way to the now universally held belief in the total authority of the **Guru Granth**, the recorded words of the Guru in the scripture.

**Sikh worship** The meditative worship Guru Nanak commended is a part of the life of every devout Sikh today, who starts each day with private meditation and a recitation of the verses of Guru Nanak himself, the *Japji*. However, from the time of the third Guru, Sikhs have also worshipped as congregations in Gurudwaras ('gateways to the Guru'). The Golden Temple in Amritsar, built at the end of the 16th century, is the holiest site of Sikhism.

The present institutions of Sikhism owe their origins to 19th-century reform movements. Under the Sikh Gurudwaras Act of 1925 all temples were restored to the management of a Central Gurudwara Management Committee, thereby removing them from the administrative control of the Hindus under which many had come. This body has acted as the religion's controlling body ever since.

## Christianity

There are about 24 million Christians in India. Christianity ranks third in terms of religious affiliation after Hinduism and Islam and there are Christian congregations in all the major towns of India. The great majority of the Protestant Christians in India are now members of the Church of South India, formed from the major Protestant denominations in 1947, or the Church of North India, which followed suit in 1970. Together they account for approximately half the total number of Christians. Roman Catholics make up the majority of the rest. Many of the church congregations, both in towns and villages, are active centres of Christian worship.

**Origins** Some of the churches owe their origin either to the modern missionary movement of the late 18th century onwards, or to the colonial presence of the European powers. However, Christians probably arrived in India during the first century after the birth of Christ. There is evidence that one of Christ's Apostles, **Thomas**, reached India in 52 AD, only 20 years after Christ was crucified. He settled in Malabar and then expanded his missionary work to China. It is widely believed that he was martyred in Tamil Nadu on his return to India in AD 72 and is buried in Mylapore, in the suburbs of modern Chennai. St Thomas' Mount, a small rocky hill just north of Chennai airport, takes its name from him. Today there is still a church of Thomas Christians in Kerala.

**Northern missions** Protestant missions in Bengal from the end of the 18th century had a profound influence on cultural and religious development. In November 1793 the Baptist missionary **William Carey** reached the Hugli River. Although he went to India to preach, he was also interested in languages and education and the work of 19th-century missions rapidly widened to cover educational and medical work as well.

Converts were made most readily among the backward castes and in the tribal areas. The Christian populations of the tribal hill areas of Nagaland and Assam stem from such late 19th-century and 20th-century movements. But the influence of Christian missions in education and medical work was greater than as a proselytizing force. Education in Christian schools stimulated reformist movements in Hinduism itself, and mission hospitals supplemented government-run hospitals, particularly in remote areas. Some of these Christian-run hospitals, such as that at Vellore, continue to provide high-class medical care.

**Christian beliefs** Christian theology had its roots in Judaism, with its belief in one God, the eternal Creator of the universe. Judaism saw the Jewish people as the vehicle for God's salvation, the 'chosen people of God' and pointed to a time when God would send his Saviour, or Messiah. Jesus, whom Christians believe was 'the Christ' or Messiah, was born in the village of Bethlehem, some 20 km south of Jerusalem. Very little is known of his early life except that he was brought up in a devout Jewish family. At the age of 29 or 30 he gathered a small group of followers and began to preach in the region between the Dead Sea and the Sea of Galilee. Two years later he was crucified in Jerusalem by the authorities on the charge of blasphemy – that he claimed to be the son of God.

Christians believe that all people live in a state of sin, in the sense that they are separated from God and fail to do his will. They believe that God is personal, 'like a father'. As God's son, Jesus accepted the cost of that separation and sinfulness himself through his death on the cross. Christians believe that Jesus was raised from the dead on the third day after he was crucified and that he appeared to his closest followers. They believe that his spirit continues to live today and that he makes it possible for people to come back to God.

The New Testament of the Bible, which, alongside the Old Testament, is the text to which Christians refer as the ultimate scriptural authority, consists of four 'Gospels' (meaning 'good news') and a series of letters by several early Christians referring to the nature of the Christian life.

**Christian worship** Although Christians are encouraged to worship individually as well as together, most forms of Christian worship centre on the gathering of the church congregation for praise, prayer and the preaching of God's word. Different denominations place varying emphases on the main elements of worship, but in most church services today the congregation will take part in singing hymns (songs of praise), prayers will be led by the minister, priest or a member of the congregation, readings from the Bible will be given and a sermon preached. For many Christians the most important service is the act of Holy Communion (Protestant) or Mass (Catholic) which celebrates the death and resurrection of Jesus in sharing bread and wine, which are held to represent Christ's body and blood given to save people from their sin.

## Zoroastrianism

The first Zoroastrians arrived on the west coast of India in the mid-eighth century AD, forced out from their native Iran by persecution of the invading Islamic Arabs. Until 1477 they lost all contact with Iran and then for nearly 300 years maintained contact with Persian Zoroastrians through a continuous exchange of letters. They became known by their now much more familiar name, the **Parsis** (or Persians).

Although they are a tiny minority (approximately 100,000), even in the cities where they are concentrated, they have been a prominent economic and social influence, especially in West India. Parsis adopted westernized customs and dress and took to the new economic opportunities that came with colonial industrialization. Families in West India such as the Tatas continue to be among India's leading industrialists, just part of a community that in recent generations has spread to Europe and North America.

**Origins** Zoroastrians trace their beliefs to the prophet Zarathustra, who lived in Northeast Iran around the seventh or sixth century BC. His place and even date of birth are uncertain, but he almost certainly enjoyed the patronage of the father of Darius the Great. The passage of Alexander the Great through Iran severely weakened support for Zoroastrianism, but between the sixth century BC and the seventh century AD it was the major religion of peoples living from North India to central Turkey. The spread of Islam reduced the number of Zoroastrians dramatically and forced those who did not retreat to the desert to emigrate.

**Parsi beliefs** The early development of Zoroastrianism marked a movement towards belief in a single God. **Ahura Mazda**, the Good Religion of God, was shown in rejecting evil and in purifying thought, word and action. Fire plays a central and symbolic part in Zoroastrian worship, representing the presence of God. There are eight *Atash Bahram* – major fire temples – in India; four are in Mumbai, two in Surat and one each in Navsari and Udwada. There are many more minor temples, where the rituals are far less complex – perhaps 40 in Mumbai alone.

Earth, fire and air are all regarded as sacred, while death is the result of evil. Dead matter pollutes all it touches. Where there is a suitable space therefore, dead bodies are simply placed in the open to be consumed by vultures, as at the Towers of Silence in Mumbai. However, burial and cremation are also common.

# Indian Himalayan land and environment

## Geography

### The origins of India's landscapes
Only 100 million years ago the Indian Peninsula was still attached to the great land mass called 'Pangaea' alongside South Africa, Australia and Antarctica. Then as the great plates on which the earth's southern continents stood broke up, the Indian Plate started its dramatic shift northwards, eventually colliding with the Asian Plate. As the Indian Plate continues to be pushed under the Tibetan Plateau so the Himalaya continue to rise. Northeast India falls into two major geological regions. The north is enclosed by the great arc of the Himalaya, while along their southern flank lie the alluvial plains of the Ganga.

**The Himalaya** The Himalaya dominate the northern borders of India, stretching 2500 km from northwest to southeast. Of the 94 mountains in Asia above 7300 m, all but two are in the Himalaya. Nowhere else in the world are there mountains as high. The Himalaya proper, stretching from the Pamirs in Pakistan to the easternmost bend of the Brahmaputra in Assam, can be divided into three broad zones. On the southern flank are the Shiwaliks, or Outer Ranges. To their immediate north run the parallel Middle Ranges of Pir Panjal and Dhauladhar and to the north again is the third zone, the Inner Himalaya, which has the highest peaks, many of them in Nepal. The central core of the Himalayan ranges did not begin to rise until about 35 million years ago. The latest mountain building period, responsible for the Shiwaliks, began less than five million years ago and is still continuing, raising some of the high peaks by as much as 5 mm a year. Such movement comes at a price and the boundary between the plains and the Himalayan ranges is a zone of continuing violent earthquakes and massive erosion.

**The Gangetic plains** As the Himalaya began their dramatic uplift, the trough that formed to the south of the newly emerging mountains was steadily filled with the debris washed down from the hills, creating the Indo-Gangetic plains. Today the alluvium reaches depths of over 3000 m in places (and over 22 km at the mouth of the Ganga in Bangladesh), and contains some of the largest reserves of underground water in the world. These have made possible extensive well irrigation, especially in Northwest India, contributing to the rapid agricultural changes that have taken place.

The Indo-Gangetic plains are still being extended and modified. The southern part of Bengal emerged from the sea only during the last 5000 years. The Ganga and the Indus have each been estimated to carry over one million tonnes of silt every year – considerably more than the Mississippi. The silts washed down from the Himalaya have made it possible for intensive rice cultivation to be practised continuously for hundreds of years, though they cause problems for modern irrigation development. Dams in the Himalayan region are being rapidly filled by silt, over 33 million tonnes being deposited behind the Bhakra Dam on the Sutlej River alone.

## Vegetation

India's tropical location and its position astride the wet monsoonal winds ensured that 16 different forest types were represented in India. The most widespread was tropical dry deciduous forest. Areas with more than 1700 mm of rainfall had tropical moist deciduous, semi-evergreen or wet evergreen forest, while much of the remainder had types ranging from tropical dry deciduous woodland to dry alpine scrub, found at high altitudes. However, today forest cover has been reduced to about 13% of the surface area.

**Deciduous forest** Two types of deciduous tree remain particularly important, **sal** (*Shorea robusta*), now found mainly in eastern India, and **teak** (*Tectona grandis*). Most teak today has been planted. Both are resistant to burning, which helped to protect them where people used fire as a means of clearing the forest.

**Mountain forests and grassland** At between 1000-2000 m in the eastern hill ranges of India and in Bhutan, for example, wet hill forest includes evergreen oaks and chestnuts. Further west in the foothills of the Himalaya are belts of subtropical pine at roughly the same altitudes. Deodars (*Cedrus deodarus*) form large stands and moist temperate forest, with pines, cedars, firs and spruce, is dominant, giving many of the valleys a beautifully fresh, alpine feel. Between 3000-4000 m alpine forest predominates. Rhododendron are often mixed with other forest types. Birch, juniper, poplars and pine are widespread.

There are several varieties of coarse grassland along the southern edge of the Terai and alpine grasses are important for grazing above 2000 m. A totally distinctive grassland is the **bamboo** (*Dendo calamus*) region, which is found in the eastern Himalaya.

## Trees
**Flowering trees** Many Indian trees are planted along roadsides to provide shade and they often also produce beautiful flowers. The **silk cotton tree** (*Bombax ceiba*), up to 25 m in height, is one of the most dramatic. The pale greyish bark of this buttressed tree usually bears conical spines. It has wide spreading branches and keeps its leaves for most of the year. The flowers, which appear when the tree is leafless, are cup-shaped, with curling, rather fleshy red petals up to 12 cm long while the fruits produce the fine, silky cotton that gives it its name.

Other common trees with red or orange flowers include the dhak (also called 'Flame of the forest' or *Palas*), the Gulmohur, the Indian coral tree and the tulip tree. The smallish (6m) deciduous **dhak** (*Butea monosperma*), has light grey bark, a gnarled, twisted trunk and thick, leathery leaves. The large, bright orange and sweet pea-shaped flowers appear on leafless branches. The 8-9-m-high umbrella-shaped **gulmohur** (*Delonix regia*), a native of Madagascar, is grown as a shade tree in towns. The fiery-coloured flowers make a magnificent display after the tree has shed its feathery leaves. The scarlet flowers of the **Indian coral tree** (*Erythrina indica*) appear when its branches with thorny bark are leafless. The tall **tulip tree** (*Spathodea campanulata*) (not to be confused with the North American one) has a straight, darkish brown, slender trunk. It is usually evergreen except in the drier parts of India. The scarlet bell-shaped, tulip-like flowers grow in profusion at the ends of the branches from November to March.

Often seen along roadsides, the **jacaranda** (*Jacaranda mimosaefolia*), has attractive feathery foliage and purple-blue thimble-shaped flowers up to 40 mm long. When not in flower it resembles a gulmohur, but differs in its general shape. The valuable **tamarind** (*Tamarindus indica*), with a short straight trunk and a spreading crown, often grows along the roadside. An evergreen with feathery leaves, it bears small clusters of yellow and red flowers. The noticeable fruit pods are long, curved and swollen at intervals. In parts of India, the rights to the fruit are auctioned off annually for up to Rs 4000 (US$100) per tree.

Of these trees, the silk cotton, the dhak and the Indian coral are native to India. Others were introduced mostly during the last century: the tulip tree from East Africa, the jacaranda from Brazil and the tamarind, possibly from Africa.

**Fruit trees** The familiar apple, plum, apricot and cherry grow in the cool upland areas of India. In the warmer plains tropical fruits flourish. The large, spreading **mango** (*Mangifera indica*) bears the delicious, distinctively shaped fruit that comes in hundreds of varieties. The evergreen **jackfruit** (*Artocarpus heterophyllus*) has dark green leathery leaves. The huge fruit (up to 90 cm long and 40 cm thick), growing from a short stem directly off the trunk and branches, has a rough, almost prickly skin and is almost sickly sweet. The **banana** (*Musa*), actually a gigantic herb (up to 5 m high) arising from an underground stem, has very large leaves which grow directly off the trunk. Each large purplish flower produces a bunch of up to 100 bananas. The **papaya** (*Carica papaya*) grows to about 4 m with the large hand-shaped leaves clustered near the top. Only the female tree bears the fruit, which hang down close to the trunk just below the leaves.

**Palm trees** Coconut palms (*Cocos nucifera*) are extremely common all round the coast of India. It has tall (15-25 m), slender, unbranched trunks, feathery leaves and large green or golden fruit with soft white flesh filled with milky water, so different from the brown fibre-covered inner nut that makes its way to Europe. The 10-15 m high **palmyra palms** (*Borassus flabellifer*), indigenous to South and East India, have very distinctive fan-like leaves, as much as 150 cm across. The fruit, which is smaller than a coconut, is round, almost black and very shiny. The **betel nut palm** (*Areca catechu*) resembles the coconut palm, its slender trunk bearing ring marks left by fallen leaf stems. The smooth, round nuts, only about 3 cm across, grow in large hanging bunches. **wild date palms** (*Phoenix sylvestris*), originally came from North Africa. About 20-25 m tall, the trunks are also marked with the ring bases of the leaves that drop off. The distinctive leaflets, which stick out from the central vein, give the leaf a spiky appearance. Dates are borne only by the female tree.

All these palm trees are of considerable **commercial importance**. From the fruit alone the coconut palm produces coir from the outer husk and copra from the fleshy kernel, from which coconut oil or coconut butter is extracted, in addition to the desiccated coconut and coconut milk. The sap is fermented to make a drink called toddy. A similar drink is produced from the sap of the wild date and the palmyra palms, which are also important for sugar production. The fruit of the betel nut palm is wrapped in a special leaf and chewed. The trunks and leaves of all the palms are widely used in building and thatching.

**Other trees** Of all Indian trees the **banyan** (*Ficus benghalensis*) is probably the best known. It is planted by temples, in villages and along roads. The seeds often germinate in the cracks of old walls, the growing roots splitting the wall apart. If it grows in the bark of another tree, it sends down roots towards the ground. As it grows, more roots appear from the branches, until the original host tree is surrounded by a 'cage' which eventually strangles it. The famous one in Kolkata's Botanical Gardens is more than 400 m in circumference.

Related to the banyan, the **pipal** or peepul (*Ficus religiosa*), also cracks open walls and strangles other trees with its roots. With a smooth grey bark, it too is commonly found near temples and shrines. You can distinguish it from the banyan by the absence of aerial roots and its large, heart-shaped leaf with a point tapering into a pronounced 'tail'. It bears abundant 'figs' of a purplish tinge and about 1 cm across.

The **ashok** or **mast** (*Polyalthia longifolia*) is a tall evergreen that can reach 15 m or more in height. One variety, often seen in avenues, is trimmed and tapers towards the top. The leaves are long, slender and shiny and narrow to a long point.

**Acacia** trees with their feathery leaves are fairly common in the drier parts of India. The best known is the **babul** (*Acacia arabica*) with a rough, dark bark. The leaves have long silvery white thorns at the base and consist of many leaflets while the flowers grow in golden balls about 1 cm across.

The **eucalyptus** or **gum tree** (*Eucalyptus grandis*), introduced from Australia in the 19th century, is now widespread and is planted near villages to provide both shade and firewood. There are various forms but all may be readily recognized by their height, their characteristic long, thin leaves, which have a pleasant fresh smell, and the colourful peeling bark.

The wispy **casuarina** (*Casuarina*) grows in poor sandy soil, especially on the coast and on village waste land. It has the typical leaves of a pine tree and the cones are small and prickly to walk on. It is said to attract lightning during a thunderstorm.

**Bamboo** (*Bambusa*) strictly speaking is a grass, which can vary in size from small ornamental clumps to the enormous wild plant whose stems are so strong and thick that they are used for construction and for scaffolding and as pipes in rural irrigation schemes.

## Flowering plants

Common in the Himalaya is the beautiful **rhododendron**, a flowering shrub or tree that can be as tall as 12 m and is indigenous to this region. In the wild the commonest colour of the flowers is crimson, but other colours such as pale purple occur too. From March to May the flowers are very noticeable on the hillsides. Another common wild flowering shrub is **lantana**. This is a fairly small untidy-looking bush with rough, toothed oval leaves, which grow in pairs on the square and prickly stem. The flowers grow together in a flattened head, the ones near the middle being usually yellowish, while those at the rim are pink, pale purple or orange. The fruit is a shiny black berry.

Many other flowering plants are cultivated in parks, gardens and on roadside verges. The attractive **frangipani** (*Plumeria acutifolia*) has a rather crooked trunk and stubby branches, which if broken give out a white milky juice that can be irritating to the skin. The big, leathery leaves taper to a point at each end and have noticeable parallel veins. The sweetly scented waxy flowers are white, pale yellow or pink. The **bougainvillea** grows as a dense bush or climber with small oval leaves and rather long thorns. The brightly coloured part which can be pinkish-purple, crimson, orange, yellow, etc) looks like a flower but is not formed of petals, which are quite small and undistinguished, but by large papery bracts.

The trumpet-shaped flower of the **hibiscus**, as much as 7 or 8cm across, has a very long 'tongue' growing out from the centre and varies in colour from scarlet to yellow or white. The leaves are somewhat oval or heart-shaped with jagged edges. In municipal flowerbeds the commonest planted flower is probably the **canna lily**. It has large leaves, which are either green or bronzed, and lots of large bright red or yellow flowers. The plant can be more than 1 m high.

On many ponds and tanks the floating plants of the **lotus** (*Nelumbo nucifera*) and the **water hyacinth** (*Eichornia crassipes*) are seen. Lotus flowers, which rise on stalks above the water, can be white, pink or a deep red and up to 25 cm across. The very large leaves either float on the surface or rise above the water. Many dwarf varieties are cultivated. The rather fleshy leaves and lilac flowers of the water hyacinth float to form a dense carpet, often clogging the waterways.

## Crops

Of India's enormous variety, the single most widespread crop is **rice** (commonly *Orysa indica*). This forms the most important staple in South and East India, though other cereals and some root crops are also important elsewhere. The rice plant grows in flooded fields called *paddies* and virtually all planting or harvesting is done by hand. Millets are favoured in drier areas inland, while wheat is the most important crop in the Northwest.

There are many different sorts of millet, but the ones most often seen are finger millet, pearl millet and sorghum. **Finger millet**, commonly known as ragi (*Eleusine corocana*), is so-called because the ear has several spikes which radiate out, a bit like the fingers of a hand. Usually less than 1 m high, it is grown extensively in the south. Both **pearl millet** (*Pennisetum typhoideum*, known as *bajra* in the north) and **sorghum** (*Sorghum vulgare*, known as *jowar* in the north) look superficially similar to the more familiar maize, though each can be easily distinguished when the seed heads appear. Pearl millet, mainly grown in the north, has a tall single spike which gives it its other name of bulrush millet. Sorghum bears an open ear at the top of the plant.

**Tea** (*Camellia sinensis*) is grown on a commercial scale in tea gardens in areas of high rainfall, often in highland regions. Over 90% comes from Assam and West Bengal in the Northeast and Tamil Nadu and Kerala in the South. Left to itself tea grows into a tree 10 m tall. In the tea gardens it is pruned to waist height for the convenience of the tea pluckers and forms flat-topped bushes, with shiny bright green oval leaves.

**Coffee** (*Coffea*) is not as widely grown as tea, but high quality arabica is an important crop in parts of South India. Coffee is also a bush, with fairly long, shiny dark green leaves. The white, sweet-smelling flowers, which yield the coffee berry, grow in groups along the stems. The coffee berries start off green and turn red when ripe.

**Sugar cane** (*Saccharum*) is another important crop. It looks like a large grass, standing up to 3 m tall. The crude brown sugar is sold as jaggery and tastes like molasses.

Of the many spices grown in India, the two climbers pepper and vanilla and the grass-like cardamom are the ones most often seen. The **pepper** vine (*Piper Nigrum*) is indigenous to India where it grows in the warm moist regions. As it is a vine it needs support such as a trellis or a tree. It is frequently planted up against the betel nut palm and appears as a leafy vine with almost heart-shaped leaves. The peppercorns cluster along hanging spikes and are red when ripe. Both black and white pepper is produced from the same plant, the difference being in the processing.

**Vanilla** (*Vanilla planifolium*), which belongs to the orchid family, also grows up tree for support and attaches itself to the bark by small roots. It is native to South America, but grows well in India in areas of high rainfall. It is a rather fleshy-looking plant, with white flowers and long slender pods.

**Cardamom** (*Elettaria cardomomum*) is native to India and is planted under shade. It grows well in highland areas such as Sikkim and the Western Ghats. It is a herbaceous plant looking like a big clump of grass, with long leafy shoots springing out of the ground up to 2-3 m. The white flowers grow on shoots that can be upright but usually sprawl on the ground. It is from these flowers that the seed-bearing capsules grow.

The **cashew nut** tree (*Anacardium occidentale*) was introduced into India, but now grows wild as well as being cultivated. It is a medium-sized tree with bright green, shiny rounded leaves. The nut grows on a fleshy fruit called a cashew apple and hangs down below this. **Cotton** (*Gossypium*) is important in parts of the West and South. The cotton bush is a small knee-high bush and the cotton boll appears after the flower has withered. This splits when ripe to show the white cotton lint inside.

The **castor oil** plant (*Ricinus Communis*) is cultivated as a cash crop and is planted in small holdings among other crops and along roads and paths. It is a handsome plant up to about 2 m in height, with very large leaves divided into some 12 'fingers'. The young stems are reddish and shiny. The well known castor oil is extracted from the bean, which is a mottled brown in colour.

## Wildlife

India has an extremely rich and varied wildlife, though many species survive only in very restricted environments. Alarmed by the rapid loss of wildlife habitat, the Indian government established the first conservation measures in 1972, followed by the setting up of national parks and reserves. Some 25,000 sq km were set aside in 1973 for Project Tiger. Tigers are reported to be increasing steadily in several game reserves but threats to their survival continue, mainly due to poaching. The same is true of other less well-known species. The natural habitat has been destroyed both by people and by domesticated animals. There are now nearly 70 national parks and 330 sanctuaries, as well as programmes of afforestation and coastline preservation. Most sanctuaries and parks are open October-March.

### The animals
**The big cats** Of the three Indian big cats the Asiatic lion is virtually confined to a single reserve. The other two, the tiger and leopard, occasionally occur outside. The **tiger** (*Panthera tigris*), which prefers to live in fairly dense cover, is most likely to be glimpsed as it lies in long grass or in dappled shadow or in the mangroves of the Sunderbans. The **leopard** or **panther**, as it is often called in India (*Panthera pardus*), is far more numerous than the tiger, but is even more elusive. The all-black form is not uncommon in areas of higher rainfall in Northeast India, though the typical form is seen more often.

**Elephant and rhino** The **Indian elephant** (*Elephas maximus*) has been domesticated for centuries and today it is still used as a beast of burden. In the wild it inhabits hilly country with forest and bamboo, where it lives in herds that can number as many as 50 or more individuals. They are adaptable animals and can live in all sorts of forest, except in dry areas. Wild elephants are mainly confined to reserves, but occasionally move out into cultivation, where they cause great damage. The **great Indian one-horned rhinoceros** (*Rhinoceros unicornis*) has folds of skin that look like rivet-covered armour plating. It stands it up to 170 cm at the shoulder.

**Deer, antelope, oxen and their relatives** Once widespread, these animals are now largely confined to the reserves. The male deer (stags) carry antlers that are branched, each 'spike' on the antler being called a tine. Antelopes and oxen, on the other hand, have horns that are not branched. There are several deer species in India, mainly confined to very restricted ranges. Three species are quite common. The largest, and one of the most widespread, is the magnificent **sambar** (*Cervus unicolor*) which can be up to 150 cm. It has a noticeably shaggy coat, which varies in colour from brown with a yellow or grey tinge through to dark, almost black, in the older stags. The sambar is often found on wooded hillsides and lives in groups of up to 10, though solitary individuals are also seen. The **barasingha** or **swamp deer** (*Cervus duvauceli*), standing about 130 cm at the shoulder, is also quite common. The females are usually lighter and some are spotted, as are the young. The antlers are much more complex than those of the sambar, having as many as 20 tines, but 12 is more usual. Barasingha prefer swampy habitat, but are also seen in grassy areas, often in large herds. The small **chital** or **spotted deer** (*Axis axis*), only about 90 cm tall, are seen in herds of 20 or so, in grassy areas. The bright rufous coat spotted with white is unmistakable; the stags carry antlers with three tines.

These animals live in open grasslands, never too far from water. The beautiful **blackbuck** or **Indian antelope** (*Antilope cervicapra*), up to 80 cm at the shoulder, occurs in large herds. The distinctive colouring and the long spiral horns make the stag easy to identify. The coat is chocolate brown above, sharply demarcated from the white of the underparts. The females do not usually bear horns and like the young, have yellowish brown coats. The larger, heavier **nilgai** or **blue bull** (*Boselaphus tragocamelus*) is about 140 cm at the shoulder and has a horse-like sloping back. The male has a dark grey coat; the female is sandy coloured. Both sexes have two white marks on the cheek, white throats and a white ring above each hoof. The male carries short, forward-curving horns and has a tuft of long black hairs on the front of the neck.

The very graceful **chinkara** or **Indian gazelle** (*Gazella gazella*) is only 65 cm at the shoulder. The light russet colour of the body has a distinct line along the side where the paler underparts start. Both sexes carry slightly S-shaped horns. Chinkara live in small groups in rather broken hilly countryside.

The commonest member of the oxen group is the **Asiatic wild buffalo** or water buffalo (*Bubalus bubalis*). About 170 cm at the shoulder, the wild buffalo, which can be aggressive, occurs in herds on grassy plains and swamps near rivers and lakes. The black coat and wide-spreading curved horns, carried by both sexes, are distinctive.

In the high Himalaya, the **yak** (*Bos grunniens*) is domesticated. The wild yak, found on bleak Himalayan hillsides, has a shaggy, blackish brown coat and large horns; the domesticated animals are often piebald and the horns much smaller.

The **Indian bison** or **gaur** (*Bos gaurus*) can be up to 200 cm at the shoulder with a heavy muscular ridge across it. Both sexes carry curved horns. The young gaur is a light sandy colour, which darkens with age, the old bulls being nearly black with pale sandy coloured 'socks' and a pale forehead. Basically hill animals, they live in forests and bamboo clumps and emerge from the trees to graze.

The rare **Asiatic wild ass** (*Equus hemionus*) is confined to the deserts of the Little Rann of Kachchh. The **wild boar** (*Sus scrofa*) has a mainly black body and a pig-like head; the hairs thicken down the spine to form a sort of mane. A mature male stands 90 cm at the shoulder and, unlike the female, bears tusks. The young are striped. Quite widespread, they can often cause great destruction among crops.

One of the most important scavengers of the open countryside, the **striped hyena** (*Hyena hyena*) usually comes out at night. It is about 90 cm at the shoulder with a large head with a noticeable crest of hairs along its sloping back.

The **common giant flying squirrel** (*Petaurista petaurista*) are common in the large forests of India, except in the northeast. The body can be 45 cm long and the tail another 50 cm. They glide from tree to tree using a membrane stretching from front leg to back leg, which acts like a parachute.

**In towns and villages** The **common langur** (*Presbytis entellus*), 75 cm, is a long-tailed monkey with a distinctive black face, hands and feet. Usually a forest dweller, it is found almost throughout India. The **rhesus macaque** (*Macaca mulatta*), 60 cm, is more solid looking with shorter limbs and a shorter tail. It can be distinguished by the orange-red fur on its rump and flanks.

**Palm squirrels** are very common. The **five-striped** (*Funambulus pennanti*) and the **three-striped palm squirrel** (*Funambulus palmarum*), are both about the same size (30 cm long, about half of which is tail). The five-striped is usually seen in towns.

The two bats most commonly seen in towns differ enormously in size. The larger so-called **flying fox** (*Pteropus giganteus*) has a wing span of 120 cm. These fruit-eating bats found throughout, except in the driest areas, roost in large noisy colonies where they look like folded umbrellas hanging from the trees. In the evening they can be seen leaving the roost with slow measured wing beats. The much smaller **Indian pipistrelle** (*Pipistrellus coromandra*), with a wing span of about 15 cm, is an insect eater. It comes into houses at dusk, roosting under eaves, and has a fast, erratic flight.

The **jackal** (*Canis aureus*), a lone scavenger in towns and villages, looks like a cross between a dog and a fox and varies from brown to black. The bushy tail has a dark tip.

The **common mongoose** (*Herpestes edwardsi*) lives in scrub and open jungle. It kills snakes, but will also take rats, mice and chicken. Tawny coloured with a grey grizzled tinge it is about 90 cm in length, of which half is pale-tipped tail.

The **sloth bear** (*Melursus ursinus*), about 75 cm at the shoulder, lives in broken forest but may be seen on a lead accompanying a street entertainer who makes it 'dance' to music as a part of an act. It has a long snout, a pendulous lower lip and a shaggy black coat with a yellowish V-shaped mark on the chest.

If you take a boat trip on the Ganga or the Brahmaputra Rivers, look out for the freshwater **gangetic dolphin** (*Platanista gangetica*) as it comes to the surface to breathe.

## Birds

**Town and village birds** Some birds perform a useful function scavenging and clearing refuse. One of the most widespread is the brown **pariah kite** (*Milvus migrans*, 65 cm). The more handsome chestnut and white **brahminy kite** (*Haliastur indus*, 48 cm) is largely confined to the waterside. The common brown **white-backed vulture** (*Gyps bengalensis* 90 cm) looks ungainly and has a bare and scrawny head and neck. The smaller **scavenger vulture** (*Neophron percnopterus*, 65 cm) is mainly white, but often has dirty-looking plumage and the bare head and neck of all vultures. In flight its wedge-shaped tail and black and white colouring are characteristic.

The **house crow** (*Corvus splendens*, 45 cm) on the other hand is a very smart-looking bird with a grey body and black tail, wings, face and throat. It occurs in almost every town and village in India. The **jungle crow** (*Corvus macrorhynchos*, 50 cm) originally a bird of the countryside, has started to move into populated areas and in the hill stations tends to replace the house crow. Unlike the house crow it is a glossy black all over and has a much deeper, hoarser caw.

The **feral pigeon**, or **blue rock dove** (*Columba livia*, 32 cm), found throughout the world, is generally a slaty grey in colour. It invariably has two dark bars on the wing and a white rump. The **little brown dove** (*Streptopelia senegalensis*, 25 cm) is bluey grey and brown above, with a pink head and underparts and a speckled pattern on the neck. The collared dove (*Streptopelia decaocto*, 30 cm) with a distinct half collar on the back of its neck, is common, especially in the drier parts of India.

Bulbuls are common in gardens and parks. The **red-vented bulbul** (*Pycnonotus cafer*, 20 cm), a mainly brown bird, can be identified by the slight crest and a bright red patch under the tail. The **house sparrow** (*Passer domesticus*, 15 cm) can be seen in towns. The ubiquitous **common myna** (*Acridotheres tristis*, 22 cm), feeds on lawns, especially after rain or watering. Look for the white under the tail and the bare yellow skin around the eye, yellow bill and legs and in flight the large white wing patch.

A less common, but more striking bird, also seen feeding in open spaces, is the **hoopoe** (*Upupa epops*, 30 cm), easily identified by its sandy plumage with black and white stripes and long thin curved bill. The marvellous fan-shaped crest is sometimes raised. Finally there is a member of the cuckoo family, which is heard more often than seen. The **koel** (*Eudynamys scolopacea*, 42 cm) is commonly heard during the hot weather: kuoo-kuoo-kuoo, the double note starts off low and flute-like, rises in pitch and intensity, then suddenly stops, only to start all over again. The male is all black with a greenish bill and a red eye; the female streaked and barred.

**Water and waterside birds** The *jheels* (marshes or swamps) of India form one of the richest bird habitats in the world. Cormorants abound; the commonest, the **little cormorant** (*Phalacrocorax niger*, 50 cm) is found on most inland waters. An almost entirely black bird with just a little white on the throat, it has a long tail and a hooked bill. The **coot** (*Fulica atra*, 40 cm), another common black bird seen especially in winter, has a noticeable white shield on the forehead.

The magnificent **sarus crane** (*Grus antigone*, 150 cm) is one of India's tallest birds. It is widespread year round across northern India, usually in pairs. The bare red head and long red legs combined with its height and grey plumage make it easy to identify. The commonest migrant crane is the **common crane** (*Grus grus*, 120 cm), present only in winter, often in flocks. It has grey plumage with a black head and neck. There is a white streak running down the side of the neck and above the eye is a tuft of red feathers.

The **openbill stork** (*Anastomus oscitans*, 80 cm) and the **painted stork** (*Ibis leucocephalus*, 100 cm) are common too and breed in large colonies. The former is white with black wing feathers and a curiously shaped bill. The latter, mainly white, has a pinkish tinge on the back and dark marks on the wings and a broken black band on the lower chest. The bare yellow face and yellow down-curved bill are conspicuous.

By almost every swamp, ditch or rice paddy up to about 1200 m you will see the **paddy bird** (*Ardeola grayii*, 45 cm). An inconspicuous, buff-coloured bird, it is easily overlooked as it stands hunched up by the waterside. As soon as it takes off, its white wings and rump make it very noticeable. The **bronze-winged jacana** (*Metopidius indicus*, 27 cm) has very long toes, which enable it to walk on the floating leaves of water-lilies, and there is a noticeable white streak over and above the eye. Village ponds often have their resident bird.

The commonest and most widespread of the Indian kingfishers is the jewel-like **common kingfisher** (*Alcedo atthis*, 18 cm). With its brilliant blue upperparts and orange breast it is usually seen perched on a twig or a reed beside the water.

**Open grassland, light woodland and cultivated land** The **cattle egret** (*Bubulcus ibis*, 50 cm), a small white heron, is usually seen near herds of cattle, frequently perched on the backs of the animals. Equal in height to the sarus crane is the impressive but ugly **adjutant stork** (*Leptopilos dubius*, 150 cm). This often dishevelled bird is a scavenger and is thus seen near rubbish dumps and carcasses. It has a naked red head and neck, a huge bill and a large fleshy pouch which hangs down the front of the neck.

The **rose-ringed parakeet** (*Psittacula krameri*, 40 cm) is found throughout India up to about 1500 m while the **pied myna** (*Sturnus contra*, 23 cm) is restricted to northern and central India. The rose-ringed parakeet often forms huge flocks, an impressive sight coming in to roost. The long tail is noticeable both in flight and when the bird is perched. They can be very destructive to crops, but are attractive birds which are frequently kept as pets. The pied myna, with its smart black and white plumage, is conspicuous, usually in small flocks in grazing land or cultivation. It feeds on the ground and on village rubbish dumps. The all-black **drongo** (*Dicrurus adsimilis*, 30 cm) is invariably seen perched on telegraph wires or bare branches. Its distinctively forked tail makes it easy to identify.

Weaver birds are a family of mainly yellow birds, all remarkable for the intricate nests they build. The most widespread is the **baya weaver** (*Ploceus philippinus*, 15 cm) which nests in large colonies, often near villages. The male in the breeding season combines a black face and throat with a contrasting yellow top of the head and a yellow breast band. In the non-breeding season both sexes are brownish sparrow-like birds.

**Hill birds** Land above 1500 m supports different species, although some, such as the ubiquitous **common myna**, are found in the highlands as well as in lower-lying terrain.

The highland equivalent of the red-vented bulbul is the **white-cheeked bulbul** (*Pycnonotus leucogenys*, 20 cm) which is found in gardens and woodland in the Himalaya up to about 2500 m. It has white underparts with a yellow patch under the tail. The black head and white cheek patches are distinctive. The crest varies in length and is most prominent in birds found in Kashmir, where it is very common in gardens. The **red-whiskered bulbul** (*Pycnonotus jocosus*, 20 cm) is widespread in the Himalaya and the hills of South India up to about 2500 m. Its pronounced pointed crest, which is sometimes so long that it flops forward towards the bill, white underparts and red and white 'whiskers' serve to distinguish it. It has a red patch under the tail.

In the summer the delightful **verditer flycatcher** (*Muscicapa thalassina*, 15 cm) is a common breeding bird in the Himalaya up to about 3000 m. It is tame and confiding, often builds its nest on verandas and is seen perching on telegraph wires. In winter it is more widely distributed throughout the country. It is an active little bird that flicks its tail up and down in a characteristic manner. The male is all bright blue-green with darker wings and a black patch in front of the eyes. The female is similar, but duller.

Another species associated with people is the **white wagtail** (*Motacilla alba*, 21 cm), very common in the Himalayan summer up to about 3000 m. It is found near water, but

treams and lakes, on floating vegetation and among the houseboats in Kashmir. Its black
and white plumage and constantly wagging tail make it easy to identify.

Yet another species common in Kashmir and in other Himalayan hill stations is the
**ed-billed blue magpie** (*Urocissa erythrorhyncha*, 65 cm). With a long tail and pale blue
plumage, contrasting with its black head, it is usually seen in small flocks as it flies from
ree to tree. Its habitats of choice are tea gardens, open woodland and cultivation.

The highlands of India, especially the Himalaya, are the home of the ancestors of
**domestic hens** and also of numerous beautiful **pheasants**. These are mainly forest
dwellers and are not easy to see as they tend to be shy and wary of people.

Last but not least is India's national bird, the magnificent **peafowl** (*Pavo cristatus*,
male 210 cm, female 100 cm), which is more commonly known as the peacock. Semi-
domesticated birds are commonly seen and heard around towns and villages, especially in
he northwest of India. In the wild it favours hilly jungles and dense scrub.

## Reptiles and amphibians

ndia is famous for its reptiles, especially its snakes, which feature in many stories
and legends. One of the most common is the **Indian rock python** (*Python molurus*) a
constrictor' that kills it's prey by suffocation. Usually about 4 m in length, they can be
much longer. Their docile nature make them favourites of snake handlers.

The other large snakes favoured by street entertainers are cobras. The various species
all have a hood, which is spread when the snake draws itself up to strike. They are all highly
venomous and the snake charmers prudently de-fang them to render them harmless. The
best known is probably the **spectacled cobra** (*Naja naja*), which has a mark like a pair of
spectacles on the back of its hood. The largest venomous snake in the world is the **king
cobra** (*Ophiophagus hannah*) which is 5 m in length. It is usually brown, but can vary from
cream to black and lacks the spectacle marks of the other. In their natural state cobras are
generally inhabitants of forest regions.

Equally venomous, but much smaller, the **common krait** (*Bungarus caeruleus*) is just
over 1 m long. The slender, shiny, blue-black snake has thin white bands. They are found all
over the country except in the northeast where the cannibalistic **banded krait** with bold
yellowish and black bands have virtually eradicated them.

In houses everywhere you cannot fail to see the **gecko** (*Hemidactylus*). This small,
harmless lizard is active after dark. It lives in houses behind pictures and curtain rails and
at night emerges to run across the walls and ceilings to hunt insects. It is not usually more
than about 14 cm long, with a transparent, pale yellowish brown body.

At the other end of the scale is the **monitor lizard** (*Varanus*), which can grow to 2 m in
length. They can vary from a colourful black and yellow, to plain or speckled brown. They
live in different habitats from cultivation and scrub to waterside places and desert.

The most widespread crocodile is the freshwater **mugger** or Marsh crocodile (*Crocodilus
palustrus*) which grows to 3-4 m in length. The only similar freshwater species is the
**gharial** (*Gavialis gangeticus*) which lives in large, fast-flowing rivers. Twice the length of
the mugger, it is a fish-eating crocodile with a long thin snout and, in the case of the male,
an extraordinary bulbous growth on the end of the snout.

The huge, aggressive **estuarine** or **saltwater crocodile** (*Crocodilus porosus*) is restricted
to the brackish waters of the Sundarbans on the east coast and in the Andaman and
Nicobar Islands. It grows to 7 m in length and is sleeker than the mugger.

# Books on the Indian Himalaya

The literature on India is as huge and varied as the subcontinent itself. India is a good place to buy English language books as foreign books are often much cheaper than the published price. There are also cheap Indian editions and occasionally reprints of out-of-print books. There are excellent bookshops in all the major Indian cities. Below are a few suggestions.

## Art and architecture

**Cooper, I and Dawson, B** *Traditional Buildings of India*, Thames & Hudson.
**Tillotson, G** *Mughal Architecture*, London, Viking, 1990; *The Tradition of Indian Architecture*, Yale 1989. Superbly clear writing on Indian architecture under Rajputs, Mughals and the British.

## Cities, sites and places

### Delhi
**Kaul, H, Ed** *Historic Delhi: an anthology*. Delhi, OUP, 1985.
**Liddle, S** *Delhi: 14 Historic Walks*, Westland Ltd, 2011. Well-paced walks with informative text.
**Miller, S** *Delhi: Adventures in a Megacity*. Penguin 2008. A non-fiction bestseller.
**Peck, L** *Delhi: A Thousand Years of Building*, Intach, 2005. Fascinating read, covers all monuments, plus maps and history.

### Dharamshala
**Avedon** *In Exile from the Land of the Snows*.
**Dalai Lama** *My Land and my People* and *Freedom in Exile*.
**Sogyal Rinpoche** *The Tibetan Book of Living and Dying*.

### Kolkata
**Humphrey, K** *Walking Calcutta*, Grosvenor House, 2009. One of the best ways to discover the city and its inhabitants, off the tourist trail.
**Moorhouse, G** *Calcutta*, 1971. It has dated somewhat, but is still a classic appraisal of the city. Written during Calcutta's bleaker moments.
**Winchester, S** *Lonely Planet*, 2004. Engaging essays by father and son, utilizing many worthy sources of travel literature.

### Kullu
**Chetwode, P** *Kulu, to the end of the habitable world*, Times Books Intl, 1989. Chronicles her travels from Narkanda to Ani and over the Jalori Pass to Banjar and Aut in the Tirthan valley. Penelope passed away near Khanag in the 1990s.

### Ladakh
**Harvey, A** *A Journey in Ladakh: Encounters with Buddhism*, Mariner Books, 2000.
**Norberg-Hodge, H** *Ancient Futures: Learning from Ladakh*, Sierra Club Books, 2009.
**Shipton, E** *That Untravelled World*, Charles Scribner's Sons, 1969.

## Current affairs and politics

**French, P** *Liberty or Death*, Harper Collins, 1997. Well researched, serious, but very readable.
**Granta 57** *India: the Golden Jubilee*. Superb edition devoted to India's 50th anniversary of Independence, 22 international writers give brilliant snapshot accounts.
**Silver, RB and Epstein, B** *India: a Mosaic*. New York, NYRB, 2000. Distinguished essays on history, politics and literature. Amartya Sen on Tagore, Pankaj Mishra on nuclear India.
**Tully, M** *No Full Stops in India*, Viking, 1991. An often superbly observed but controversially interpreted view of contemporary India.

## History: medieval and modern

**Beames, J** *Memoirs of a Bengal Civilian.* A readable insight into the British Raj in the post-Mutiny period, London, Eland, 1991.

**Edwardes, M** *The Myth of the Mahatma*, Constable 1986. Presents Gandhi in a whole new light.

**French, P** *India – a Portrait*, 2012.

**Gandhi, R** *The Good Boatman* Viking/Penguin 1995. An excellent biography by one of Gandhi's noted grandsons.

**Gascoigne, B** *The Great Moghuls*, London, Cape, 1987.

**Keay, J** *India: a History*, Harper Collins, 2000. A major popular history of the subcontinent.

## Language

**Snell, R and Weightman, S** *Teach Yourself Hindi.* An excellent, accessible teaching guides with CDs.

**Yule, H and Burnell, AC** (eds) *Hobson-Jobson: the Anglo-Indian Dictionary*, 1886. Paperback edition, 1999. A delightful insight into Anglo-Indian words and phrases.

## Literature

**Anand, Mulk Raj** *Untouchable.* Penguin Classics, 1935. A day in the life of a casteless toilet-sweeper.

**Chatterjee, U** *English August.* London, Faber, 1988. A wry account of an Indian civil servant's year in a rural posting.

**Chaudhuri, N** Vivid, witty and often sharply critical accounts of India across the 20th century. *The Autobiography of an Unknown Indian*, Macmillan, London; *Thy Hand, Great Anarch!*, London, Chatto & Windus, 1987.

**Desai, Kiran** *The Inheritance of Loss*, Hamish Hamilton 2006. Set in Kalimpong in the 1980s during the Gorkha uprising.

**Farrell, JG** *The Siege of Krishnapur*, 1973. Comic, horrific and gripping fiction about the 1857 mutiny.

**Farrell, JG**, *The Hill Station.* This last, unfinished novel describes colonial Simla of 1871.

**Lapierre, Dominique** *City of Joy*, 1985. It's no great work of literature, but every volunteer in Kolkata will find themselves reading this story of a rickshaw-wallah and a priest. There's also a film, starring the late P Swayze.

**Mistry, R** *A Fine Balance.* Faber, 1995. A tale of the struggle to survive in the modern Indian city.

**Naipaul, VS** *A Million Mutinies now,* Penguin, 1992. 'Revisionist' account of India turns away from the despondency of his earlier books (*An Area of Darkness* and *India: a Wounded Civilisation*).

**Rushdie, S** *Midnight's Children*, London, Picador, 1981. India since Independence, with funny and sharp critiques of South Asian life in the 1980s. *The Moor's Last Sigh*, Viking, 1996, is of particular interest to those travelling to Kochi and Mumbai.

**Scott, P** *The Raj Quartet*, London, Panther, 1973; *Staying On*, Longmans, 1985. Outstandingly perceptive novels of the end of the Raj.

**Scott, P** *Staying On.* Heinemann, 1977. Very funny, very poignant evocation of life in a hill station. Won the Booker Prize.

**Seth, V** *A Suitable Boy*, Phoenix House London, 1993. Prize-winning novel of modern Indian life.

## People

**Bijapurkar, R** *We are like that only*, Penguin Books India 2008. To understand consumer India.

**Bumiller, E** *May you be the mother of one hundred sons*, Penguin, 1991. An American woman journalists' account of coming to understand the issues that face India's women.

**Holmstrom, L** *The Inner Courtyard.* A series of short stories by Indian women, translated into English, Rupa, 2001.

**Lloyd, S** *An Indian Attachment*, London, Eland, 1992. A very personal and engaging account of time spent in an Indian village.

**Varma, PK** *Being Indian: Inside the Real India.* Arrow 2006.

## Religion

**Doniger O'Flaherty, W** *Hindu Myths*, Penguin Classics, 2004. A sourcebook translated from the Sanskrit.
**Rahula, W** *What the Buddha Taught.* Grove Press 1974.
**Waterstone, R** *India (The cultural companion)*, Barnes and Noble 2005. India's spiritual traditions brought up to date, well illustrated.

## Travelogues

**Dalrymple, W** *City of Djinns*, 1994. Fascinating and personal account of Delhi and its history, the perfect read when in the city.
**Dalrymple, W** *Nine Lives: In Search of the Sacred in Modern India*, 2009. The early days of the East India Company, classic Dalrymple, readable
**Dalrymple, W** *White Moghuls*, Harper-Collins 2002. The early days of the East India Company, classic Dalrymple.
**Frater, A** *Chasing the Monsoon*, London, Viking, 1990. Prize-winning account of the human impact of the monsoon's sweep across India.

**Keay, J** *Into India*, London, John Murray, 1999. Seasoned traveller's introduction to understanding and enjoying India.
**Parkes, Fanny** *Begums, Thugs and White Moghuls*. Eland, 2001. The jounals of this interpid lady who immersed herself in Indian culture during the early years of the Raj are honest, illuminating and immensely readable.

## Trekking

**Hardy, J** *The Ochre Border,* Constable, 1995. An account of crossing the Puri Parvati Pass from Kullu to Spiti. Hard to get hold of a copy.
**Hillary, E** *High Adventure*, Oxford University Press, USA 2003. Classic account of Himalayan climbs in the 1950s.
**Khosla, GD** *Himalayan Circuit*, 1989, OUP. An early account of travel into the then virtually unknown region of Kinnaur and Spiti.
**Loram, C** *Trekking in Ladakh*, Trailblazer, 2004, 3rd edition.

## Wildlife

**Grimmett R** *Birds of the Indian Subcontinent*, Christopher Helm, 2013.
**Pfister O** *Birds and Mammals of Ladakh*, Oxford University Press USA, 2004.

# Contents

Footnotes

# Basic Hindi words and phrases

**Pronunciation**: 'a' as in *ah*; 'i' as in *bee*; 'o' as in *oh*; 'u' as *oo* in *book*
**Hello** *namaste/nomoshkar*
**Thank you/no thank you** *dhanyavad or shukriya/nahin shukriya*
**Yes/no** *ji han/ji nahin*
**What is your name?** *apka nam kya hai?*
**My name is...** *mera nam... hai*
**How are you?** *kya hal hai?*
**I am well, thanks, and you?** *main thik hun, aur ap?*
**How much?** *kitna?*
**That is very expensive!** *bahut mahanga hai!*

# Food and drink glossary

## Meat and fish
| | |
|---|---|
| gosht, mas | meat, usually mutton (sheep) |
| jhinga | prawns |
| macchli | fish |
| murgh | chicken |

## Vegetables (sabzi)
| | | | |
|---|---|---|---|
| aloo | potato | khumbhi | mushroom |
| baingan | aubergine | matar | peas |
| band gobi | cabbage | piaz | onion |
| bhindi | okra, ladies' fingers | phool gobi | cauliflower |
| gajar | carrots | sag | spinach |

## Styles of cooking
Many items on restaurant menus are named according to methods of preparation, roughly equivalent to terms such as 'Provençal' or 'sauté'.

**bhoona** in a thick, fairly spicy sauce
**chops** minced meat, fish or vegetables, covered with mashed potato, crumbed and fried
**cutlet** minced meat, fish, vegetables formed into flat rounds or ovals, crumbed and fried (eg prawn cutlet, flattened king prawn)
**do piaza** with onions (added twice during cooking)
**dum pukht** steam baked
**jhal frazi** spicy, hot sauce with tomatoes and chillies
**jhol** thin gravy (Bengali)
**Kashmiri** cooked with mild spices, ground almonds and yoghurt, often with fruit
**kebab** skewered (or minced and shaped) meat or fish; a dry spicy dish cooked on a fire
**kima** minced meat (usually 'mutton')
**kofta** minced meat or vegetable balls
**korma** in fairly mild rich sauce using cream /yoghurt
**masala** marinated in spices (fairly hot)
**Madras** hot

makhani  in butter rich sauce
moli  South Indian dishes cooked in coconut milk and green chilli sauce
Mughlai  rich North Indian style
Nargisi  dish using boiled eggs
navratan curry  ('9 jewels') colourful mixed vegetables and fruit in mild sauce
Peshwari  rich with dried fruit and nuts (Northwest Indian)
tandoori  baked in a tandoor (special clay oven) or one imitating it
tikka  marinated meat pieces, baked quite dry
vindaloo  hot and sour Goan meat dish using vinegar

## Typical dishes

aloo gosht  potato and mutton stew
aloo gobi  dry potato and cauliflower with cumin
aloo, matar, kumbhi  potato, peas, mushrooms in a dryish mildly spicy sauce
bhindi bhaji  lady's fingers fried with onions and mild spices
boti kebab  marinated pieces of meat, skewered and cooked over a fire
dhal makhani  lentils cooked with butter
dum aloo  potato curry with a spicy yoghurt, tomato and onion sauce
matar panir  curd cheese cubes with peas and spices (and often tomatoes)
murgh massallam  chicken in creamy marinade of yoghurt, spices and herbs with nuts
nargisi kofta  boiled eggs covered in minced lamb, cooked in a thick sauce
rogan josh  rich, mutton/beef pieces in creamy, red sauce
sag panir  drained curd (panir) sautéed with chopped spinach in mild spices
sarson-ke-sag and makkah-ki-roti  mustard leaf cooked dry with spices served with maize
flour roti from Punjab
shabdeg  a special Mughlai mutton dish with vegetables
yakhni  lamb stew

## Rice

bhat/sada chawal  plain boiled rice
biriyani  partially cooked rice layered over meat and baked with saffron
khichari  rice and lentils cooked with turmeric and other spices
pulao/pilau  fried rice cooked with spices (cloves, cardamom, cinnamon) with dried fruit,
nuts or vegetables. Sometimes cooked with meat, like a biriyani

## Roti – breads

chapati (roti)  thin, plain, wholemeal unleavened bread cooked on a tawa (griddle), usually
made from ata (wheat flour). Makkaikiroti is with maize flour.
nan  oven baked (traditionally in a tandoor) white flour leavened bread often large and
triangular; sometimes stuffed with almonds and dried fruit
paratha  fried bread layered with ghi (sometimes cooked with egg or with potatoes)
poori  thin deepfried, puffed rounds of flour

## Sweets

These are often made with reduced/thickened milk, drained curd cheese or powdered
lentils and nuts. They are sometimes covered with a decorative, edible silver leaf.
barfi  fudgelike rectangles/diamonds
gulab jamun  dark fried spongy balls, soaked in syrup

**halwa**  rich sweet made from cereal, fruit, vegetable, nuts and sugar
**khir, payasam, paesh**  thickened milk rice/vermicelli pudding
**kulfi**  cone-shaped Indian ice cream with pistachios/almonds, uneven in texture
**jalebi**  spirals of fried batter soaked in syrup
**laddoo**  lentil based batter 'grains' shaped into rounds
**rasgulla (roshgulla)**  balls of curd in clear syrup
**sandesh**  dry sweet made of curd cheese

## Snacks

**bhaji, pakora**  vegetable fritters (onions, potatoes, cauliflower etc) deep-fried in batter
**chat**  sweet and sour fruit and vegetables flavoured with tama rind paste and chillis
**chana choor, chioora ('Bombay mix')**  lentil and flattened rice snacks mixed with nuts and dried fruit
**dosai**  South Indian pancake made with rice and lentil flour; served with a mild potato and onion filling (masala dosai) or without (ravai or plain dosai)
**iddli**  steamed South Indian rice cakes, a bland breakfast given flavour by spiced accompaniments
**kachori**  fried pastry rounds stuffed with spiced lentil/ peas/potato filling
**momos**  Tibetan stuffed pastas
**samosa**  cooked vegetable or meat wrapped in pastry triangles and deep fried
**utthappam**  thick South Indian rice and lentil flour pancake cooked with spices, onions/tomatoes
**vadai**  deep fried, small savoury lentil 'doughnut' rings. **Dahi vada** are similar rounds in yoghurt

# Glossary

Words in *italics* are common elements of words, often making up part of a place name.

## A

**aarti** (arati) Hindu worship with lamps

*abad* peopled

**acharya** religious teacher

**Adi Granth** Guru Granth Sahib, holy book of the Sikhs

**Adinatha** first of the 24 Tirthankaras, distinguished by his bull mount

**agarbathi** incense

**Agni** Vedic fire divinity, intermediary between gods and men; guardian of the Southeast

**ahimsa** non-harming, non-violence

**amrita** ambrosia; drink of immortality

**ananda** joy

**Ananda** the Buddha's chief disciple

**Ananta** a huge snake on whose coils Vishnu rests

**anna** (ana) 1/16 of a rupee

**Annapurna** Goddess of abundance; one aspect of Devi

**apsara** celestial nymph

**Ardhanarisvara** Siva represented as half-male and half-female

**Arjuna** hero of the Mahabharata, to whom Krishna delivered the Bhagavad Gita

**arrack** alcoholic spirit fermented from potatoes or grain

**asana** a seat or throne (Buddha's) pose

**ashram** hermitage or retreat

**Ashta Matrikas** The eight mother goddesses who attended on Siva or Skanda

**astanah** threshold

**atman** philosophical concept of universal soul or spirit

**aus** summer rice crop (Apr-Aug) Bengal

**Avalokiteshwara** Lord who looks down; Bodhisattva, the Compassionate

**avatara** 'descent'; incarnation of a divinity

**ayah** nursemaid

## B

**babu** clerk

*bagh* garden

**bahadur** title, meaning 'the brave'

**baksheesh** tip 'bribe'

**Balabhadra** Balarama, elder brother of Krishna

**bandh** a strike

**Bangla** (Bangaldar) curved roof, based on thatched roofs in Bengal

**bania** merchant caste

**basti** Jain temple

**bazar** market

**begum** Muslim princess/woman's courtesy title

**Bhagavad-Gita** Song of the Lord; section of the Mahabharata

**Bhagiratha** the king who prayed to Ganga to descend to earth

**bhai** brother

**Bhairava** Siva, the Fearful

**bhakti** adoration of a deity

**bhang** Indian hemp

**Bharata** half-brother of Rama

**bhavan** building or house

**bhikku** Buddhist monk

**Bhima** Pandava hero of the Mahabharata, famous for his strength

**Bhimsen** Deity worshipped for his strength and courage

**bidi** (beedi) Indian cigarette, tobacco wrapped in tendu leaves

**bo-tree** (or Bodhi) *Ficus religiosa*, pipal tree associated with the Buddha

**Bodhisattva** Enlightened One, destined to become Buddha

**bodi** tuft of hair on back of the shaven head (also *tikki*)

**Brahma** Universal self-existing power; Creator in the Hindu Triad.

**Brahmachari** religious student, accepting rigorous discipline (eg chastity)

**Brahman** (Brahmin) highest Hindu (and Jain) caste of priests

**Brahmanism** ancient Indian religion, precursor of modern Hinduism

**bundh** (literally closed) a strike

**burqa** (burkha) over-dress worn by Muslim women observing purdah

**bustee** slum

## C

**cantonment** planned military or civil area in town

**chaam** Himalayan Buddhist masked dance

**chadar** sheet worn as clothing

**chai** tea

**chakra** sacred Buddhist wheel of the law; also Vishnu's discus

**chala** Bengali curved roof

**Chamunda** terrifying form of the goddess Durga

**Chandra** Moon; a planetary deity

**char bagh** formal Mughal garden, divided into quarters

**char bangla** (char-chala) 'four temples' in Bengal, built like huts

**charpai** 'four legs' – wooden frame string bed

**chatt(r)a** ceremonial umbrella on stupa (Buddhist)

**chaukidar** (chowkidar) night-watchman; guard

**chhang** strong mountain beer of fermented barley maize rye or millet or rice

**chhatri** umbrella shaped dome or pavilion

**chhetri** (kshatriya) Hindu warrior caste

**chikan** shadow embroidery on fine cotton

**chogyal** heavenly king (Sikkim)

**choli** blouse

**chorten** Himalayan Buddhist relic shrine or a memorial stupa

**chowk** (chauk) a block; open place in a city where the market is held

**coir** fibre from coconut husk

**crore** 10 million

## D

**dacoit** bandit

**dada** (dadu) grandfather; elder brother

**dahi** yoghurt

**dak** post

**dakini** sorceress

**Dakshineshvara** Lord of the South; name of Siva

**dan** gift

**dandi** wooden 'seat' carried by bearers

**darbar** (durbar) a royal gathering

**darshan** (darshana) viewing of a deity or spiritual leader

**darwaza** gateway, door

**deodar** Himalayan cedar; from *deva-daru*, the 'wood of the gods'

**dervish** member of Muslim brotherhood, committed to poverty

**deul** in Bengal and Orissa, generic name for temple; the sanctuary

**devala** temple or shrine (Buddhist or Hindu)

**Devi** Goddess; later, the Supreme Goddess

**dhaba** roadside restaurant

**dharamshala** pilgrims' rest house

**dharma** moral and religious duty

**dharmachakra** wheel of 'moral' law (Buddhist)

**dhobi** washerman

**dhol** drums

**dhooli** (dhooli) swinging chair on a pole, carried by bearers

**dhoti** loose loincloth worn by Indian men

**dhyana** meditation

**digambara** literally 'sky-clad' Jain sect in which the monks go naked

*dighi* village pond (Bengal)

**dikshitar** person who makes oblations or offerings

**divan (diwan)** smoking-room; also a chief minister

**Diwali** festival of lights (Oct-Nov)

**diwan** chief financial minister

**diwan-i-am** hall of public audience

**diwan-i-khas** hall of private audience

**Draupadi** wife-in-common of the five Pandava brothers in the Mahabharata

**duar** (dwar) door, gateway

**dun** valley

**dupatta** long scarf worn by Punjabi women

**Durga** principal goddess of the Shakti cult

**durrie** (dhurrie) thick handloom rug

## E

**ek** the number 1, a symbol of unity

**ekka** one horse carriage

## F

**firman** edict or grant issued by a sovereign

## G

**gaddi** throne

**gadi/gari** car, cart, train

**gali** (galli) lane; an alley

**gana** child figures in art

**Ganesh** (Ganapati) elephant- headed son of Siva and Parvati

**Ganga** goddess personifying the Ganges

*ganj* market

**ganja** Indian hemp

*gaon* village

**garbhagriha** literally 'womb- chamber'; a temple sanctuary

*garh* fort

**Garuda** Mythical eagle, half-human Vishnu's vehicle

**Gauri** 'Fair One'; Parvati, consort of Shiva.

**Gaurishankara** Siva with Parvati

**ghagra** (ghongra) long flared skirt

**ghanta** bell

**ghat** hill range, hill road; landing place; steps on the river bank

**ghazal** Urdu lyric poetry/love songs, often erotic

**ghee** clarified butter for cooking

**gherao** industrial action, surrounding home or office of politician or industrial manager

**giri** hill

**godown** warehouse

**gola** conical-shaped storehouse

**gompa** Tibetan Buddhist monastery

**Gopala** (Govinda) cowherd; a name of Krishna

**Gopis** cowherd girls; milk maids who played with Krishna

**Gorakhnath** historically, an 11th-century yogi who founded a Saivite cult; an incarnation of Siva

**gosain** monk or devotee (Hindi)

**gram** chick pea, pulse

*gram* village; gramadan, gift of village

**gumbaz** (gumbad) dome

**gur gur** salted butter tea (Ladakh)

**gurudwara** (literally 'entrance to the house of God'); Sikh religious complex

## H

**Haj** (Hajj) annual Muslim pilgrimage to Mecca

**hakim** judge; a physician (usually Muslim)

**halwa** a special sweetmeat

**Hanuman** Monkey devotee of Rama; bringer of success to armies

**Hara** (Hara Siddhi) Siva

**Hari** Vishnu Harihara, Vishnu-Siva as a single divinity

**hartal** general strike

**hat** (haat) market

**hathi** (hati) elephant

**hathi pol** elephant gate

**hauz** tank or reservoir

**haveli** a merchant's house usually in Rajasthan

**havildar** army sergeant

**hindola** swing

**hiti** a water channel; a bath or tank with water spouts

**Holi** spring festival (Feb-Mar)

**hookah** 'hubble bubble' or smoking vase

**howdah** seat on elephant's back, sometimes canopied

**hundi** temple offering

**huzra** a Muslim tomb chamber

## I

**Iat** pillar, column

**Id** principal Muslim festivals

**Idgah** open space for Id prayers

**ikat** 'resist-dyed' woven fabric

**imam** Muslim religious leader

**imambara** tomb of a Shiite Muslim holy man; focus of Muharram procession

**Indra** King of the gods; God of rain; guardian of the East

**Ishana** Guardian of the North East

**Ishvara** Lord; Siva

**iwan** main arch in mosque

## J

**jadu** magic

**jaga mohan** audience hall or ante-chamber of an Orissan temple

**Jagadambi** literally Mother of the World; Parvati

**Jagannath** literally Lord of the World; particularly, Krishna worshipped at Puri

**jagati** railed parapet

**jaggery** brown sugar, made from palm sap

**jahaz** ship: building in form of ship

**Jambudvipa** Continent of the Rose-Apple Tree; the earth

**Jami masjid** (Jama, Jumma) Friday mosque, for congregational worship

**Jamuna** Hindu goddess who rides a tortoise; river

**Janaka** Father of Sita

**jangha** broad band of sculpture on the outside of the temple wall

**jarokha** balcony

**jataka stories** accounts of the previous lives of the Buddha

**jatra** Bengali folk theatre

**jawab** literally 'answer,' a building which duplicates another to provide symmetry

**jawan** army recruit, soldier

**jheel** (jhil) lake; a marsh; a swamp

**jhilmil** projecting canopy over a window or door opening

**-ji** (jee) honorific suffix added to names out of reverence and/or politeness; also abbreviated 'yes' (Hindi/Urdu)

**Jina** literally 'victor'; spiritual conqueror or Tirthankara, after whom Jainism is named

**Jogini** mystical goddess

**jorbangla** double hut-like temple in Bengal

**Jyotirlinga** luminous energy of Siva manifested at 12 holy places, miraculously formed lingams

**K**

**kabigan** folk debate in verse

**kacheri** (kutchery) a court; an office for public business

**Kailasa** mountain home of Siva

**Kali** literally 'black'; terrifying form of the goddess Durga, wearing a necklace of skulls/heads

**Kalki** future incarnation of Vishnu on horseback

**kalyanamandapa** marriage hall

**kameez** women's shirt

**kanga** comb (one of five Sikh symbols)

**kantha** Bengali quilting

**kapok** the silk cotton tree

**karma** impurity resulting from past misdeeds

**Kartikkeya** (Kartik) Son of Siva, God of war

**kati-roll** Muslim snack of meat rolled in a 'paratha' bread

**khadi** cotton cloth made from home-spun cotton (or silk) yarn

**khal** creek; a canal

*khana* food or meal, also suffix for room/office/place

**khanqah** Muslim (Sufi) hospice

*khet* field

**khola** river or stream in Nepal

**khondalite** crudely grained basalt

**khukri** traditional curved Gurkha weapon

**kirti-stambha** 'pillar of fame,' free standing pillar in front of temple

**kos minars** Mughal 'mile' stones

**kot** (kota/kottai/kotte) fort

**kothi** house

**kotla** citadel

**Kubera** chief yaksha; keeper of the treasures of the earth, Guardian of the North

**kumar** a young man

**Kumari** virgin; Durga

**Kumbhayog** auspicious time for bathing to wash away sins

**kumhar** (kumar) potter

**kund** lake, well or pool

**kurta** Punjabi shirt

**kurti-kanchali** small blouse

**kutcha** (cutcha/kacha) raw; crude; unpaved; built with sun-dried bricks

**kwabgah** bedroom; literally 'palace of dreams'

**L**

*la* Himalayan mountain pass

**lakh** 100,000

**Lakshmana** younger brother of Rama

**Lakshmi** Goddess of wealth and good fortune, consort of Vishnu

**lama** Buddhist priest in Tibet

**lassi** iced yoghurt drink

**lathi** bamboo stick with metal bindings, used by police

**lena** cave, usually a rock-cut sanctuary

**lingam** (linga) Siva as the phallic emblem

**Lingaraja** Siva worshipped at Bhubaneswar

**Lokeshwar** 'Lord of the World', Avalokiteshwara to Buddhists and form of Siva to Hindus

**lungi** wrapped-around loin cloth, normally checked

# M

**madrassa** Islamic theological school or college

**maha** great

**Mahabharata** Sanskrit epic about the battle between the Pandavas and Kauravas

**Mahabodhi** Great Enlightenment of Buddha

**Mahadeva** 'Great Lord'; Siva

**mahal** palace, grand building

**mahalla** (mohulla) division of a town; a quarter; a ward

**mahant** head of a monastery

**maharaja** great king

**maharani** great queen

**maharishi** (Maharshi) literally 'great teacher'

**Mahavira** literally 'Great Hero'; last of the 24 Tirthankaras, founder of Jainism

**Mahayana** The Greater Vehicle; form of Buddhism practised in East Asia, Tibet and Nepal

**Mahesha** (Maheshvara) Great Lord; Siva

**mahout** elephant driver/keeper

**mahseer** large freshwater fish found especially in Himalayan rivers

**maidan** large open grassy area in a town

**Maitreya** the future Buddha

**makara** crocodile-shaped mythical creature symbolizing the river Ganga

**makhan** butter

**mali** gardener

**Manasa** Snake goddess; Sakti

**mandala** geometric diagram symbolizing the structure of the Universe

*mandi* market

**mandir** temple

**mani** stones with sacred inscriptions at Buddhist sites

**Mara** Tempter, who sent his daughters (and soldiers) to disturb the Buddha's meditation

**marg** wide roadway

**masjid** literally 'place of prostration'; mosque

**mata** mother

**math** Hindu or Jain monastery

**maulana** scholar (Muslim)

**maulvi** religious teacher (Muslim)

**maund** measure of weight about 20 kg

**maya** illusion

**meena** enamel work

**mela** festival or fair, usually Hindu

**memsahib** married European woman, term used mainly before Independence

**Meru** mountain supporting the heavens

**mihrab** niche in the western wall of a mosque

**mimbar** pulpit in mosque

**Minakshi** literally 'fish-eyed'; Parvati

**minar** (minaret) slender tower of a mosque

**mitthai** Indian sweets

**mithuna** couple in sexual embrace

**mofussil** the country as distinct from the town

**moksha** salvation, enlightenment; literally 'release'

**mudra** symbolic hand gesture

**muezzin** mosque official who calls the faithful to prayer

**Muharram** period of mourning in remembrance of Hasan and Hussain, murdered sons of Ali

**mullah** religious teacher (Muslim)

**musalla** prayer mat

**muthi** measure equal to 'a handful'

# N

**nadi** river

**Naga** (nagi/nagini) Snake deity; associated with fertility and protection

**nagara** city, sometimes capital

**nallah** (nullah) ditch, channel

**namaaz** Muslim prayers, worship

**namaste** Hindu greeting (with joined palms) translated as: 'I salute all divine qualities in you'

**namda** rug

**Nandi** a bull, Siva's vehicle and a symbol of fertility

**Narayana** Vishnu as the creator of life

**Nataraja** Siva, Lord of the cosmic dance

*nath* literally 'place' eg Amarnath

**natya** the art of dance

**nautch** display by dancing girls

**navagraha** nine planets, represented usually on the lintel or architrave of the front door of a temple

**navaranga** central hall of temple

**navaratri** literally '9 nights'; name of the Dasara festival

**nawab** prince, wealthy Muslim, sometimes used as a title

**niwas** small palace

**nritya** pure dance

**P**

**pada** foot or base

**padam** dance which tells a story

**padma** lotus flower, Padmasana, lotus seat; posture of meditating figures

**paga** projecting pilaster-like surface of an Orissan temple

*pahar* hill

**paisa** (poisa) one hundredth of a rupee

**palanquin** covered litter for one, carried on poles

**pali** language of Buddhist scriptures

*palli* village

**pan** leaf of the betel vine; sliced areca nut, lime and other ingredients wrapped in leaf for chewing

**panchayat** a 'council of five'; a government system of elected councils

**pandal** marquee made of bamboo and cloth

**pandas** temple priests

**pandit** teacher or wise man; a Sanskrit scholar

**pankah** (punkha) fan, formerly pulled by a cord

**Parinirvana** the Buddha's state prior to nirvana, shown usually as a reclining figure

**parishads** political division of group of villages

**Parsi** (Parsee) Zoroastrians who fled from Iran to West India in the 8th century to avoid persecution

**Parvati** daughter of the Mountain; Siva's consort

**Pashupati** literally Lord of the Beasts; Siva

**pata** painted hanging scroll

*patan* town or city (Sanskrit)

**patel** village headman

**pattachitra** specially painted cloth (especially Orissan)

**pau** measure for vegetables and fruit equal to 250 g

**peon** servant, messenger (from Portuguese *peao*)

**pida** (pitha) basement

**pida deul** hall with a pyramidal roof in an Orissan temple

**pinjrapol** animal hospital (Jain)

**pipal** Ficus religiosa, the Bodhi tree

**pir** Muslim holy man

**pithasthana** place of pilgrimage

**pralaya** the end of the world

**prasadam** consecrated temple food

**prayag** confluence considered sacred by Hindus

**puja** ritual offerings to the gods; worship (Hindu)

**pujari** worshipper; one who performs puja (Hindu)

**pukka** literally 'ripe' or 'finished'; reliable; solidly built

**punya** merit earned through actions and religious devotion (Buddhist)

**Puranas** literally 'the old' Sanskrit sacred poems

**purdah** seclusion of Muslim women from public view (literally curtains)

**pushkarani** sacred pool or tank

**Q**

**qabr** Muslim grave

**qibla** direction for Muslim prayer

**qila** fort

**qutb** axis or pivot

**R**

**rabi** winter/spring season crop

**Radha** Krishna's favourite consort

**raj** rule or government

**raja** king, ruler (variations include rao, rawal)

**rajbari** palaces of a small kingdom

**Rajput** dynasties of western and central India

**Rakshakas** Earth spirits

**Rama** Seventh incarnation of Vishnu

**Ramayana** Sanskrit epic – the story of Rama

**Ramazan** (Ramadan) Muslim month of fasting

**rana** warrior (Nepal)

**rani** queen

**rath** chariot or temple car

**Ravana** Demon king of Lanka; kidnapper of Sita

**rawal** head priest

**Rig (Rg) Veda** oldest and most sacred of the Vedas

**Rimpoche** blessed incarnation; abbot of a Tibetan Buddhist monastery (gompa)

**rishi** 'seer'; inspired poet, philosopher

**ryot** (rayat/raiyat) a subject; a cultivator; a farmer

**S**

**sabha** columned hall (sabha mandapa, assembly hall)

**sabzi** vegetables, vegetable curry

**sadar** (sadr/saddar) chief, main especially Sikh

**sadhu** ascetic; religious mendicant, holy man

**sagar** lake; reservoir

**sahib** title of address, like 'sir'

**Saiva** (Shaiva) the cult of Siva

**sal** a hall

**sal** hardwood tree of the lower slopes of the Himalayan foothills

**salaam** literally 'peace'; greeting (Muslim)

**salwar** (shalwar) loose trousers (Punjab)

**samadh(i)** literally concentrated thought, meditation; a funerary memorial

**samsara** transmigration of the soul

**samudra** large tank or inland sea

**sangam** junction of rivers

**sangarama** monastery

**sangha** ascetic order founded by Buddha

**sankha** (shankha) the conch shell (symbolically held by Vishnu); the shell bangle worn by Bengali women

**sanyasi** wandering ascetic; final stage in the ideal life of a man

**sarai** caravansarai, halting place

**saranghi** small four-stringed viola shaped from a single piece of wood

**Saraswati** wife of Brahma and goddess of knowledge

**sarkar** the government; the state; a writer; an accountant

**sarod** Indian stringed musical instrument

**sarvodaya** uplift, improvement of all

**sati** (suttee) a virtuous woman; act of self-immolation on a husband's funeral pyre

**Sati** wife of Siva who destroyed herself by fire

**satyagraha** 'truth force'; passive resistance

**seer** (ser) weight (about 1 kg)

**sepoy** (sepai) Indian soldier, private **serow** a wild Himalayan antelope

**seth** merchant, businessman

**seva** voluntary service

**shahtush** very fine wool from the Tibetan antelope

**Shakti** Energy; female divinity often associated with Siva

**Shankara** Siva

**sharia** corpus of Muslim theological law

**shastras** ancient texts defining temple architecture

**shastri** religious title (Hindu)

**sheesh mahal** palace apartment with mirror work

**sherwani** knee-length coat for men

**Shesha** (Sesha) serpent who supports Vishnu

**shikar** hunting

**shloka** (sloka) Sanskrit sacred verse

**sindur** vermilion powder used in temple ritual; married women mark their hair parting with it (East India)

**singh** (sinha) lion; Rajput caste name adopted by Sikhs

**Sita** Rama's wife, heroine of the Ramayana epic

**sitar** classical stringed musical instrument with a gourd for soundbox

**Siva** (Shiva) The Destroyer in the Hindu triad of Gods

**Sivaratri** literally 'Siva's night'; a festival (Feb-Mar)

**soma** sacred drink mentioned in the Vedas

**sri** (shri) honorific title, often used for 'Mr'; a sign of great respect

**stupa** hemispheric Buddhist funerary mound

**subahdar** (subedar) the governor of a province; viceroy under the Mughals

**sudra** lowest of the Hindu castes

**sufi** Muslim mystic; sufism, Muslim mystic worship

**Surya** Sun; Sun God

**svami** (swami) holy man; a suffix for temple deities

**svastika** (swastika) auspicious Hindu/ Buddhist cross-like sign

**swadeshi** home-made goods

**swaraj** home rule

**swatantra** freedom

## T

**tabla** a pair of drums
**tahr** wild goat
**takht** throne
**talao** (*tal*, talar) water tank
**taluk** administrative subdivision of a district
**tamasha** spectacle; festive celebration
**tandava** (dance) of Siva
**tapas** (tapasya) ascetic meditative self-denial
**Tara** literally 'star'; a goddess
**tarkashi** Orissan silver filigree
**Teej** Hindu festival
**tehsil** subdivision of a district (North India)
**tempo** three-wheeler vehicle
**terai** narrow strip of land along Himalayan foothills
**thakur** high Hindu caste; deity (Bengal)
**thakur bari temple** sanctuary (Bengal)
**thana** a police jurisdiction; police station
**thangka** (thankha) cloth (often silk) painted with a Tibetan Mahayana deity
**tiffin** snack, light meal
**tika** (tilak) vermilion powder, auspicious mark on the forehead; often decorative
**tirtha** ford, bathing place, holy spot (Sanskrit)
**Tirthankara** literally 'ford-maker'; title given to 24 religious 'teachers', worshipped by Jains
**Tollywood** the Bengali film industry
**tonga** two-wheeled horse carriage
**Trimurti** the Hindu Triad, Brahma, Vishnu and Siva
**trisul** the trident chief symbol of the god Siva
**triveni** triple-braided
**tsampa** ground, roasted barley, eaten dry or mixed with milk, tea or water (Himalayan)
**tulsi** sacred basil plant

## U

**Uma** Siva's consort in one of her many forms
**untouchable** 'outcastes', with whom contact of any kind was believed by high caste Hindus to be defiling
**Upanishads** ancient Sanskrit philosophical texts, part of the Vedas
**ustad** master
**uttarayana** northwards

## V

**vahana** 'vehicle' of the deity
**vaisya** the 'middle-class' caste of merchants and farmers
**Valmiki** sage, author of the Ramayana epic
**Vamana** dwarf incarnation of Vishnu
**vana** grove, forest
**Varaha** boar incarnation of Vishnu
**varna** 'colour'; social division of Hindus into Brahmin, Kshatriya, Vaishya and Sudra
**Varuna** Guardian of the West, accompanied by Makara
**Veda** (Vedic) oldest known Hindu religious texts
**vedi** (bedi) altar, also a wall or screen
**vihara** Buddhist or Jain monastery with cells around a courtyard
**Vishnu** a principal Hindu deity; the Preserver (and Creator)

## W

**-wallah** suffix often used with a occupational name, eg rickshaw-wallah
**wazir** chief minister of a raja (from Turkish 'vizier')

## Y

**yagya** (yajna) major ceremonial sacrifice
**Yaksha** (Yakshi) a demi-god, associated with nature
**Yama** God of death, judge of the living
**yantra** magical diagram used in meditation; instrument
**yatra** pilgrimage
**Yellow Hat** Gelugpa Sect of Tibetan Buddhism – monks wear yellow headdress
**yoni** a hole symbolizing female sexuality; vagina

## Z

**zamindar** a landlord granted income under the Mughals
**zari** silver and gold thread for weaving or embroidery
**zarih** cenotaph in a Muslim tomb
**zenana** segregated women's apartments
**ziarat** holy Muslim tomb
**zilla** (zillah) district

# Index → Entries in **bold** refer to maps

# Advertisers' index

# Credits

**Footprint credits**
**Editor**: Jo Williams
**Production and layout**: Emma Bryers
**Maps**: Kevin Feeney
**Colour section**: Angus Dawson

**Publisher**: Patrick Dawson
**Managing Editor**: Felicity Laughton
**Advertising**: Elizabeth Taylor
**Sales and marketing**: Kirsty Holmes

**Photography credits**
**Front cover**: Leh City at night f9photoes/
Shutterstock.com
**Back cover**: Maitreya temple, Basgo
Natalia Davidovich/Shutterstock.com

**Colour section**
page 1: Dmitry Rukhlenko/Dreamstime;
page 2: S4sanchita/Dreamstime;
page 6 top: Federico Donatini/Dreamstime;
page 6 bottom: Naveen Kumar Arora/
Dreamstime; page 7: Pius Lee/Dreamstime;
page 8 top: Digitalfestival/Dreamstime;
page 8 bottom: Straannick/Dreamstime;
page 9: Matej Hudovernik/Dreamstime;
page 10 top: Andrey Armyagov/Dreamstime;
page 10 bottom: Pius Lee/Dreamstime

Printed in India by Replika Press Pvt Ltd

**Publishing information**
Footprint Indian Himalaya
3rd edition
© Footprint Handbooks Ltd
March 2014

ISBN: 978 1 907263 88 0
CIP DATA: A catalogue record for this book
is available from the British Library

® Footprint Handbooks and the Footprint
mark are a registered trademark of
Footprint Handbooks Ltd

Published by Footprint
6 Riverside Court
Lower Bristol Road
Bath BA2 3DZ, UK
T +44 (0)1225 469141
F +44 (0)1225 469461
footprinttravelguides.com

Distributed in the USA by Globe Pequot
Press, Guilford, Connecticut

Every effort has been made to ensure that
the facts in this guidebook are accurate.
However, travellers should still obtain advice
from consulates, airlines, etc about travel
and visa requirements before travelling.
The authors and publishers cannot
accept responsibility for any loss, injury
or inconvenience however caused.

# Footprint Mini Atlas
# Indian Himalaya

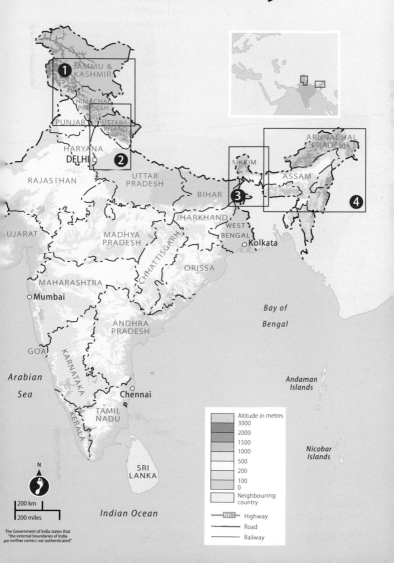

JAMMU &
KASHMIR

HIMACHAL
PRADESH

PUNJAB UTTARA
KHAND

HARYANA

DELHI

RAJASTHAN

UTTAR
PRADESH

BIHAR

SIKKIM

ARUNACHAL
PRADESH

ASSAM

JHARKHAND

GUJARAT

MADHYA
PRADESH

CHHATTISGARH

WEST
BENGAL

○ Kolkata

ORISSA

MAHARASHTRA

○ Mumbai

ANDHRA
PRADESH

GOA

KARNATAKA

Bay of
Bengal

Arabian
Sea

○ Chennai

Andaman
Islands

TAMIL
NADU

KERALA

N

SRI
LANKA

Nicobar
Islands

Altitude in metres
3000
2000
1500
1000
500
200
100
0
Neighbouring
country

200 km

200 miles

Indian Ocean

NH1 — Highway
— Road
— Railway

The Government of India states that
"the external boundaries of India
are neither correct nor authenticated"

# Map 1

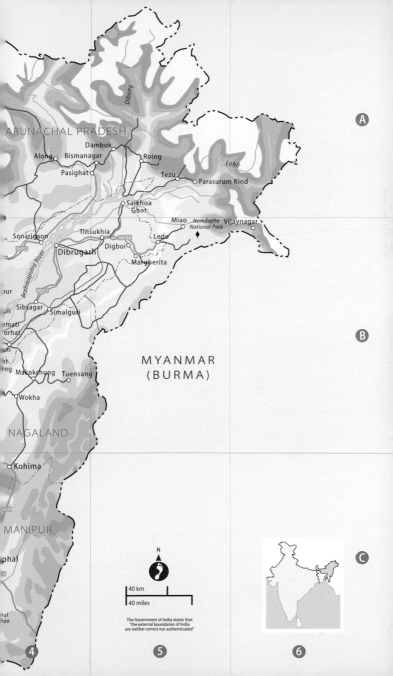

ARUNACHAL PRADESH

Dibong

Lohit

Along
Bismanagar
Dambuk
Roing
Pasighat
Tezu
Parasurum Kind

Saikhoa
Ghat

Miao
Namdaphe
National Park
Vijaynagar

Sonaridaon
Tinsukhia
NH38
Ledo
Brahmaputra River
NH52
Dibrugarh
Digboi
Margherita

pur

NH17
Sibsagar
Simalguri

emati
orhat

ng

Makokchung
Tuensang

Wokha

NAGALAND

Kohima

MYANMAR
(BURMA)

H39

MANIPUR

phal

2

pul
ao

A

B

C

4

5

6

N

40 km
40 miles

The Government of India states that
"the external boundaries of India
are neither correct nor authenticated"

# Map symbols

- □ Capital city
- ○ Other city, town
- International border
- Regional border
- ⊖ Customs
- Contours (approx)
- ▲ Mountain, volcano
- Mountain pass
- Escarpment
- Glacier
- Salt flat
- Rocks
- Seasonal marshland
- Beach, sandbank
- Waterfall
- Reef
- Motorway
- Main road
- Minor road
- Track
- Footpath
- Railway
- Railway with station
- ✈ Airport
- Bus station
- Ⓜ Metro station
- Cable car
- Funicular
- Ferry
- Pedestrianized street
- Tunnel
- One way-street
- Steps
- Bridge
- Fortified wall
- Park, garden, stadium
- Sleeping
- Eating
- Bars & clubs

- Building
- Sight
- Cathedral, church
- Chinese temple
- Hindu temple
- Meru
- Mosque
- Stupa
- Synagogue
- Tourist office
- Museum
- Post office
- Police
- Bank
- @ Internet
- ♪ Telephone
- Market
- Medical services
- Parking
- Petrol
- Golf
- Archaeological site
- National park, wildlife reserve
- Viewing point
- Campsite
- Refuge, lodge
- Castle, fort
- Diving
- Deciduous, coniferous, palm trees
- Mangrove
- Hide
- Vineyard, winery
- Distillery
- Shipwreck
- Historic battlefield
- Related map

# Join us online...

Follow us on **Twitter** and **Facebook** – ask us questions, speak to our authors, swap your stories, and be kept up to date with travel news and exclusive discounts and competitions.

Upload your travel pics to our **Flickr** site – inspire others on where to go next, and have your photos considered for inclusion in Footprint guides.

And don't forget to visit us at  footprinttravelguides.com

# Footprint story

### It was 1921

Ireland had just been partitioned, the British miners were striking for more pay and the federation of British industry had an idea. Exports were booming in South America – how about a handbook for businessmen trading in that far away continent? The Anglo-South American Handbook was born that year, written by W Koebel, the most prolific writer on Latin America of his day.

### 1924

Two editions later the book was 'privatized' and in 1924, in the hands of Royal Mail, the steamship company for South America, it became The South American Handbook, subtitled 'South America in a nutshell'. This annual publication became the 'bible' for generations of travellers to South America and remains so to this day. In the early days travel was by sea and the Handbook gave all the details needed for the long voyage from Europe. What to wear for dinner; how to arrange a cricket match with the Cable & Wireless staff on the Cape Verde Islands and a full account of the journey from Liverpool up the Amazon to Manaus: 5898 miles without changing cabin!

### 1939

As the continent opened up, the South American Handbook reported the new Pan Am flying boat services, and the fortnightly airship service from Rio to Europe on the Graf Zeppelin. For reasons still unclear but with extraordinary determination, the annual editions continued through the Second World War.

### 1970s

Many more people discovered South America and the backpacking trail started to develop. All the while the Handbook was gathering fans, including literary vagabonds such as Paul Theroux and Graham Greene (who once sent some updates addressed to "The publishers of the best travel guide in the world, Bath, England").

### 1990s

During the 1990s the company set about developing a new travel guide series using this legendary title as the flagship. By 1997 there were over a dozen guides in the series and the Footprint imprint was launched.

### 2000s

The series grew quickly and there were soon Footprint travel guides covering more than 150 countries. In 2004, Footprint launched its first thematic guide: *Surfing Europe*, packed with colour photographs, maps and charts. This was followed by further thematic guides such as *Diving the World*, *Snowboarding the World*, *Body and Soul escapes*, *Travel with Kids* and *European City Breaks*.

### 2014

Today we continue the traditions of the last 93 years that have served legions of travellers so well. We believe that these help to make Footprint guides different. Our policy is to use authors who are genuine experts who write for independent travellers; people possessing a spirit of adventure, looking to get off the beaten track.